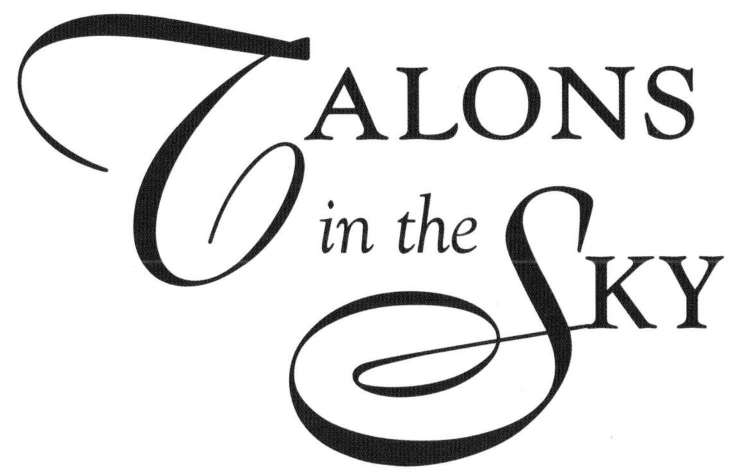

The Great Gallery of Eagles, Hawks and Owls

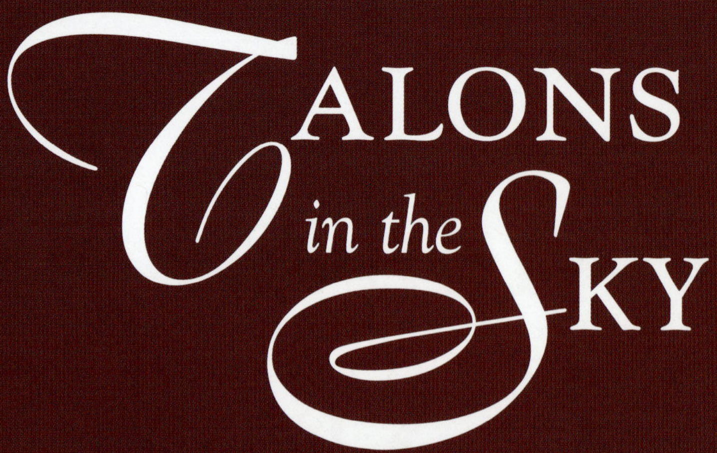

The Great Gallery of
Eagles, Hawks and Owls

Photographs by
STEVE MASLOWSKI

Foreword by
FLOYD SCHOLZ

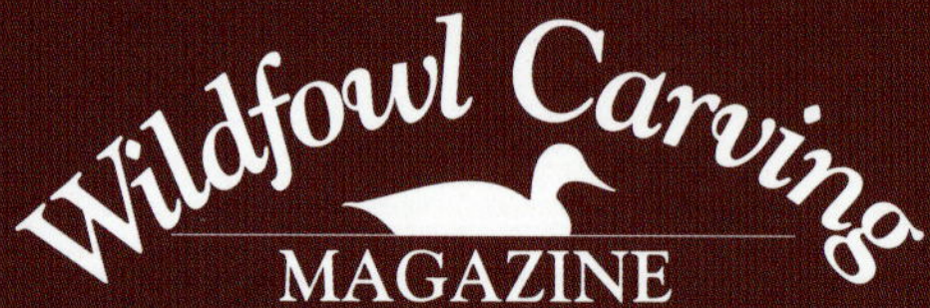

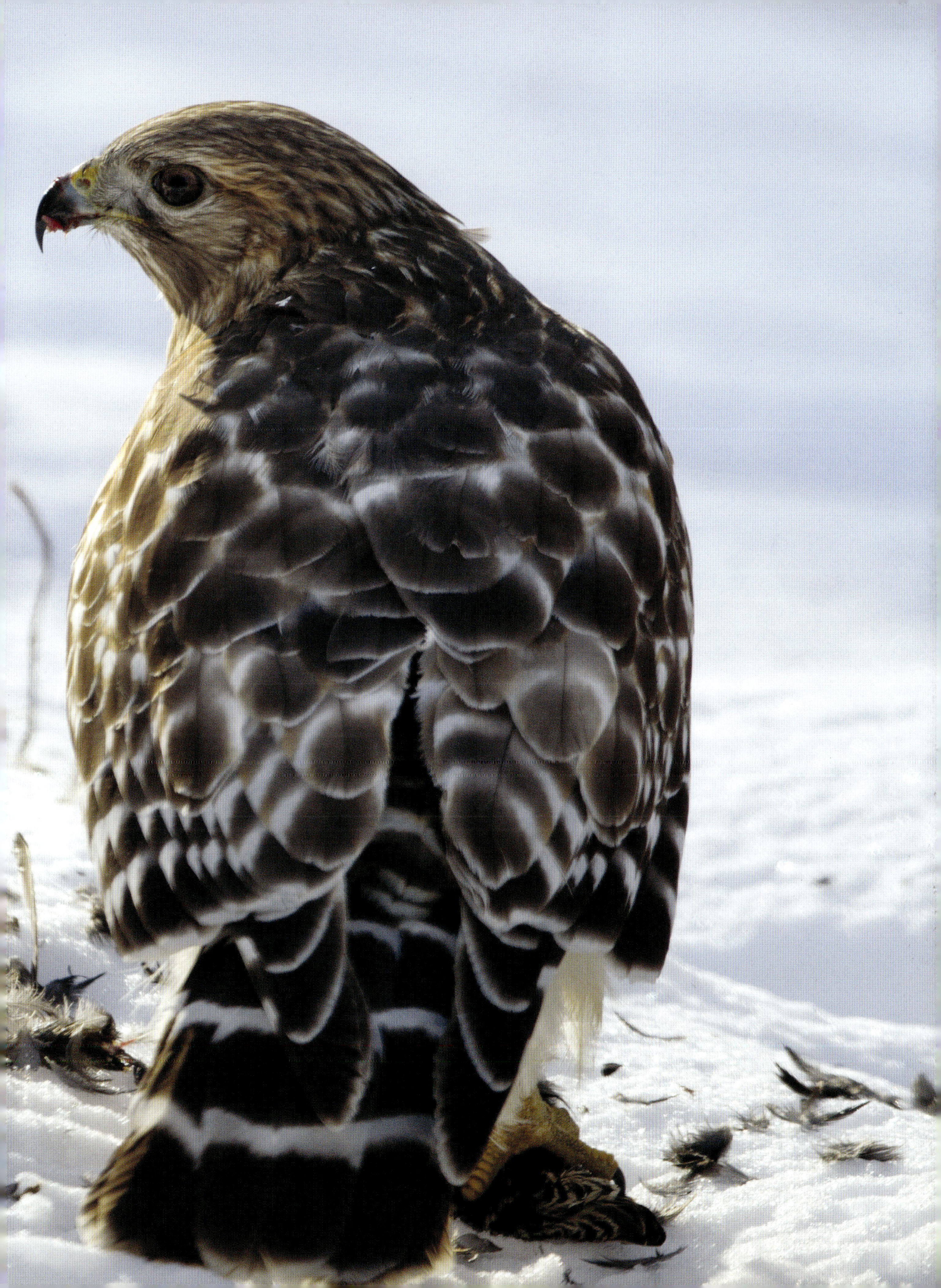

Published by

Ampry Publishing, LLC

3400 Dundee Rd., Suite 220

Northbrook, IL 60062

Customer Service (877) 762–8034 (U.S.); (866) 375–7257 (Canada)

www.wildfowl-carving.com

Printed in United States of America

10 9 8 7 6 5 4 3 2 1

Cover design by Cher Williams

ISBN 978-1-945550-00-3

Library of Congress Control Number: 2016953901

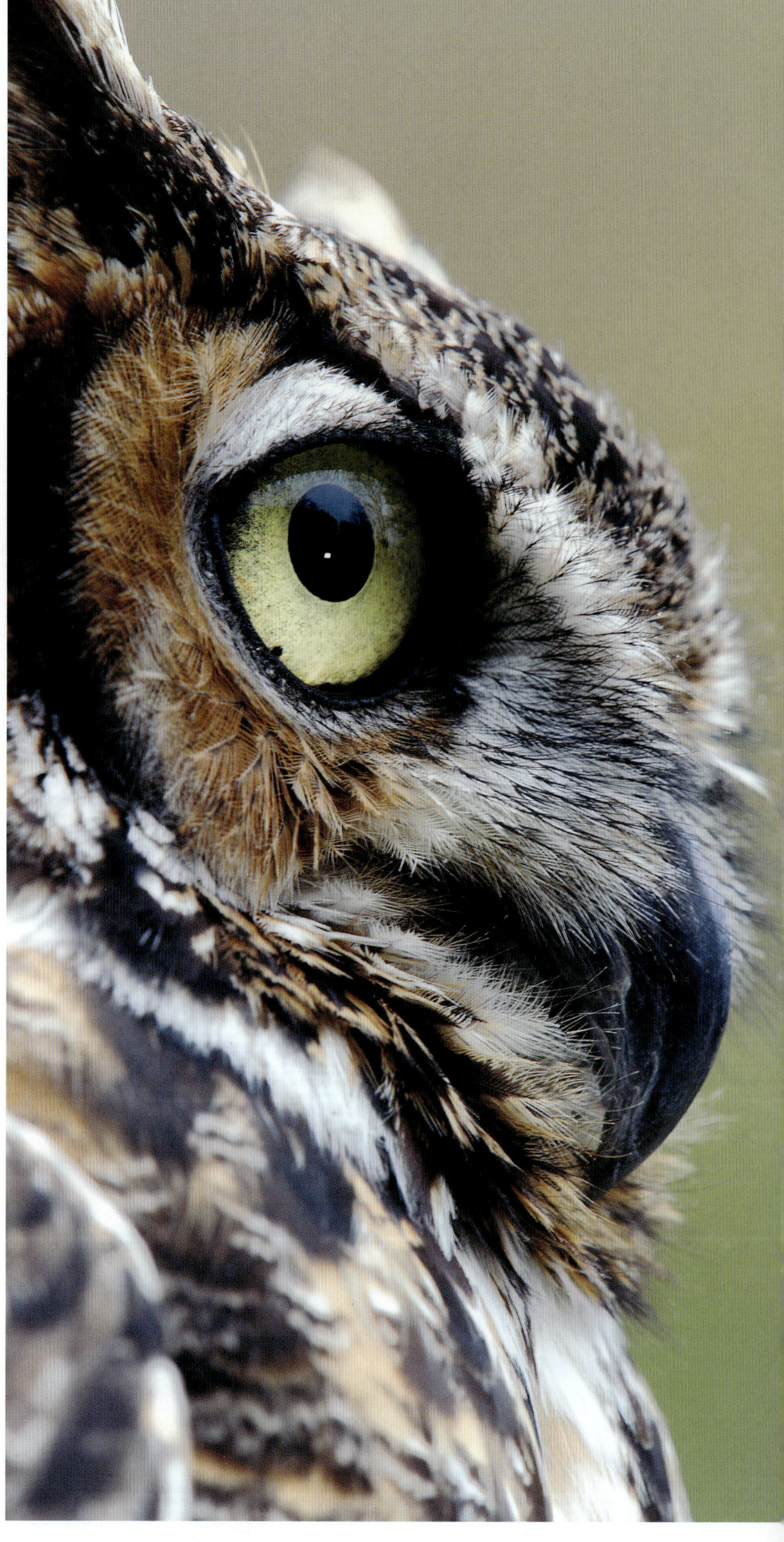

Acknowledgments

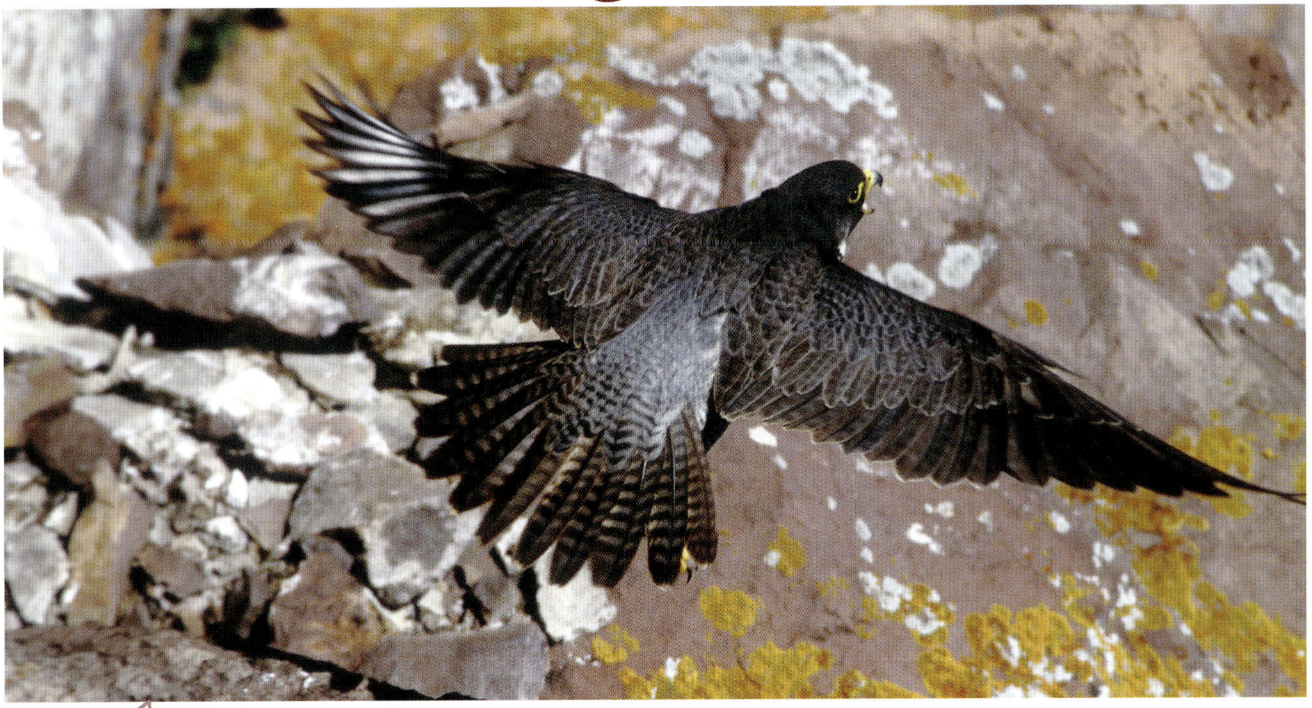

I could not have taken the photographs for this book without the assistance and generosity of many mentors, friends, and acquaintances. Most deserve far more credit than this brief acknowledgment.

Foremost mention goes to my late father, Karl Maslowski, who displayed infinite patience while I learned photography under his tutelage. I should also mention his friend and frequent collaborator, the late Ron Austing. Ron's knowledge of hawks and owls was unsurpassed, and his photo techniques were innovative.

Jack Holt offered remarkable insight into the world of great horned owls and other raptors. Tom Uhlman contributed a number of photos for the book. Greg and Linda McMillan provided essential help in California, as did Terry Peterson. Anthony Mercica was generous with his knowledge. Troy Utterback offered a memorable experience with south Texas raptors in a very special setting. Cindy Alverson, Jerry Meyer and Raptor, Inc., of Cincinnati were helpful in many ways. The Desert Museum near Tucson has a wonderful program on raptors. Years ago the late Worth Randle introduced falconry into an Ohio neighborhood, opening many young eyes to the majesty of raptors. Dave Tepe's falconry skills verged on art. Glenn and Trish Warner of the Bathurst Inlet Lodge in the Arctic regions of Canada provided amazing views of birds in that beautiful and remote region. My brother Dave played a big role in this book's photography. And WILDFOWL CARVING MAGAZINE editor Tom Huntington's creative skills changed a buzzard into an eagle.

Most importantly, Karen and the kids successfully managed to learn to hunt for themselves while I was away capturing elusive images.

Thanks to all!

Steve Maslowki

Contents

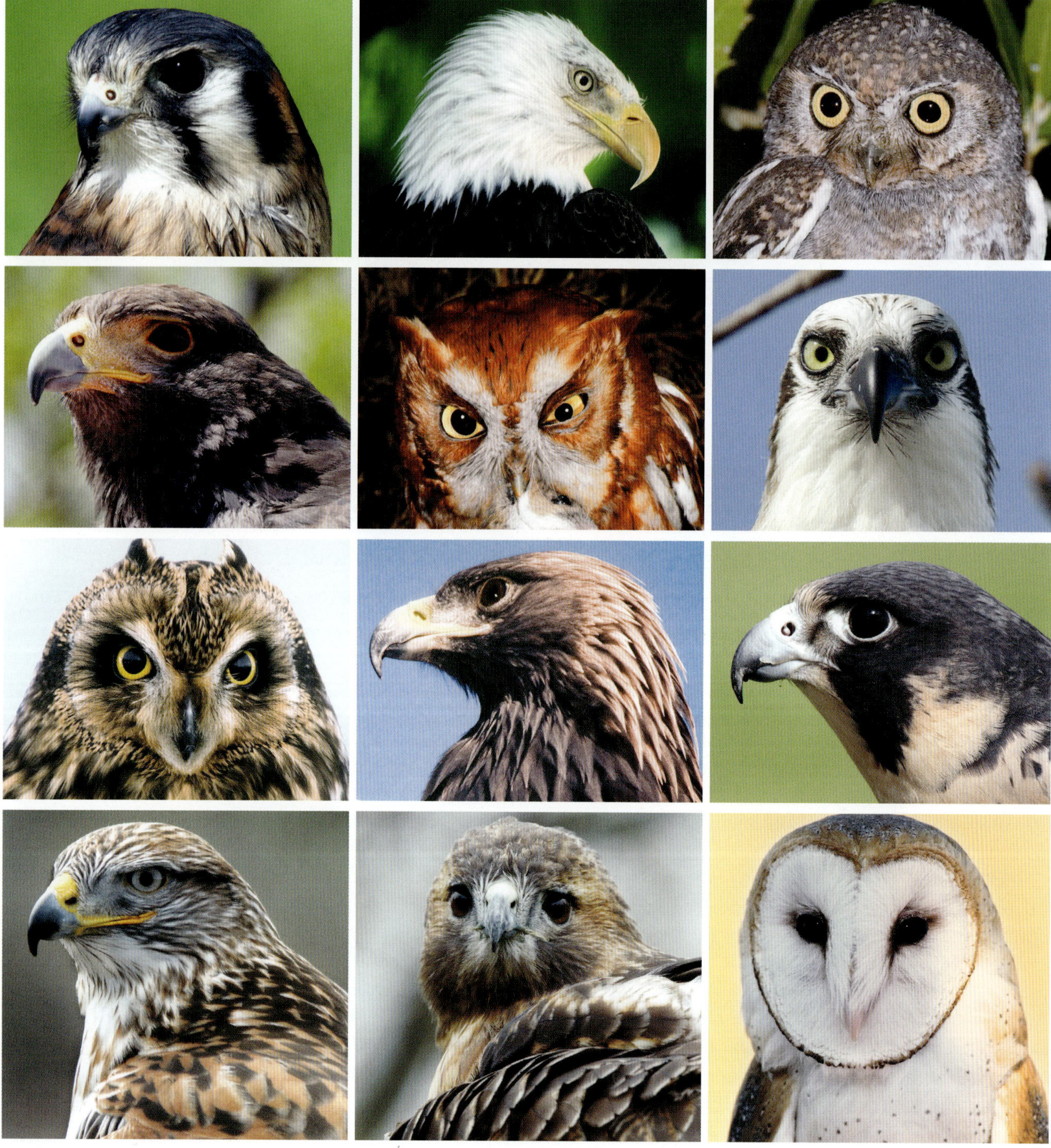

RAPTORS

OWLS

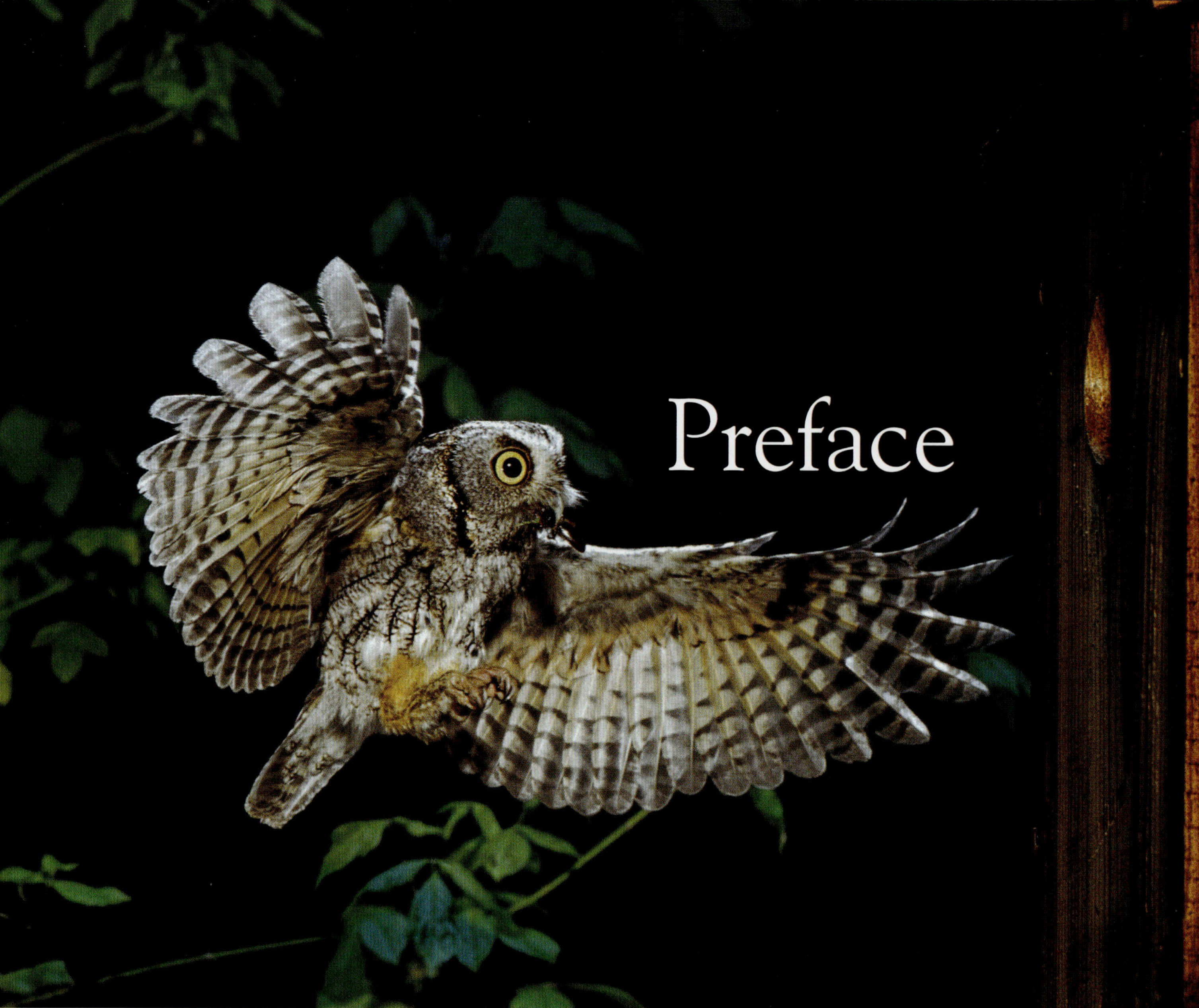

Preface

This book is a sequel of sorts to *Wings on the Water: The Great Gallery of Ducks, Geese and Loons*. Like that book, this one reprints the words from reference articles that appeared in WILDFOWL CARVING MAGAZINE over the years and supplements them with images by award-winning photographer Steve Maslowski.

There's one big difference, though. Many of the birds in this book would eat the ones that appeared in the previous one.

Talons in the Sky takes a close look at eagles, hawks, falcons, and owls—birds with razor-sharp claws and strong snapping beaks. Not to mention the powerful wings that hold them aloft. They are exciting and dynamic creatures, and popular subjects for wildfowl carvers. Does anybody wonder why? Owls, with their air of solemn mystery, have long been the subject of enduring fascination. The great eagles and hawks, those majestic aerial hunters, are equally captivating. Rendering any of these birds in wood is a challenge indeed.

But this book will dazzle even those who have never whittled a stick, much less carved an eagle. Bird enthusiasts and nature lovers alike will thrill to Steve's breathtaking photography and learn something from the accompanying texts. These pages are the next best thing to soaring among the clouds with these stunning birds.

Tom Huntington
Editor, WILDFOWL CARVING MAGAZINE
and COMPETITION

Foreword

WHAT'S IN A NAME?

When it comes to christening some of history's groundbreaking, powerful, and record-setting machines, the answer is, a lot!

Think about it. When Neil Armstrong and Buzz Aldrin landed on the moon's rock-strewn surface back in 1969, Armstrong uttered four words that have become part of the twentieth century lexicon. "The *Eagle* has landed," he said. Not the Turkey. Not the Chickadee. The *Eagle*.

From the iconic P-40 Warhawk of World War II through the F-16 Fighting Falcon and today's F-22 Raptor, humans have referenced birds of prey when they sought names that project strength, integrity, and power for some of their most formidable and deadly machines.

There's a reason for that, and you understand it when you encounter a bird of prey up close for the first time. It's impossible not to feel impressed—even awe-struck. These birds radiate coiled power and grace just by being themselves. They are in a class of their own. It's easy to see why, as I've often stated, these birds are indeed feathered royalty.

I can trace my fascination with these majestic creatures back to my childhood. When I was young, I often wandered the fields and forests near my home. Occasionally I would gaze skyward and receive a thrill from the sight of a hawk or eagle circling high above. During my preteen and teenage years, countless trips to the local Audubon Society fueled my growing interest and curiosity about these elusive, beautiful birds. When I started bird carving, my fledgling hobby provided me with an outlet to express my deep admiration for these birds of prey. Decades later, I'm still channeling my love of these magnificent creatures into my work.

How fortunate we raptor lovers are to live in North America, where we have such a varied and unique selection of owls, hawks, falcons, and eagles to admire. From the rugged coastlines of Maine and maritime Canada to the expansive Pacific shores of the West Coast, we are truly blessed to have so many different raptors sharing the continent with us. From the diminutive yet fierce American kestrel and saw-whet owl up to the mighty great horned owl and golden eagle, this expanded family of meat-eating, winged hunters occupies a special place in nature's grand balance as apex predators.

Whether you use this book as a valuable reference tool or just enjoy it for the inherent beauty of Steve Maslowski's photography, by the time you reach the last page you should have a deep respect and admiration for the fantastic, yet fragile family of winged hunters. Hopefully, this book won't be the end of your journey, but will inspire you to enrich your understanding of and desire to learn more about the compelling family of birds known as raptors.

As an artist and author who has devoted my life to celebrating the majesty of these great birds in sculpture and text, I also hope that you, the reader, will take a moment to reflect on our changing world and consider what steps you can take to preserve wild places and wild things. As Henry David Thoreau so aptly stated, "In wildness is the preservation of the world."

Floyd Scholz is a world-renowned bird carver and the author of several books, including Birds of Prey *and* Owls.

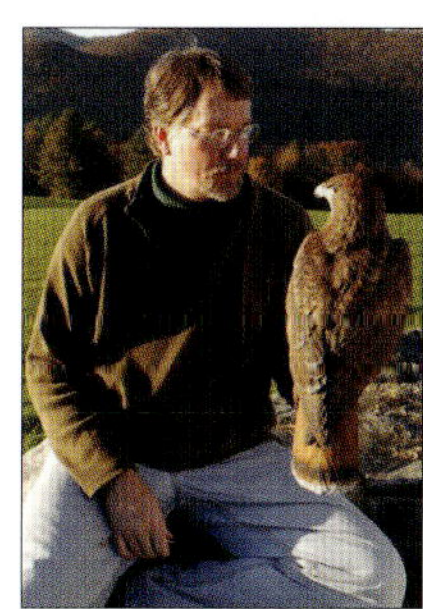

BY STEVE MASLOWSKI

Introduction

You can't ignore raptors. With their hooked beaks, piercing eyes, blood-stained talons, and imperious bearing, they perch at the top of the food chain. One thing that sparks our imagination about them is the knowledge that these creatures live by killing—and they are very good at it.

For most of us, the killing remains something of a mystery. Many people have never seen a hawk or owl capture prey, and those that have probably witnessed it rarely. Maybe an accipiter swooped through the yard at breakneck speed to pluck a finch off the bird feeder. People who live near a coast or waterway might have seen ospreys and eagles plunge for fish. More inland, sparrow hawks sitting on utility wires not infrequently make forays into the grass below for mice or grasshoppers. Still, for the most part, the ways hawks and owls actually hunt and kill stir the imagination.

In the course of shooting the photographs in this book I witnessed predation directly or indirectly on a few special occasions. The most memorable occurred years ago in the middle of winter north of Duluth, Minnesota. The temperature seemed cold enough to freeze the underworld, the wind howled, and snow reached my belt buckle. If I had fallen into some of the drifts, nobody would have found me until spring.

A great gray owl sitting atop a stunted, isolated spruce 30 yards away from me seemed unfazed by either the weather or my presence. The big, fluffy bird made a couple of half-hearted forays over the snow-pack, only to quickly return to the perch. I really wasn't sure what it was doing, since the ground lay 30 inches or so beneath the snow. Then the owl suddenly lifted 30 feet up into the air, carried by the wind, and plunged—*kerplunk!*—belly deep into the snow. A second later a meadow mouse scurried out from beneath the owl, turned, stood up, and squared off to face the bird looming over it. Had the wind not been blowing so hard, I surely would have heard that mouse cussing like a sailor at the owl. The owl did a double-take, reached out with sharp talons, and promptly ended that rodent's last great act of defiance. I can't figure out if the event was a comedy, a tragedy, or simply one of those win-lose situations.

I'm aware of the details of the capture because I happened to be shooting movies at the time, and I have replayed the footage numerous times. It still amazes me that the owl found the mouse. The rodent must have tunneled up through the snow to reach a weed seedpod at the surface. The owl detected movement, but was not quite sure where the mouse was. When the owl struck, it missed the mouse, but the startled rodent jumped and broke through the snow.

Perhaps for the great grays of the world, every catch includes an element of serendipity.

In a warmer place—central California—I was delighted to witness—albeit indirectly—the hunting prowess of barn owls, specifically a pair I observed nesting in a hayloft. I should point out that by nature I am more of a diurnal hawk than a nocturnal owl. I like daylight, and I am ready to roost once the sun goes down. So it was with some dread that I climbed into the blind for the first night of photography at the barn owl's nest. Happily, no more than half an hour after dark an adult arrived with a pocket gopher for the nestlings. An owlet quickly grabbed the gopher, turned its back to the others so they could not get to it, and spent the next few minutes swallowing the carcass in a series of massive gulps. (Owls generally tend to eat things whole, while hawks tear prey apart into more mannerly bites.) After consuming the pocket gopher, the owlet settled down and fell asleep.

There were five young in the nest, and about every half-hour thereafter another pocket gopher was delivered and devoured, and the sated consumer went to sleep. By 10 o'clock, I was the only one still awake, but barely. So I followed the owlets' example—without, I should add, eating a pocket gopher.

The same feeding schedule took place every time I sat in the blind. The adult owls were like machines, efficient and dependable. I saw pocket gophers only

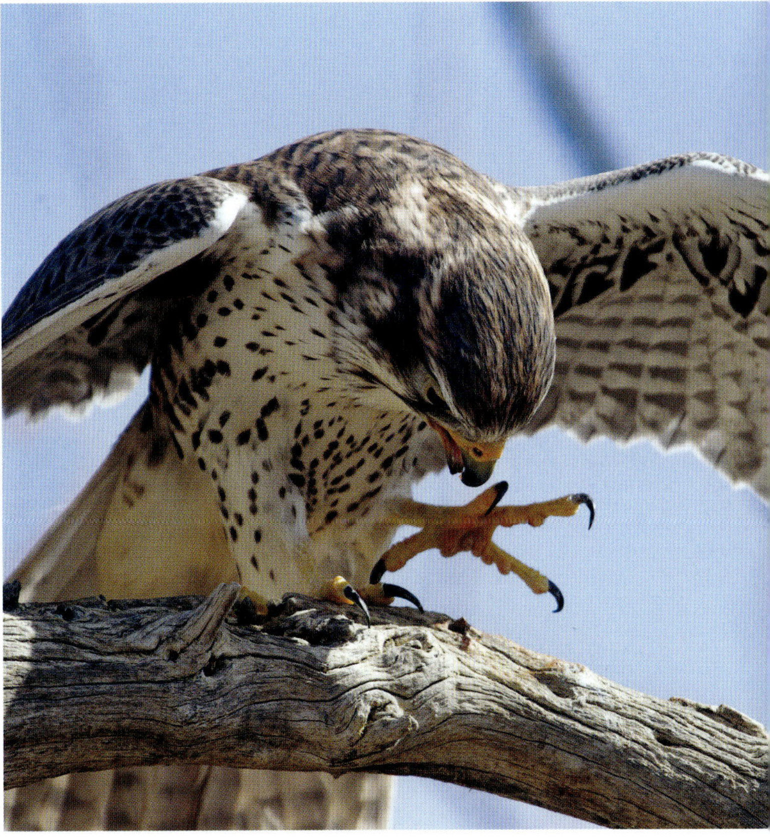

rarely during the day, but the place must have crawled with them at night. Of course I was never awake to see them.

While the barn owls seemed to live on pocket gophers exclusively, a pair of screech owls I photographed in Ohio were far more flexible. The nest was in a suburb, and on warm nights I could watch the owls hunt below street lamps to catch moths and beetles. On wet nights, the owls often caught night crawlers, which stretched across the grass in some sort of courtship activity. And on cold nights when neither bug nor worm moved much, the owls visited a nearby creek and caught three-inch stoneroller minnows. In addition, they caught an occasional mouse or bird, and one evening dinner even included a starling. The starling was almost as big as the owl, and you could almost hear the labored breath of the raptor as it airlifted that heavy package.

Of course, I watched hawks, too. A pair of red-shoulders in my suburban neighborhood delivered all manner of snakes and frogs from an area that seemed bereft of them. In Montana, I watched harriers course over hayfields. Most of the time the raptors disappeared into the grass, only to emerge after a considerable while. Had the predators been eating or resting? However, on some occasions a hawk lifted off immediately with a squirming mouse in its clutches.

Also in Montana, I encountered an amazing collection of raptor nests amidst a plain of plenty. The local countryside featured rolling grassland where some dry-grain farming took place. The rich, loose, silty soil must have been perfect for burrowing rodents. This probably generated more food for the local Swainson's and ferruginous hawks than they could eat. The problem was, the landscape was almost empty of trees. The birds had a surplus of food for themselves and their young, but they lacked nesting places. So it appeared they lowered their standards. They built nests in small, scraggly trees sometimes barely eight feet off the ground. Every other tree seemed to have its carefully tended pile of sticks, and each nest usually sheltered the maximum-sized clutch or brood, well-fed. This high-density housing stretched along a highway for about 25 miles.

While raptors' claim to fame is their reputation as killing machines, I think one of the more surprising features about them is their variety. For sure, there are too many North American varieties to cover in this book. There are about 15 species of owls, while daylight skies fill with more than 35 kinds of diurnal raptors, which include vultures, hawks, falcons, eagles, ospreys, and the like. Each species seems to have its own temperament. For example, red-tails are patient, but determined, while Cooper's are high-strung and active. Peregrine falcons dive-bomb birds in mid-air, while prairie falcons dive-bomb prey on or near the ground. Burrowing owls think the best place to nest is in an old ground squirrel den, while barn owls—the world's most widespread owl species—thrive in the presence of rural humans who maintain farm buildings amidst pastures and grasslands. Swainson's hawks don't like the cold and live in the United States only during spring and summer, while snowy owls avoid the heat and come to the lower 48 just in the severest days of winter.

Raptors are no less varied and specialized in size, shape, and color. They all share hooked beaks, sharp talons, amazing eyes, and that imperious bearing. It is no small task to capture the essence of a raptor, whether on film or in wood. But it is certainly worth the try. And dinner doesn't depend on it.

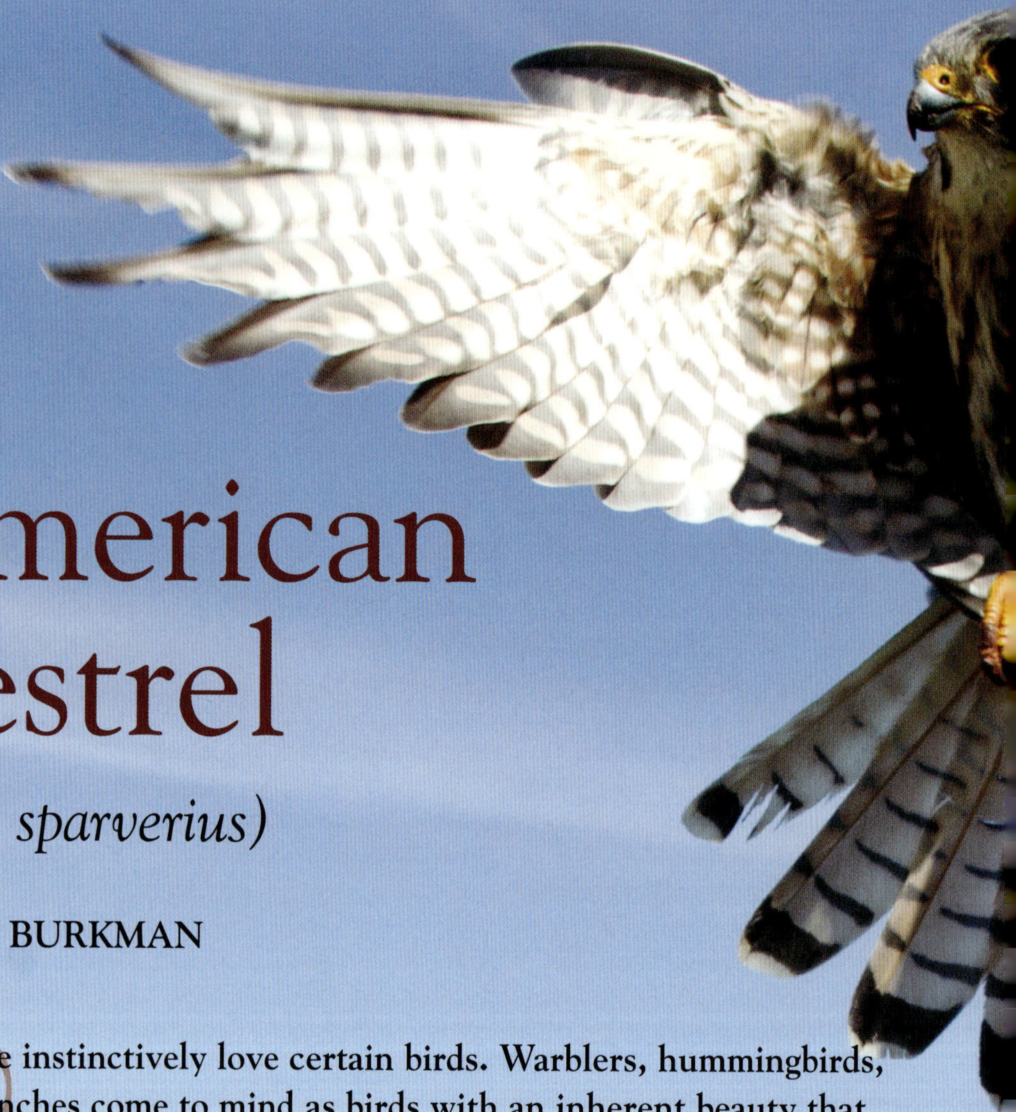

American Kestrel

(Falco sparverius)

BY RICK BURKMAN

People instinctively love certain birds. Warblers, hummingbirds, and finches come to mind as birds with an inherent beauty that endears them to many. Then there are birds that people tolerate but claim not to like too much, despite their obvious allure. These include gulls, jays, and anything with an abundance of black feathers. However, there are some birds that, by their very nature, command admiration, respect, and even a degree of reverence. They are beautiful, strong birds of nobility—the graceful and awe-inspiring falcons.

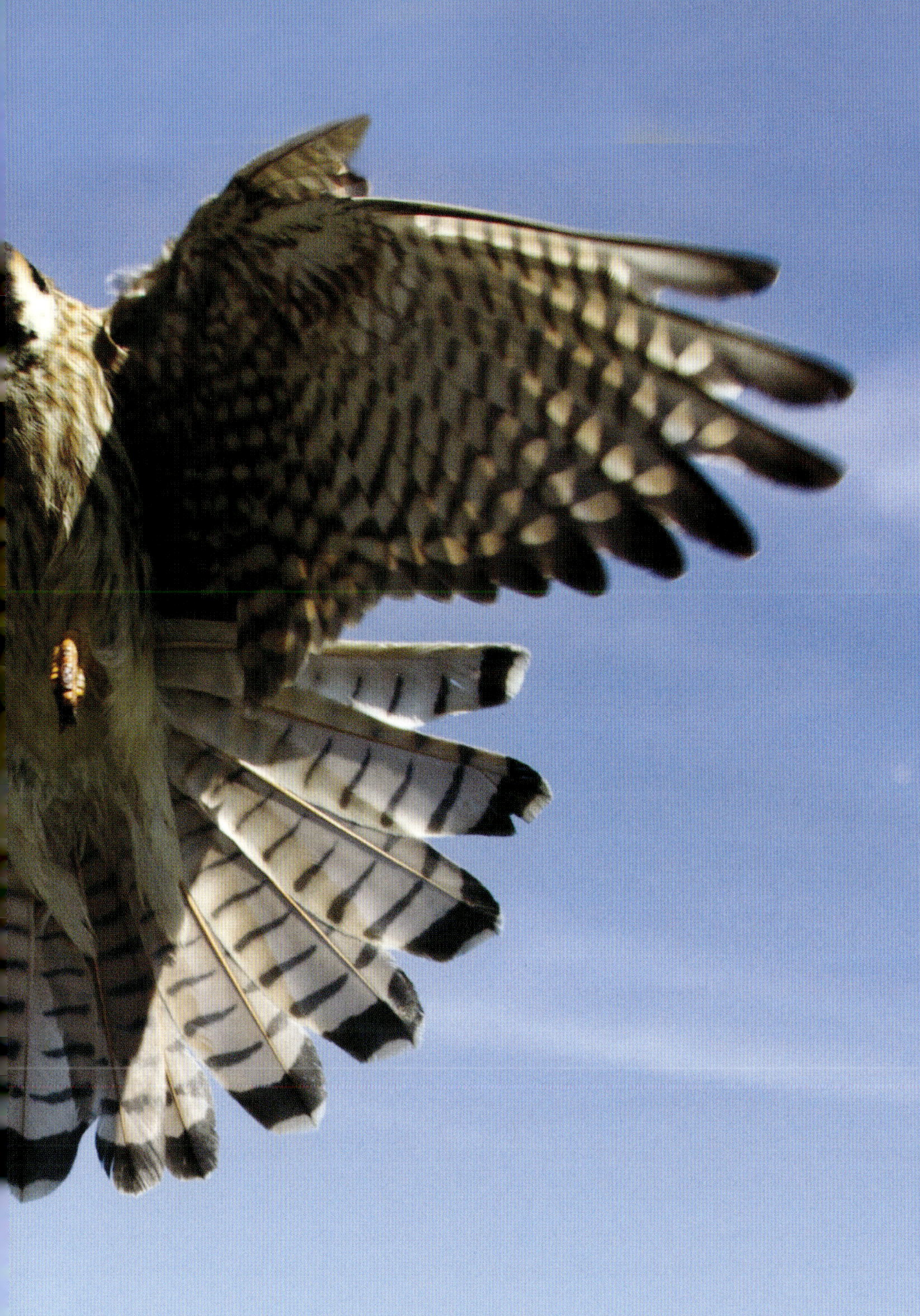

An American kestrel reveals its barred underparts as it swoops in for a landing. These little falcons are commonly known as sparrow hawks.

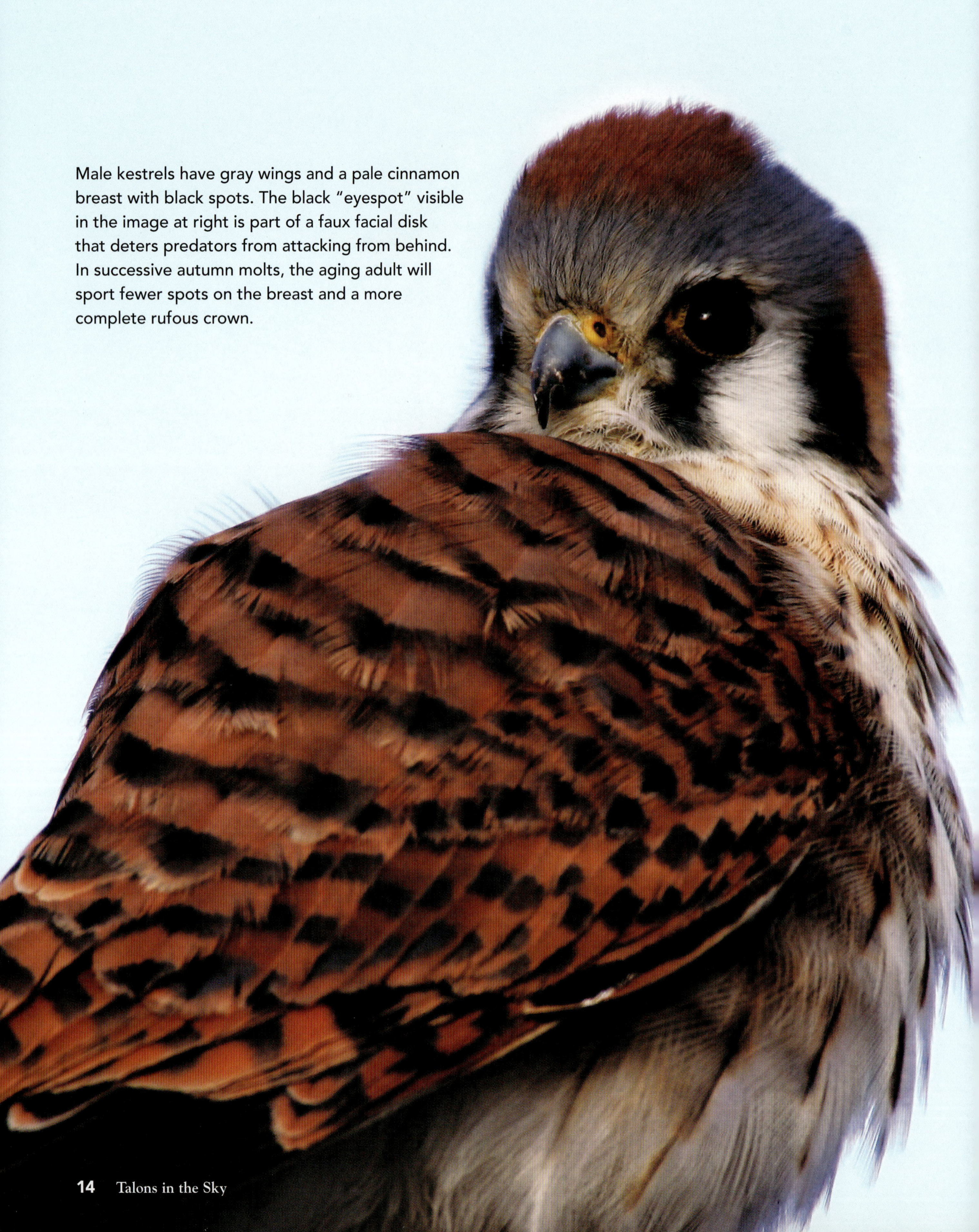

Male kestrels have gray wings and a pale cinnamon breast with black spots. The black "eyespot" visible in the image at right is part of a faux facial disk that deters predators from attacking from behind. In successive autumn molts, the aging adult will sport fewer spots on the breast and a more complete rufous crown.

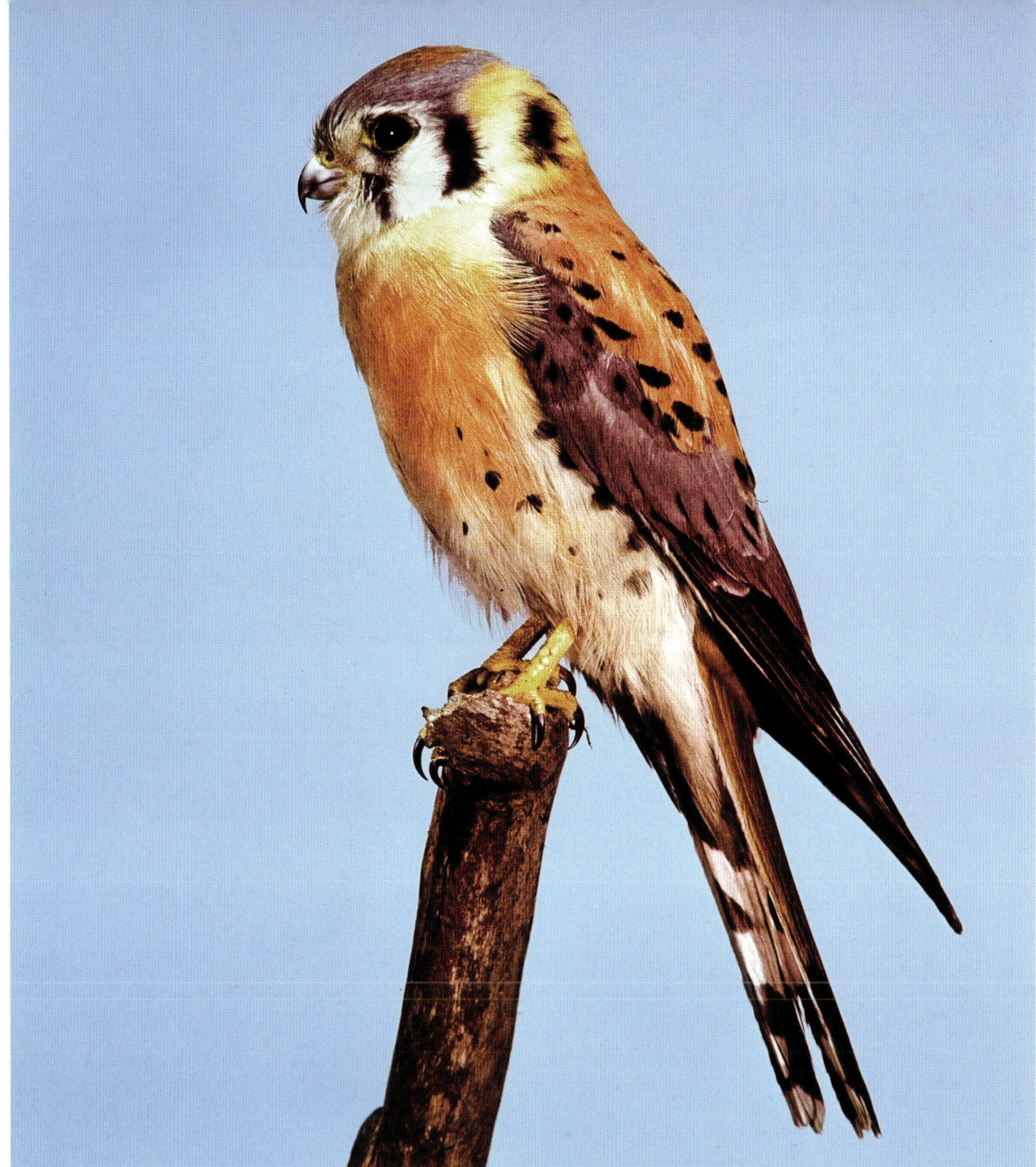

North American falcons range from large and powerful hunters such as the arctic-loving gyrfalcon, capable of capturing geese and grouse as it cruises the tundra; to the robin-size American kestrel, which can hover effortlessly over freshly plowed fields before dropping onto an unsuspecting grasshopper or field mouse.

Once known as the sparrow hawk, the American kestrel (*Falco sparverius*) is one of the world's smallest falcons. But don't be misled by their size—these birds are skilled hunters with finely tuned senses to seek and capture prey.

Fortunately, the prey the kestrel chooses is appropriate to its size. Grasshoppers are a perennial favorite, but beetles, butterflies, dragonflies, and moths are also taken. Like most wild creatures, kestrels are opportunistic and cosmopolitan when choosing prey, so their diet is not restricted to insects. Mice, shrews, voles, and even bats, as well as fish, lizards, snakes, and small birds are all part of the kestrel diet.

Kestrels like to hunt and nest where humans live and play. They are commonly seen perched on power lines and fence posts and hunting agricultural fields, golf courses, and roadsides. Kestrels sit on elevated

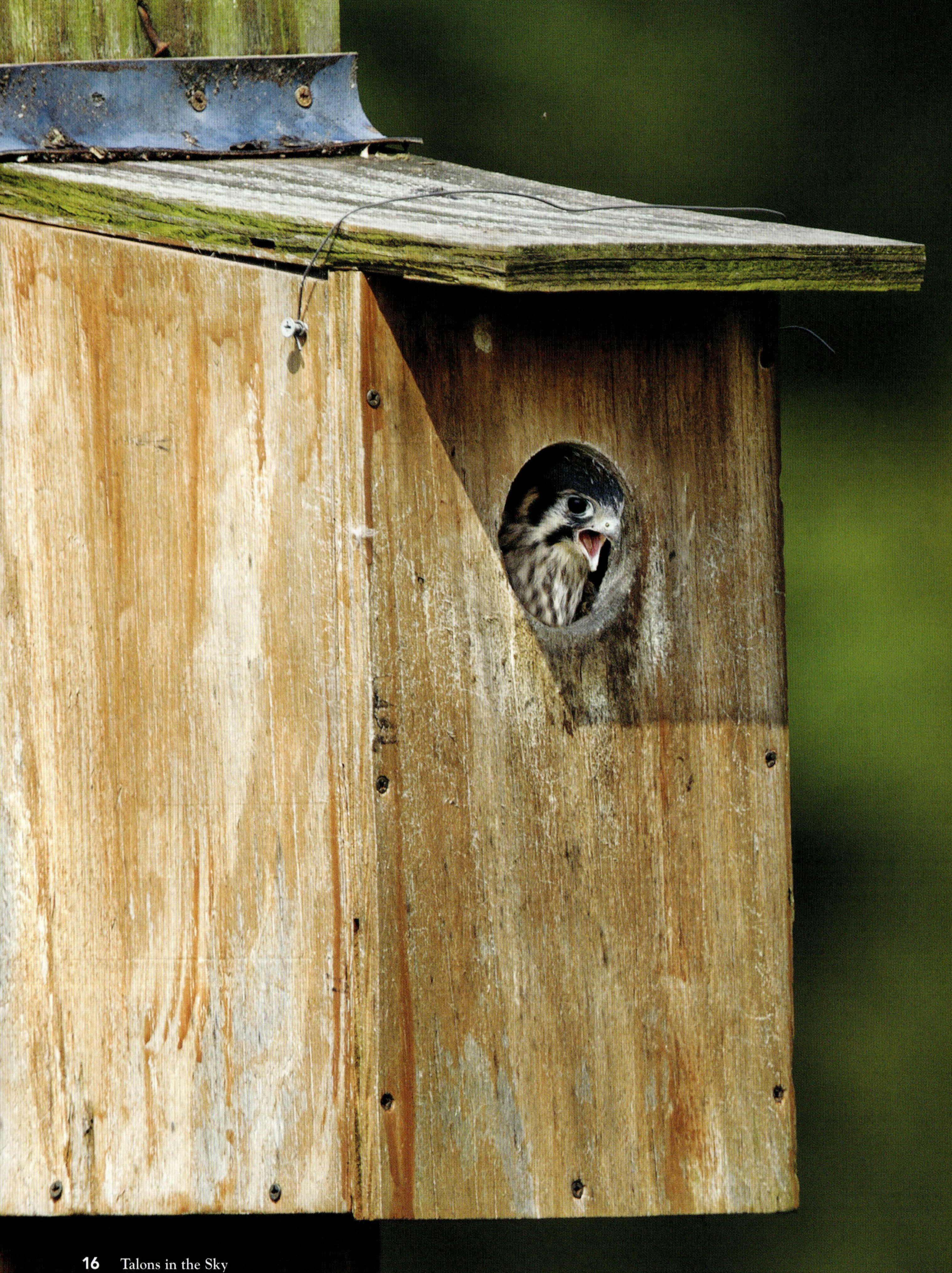

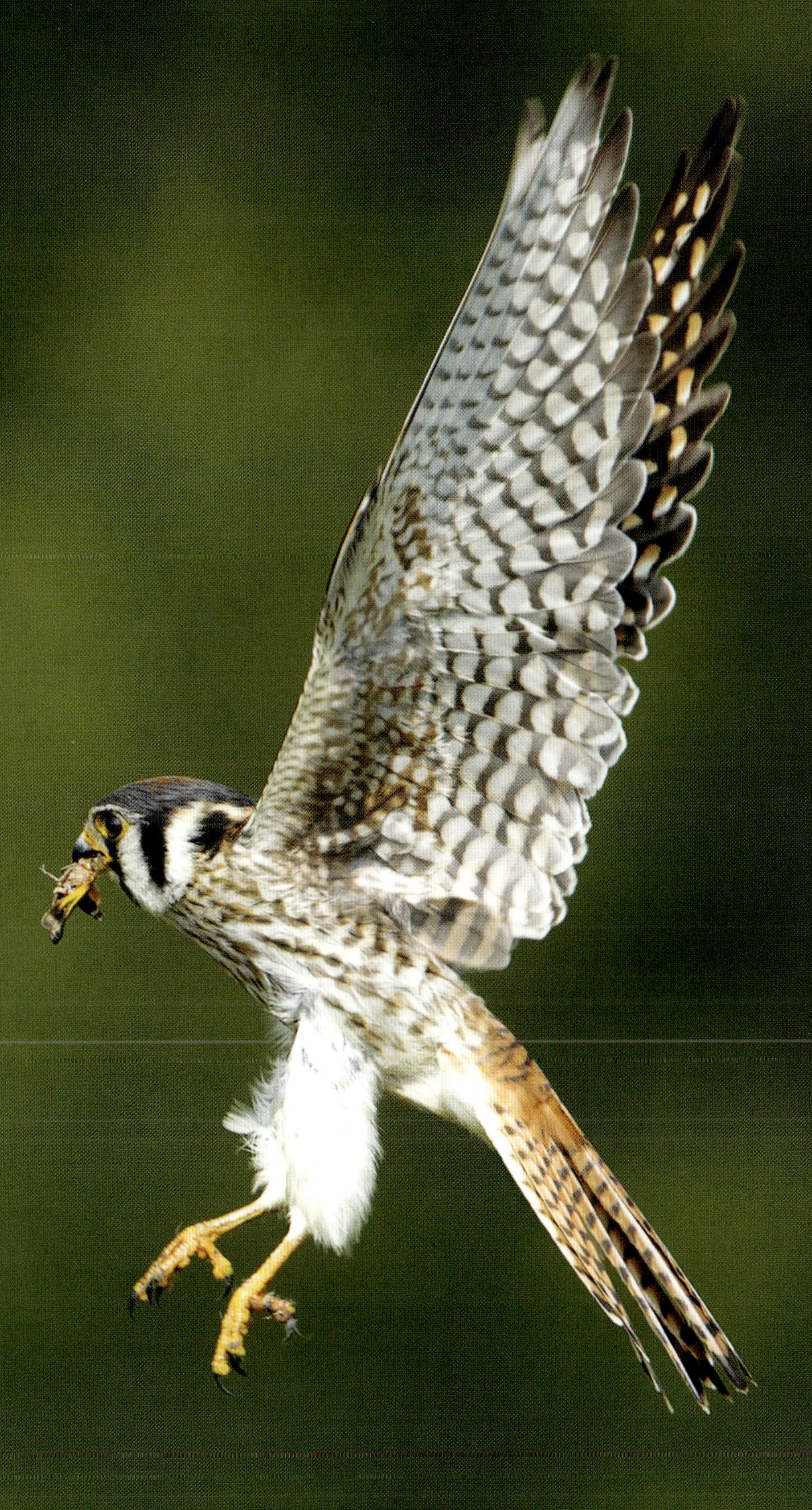

A kestrel brings a cricket back to its nest box. Kestrels have long toes with strong, curved talons. Unlike larger raptors, kestrels don't use their feet as their primary killing tools. Instead, they use them to capture prey on the wing or, more commonly, to knock it off balance for an easier capture. The bird uses its notched bill, not its talons, to dispatch prey.

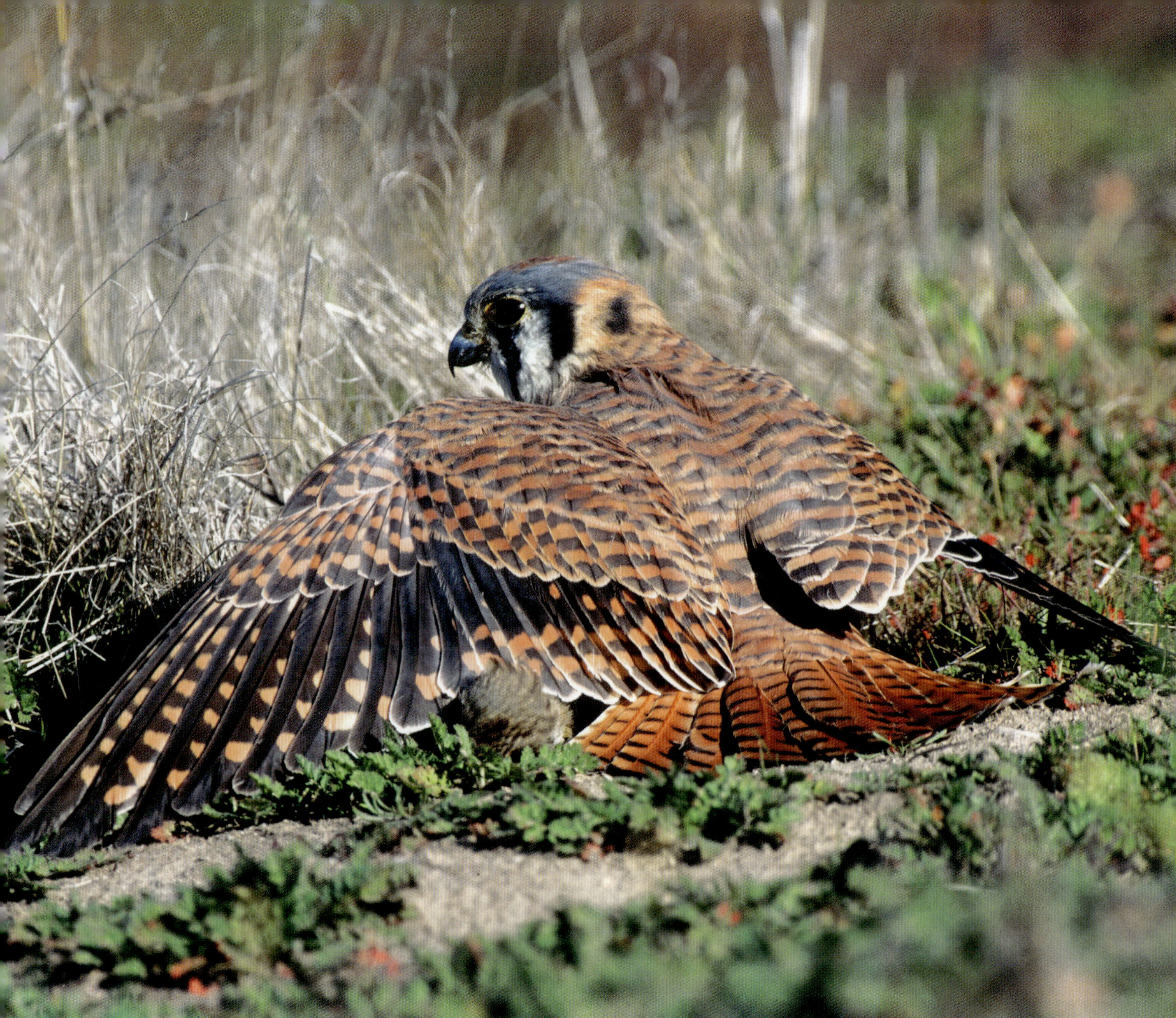

perches, intently scanning the ground below. If an elevated perch is not available, a hunting kestrel will hover over open ground, flapping its wings and adjusting its tail to ride the air currents as it holds its head still and pointed into the wind. (This behavior has given rise to one of its common names, windhover.)

They use their exceptional eyesight to spy a rustle in the leaves or the twitching of a single blade of grass, subtle clues to the presence of a tasty morsel. A hunting kestrel focuses on any area of movement, bobbing its head to pinpoint the exact location of its prey. After it zeroes in on its target, it pounces and grabs the hapless creature with its needle-sharp talons. The falcon then bites the prey's neck using its maxillary toma, a characteristic area of downward curvature on the bill of falcons designed to sever a victim's spinal cord.

Kestrels will eat small prey immediately, but usually take a larger animal to a nearby perch. They cache leftovers in fence posts, clumps of grass, or nearby trees for eating another day. During the breeding season, the tierce (male falcon) will capture food and present it to the female as a courting gift. This is the raptor version of a box of chocolates.

Although kestrels have adapted to man-made habitats, like other birds of prey, they have also suffered at the hands of men.

During the decades of agricultural experimentation, tilled fields provided ideal places for kestrels to hunt. Persistent pesticides, such as DDT, used to control agricultural pests were poison not only to the bugs, but also to the animals and birds that ate them.

For many years, all birds of prey were viewed as com-

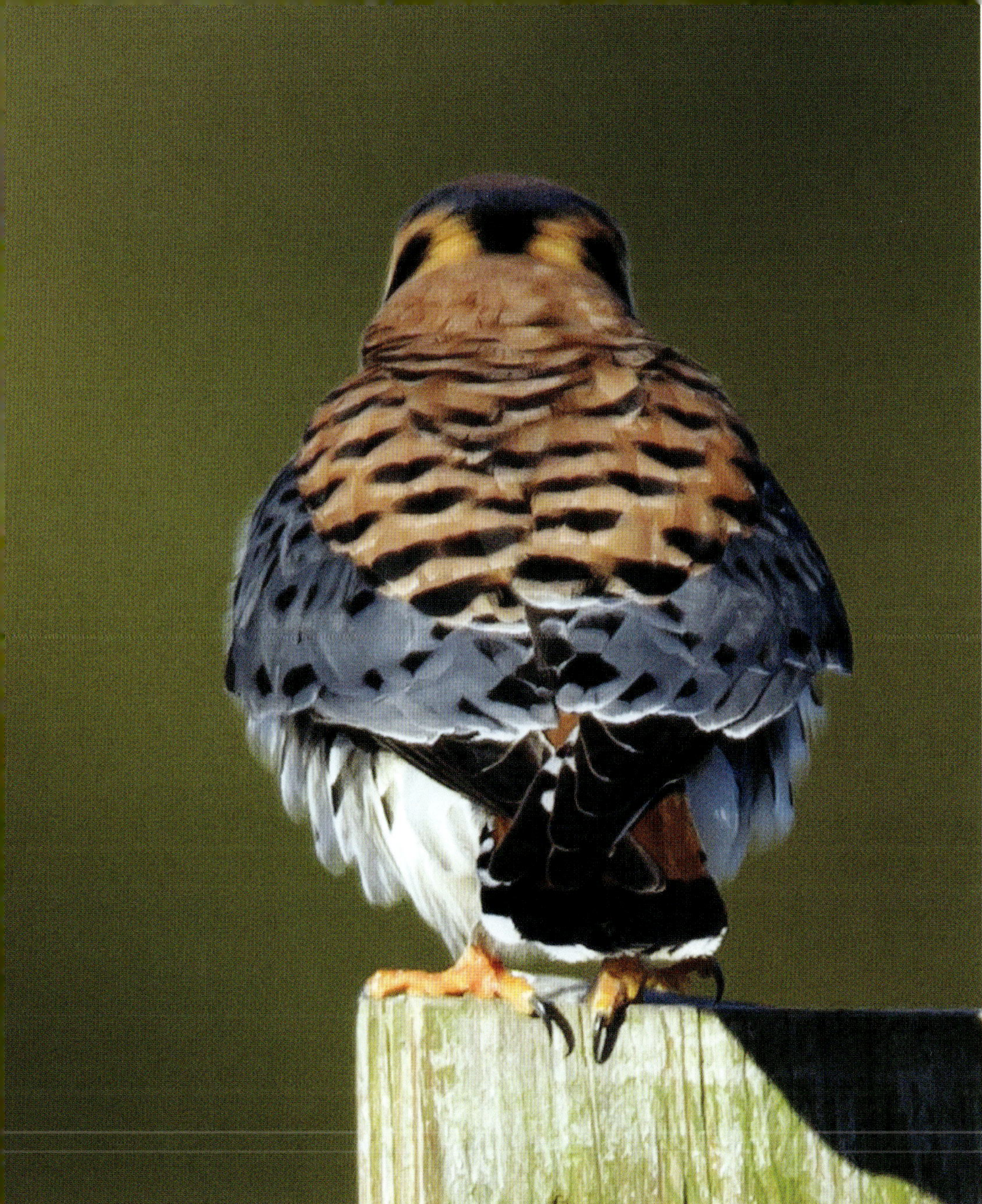

OPPOSITE PAGE: A female kestrel "mantles" over her prey. The dramatic black markings on the head are similar to those on the male. **LEFT:** The tail feathers on the male have a light fringe with a dark subterminal band. The "face" on the back of the head is obvious here.

petitors for animals that men liked—gamebirds, small game animals, and songbirds. Raptors were hunted relentlessly. At migration funnels around the country, hunters would line up during the migration season to randomly shoot birds of prey as they passed. Hundreds of hawks, kestrels included, were killed during these hunting trips.

But during these periods, bird lovers and hunters kept another sport alive—the sport of kings—falconry. There's a certain thrill in training another creature to hunt at the will of the hunter.

But unlike our better-known hunting companion, the dog, raptors have no affinity for the people with whom they hunt. Dogs live to please, but given a chance, any bird of prey will fly off with no regrets or sense of loss. This bit of independence and wildness is one of the endearing qualities of birds of prey. You can take the bird out of the wild, but the wild always stays in the bird.

Kestrels continue to play a vital role in the world of falconry. Their small size makes them relatively easy to handle, so they have become great first birds for beginning falconers. And, because of their affinity for nesting near human habitations, they're relatively easy to capture. Unlike some wild animals, kestrels adapt relatively well to captivity, making them favorite exhibits at zoos and wilderness parks.

Although they have adapted to human environs, kestrels are not always tolerant of humans in the vicinity. They scream their "killy, killy, killy" cry when people venture too close to their nests, but people fare better than typical kestrel competitors.

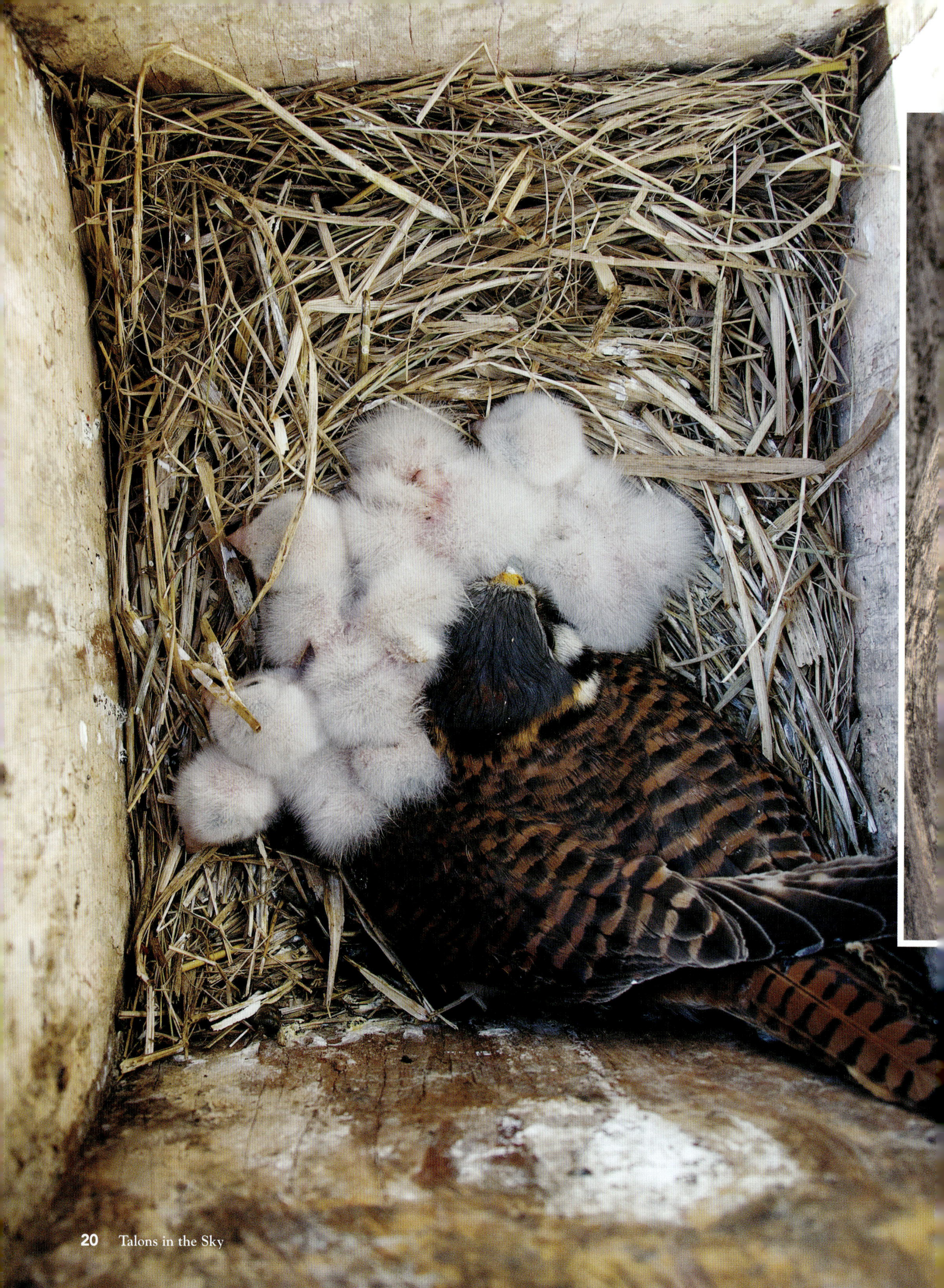

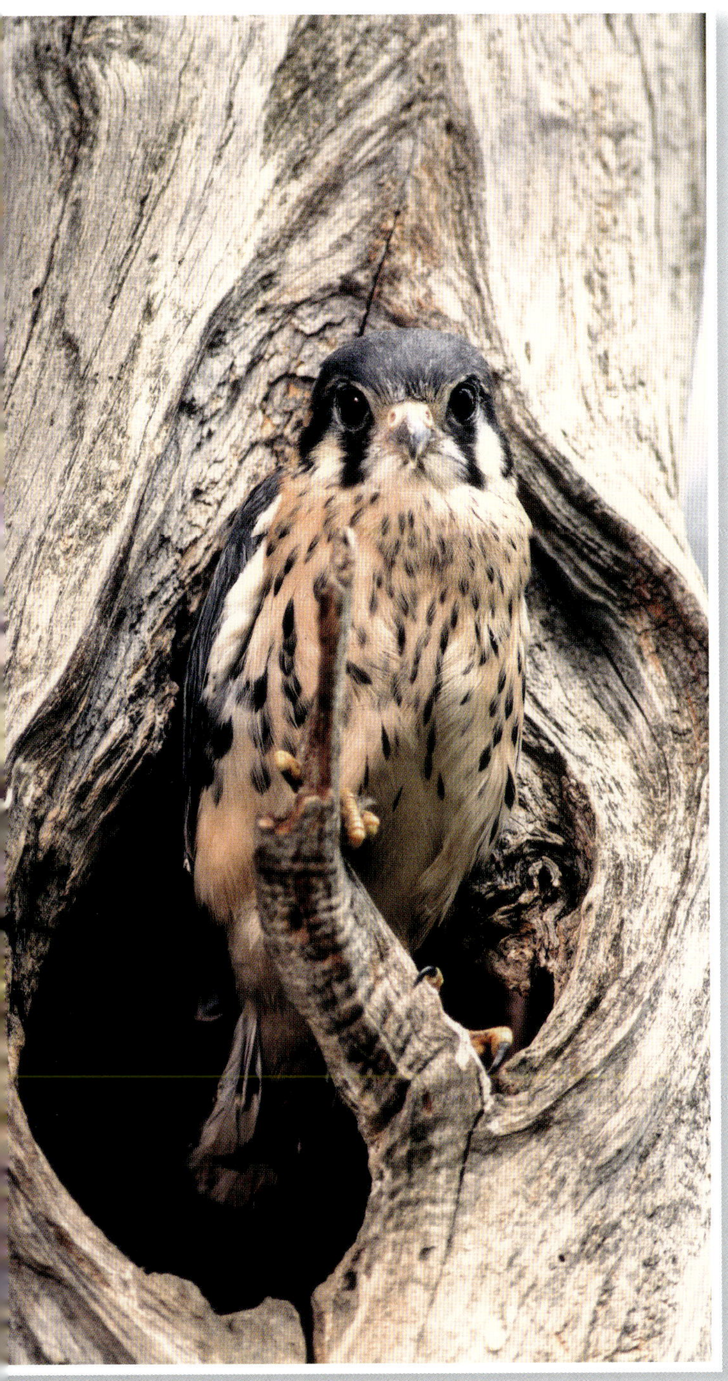

OPPOSITE: A female kestrel huddles with her young in a nest box. The female lays three to seven eggs per brood and spends 27 to 30 days incubating them. **ABOVE:** Kestrels do not build stick nests. Instead, they use abandoned cavities to lay their eggs with little to no nesting material. This makes them natural candidates for artificial nest boxes.

Couples actively defend territories during the breeding season—chasing and harassing crows, hawks, ravens, and other kestrels, sometimes leading to malicious attacks to the point of locking talons with intruding kestrels and tumbling through the air.

Once a kestrel bonds to a mate, the business of raising a family begins. Unlike other falcons, the kestrel likes to use cavities with small entrance holes in broken or hollow trees and cacti for nest sites. The male searches his territory for appropriate nesting spots. As he finds them, he presents them to his mate. She may choose one of the selected cavities, or, in rare cases, she may lay her eggs in the abandoned stick nests of red-tailed hawks, merlins, or crows.

Once the nest cavity is chosen, nest building is over. The pair makes a small scrape on the cavity floor but adds nothing to enhance the softness or insulative value of the cavity. Because they need little more than a cavity for a nest, they readily accept man-made nest boxes. However, if you build one, make sure to add a layer of sawdust or other insulating material, or the birds will lay their eggs directly on the hard floor, reducing the chances of survival.

Once the nest site is chosen, the female lays her eggs. She lays between three and seven dull white or cream-colored oval eggs, some with violet or brown splotches, over a period of one or two weeks. There is occasionally some confusion over the ownership of a nest cavity. Kestrel eggs have been found mixed with clutches of screech owl eggs, and kestrels have been seen incubating wood duck eggs. In another instance, a bufflehead egg was found in a kestrel nest.

When all the eggs are laid, incubation begins. The mother sits on the eggs for 27 to 30 days. The male provides occasional breaks, but it's largely the female's duty to keep the eggs warm as they mature. The tierce is not an absentee parent during the process. Instead, he fiercely guards the territory, chasing encroaching enemies away from the nesting area.

When not patrolling for intruders, he is the primary provider for the family. Each day, he delivers food, first to the nesting female, then, after the eggs hatch, to the voracious young.

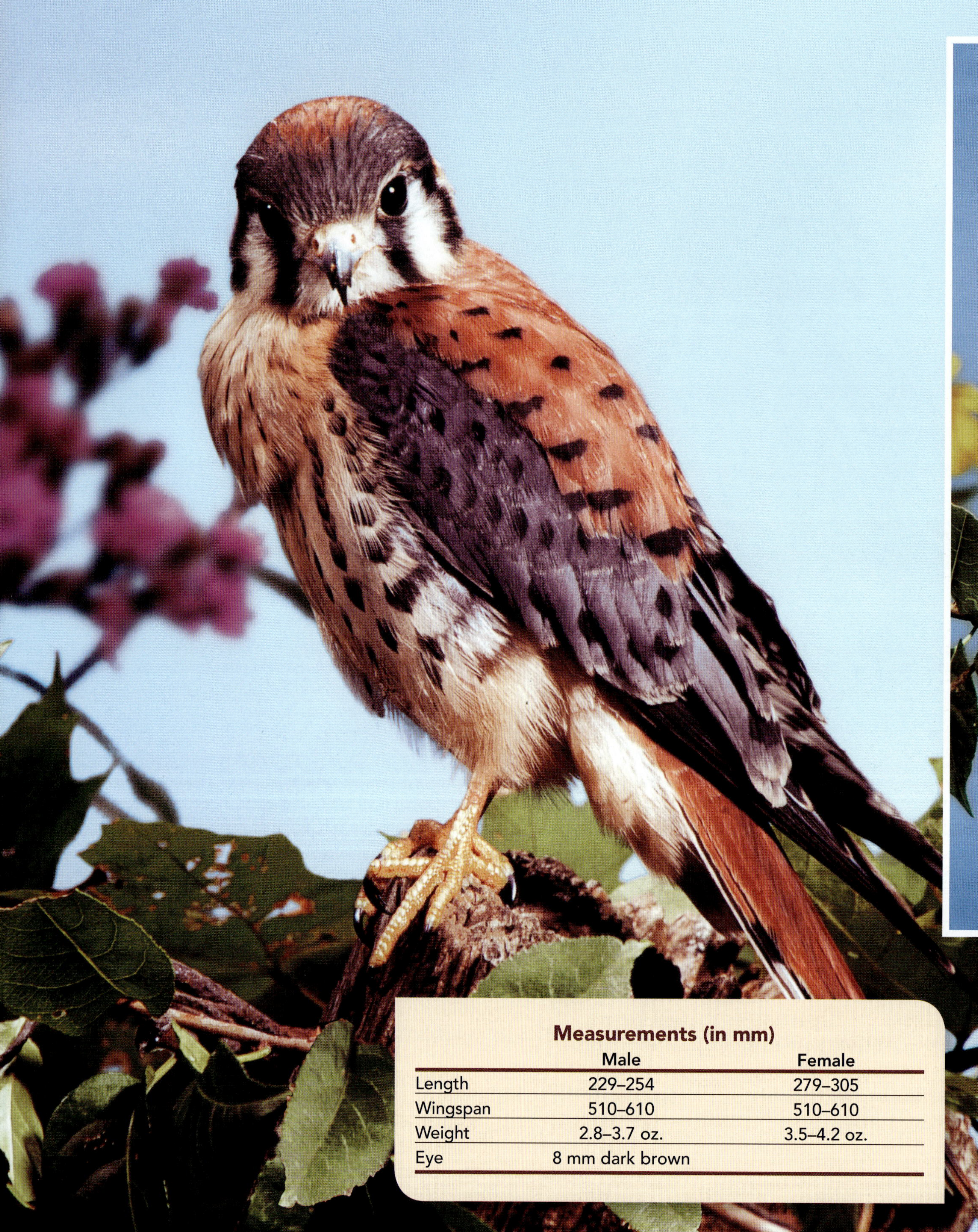

Measurements (in mm)	Male	Female
Length	229–254	279–305
Wingspan	510–610	510–610
Weight	2.8–3.7 oz.	3.5–4.2 oz.
Eye	8 mm dark brown	

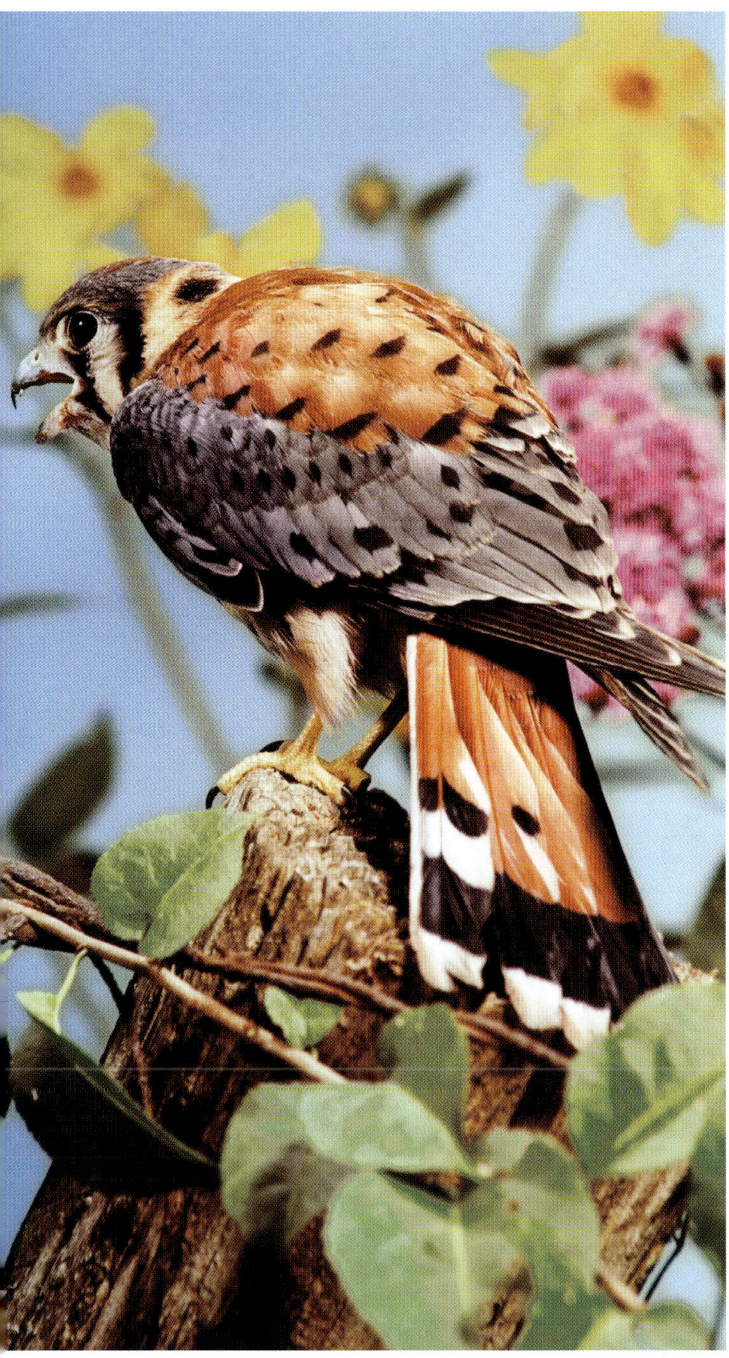

LEFT: This male's open beak shows the notch in the lower mandible, which helps secure prey while the "tooth" of the upper mandible provides deadly, shearing pressure. **OPPOSITE PAGE:** Examine the serious brow in head-on photos of the kestrel. It's a serious, no-nonsense attitude. The full rufous crown indicates that this is an older bird.

The first egg laid is the first to hatch; the rest of the chicks emerge over a period of three to four days. The female becomes excited when the eggs are about to hatch, and she occasionally helps free the struggling chicks by tugging and breaking pieces of the shell. Eggshells are eaten or dropped in the nest where they are stepped on and broken to eventually become part of the cavity floor.

Newly emerged young are helpless creatures covered in white down. They are so weak from the confinement in their shells that they cannot yet lift their heads to beg for food. However, their dutiful parents provide a protein-rich diet, and the chicks grow rapidly. Within a week, an eyass (young bird of prey) in the nest has the strength and muscle coordination to roll over and make a show of defending itself with needle-sharp talons and a cutting beak.

After two weeks, feathers cover their bodies, and males can be distinguished from females by their color patterns. Thirty days after hatching, the young have fledged. They may return to the nest for nighttime protection for the next few weeks, but the nest quickly becomes too crowded for comfort. Soon the young birds are hunting for themselves and getting ready for lives of their own.

The eyasses quickly morph into their adult plumage. Both males and females are exquisitely colored in shades of blue gray, cinnamon, and buff. Males have a blue-gray crown, white cheeks, and two black moustache marks on each side of the face. Their backs are rufous-colored with black bars on the lower half; the breast is white to rufous; and the tail is rufous with a black terminal band.

Females are equally colorful, but with a different pattern. They are approximately 10 percent larger than males, and their heads are similar in color, but paler. Their backs are reddish brown with dark brown barring; the breast is cream-colored with reddish-brown streaks; and the tail is reddish brown with eight dark brown bands and a wide subterminal band.

Although tiny in the world of predators, this sharp-taloned dynamo is a colorful and worthy representative of the falcon world—a touch of the wild in our own backyards.

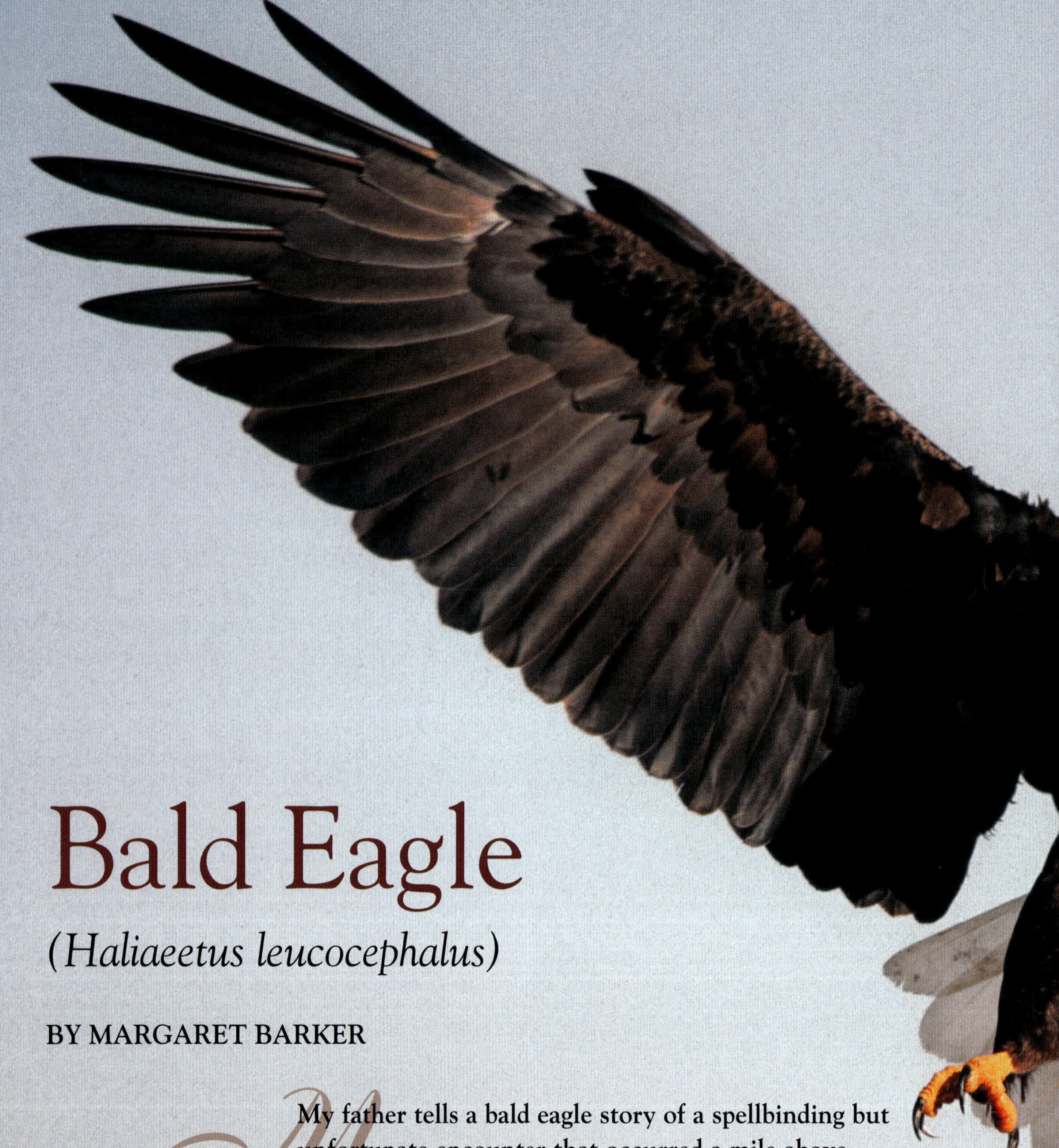

Bald Eagle

(Haliaeetus leucocephalus)

BY MARGARET BARKER

My father tells a bald eagle story of a spellbinding but unfortunate encounter that occurred a mile above the earth. It is one of my earliest recollections of this magnificent bird.

Back in the fall of 1945, my dad was ferrying a B-17 from Independence, Kansas, to the "airplane graveyard" in Kingman, Arizona. En route over Shamrock, Texas, at an altitude of 5,600 feet, his view was all clear blue sky—that is, until he saw the eagle just ahead of him. "I came on that beautiful, soaring bird so fast. No time to steer away. It

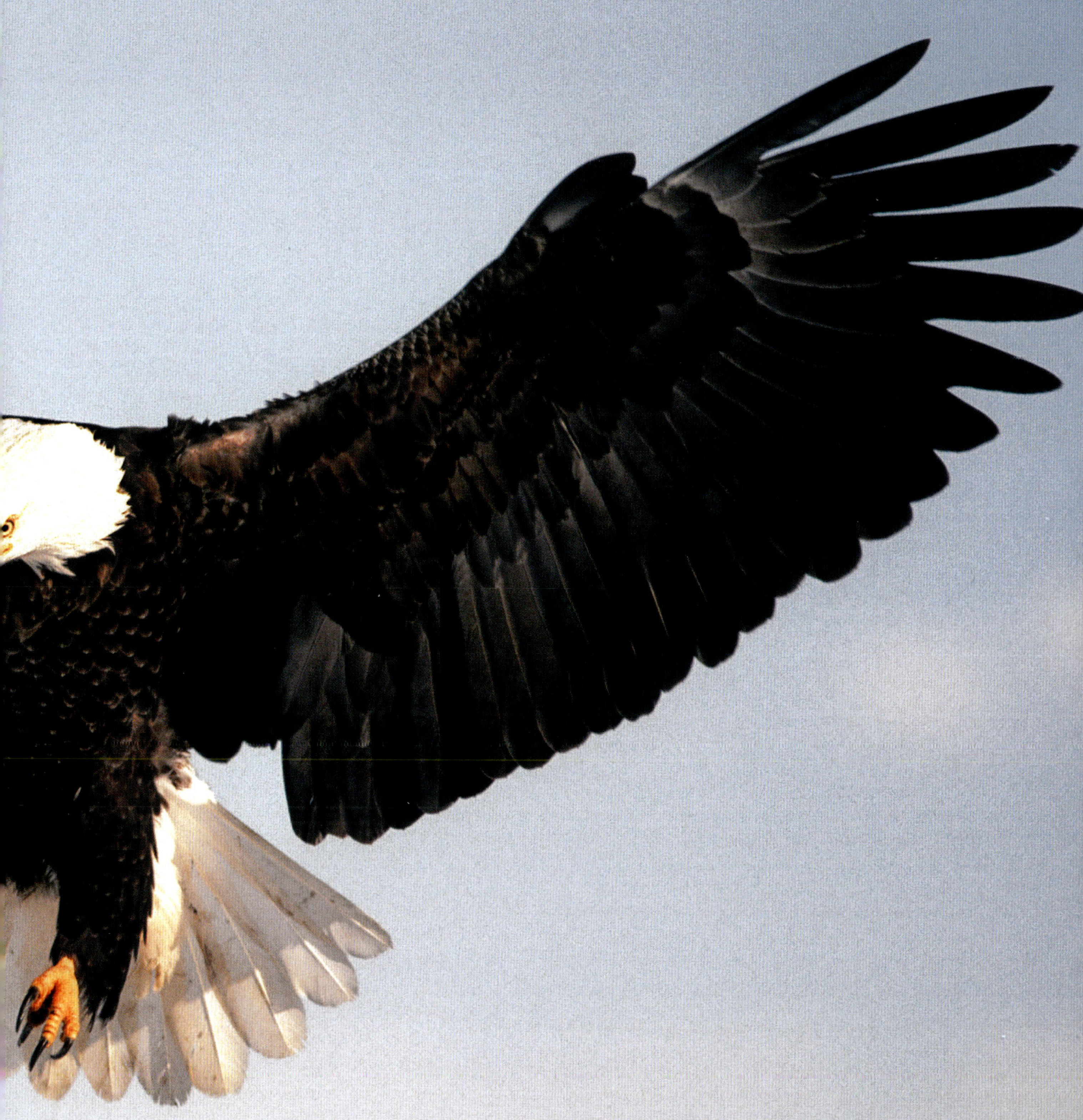

With a wingspan that can stretch seven feet, a bald eagle in the air is an awe-inspiring sight. The alulas, roughly equivalent to the bird's "thumbs," are very evident in this image. These feathers are very important to the bird aerodynamically during slow flight.

must have been the engine's roar, because, just before we hit, it turned its head backward over its right shoulder and fixed its bright yellow eye straight on me. I saw it immediately extend its legs, maybe trying to maneuver, or slow down or change direction. That was an 'oh, expletive' moment, really terrifying. I think for us both." The plane was cruising at 150 mph, and the bird smashed into the copilot's window, behind which my father, though piloting, was sitting—a habit acquired while flying B-24s in World War II. The windshield cracked but remained intact, allowing my dad and the crew to land safely in Amarillo.

I've heard this story since I was a girl, and I've never failed to say, "And tell me more. What did that bird look like so close, up so high?" Each time, my father describes a big bird "sailing along due west just like we were, its wings as wide as your arms." But he skips the rest of the description—the dark body, bright white tail-and-head part—and gets right to where he saw that bird's "big, yellow eye." The moment he and the eagle looked knowingly at each other still haunts him. The image is vivid in my own story-filled memory.

It is rare to see a bald eagle from an airplane. There are plenty of earthbound views, however. During spring and fall migrations, look for bald eagles catching winds along mountain ranges. Hawk Ridge, near Duluth, Minnesota, is a particularly reliable place to view them. The largest gathering of bald eagles in the world happens each fall along a five-mile stretch of the Chiklat River near Haines, Alaska. As many as 4,000 bald eagles gather there each November to feast on salmon.

In fact, fish, water, and bald eagles go together. Fish, dead or alive, are the eagle's main food source, though eagles will also eat small birds, mammals, and turtles. The eagles nest near water from northern Alaska to southeast Quebec and Newfoundland; south to Baja, California; Arizona; Texas; along the Gulf Coast; and Florida. While many bald eagles migrate south, you can find them throughout their breeding range in winter.

The bald eagle has historically ranged throughout North America except in extreme northern Alaska and Canada, and central and southern Mexico. Loss of habitat due to human development has been a continuing threat to these birds, especially in the twentieth century. Bald eagles defend large territories around their nests. Prime habitat includes clean water and mature trees.

Surprisingly, little is known for certain about bald eagle courtship. There is some evidence that they mate for life, or until one of the pair dies. Some aerobatic maneuvers may be associated with courtship. One bird dives at another in mid-air. The attacked bird rolls over and shows its talons. Copulation takes place in or near the nest. Some interactions, such as touching bills and preening the other bird, may take place. Depending on how far north or south the birds are, courtship, nest building, and breeding can take place from late winter to early fall.

Nests are big (and that's an understatement), from an average of six up to 10 feet across. Both the male and the female help to build it. Over time, each will carry hundreds of pounds of sticks, creating a huge circular nest, usually in the crotch of a very large tree located near some body of water or wetlands. The birds line the nest with soft materials such as mosses, pine needles, and feathers. Mated bald eagle pairs are known to use the same nest year after year, occasionally adding to it.

Female eagles usually lay a clutch of two eggs. These hatch after a 35-day incubation. At three weeks, eaglets have full-grown eyes, beaks, and feet, but possess disproportionately stubby wings and a short, plump, grayish down body. At nine to 14 weeks, with juvenile plumage already in place, the older, sleeker birds are up and flying. At about four months, they leave the nest for good to feed and defend themselves.

Due in large part to poor hunting strategies, only about half of bald eagle young in a given year are expected to survive. Those that do, however, can expect long lives. Various sources report them living up to 30 years in the wild. In captivity, one individual in New York State was reported to be nearly 50 years old.

The bald eagle is a member of the hawk family, all of which possess keen eyesight, perhaps the best of all the creatures on Earth. In fact, eagles often have eyes larger than a human's, although much of the eye is

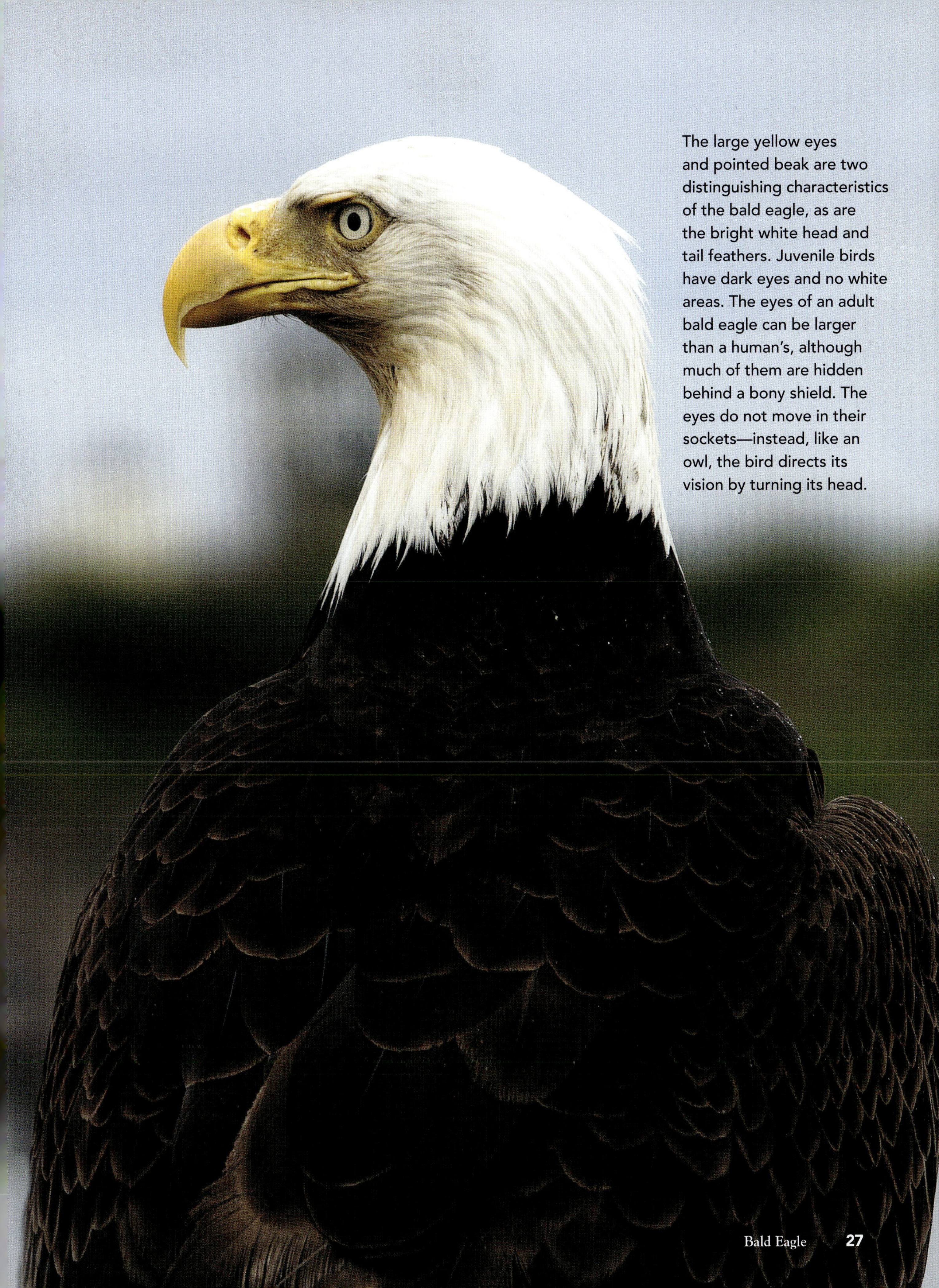

The large yellow eyes and pointed beak are two distinguishing characteristics of the bald eagle, as are the bright white head and tail feathers. Juvenile birds have dark eyes and no white areas. The eyes of an adult bald eagle can be larger than a human's, although much of them are hidden behind a bony shield. The eyes do not move in their sockets—instead, like an owl, the bird directs its vision by turning its head.

often hidden by the skull. The eyes of a bald eagle are so large that they don't move in their sockets. Instead, like an owl, the bird directs its vision by turning its head. An eagle skeleton will reveal a bony shield over the eyes, which helps to conceal the eyes and results in the living bird's characteristic fierce look.

Eagle eyes are set further forward than those of many other bird species, such as ducks. This placement allows it a wider range of binocular vision. But, as a trade-off, to look behind, the eagle has to turn its head.

Eye color in the bald eagle changes as the bird matures. Young eaglets have deep brown eyes. By the end of the third year, a bald eagle's eyes will have turned to light brown or hazel. In the fourth year, the iris turns pale yellow.

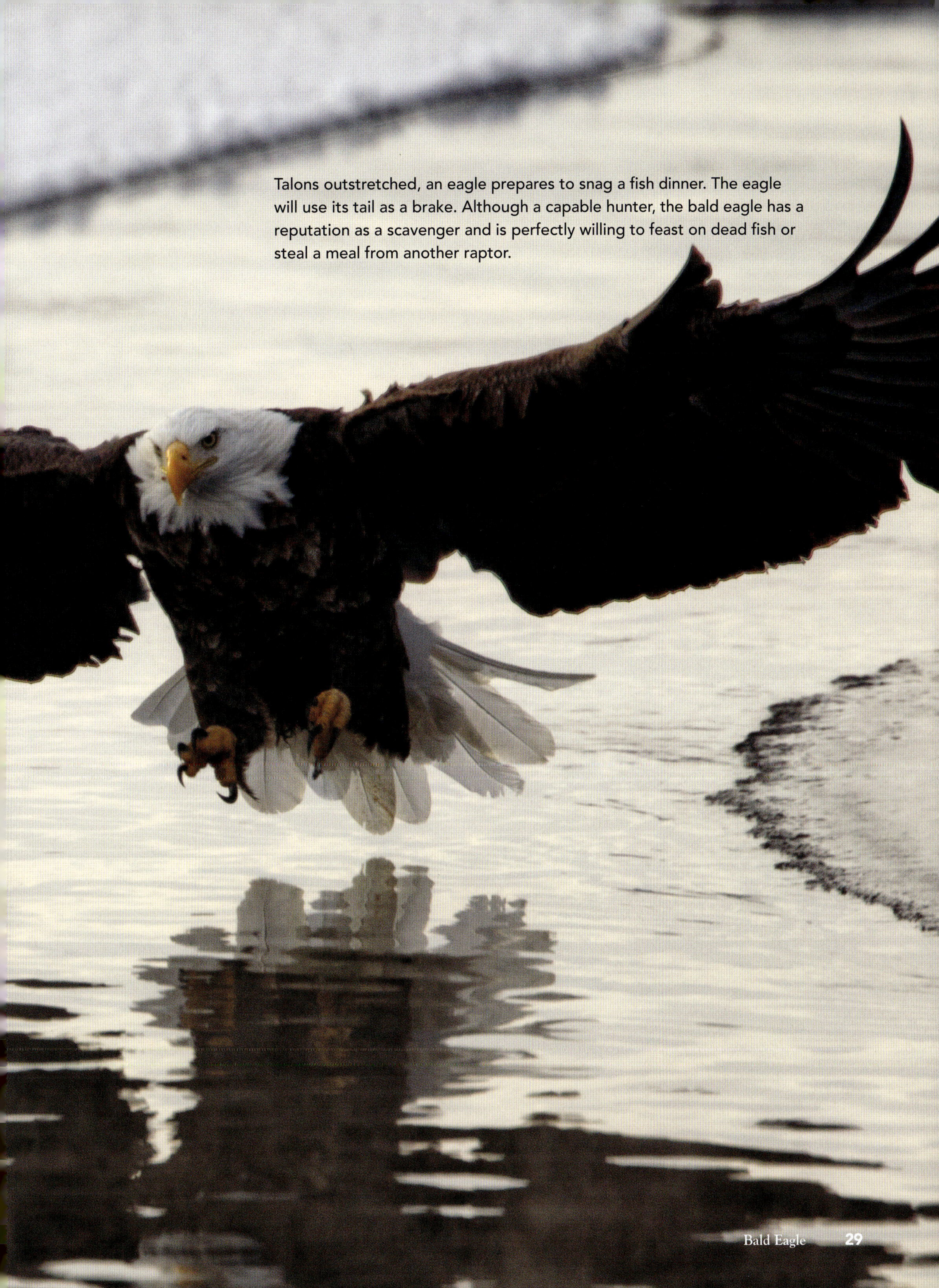

Talons outstretched, an eagle prepares to snag a fish dinner. The eagle will use its tail as a brake. Although a capable hunter, the bald eagle has a reputation as a scavenger and is perfectly willing to feast on dead fish or steal a meal from another raptor.

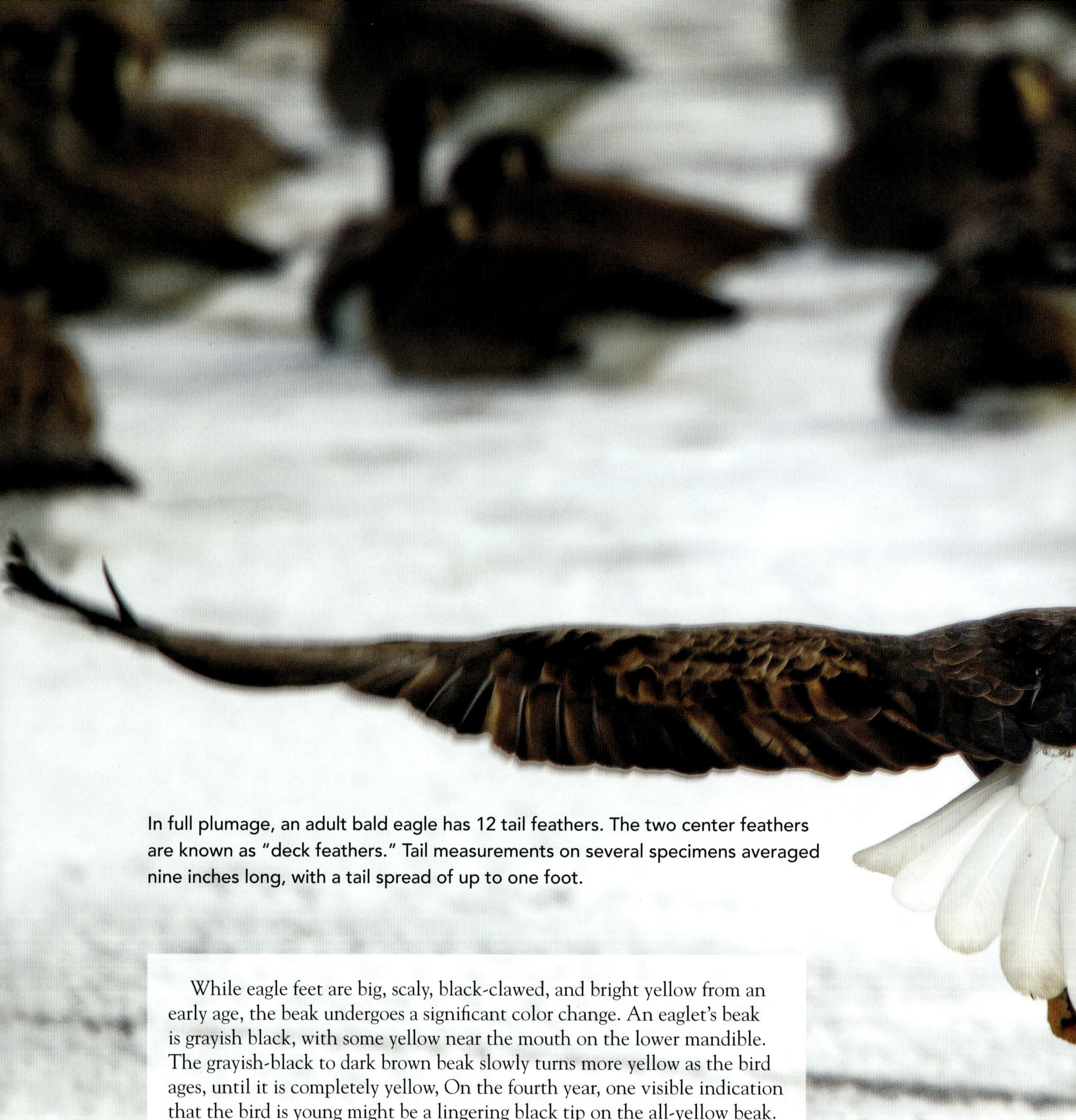

In full plumage, an adult bald eagle has 12 tail feathers. The two center feathers are known as "deck feathers." Tail measurements on several specimens averaged nine inches long, with a tail spread of up to one foot.

While eagle feet are big, scaly, black-clawed, and bright yellow from an early age, the beak undergoes a significant color change. An eaglet's beak is grayish black, with some yellow near the mouth on the lower mandible. The grayish-black to dark brown beak slowly turns more yellow as the bird ages, until it is completely yellow, On the fourth year, one visible indication that the bird is young might be a lingering black tip on the all-yellow beak.

Bald eagle beaks have two distinct parts. The sometimes slightly lighter colored cere, which is closest to the head, contains the nostrils. The smooth hooked part curves downward, hanging about half an inch over the lower mandible. Dr. Kevin McGowan, curator of the bird skins collection at Cornell University, notes that the beak curvature doesn't start until just before the tip of the lower mandible and then turns directly down at the end by almost 90 degrees. The bald eagle's beak is bigger and broader than that of the golden eagle.

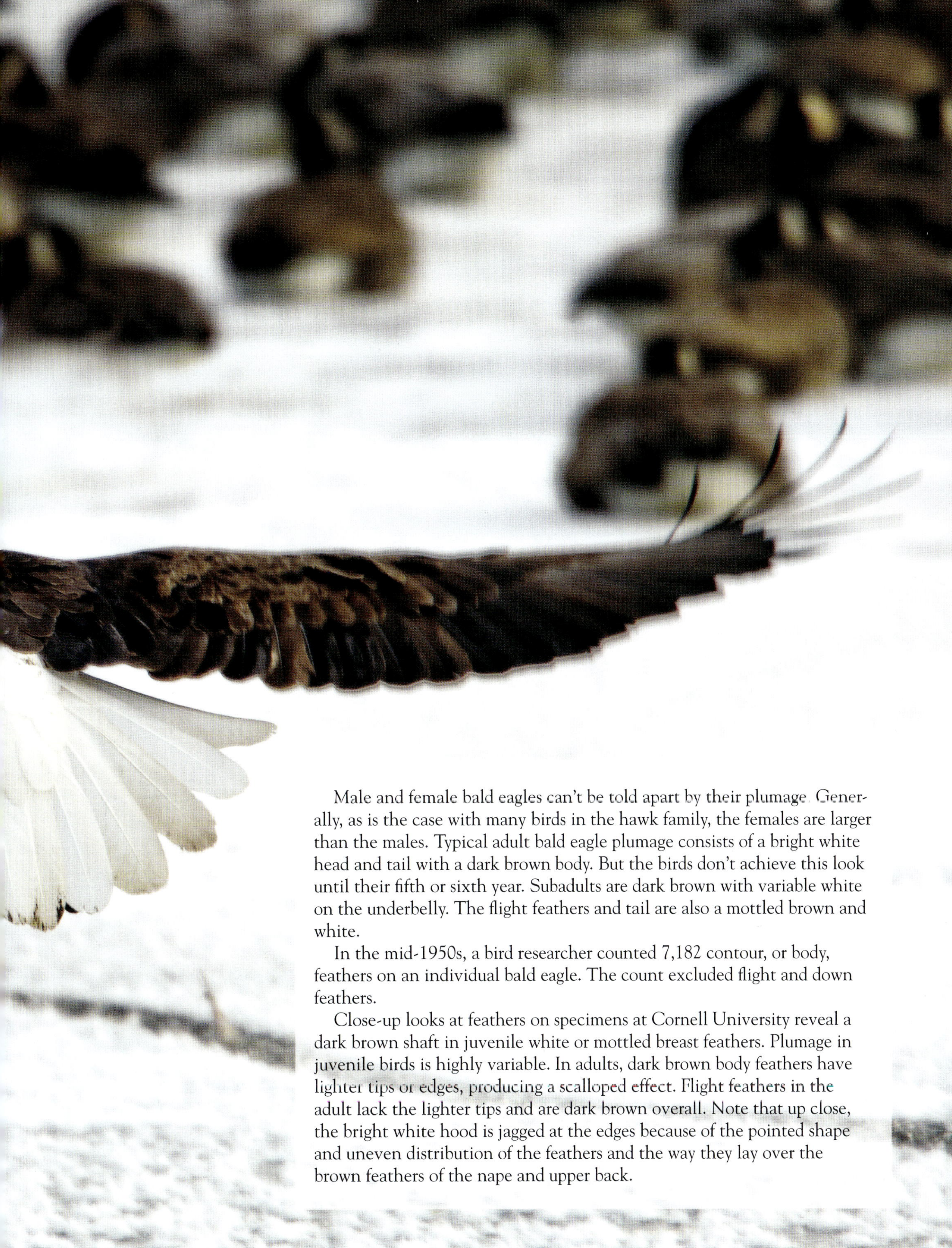

Male and female bald eagles can't be told apart by their plumage. Generally, as is the case with many birds in the hawk family, the females are larger than the males. Typical adult bald eagle plumage consists of a bright white head and tail with a dark brown body. But the birds don't achieve this look until their fifth or sixth year. Subadults are dark brown with variable white on the underbelly. The flight feathers and tail are also a mottled brown and white.

In the mid-1950s, a bird researcher counted 7,182 contour, or body, feathers on an individual bald eagle. The count excluded flight and down feathers.

Close-up looks at feathers on specimens at Cornell University reveal a dark brown shaft in juvenile white or mottled breast feathers. Plumage in juvenile birds is highly variable. In adults, dark brown body feathers have lighter tips or edges, producing a scalloped effect. Flight feathers in the adult lack the lighter tips and are dark brown overall. Note that up close, the bright white hood is jagged at the edges because of the pointed shape and uneven distribution of the feathers and the way they lay over the brown feathers of the nape and upper back.

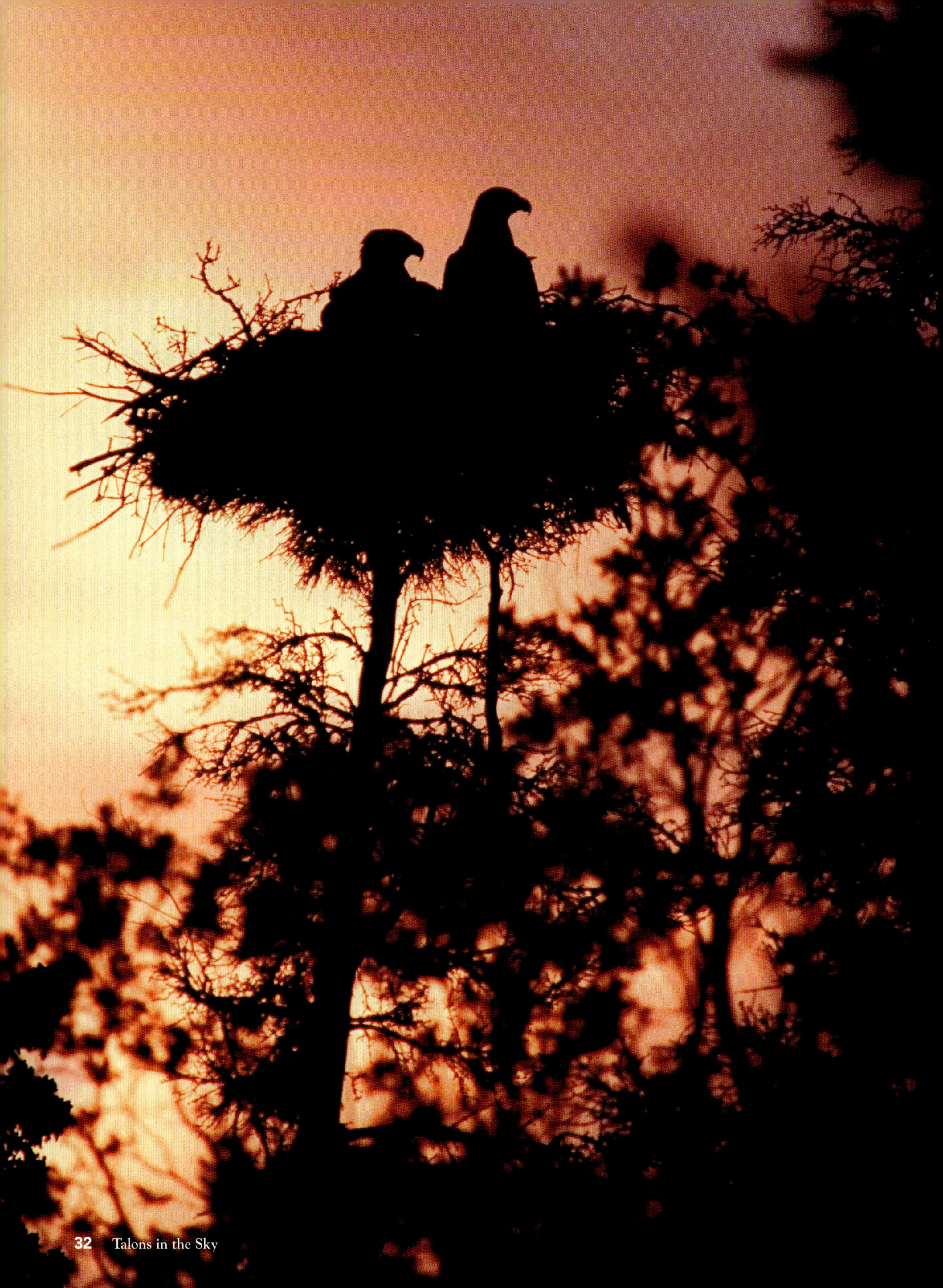

Immature bald eagle plumage looks similar to adult golden eagle plumage, but there are some differences. For example, you'll find white on the belly of only the young bald eagle. Golden eagles have wider wings and longer tails than bald eagles of the same size. A bald eagle's legs and feet are less feathered than a golden eagle's. Beaks of the immature bald and adult golden eagles, while similar in color, are slightly different in shape.

From February 14, 1978, until August 11, 1995, the U.S. Fish and Wildlife Service classified the bald eagle as an endangered species in 43 states under the Endangered Species Act; the exceptions were Minnesota, Michigan, Wisconsin, Washington, and Oregon, where it was listed as a threatened species. Hawaii has no bald eagles. Alaska's bald eagle population was strong, numbering in the tens of thousands. On August 11, 1995, the bird's status was reclassified as threatened in all of the lower 48 states. On August 9, 2007, the eagle populations had recovered so well that the bird was removed from the threatened list.

Before the Endangered Species Act, the loss of habitat and the killing of bald eagles prompted passage of the 1940 Bald and Golden Eagle Protection Act. This law made it illegal to kill, harm, harass, or possess bald eagles (dead or alive) or their eggs, feathers, and nests. But just when there were signs that bald eagle populations were recovering, people started using DDT (dichloro-diphenyl-trichloroethane) as a mosquito control. For decades after, a byproduct of DDT built up in the fatty tissues of adult females. The chain of events was devastating to bald eagle and other

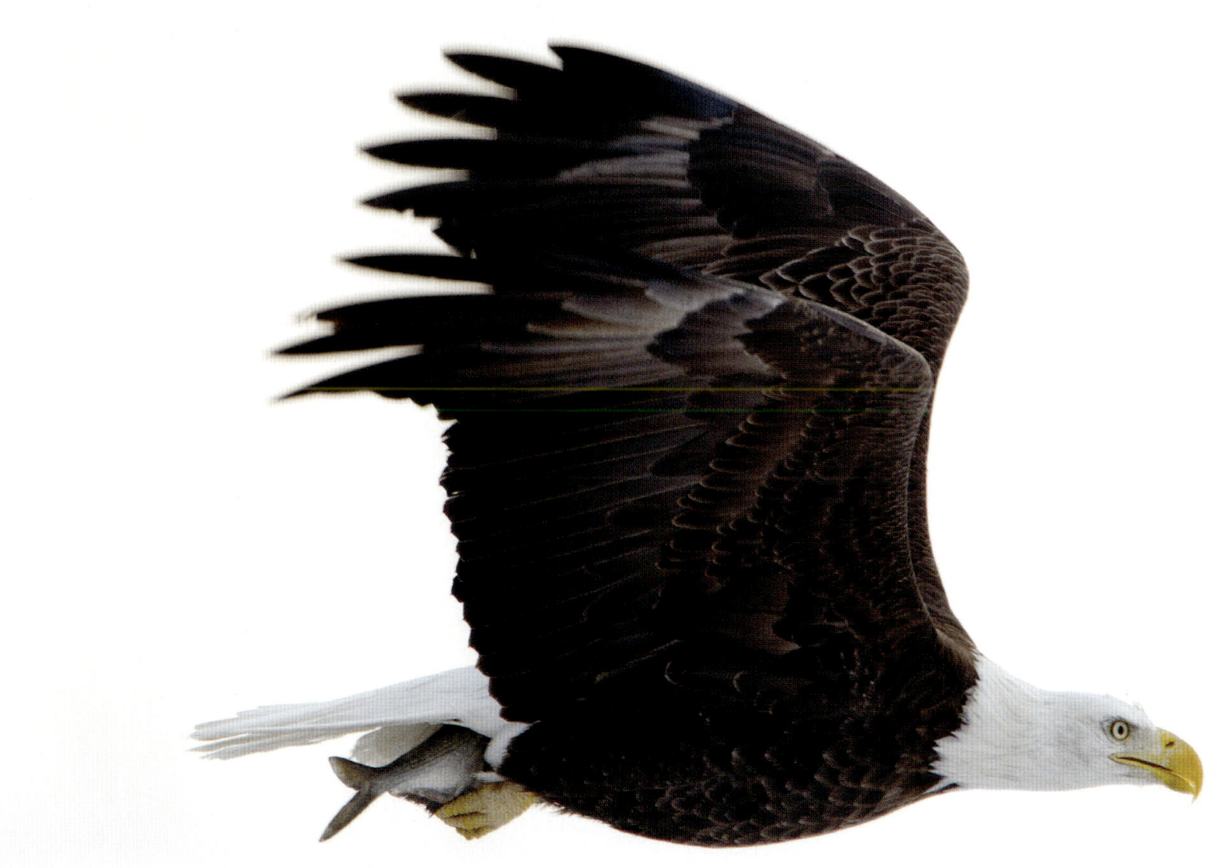

LEFT: Bald eagles build stick nests, and both members of a breeding pair will carry hundreds of pounds of sticks to create the large circular nest. It is usually in the crotch of a large tree near a body of water. **ABOVE:** Once the nestlings hatch, it's largely the duty of the male to bring food to the nest, and the meals are usually fish. The female will tear small pieces from the prey the male delivers, and feed them to the nestlings.

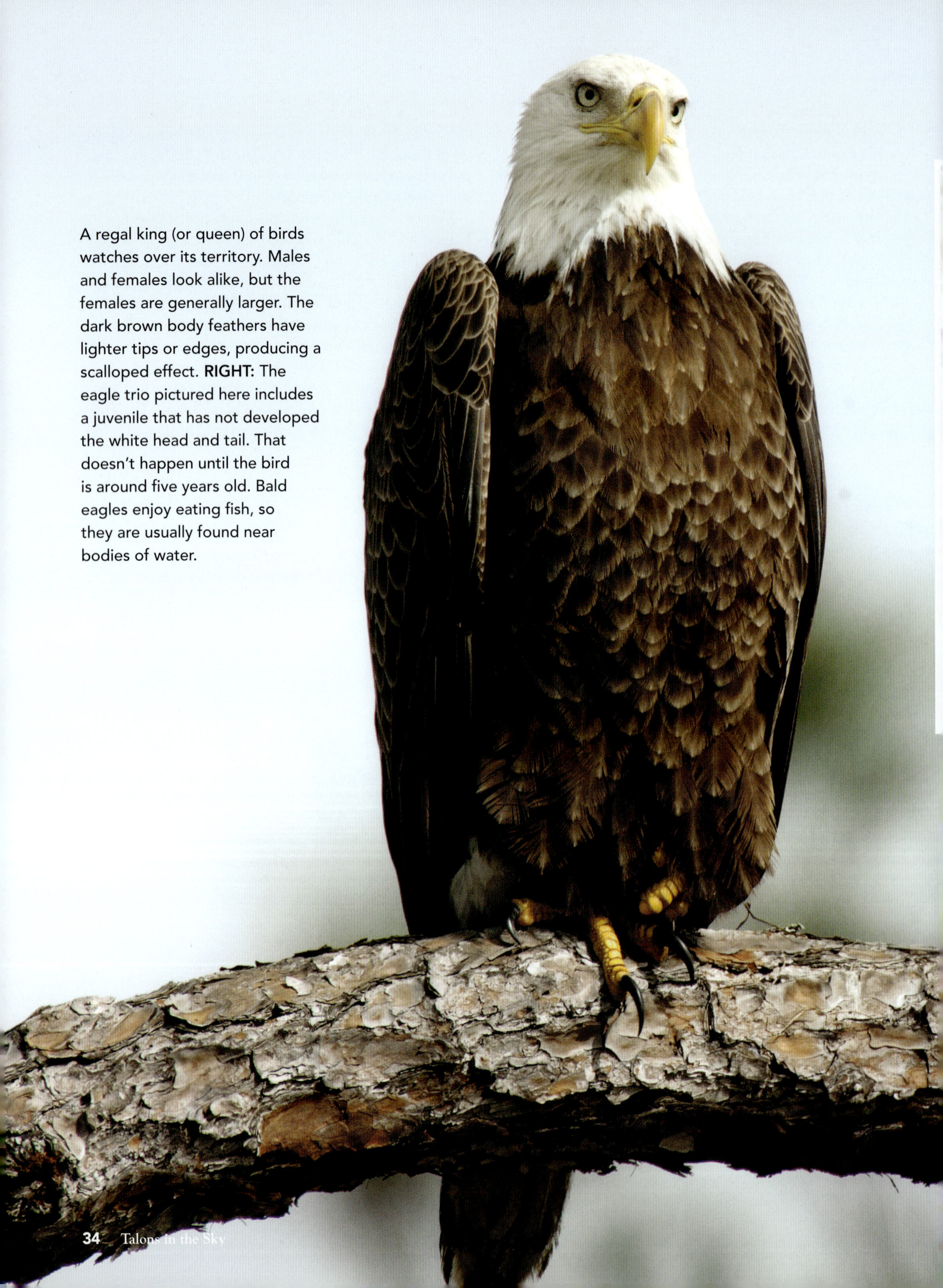

A regal king (or queen) of birds watches over its territory. Males and females look alike, but the females are generally larger. The dark brown body feathers have lighter tips or edges, producing a scalloped effect. **RIGHT:** The eagle trio pictured here includes a juvenile that has not developed the white head and tail. That doesn't happen until the bird is around five years old. Bald eagles enjoy eating fish, so they are usually found near bodies of water.

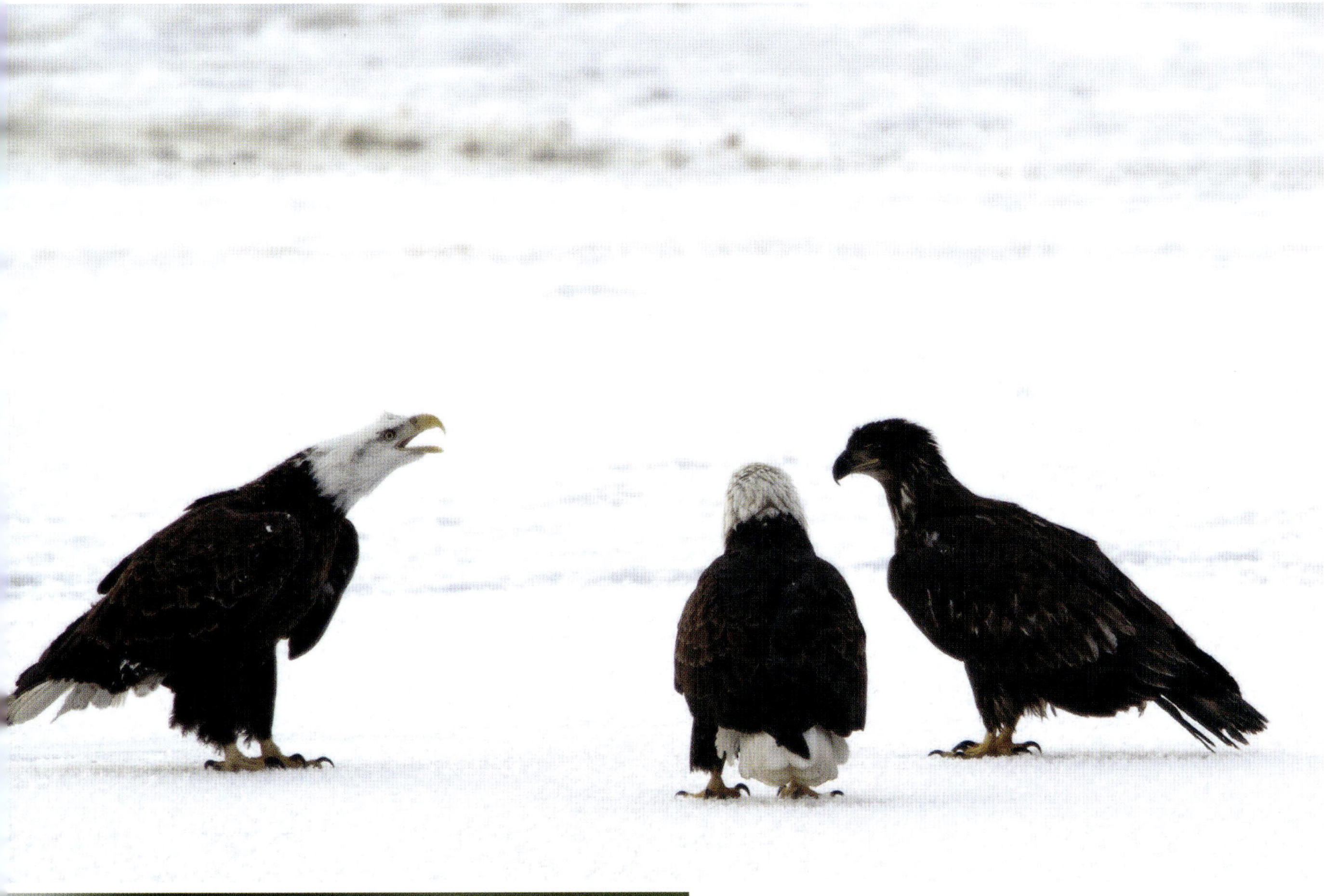

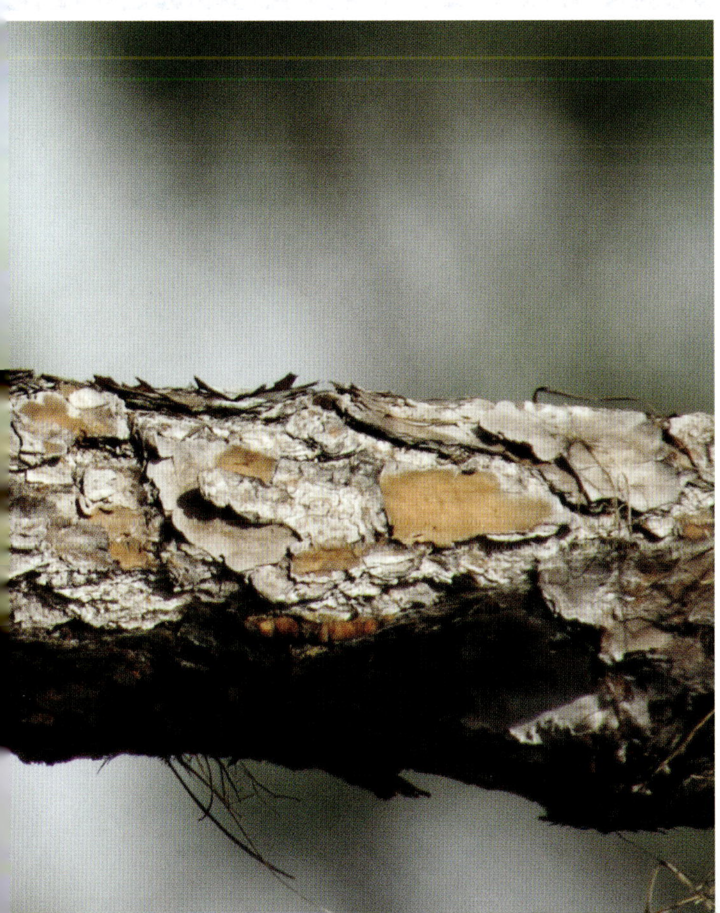

bird populations. The females could not add enough calcium to their eggs. The weakened eggs cracked. As a consequence, populations declined. While the birds were given more attention and protection under the Endangered Species Preservation Act of 1966, DDT was still in use. It wasn't banned until December 31, 1972. Since then, bald eagle populations have continued to rebound.

One cannot be in the presence of the bald eagle without being in awe of its power, beauty, and grace. What better symbol could there be for a young nation seeking a place in the world? Though Benjamin Franklin pointed out the attributes of the wild turkey, the bald eagle became the symbol of our forming nation in 1782.

But the eagle did not hold a place only in the minds and hearts of European immigrants. The bald eagle is a prevalent ceremonial and religious symbol in Native American culture. In a 1995 Associated Press article, Wallace Coffey, speaking on behalf of the Cammanche

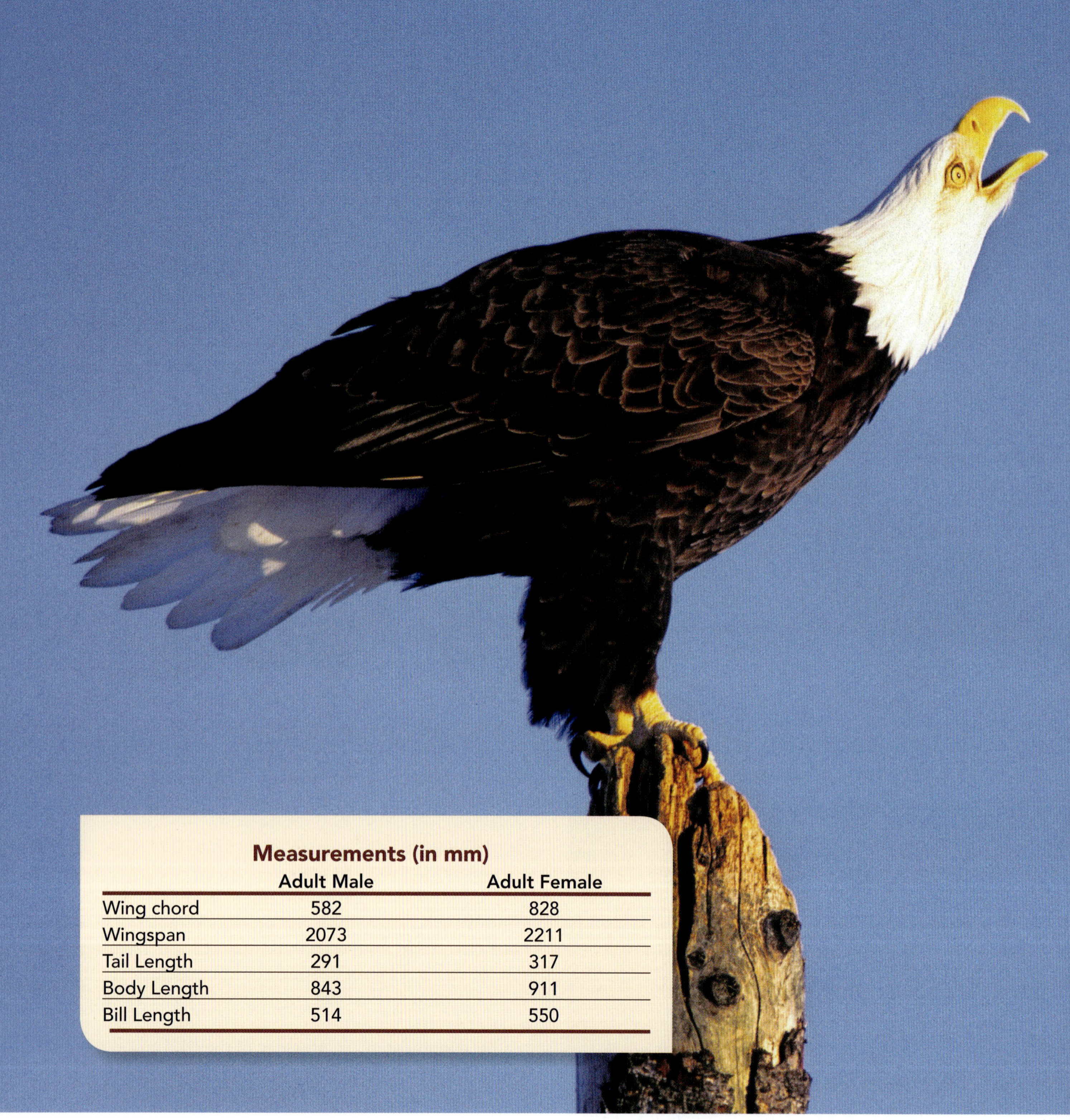

Measurements (in mm)	Adult Male	Adult Female
Wing chord	582	828
Wingspan	2073	2211
Tail Length	291	317
Body Length	843	911
Bill Length	514	550

Tribe in Oklahoma, explained that to many Native Americans, the bald eagle is holy. "Even just to see it is a blessing," he said.

Carcasses from birds that are killed by powerlines and cars, or that were illegally shot or poisoned by poachers, end up at the U.S. Fish and Wildlife's National Eagle Repository near Denver. The service receives 2,000 requests a year for eagle items for use by Native Americans for "recognized religious, cultural and ceremonial purposes."

We can be thankful that the bald eagle did not follow the passenger pigeon and the dodo into extinction, and that this amazing bird will continue to be an awe-inspiring sight for years to come.

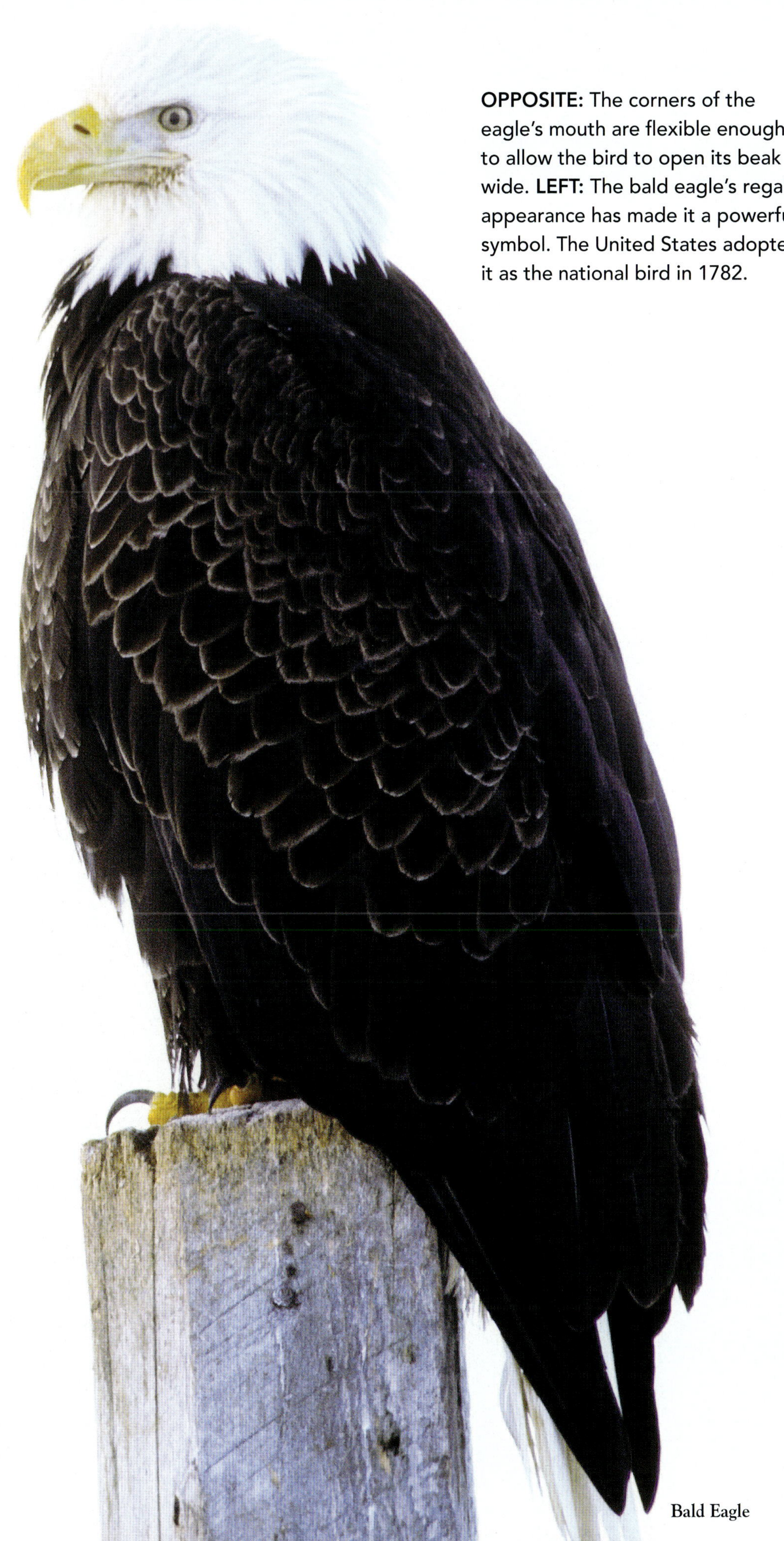

OPPOSITE: The corners of the eagle's mouth are flexible enough to allow the bird to open its beak wide. **LEFT:** The bald eagle's regal appearance has made it a powerful symbol. The United States adopted it as the national bird in 1782.

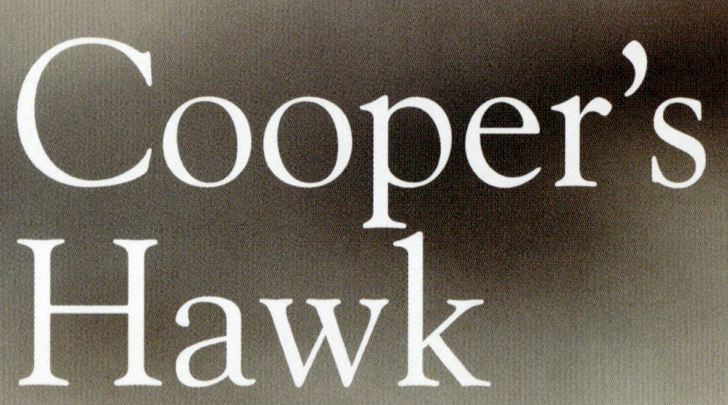

Cooper's Hawk

(Accipiter cooperi)

Sharp-shinned Hawk

(Accipiter striatus)

BY RICK BURKMAN

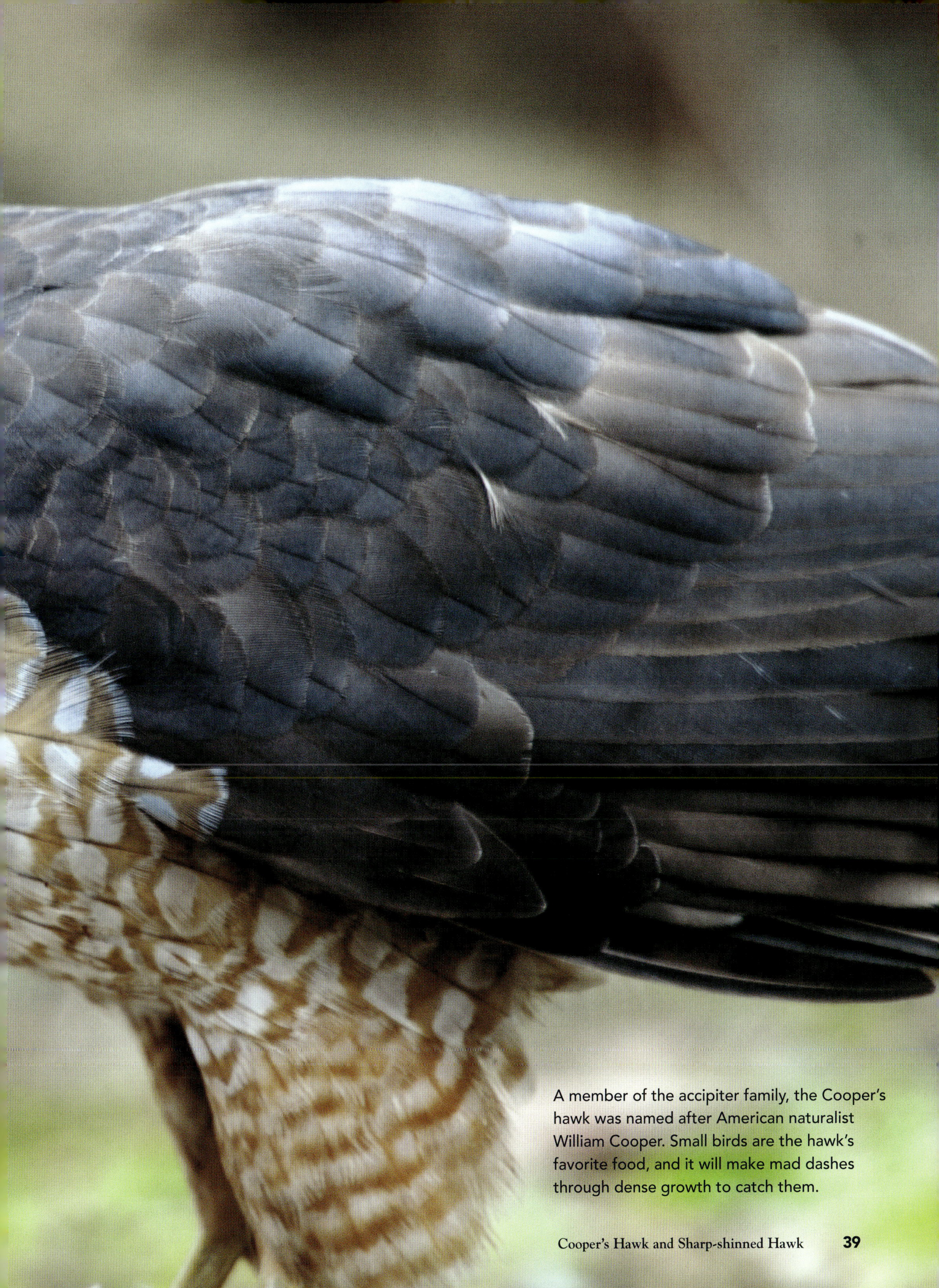

A member of the accipiter family, the Cooper's hawk was named after American naturalist William Cooper. Small birds are the hawk's favorite food, and it will make mad dashes through dense growth to catch them.

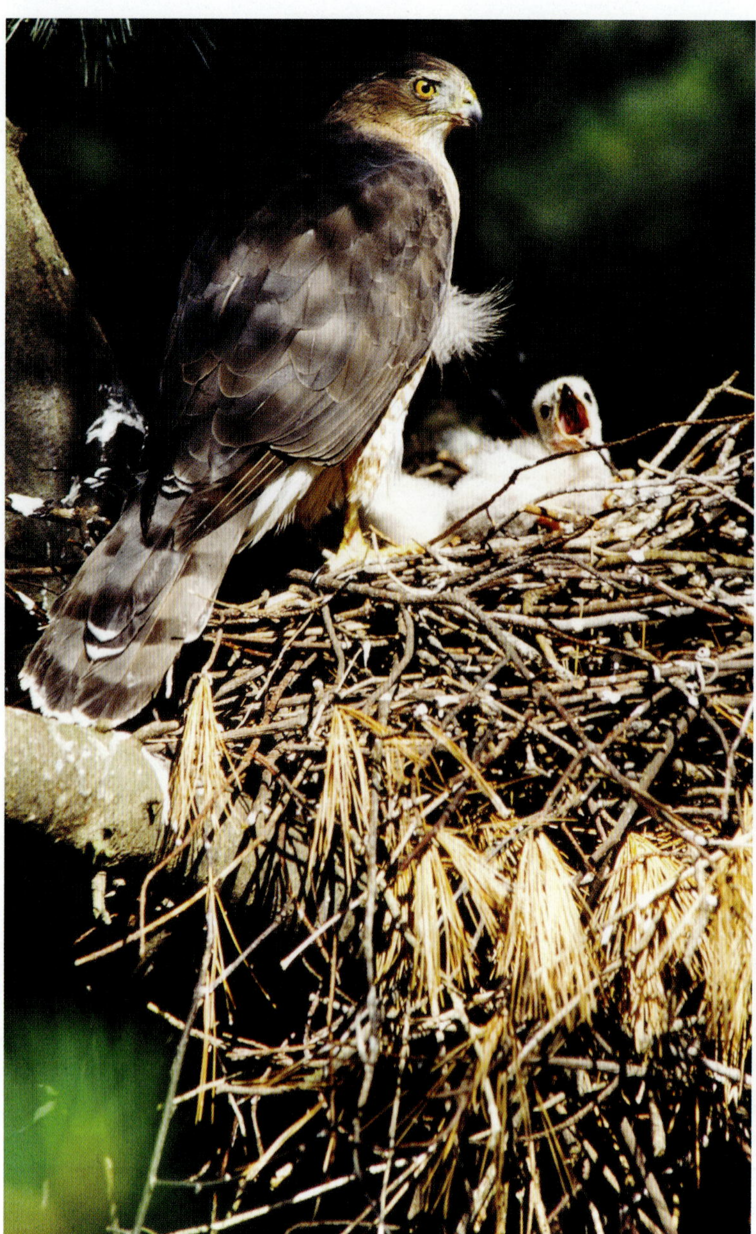

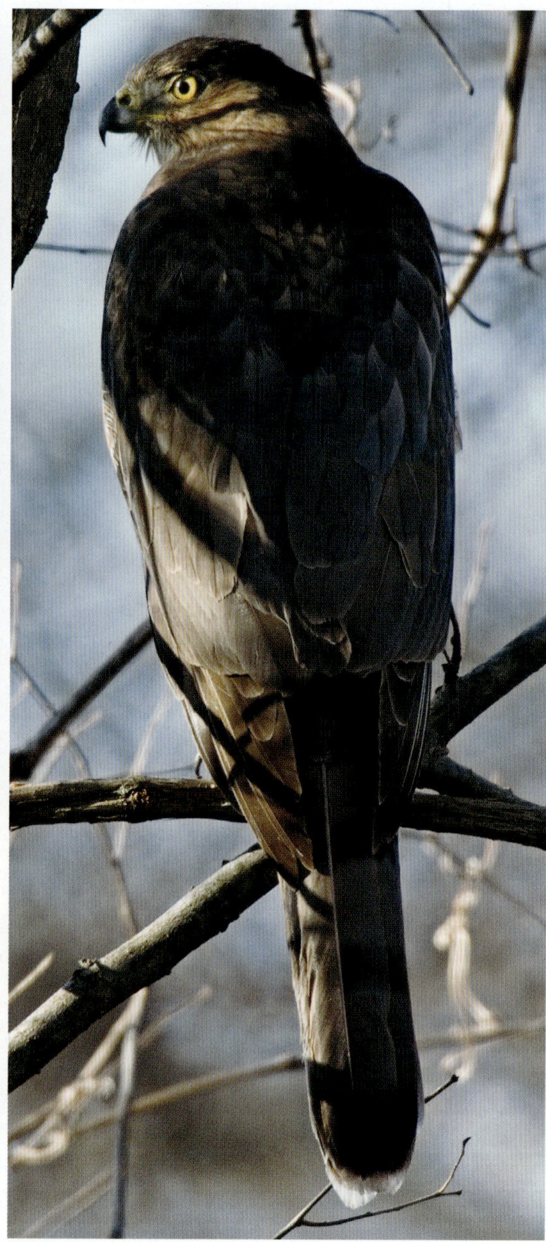

Fiery red eyes peer with intelligent intent out of a body armored in feathers of blue-gray steel and rust. This is an apt description of two of the most graceful, powerful, and deadly hunters of the deep woods, the sharp-shinned hawk (*Accipiter striatus*) and the Cooper's hawk (*Accipiter cooperi*). (The third North American member of this group is the northern goshawk.) Although these birds can be quiet and difficult to find unless they are migrating, they are widely admired. As award-winning carver Floyd Scholz wrote elegantly in his book *Birds of Prey*, "The Cooper's is an incredibly beautiful creature, extremely well proportioned, a seemingly perfect combination of size, color, and form." What more is there to say, except that its cousin, the sharpie, is equally stunning?

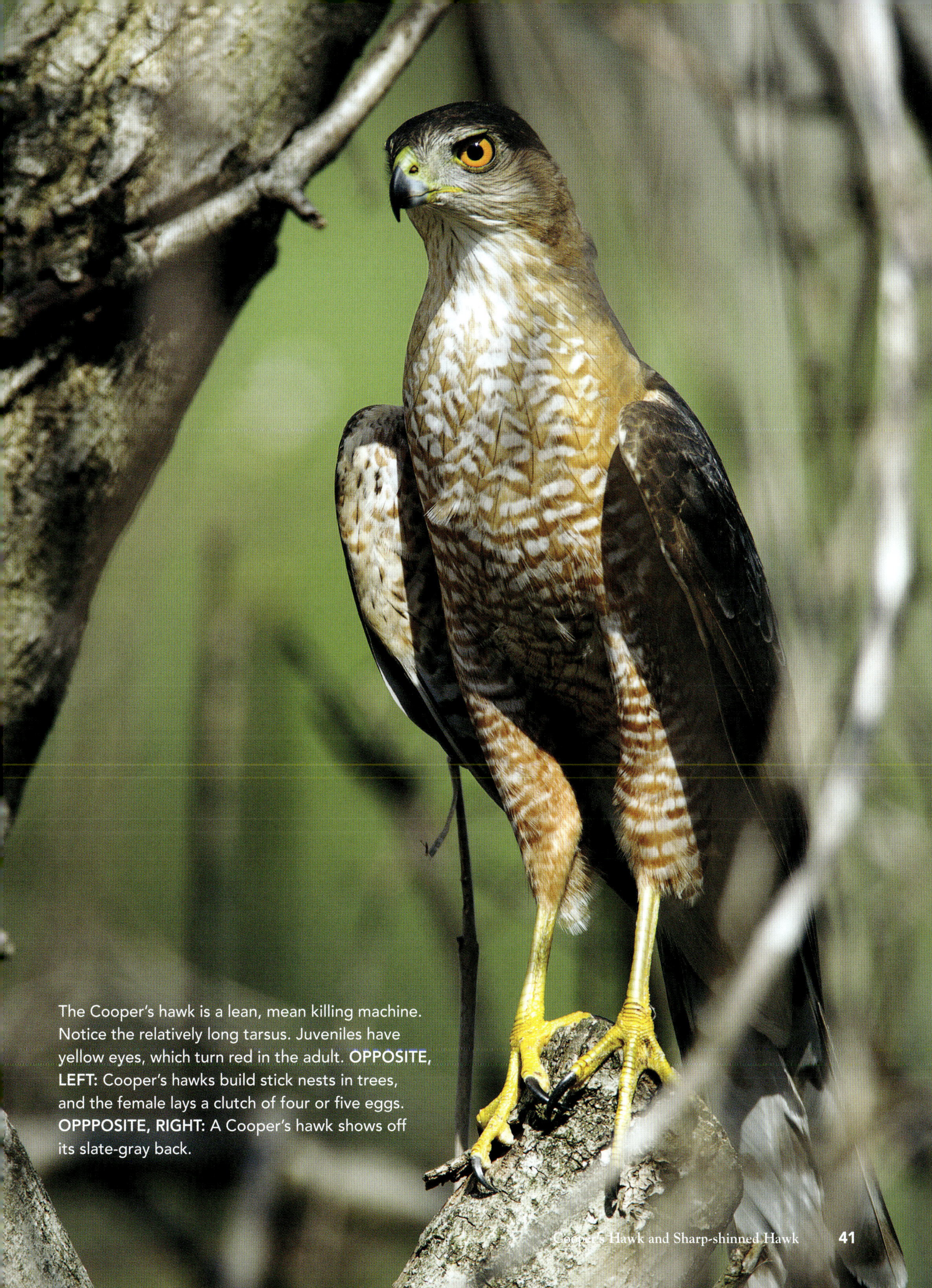

The Cooper's hawk is a lean, mean killing machine. Notice the relatively long tarsus. Juveniles have yellow eyes, which turn red in the adult. **OPPOSITE, LEFT:** Cooper's hawks build stick nests in trees, and the female lays a clutch of four or five eggs. **OPPPOSITE, RIGHT:** A Cooper's hawk shows off its slate-gray back.

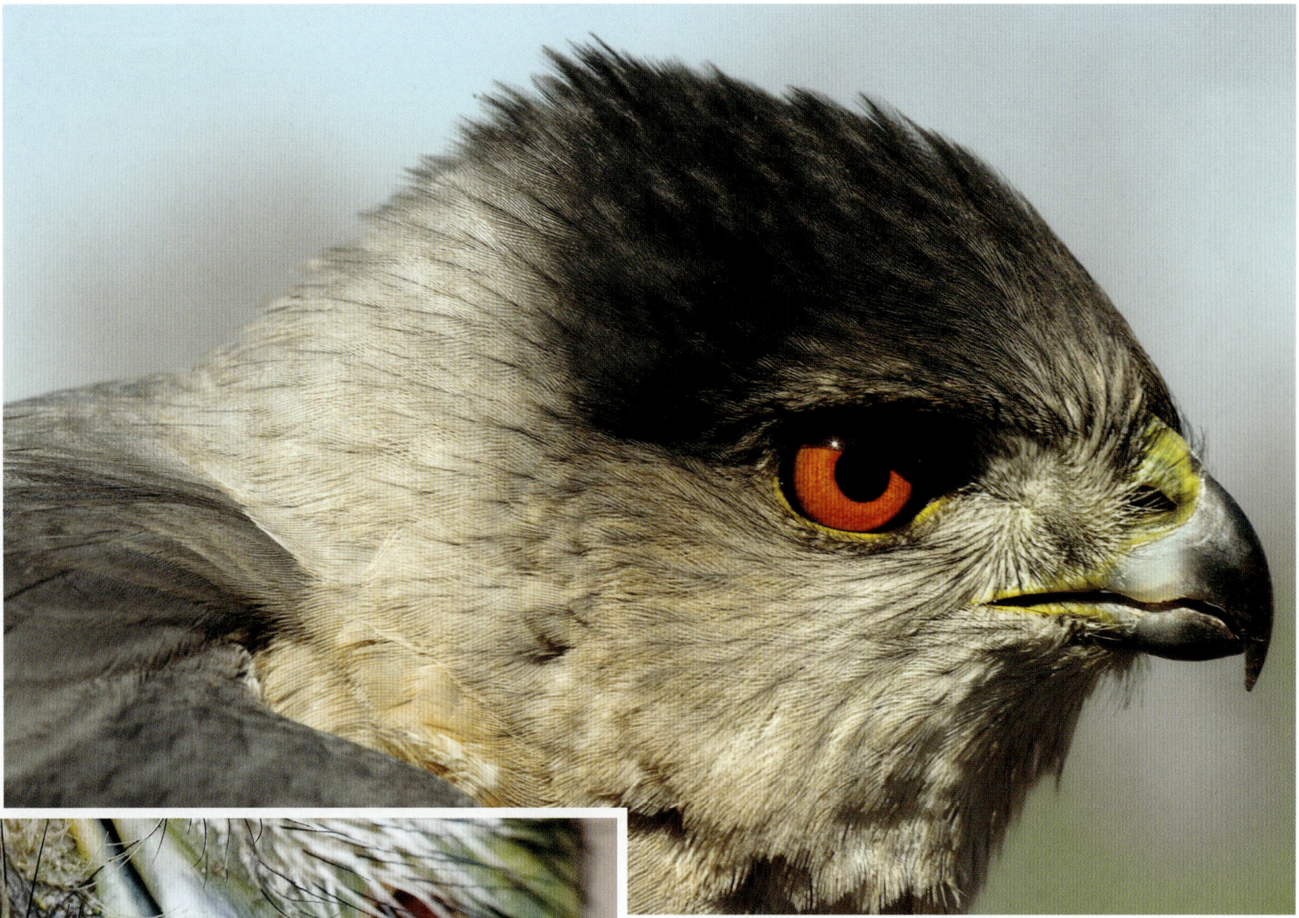

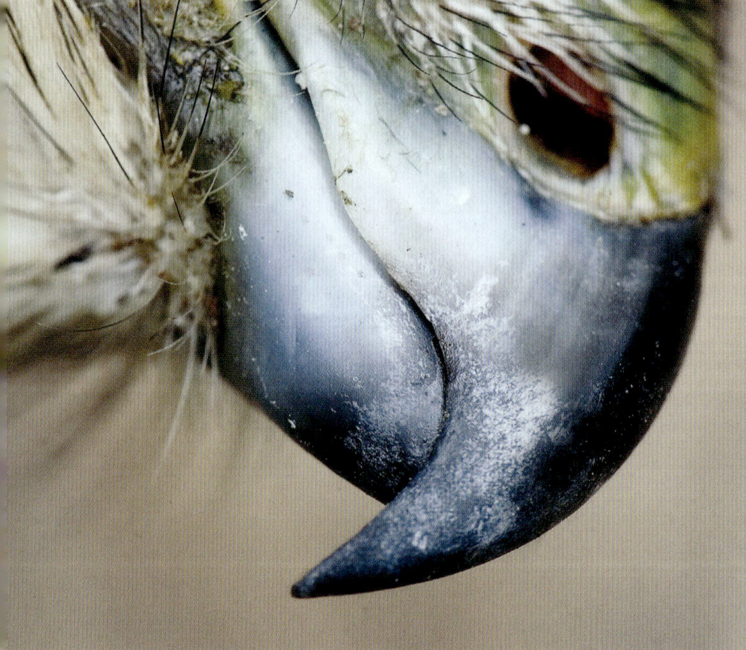

Sharp-shinned and Cooper's hawks look a lot alike. They have slate-blue or gray backs with brown tints, along with rusty-colored barring on their whitish chests and abdomens, coloring that provides perfect camouflage in the deep cover of trees. Ruby-red hunter's eyes stare over sharply hooked, dark gray beaks and contrasting yellow ceres. The sharp-shinned's eyes appear to bulge a little more because of a comparatively smaller head, while the Cooper's hawk has a slightly darker crown that contrasts with a lighter nape, but these distinctions are subtle, and even experts can be fooled when viewing these birds from a distance. Both come equipped with weapons in the form of long, black, needle-sharp talons at the tips of strong, wiry, yellow legs and toes. Like many birds, juveniles look different from their parents. They are cloaked in streaks of brown, making them even more difficult to identify. The weapons, however, remain the same.

Size can help to differentiate these birds in the field, but it is not always a reliable indicator. Sharp-shinned hawks are commonly described as being a little larger than a blue jay, and Cooper's hawks about the size of a crow, but those are just rough comparisons. Females are always larger than the males and a large sharp-shinned hen can be close to the size of small Cooper's tiercel, making positive identification a challenge.

Some ornithologists believe that the size difference between genders helps ensure proper egg incubation and nest defense, but others believe the extra bulk protects the hen during copulation. When mating, the male is always on the hen's back, grasping her with

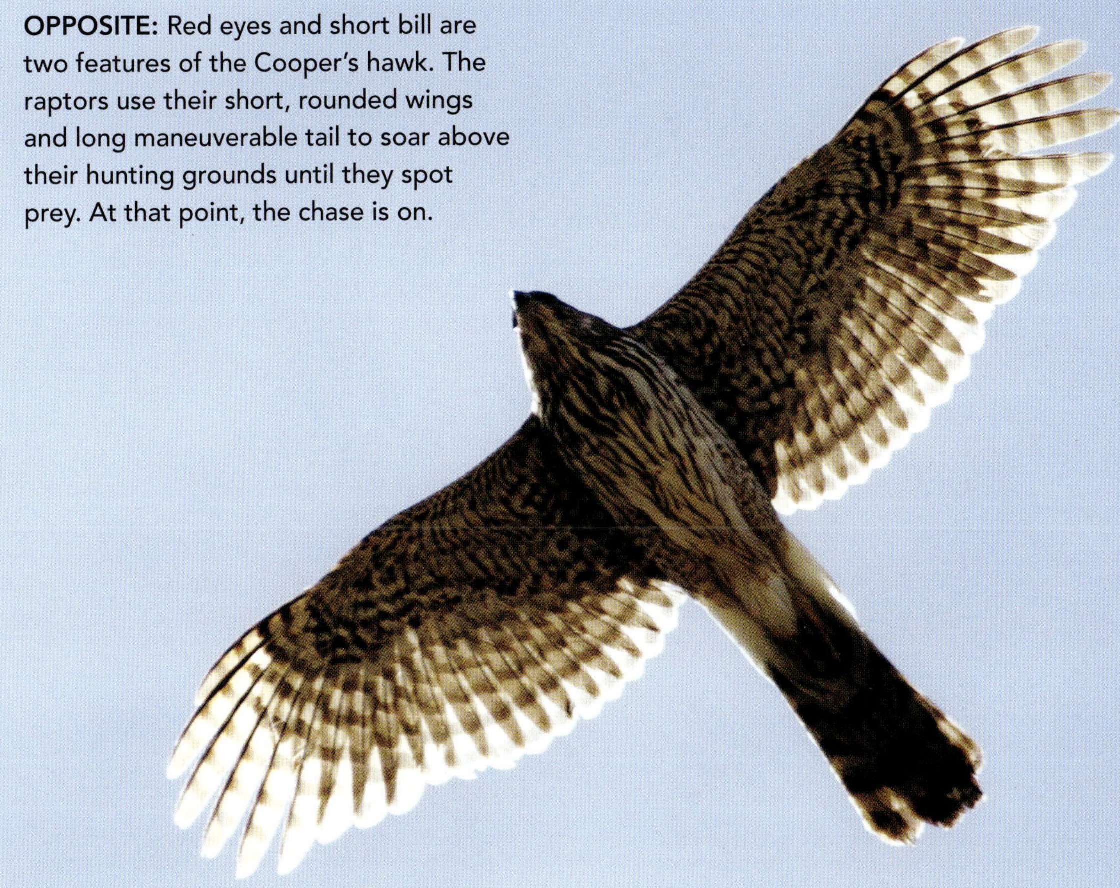

OPPOSITE: Red eyes and short bill are two features of the Cooper's hawk. The raptors use their short, rounded wings and long maneuverable tail to soar above their hunting grounds until they spot prey. At that point, the chase is on.

his deadly talons. These curved needles are positioned much the same as they are when the hawk grabs its favorite prey, smaller birds, making the hen vulnerable to an unappreciated coital death squeeze. So females have evolved to appear large and intimidating enough to avoid being killed during the male's blissful afterglow. Whatever the reason for the size difference, it works for these birds.

Despite their strength, the accipiters like to spend their days hiding, waiting in ambush until a small bird passes within view. The hunt is short and fast—a panicked songbird races for its life in a flurry of feathers as the hunter explodes through branches and leaves in single-minded pursuit. Short, rounded wings and a long, maneuverable tail keep the hunter on target, while long yellow legs guided by exquisite eyesight reach out with lightning-like speed to grasp the target in a death grip. The talon-tipped toes squeeze the hapless victim and, if that is not enough to quickly dispatch their prey, the hawks may drown their quarry in a nearby pond or puddle. Smaller birds comprise more than 90 percent of the hawks' diet with an occasional chipmunk, mouse, red squirrel, or snake rounding out the menu.

One unfortunate sharp-shinned hawk banded at the Whitefish Point Bird Observatory in Michigan had porcupine quills embedded in its foot. We will never know whether the quills were the result of the hawk's hubris or hunger.

Despite their skill, these avian hunters are successful less than 20 percent of the time, which probably means that they capture only one or two songbirds each day. Nevertheless, some early naturalists declared these predators the enemies of all small birds. Hunters and sport shooters sharpened their skills at spring and autumn migration points by shooting thousands of passing hawks. Population numbers dropped. And that wasn't all the bad news. Widespread use of agricultural pesticides caused egg shell thinning and nest failures in top-level avian predators. Raptors, including the Cooper's and sharp-shinned hawks, were in trouble.

Fortunately, environmental and conservation awareness increased, and in 1972 raptors were internationally protected for the first time under the Migratory Bird Treaty Act. That same year the widespread use of DDT and other agricultural pesticides was federally regulated and bird populations began their slow road to recovery. There have been ups and downs in the intervening

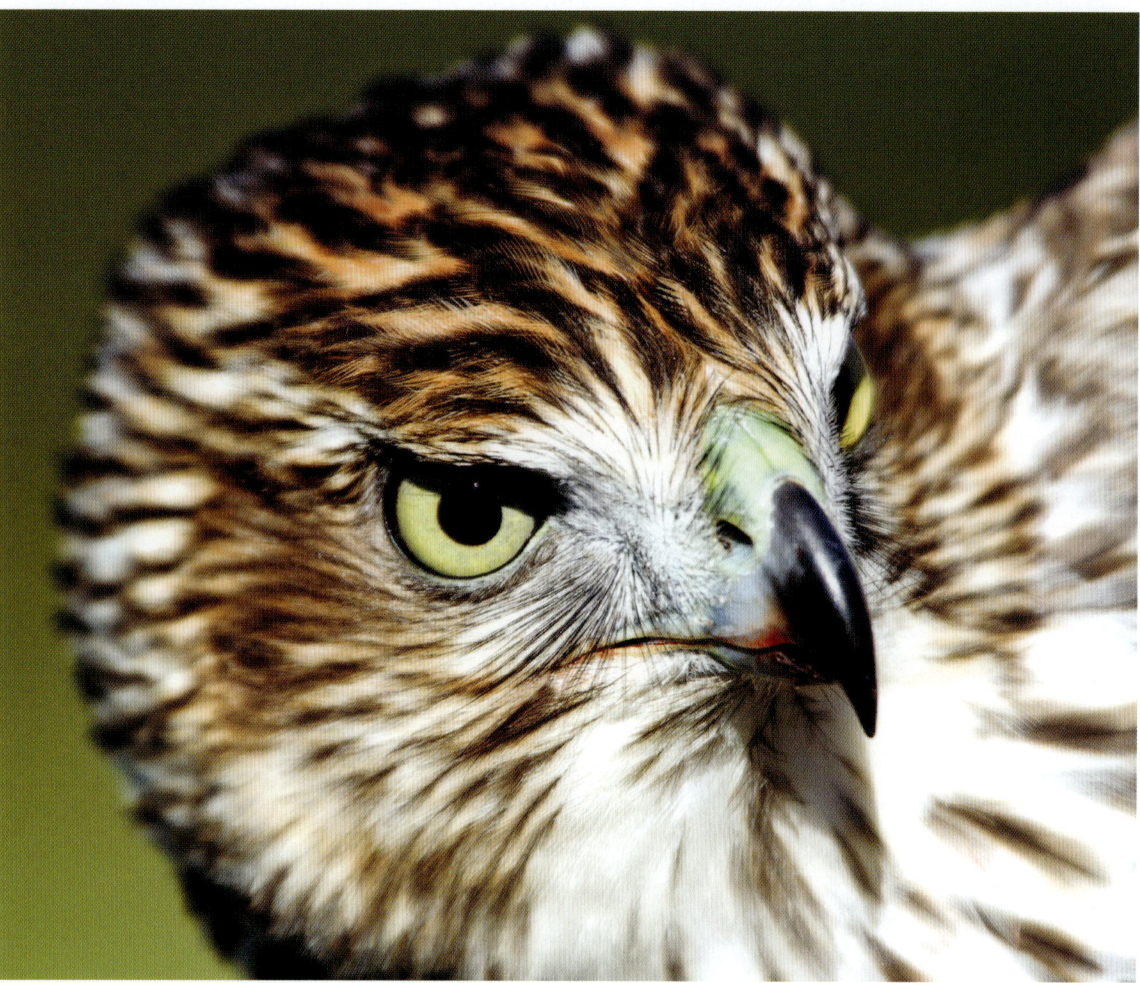

years, but the overall trend for accipiters is improving. Cooper's and sharp-shinned hawks are still being hunted, but now it is with binoculars instead of shotguns, during both spring and fall raptor migration counts.

The spring migration is particularly important for these normally solitary birds because the end of the trip marks the start of the nesting season. The hawks reuse their territories from year to year, but their secretiveness means we still have gaps in their life histories. For example, it is not clear whether the male or the female arrives at the territory first, and there are conflicting reports about which of the pair chooses the nest site. It does seem that the sharp-shinned hen does most of the nest construction, while the male Cooper's hawk is the primary builder. We are learning more about the Cooper's habits because they have been adapting to human environments, occasionally nesting in parks and woodlots in urban areas. The sharpies are staying wild, sticking to remote, difficult-to-access boreal forests.

Both species build flat stick nests, hiding them close to tree trunks in the dense forest canopy. Some birds add a few bark chips as lining. A hen lays one egg every other day until she has a clutch of about four or five whitish or bluish eggs, some with brown, red, or violet splotching. She starts incubating the clutch after laying the third egg. Sharp-shinned hawks sit on the eggs for about four weeks; Cooper's hawk incubation lasts a few days longer. When they are ready to emerge, chicks pip their shells from the inside then push and strain for up to a day before breaking into the world. Their short white down is wet, but dries and fluffs quickly when exposed to air.

Nestlings need warmth and protection from the elements for the first several days of life, so the hen broods while the male delivers food for the newly hatched family. At first he brings food to the hen on the nest, who promptly eats the head and then serves bits and pieces of the remainder to the jostling nestlings. Although accipiters are sit-and-wait hunters, a month of incubation duties makes the hen restless. Before long she starts flying out to greet the male as he brings food. She starts by meeting him at a trading branch, a regularly visited nearby perch, but the pair soon does mid-air transfers above the tree canopy as they pass

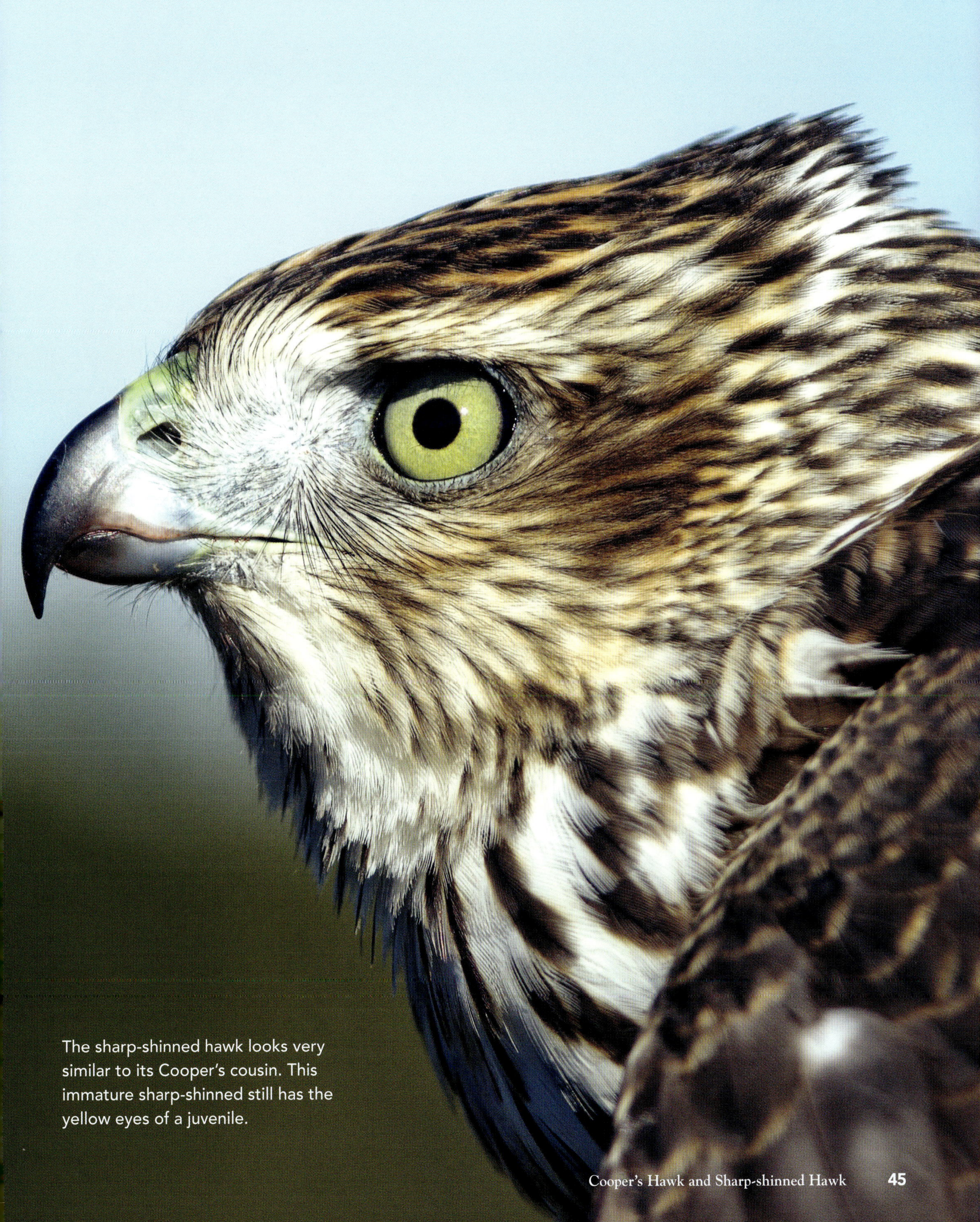

The sharp-shinned hawk looks very similar to its Cooper's cousin. This immature sharp-shinned still has the yellow eyes of a juvenile.

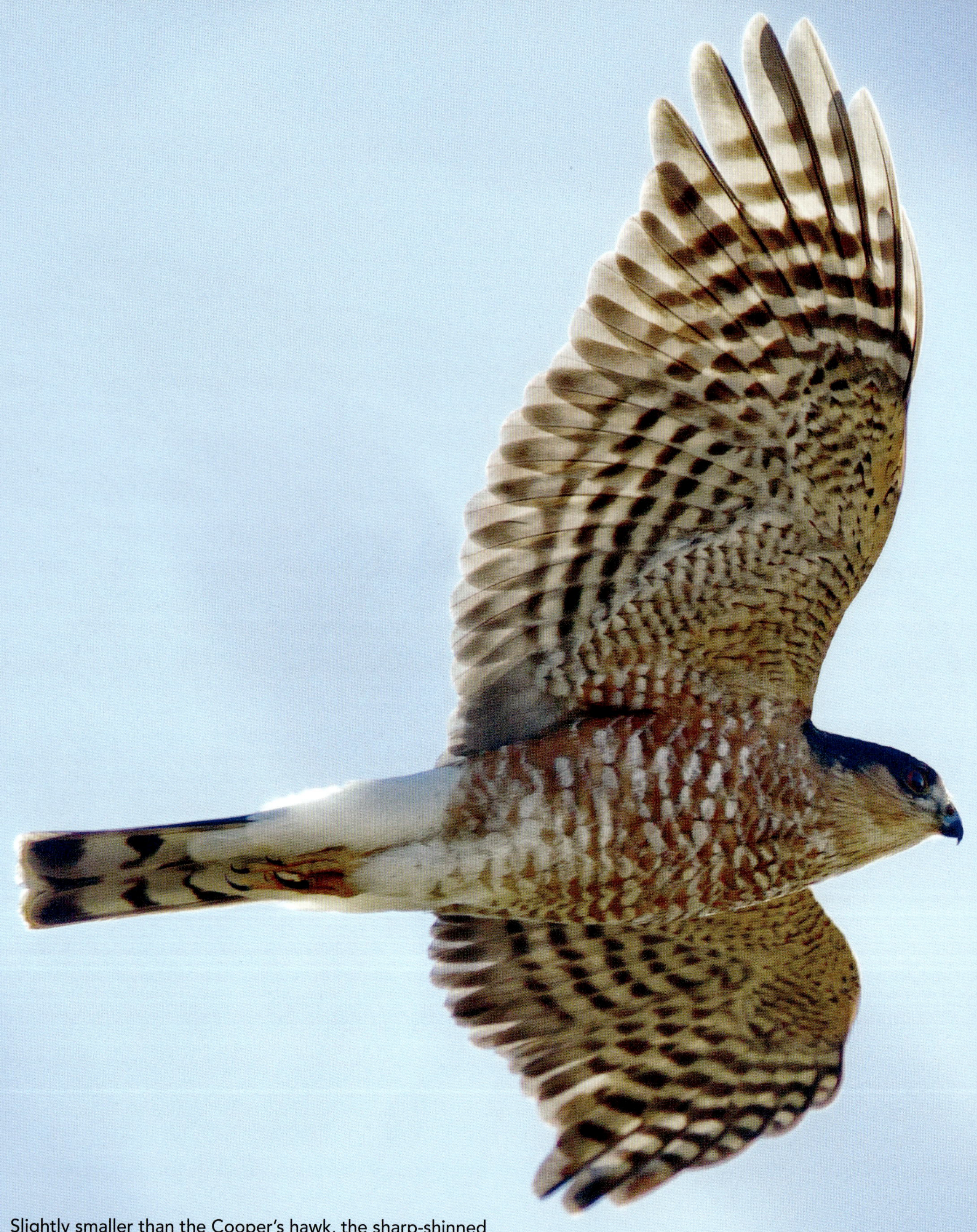

Slightly smaller than the Cooper's hawk, the sharp-shinned also has a more squared-off tail. As is the case with many raptors, the females are larger than the males. **OPPOSITE:** A perching sharp-shinned hawk displays the chest patterning and red eyes of an adult.

one another in flight.

Within a month of hatching, the young birds have grown from nestlings to fledglings and begin exploring the area around their nest. At this age the males, despite their smaller size, are the more adventurous gender and usually leave the nest before their sisters, even if hatched later. The young birds climb and flap to nearby branches, expanding their world as they strengthen and learn to control their rapidly growing muscles.

Parents continue to feed the fledglings as they flap and toddle through the neighboring trees. Fitful flapping leads to controlled flying, and soon the young birds are competing to be the first to spot a parent returning with food. The first one to see the incoming prize flies to meet the parent with the other juveniles in hot pursuit. The parents hand the food directly to the grasping talons of the young as they pass in flight. Improving skills means increasing challenges, and it is not long before the parents are tossing the prey to the young as they fly by, forcing the adolescents to improve their acrobatic skills by snatching their dinner out of the air.

As summer wanes, so do the family ties. Family groups break up and the birds become more and more solitary as they begin their autumnal drift. While southern birds may stay on their territories year round, northern birds move south for the winter, but their migratory patterns seem to be changing. Some do not travel as far south as they did in the past. They are "short-stopping," an ornithologists' term meaning they take advantage of concentrations of prey species such as doves, robins, sparrows, and starlings around rural and suburban bird feeders rather than traveling farther south.

Or maybe they are simply returning to habits from the times before the populations crashed, filling niches left empty for decades. The natural world has a way of self-correcting and bringing balance back to disrupted systems. Even though our accipiters experienced some trying times, they are recovering and adding their unique version of grace, beauty, elegance, and strength to the wilderness—in the far north and our own backyards.

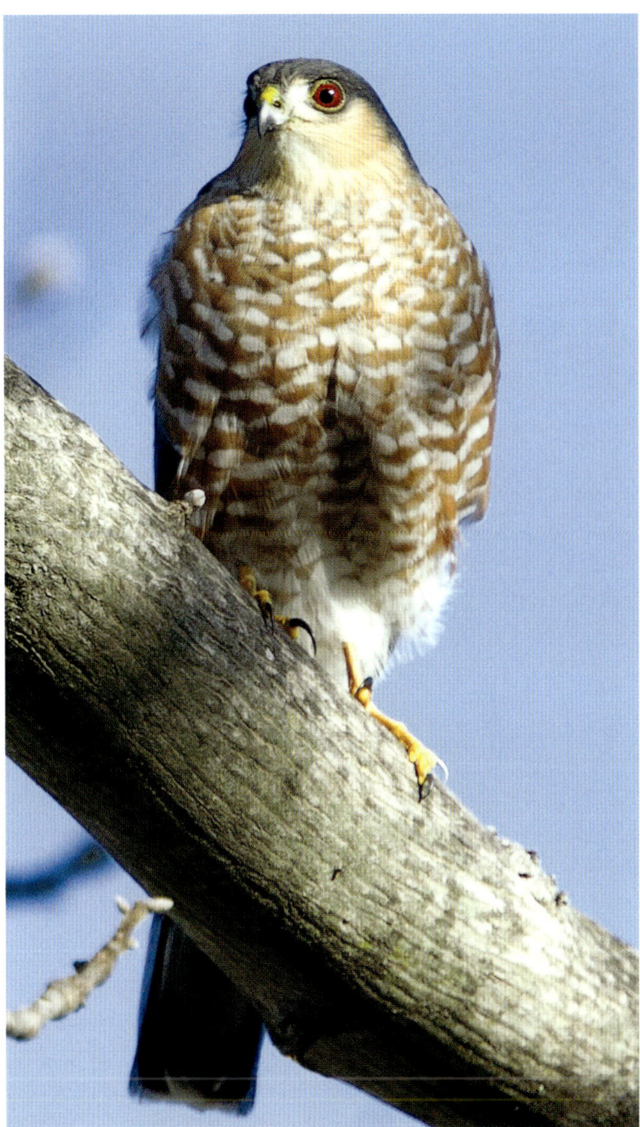

Measurements (in mm)

	Male	Female
Cooper's Hawk		
Culmen	15.6	20.0
Tail	170.0	205.0
Tarsus	60.0	73.6
Wing Chord	214	278

	Male	Female
Sharp-shinned Hawk		
Culmen	9.8	12.1
Tail	131.1	157.9
Tarsus	45.0	59.0
Wing Chord	170.9	201.5

Golden Eagle

(Aquila chrysaetos)

BY RICK BURKMAN

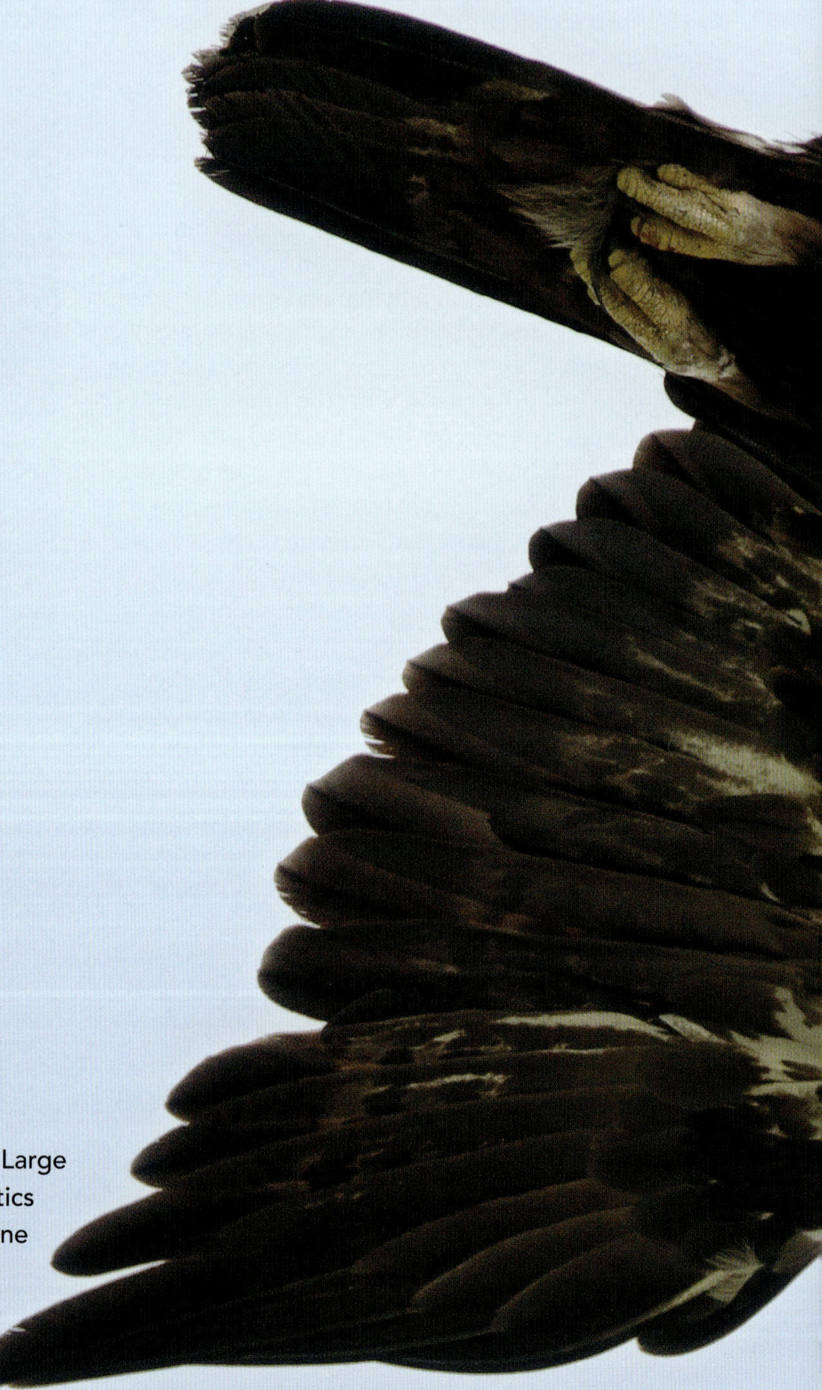

The Aquila chrysaetos adds the "regal" to eagle. Large eyes and big beak are two prominent characteristics of the golden eagle. Doing a life-size carving of one of these magnificent birds is a challenge indeed.

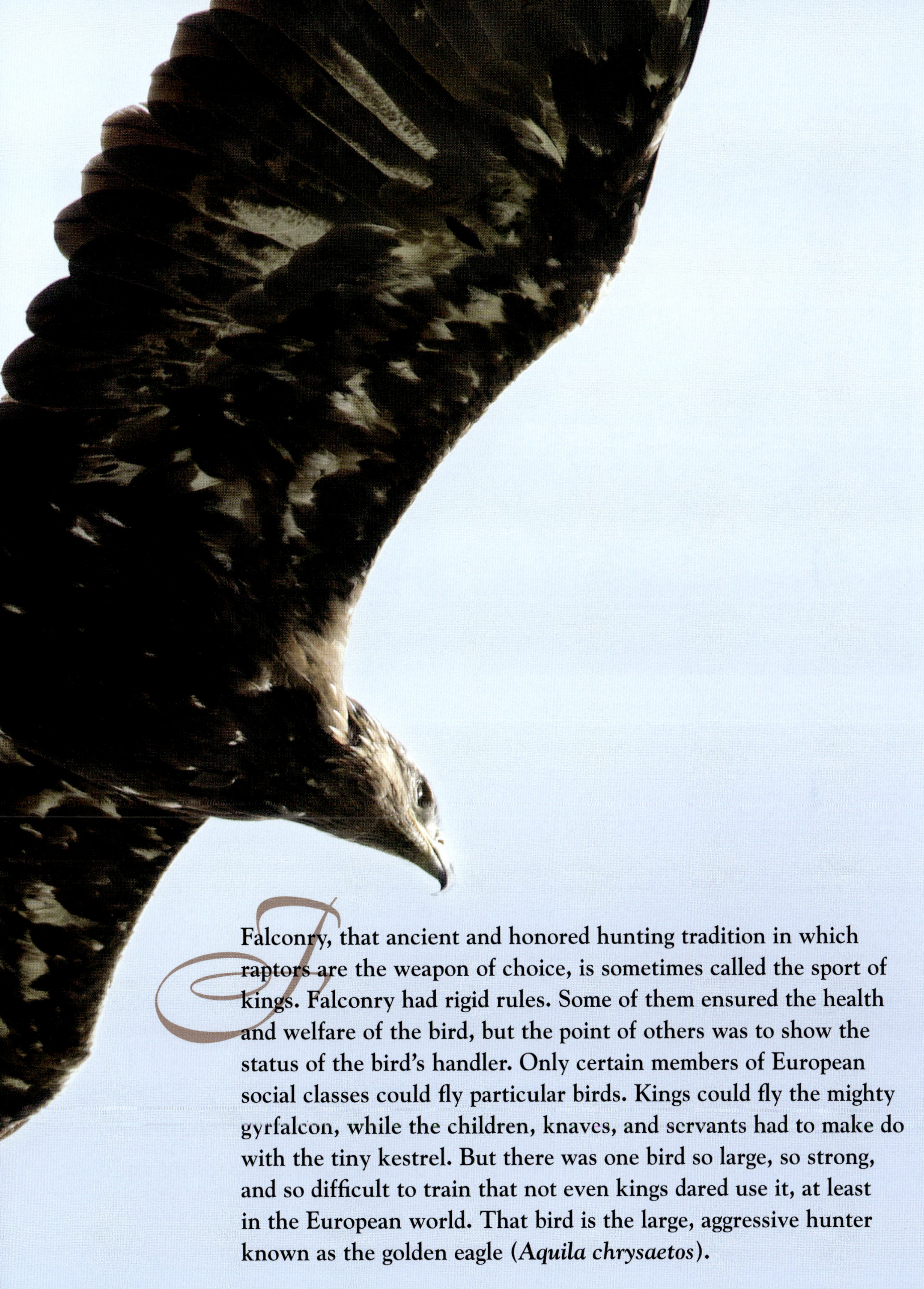

Falconry, that ancient and honored hunting tradition in which raptors are the weapon of choice, is sometimes called the sport of kings. Falconry had rigid rules. Some of them ensured the health and welfare of the bird, but the point of others was to show the status of the bird's handler. Only certain members of European social classes could fly particular birds. Kings could fly the mighty gyrfalcon, while the children, knaves, and servants had to make do with the tiny kestrel. But there was one bird so large, so strong, and so difficult to train that not even kings dared use it, at least in the European world. That bird is the large, aggressive hunter known as the golden eagle (*Aquila chrysaetos*).

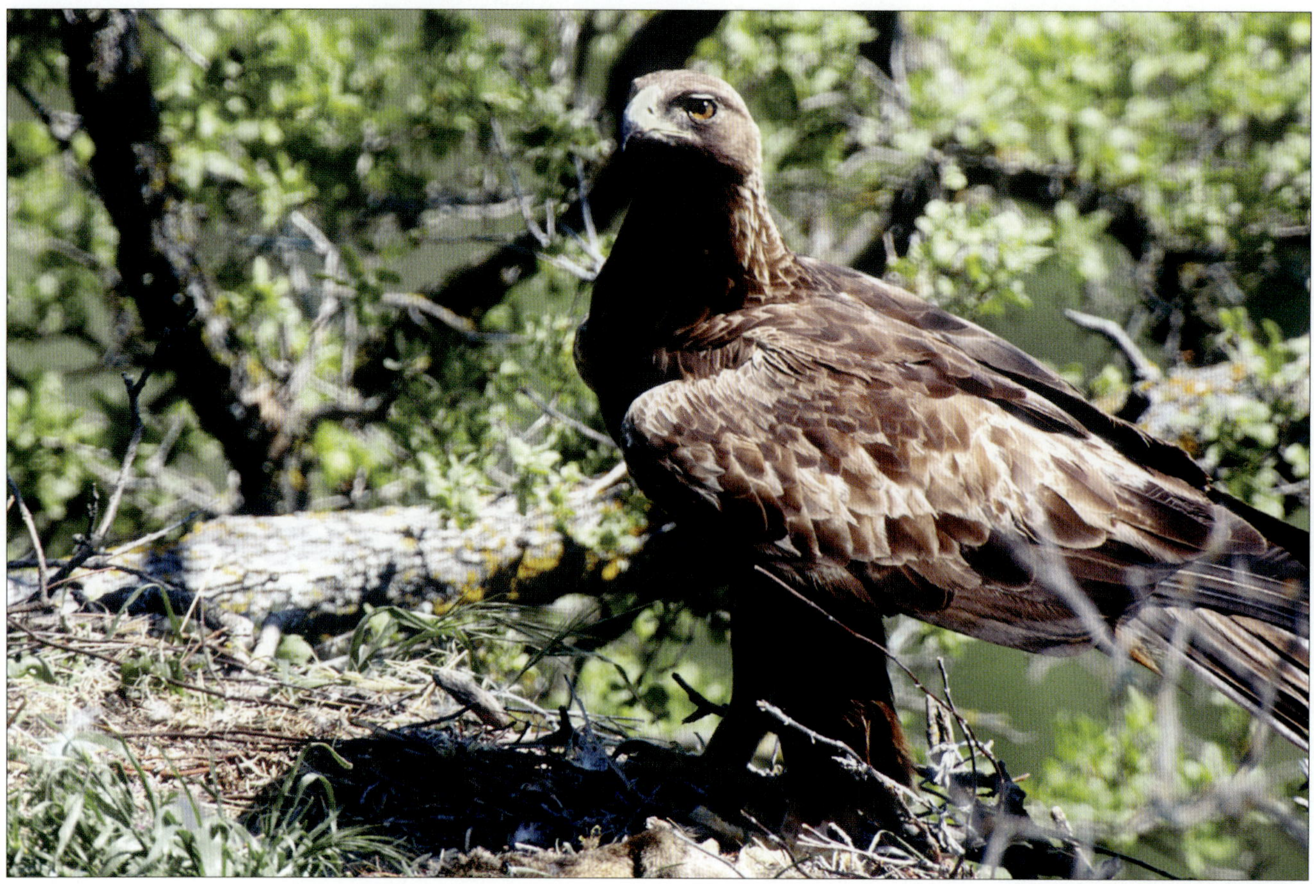

People revered the golden eagle then and they still do today. It is the national bird for five countries: Albania, Austria, Germany, Kazakhstan, and Mexico. The golden eagle also appears in the coat of arms of Egypt, Iraq, Palestine, and Romania. It's easy to understand why. The birds are awe inspiring. They grace the air with wingspans that can reach seven feet. (As is the case with other raptors, the female is larger than the male.) Golden eagles are not only big, they are powerful, capable of killing prey as large as deer and mountain goats. A 12-pound ball of feathered terror with sharp eyes zeroed in on its prey and needle-sharp talons extended in an obvious intent to kill, the golden eagle is a dangerous and deadly adversary, no matter how big or strong its target.

When their normal prey—ground squirrels, hares, marmots, for instance—is scarce, golden eagles have even attacked caribou. In at least one recorded instance, a golden eagle killed and left the scene with a brown bear cub. These birds can take their toll on livestock; in some places people use them to hunt foxes, coyotes, and wolves. Not only do golden eagles possess arrow-like precision to take land-based prey, they are agile enough to round out their diets with birds as small as jays and as large as swans and cranes. Few creatures can feel safe when a hungry golden is on the hunt.

The people of central Asia's northern steppes revere the golden eagle's large size and aggressive hunting abilities and pass that respect from generation to

Golden eagles are not only big, they are powerful, capable of killing prey as large as deer and mountain goats. A 12-pound ball of feathered terror with sharp eyes zeroed in on its prey and needle-sharp talons in a obvious intent to kill, the golden eagle is a dangerous and deadly adversary, no matter how big or strong its target.

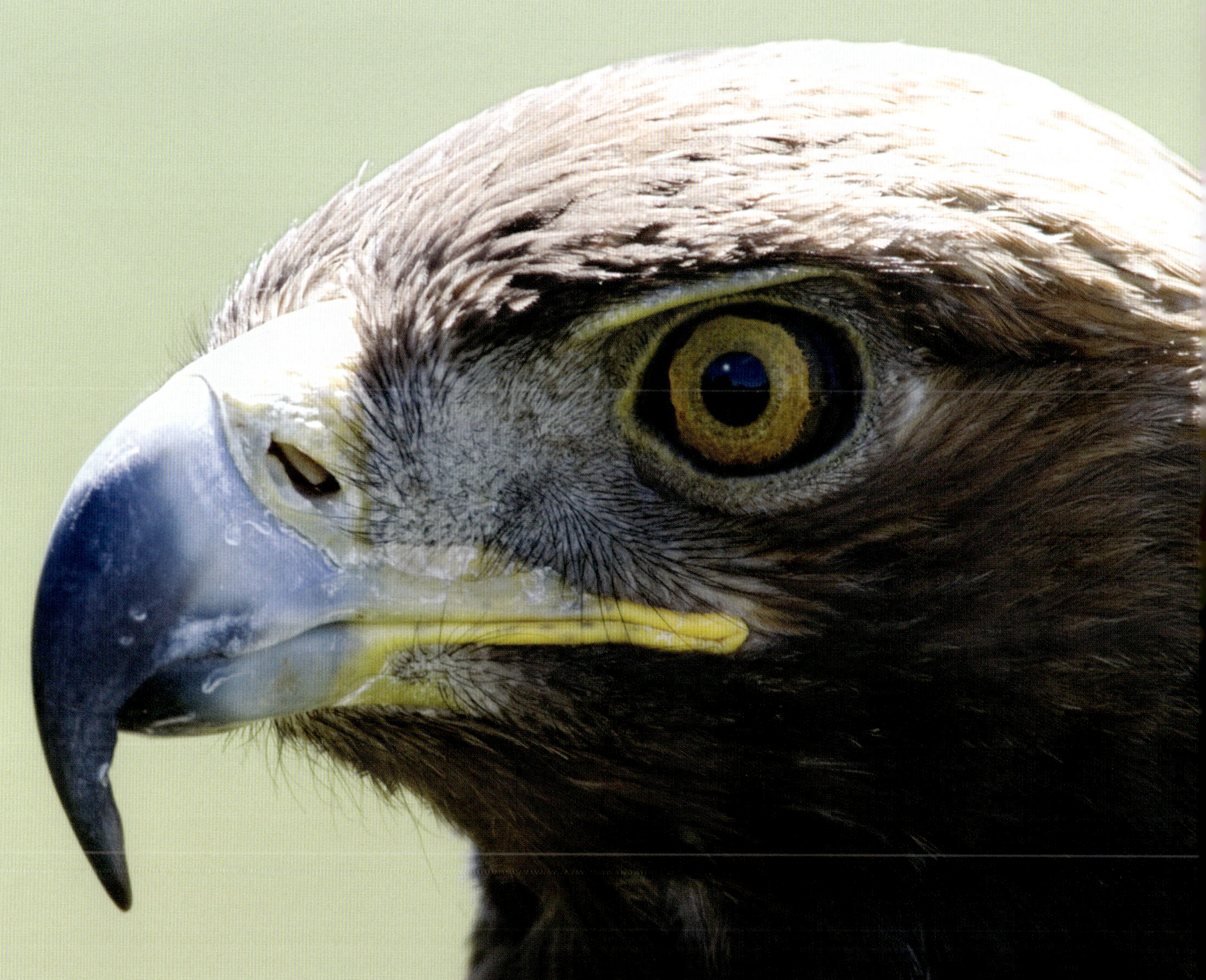

OPPOSITE: Golden eagles are ambitious nest builders and will continue adding sticks—and sometimes bones and antlers—to the dwelling throughout the year. **THIS PAGE:** The eagle's sharply hooked beak spells doom for the bird's prey. The ridges over the eyes give the eagle a particularly menacing expression that adds to its fierce reputation.

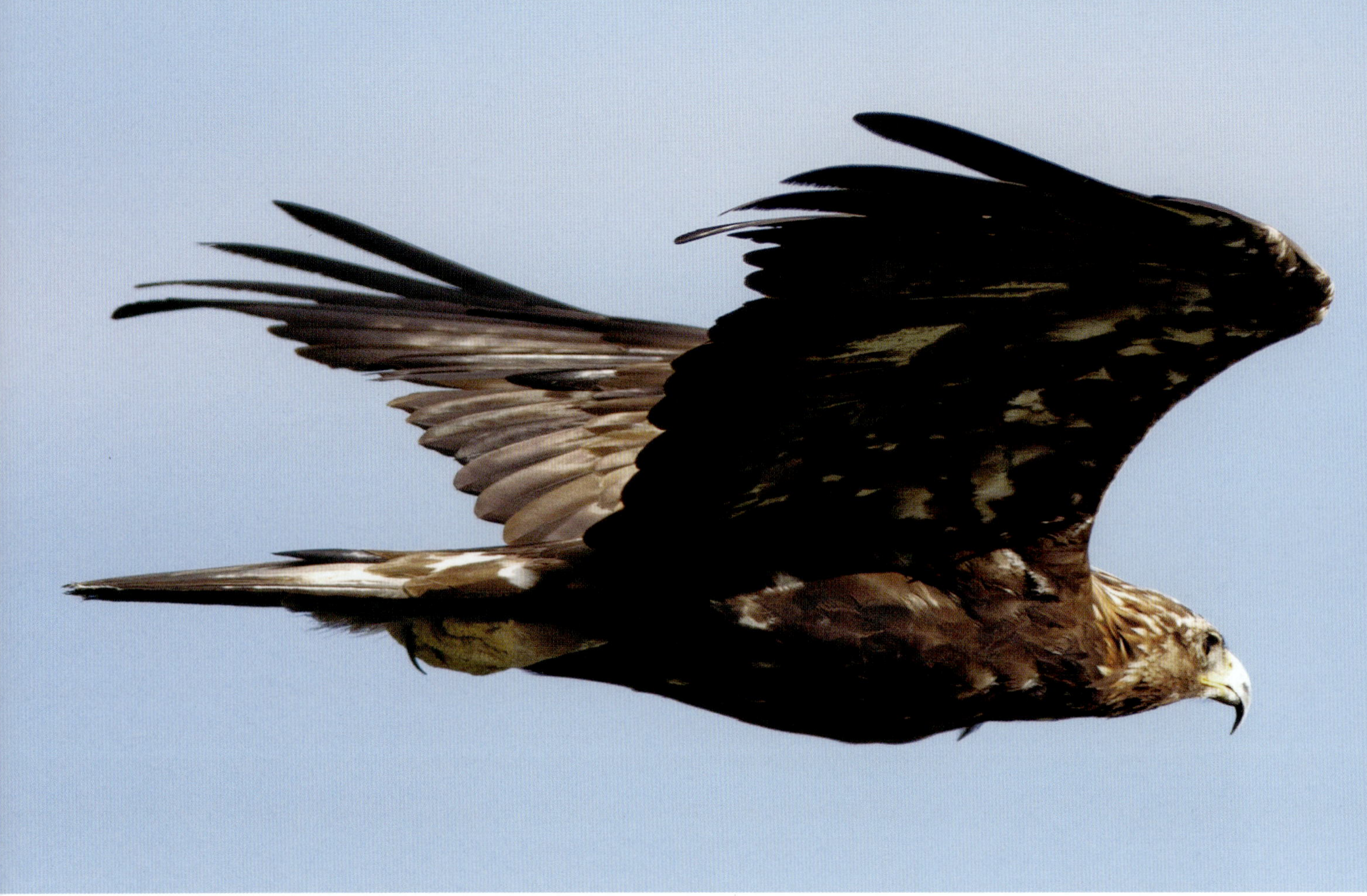

ABOVE: Equipped with large wings, golden eagles can soar for hours, but then swoop with deadly speed and accuracy down to the next meal. **OPPOSITE:** Although the golden eagle may appear similar in appearance to the bald eagle, it is actually more closely related to buteo hawks such as the red-tailed.

generation. A Berkutchi, a traditional native falconer who specializes in hunting with golden eagles, is a privileged member of society that is believed to have mystical powers of strength and fertility. Aged masters train their young apprentices in the methods of rearing and training these birds. When the eagles are ready, the Berkutchi use them to hunt the foxes and wolves that provide the furs that are so important in these cold regions. The sport is an honored one, but the bird's size and unpredictability add elements of danger, so the Berkutchi closely guard their secrets for selection, training, and nurturing. As is the case with all things of great import and consequence, the Berkutchi uphold these traditions with the utmost veneration and respect.

As with most raptors, pair bonding with golden eagles begins before the female lays eggs and the eaglets hatch. During their mating rituals, golden eagles use their flying prowess to create aerial displays, show their strength and home-making ability by carrying large sticks, and call to one another with strong songs reminiscent of other large buteos, to which they are closely related. (Despite their size and appearance they are not closely related to the bald eagle, which belongs with the sea eagles.) Once the birds form a pair bond, they may remain on their territory for their entire lives. It takes a big territory to nurture two birds of this size, and an eagle pair may defend an area of up to 11.6 square miles (30 square kilometers) from other golden eagles and large raptors.

They build large nests of sticks within their territorial boundaries, and they add sticks all year, as long as food holds out and the weather does not become too inclement. Some pairs have built up to 14 nests in trees, on rock ledges, and on outcroppings. They may favor one nest over another from year to year, likely an evolved strategy to eliminate an overabundance of feather lice and other vermin. Or maybe they just want to change the view. After the birds choose their nest for the year they add new material, weaving in sticks

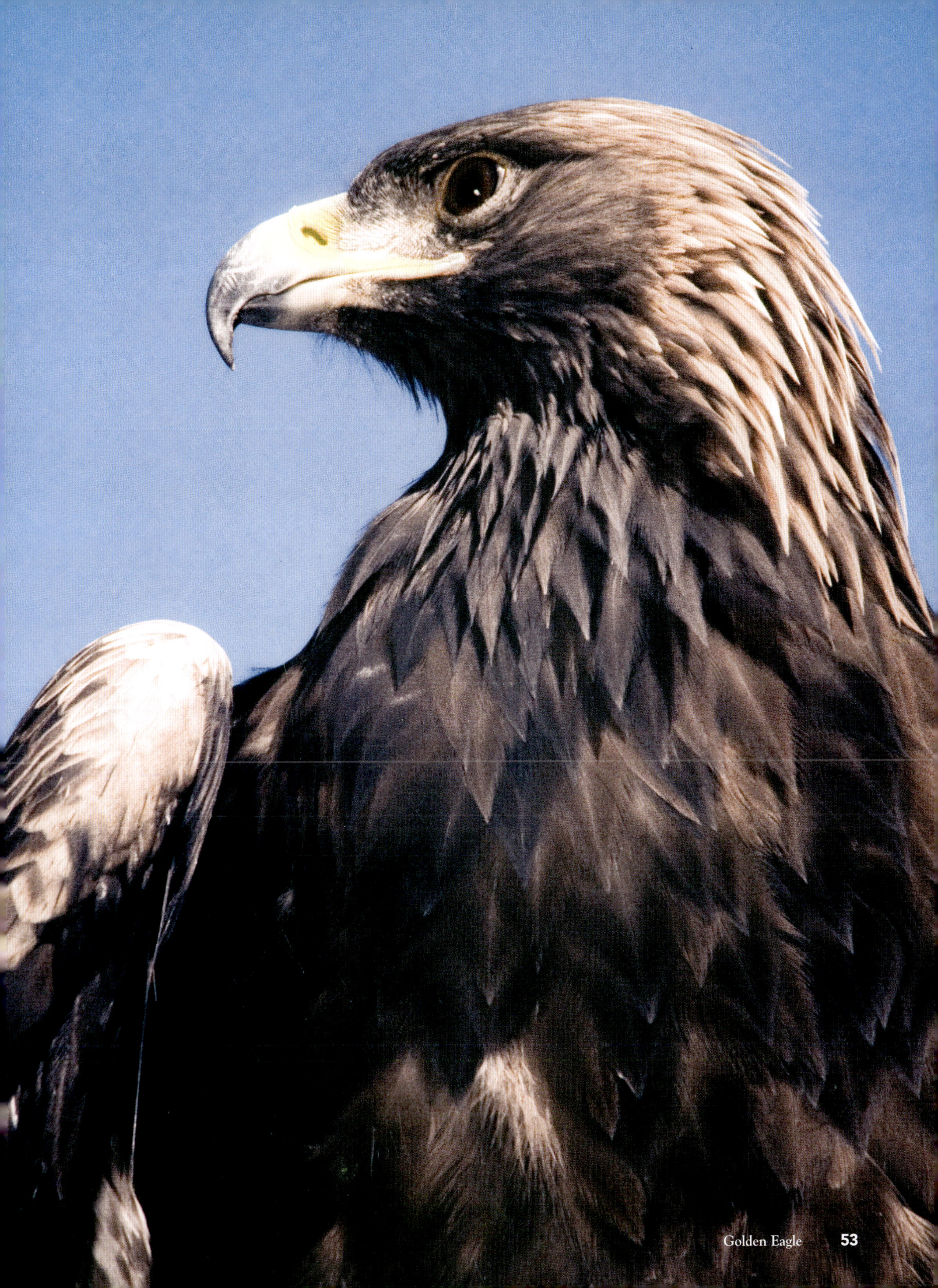

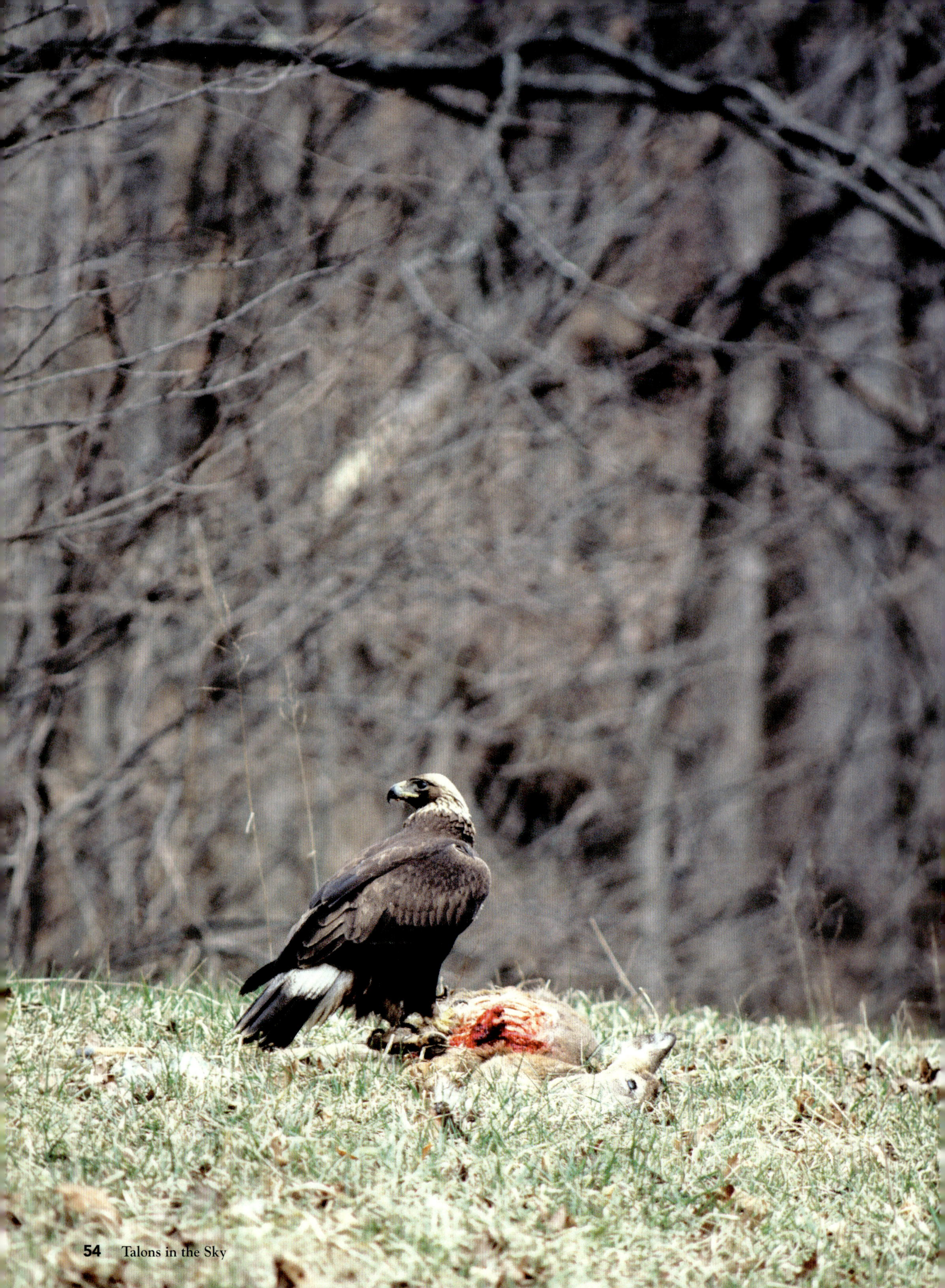

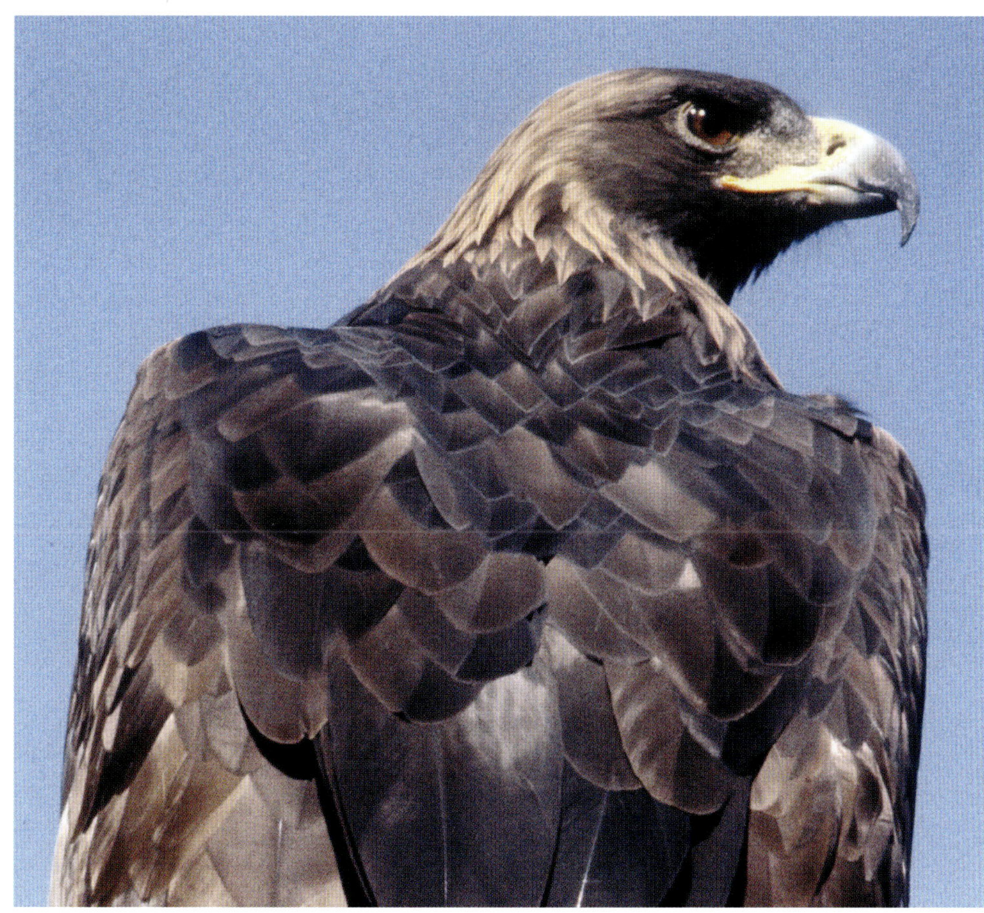

LEFT: The golden, crescent-shaped feathers on the bird's nape are a distinctive feature and give the bird its name. **OPPOSITE:** An eagle feasts on the carcass of a white-tailed deer. Unlike the bald eagle, which scavenges as much as it hunts, the golden is adept at taking live prey.

and limbs and even animal bones and antlers. They make a bowl in the center of the stick edifice and line it with softer materials, such as bark, grasses, leaves, lichens, mosses, shredded yucca, and even shreds of fur or feathers.

Once the eagles have prepared the nest the female takes a week to lay up to three white or cream-colored eggs that are evenly marked with small dots. Both males and females share the incubation duties and despite their large size and stern gazes they are caring and attentive parents—as long as the food is abundant. When prey proves scarce the parents may abandon the nest and eggs and wait until the following year to raise a brood. If all goes well, the incubation lasts for just under six weeks. The eaglets can take up to three days to break free of their shells, with one chick usually breaking free several days before the next emerges. This makes for a large variation in eaglet sizes, not always a positive for the smaller sibling. The bigger eaglets may force the smallest bird from the nest, harass it until it dies, or even make a meal of it. Sometimes the Berkutchi capture a possibly doomed smaller chick from a nest where two or more young birds have hatched. In such cases it does not seem cruel or detrimental to raise those birds in captivity.

As the eaglets grow the adults dutifully bring food to the nest and the youngsters voraciously consume it. After six weeks the eaglets begin exploring the world around them. First they walk about the immense stick nest, flapping and stretching their oversized wings. Then they explore nearby branches and, as their bravery increases, they begin to hop from branch to branch and then make their first flights from tree to tree. Soon the young eagles learn to spot prey with their incredibly enhanced vision. They begin to fly and swoop, and before long they can grab their victims with agility and ease. They have become lords of the sky. And after six months on their parents' territories, the young birds leave their homes to search out new lands, seek new adventures, and create their own families as they awe and amaze those of us stuck on the ground below.

There are only a few humans—the Berkutchis and other brave falconers, or even the adventuresome climbers who scale rocky cliffs and hike narrow mountain trails—who can, perhaps just for a moment, understand the sense of freedom and serenity of flying as the king of birds.

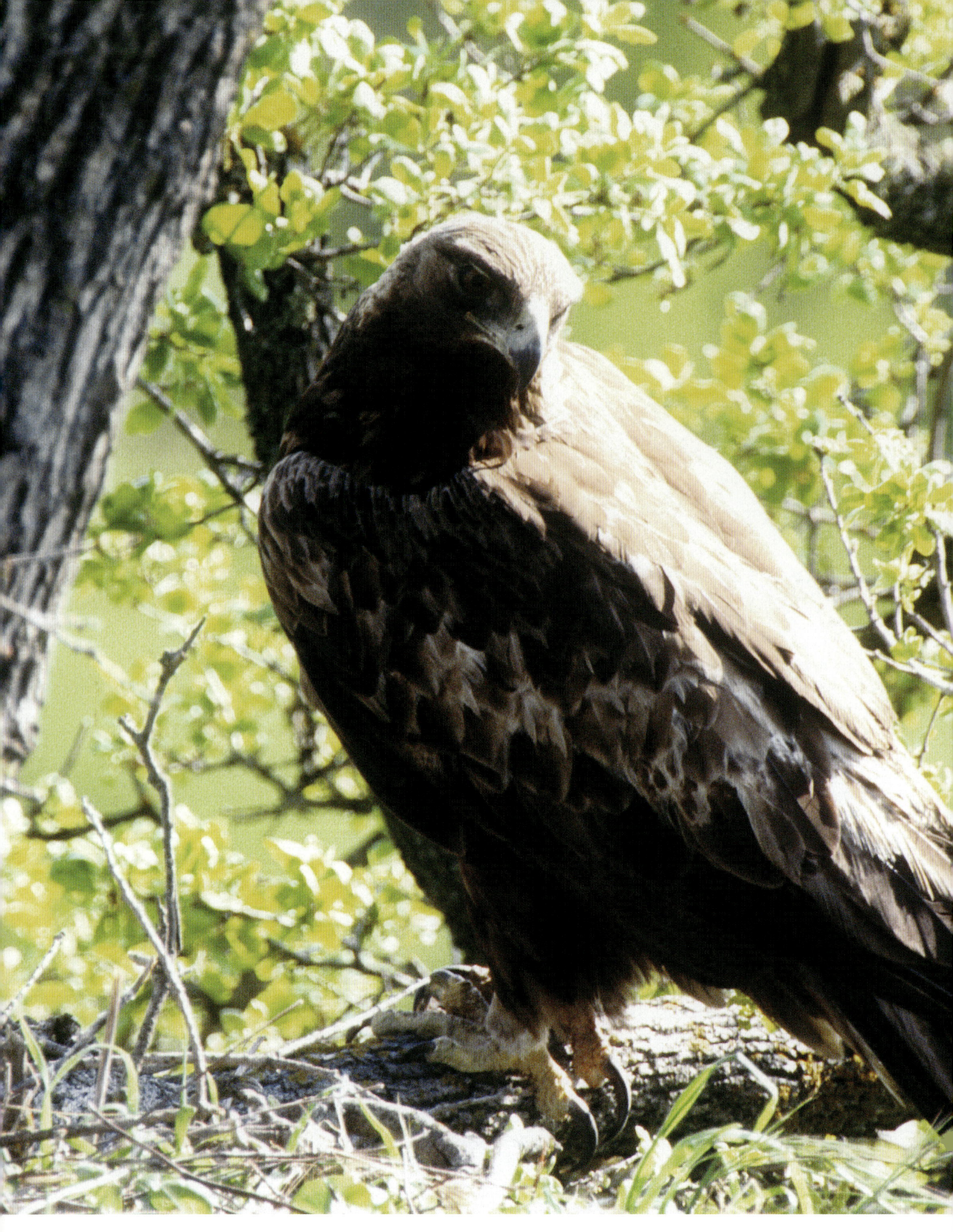

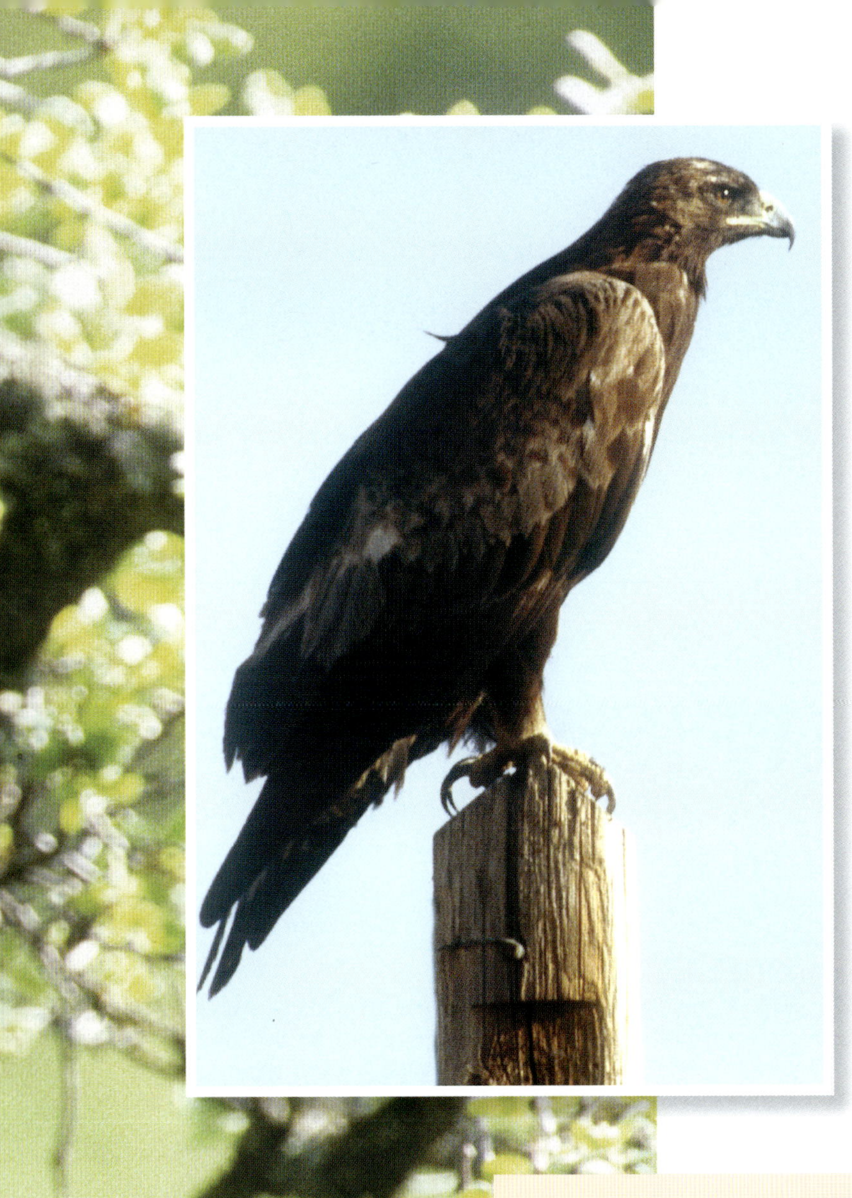

Note the large and powerful talons and the heavily feathered legs. The eagles use their talons to take down a wide variety of game, including foxes, coyotes, and wolves. Little wonder that the golden eagle has been an object of human fascination for centuries.

Measurements (in mm)

Variable/age class	Male	Female
Wing Chord (unflattened)		
Adult	595.0	640.4
Immature	585.9	632.2
Tail Length		
Adult	286.5	307.2
Immature	297.7	322.0
Culmen Length		
Adult	40.6	44.2
Immature	39.4	43.3
Foot Pad		
Adult/immature	131.6	145.4
Hallux-clawLength		
Adult	49.4	55.7
Immature	47.8	54.0

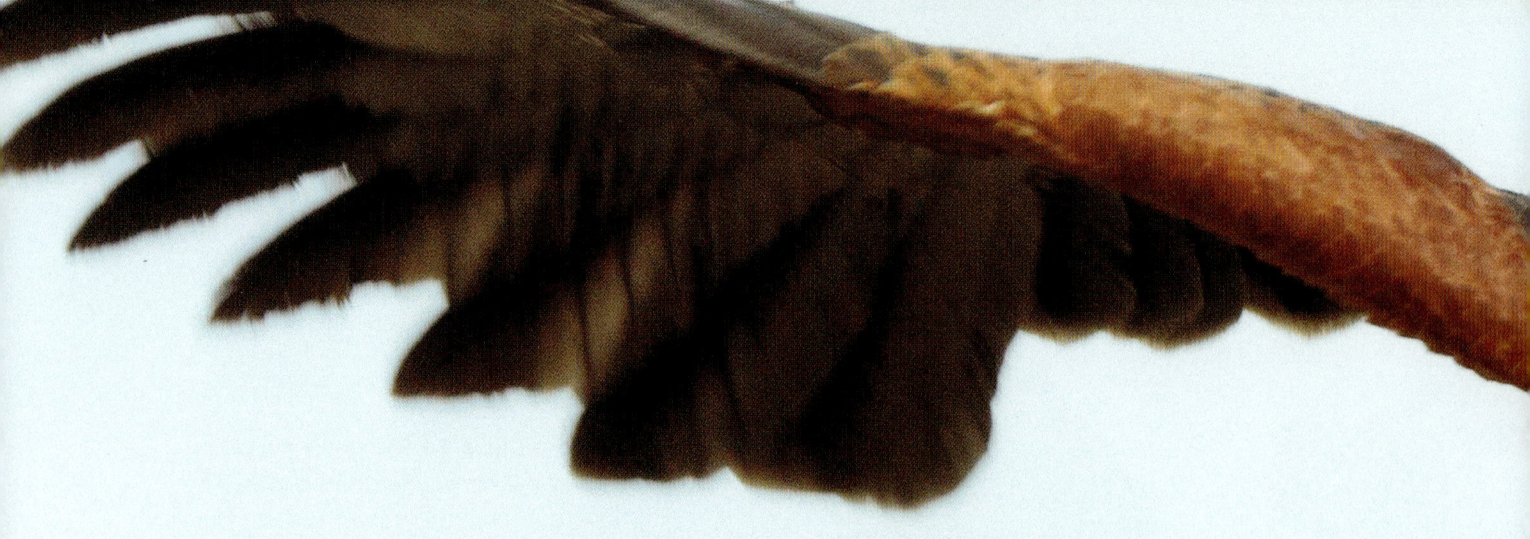

Harris's Hawk

(Parabuteo unicinctus)

BY KURT ROBINETTE

As the first rays of the sun begin to streak across the desert landscape, long shadows add contrast to the sand of the Sonoran. Tall saguaro cacti stand as sentinels above smaller cactis, occasional brush, and rocks. The sand quickly warms, and five black hawks position themselves along the tops of several saguaro. A few head bobs later, a large female Harris's hawk powers into the sky on a direct flight over nearby vegetation. With a shrill call and a blast of wings, a covey of Gambel's quail scatter in all directions. Undeterred, the hawk continues a steady climb above several stragglers. The other four hawks now launch from their perches and pump across the landscape. As several quail dive into cover, the female raptor circles around and lands on a nearby cactus, waiting for the other hawks to catch up. One young male lands on the ground near the quail and reaches his long legs into the brush to flush them out. Another launch by the quail is countered by strong flights by the other members of the pack. Quickly, the quail are dispatched, and all of the hawks land and partake of the group effort.

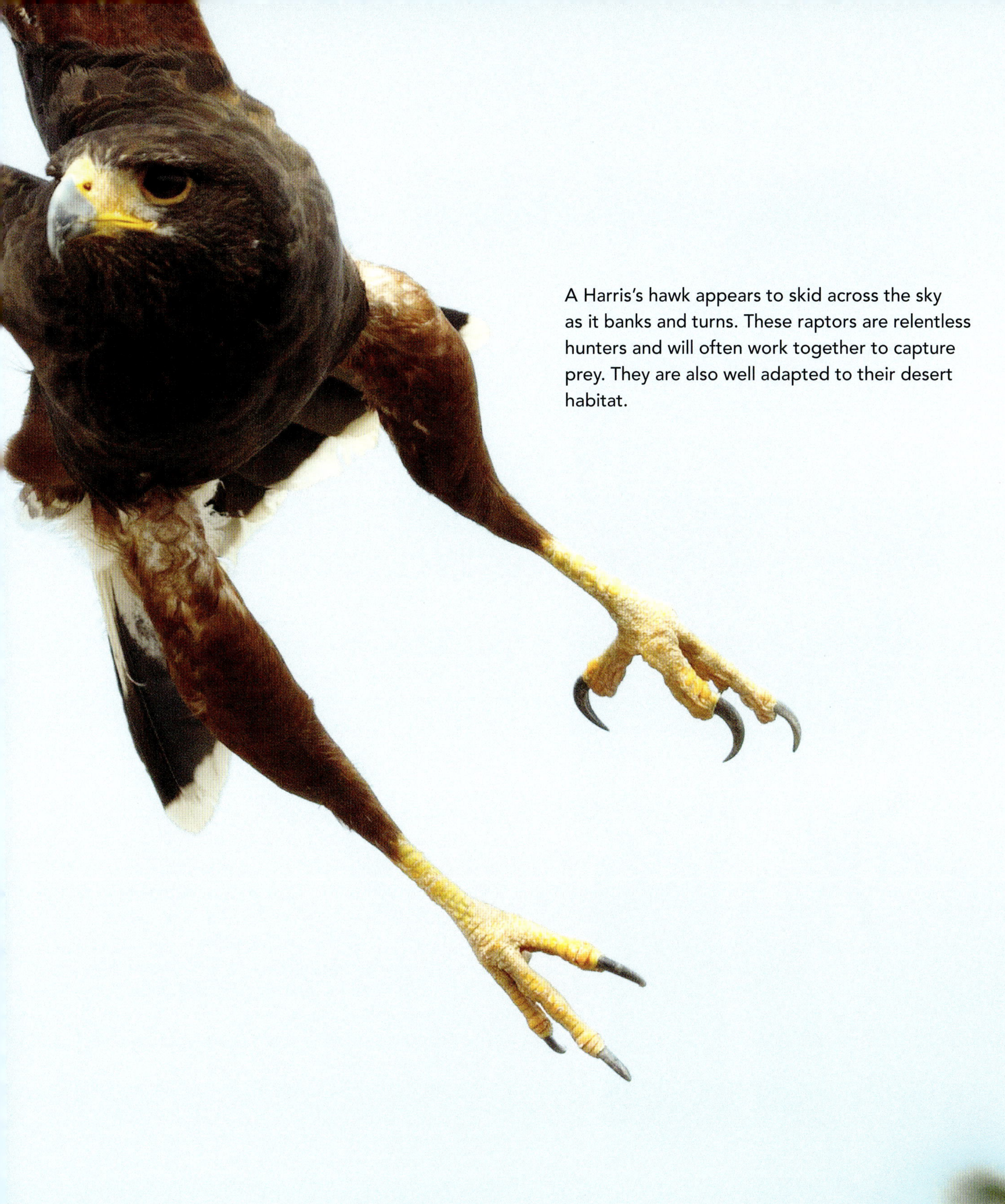

A Harris's hawk appears to skid across the sky as it banks and turns. These raptors are relentless hunters and will often work together to capture prey. They are also well adapted to their desert habitat.

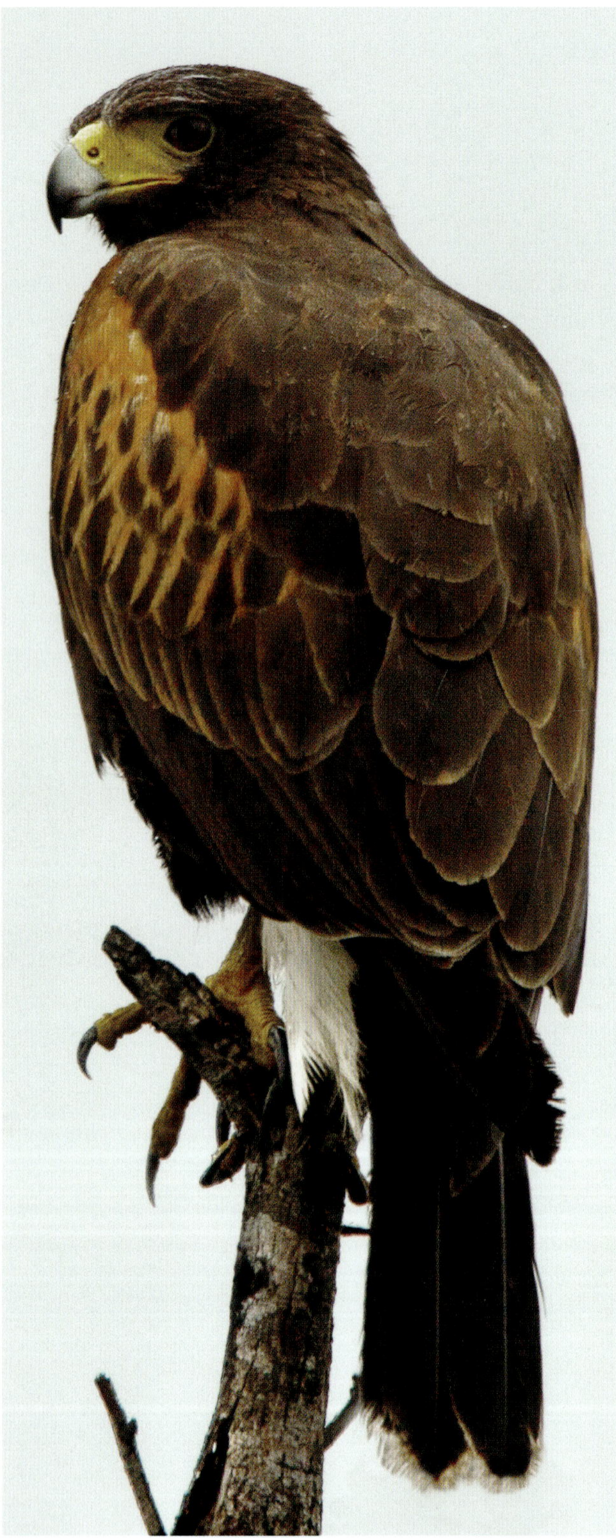

ABOVE: John James Audubon named this bird "Harris's" after a friend, but some people call this the bay-winged hawk because of the chestnut-colored shoulder patches. **OPPOSITE:** The bird's cere and eyelids are bright yellow; the beak is bluish with a black tip. The eyes (11 to 12 mm) are a light brown.

The Harris's hawk (*Parabuteo unicinctus*) was named by John James Audubon in honor of his friend, Edward Harris. Another name for the Harris's is the bay-winged hawk, from the bird's chestnut shoulder patches.

The lone member of the parabuteo family, the Harris's hawk is a sleek, lean-looking bird. Compared to a typical buteo, the parabuteo has a faster wingbeat, a very long tail, and is highly adapted to the hot desert environment. These birds tolerate heat very well with their sleek feathers and long legs that assist in heat dispersion. Consequently, the Harris's has a low tolerance of cold, and frostbite of toes easily occurs if temperatures go much below freezing.

From a distance, the hawk looks black. Close up, however, this tri-colored hawk becomes rather striking. Although there appear to be two subspecies of Harris's, the colorations are so much alike that it is generally only where they are found in the world that readily distinguishes them. The Texan Harris's (*Parabuteo unicinctus harrisi*) is observed from Texas to the far tip of South America. The Sonoran or Arizona Harris's (*Parabuteo unicinctus superior*) ranges from southern California and Arizona to Baja and western Mexico. The Sonoran is generally considered a larger bird, though there is so much overlapping in sizes that most observers would have a difficult time deciding which subspecies they were looking at without a global positioning system and a map.

The adult bay-winged hawk is generally a blackish or sooty brown overall color with shoulders, underwing coverts, and thighs a bright chestnut. Upper- and under-tail coverts and a tip about one inch in width on the tail are white. Cere, eyelids, and legs are bright yellow. The immature Harris's is similar to the adult except that its underparts are streaked with whitish to gold markings. The thighs are barred with white. Upper parts are more or less edged with rufous, the outer tail feathers are obscurely barred, and the feet, cere, and eyelids are a pale yellow. Sexes appear similar. Females are generally larger, but occasionally a large male will be the same size as a small female. Females have a 10-inch tail, while males' are eight inches in

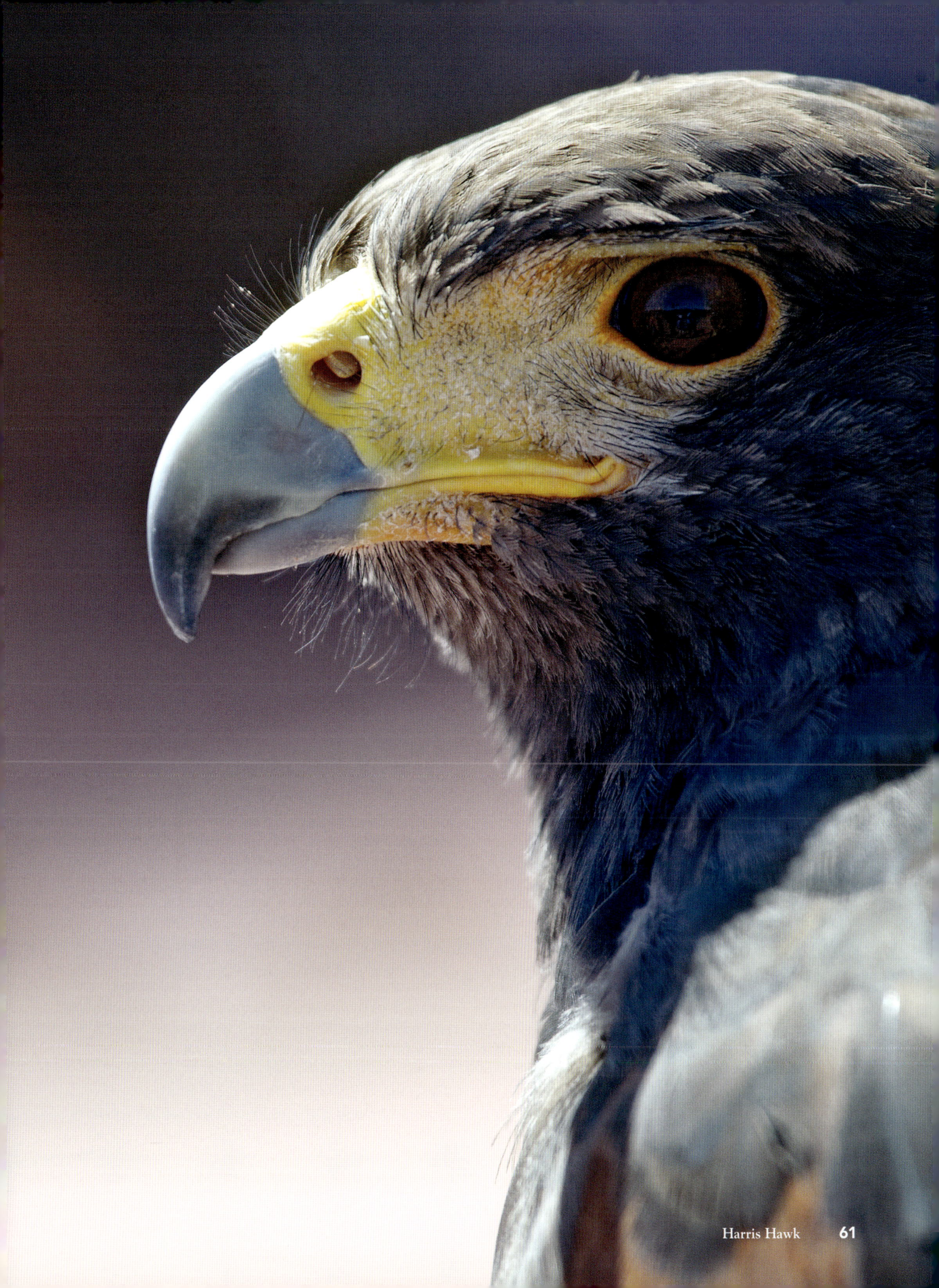

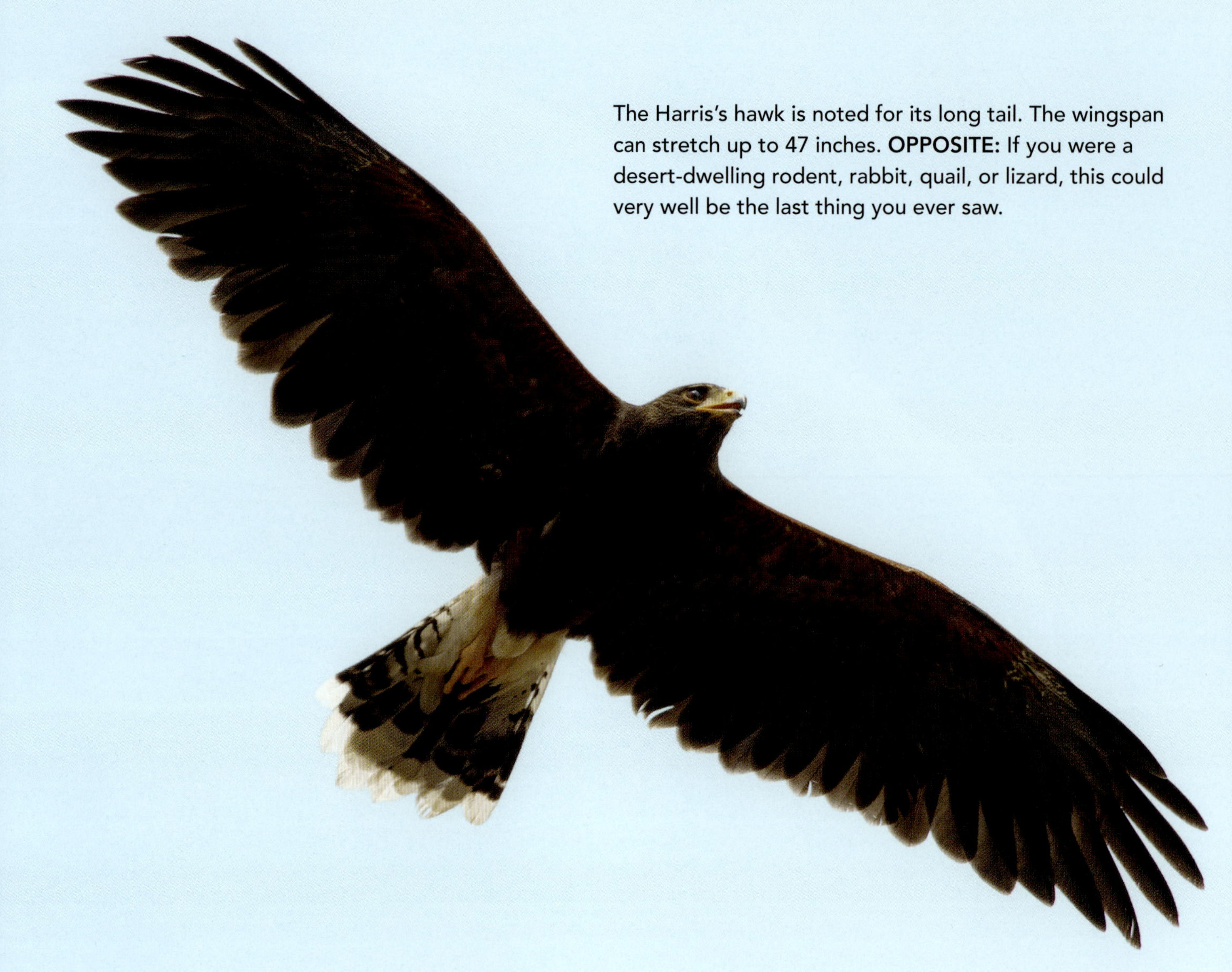

The Harris's hawk is noted for its long tail. The wingspan can stretch up to 47 inches. **OPPOSITE:** If you were a desert-dwelling rodent, rabbit, quail, or lizard, this could very well be the last thing you ever saw.

length. The eyes are a medium brown (11 to 12 mm). The beak is bluish with a black tip. The Harris's hawk has a wingspan of 40 to 47 inches and is 18 to 23 inches in length. Its plumage is unbelievably hardy and can withstand the abuse that desert hunting requires. The tip of a Harris's tail feather can bend all the way to the barb without breaking. No other raptor has such a durable outfit.

Most observers quickly notice how long the tail appears when compared to the rest of the bird, and the extremely long legs, which are emphasized by their bright yellow color. The Harris's is adept on the ground, can run fairly quickly, and will walk into tight areas in pursuit of quarry. Those lengthy legs also come in handy for reaching prey that feels it is safely out of reach. It is not uncommon to see a Harris's reach into a rabbit hole and "bring a rabbit out of a hat" successfully.

This hawk has a long, harsh, buteo-like scream when warning others. First-year birds are extremely vocal and have a high-pitched squawk that they use almost every waking moment. Perhaps this behavior is to help the others keep track of the youngsters' whereabouts. There are also a series of squawks and notes that the birds apparently use to communicate with each other. In the raptor world, intelligence varies among the different species. Surprising to many, owls are the least intelligent, with eagles among the most intelligent. Harris's hawks are considered to be the smartest of the hawks, and many feel that they show more intelligence than eagles. In the hunt, one can see their problem-solving intellect in action.

This highly adaptable hawk will soar overhead like a buteo, power off a high perch like a goshawk, stoop from high altitudes like a falcon, crash recklessly through trees and brush, and even chase its prey on foot. Males appear to be more aerial in nature and can climb faster than the steady and powerful females. A

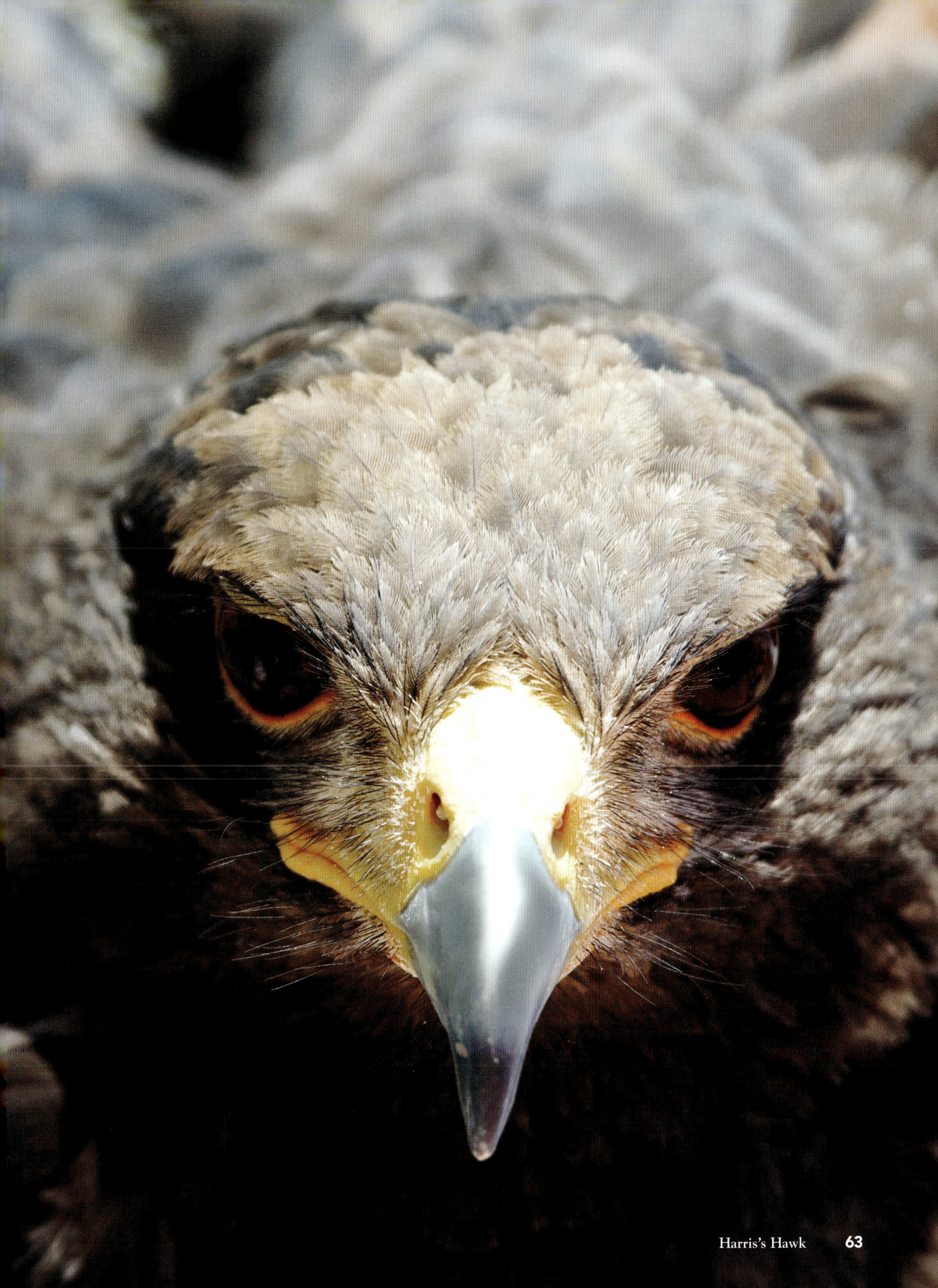

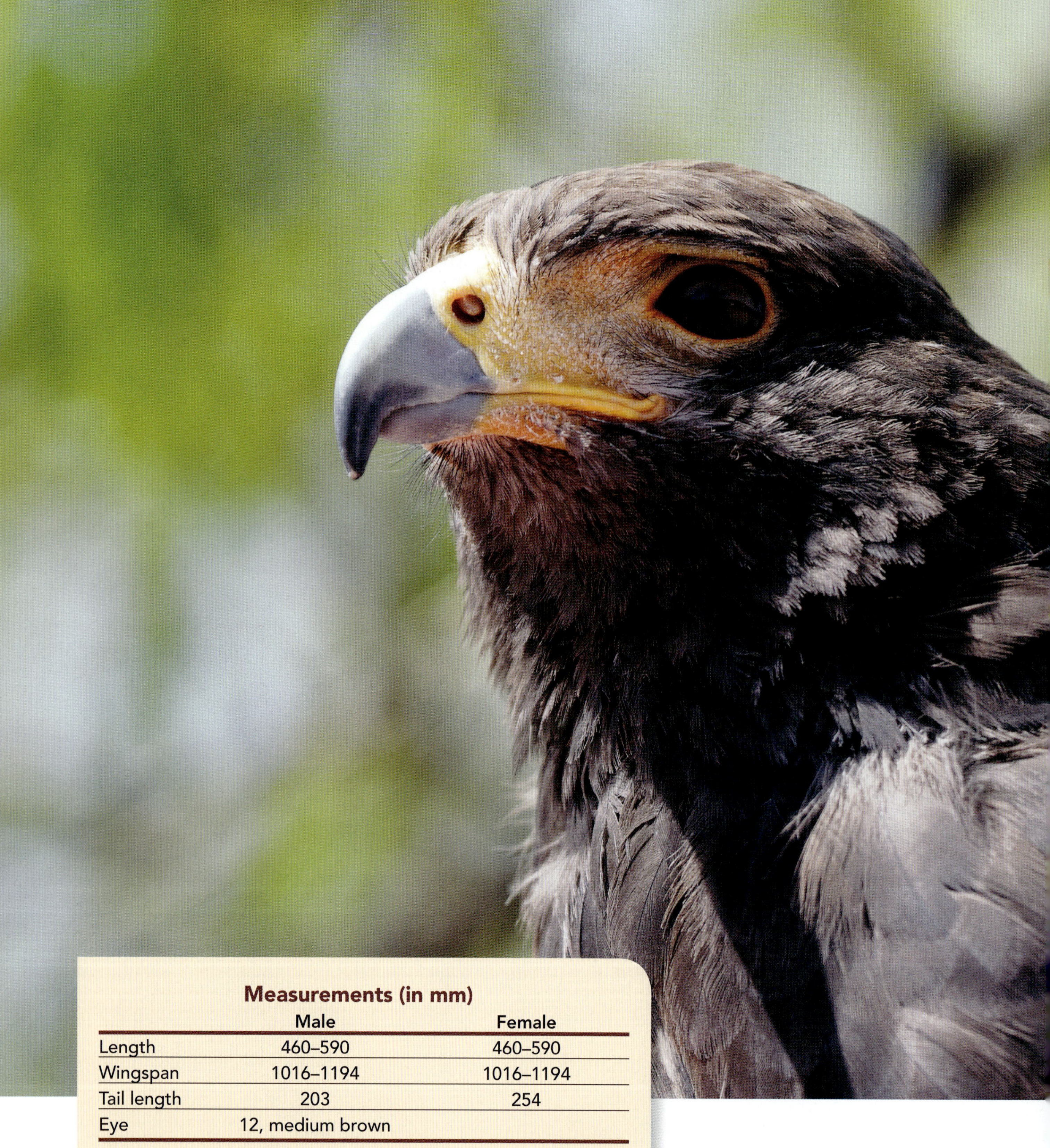

Measurements (in mm)

	Male	Female
Length	460–590	460–590
Wingspan	1016–1194	1016–1194
Tail length	203	254
Eye	12, medium brown	

Females are generally larger, but occasionally a large male will be the same size as a small female. Females have a 10-inch tail, while males' are eight inches in length. The eyes are a medium brown (11 to 12 mm). The beak is bluish with a black tip. The Harris's hawk has a wingspan of 40 to 47 inches and is 18 to 23 inches in length.

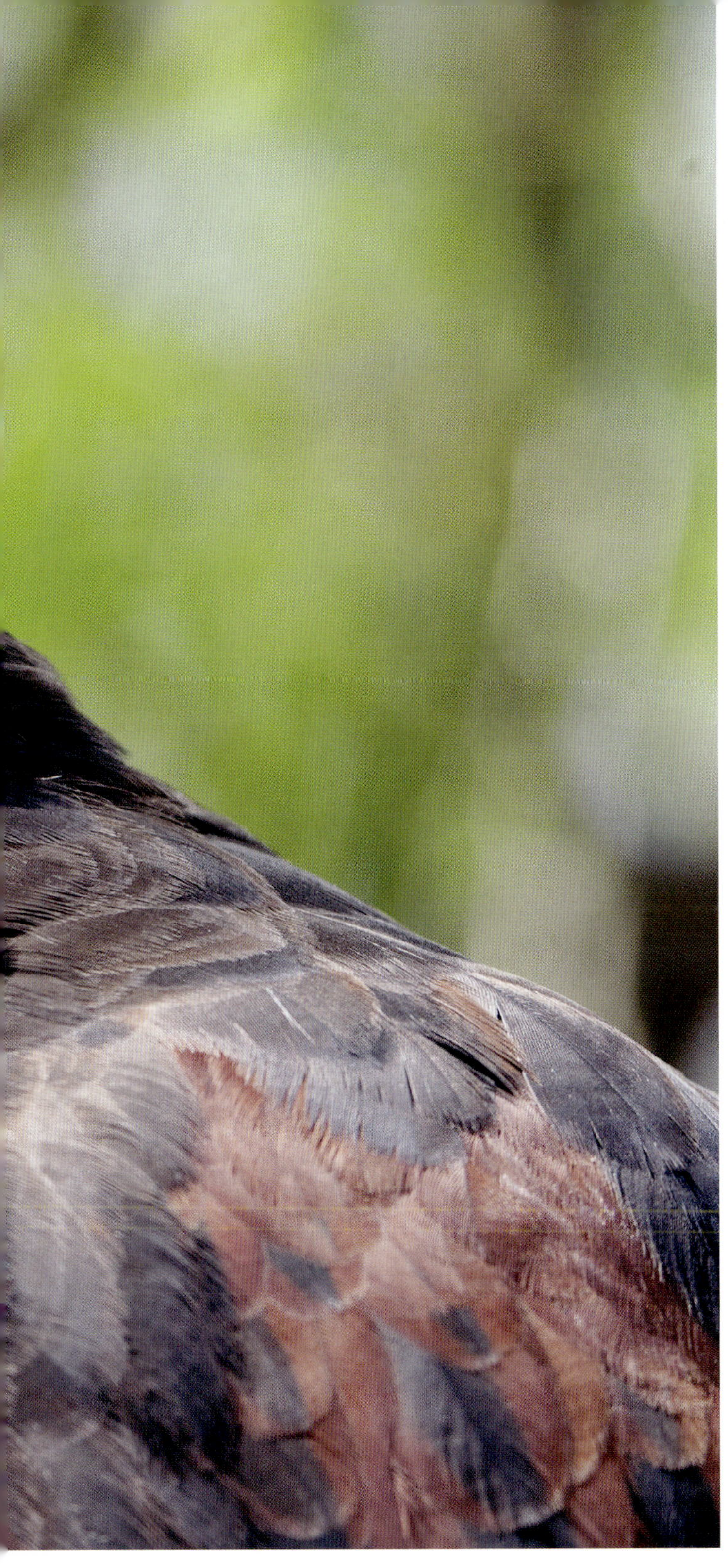

From a distance, the hawk looks black. Close up, however, this tri-colored hawk becomes rather striking.

When it comes to intelligence, the Harris's hawk appears to be at or near the top of the scale for raptors. When hunting together, the birds demonstrate problem-solving skills and appear to communicate with each other through various vocalizations.

female can capture jackrabbits without much problem. The male will usually try to capture smaller prey and is more likely to take birds than the female. Cottontail rabbits are the most common mammal taken by the Harris's, and the hawks quickly dispatch their prey with the powerful clutch of feet and talons.

Most raptors are solitary except during breeding season. The Harris's, however, is a very social bird and can be found in wolf-like packs of four to seven birds. These packs are as close to family units as can be seen in the bird world. A typical group consists of a female and two males with several sub-adults and immature youngsters. There are many advantages to this group effort. Acting as a team, all participate in the hunt. When one of the birds sights prey, it begins pursuit and gives a "come on" chirp to the others. One bird may act as a spotter, one a flusher, and others as hunters. A gang of hawks can take larger quarry. The Harris's diet includes rabbits, squirrels, wood rats, and other rodents; Gambel's quail, scaled quail, other birds; and lizards. Several researchers insist that Harris's do not eat snakes, though their environment is full of them. Once a bird captures its quarry, the individual mantles and screams defensively as others come to eat. The scream is mostly just a bluff, as the whole group gathers around the "table" and the food quickly disappears in the circle of mantling birds. With such an intimidating group, there are few enemies besides habitat loss and power lines. Owls frequently take clutches of young at night. Coyotes and bobcats also take their tolls on youngsters and adults if they get a chance. The adults are not afraid of much and, with dedication, will defend their nesting areas from intruders.

Even more atypical of other raptors, the Harris's

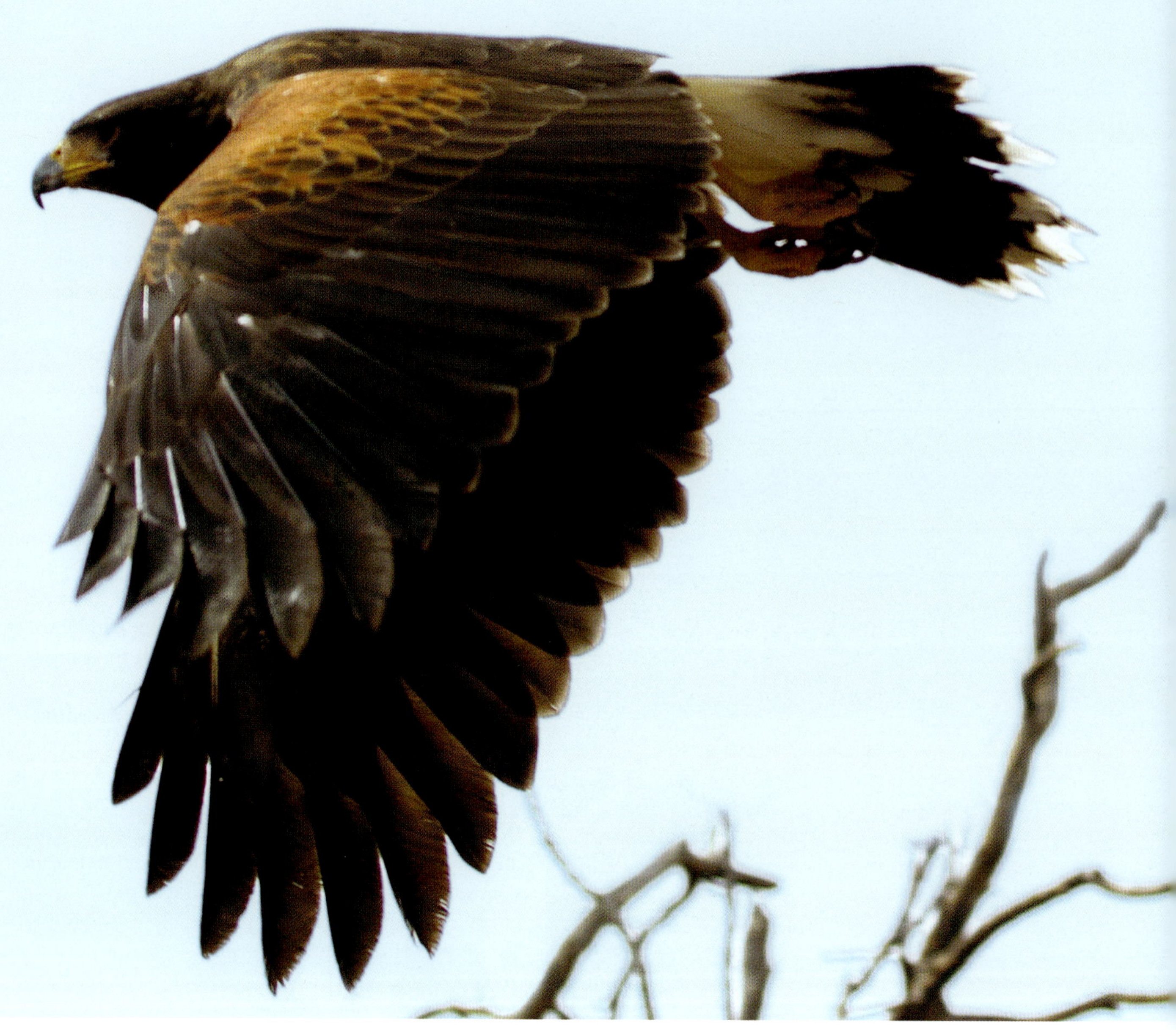

ABOVE: The adult bay-winged hawk is generally a blackish or sooty brown overall, with shoulders, underwing coverts, and thighs a bright chestnut. Upper- and under-tail coverts and a tip about one inch in width on the tail are white. **OPPOSITE:** Known for their long legs, these hawks have tough and powerful feet. They can use them to pluck rabbits from their burrows or to chase prey on foot.

appears to have monogamous, polygamous, and polyandrous nesting behaviors. The most common scenario is one dominant female with two males, and DNA samples have shown that she often breeds with both. Having two husbands has its rewards, as both males try to keep her happy by providing food for the group.

Nesting activity usually begins anywhere from mid-January through August, with the majority of nests becoming active from April through June. Many groups have more than one clutch of young in a year, and the first clutch often participates in rearing their younger siblings. Most Harris's nests are eight to 30 feet off the ground in Spanish bayonet, paloverde, yucca, mesquite, cactus, hackberry, and other low trees. The nest is compactly made—a platform of sticks, twigs, weeds, and roots. It can be lined with grass, bark, elm shoots, Spanish moss, and green mesquite. The female generally lays between three to five eggs in intervals over several days. The eggs are dull white and usually unmarked. Incubation takes 33 to 36 days and is done by both sexes and many members of the clan. Newly hatched hawks are fed every few hours during daylight.

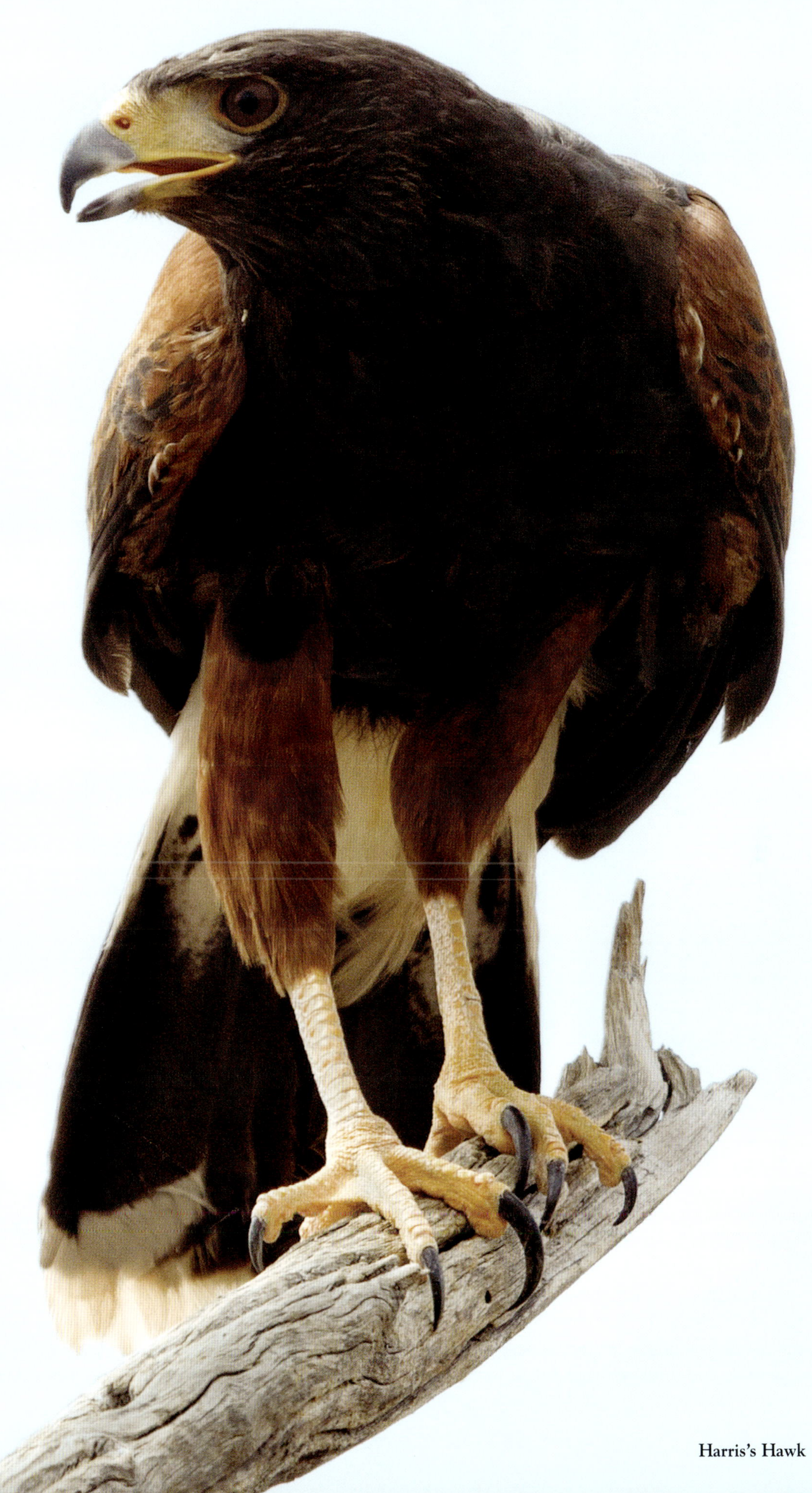

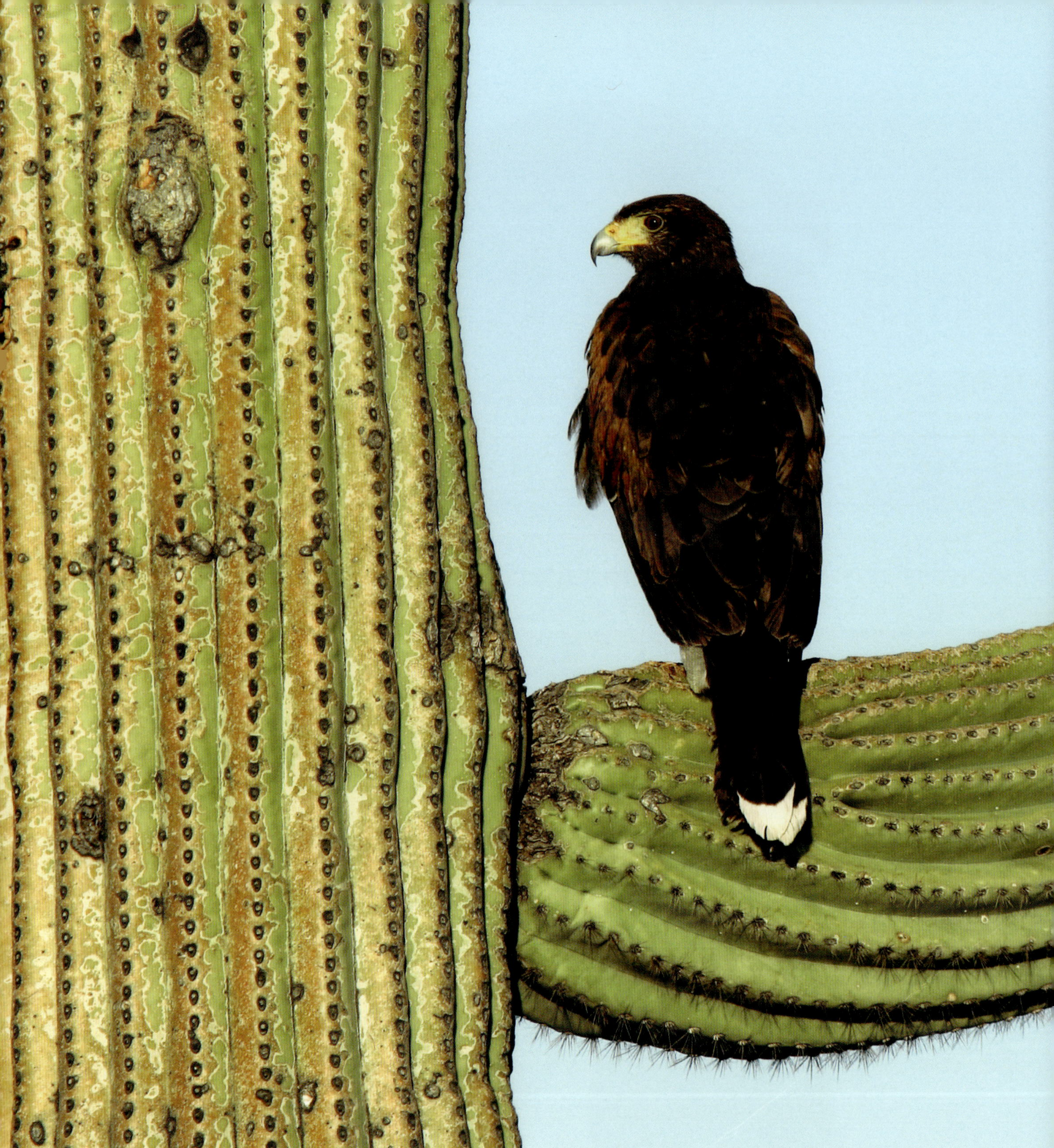

Fledglings are in the nest for 40 to 45 days. The young birds usually remain in the area for at least two to three months after gaining the ability to fly.

Most raptors suffer a very high mortality rate, with only one in four youngsters surviving the first year. Harris's hawks average much better because of the family protection and hunting techniques. No doubt, the young birds learn to hunt from their parents and quickly learn to provide for others. Wild Harris's hawks live up to 12 years. In captivity, birds over 24 years have been noted.

Drastic alteration of environment is devastating to all forms of wildlife. The disappearance of many desert areas is having an effect on the Harris's population.

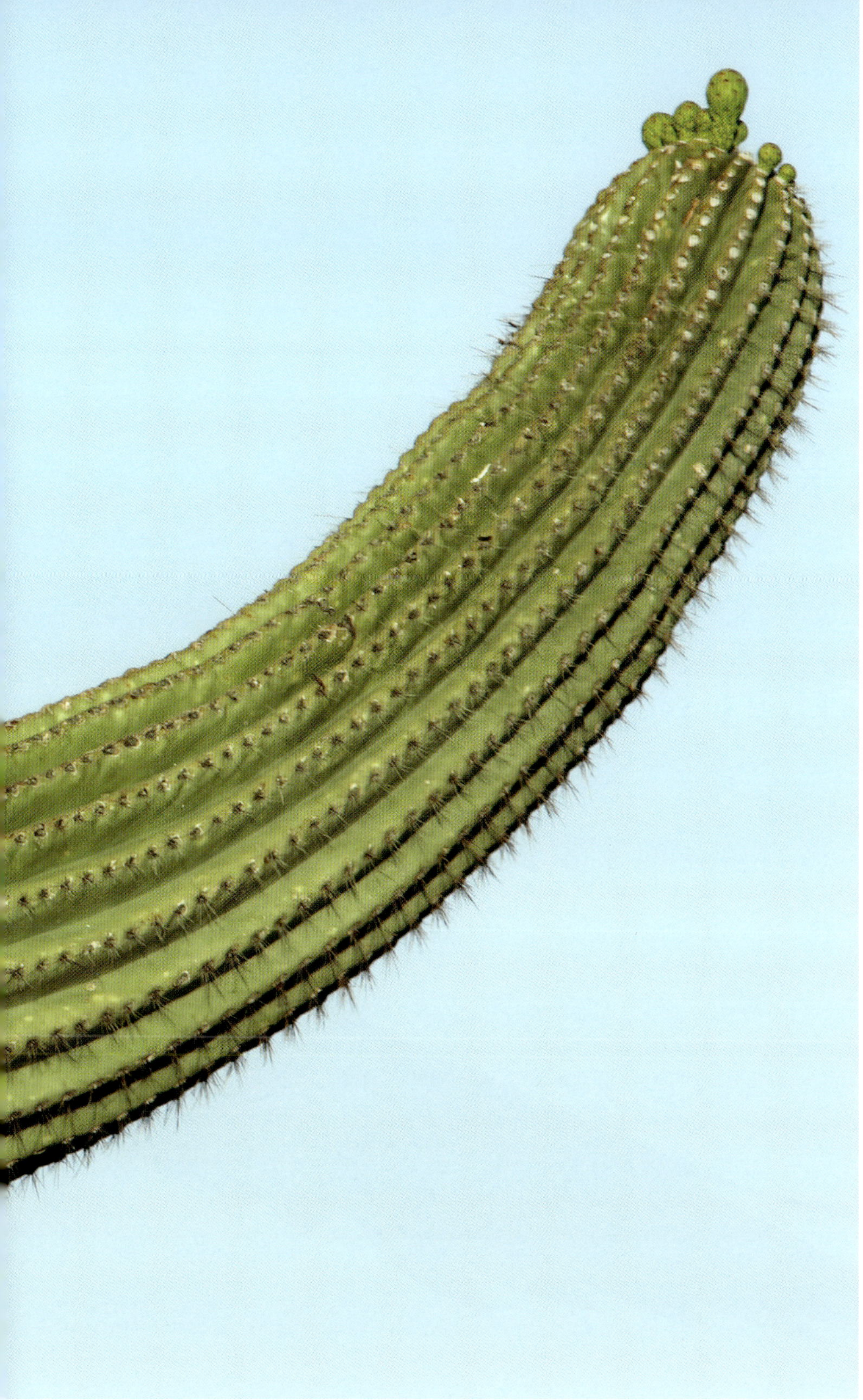

TOM UHLMAN

Harris's hawks are often spotted atop cacti, resting or watching for prey. The sleek feathers and long legs assist in heat dispersion during the hot desert days, but the hawks do not handle cold temperatures as well.

Several factors, such as dam construction, dredging operations, and increased recreational disturbances, as well as nest destruction, have taken their toll. The Arizona population is shrinking mostly from urban sprawl. By far, the largest population in the United States is in Texas. It also appears to be shrinking, although awareness about the birds appears to be helping reverse the downward trend. The adaptability of the hawks also helps, as the birds sometimes use golf courses and even mall parking lots for hunting areas.

The bay-winged hawk is a noble and intelligent bird full of courage. With help from those who care about our environment, we will continue to enjoy the bird for many years to come.

Kites

Mississippi Kite

(Ictinia mississippiensis)

Swallow-tailed Kite

(Elanoides forficatus)

BY RICK BURKMAN

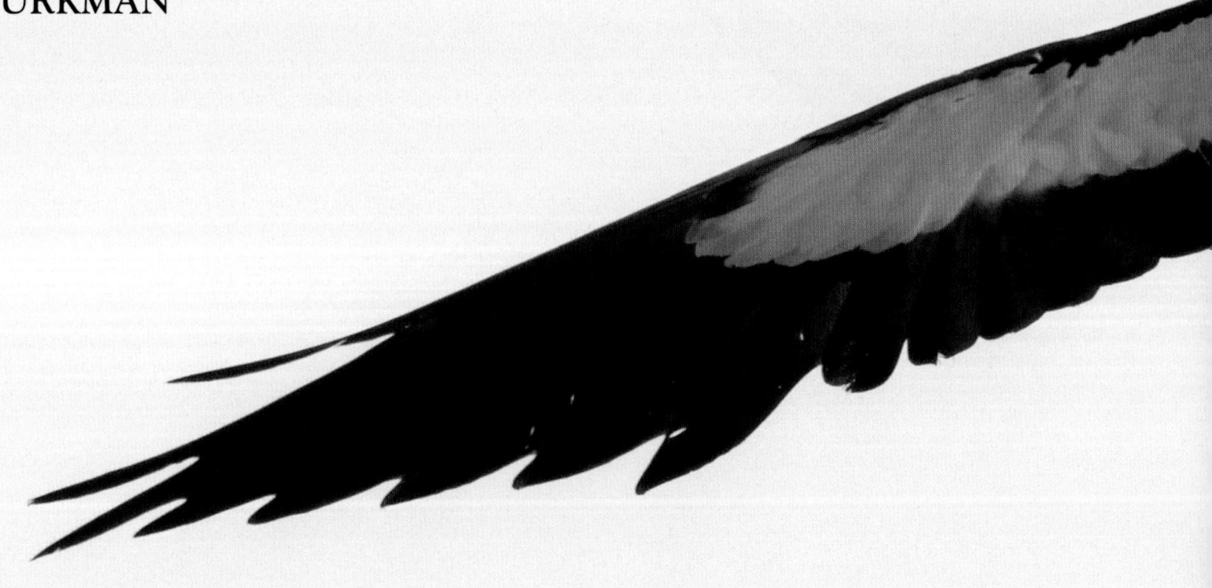

Swallow-tailed kites got the name not only by their ease in the air, but also from the distinctive forked tails, which seem better suited for members of the swallow family. This kite has captured a small frog.

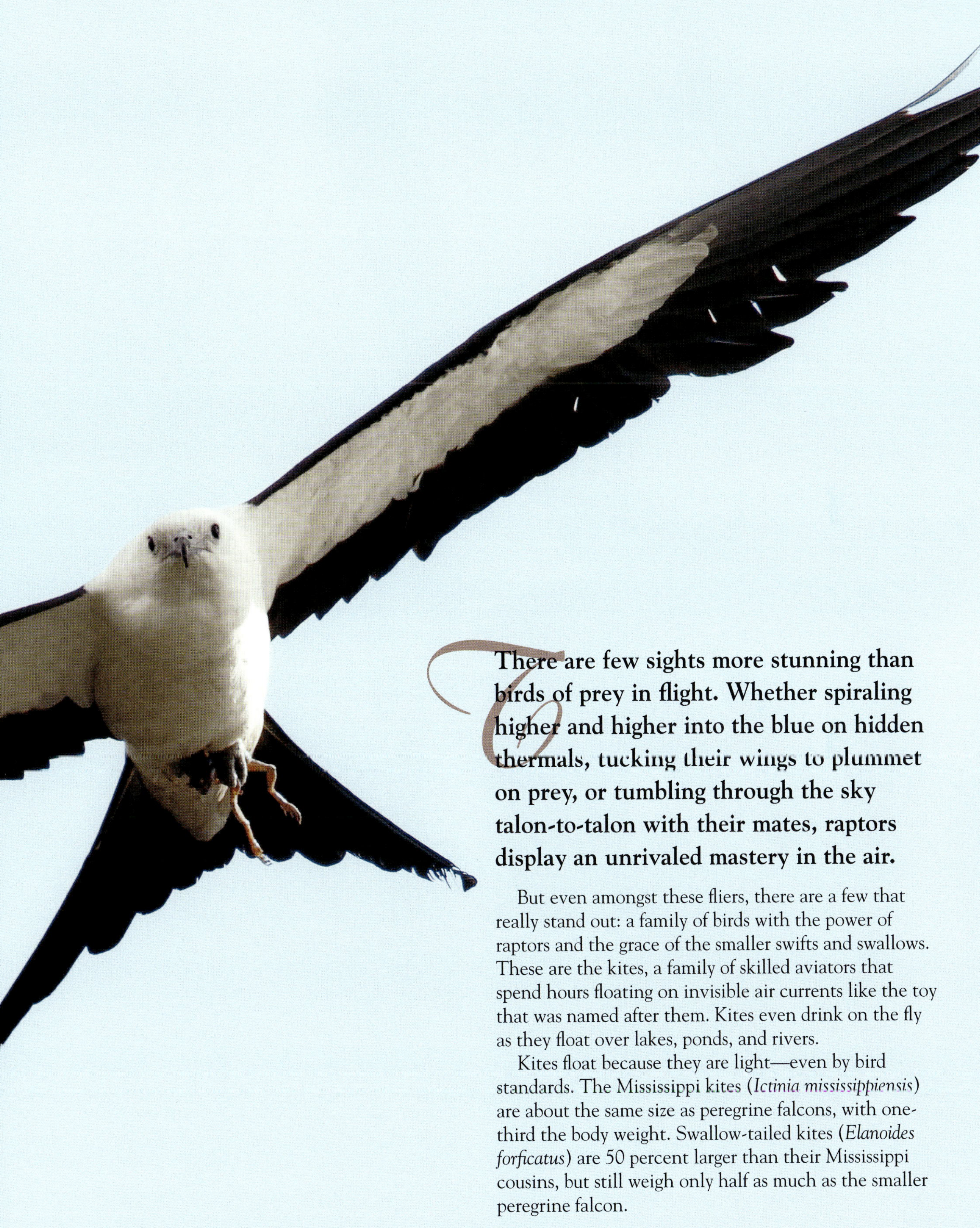

There are few sights more stunning than birds of prey in flight. Whether spiraling higher and higher into the blue on hidden thermals, tucking their wings to plummet on prey, or tumbling through the sky talon-to-talon with their mates, raptors display an unrivaled mastery in the air.

But even amongst these fliers, there are a few that really stand out: a family of birds with the power of raptors and the grace of the smaller swifts and swallows. These are the kites, a family of skilled aviators that spend hours floating on invisible air currents like the toy that was named after them. Kites even drink on the fly as they float over lakes, ponds, and rivers.

Kites float because they are light—even by bird standards. The Mississippi kites (*Ictinia mississippiensis*) are about the same size as peregrine falcons, with one-third the body weight. Swallow-tailed kites (*Elanoides forficatus*) are 50 percent larger than their Mississippi cousins, but still weigh only half as much as the smaller peregrine falcon.

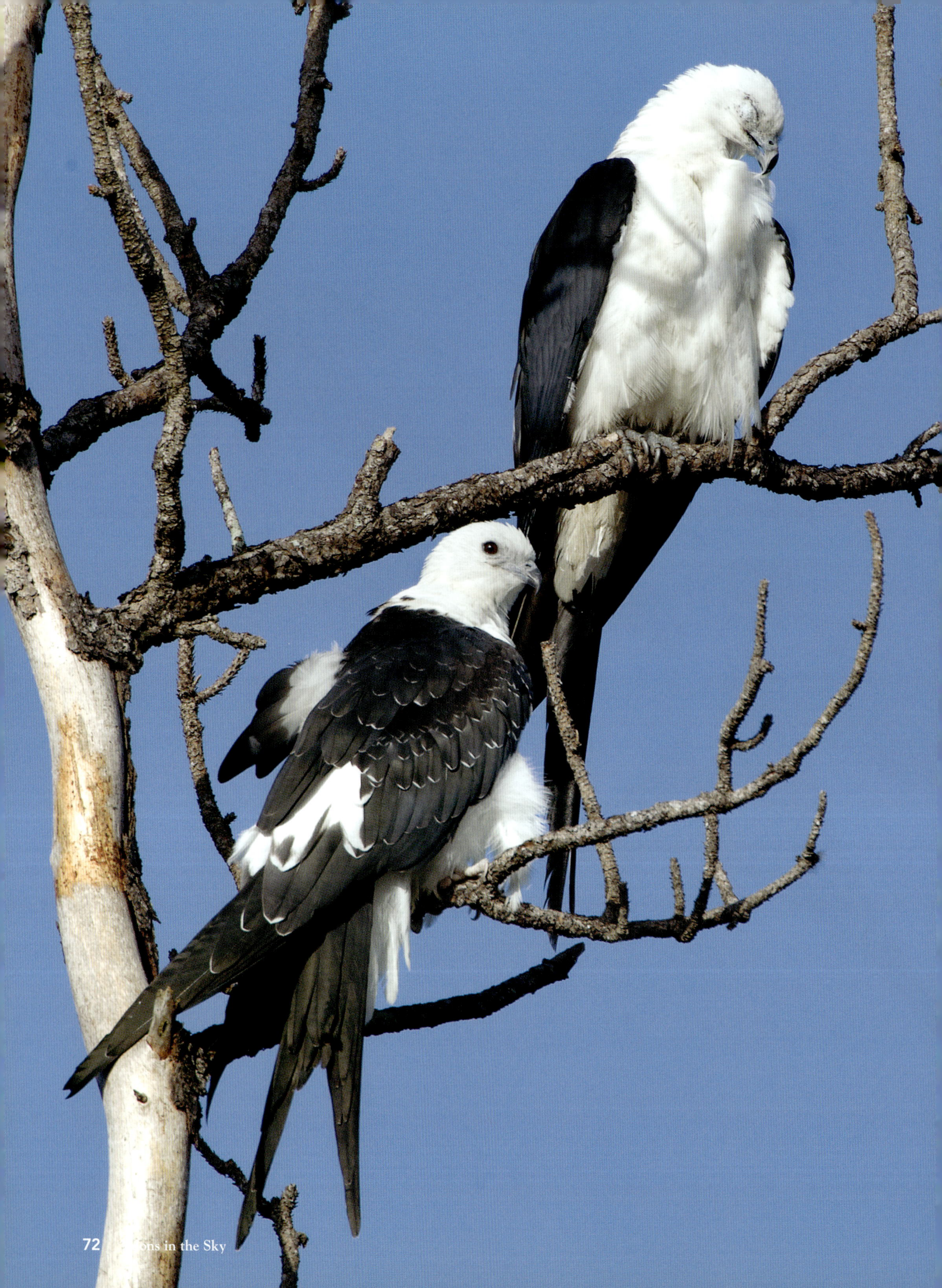

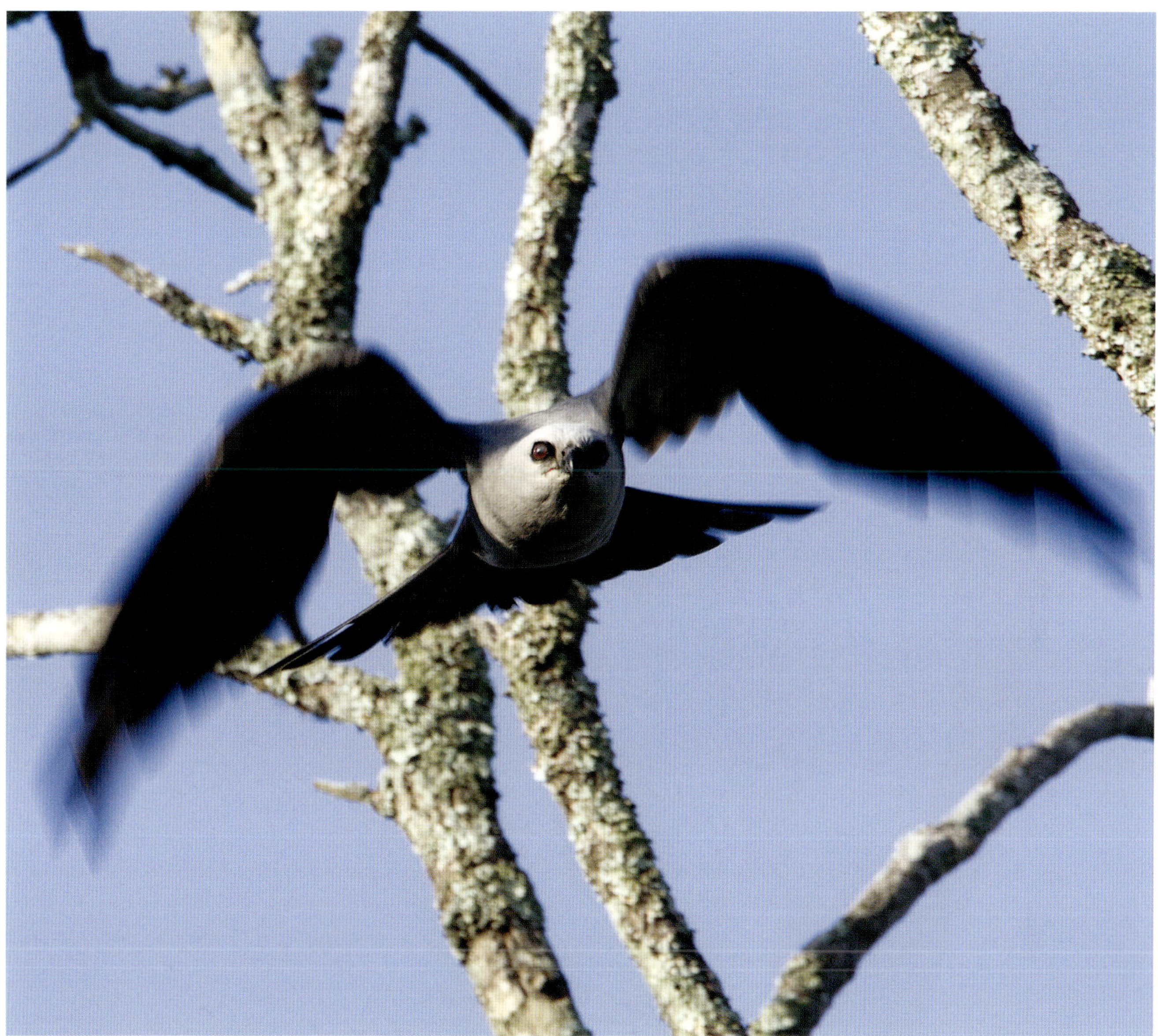

OPPOSITE: A pair of swallow-tailed kites takes a break from flying. When they nest, these birds build their homes in the outermost branches of large trees, exposed positions that can result in nest damage or loss. **ABOVE:** The Mississippi kite looks quite different from its swallow-tailed cousin, but it shares the same mastery of the air.

Both the Mississippi kite and the swallow-tailed kite make their summer homes in the warm climes of the southern Great Plains, east to the Atlantic and south to the Gulf of Mexico. Mississippi kites are easily recognized, slate-gray birds with yellow legs and piercing red eyes. Long black-and-gray tails and wings, almost falcon-like, complete the dress. As is the case with the other birds of prey, the females are larger than the males.

Swallow-tailed kites are even more graceful and flamboyant than the Mississippi variety. Clad in white, with pointed, jet-black wings and deeply forked tails, these raptors look like they are getting ready for the prom. Wanderers make regular appearances as far north as the Great Lakes states and, once spotted, they are rarely mistaken for any other bird.

Kites nest in tree belts or savannahs, where they build new structures of sticks or add to a previous year's construction. Mississippi kites are especially attracted to the tree belts found near subdivisions and golf courses. The bright side is that Mississippi kite populations are increasing, in part because of these

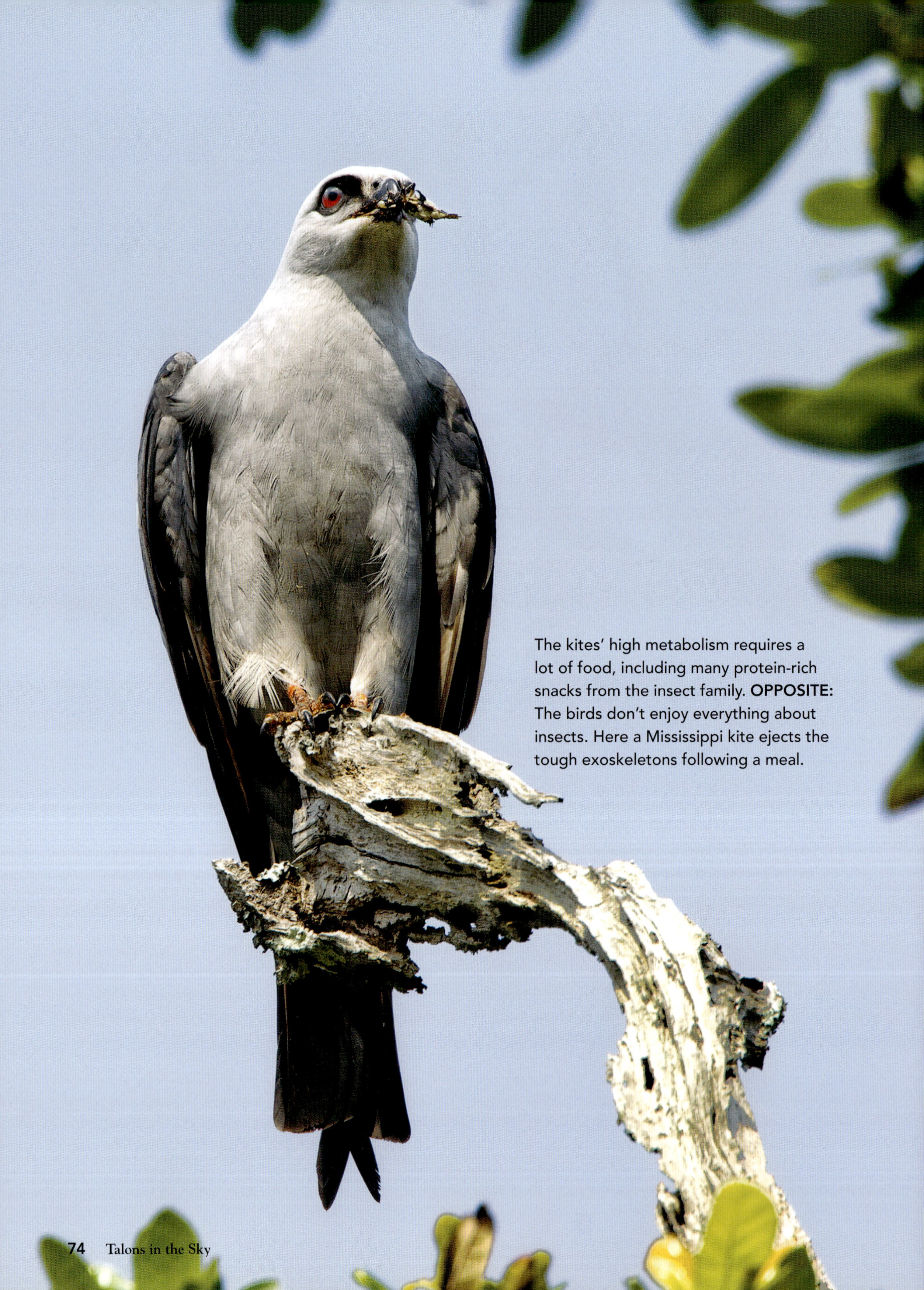

The kites' high metabolism requires a lot of food, including many protein-rich snacks from the insect family. **OPPOSITE:** The birds don't enjoy everything about insects. Here a Mississippi kite ejects the tough exoskeletons following a meal.

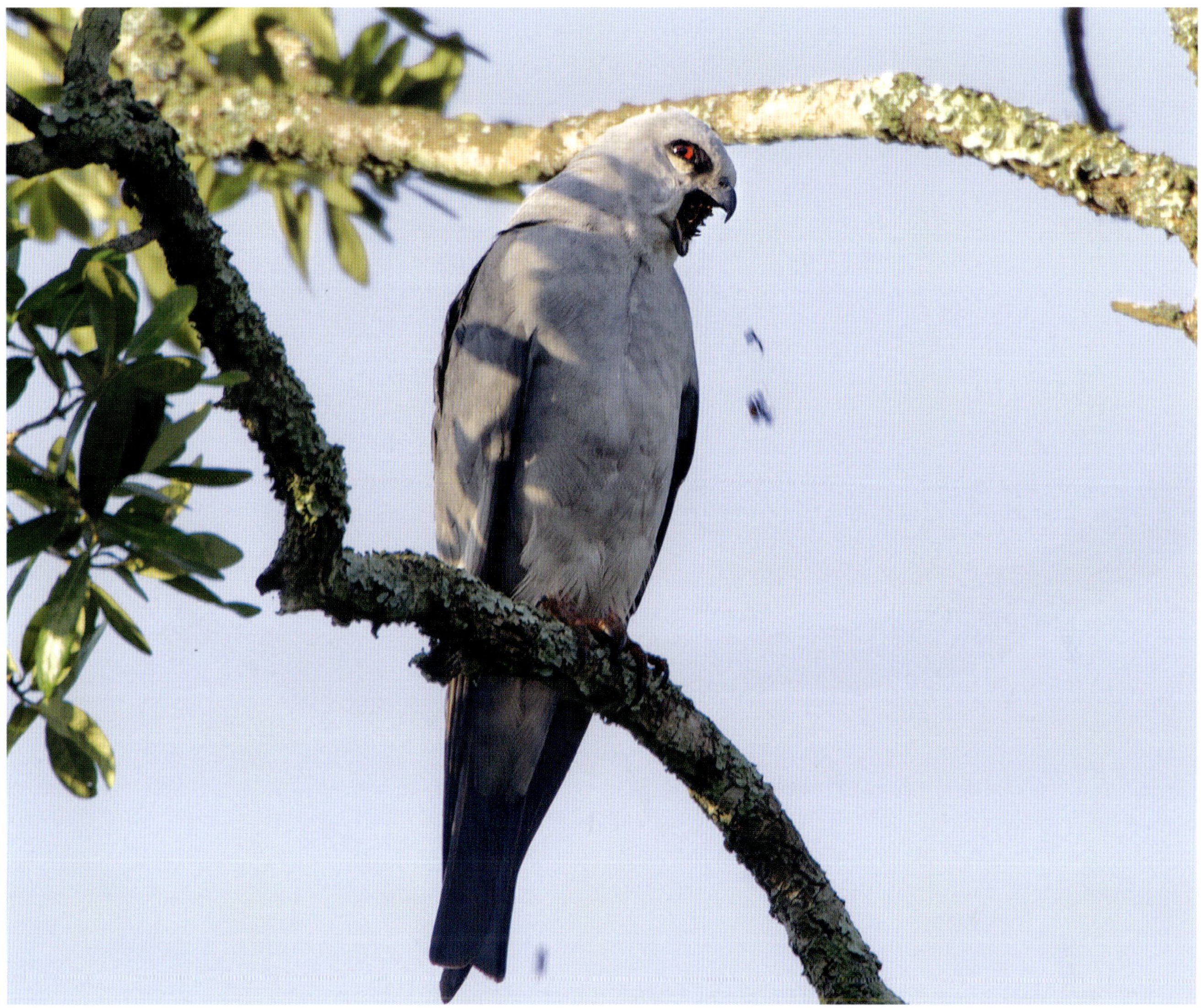

human-made habitats. On the other hand, the situation brings these fierce nest protectors into conflict with leisure-seeking humans. Both kite species aggressively defend their breeding areas and, unlike most raptors, they nest close together and allow non-nesting birds to hang out with the gang. This means that there are a lot of razor-sharp claws to drive away perceived trespassers, including unwary humans. The birds rarely make direct contact during these encounters, but just being attacked is an unnerving experience.

Both these kites start nest building as soon as they get to their breeding grounds in the spring, but they are in no hurry to complete the task. They add small branches in a leisurely fashion, and layer leaves, lichens, and Spanish moss. Mississippi kites are strong enough to snap off branches and twigs from trees in mid-flight and carry the pieces to the nest. Their nests are bulky and supported in the crotches of large trees. The swallow-tailed kites, although the larger birds, have smaller, weaker feet, and are more likely to gather already broken twigs rather than grab them in a head-on collision. Swallow-tailed kites also build on the outer branches of large trees, leaving the nest exposed to aerial predators and the vagaries of weather, but also providing them easy access, freedom from ground predators, and relief from pesky mosquitoes.

Nest failure caused by faulty construction is always a concern, and nest mortality is high, especially for the swallow-tailed kites. Thunderstorms pound on unprotected young birds, strong winds can blow them out of their nests, and predators are always hunting for an easy meal.

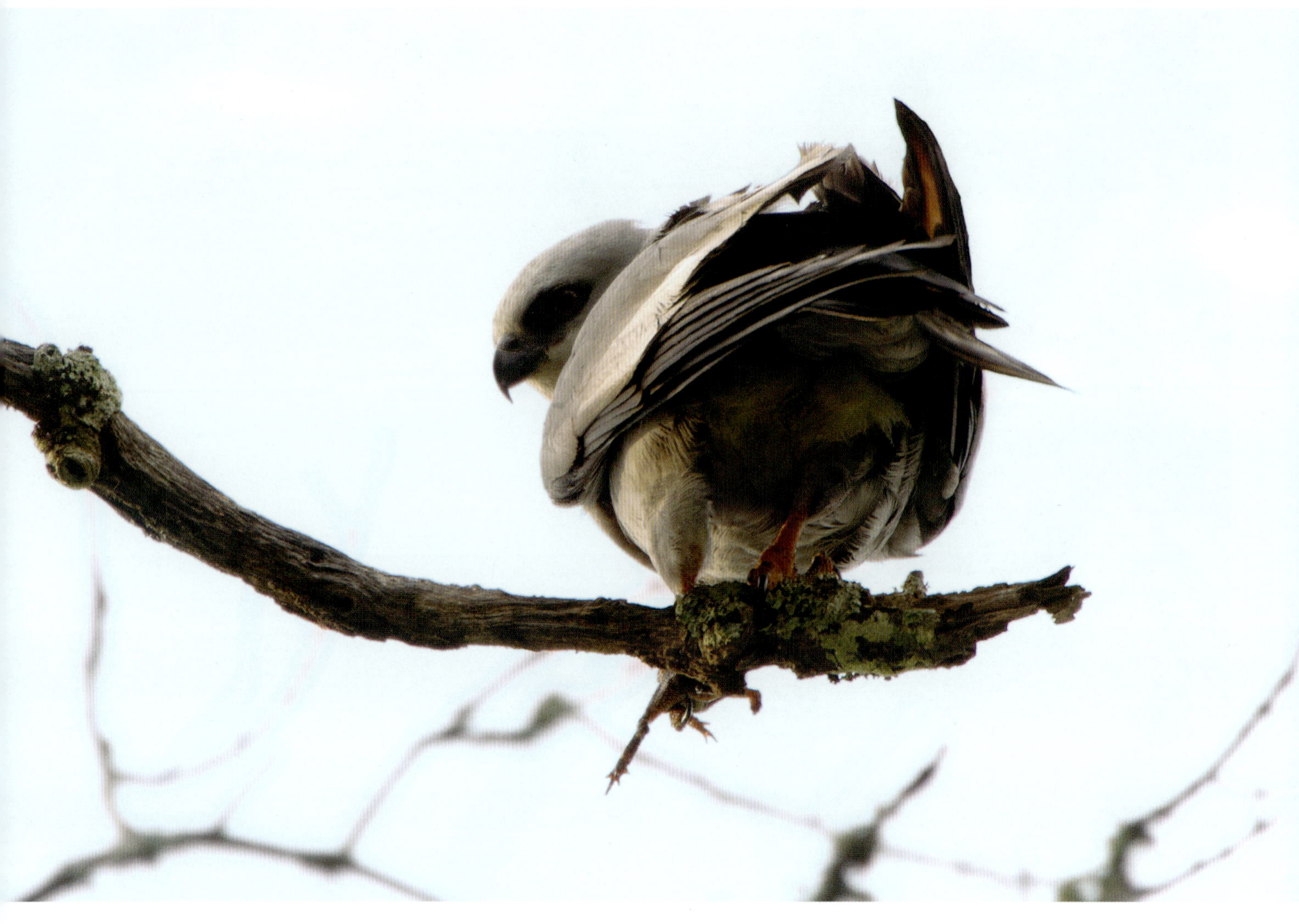

ABOVE: Although about the size of a peregrine falcon, the Mississippi kite weighs only about a third as much, one factor that aids its gliding ability. **OPPOSITE:** A Mississippi kite carries a stick for its nest. This species is strong enough to snap twigs and small branches from trees in mid-flight.

Nest completed, the hen lays two whitish or creamy-white eggs. The swallow-tailed kite's eggs are covered in reddish-brown spots, but the Mississippi kite's eggs are rarely spotted with anything but debris. An early ornithologist listed the Mississippi kites' eggs as bluish-colored, and multiple guides since then have copied that description. However, that original account appears to be an error—observers and researchers have recorded nothing but white eggs since that first published description.

The white eggs will shine like beacons to aerial predators if left unguarded. Even though these birds breed in warm, humid conditions, they do not leave their eggs exposed for more than a few moments, usually while adults are swapping incubation duties. Both adults begin brooding with the first egg laid. Males add twigs, leaves, and moss to the central nest cup during the entire incubation. Eventually so much material accumulates that the nest cup disappears, and the nest becomes a level, horizontal platform.

The eggs begin to hatch after four weeks of incubation. Young birds are covered with light-colored down and have voracious appetites. Although hungry, Mississippi kite nestlings are quiet birds. The chicks cuddle together and cower in their nest for the first several weeks of life. As they grow, they rearrange the sticks in their nest and groom one another—nurturing behavior that is unusual in the raptor world.

Their cousins the swallow-tailed kites behave completely differently. The chicks break free of their shells hungry and squawking for food. The first nestling to hatch has a head start on growth and uses its larger

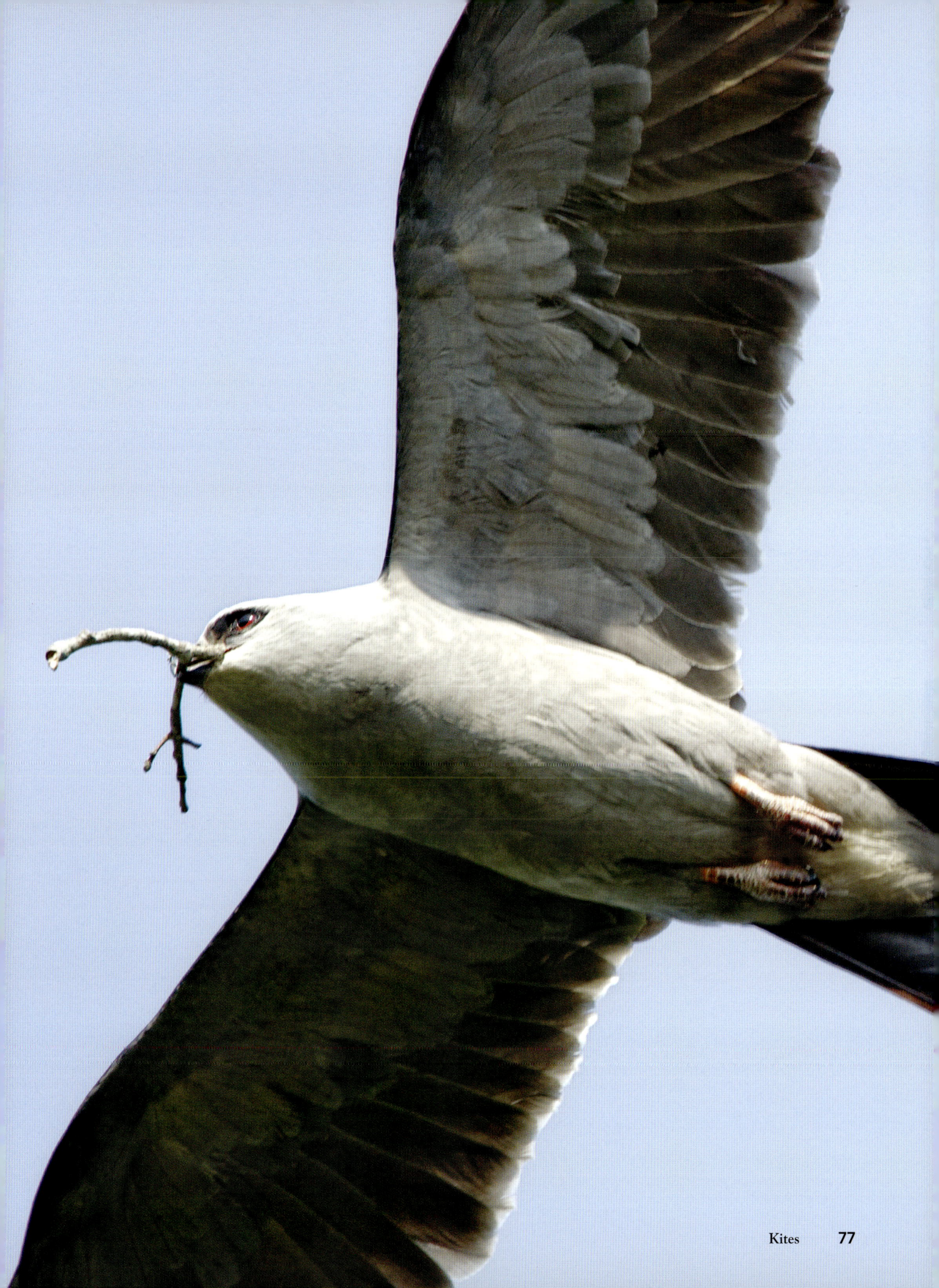

size to relentlessly bully its sibling. Instead of preening its smaller brother or sister, it pecks the younger bird and snatches the food the parents bring to the nest. The second-hatched swallow-tailed kite nestlings have brutal lives and rarely survive to adulthood.

Despite the perils, the chicks grow quickly on a mash of protein-rich regurgitated bugs. After the first month, the nest feels small and crowded. The young birds flap and stretch their newly feathered wings, exercising their muscles until the day they find themselves airborne. It takes a while for these precision flyers to perfect their skills—effortlessly floating through the sky takes a lot work. But the skills are built into the birds, and they just need a little practice to float like angels.

Although the kites are southern birds by North American standards, they head even further south with the coming of winter. They begin a circuitous journey by drifting to the Gulf of Mexico, make a westward jaunt to the Pacific coast, and then move south to South America. They head east from the west coast of South America, crossing deserts and floating over the Andes Mountains to the wilds of Brazil, where they rest and fatten on the rainforest's richness of bugs and small creatures. After only a few weeks of indulgence and relaxation, a primal urge beckons them north—and so the journey begins again to create a new generation of kites to float the skies.

Measurements (in mm)

Mississippi Kite

	Male	Female
Bill	16.0	15.1
Wing	295.0	310.0
Tail	157.1	163.0
Tarsus	35.9	38.3

Swallow-tailed Kite

	Male	Female
Wing	431.0	440.0
Tail	334.0	356.0
Tarsus	33.0	33.0

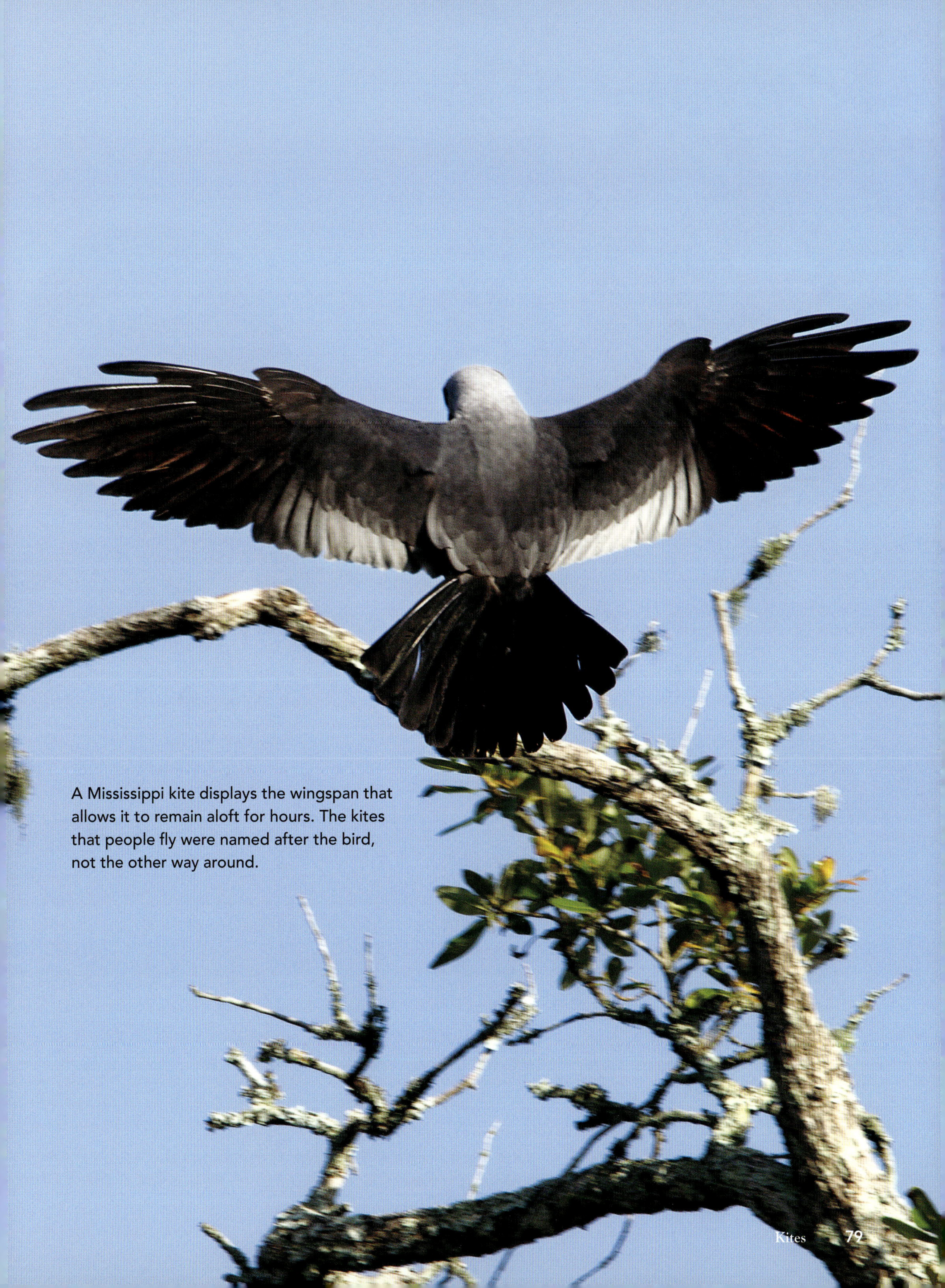

A Mississippi kite displays the wingspan that allows it to remain aloft for hours. The kites that people fly were named after the bird, not the other way around.

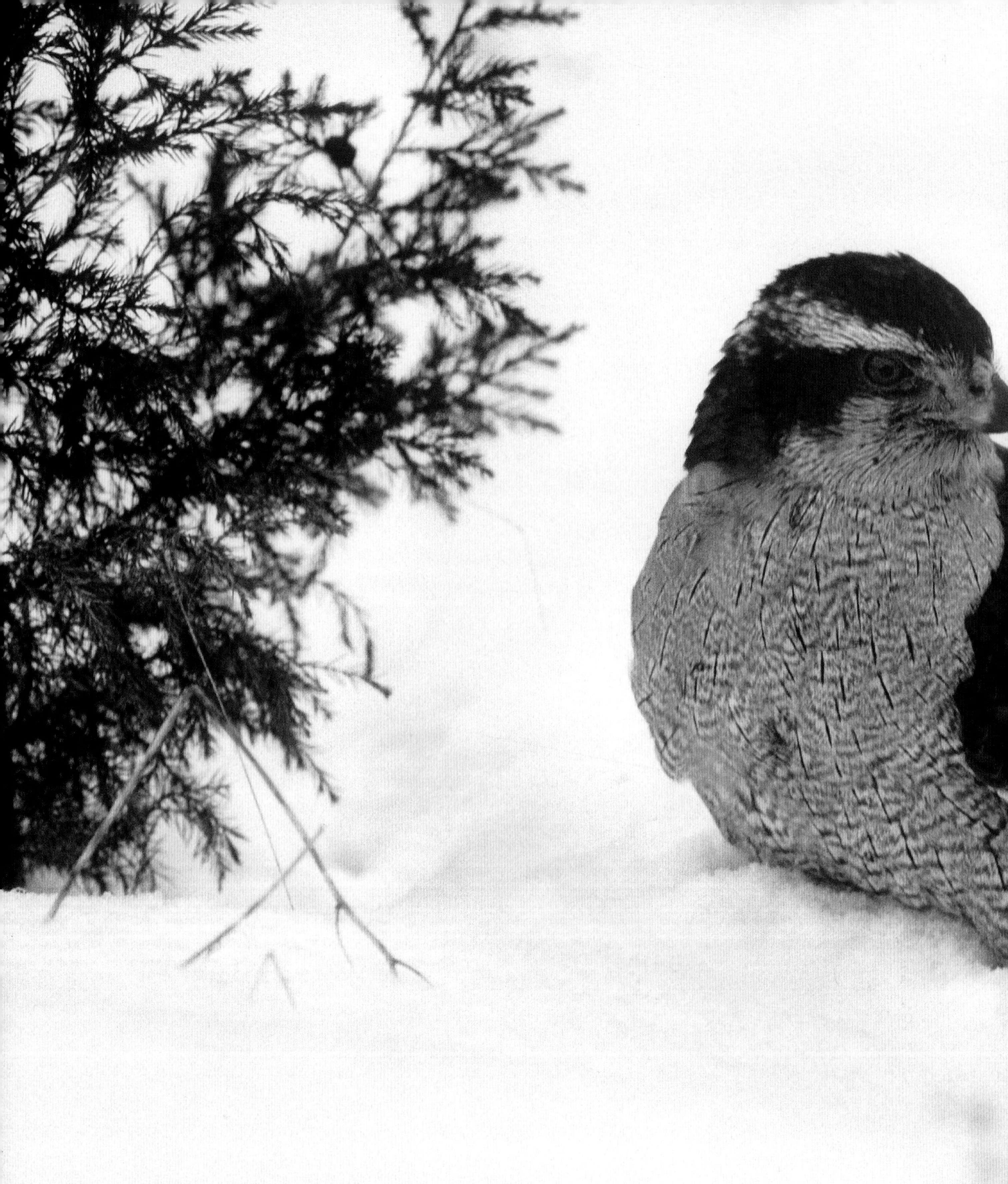

The northern goshawk is the largest of three North American accipiters, a group that includes the Cooper's and sharp-shinned hawks. Birders know that the goshawk is the most elusive of the three.

Northern Goshawk

(*Accipiter gentilis*)

BY RICK BURKMAN

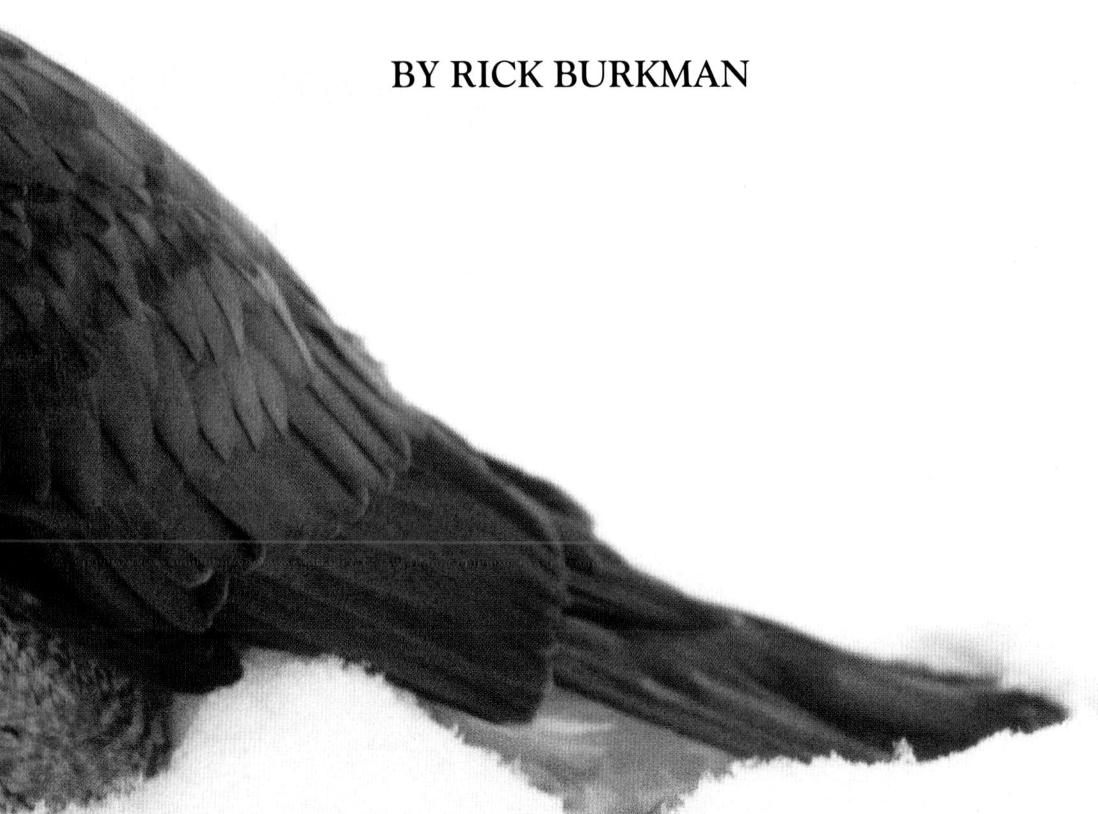

It is a wet, overcast day. A large gray bird sitting on a large gray limb is hidden in the white fog of early morning. She huddles against the dampness as she surveys her forest home with fiery red eyes. A squirrel foraging in the leaf litter catches her attention. Silently, she launches from her perch, beats her wings rapidly as she accelerates, and finally crashes through intervening shrubbery with her talons extended. She hits her unsuspecting prey and quickly carries it to her young in a nearby nest. Another day in the life of a northern goshawk (*Accipiter gentilis*) has begun.

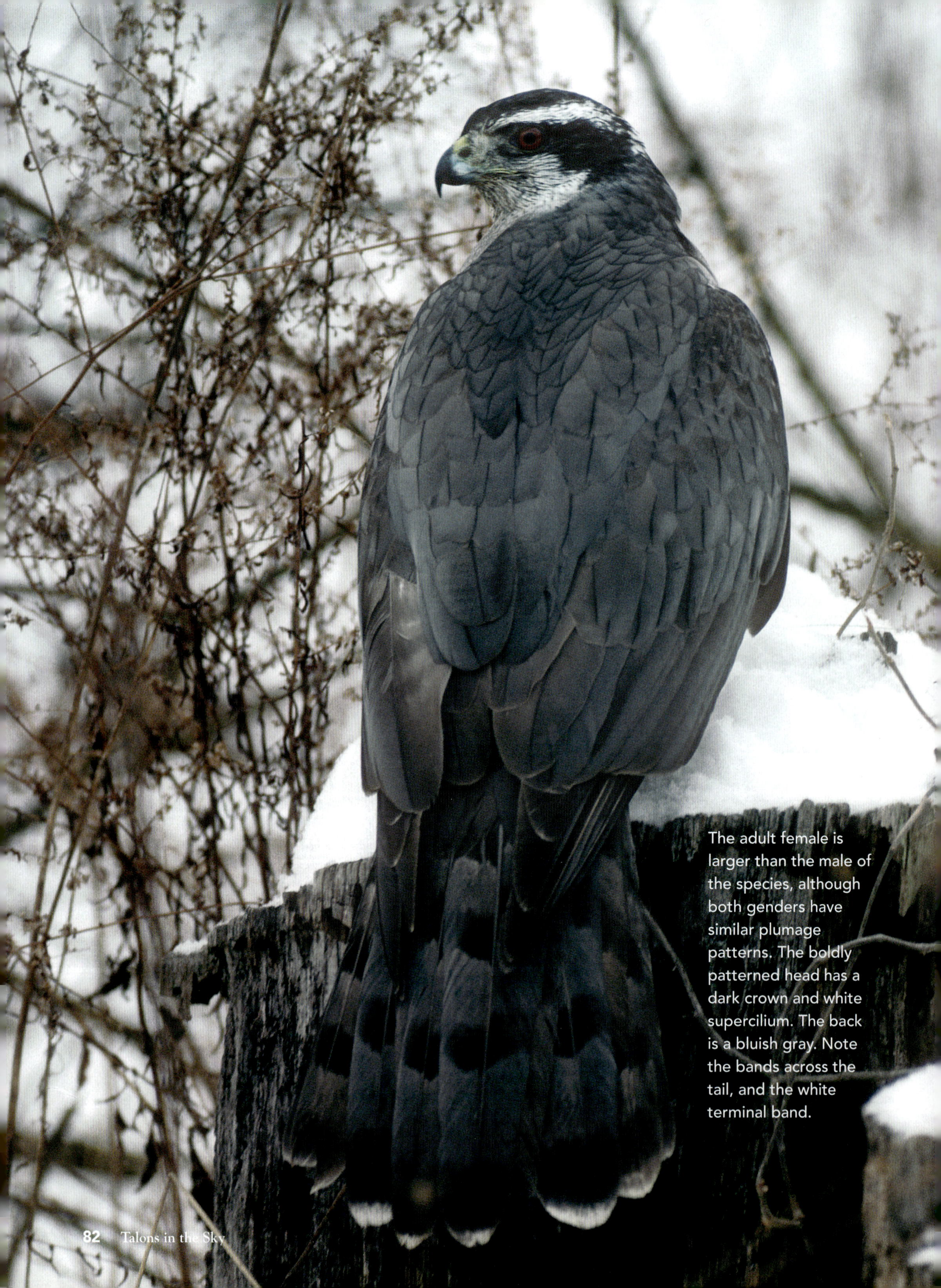

The adult female is larger than the male of the species, although both genders have similar plumage patterns. The boldly patterned head has a dark crown and white supercilium. The back is a bluish gray. Note the bands across the tail, and the white terminal band.

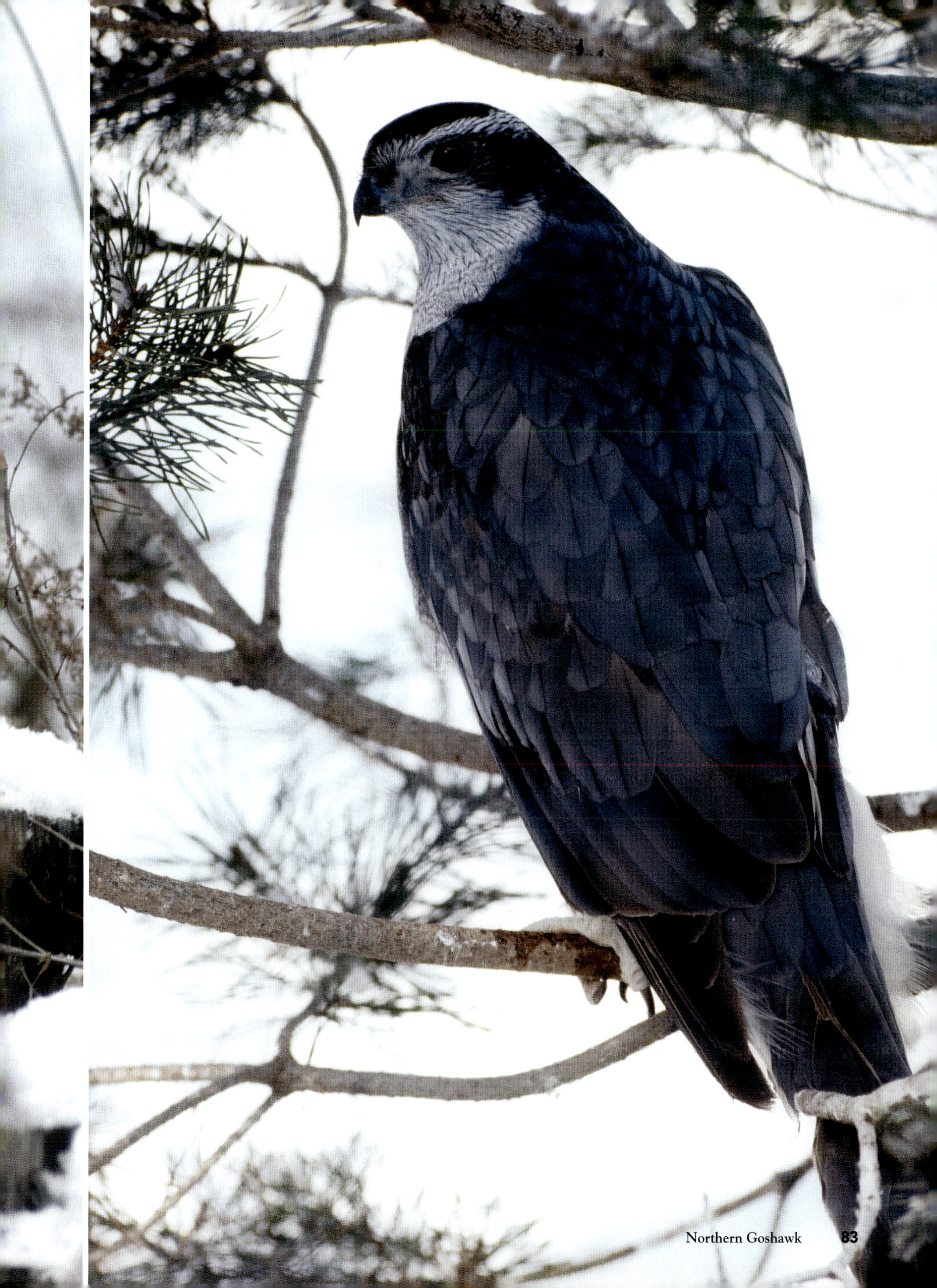

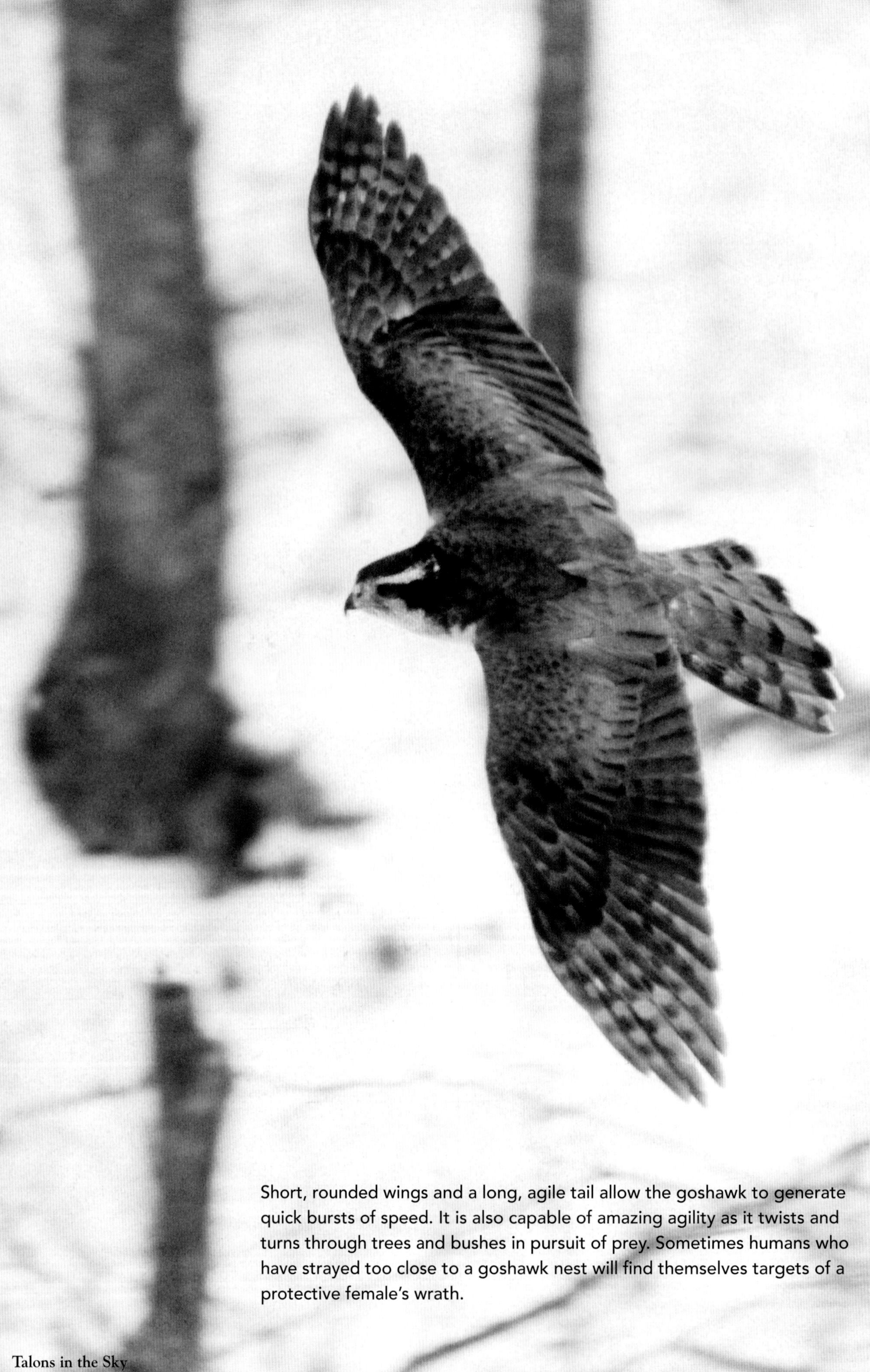

Short, rounded wings and a long, agile tail allow the goshawk to generate quick bursts of speed. It is also capable of amazing agility as it twists and turns through trees and bushes in pursuit of prey. Sometimes humans who have strayed too close to a goshawk nest will find themselves targets of a protective female's wrath.

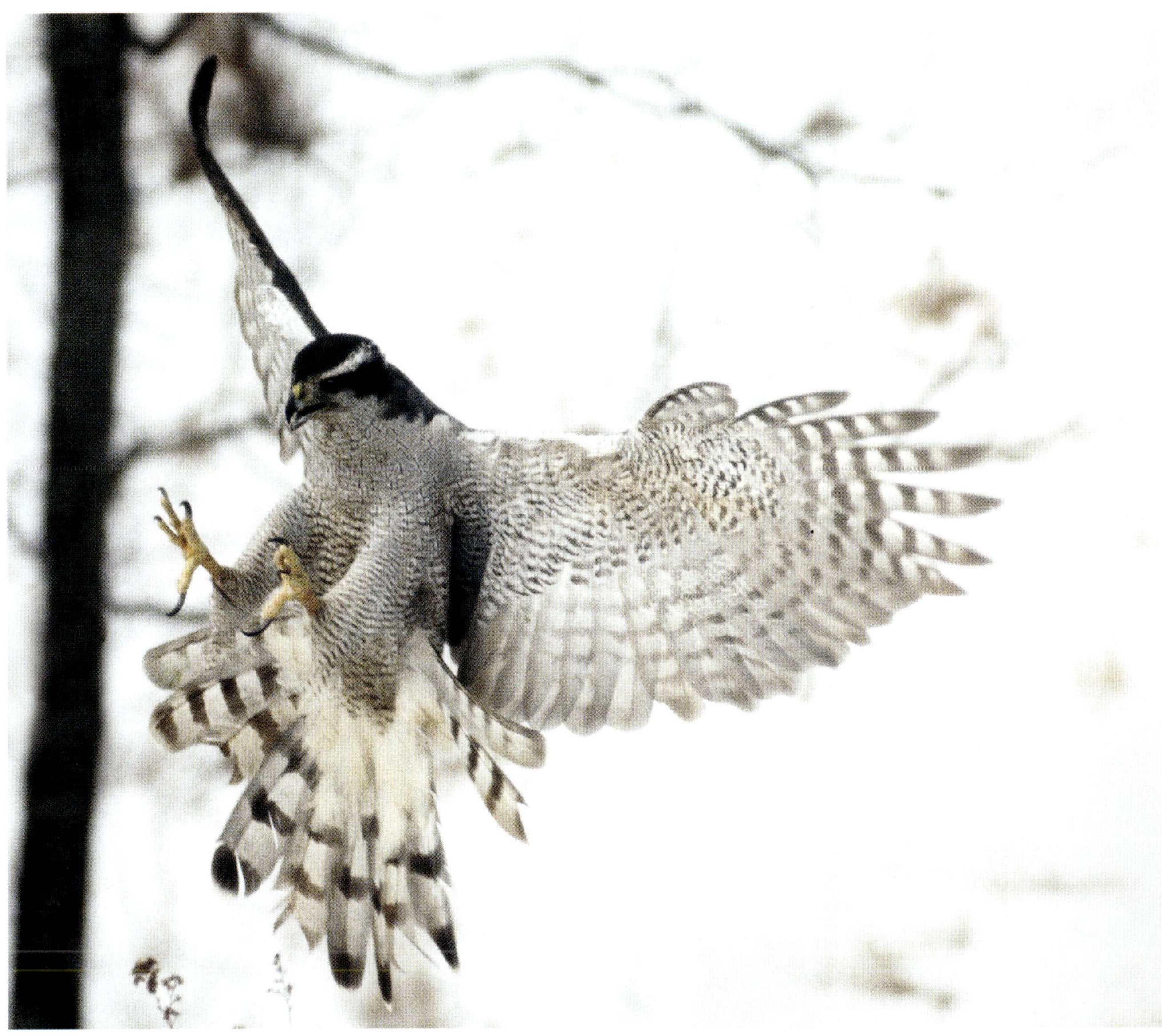

The goshawk is the largest of the three North American accipiters, a group that includes the Cooper's and sharp-shinned hawks. All three species have powerful wings and long tails that enhance their ability to maneuver when pursuing birds and other prey in their forest homes. The goshawk is easily distinguished from the others by its overall larger size and wide, buteo-like body. In fact, goshawks are sometimes mistakenly identified as one of the woodland buteos, like the red-tailed or red-shouldered hawk. Because they live in wild or inaccessible places and are difficult birds to locate, they are treasured finds for avid bird-watchers.

Although elusive, goshawks have, nevertheless, had a long relationship with humans. At times, they were allies and companions. The daring hunting style and regal beauty of these birds have endeared them to falconers for 2,000 years. In recent decades, they have gained a largely undeserved reputation as bloodthirsty and ferocious predators that compete with humans for prey. However, their malevolence is overstated and this secretive woodland raptor is gaining more and more respect for the role it plays in the ecosystem.

Goshawks are generally quiet birds, but when they're disturbed they emit a loud series of "Kek-kek-kek-kek-kek" calls. Softer, quieter recognition calls and vocalizations are used during courtship and when the female receives food from the male. Young birds will use begging sounds to elicit food from nearby adults.

The goshawk is a tenacious hunter. It begins the hunt by perching on a tree branch and observing the surroundings. The goshawk will wait and watch for the movements of an unsuspecting potential meal. If nothing appears within a few minutes, the goshawk will move to another location and try gain. Once the quarry is spotted, the hunt is on. Short, rounded wings and a long, agile tail allow the hawk to generate quick bursts of speed while twisting and turning through its wooded home in pursuit of animals or birds. The bird will chase its intended victim through the air or on the ground until the prey is either captured or manages a fortuitous escape. Shrubs and tree branches do not hamper the pursuit. The goshawk deliberately crashes through these obstacles, with all the grace of a charging bull moose, to nab a target. Unfortunately, this aggressive hunting style can occasionally backfire. A goshawk was once found with it foot firmly wedged in the fork of a tree, probably the result of a chase gone awry. Unable to free itself, the bird starved to death.

Goshawks will, occasionally, stalk their prey. While on the ground, they will stealthily move from one patch of ground cover to another until they are close enough for one final, fatal lunge. They are also persistent. A researcher once observed a goshawk pursue a snowshoe hare for an hour before capturing it. Amazingly, these three-pound birds can capture and carry animals weighing three to four pounds with relative ease.

The birds will take prey to one of several favored forest structures—a stump, fallen log, or bent tree limb—for cleaning and eating. A goshawk maintains several of these plucking perches in its territory and uses them habitually.

Goshawks build and maintain a primary nest and up to eight alternative nest sites. These monogamous birds are loyal to their breeding and hunting territory and try to maintain their home range year-round. Each year, the goshawk pair will choose a new nest from among the alternate sites, and that nest will then become the new primary nest. Rotating the nests from year to year probably reduces the amount of infestation from bird parasites such as mites and ticks.

The nests are large structures that average two and one-half feet deep and three feet in diameter. Carefully chosen sticks and bits of coniferous shrubbery serve for new construction or to maintain an already existing nest. Both the male and female contribute to nest building and maintenance. Nests are usually located in the primary crotches of large trees. In the West, goshawks prefer coniferous trees, such as lodge pole and Ponderosa pines and Douglas firs. In the Midwest and East, they generally choose large hardwoods, such as the American beech and yellow birch.

When courtship and nest construction are complete, the female will lay two to four oval, off-white, or pale bluish-white eggs. After 30 days, the first egg hatches and a dirty-white downy chick emerges. All the eggs hatch within two or three days.

A brooding female will not leave the nest for the first week after her eggs hatch. Even when threatened by a predator, she will remain tightly seated on the newly hatched young for the first seven days. During this time, it is the male's job to protect and deliver food to the nesting female. She, in turn, feeds both herself and the young. The female remains on or near the nest for several weeks.

As the young birds mature, they begin exploring their forest world. Initially, they remain in close proximity to their home, hopping from branch to branch within their nest tree. They learn to fly by vigorously flapping their wings until they can lift their bodies a few inches from their perch. As their skills improve, they become more daring. They expand their explorations to areas farther and farther from the nest. However, like human teens, freedom from the nest does not prevent them from begging for meals, and the adults will continue to feed the young until they disperse to establish their own territories.

Goshawks do not tolerate other large birds nesting within their territories, and they are adamant defenders of their chosen realms. Any large creature that has the misfortune to encroach on a goshawk's territory during this time does so at the risk of its life. Large animals are harassed until they leave the area. Birds of prey are attacked with homicidal fury. Even humans that inadvertently stumble into a nesting bird's realm may fall victim to the defensive action of their sharp talons.

As is the case with many hawks, the female goshawk is larger than the male. Both genders have similar plumage patterns. The goshawk's head is boldly patterned with a black crown and a starkly contrasting white supercilium. Dark auricular feathers and piercing ruby-red eyes give this raptor a stern and regal appear-

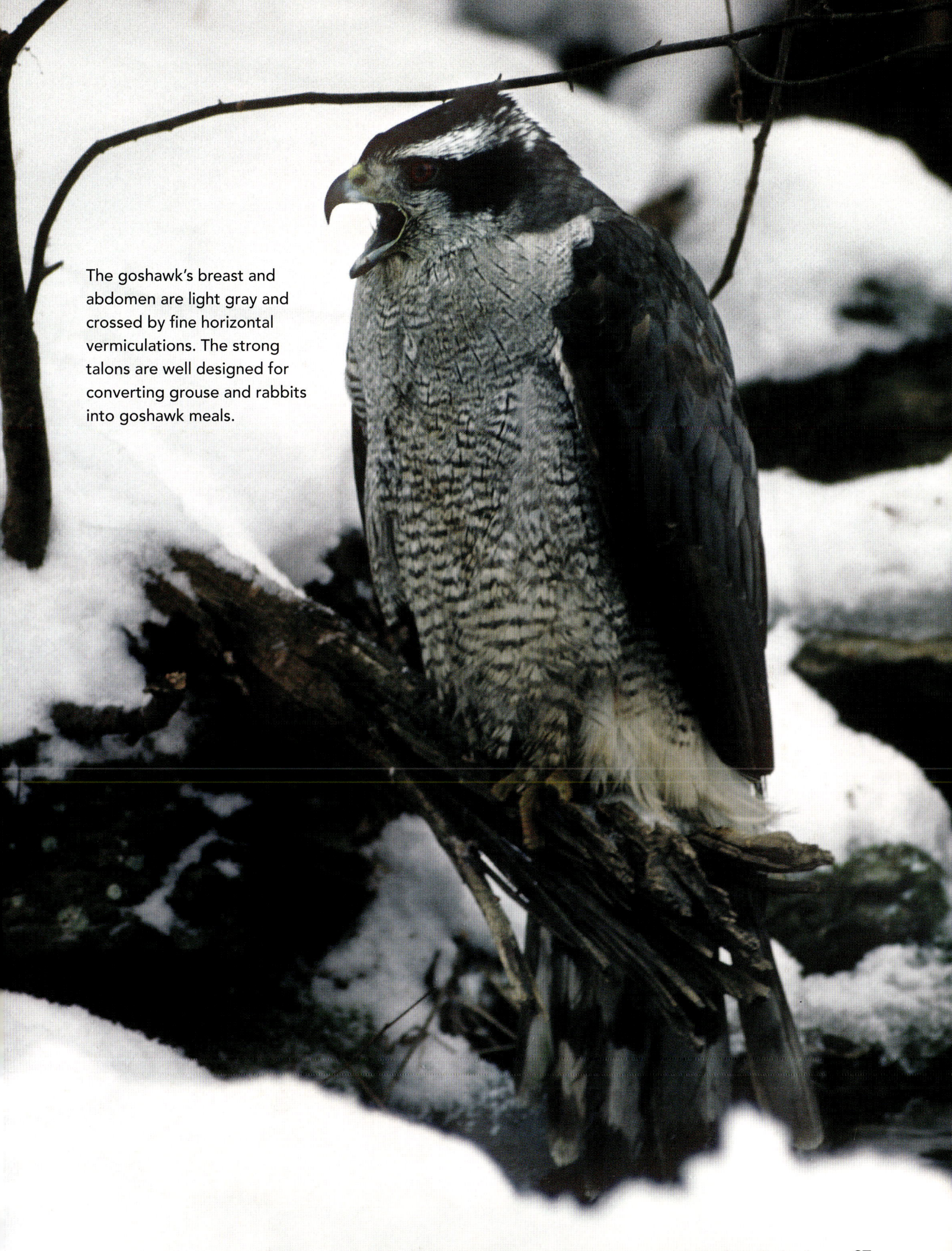

The goshawk's breast and abdomen are light gray and crossed by fine horizontal vermiculations. The strong talons are well designed for converting grouse and rabbits into goshawk meals.

ance. Its back is bluish gray, and breast and abdomen are light gray and crossed by fine horizontal vermiculations. Dark vertical streaking is also present on the abdomen and breast. Under-tail coverts are fluffy and white. The long, brownish tail is crossed by three to five dark bands and ends in a white terminal band. The terminal band usually becomes discolored and disappears completely with wear. Upper wings are the same color as the back, but the flight feathers are darker gray. Underwings are also two-toned: the area from the body to the elbow is similar to the breast color, but the flight feathers are dark. The lower extremities, cere, and lining of the mouth are all yellow.

Like many birds, juvenile goshawks are patterned and colored differently than the adults. Juveniles are buffy or brown colored overall. Their backs are dark brown with white mottling. The buffy breasts and abdomens of juveniles are heavily streaked with a deep brown color. It is possible to confuse immature goshawks with their close kin, the Cooper's hawk, but the large size and distinctive eyebrow of the goshawk are distinguishing characteristics.

Goshawks are year-round residents of northern temperate and boreal forests around the world. In North America, their range is limited to the northern tier of states and Canada and southward into the mountainous regions of Arizona, California, and New Mexico.

Specific habitat preferences vary by geographic region. Mixed forests of hardwood and hemlock are preferred in the Midwest and East. Pine forests are used in the western regions of the country, and birch forests are preferred in the interior of Alaska and Canada. Mature forests with a relatively high and complete canopy are characteristic of a goshawk's chosen territory. Small forest openings used as hunting areas or travel corridors to nest sites and plucking perches are scattered throughout the area. Open water in some form—a small stream, river, pond, or lake—is usually found nearby.

Although considered non-migratory, goshawks do occasionally leave their home ranges. Young birds disperse to establish their own territories. Goshawk populations are closely tied to the cyclic variations of their favorite prey species, like snowshoe hares and ruffed grouse. When these prey species are at the low ebb of their population cycles, goshawks will abandon their territories and journey southward in search of greener pastures.

Goshawks, while not uncommon, are rarely observed. They can fly silently and, except during the nesting season, prefer to slip quietly away from intruders rather than engage in potentially dangerous confrontation. However, these stately hunters can themselves become the hunted. Great horned owls will attack and kill goshawks if given the opportunity. Nesting goshawks and their eggs or young are hunted by pine martins and raccoons. In some regions of the country, the fisher, a large member of the weasel family, is known to prey on brooding goshawks and their young. Yet this is all part of the beauty and mystery of this noble, reclusive, and wild deep-woods raptor.

Measurements (in mm)

	Male	Female
Length	530–640	530–640
Wingspan	890–1050	1080–1270
Wing Chord	325	356
Tail	234	272
Weight	1.25–2+ pounds	1.75–3.75 pounds

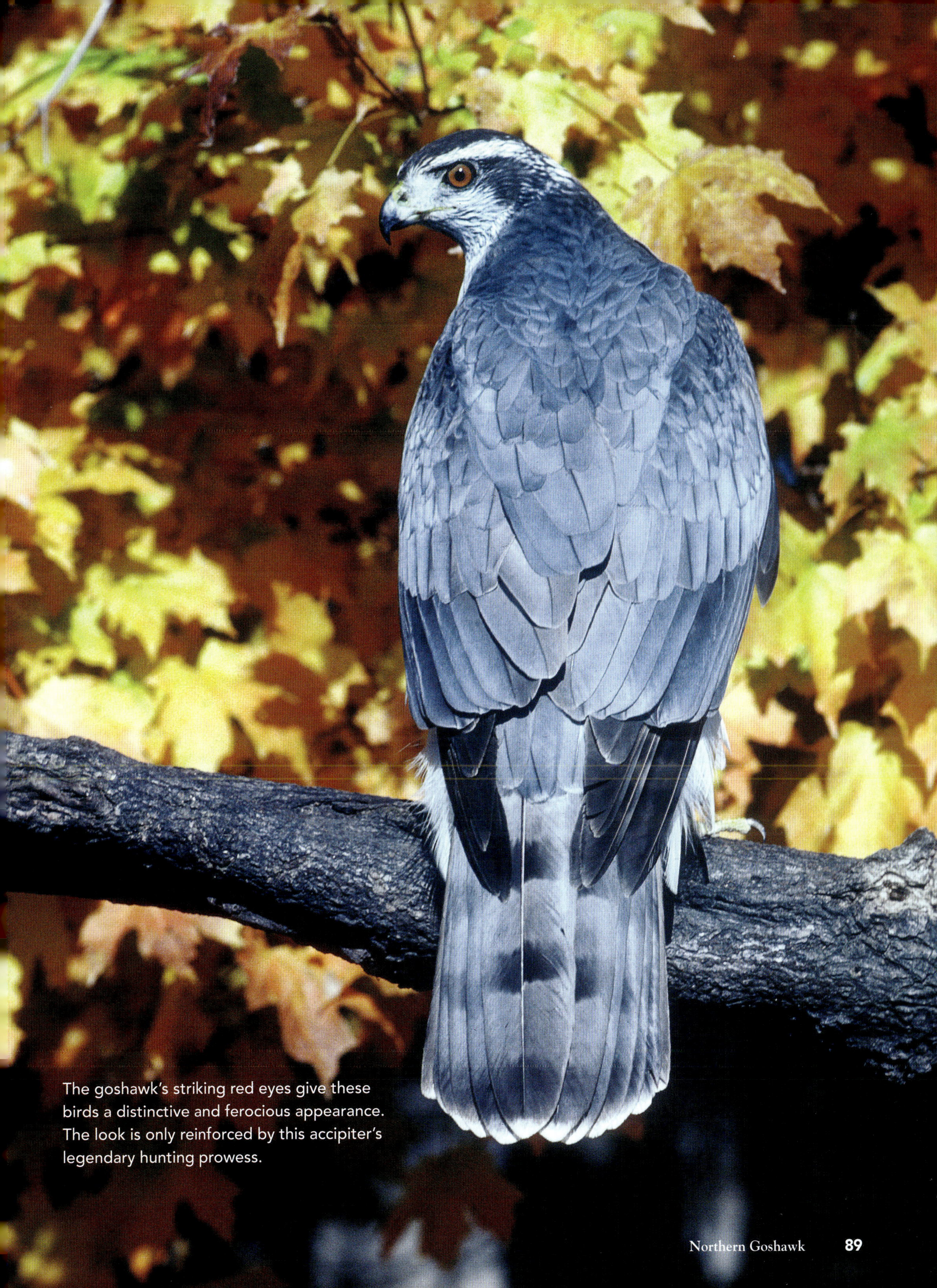

The goshawk's striking red eyes give these birds a distinctive and ferocious appearance. The look is only reinforced by this accipiter's legendary hunting prowess.

Osprey

(Pandion haliaetus)

BY TARA BOICE

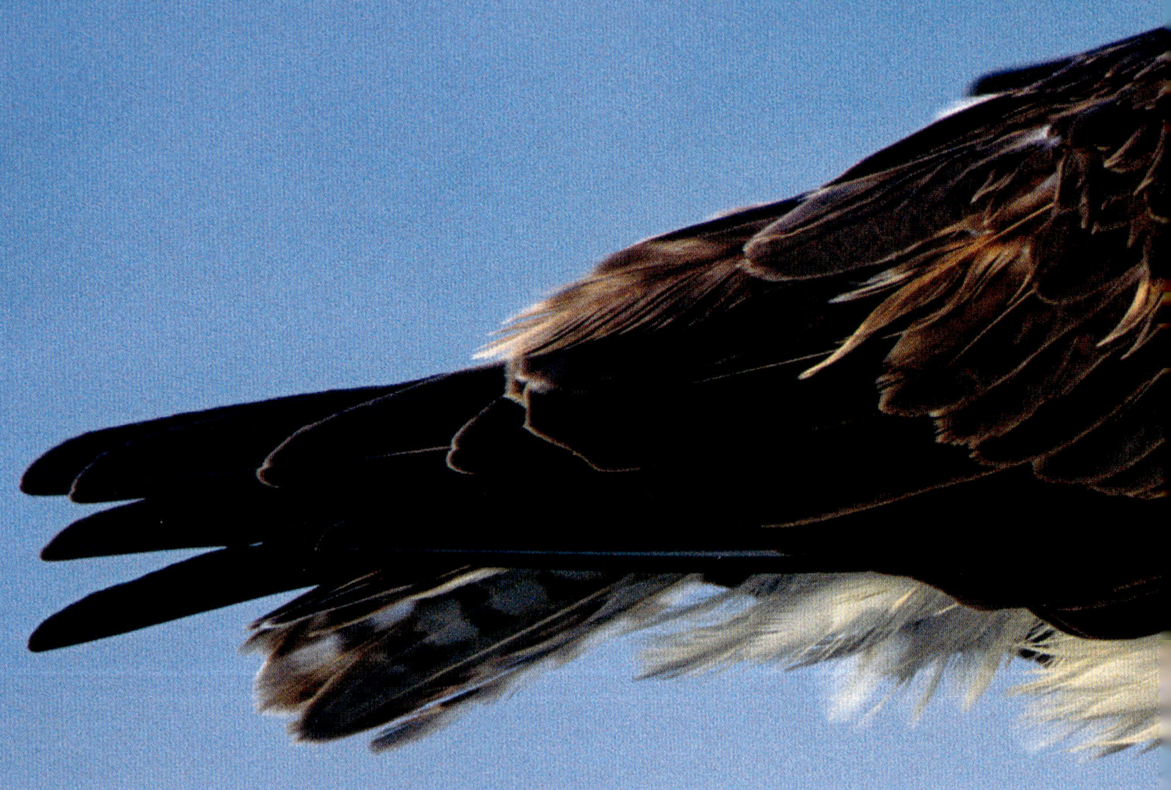

They call it the fish hawk for a reason—the osprey eats a lot of fish. The birds are found throughout North America, their populations having rebounded after a threat from DDT in the twentieth century. It is one of the easiest raptors to identify, with its snowy white crown and black eyestripe.

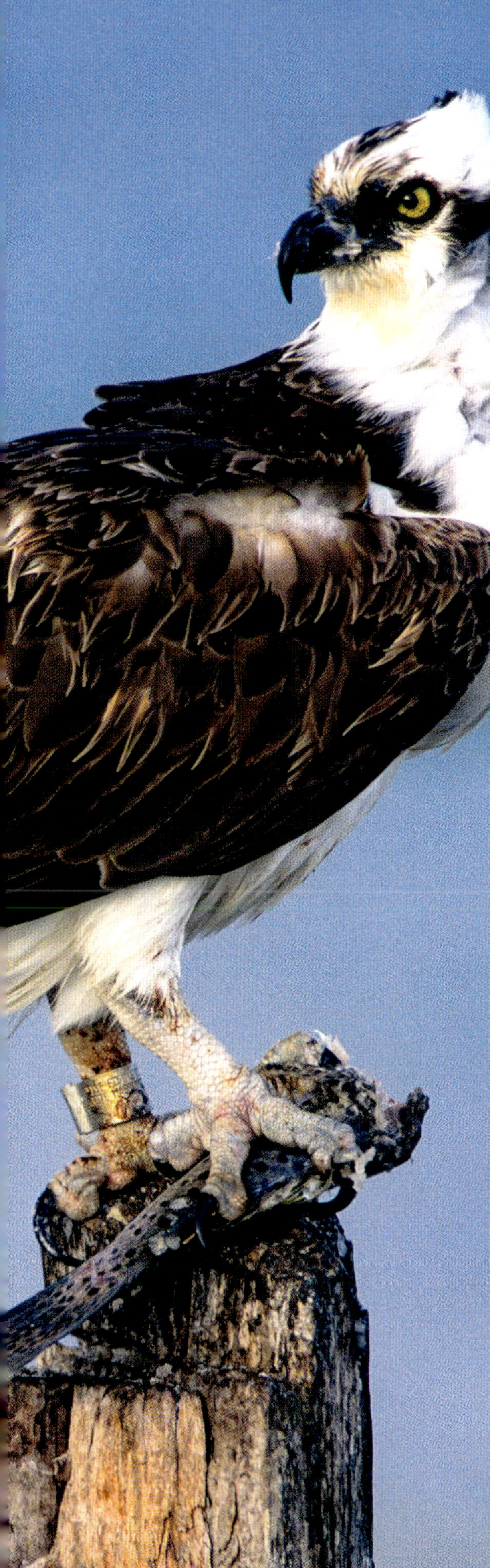

If you have ever wondered what birds reside in the huge nests perched precariously atop dead trees, telephone poles, and even channel markers—wonder no more. Those enormous nests, which measure as much as a yard across and a yard high, are "home sweet home" to the osprey (*Pandion haliaetus*), more commonly known as the fish hawk.

In continental North America, the single subspecies *P.h. carolinensis* ranges from central Alaska to the east coast of the Yucatan Peninsula. It is commonly found in Florida as well as along the Atlantic coast, especially the Chesapeake Bay, and in the Great Lakes. Virtually all of the North American population migrates south to winter in the Caribbean, Central America, and northern South America. Florida birds are resident year round, as are those few that remain along the Gulf Coast and in Southern California.

Today, Florida has one of the world's largest osprey populations despite the past use of DDT. A dangerous pesticide employed during the late 1950s through its ban in 1972, DDT's use resulted in thin-shelled eggs that cracked under the weight of brooding parents. As a result, the osprey population plummeted. Rescue efforts, such as those at the Suncoast Seabird Sanctuary, helped reestablish the population. Dedicated to the rescue, repair, and rehabilitation and release of wild land and sea birds, the Suncoast Seabird Sanctuary is a wild bird habilitation center located in Redington Shores, Florida.

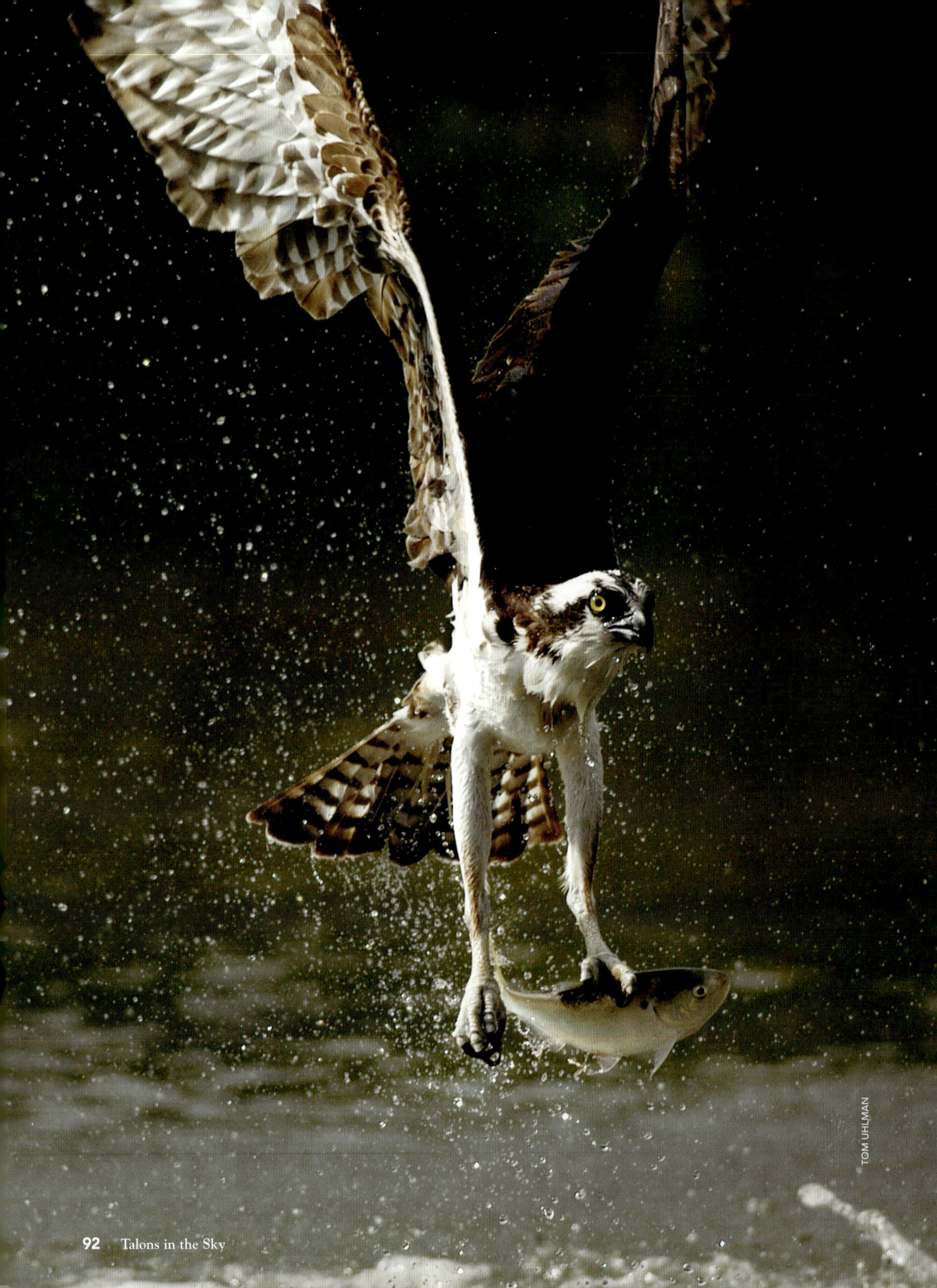
TOM UHLMAN

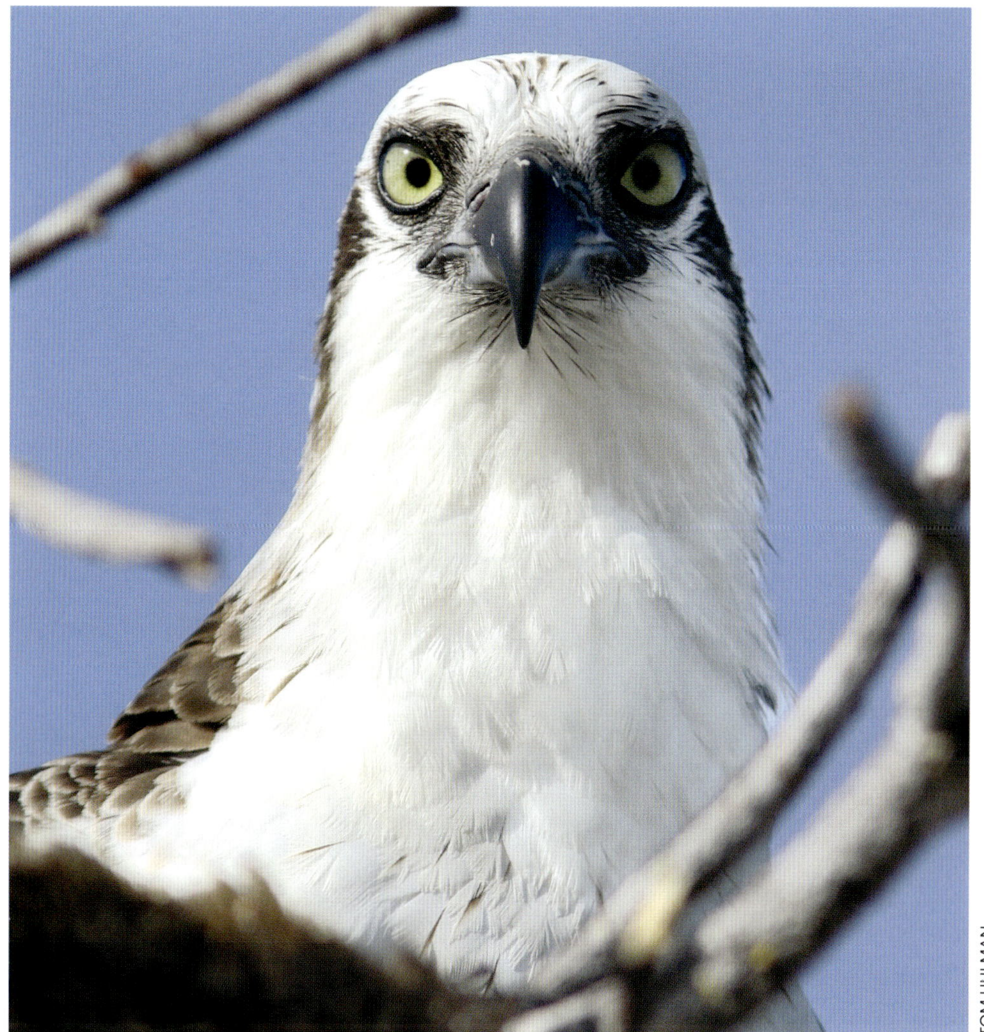
TOM UHLMAN

OPPOSITE: The osprey is well designed to catch fish, with a reversible toe that lets the bird adjust its talons so it has two forward and two back for a better grip on its slippery target. **ABOVE:** An osprey will use its hooked bill not as a weapon, but to tear apart its meal.

The efforts of the federal government, the sanctuary, and other organizations were successful—the osprey made a comeback in the United States.

Due to its distinctive wing shape in flight and equally distinctive plumage, the osprey is one of the easiest North American raptors to identify. When flying, ospreys are noted for their "crooked" wings, which bear a striking resemblance to those of a sea gull. Perched ospreys appear long-legged, and the tips of their broad, somewhat pointed wings extend beyond the tail.

The osprey is a handsome bird that has a snowy white crown and forehead; the anterior portion of the crown and middle of the nape is dark brown. Flecks of buff are often seen behind the crown, on the back of the head, and on the nape. The penetrating eye is a brilliant lemon yellow. The lore is bare and black in color. A wide black eyestripe extends from the back of the eye to the side of the neck, separating the white crown from the white throat. The hooked bill is black, and the cere and lower mandible are bluish gray.

The back and upper-wing coverts range from dark reddish brown to glossy black. The five outermost primaries are darker than the remainder of the flight feathers, as are the lesser upper-wing coverts and the interscapulars and anterior scapulars. A tawny outline narrowly edges all of the feathers. The underparts are white or occasionally a pale buff. The underwings have gray flight feathers and distinct black carpal patches.

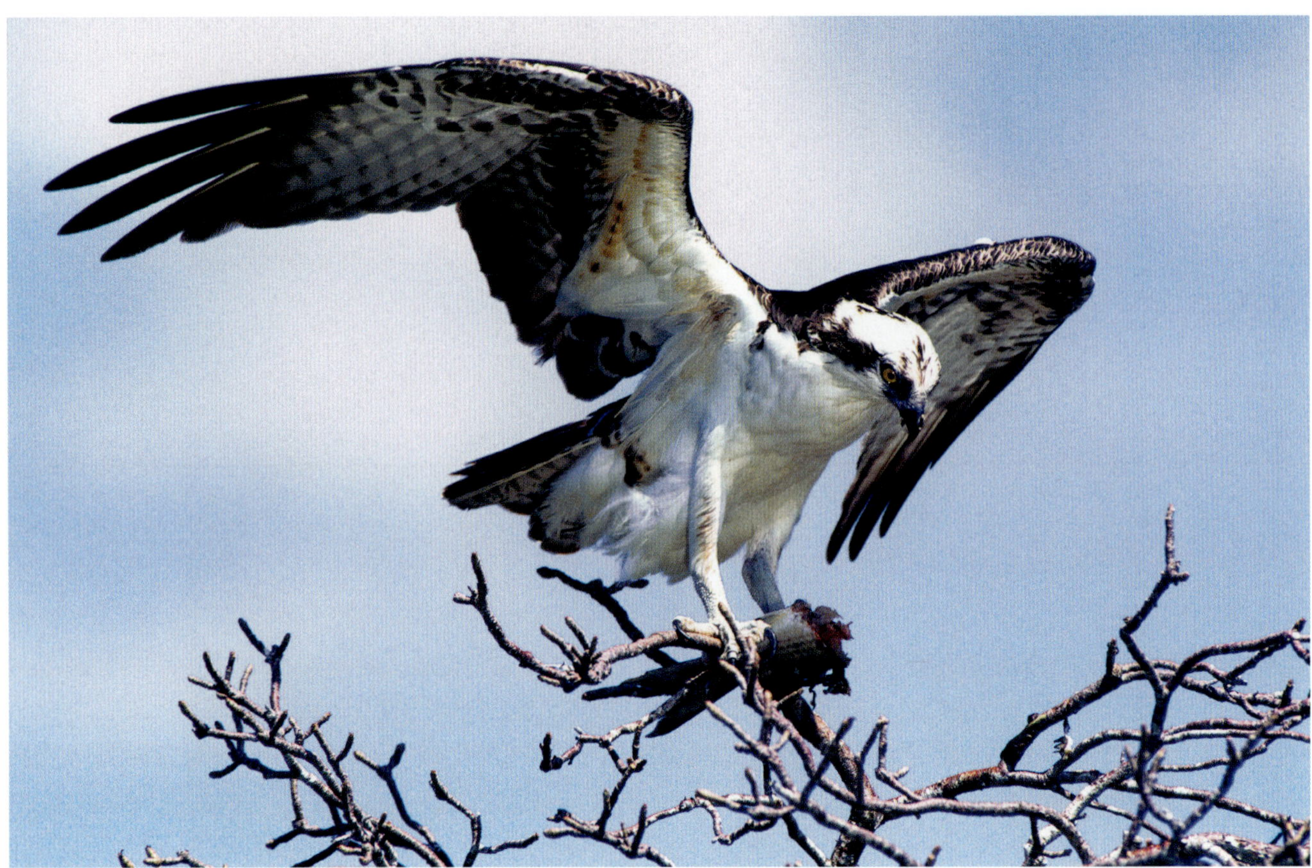

ABOVE: The average length of a female osprey's wing is 19 to 20 inches. The males, slightly smaller than the females, have a wing measurement of 18 to 20 inches. **OPPOSITE:** Don't even think of getting between this osprey and its meal.

The tail is short and banded. The tail feathers are crossed by five to seven bands of darker brown, which become quite distinct on the underside of the tail. There is little difference between the sexes in plumage, with the exception of the short brownish streaks, which resemble a necklace, on the breast of the females. The tarsi and toes are light gray to grayish blue; the claws are black.

The immature bird is very similar in appearance to the adult. The most obvious distinction is the "scaly" appearance of the juvenile due to a white border on the back and upper-wing coverts. Adults possess more dark mottling on the underwing linings than immature birds. The young bird's tail is similar to the adult's, with the exception that it has a wide white terminal band. The eyes of an immature bird range from red to orange.

Ospreys are usually spotted perched or gliding over a pond or bay searching for their favorite meal—fish. Though ospreys will sometimes prey on frogs, turtles, crustaceans, small mammals, and even birds, their unusual anatomy features specialized adaptations for catching fish. Strong, well-rounded talons aid in the attack and capture of its prey. A reversible toe, which is rotated when grasping, positions the toes with two forward and two backward, ensuring a strong grip. Sharp spicules located on the bottom of the feet help the osprey to maintain a firm hold on a slippery fish. The fiercely hooked bill is used not as a weapon, but as a tool to tear apart its food.

In a manner unlike other birds of prey, ospreys dive for fish, often completely submerging themselves during the process. The osprey hovers or glides above the water until it spots a fish near the surface. Then it dives headfirst with its wings swept back behind the tail. It adjusts its dive to compensate for the refraction in the image of the fish just below the surface. In the instant before the osprey breaks the water, it throws its feet forward in order to grasp the fish in its talons. It is able to take off from the surface and, when airborne, shakes vigorously to remove the water.

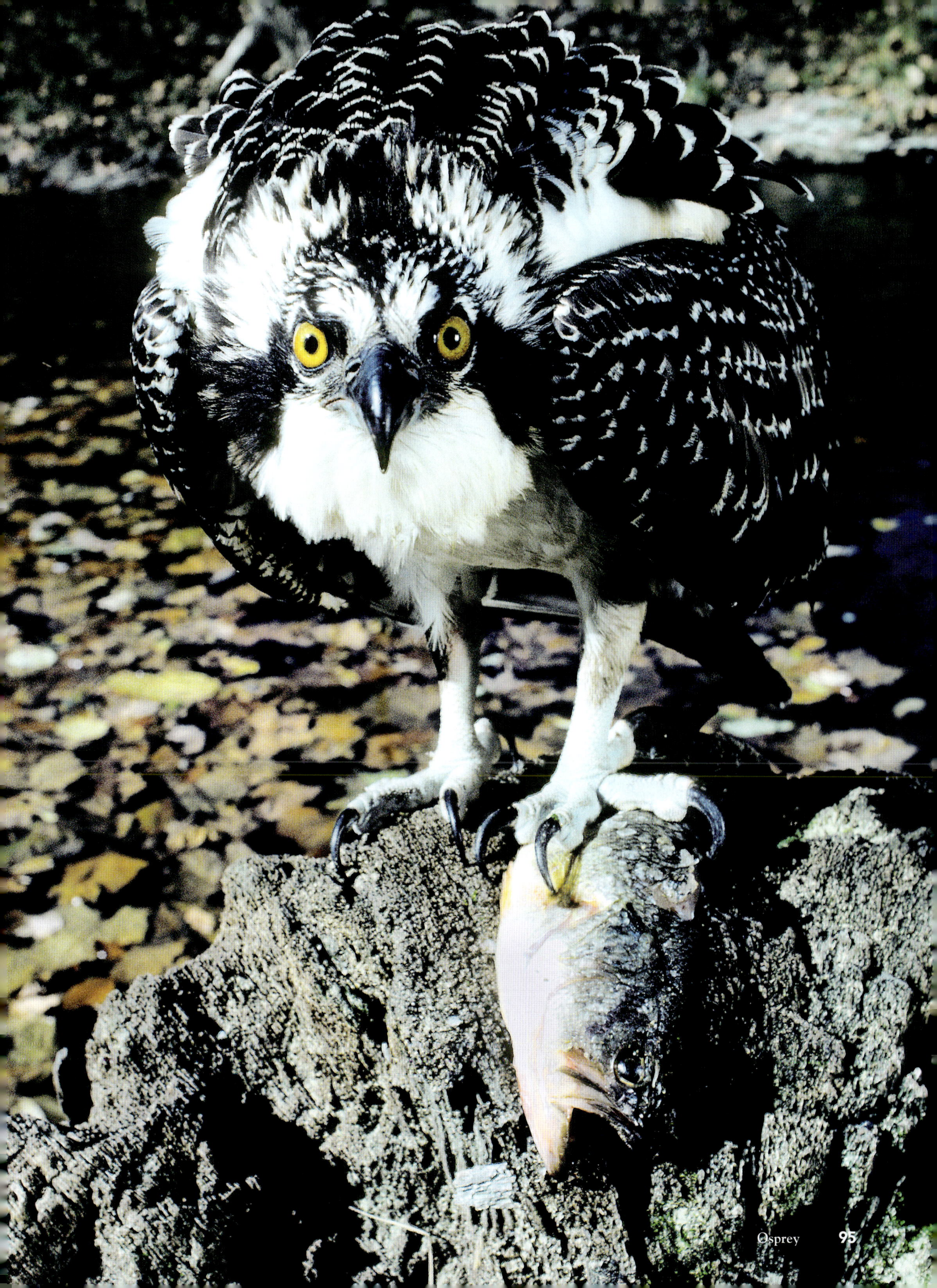

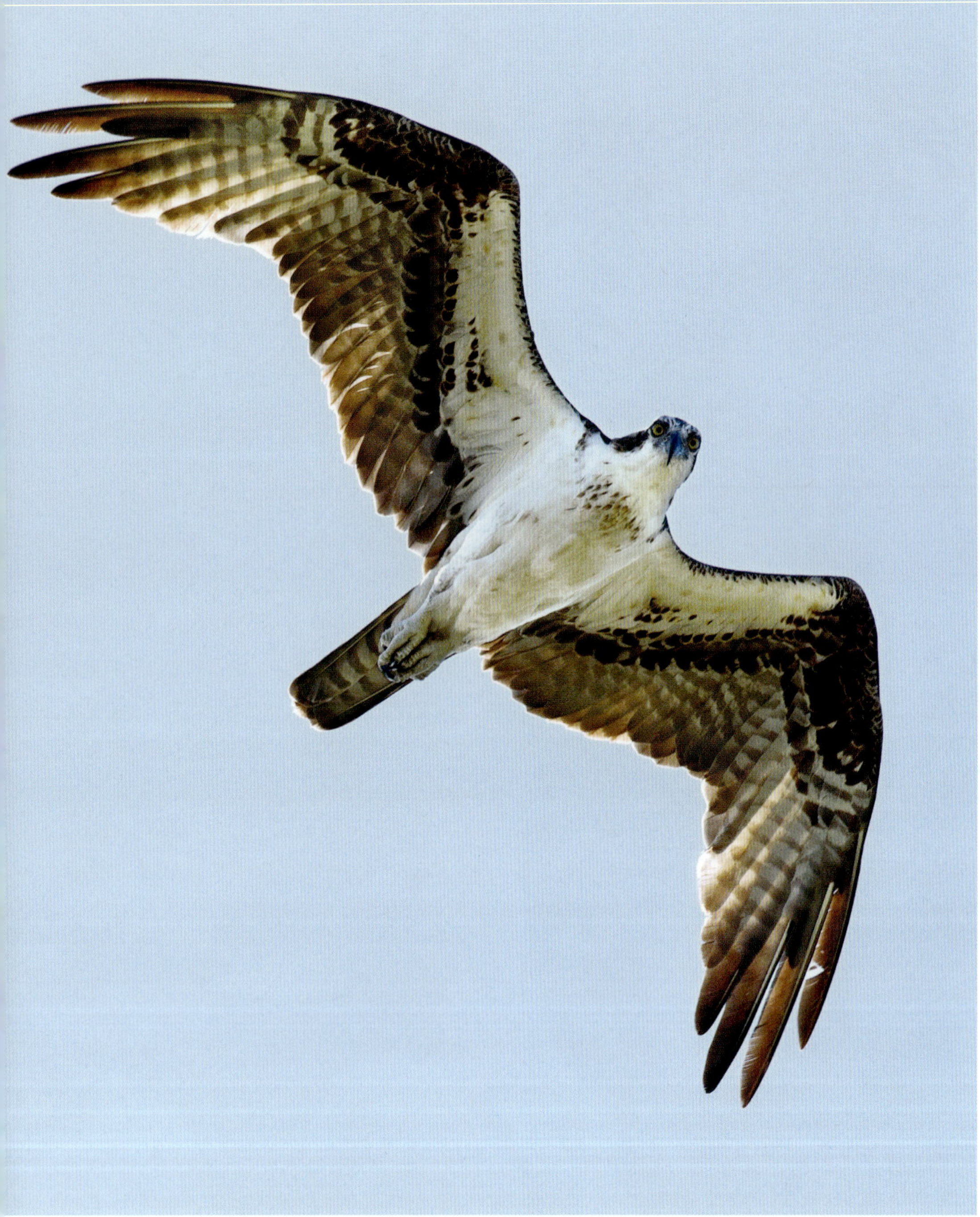

LEFT: The osprey's "crooked wings" give it a distinctive appearance in flight.

Measurements (in mm)

	Male	Female
Length	462–498	488–512
Tail Length	199–220	212–240
Culmen Length	36	36
Tarsus Length	66	66
Toe (interior)	37	37

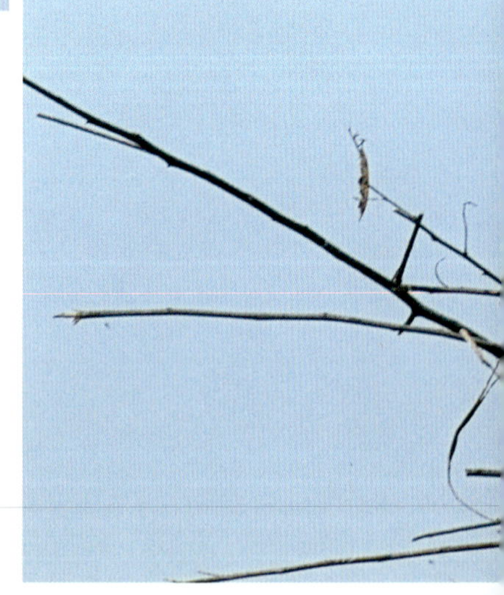

The osprey always carries the captured fish head forward—sometimes one in each claw. Weighing under four pounds, the osprey is a strong bird and can carry a fish almost its own size. It will only take live prey; if an osprey drops its catch it will not retrieve it. In addition to diving, ospreys will, in a manner similar to bald eagles, skim over the surface of the water, snatching fish with their talons.

At the sanctuary, rehabilitating ospreys is a difficult task indeed. They are nervous, highly strung birds that must be housed in an isolated area with minimum human contact. Many ospreys will not eat in captivity unless they are in the company of another osprey—competition between the two birds will often encourage them to feed.

Ospreys nest in small, loose colonies with each pair defending its nest site from intruders. Each year the ospreys return to the area where they were born to rear their own young. They will reuse the same nest year after year, refurbishing and adding to it each breeding

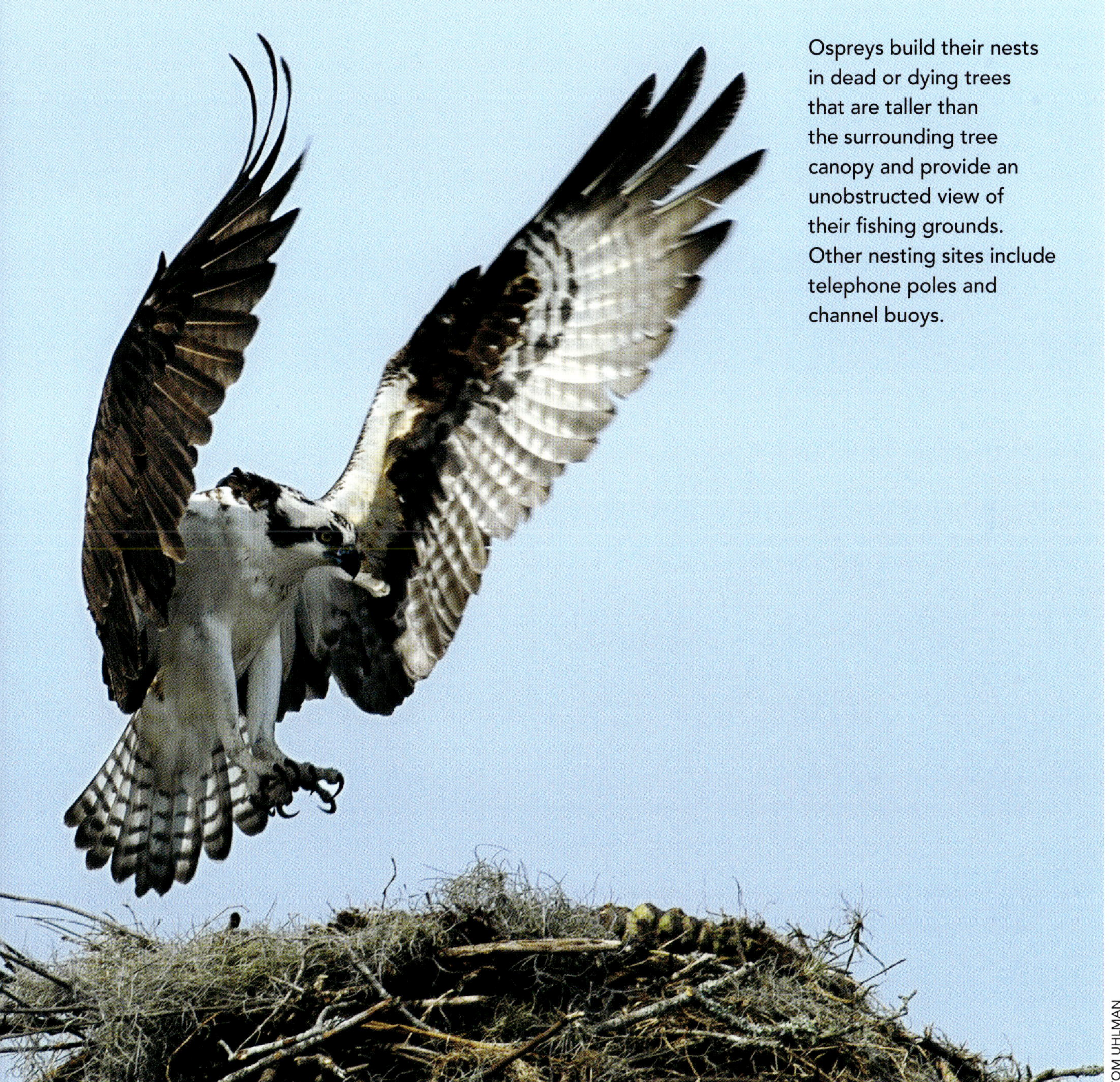

Ospreys build their nests in dead or dying trees that are taller than the surrounding tree canopy and provide an unobstructed view of their fishing grounds. Other nesting sites include telephone poles and channel buoys.

season. After several breeding seasons, a nest may collapse under its own weight.

These impressive nests are built primarily of sticks and lined with bark, grass, and vines. Ospreys prefer to nest in dead or dying trees that are taller than the surrounding tree canopy, and they tend to locate their nests at the top of the crown rather than below it. Ospreys adapt well to man-made structures and will often build their aeries on channel buoys, telephone poles, and other tall structures if their preferred nesting sites are unavailable.

The osprey is a monogamous bird for the most part; a pair bond usually lasts through several breeding seasons. The male returns to the nesting site a few days before the female. During the time, the male will make soaring climbs up to 1,000 feet, with either a fish or nesting material clutched in its talons, followed by a dramatic dive. This display often begins and ends at the aerie and, according to Johnsgard in *Hawks, Eagles & Falcons of North America*, is called the "sky dance song flight."

The sky dance is performed alone or in the presence of a female. The dance appears to serve two purposes: to attract a mate and to claim ownership to a nesting site. The sky dance reaches its climax with the arrival of the female. The pair then begins the yearly ritual of repairing and modifying the nest. At this time, the pair engages in courtship feeding behavior. From pair formation to egg laying, males supply food for both themselves and their mates.

Ospreys copulate soon after returning to the nest. The female normally lays eggs in intervals of one to three days; once she begins laying she will not leave the nest at all. An average of three pinkish-white eggs covered with reddish spots are laid each season. The eggs can range from oval to elliptical in shape and measure about 61 by 45.6 mm. Females are predominantly responsible for incubating the eggs, although the males participate to some degree. The incubation period lasts about five weeks, after which time the down-covered chicks begin to struggle free.

The chicks are pinkish in color at birth, but they soon darken to blend in with their surroundings, effectively camouflaging them from predators. Chicks depend on their parents for food and protection for about three months. After this period, the chicks will be independent, and a new generation of young ospreys will grace the skies.

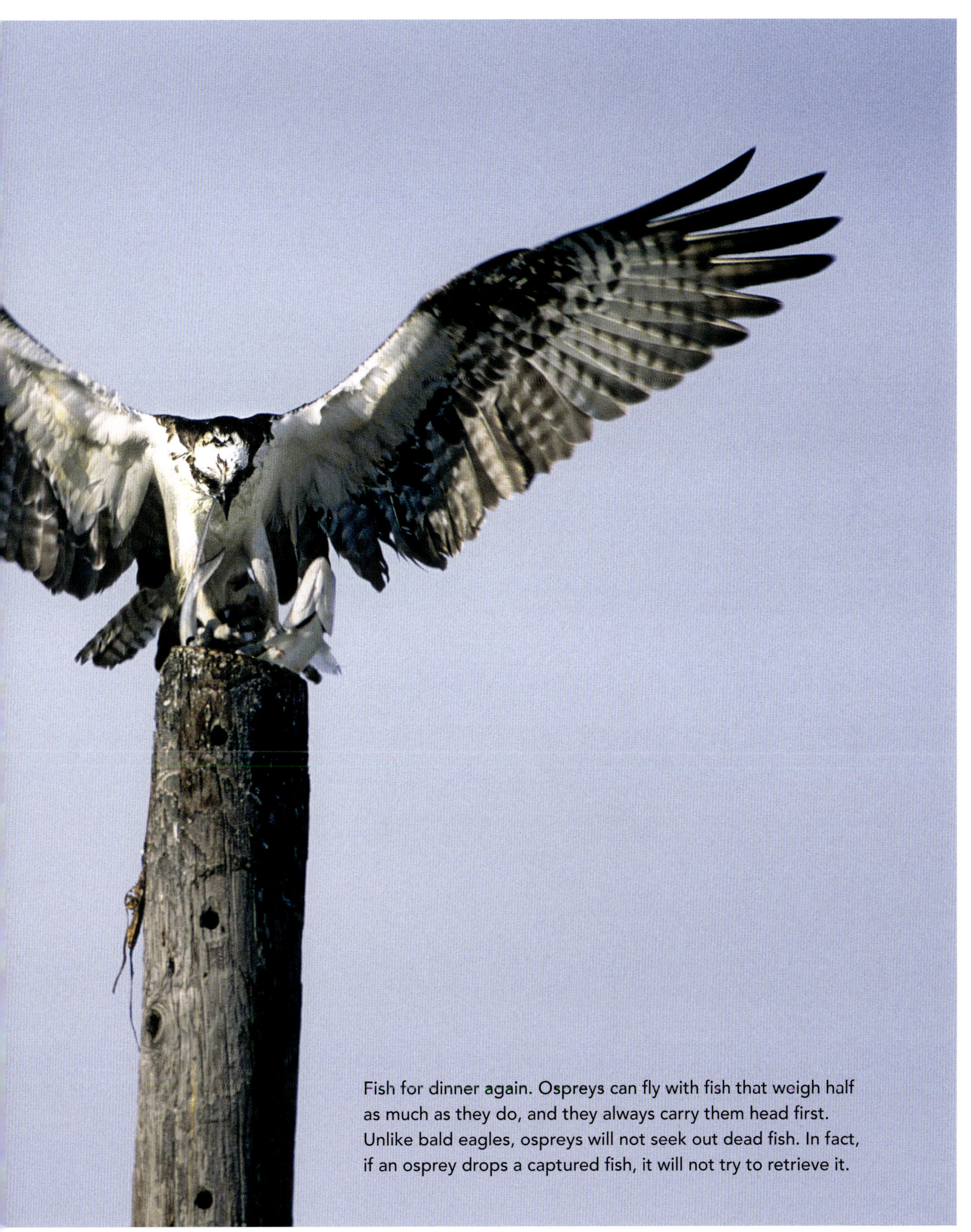

Fish for dinner again. Ospreys can fly with fish that weigh half as much as they do, and they always carry them head first. Unlike bald eagles, ospreys will not seek out dead fish. In fact, if an osprey drops a captured fish, it will not try to retrieve it.

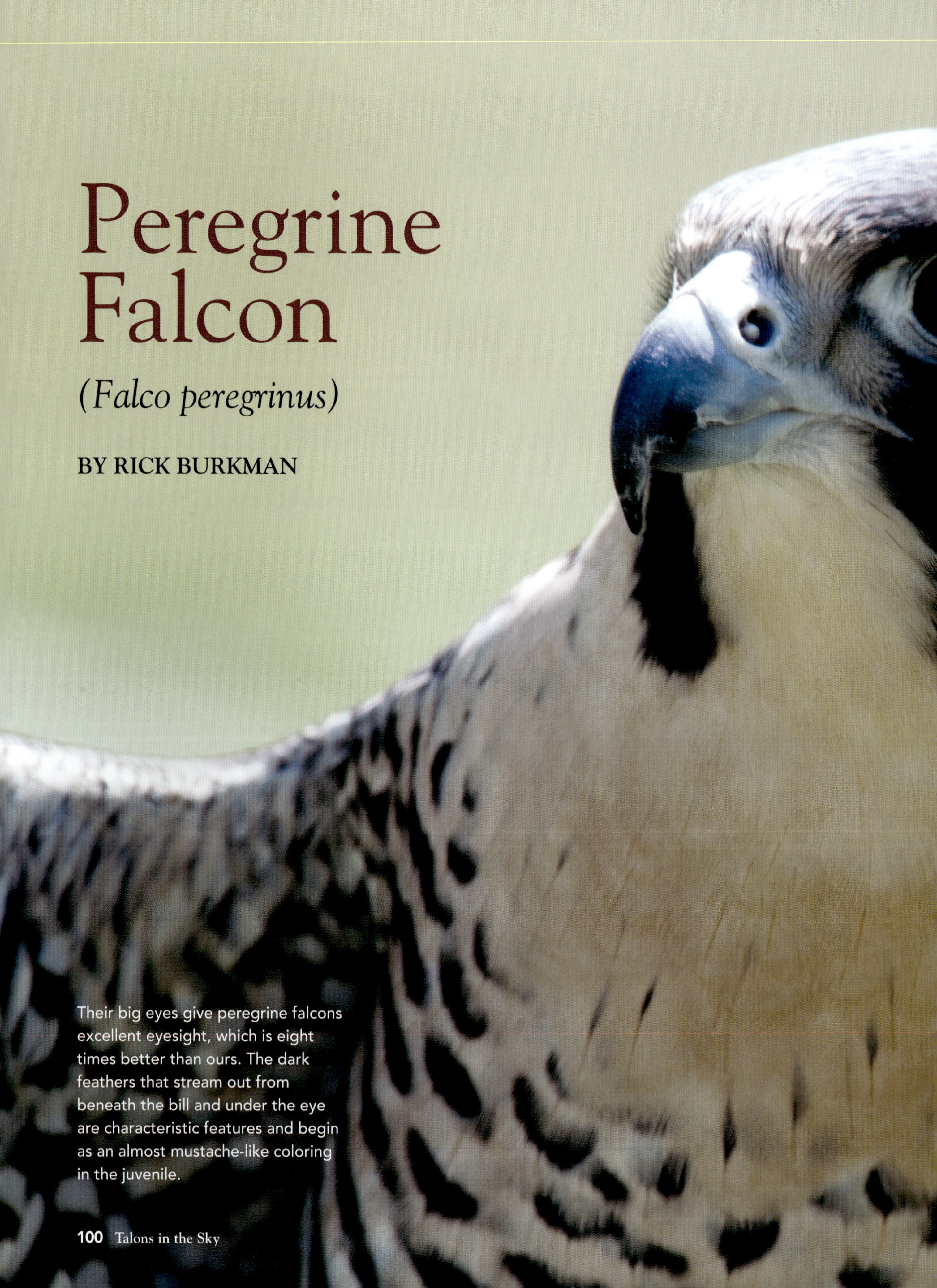

Peregrine Falcon

(*Falco peregrinus*)

BY RICK BURKMAN

Their big eyes give peregrine falcons excellent eyesight, which is eight times better than ours. The dark feathers that stream out from beneath the bill and under the eye are characteristic features and begin as an almost mustache-like coloring in the juvenile.

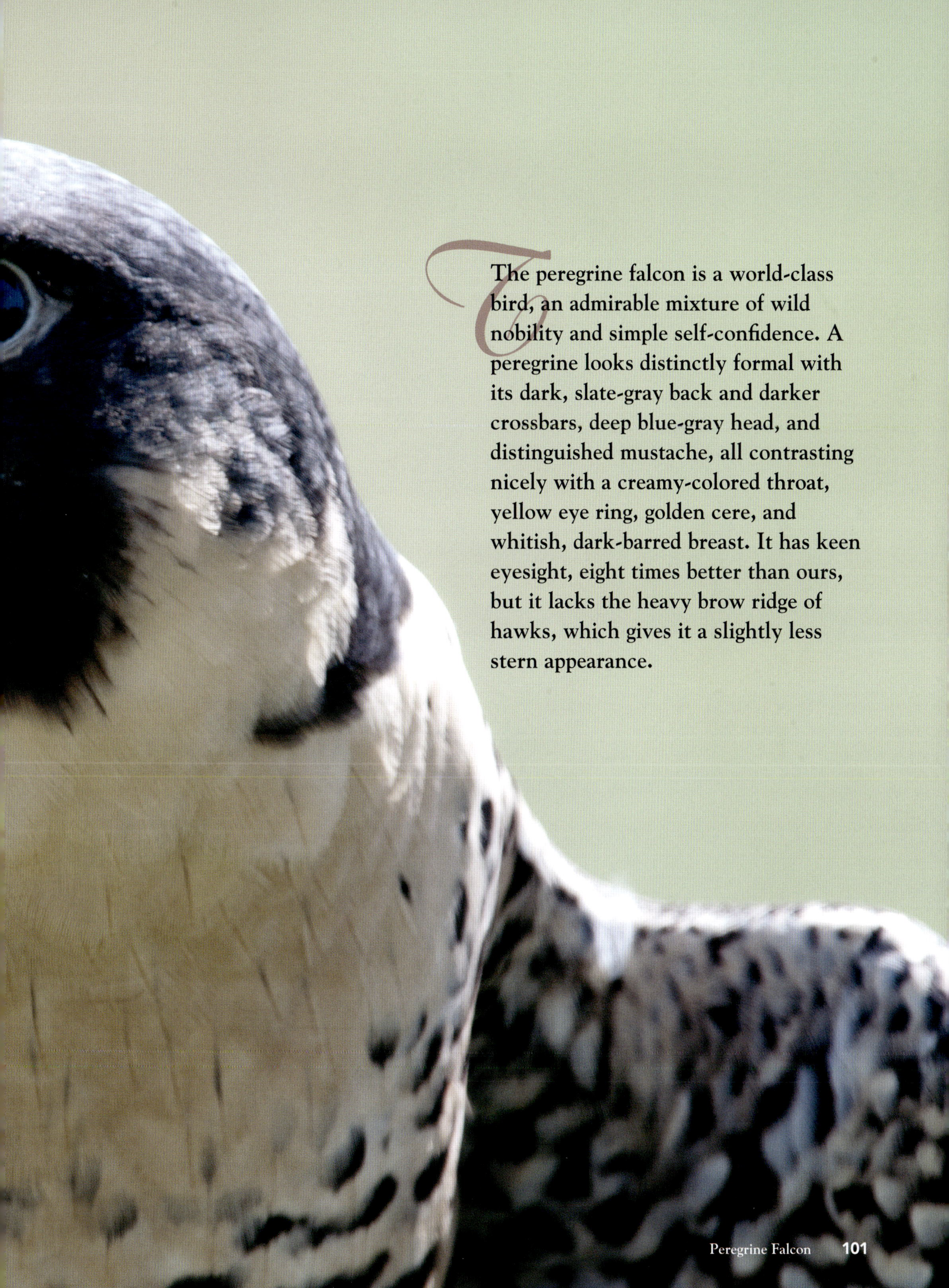

The peregrine falcon is a world-class bird, an admirable mixture of wild nobility and simple self-confidence. A peregrine looks distinctly formal with its dark, slate-gray back and darker crossbars, deep blue-gray head, and distinguished mustache, all contrasting nicely with a creamy-colored throat, yellow eye ring, golden cere, and whitish, dark-barred breast. It has keen eyesight, eight times better than ours, but it lacks the heavy brow ridge of hawks, which gives it a slightly less stern appearance.

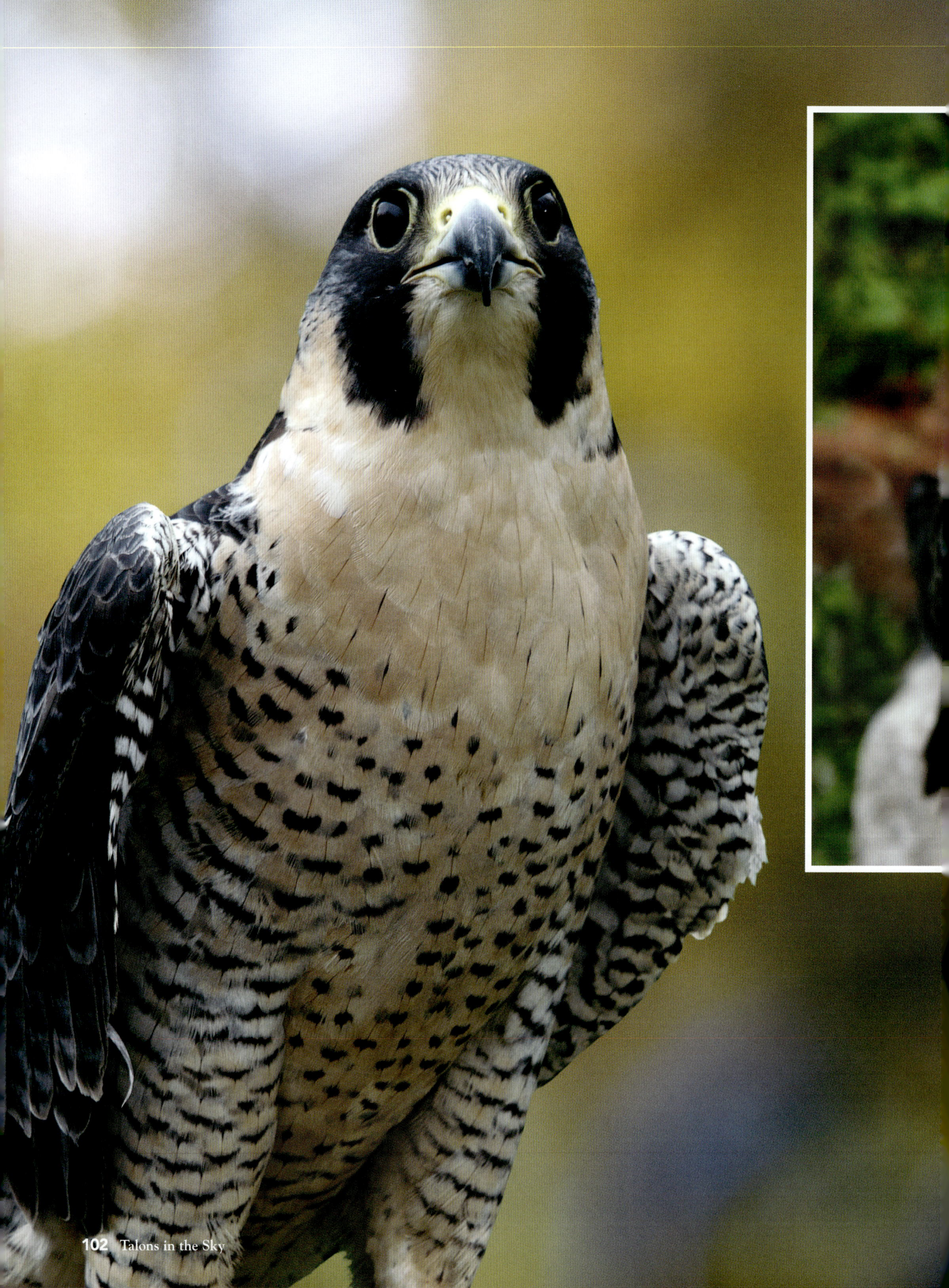

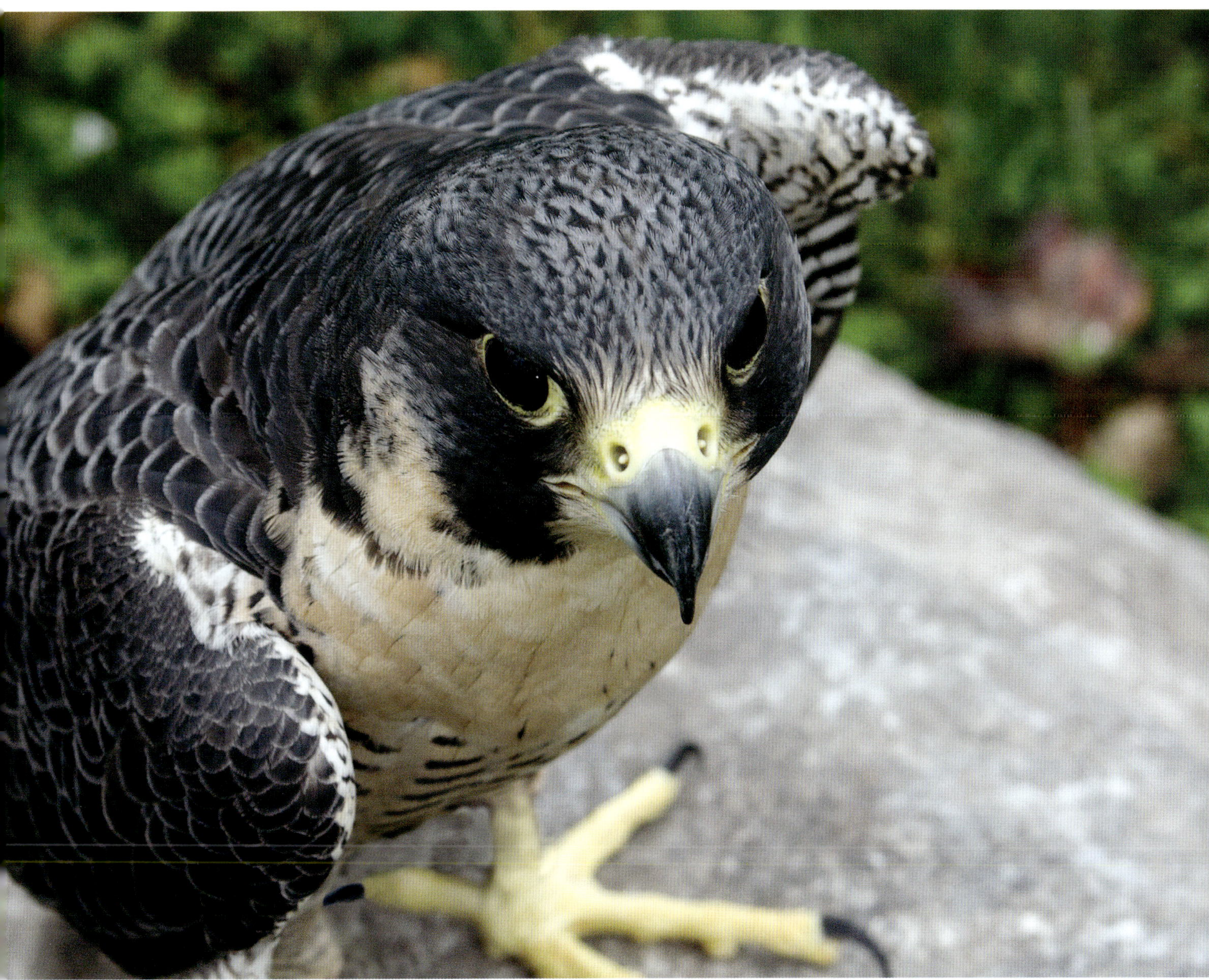

With a stocky, powerful body and a bill that's ideal for tearing into its prey, the peregrine falcon is a feathered killing machine. From any angle, it is a magnificent bird and a challenging subject for the wildfowl carver.

Peregrines are raptors, so their gentler gaze is backed by a stocky body that exudes power and strength. Maybe we relate to peregrines so well because, despite their obvious prowess, they also seem a little self-deprecating. After all, the birds' seriousness is slightly undercut by their distinctly barred "flags," the falconers' term for the leg feathers that make it appear that peregrines are wearing a pair of old-time golf knickers or pantaloons.

Flags aside, peregrines appear noble enough when perched. Their real beauty though, comes in the air. The birds can soar effortlessly above the trees and through mountain passes on long-distance migrations, floating like kites on warm updrafts and drifting toward their destinations. Some peregrines travel more than 15,000 miles on their annual journeys. (The Latin word *peregrinus* means "wanderer.") Not only can they drift with little effort, when they dive the birds can also accelerate to speeds that have been clocked at more than 200 miles per hour. In ground-hugging pursuits a peregrine resembles a jet fighter at full afterburner. Peregrine falcons also glide above coastal shorelines, plummet into dry deserts, and rest and roost

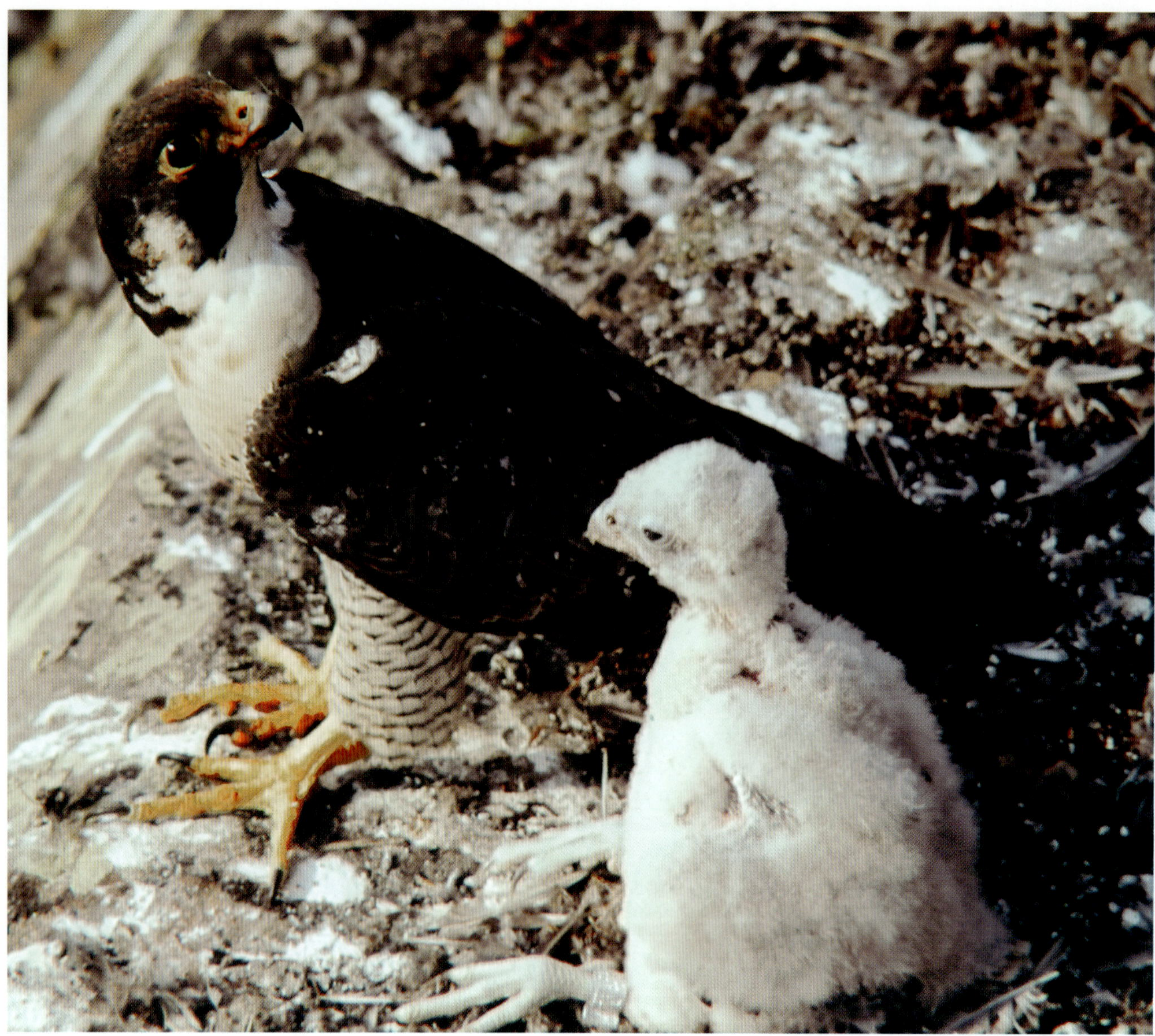

ABOVE: The young falcons may look like adorable, if somewhat awkward, balls of fluff in the beginning, but they will soon become very effective aerial hunters. **OPPOSITE:** When it comes to nest sites, the peregrine prefers a cliff or ledge that provides a good view of its territory.

on mountain cliffs and city skyscrapers. Wherever they live, peregrines are predators of the air and they own the skies that they call home.

Because of their relative abundance, distinctive looks, readily observable aerial prowess, and remote homes, the peregrine has earned positions in ancient myths. Some Native American societies considered the peregrine falcon a younger brother to the powerful eagle and the embodiment of the god of war; ancient desert Egyptians worshipped Horus, the falcon-headed sun god and god of war; and the near-Arctic dwelling Vikings had Odin, the king of the Norse gods, who was said to visit the earth in the shape of a falcon.

Today, we know that falcons are not gods, but they do provide a reflection of the lands in which they live. The healthier the land, the more stable its peregrine falcon population. In North America, peregrine falcons are part of a well-known success story, albeit one that came on the heels of a near-disaster when the pesticide DDT and its chemical relatives nearly decimated the species. These early pesticides were extremely effective at protecting agricultural crops, but the chemicals caused the falcons to lay eggs with thin shells. The fragile eggs broke in the nest and generations of birds

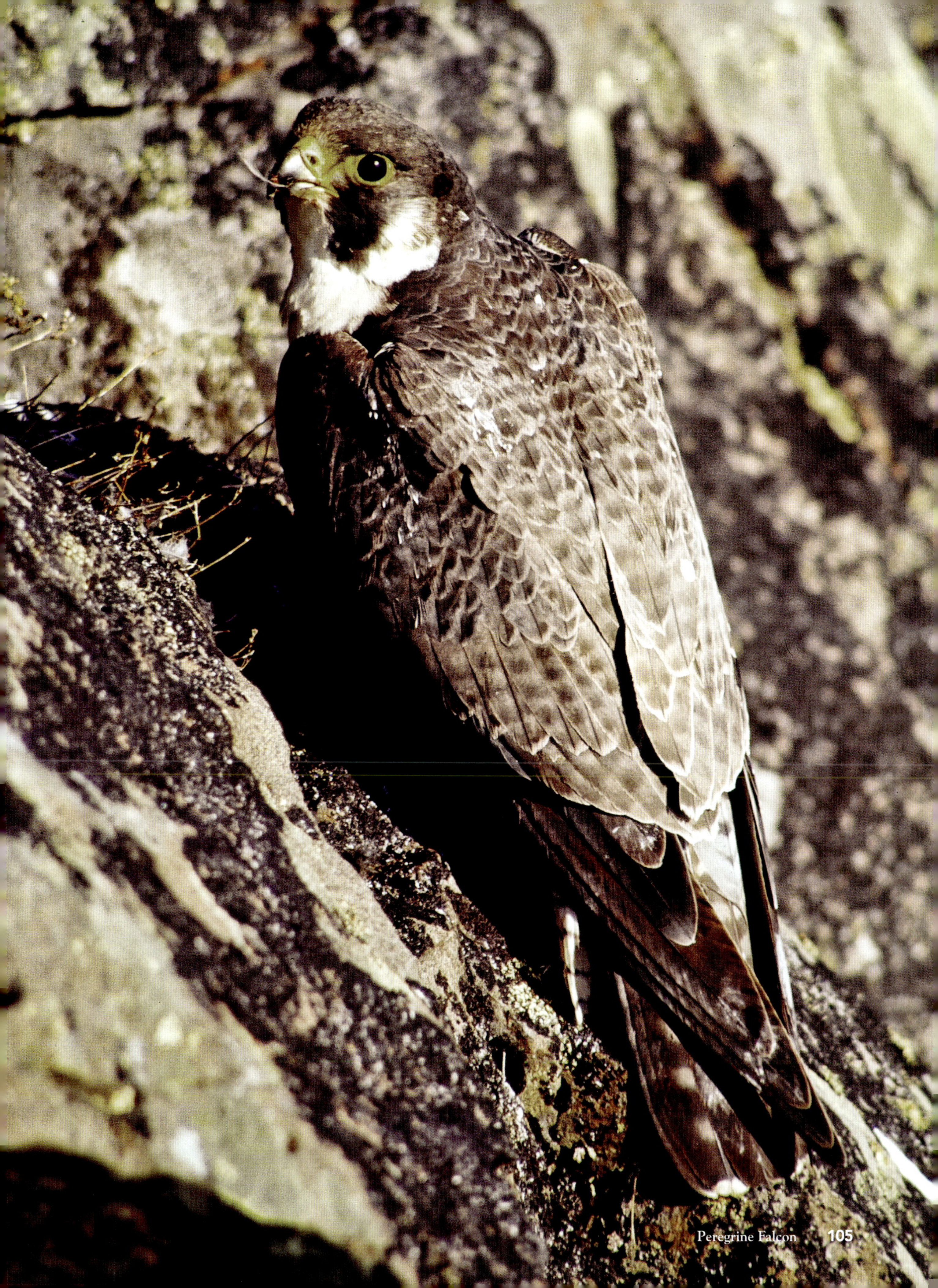

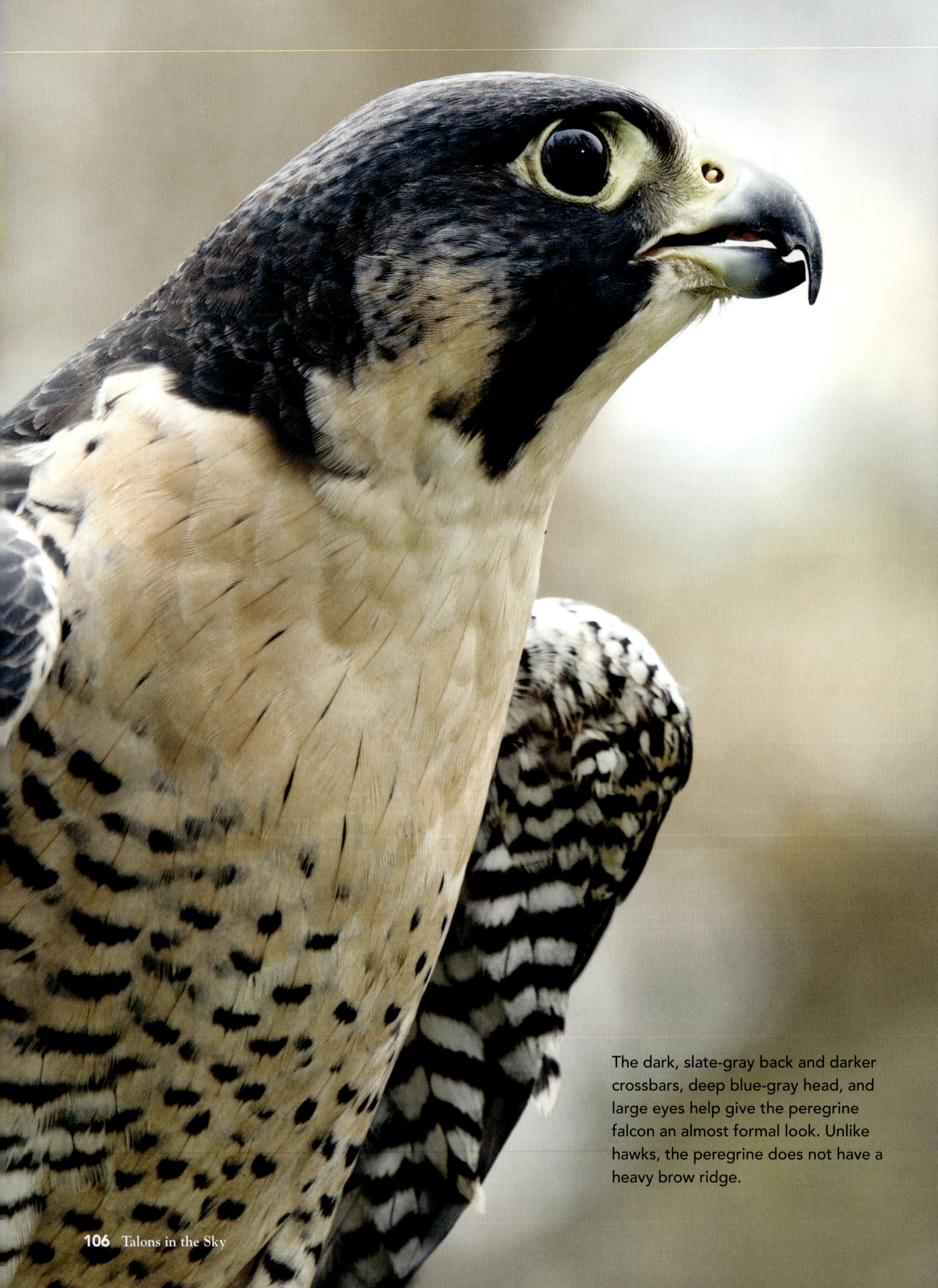

The dark, slate-gray back and darker crossbars, deep blue-gray head, and large eyes help give the peregrine falcon an almost formal look. Unlike hawks, the peregrine does not have a heavy brow ridge.

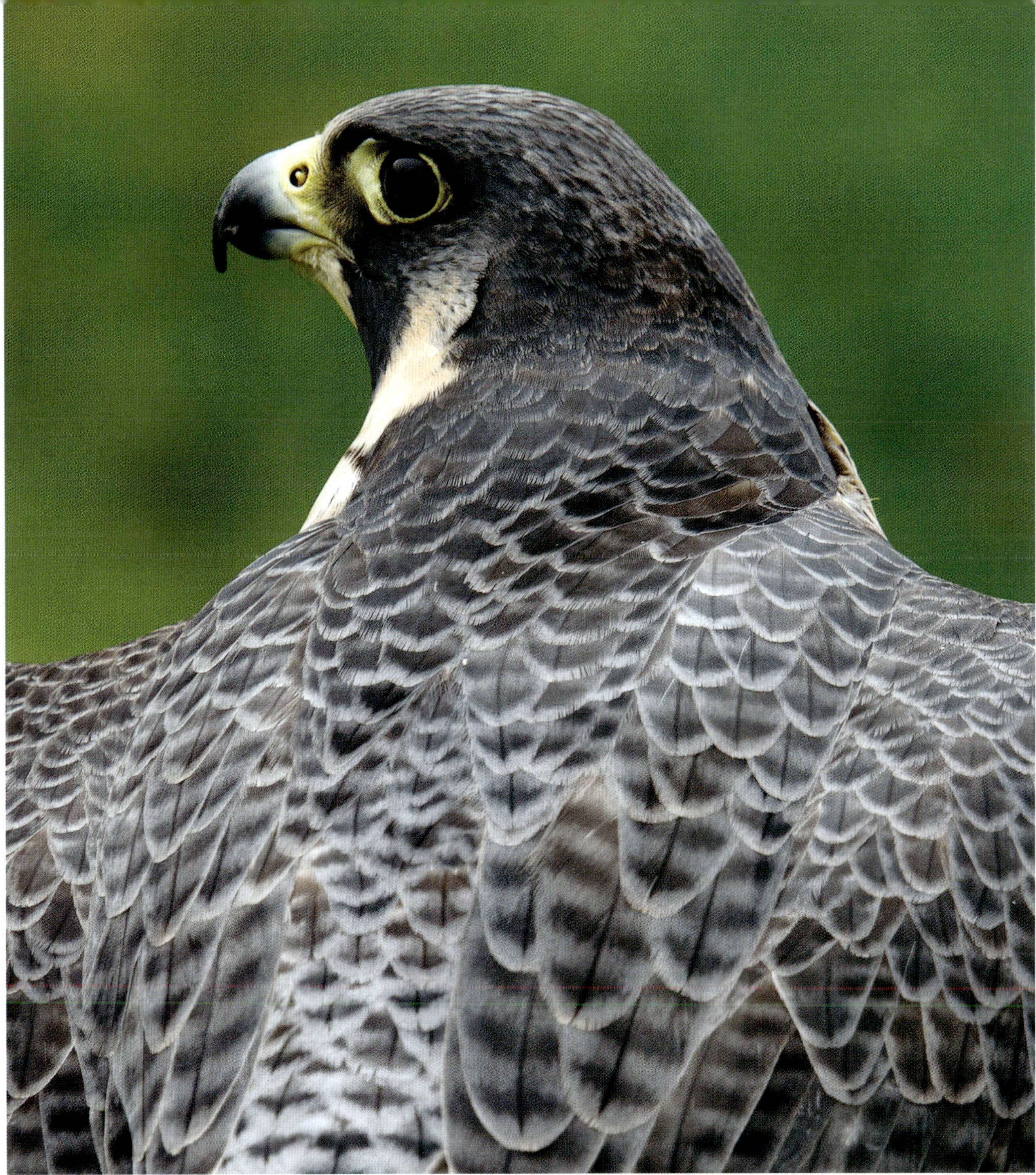

were lost. Although peregrine populations far from the reach of agricultural chemicals were not in imminent danger, portions of the North American peregrine falcon population plummeted—by 1965 there were no breeding peregrines east of the Mississippi River.

The loss of the peregrine, along with the noticeable decline of many other raptor species, prompted land managers, agricultural specialists, and politicians to reconsider their practices and ban DDT-like compounds from routine, large-scale use. It worked. Limiting chemicals in the environment allowed these birds to survive, and reintroduction efforts allowed them to thrive. Peregrine falcons, long a favorite of falconers, were once again hunting the skies.

It is easy to see why falconers and others enjoy the peregrine. This raptor's most famous hunting technique is a demonstration of pure physicality and exquisite muscle control. When a peregrine spots a smaller bird, sometimes from a mile or more away, it takes to the air, rocketing into the sky until it reaches a point above its target but still within striking range. At this critical height the bird tips its head downward. Now aiming toward its prey, the peregrine flaps its wings and accelerates. Then it tucks its wings and allows gravity to

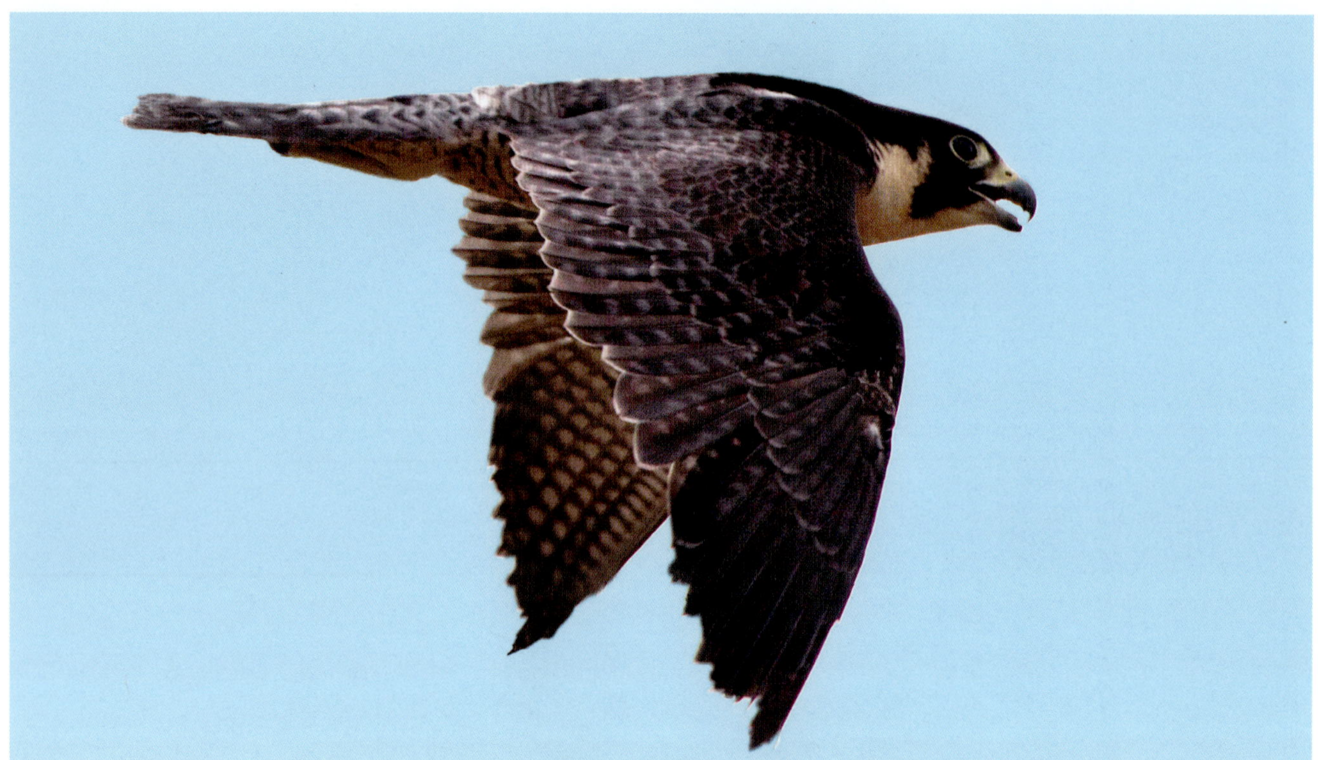

Once known as the duck hawk, no doubt because of its skill at hunting waterfowl, the peregrine falcon is a master of the skies. Once they target prey, the birds dive like missiles to make bone-crunching impact. The peregrine's wingspan can be up to 41 inches. Females are larger than males.

drive it the rest of the way. It is now a killing projectile capable of intelligently adjusting its trajectory with subtle adjustments to its tail, wings, and head.

Peregrines have been clocked diving at 243 miles per hour and they may fly even faster. Special adaptations keep the falcons alive at speeds that could kill an unprotected human. It has nictitating membranes, a type of semi-rigid lens cap that protects the eyes from wind and dust, and it has a tubercle in the nostril that changes the air pressure around the nasal opening as the falcon dives, allowing the bird to breathe rather than have air sucked out of its lungs at high speeds. The peregrine is agile enough, even at these velocities, to snatch small birds out of the air and strong enough to overtake and overpower ducks and small geese. At one time people believed the peregrine smacked its prey with a fist made of closed talons, knocking it from the sky. High speed photography has since revealed that the falcon hits its prey with feet outstretched and talons exposed, with the intent to capture or slash and maim. The falcons will grab small birds and bats and eat them in the air. Larger birds, such as gulls, grebes, and puffins, may be too large to snatch at full speed. However, these species often suffer mortal wounds from the first impact. The peregrine circles, plucking its meal out of the air or following it to the ground where it can kill its prey with a bite to the neck. Peregrines prefer birds but they will not turn down a meal of squirrel or rabbit when opportunities present themselves. They adapt their hunting style to match the currently abundant prey, so it is not uncommon for them to hunt at night, picking off bats as they leave their roosts or gulls sleeping on cliff faces. Peregrines have even been seen snatching fish breaking the water's surface.

Peregrines occasionally join forces to hunt together in pairs. When they encounter flocking birds, such as large groups of shorebirds or blackbirds, one falcon will dive at the flock, causing it to lose cohesion and become ragged. The second falcon circles above and waits for the action to start and then targets stragglers. Although known for their daring dives through open air, these birds are also masters of stealth. Peregrines can zero in on a target by staying close to the ground and skimming over hills and hummocks in grasslands or by hugging the waves over open water, until they are close enough to ambush their quarry. Startled prey may jump up in front of a hunting falcon or freeze to the ground, hoping to evade detection. Either way,

Peregrines have been clocked diving at 243 miles per hour and they may fly even faster.

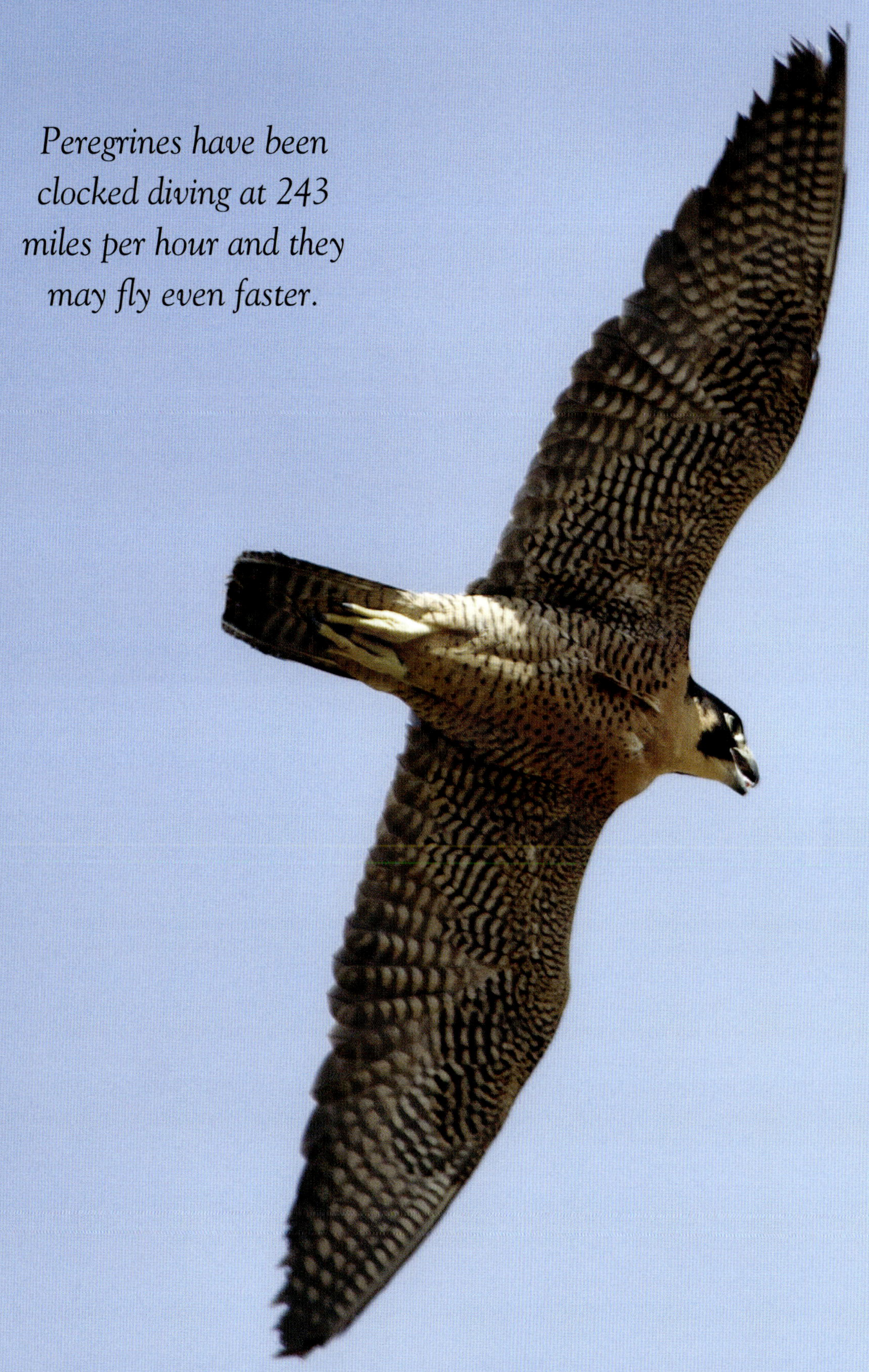

the peregrine has a good chance of winning. Even in stealth mode, peregrine falcons are dynamically perfect creatures.

Males (also called tercels or tiercels) use their flight for more than hunting. Migrating males normally arrive at their potential nest sites several days before the females. There they perform aerial displays of loops and figure eights to proclaim their title to the land where they will raise a family. They twist their bodies 180 degrees as they slash through the air, exposing their lighter abdomens to display their messages. If all goes well the male catches the interest of a passing female and she roosts within his eyesight. The birds appear nonchalant as they take stock of one another while simultaneously looking over the cliff side to determine the suitability of the neighborhood. If the female likes what she sees, she will move closer and closer to the male until the two are sitting side-by-side at the nest site. The male lowers his head, bowing to the female. She may respond in turn, repeating the performance but, like many other bird-eating raptors, she is larger and maintains the dominant position.

Once the birds choose a nesting site, the male and female will "scrape" the spot, pressing their breasts to the ground and pushing their bodies forward with their feet. This small scrape will become the resting home for the eggs. Peregrines may use successful aeries year after year. If the spot is good enough, several generations of birds may use it.

The female lays three or four eggs, one at a time with about two days between each. The cream-colored eggs may have brown or brick-red blotches. Incubation begins when the female lays the second-to-last egg (incubation can begin with the first egg in colder climates). The peregrines take turns on the nest, warming and protecting the eggs for the next four weeks.

When the time for hatching arrives the young birds start calling from inside their shells. They kick and roll around, using their egg tooth to chip and crack the shells. The hatchlings will eventually turn into fearsome adults, but at first the pink-skinned, downy-feathered babies are weak and tire quickly. They twist and turn, stopping for long periods to rest and build muscle strength. It can take two days or more for the nestlings to fully break free of their shells. Once free they are ready to face the world, and to baby birds that means immediate and insatiable hunger. Both parents feed bits and pieces of meat to the chicks. The voracious appetites fuel rapid growth spurts. Thirty days after hatching feathers have replaced half of the downy coat. By 40 days the young birds are making short flights around their aerie. Soon, they are capable of long migratory flights, but some falcons may also stay on their territory year round.

Powerful as they are, peregrine falcons can still fall prey to other predators. Golden eagles are large enough to hunt peregrines for food. Ravens and crows rob peregrine nests of eggs and young, and coyotes and raccoons attack and kill unsuspecting grounded birds. Food scarcity and competition can challenge first-year birds as they learn to live in the world. Even though life in nature is challenging, this magnificently designed bird has a survival rate of 50 percent or more in the first year. Once a peregrine passes that first-year milestone the probability of survival goes up. Adults may live for up to 20 years in the wild.

In the 1970s, reintroduction plans were developed to try to reestablish breeding populations of peregrines in the eastern United States. People gathered eggs from areas with viable peregrine populations, and human volunteers raised young birds. During the final stages of rearing, the human "parents" delivered the birds to areas that traditionally held mating pairs or that appeared to be suitable habitat. The birds were allowed to habituate to the area, and then they were released to fly, to hunt, and hopefully to return one day to raise a new family of wild peregrines.

Reintroduction plans were more successful than anticipated. A few decades ago peregrine falcons began recognizing that city skyscrapers have nooks and crannies that make ideal nesting sites for cliff-dwelling species. Birds adapted to urban environments where pigeons, cardinals, mallards, crows, and robins provided a seemingly inexhaustible food source. There are few other large birds of prey that use these urban landscapes, so there are not a lot of aerial predators to disrupt the peregrine's family life. The peregrine's comeback was so successful that they were removed from the United States Endangered Species list in 1999.

Peregrine falcons are awesome examples of aerial power and pinnacles of evolution that remind us of the wonderful and powerful aspects of a fragile nature we can find just outside the door.

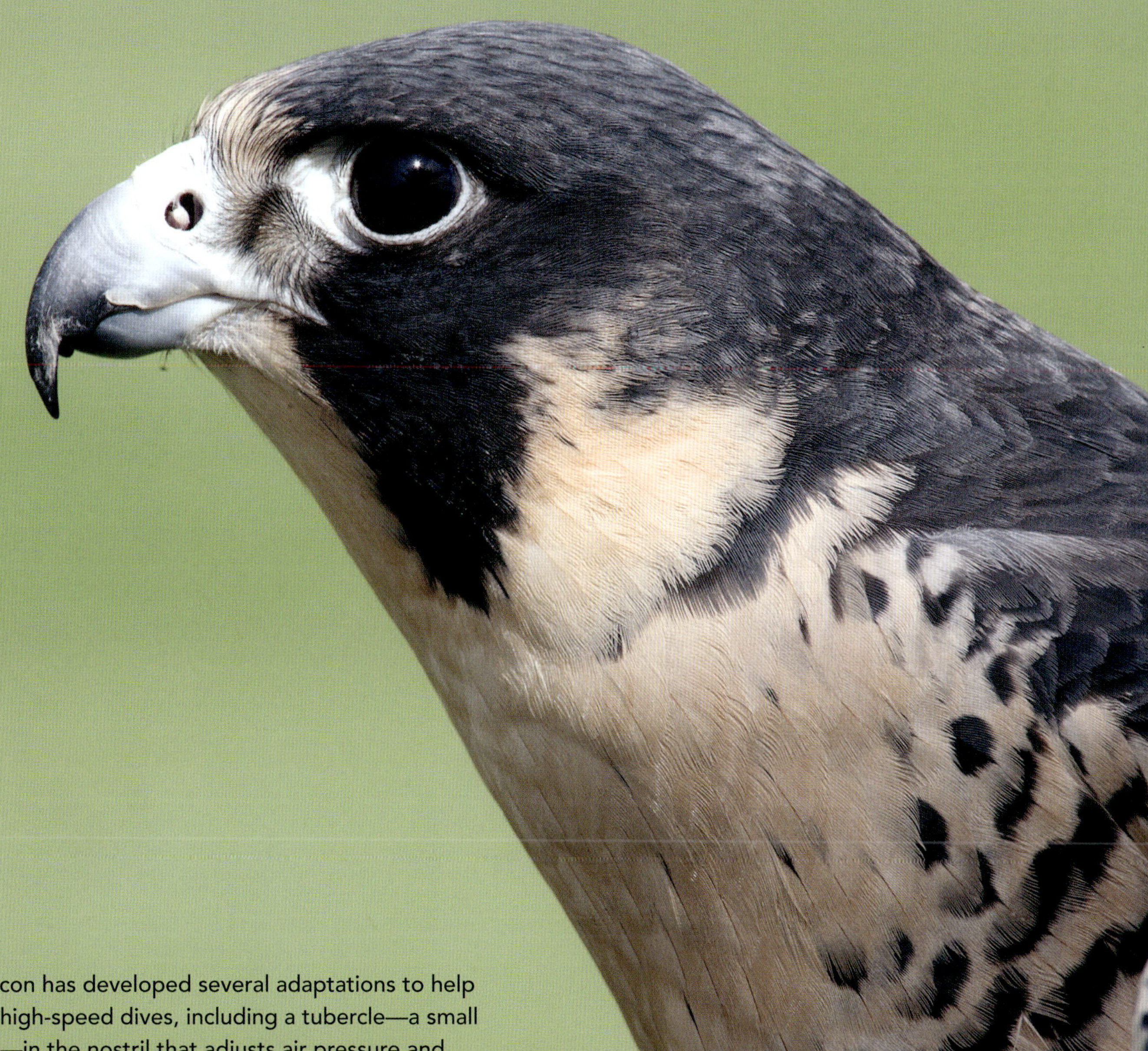

The falcon has developed several adaptations to help it with high-speed dives, including a tubercle—a small nodule—in the nostril that adjusts air pressure and nictitating membranes to protect the eyes.

Measurements (in mm)

	Male	Female
Wing-Chord	315.5	357.6
Tail	148.2	179.2
Tarsus	45.8	50.7
Toe without Claw	49.2	54.6
Culmen from Cere	19.4	23.9

Prairie Falcon

(Falco mexicanus)

BY KURT ROBINETTE

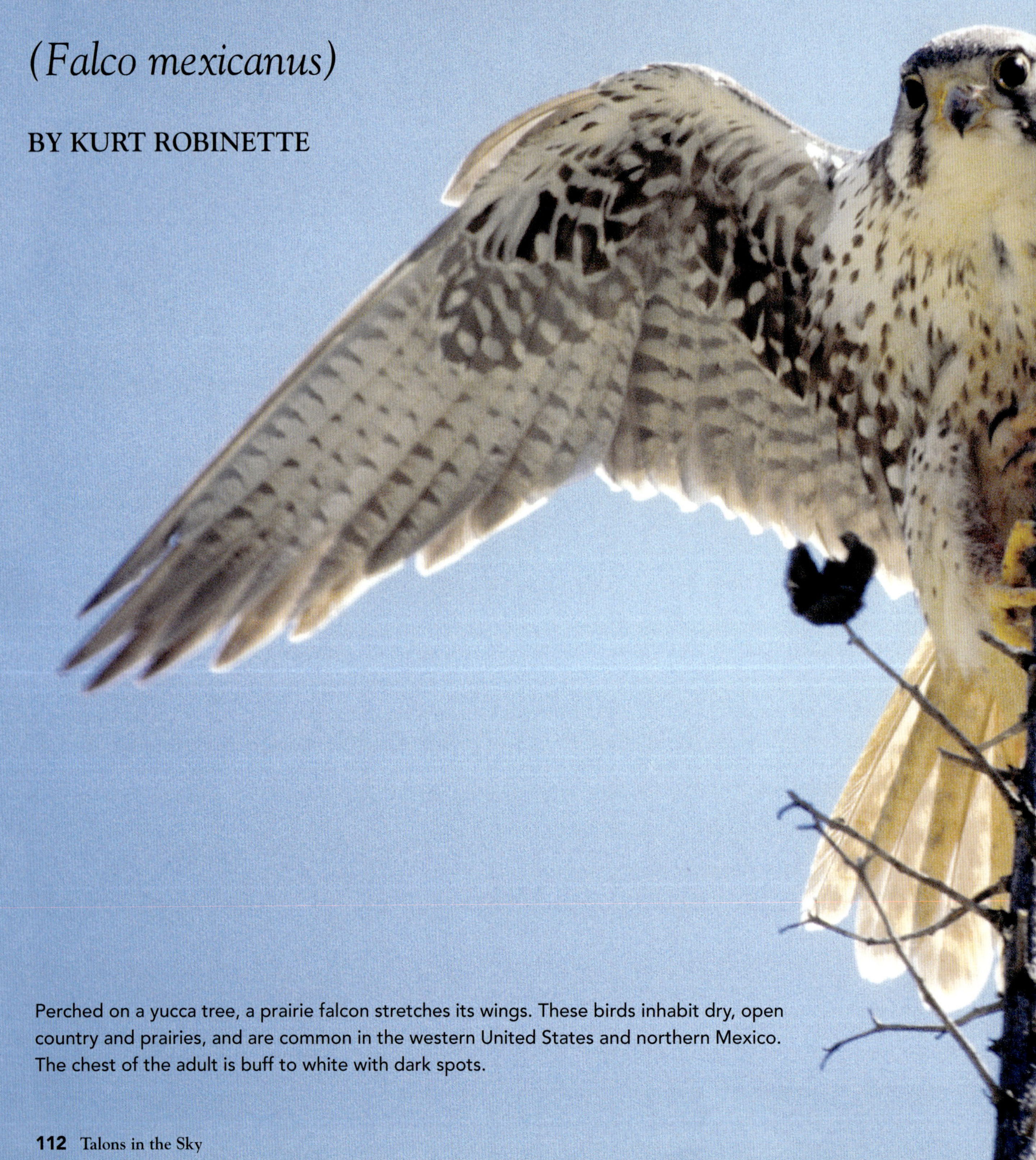

Perched on a yucca tree, a prairie falcon stretches its wings. These birds inhabit dry, open country and prairies, and are common in the western United States and northern Mexico. The chest of the adult is buff to white with dark spots.

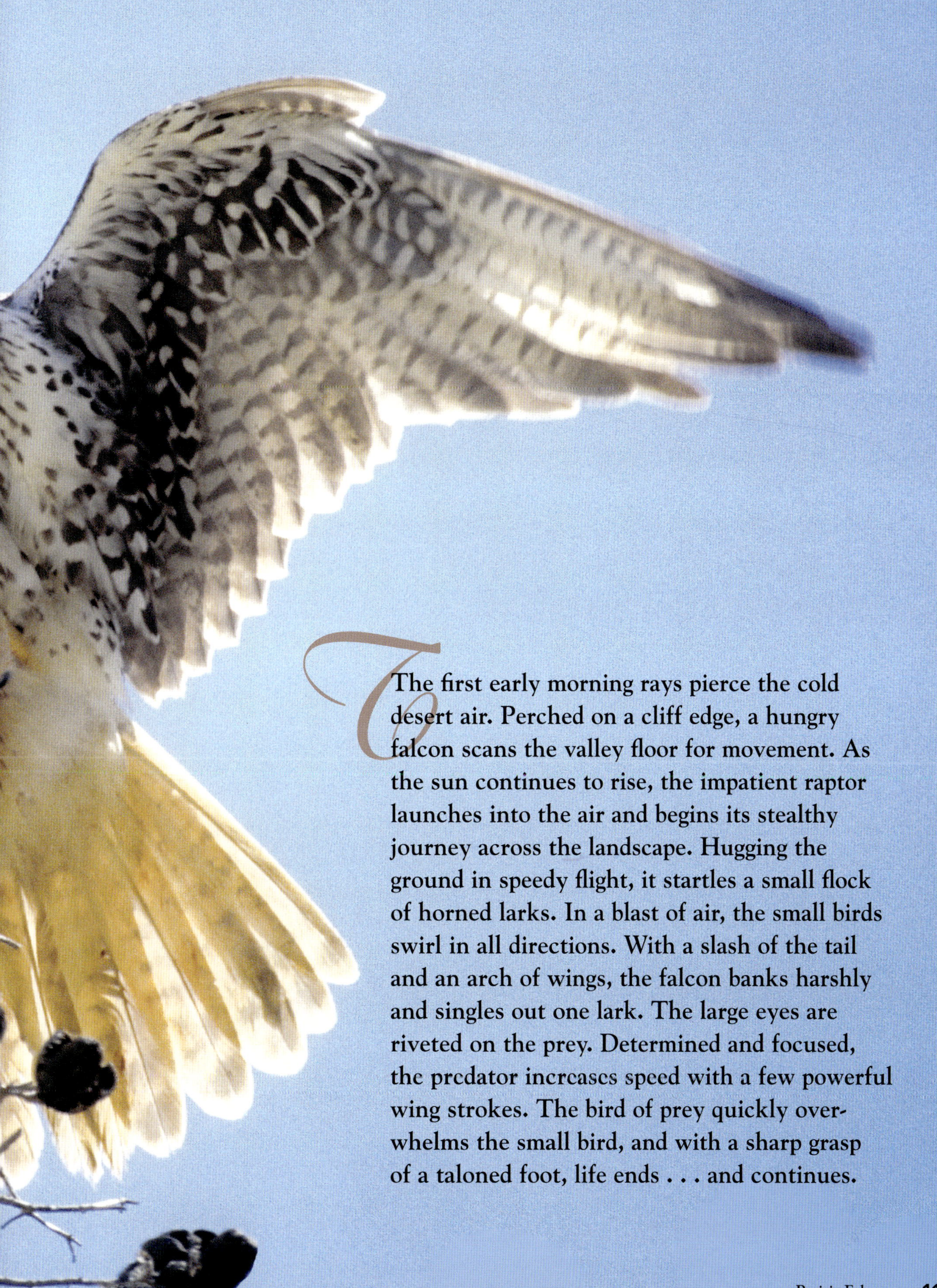

The first early morning rays pierce the cold desert air. Perched on a cliff edge, a hungry falcon scans the valley floor for movement. As the sun continues to rise, the impatient raptor launches into the air and begins its stealthy journey across the landscape. Hugging the ground in speedy flight, it startles a small flock of horned larks. In a blast of air, the small birds swirl in all directions. With a slash of the tail and an arch of wings, the falcon banks harshly and singles out one lark. The large eyes are riveted on the prey. Determined and focused, the predator increases speed with a few powerful wing strokes. The bird of prey quickly overwhelms the small bird, and with a sharp grasp of a taloned foot, life ends . . . and continues.

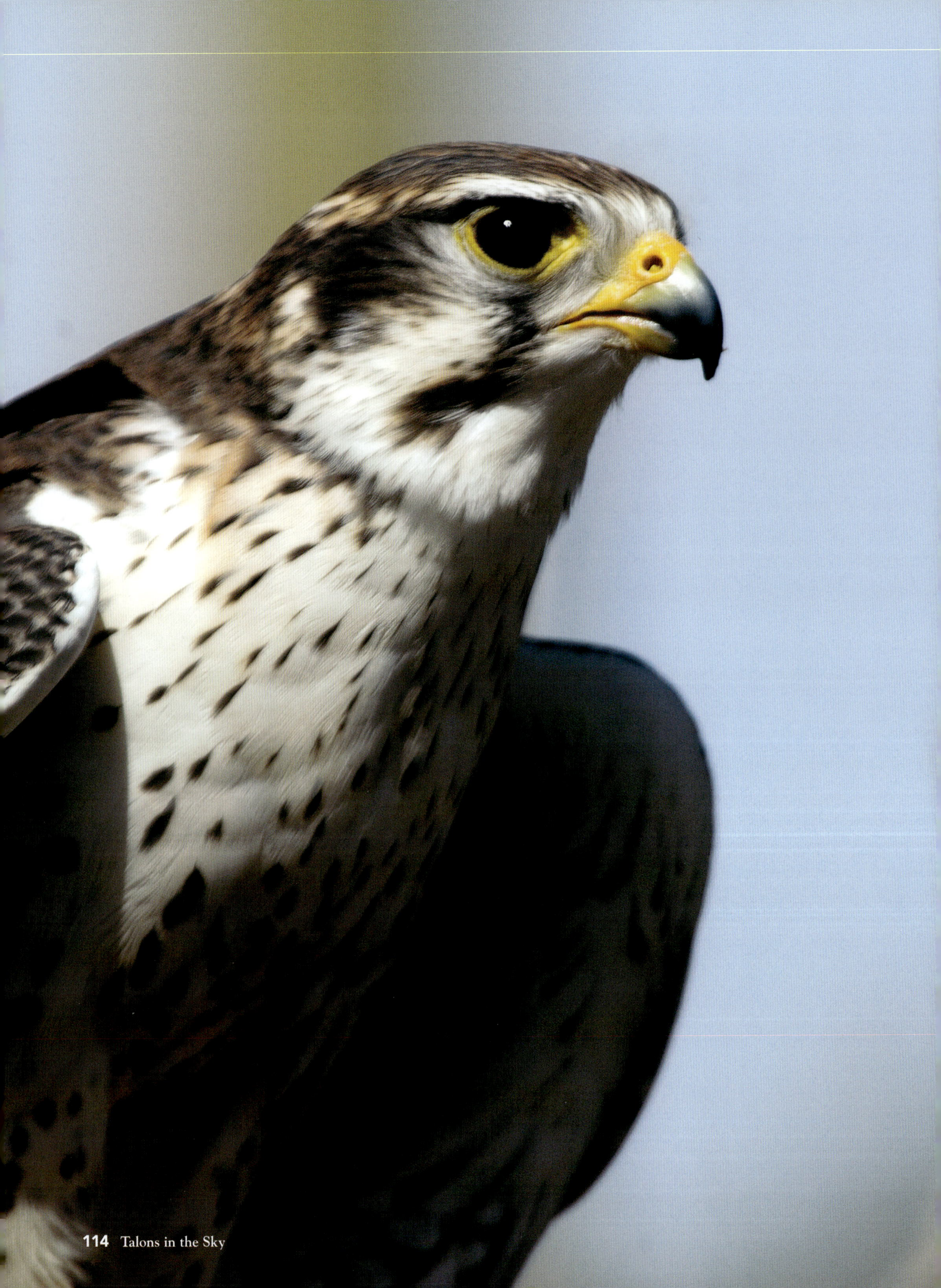

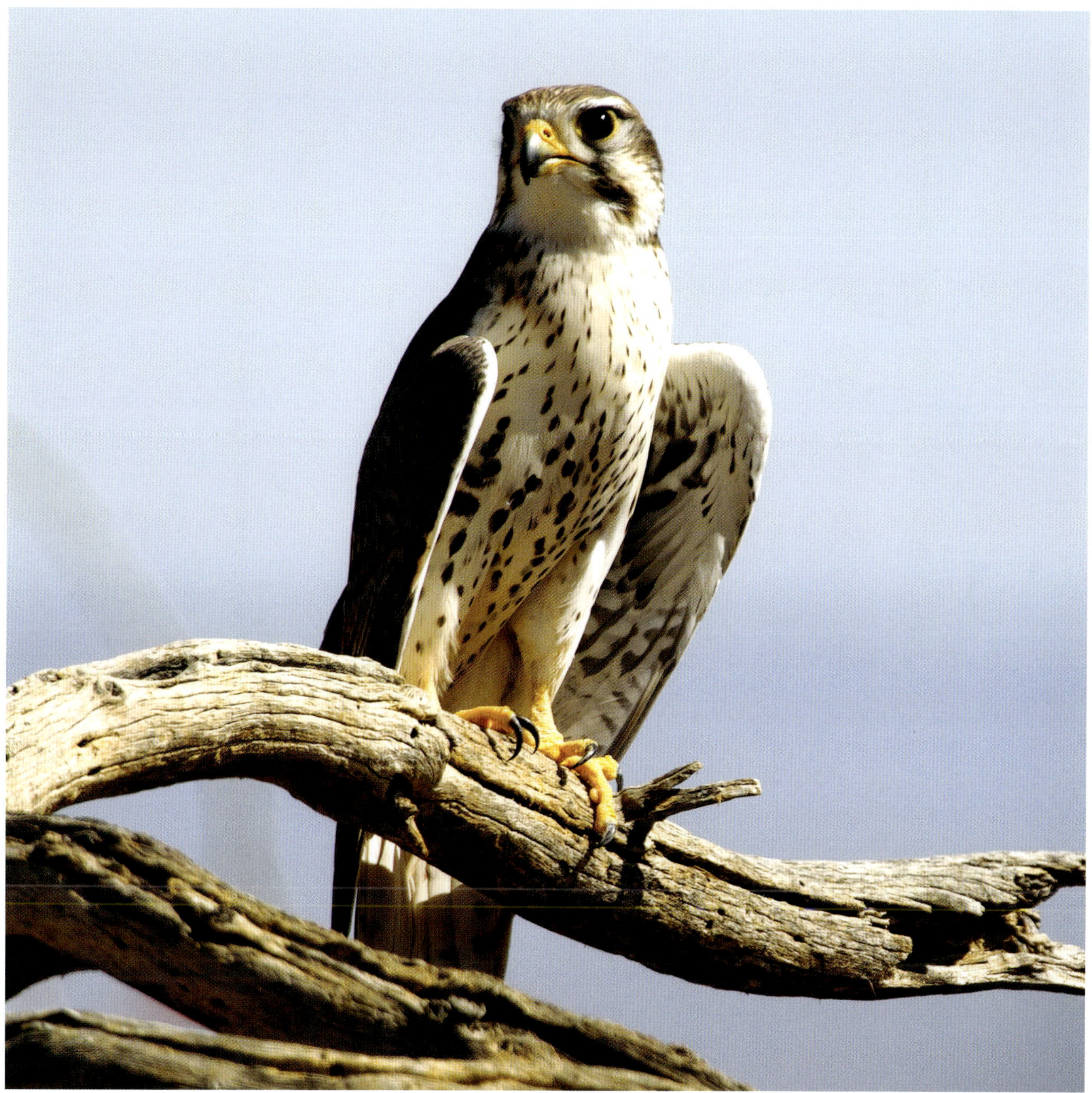

ABOVE: Prairie falcons are versatile hunters. They may flush their prey by flying low over brush, or sit and watch for an opportunity to present itself. **OPPOSITE:** The prairie falcon has a pale stripe between the dark mustache region and ear coverts. Its facial markings are narrower and the plumage paler overall than the peregrine falcon.

The prairie falcon (*Falco mexicanus*) is a raptor that breeds from southeastern British Columbia, southern Alberta, and southern Saskatchewan south in open-country habitats (mostly hilly to montane grasslands or semi-deserts) to Baja, California, western Texas, eastern Colorado, western Nebraska, and the western Dakotas; and, formerly, into northwestern Missouri. This species winters in grassland to semi-desert habitats from the breeding range in southern Canada south to central Mexico, with some birds wintering both to the east and west of the breeding range. An intermediate-sized falcon, similar in weight and size to the arctic peregrine falcon, the prairie falcon appears much slenderer than the peregrine.

The plumage of the prairie falcon varies very little from bird to bird. Adults have brown backs with pale,

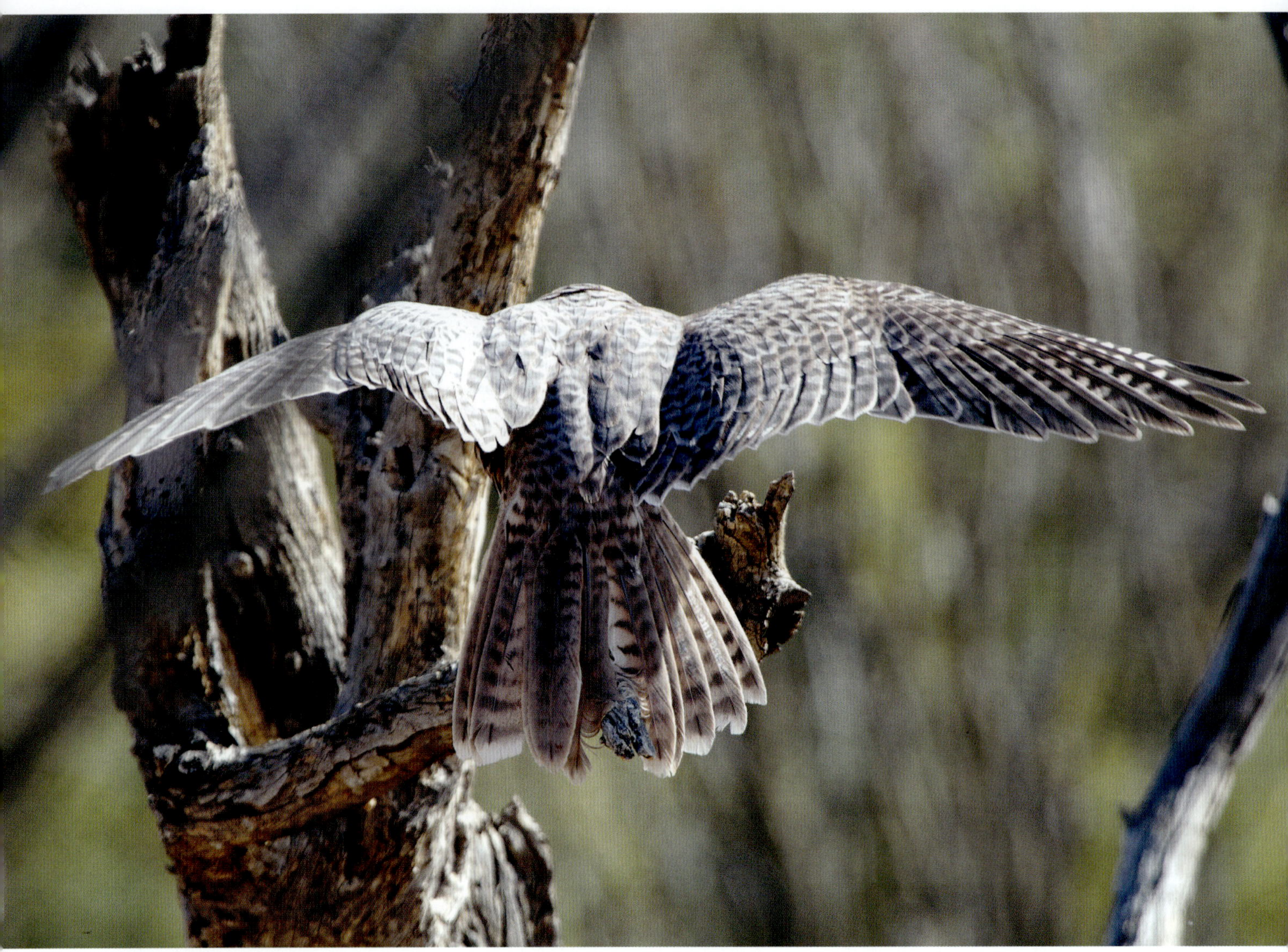

ABOVE: The prairie falcon's wings are long and narrow, with pointed tips. **OPPOSITE:** Adult birds have brown backs with pale, fluffy bands across the tertial, secondary, and scapular feathers. On older males, some of the bands will tend more to a silvery blue.

buffy bands across the tertial, secondary, and scapular feathers. Some of the bands on older males will tend toward a silvery blue. The feet and cere are pale yellow. The face has a thin, dark malar streak and light cheeks. The chest of the adult is buff to white with dark spots creating vertical lines that move into the dark brown and rusty flank feathers. The tail is long and brown with buffy barring. Immature prairie falcons have larger streaks on the chest rather than spots. The dorsal feathers are dark brown and lack barring, as does the tail. The cere and feet of a juvenile are bluish, though many do begin changing to pale yellow around midyear. Early in the summer, the chest of an immature is a pale buff and tan cast until the sun apparently bleaches the feathers into the off-white seen through most of the year. Two of the most distinctive traits of this falcon, when viewed close up, are its large, blocky head and big, owlish eyes. No other falcon has eyes as large in proportion to its body as the prairie falcon's, but the adaptive significance of the large eyes is not known. When the bird is in flight, the best field marks are the black axillaries on the undersides of the wings. They make the bird appear to have black "pits."

Like other falcons, prairie falcons have long, narrow wings with pointed tips and low camber (flat profile) reminiscent of modern jet fighters. They are equipped with a large keel on their sternums, which provides strong anchorage for their powerful flight muscles.

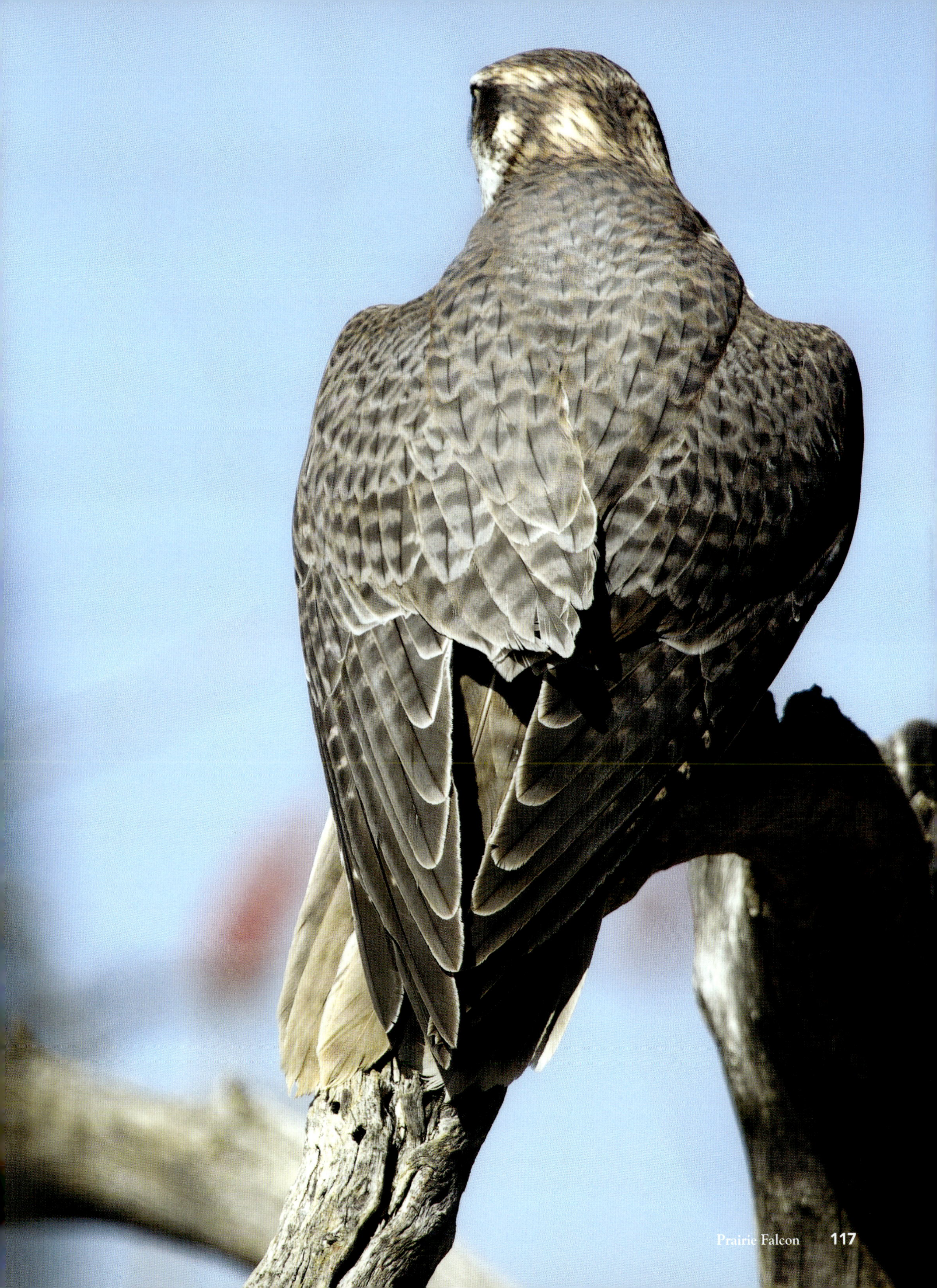

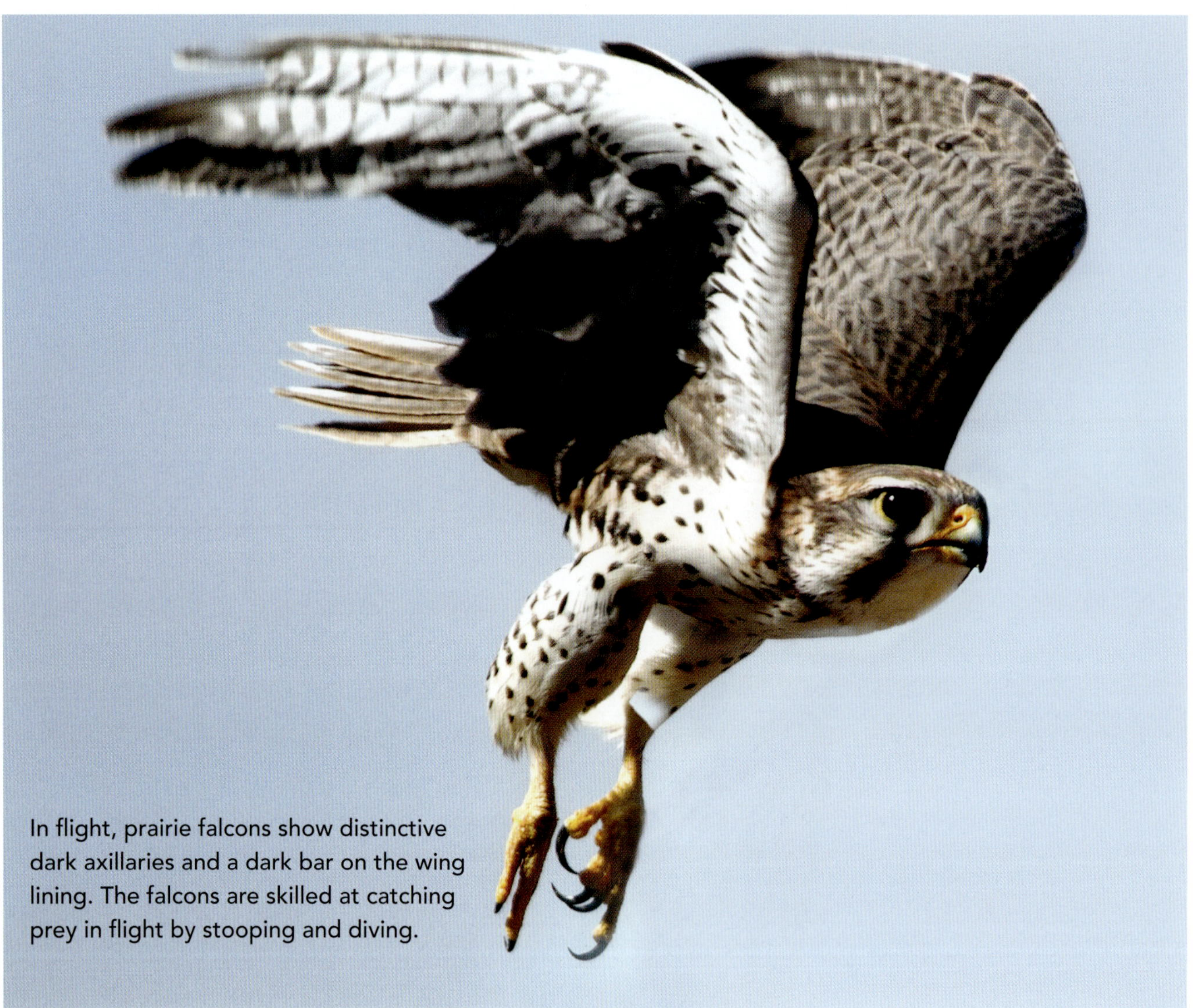
In flight, prairie falcons show distinctive dark axillaries and a dark bar on the wing lining. The falcons are skilled at catching prey in flight by stooping and diving.

Falcons also have an extra pair of bones attached at the base of the tail (pygostyle) that are unique to the family Falconidae. These bones provide a large surface area for the attachment of the powerful depressor and abductor muscles of the tail. Muscular tails are highly adaptive for birds that twist, turn, and brake sharply when pursuing quarry during high-speed chases. Similar structures occur in some hummingbirds that also depend on maneuverability and braking.

The prairie falcon is highly opportunistic and will pursue a wide variety of birds, mammals, reptiles and even insects. It is a very aggressive hunter and has been known to routinely take white-tailed jackrabbits, which weigh around 3.5 kilograms (7 lbs., 8 oz.). More common mammals taken are ground squirrels and prairie dogs. In the more severe deserts, such as the Mojave and Colorado deserts of southern California where bird life and even diurnally active rodents may be scarce, prairie falcons catch many large lizards, the principal species being the chuckwalla. Other reptiles the birds prey upon include the smaller collared lizard, leopard lizard, and desert iguana. One report even mentions shells of desert tortoises being found in aeries in the Mojave Desert.

In the Snake River Canyon of southern Idaho, a magnificent stretch of cliffs and canyon walls runs for 130 kilometers (80 miles). This area contains the largest concentration of nesting raptors in the world, more than 600 pairs representing 15 species. In some years, more than 200 pairs of prairie falcons are packed into these canyons, averaging a pair every 1,200 feet or less. The principal species of prey for the falcons here is the Townsend's ground squirrel. In 1971, the U.S. Department of the Interior set aside 40 square miles of the canyon as the Snake River Birds of Prey Natural Conservation Area. Anyone with a love of birds of

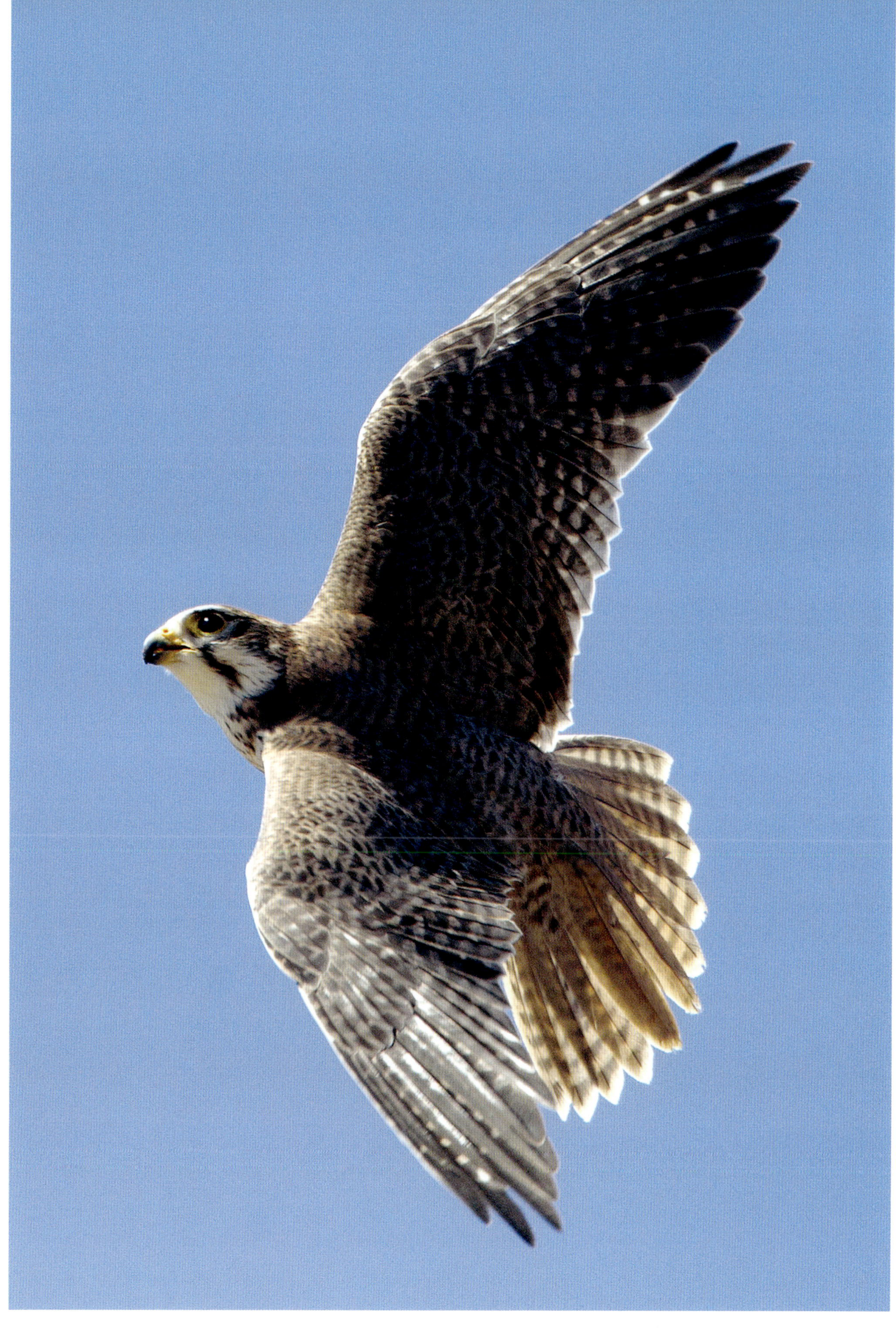

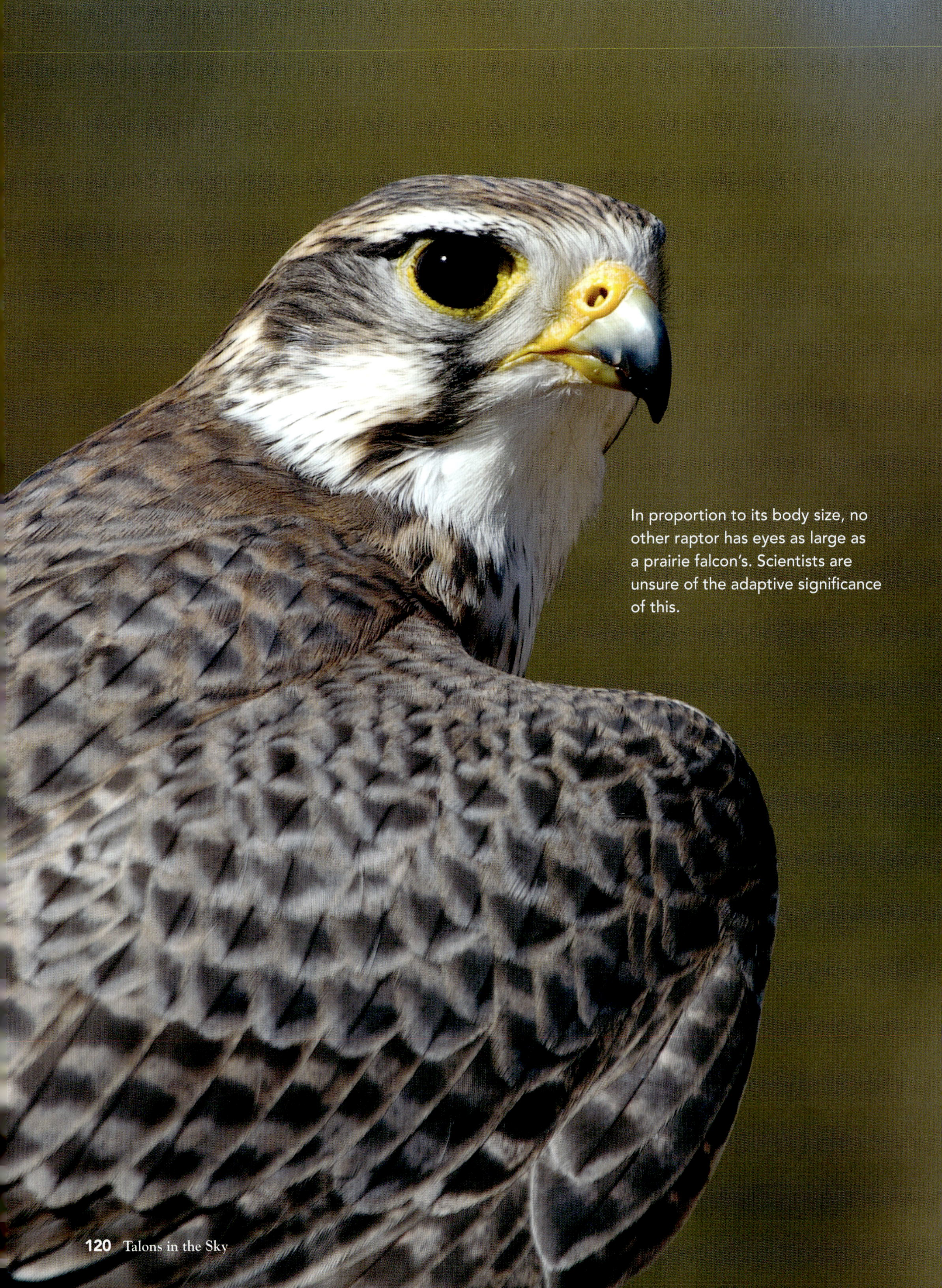

In proportion to its body size, no other raptor has eyes as large as a prairie falcon's. Scientists are unsure of the adaptive significance of this.

prey should plan a vacation that includes a guided raft trip in this area. World Center for Birds of Prey (Peregrine Fund) in Boise can give you more information.

Most prairie falcons migrate to southern areas during the winter but some do remain in the nesting vicinity. Falcons return to their nesting areas from mid-February to mid-March, with some coming as late as mid-April. Apparently, most males and females winter in separate areas, as they return at different times. Either may be first to return. Like the peregrine and gyrfalcon, the prairie falcon is a cliff-ledge nester. It prefers a pothole or well-sheltered ledge from 10 meters (33 feet) to more than 100 meters (330 feet) above the valley floor. It will often use abandoned raven nests. Courtship includes a series of head bobs and aerial displays. The male will often try to impress his mate with a series of steep dives and risky maneuvers. There are also ledge displays in the nest area.

One or both will scrape a depression in the sand on the nest ledge, sometimes using sticks. As is common among raptors, the male will bring all the food while the female does all the brooding. Generally, the first egg is laid around mid-April and is followed every other day with another egg until the female has a clutch of four or five eggs, with five being the most common number. The eggs are the same size as chicken eggs, and vary greatly in color. Most are a mottled brown with some spotting, though they can be dark brown and heavily marked to nearly white cream without markings, and these wide variations can appear in even the same clutch. Recent studies indicate that incubation begins slowly at first until the female lays the last egg. Incubation requires 29 to 33 days. Pipped eggs require 24 to 48 hours to hatch. If something happens to the nest or eggs, the pair will re-clutch in 16 days. The newly hatched downies spend 80 percent of their time sleeping and the rest eating and preening. By 35 days, they are 95 percent feathered and are nearly ready for their launch from the nest. Parents will continue to feed the young for several weeks until they are catching food for themselves.

Of all the species of falcon in North America, none is more adaptable in its hunting than the prairie falcon. It is an opportunist and uses many techniques to catch prey. Generally, there are three categories of attack. The first is a traditional high-diving falcon flight called the "stoop." Similarly to the peregrine, a prairie falcon will fly to high altitudes, especially on warm days with thermals, and watch for prey. When it spies quarry (birds in this case), the falcon will fly straight down, tucking in its wings to become a "bullet." With speeds approaching 180 miles per hour, the falcon appears like the mighty peregrine, but with a noticeable difference. The peregrine falcon will usually level out behind its prey to grab the bird and carry it off. The prairie falcon, however, is unbelievably bold and will often collide full-speed into its prey without slowing at all. Slow-speed footage reveals that this bird "punches" prey birds with a closed foot. Occasionally, prairie falcons lose their lives either in the impact or in failing to pull up after the hit in time to miss the earth. Typically, the dead quarry drops to the earth and the falcon circles for dinner.

The second hunting technique is similar to that of the other North American desert falcon, the gyrfalcon. The bird will fly at low levels to flush unsuspecting game. The last technique is to sit on a pole or cliff and watch for an opportunity to hunt.

This desert demon's evolution in the harsh desert climate has given it a high intelligence. Many falconers consider it the most intelligent of falcons. Stubborn, scrappy, and irascible, the prairie falcon can be moody and grumpy but it is always a determined hunter. The beautiful prairie falcon is one raptor that is currently doing well. May it ever be so.

Measurements (in mm)

	Male	Female
Length	370–380	450
Wingspan	950	1050
Weight	17.5–22.5 oz.	26.5–34.5 oz.

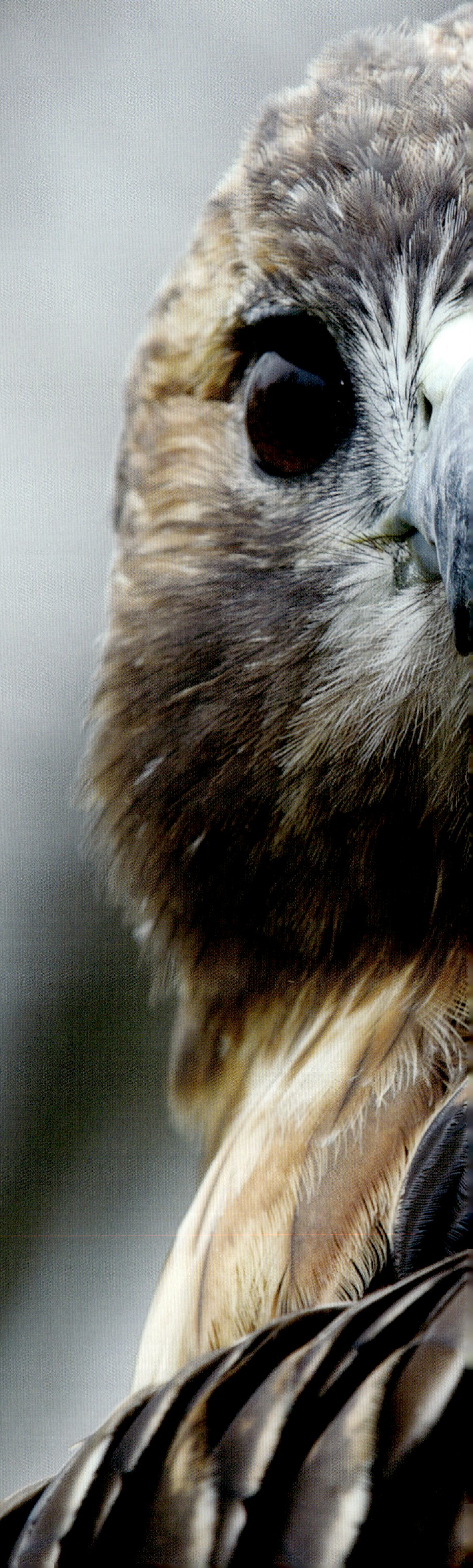

Red-tailed Hawk

(*Buteo jamaicensis*)

BY RON AUSTING

The red-tailed hawk is one of the most conspicuous of birds, occupying a stark lookout atop a dead tree snag close to the highway or soaring lazily overhead on four-foot wings. During migration in October and November, large numbers of northern residents and most immatures move south for the winter. On favorable days you can see them by the hundreds as they float effortlessly on updrafts past certain vantage points, such as Hawk Mountain Sanctuary in eastern Pennsylvania.

One of the most widespread breeding birds in North America, the red-tail nests throughout the United States, including Alaska. One of its many races, or subspecies, is represented in all environments, from arid western desert to humid eastern forest.

The red-tail is a member of the genus *Buteo*, meaning buzzard, which also includes such close relatives as the red-shouldered hawk, broad-winged hawk, and rough-legged hawk. Characterized by long, broad wings and short fan-tails, the buteos are specially designed for effortless soaring. Because they are not designed for rapid pursuit of their prey, they take almost all of it on the ground.

A general feeder, the red-tail enjoys large size and powerful build, which enable it to exploit a wide range of prey, from grasshoppers to jackrabbits. Its preference seems to be small and medium-size rodents, although snakes and other reptiles are not overlooked. Even other birds in poor condition are eagerly taken.

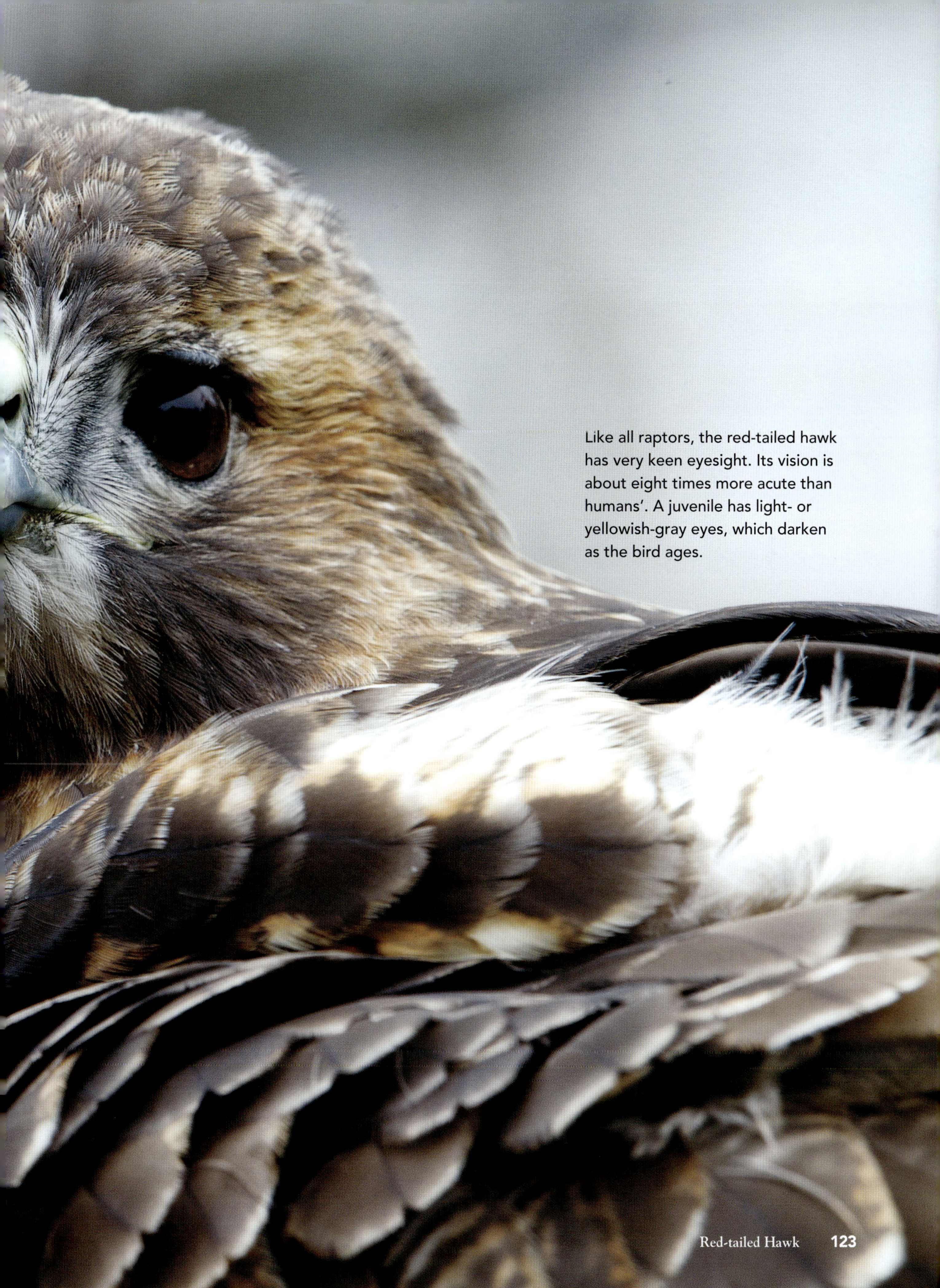

Like all raptors, the red-tailed hawk has very keen eyesight. Its vision is about eight times more acute than humans'. A juvenile has light- or yellowish-gray eyes, which darken as the bird ages.

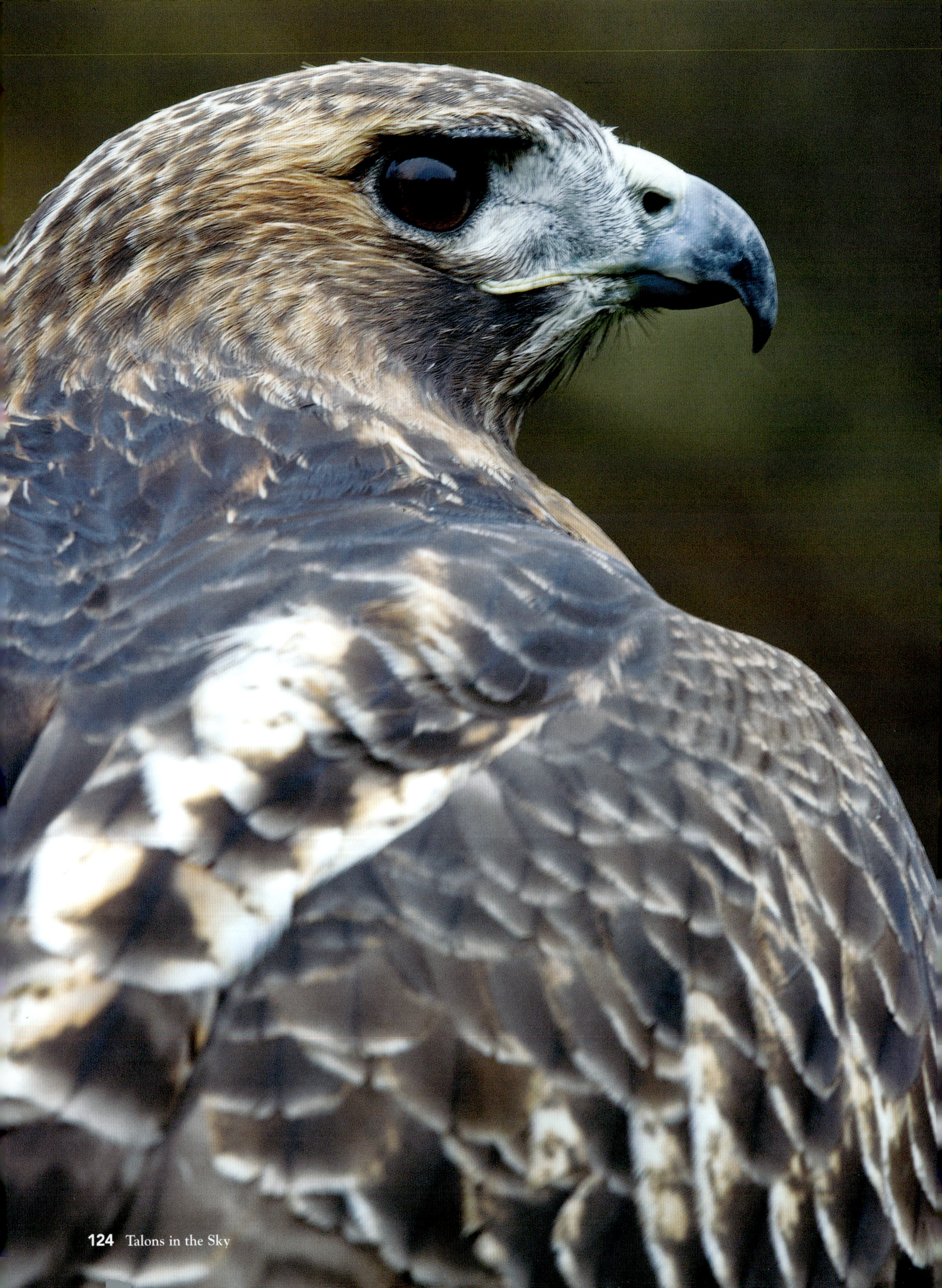

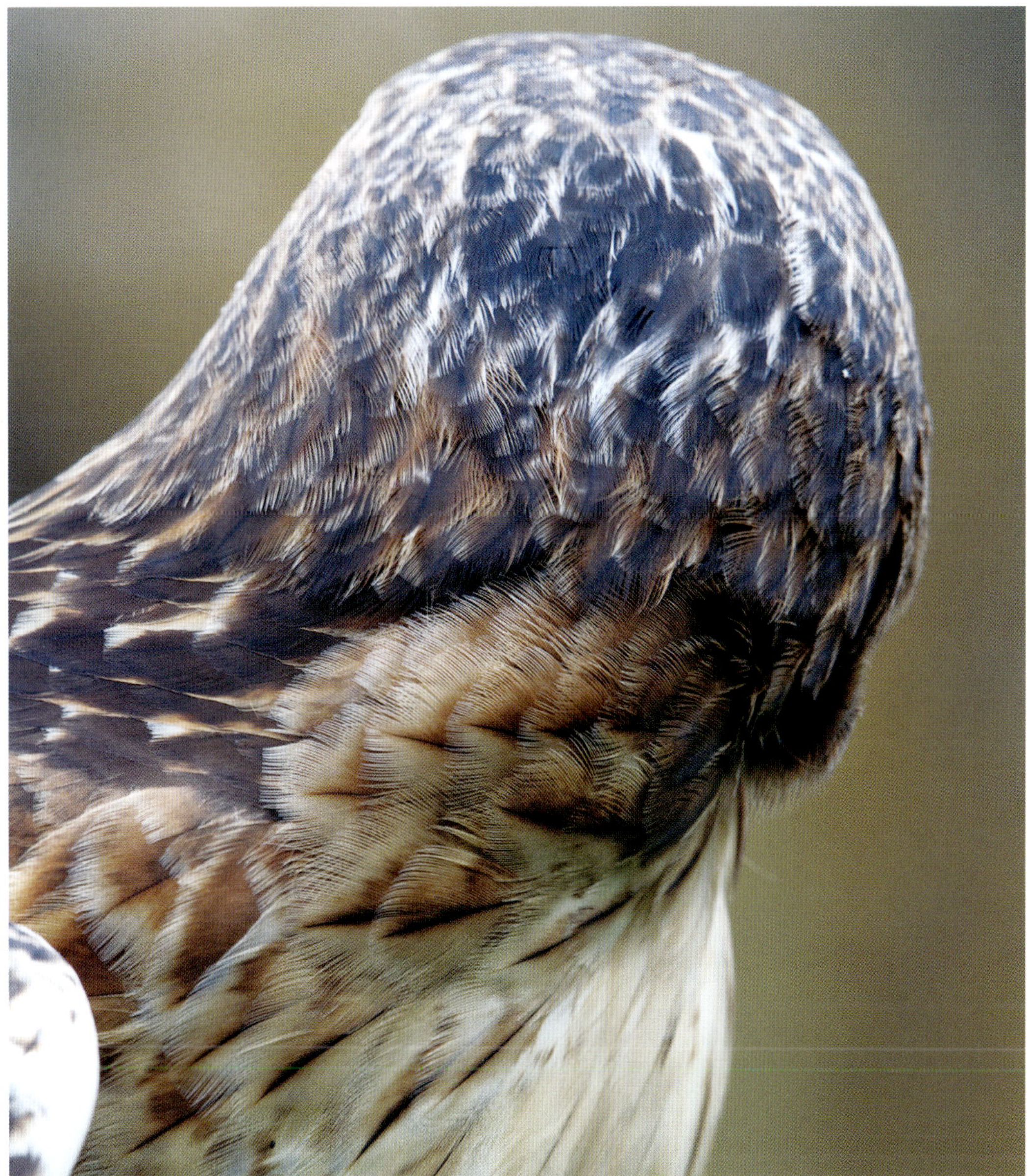

ABOVE: The back of the hawk's head displays the subtle colors and patterns that mean painting a carving of this bird can be quite a challenge. **OPPOSITE:** Note the dark ring around the outside of the eye, a unique feature of the red-tail.

As its name implies, the adult red-tail displays a rufous tail, with a narrow black subterminal band very close to the white tip. In some individuals, especially western races, this band may be wider and additional narrow bands may occur up the tail. The red pigment is primarily on the top sides of the feather; underneath is whitish. When the bird is soaring, even with a spread tail, the red may not be visible unless the sun shines through, or unless the bird banks sharply enough to expose the top. Immatures do not acquire the red tail until completion of the first molt, which takes place when they are a year old.

Perhaps the most consistent field mark of red-tails of any age is the dark belly band, often quite pronounced in immatures but sometimes lacking in older adults, especially Midwestern birds. Melanistic birds are not uncommon, especially in western races, and albinal individuals are occasionally found in the West and Midwest. A color phase of unusual redness also occurs.

One of the largest North American hawks, the red-tail is only slightly smaller than the western ferruginous hawk. Like other raptors, females are larger than males. Body weights range from two to four pounds, with males about two and one-half, and females three and

The adult red-tail displays a rufous tail, with a narrow black subterminal band very close to the white tip.

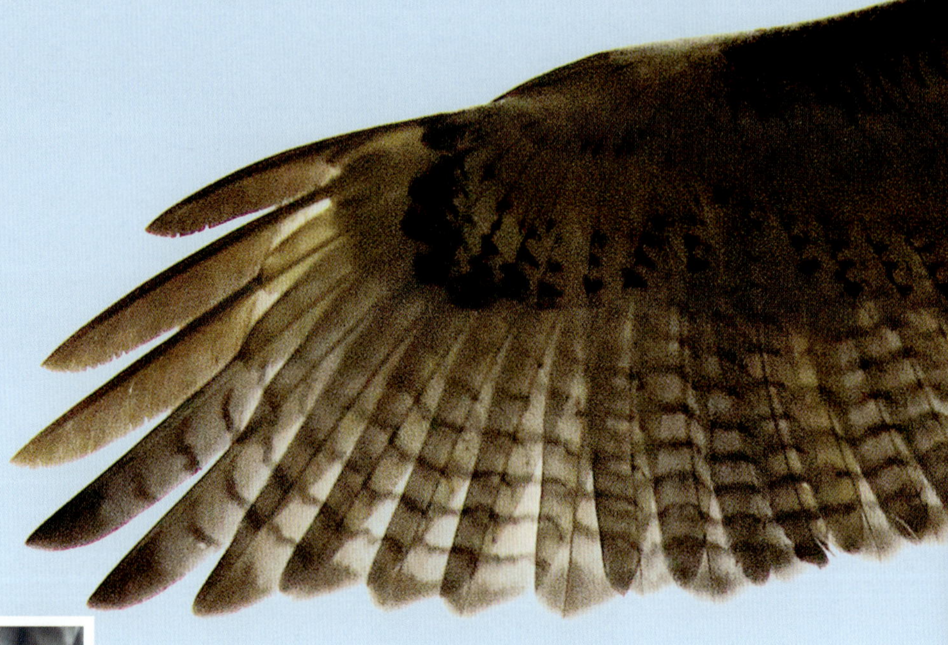

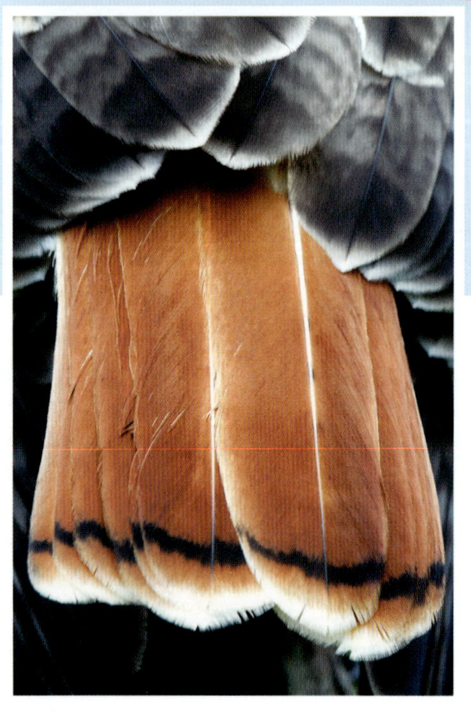

one-half. Overall length may range from 19 to 25 inches, with a wingspread of 46 to 58 inches. Fleshy parts vary from greenish or greenish yellow in the cere of immatures to greenish yellow or pale yellow in the tarsi and feet. Both areas are yellow in the adult. The iris is light gray to yellowish gray in immatures, darkening to dark brown with age. The annual molt usually occurs from May through September and is generally complete, but some individuals keep old, worn plumage.

Most red-tails mate for life and occupy a home range of roughly a square mile throughout the year.

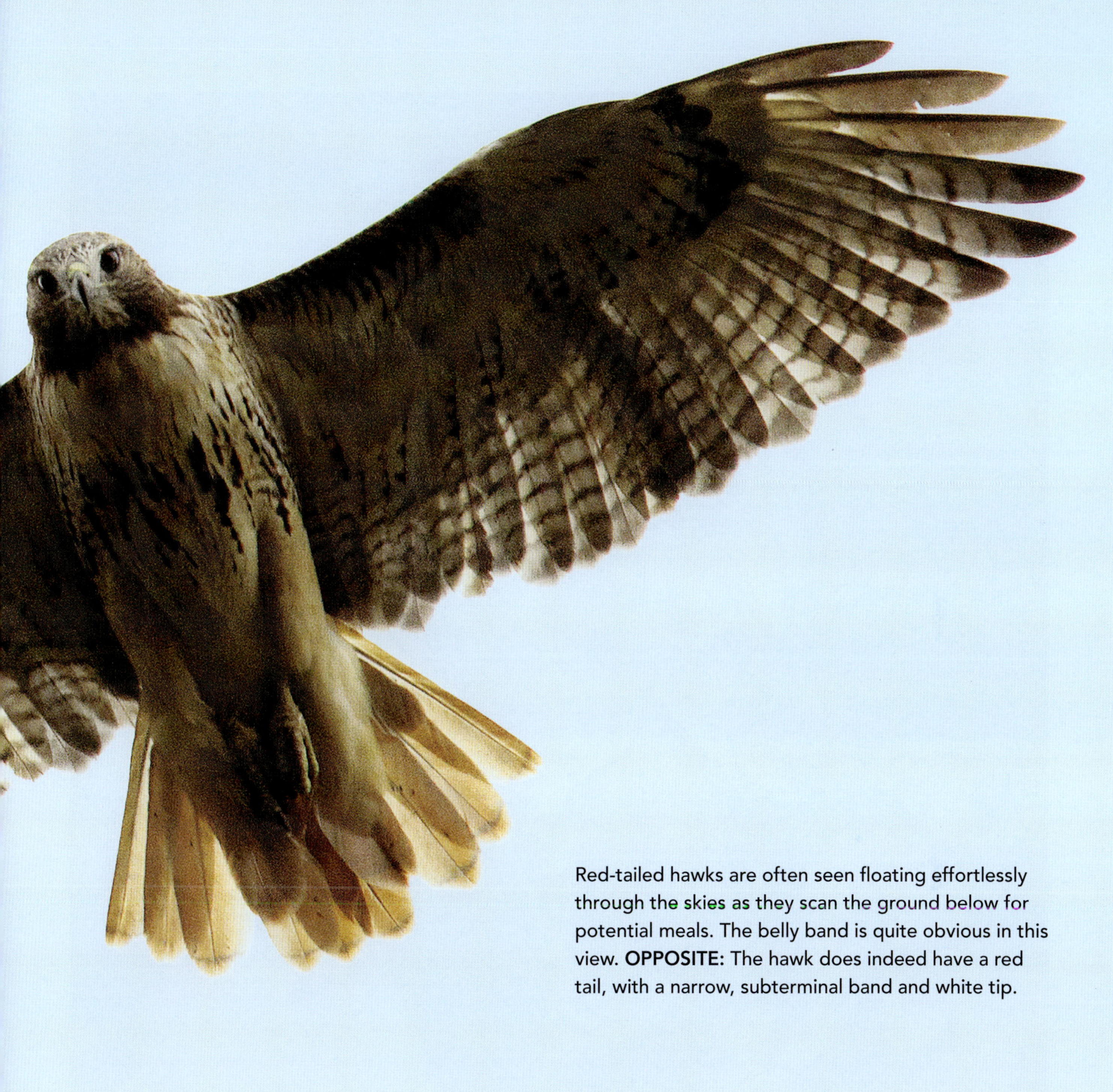

Red-tailed hawks are often seen floating effortlessly through the skies as they scan the ground below for potential meals. The belly band is quite obvious in this view. **OPPOSITE:** The hawk does indeed have a red tail, with a narrow, subterminal band and white tip.

They are usually within sight of one another and will share a kill. Other red-tails are generally not tolerated within their terrestrial range, but neighboring pairs often fly together over their ranges, especially in early spring, without aggressive displays.

Nest building begins in February (Cincinnati, Ohio area) but sometimes hawks repair old nests in the fall. They might use the same nest for several years, except when great horned owls appropriate it, leaving the hawks to build a new one. (The owls nest about two months earlier than the hawks and, like other owls, do not construct nests of their own.) The female alone incubates the two or three eggs over about 33 days. The female then tends and broods the young constantly for several weeks, with the male supplying almost all of the food. The young fledge in about eight weeks and remain nearby for several months, begging for food and being served by their parents until they develop their hunting skills.

Like many wild creatures, most young red-tails do not survive their first winter. Unoccupied habitat with sufficient food does not exist, and starvation prevails.

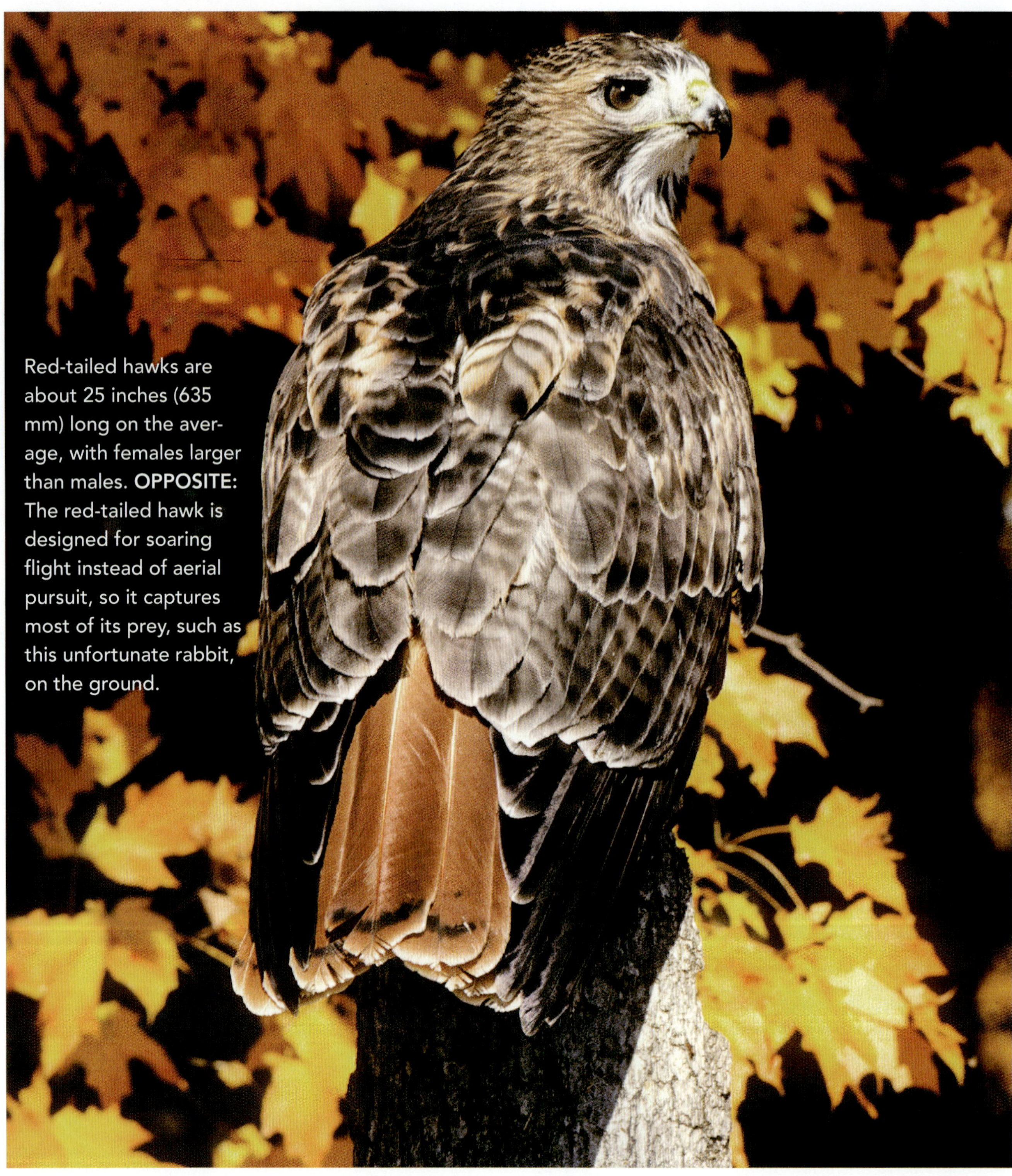

Red-tailed hawks are about 25 inches (635 mm) long on the average, with females larger than males. **OPPOSITE:** The red-tailed hawk is designed for soaring flight instead of aerial pursuit, so it captures most of its prey, such as this unfortunate rabbit, on the ground.

Resident adults constantly defend their own fertile hunting territory and youngsters eventually end up in marginal areas. We often see them in such places in winter, along roadways, watching for voles in the grassy median.

Red-tails hunt most often by taking a stand on some commanding perch, watching for quarry, then launching forth in a shallow glide at 35 to 40 miles per hour to secure it. Almost all prey is taken on the ground, including the birds found in the diet, since buteos are not designed for aerial pursuit. On breezy days, they may hang on updrafts along hillsides or ridges 200 to 300 feet aloft, or they may hover over open fields like kestrels or rough-legged hawks. Soaring hawks general-

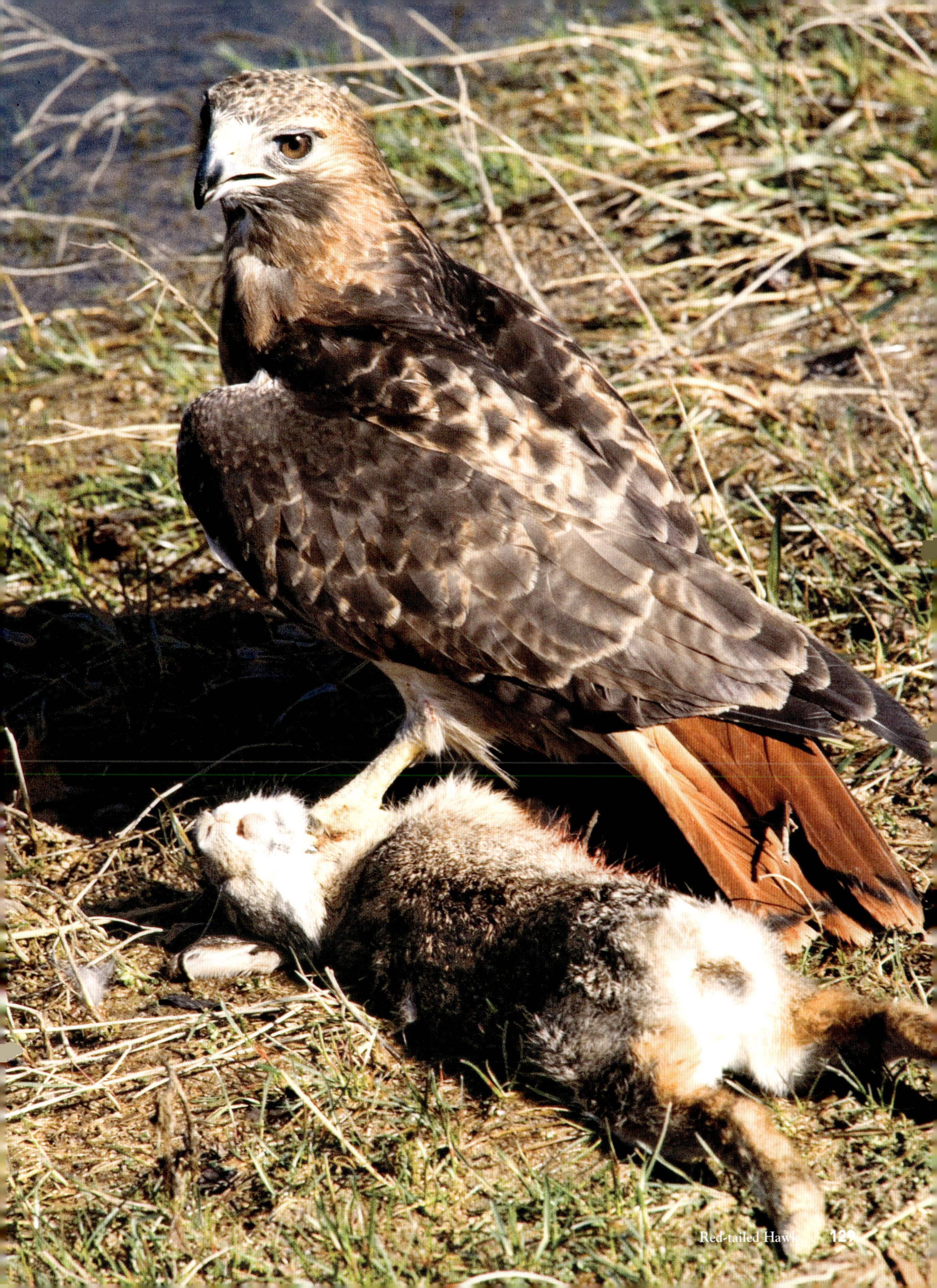

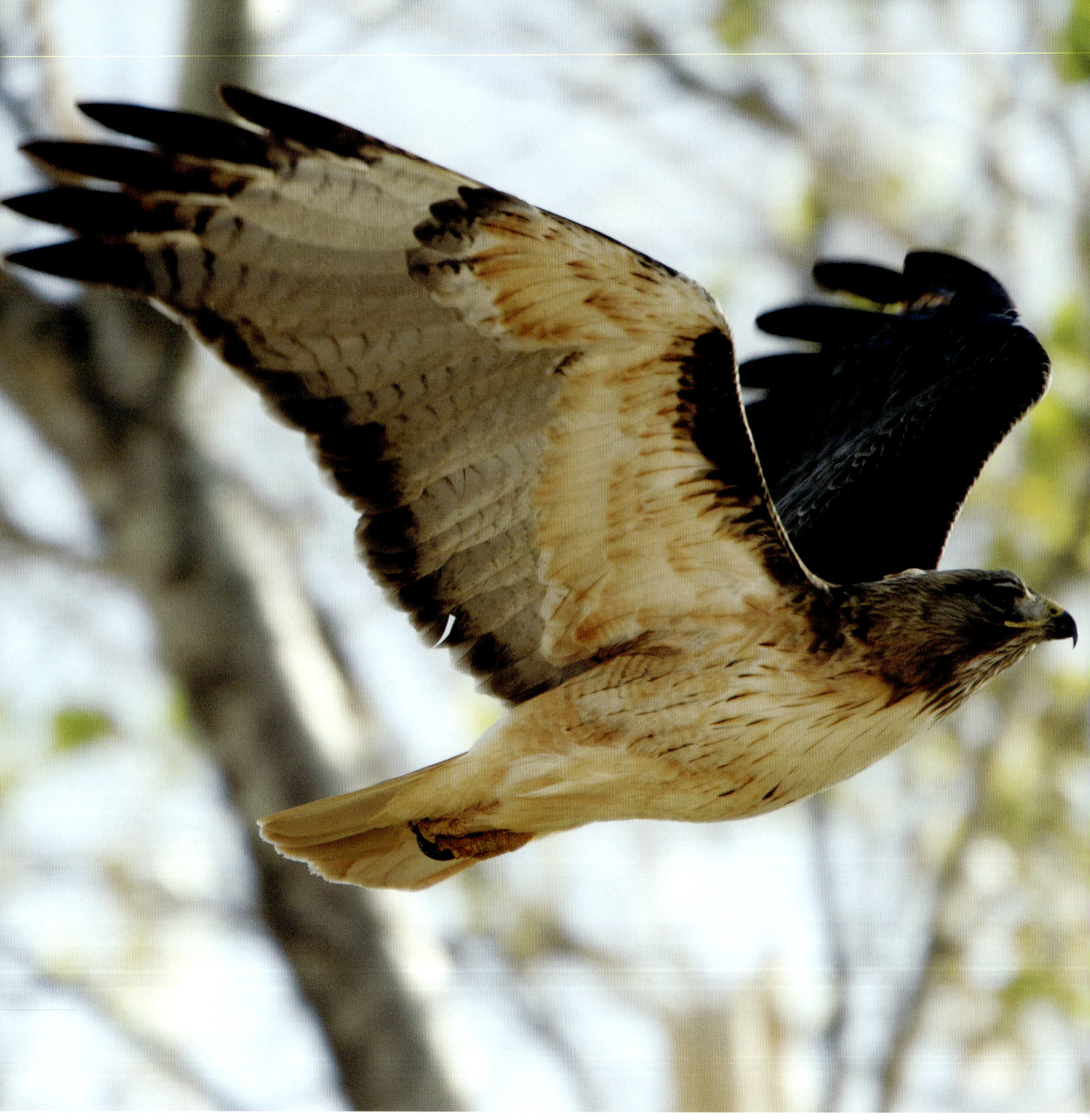

ly are not hunting. In order to be successful they must be fairly close to their prey, which does not remain visible—hence vulnerable—for very long. In winter, roadside kills are readily consumed.

Red-tails are capable of living many years; in a protected environment I would expect 40 years or more. One of my captive-bred red-tails (which suffered a minor wing injury and could not be released) was in superb condition at age 21 when he died in a freak accident. When I researched the banding data of just under 1,000 red-tails recovered from the bird-banding office in 1964, the oldest wild bird was 16.

In addition to being one of the most widespread of our raptors, the red-tail is one of the most familiar. Its large size, conspicuous habits, and generally confiding nature render it one of the easiest raptors to observe, photograph, or carve.

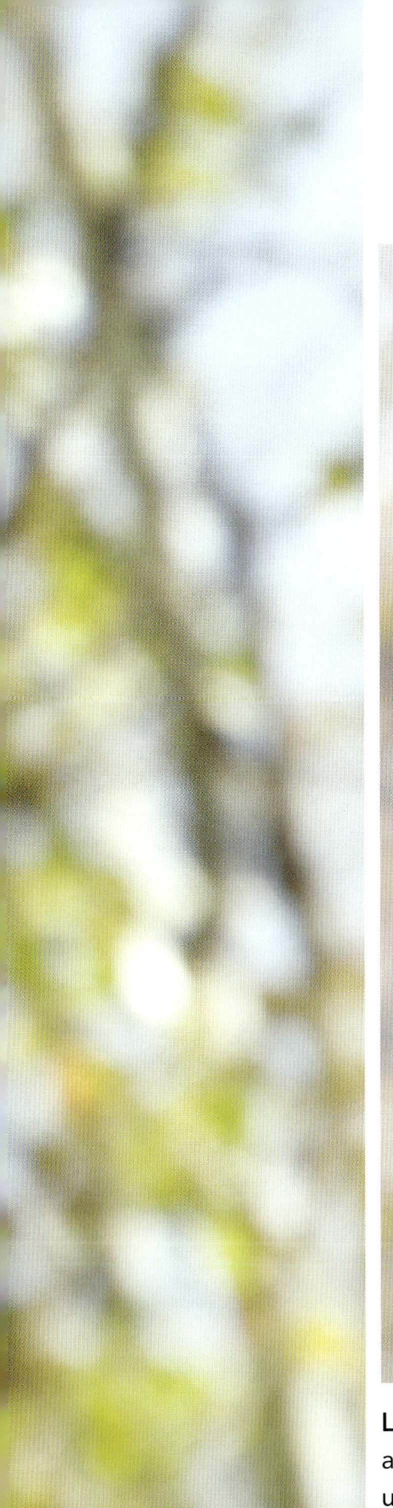

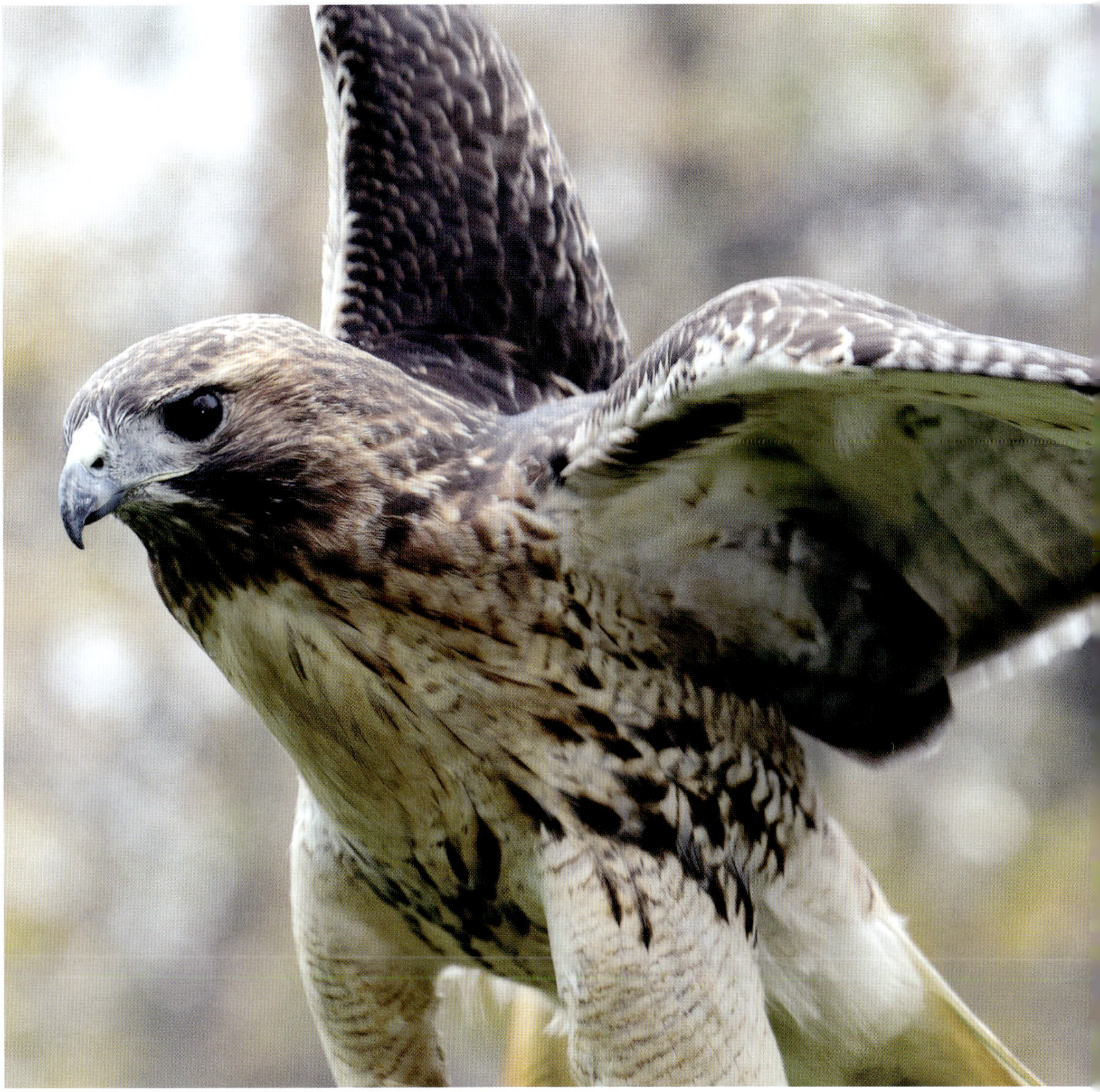

LEFT: In sustained flight, the red-tail will carry its legs and feet against the abdominal area, partially covered by the adjacent plumage. ABOVE: The underparts of these hawks are much lighter than the upper body and wings, but with dark streaking patterns.

Measurements (in mm)

	Male	Female
Length	540–600	500–650
Wingspan	1050–1350	1050–1350
Eyes	12 (brown)	12 (brown)
Weight	1.5–2.9 pounds	2–3.2 pounds

Ferruginous Hawk

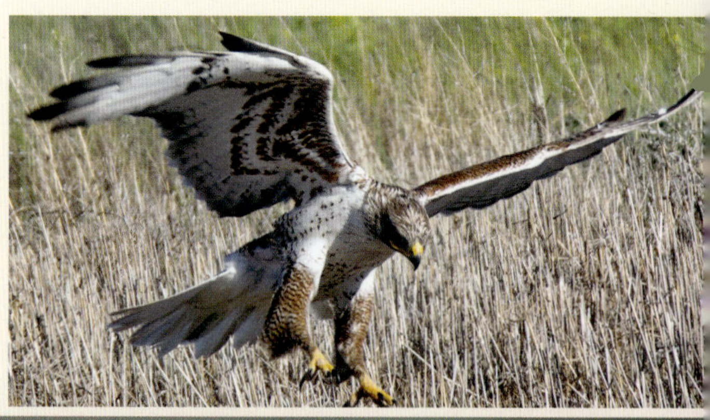

(*Buteo regalis*)

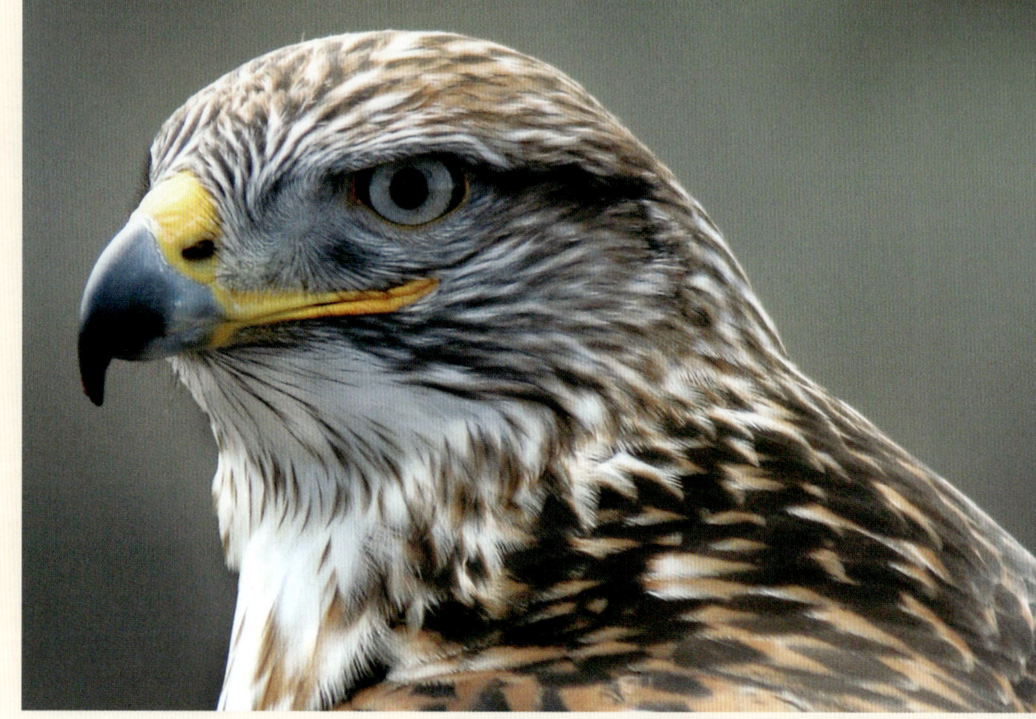

The *Buteo* genus of hawks is large and varied and includes the red-tailed (page 122) and the rough-legged (page 138). The following pages spotlight three other buteos.

The ferruginous hawk lives in the American southwest and, at up to 27 inches in length and with a wingspan of 56 inches, is North America's largest buteo. It looks as though it belongs more with the eagles than the hawks. Its Latin name means "royal hawk," and there is something regal about this large raptor. Its diet consists chiefly of the small mammals—squirrels, prairie dogs, and rabbits—that share its desert home. The name "ferruginous" refers to the rusty color of its shoulder and leg feathers. Males and females share the same markings, although females are larger.

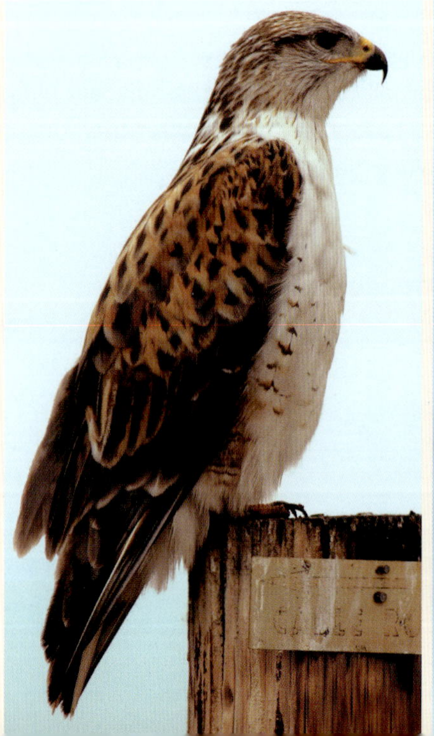

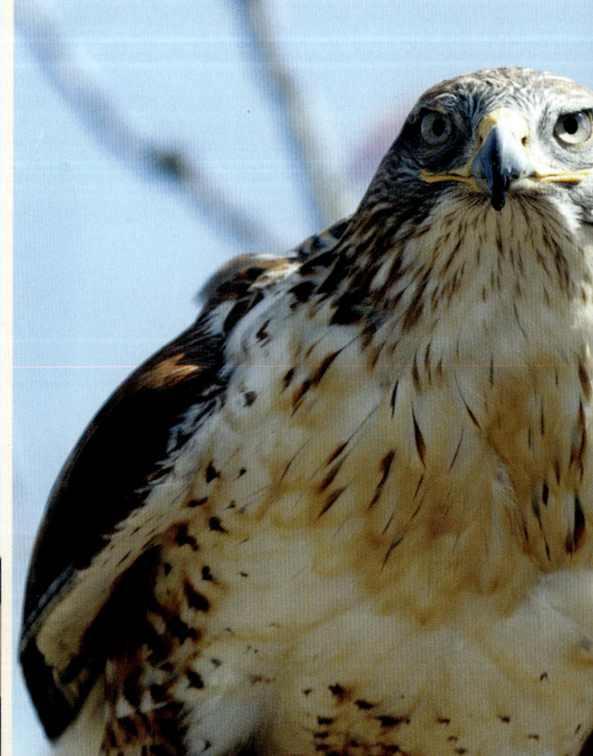

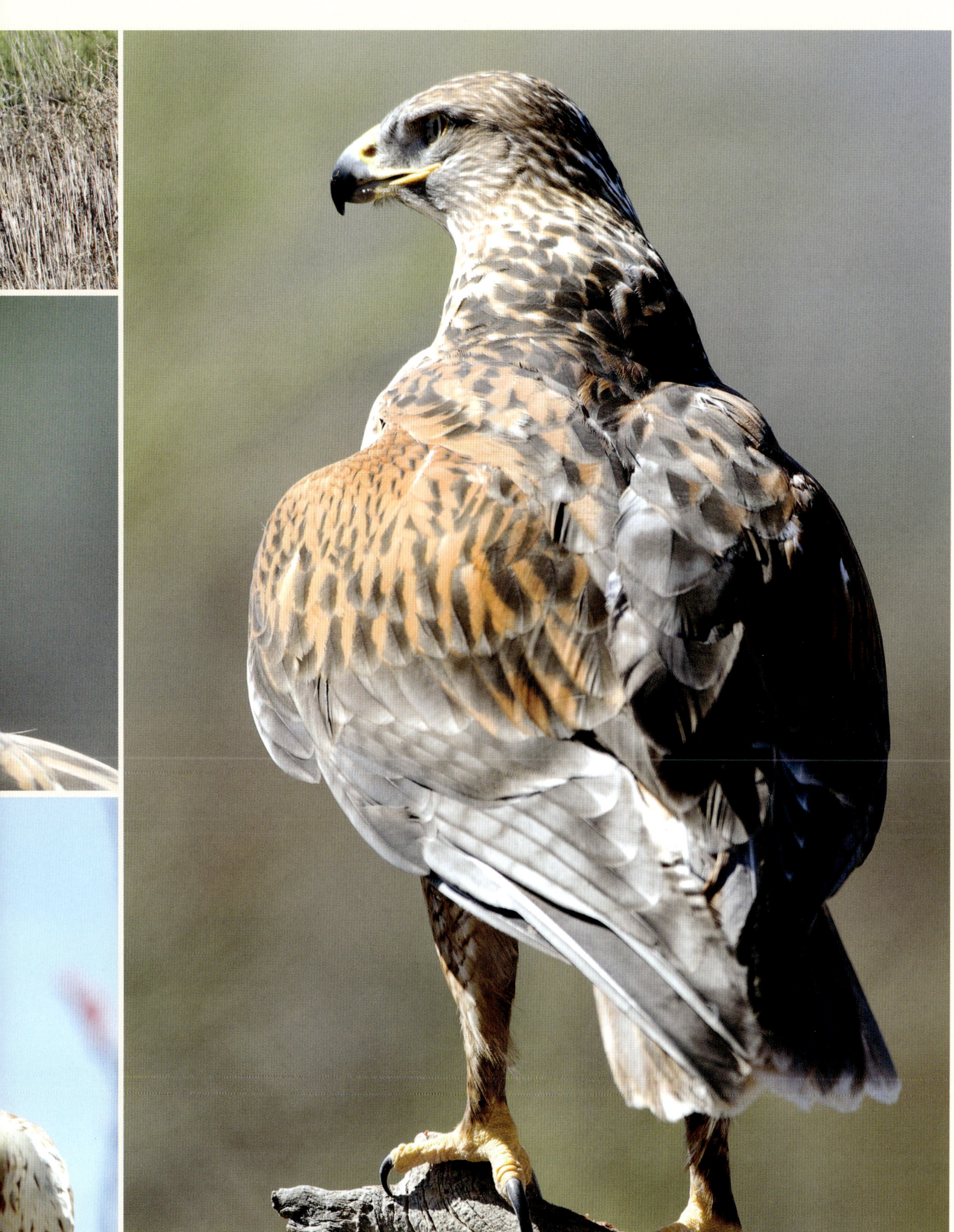

Red-shouldered Hawk

(*Buteo lineatus*)

The red-shouldered hawk is another member of the *buteo* genus, characterized by relatively narrow wings and body. Adults grow to sport the shoulder patches that give the hawk its name. The birds live in the eastern and southern parts of the United States and on the Pacific coast, although the east- and west-coast birds differ in coloration. One difference between them is the eastern adults show more barring on the breast. These woodland dwellers like to live near water. When hunting, red-shoulders are noted for their patience, and a hawk will remain perched on a tree branch for long periods as it watches for prey. They feast on small mammals but also reptiles and amphibians. John James Audubon noted that the red-shouldered is "one of the most noisy of its genus."

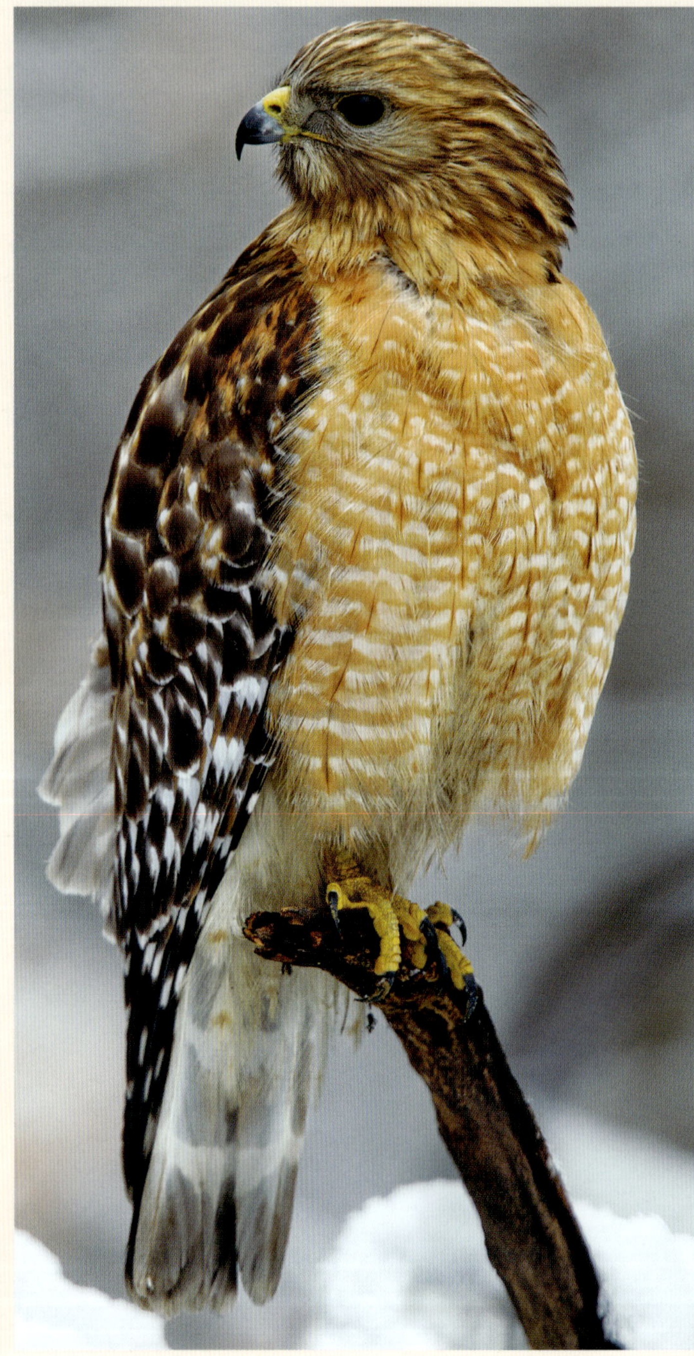

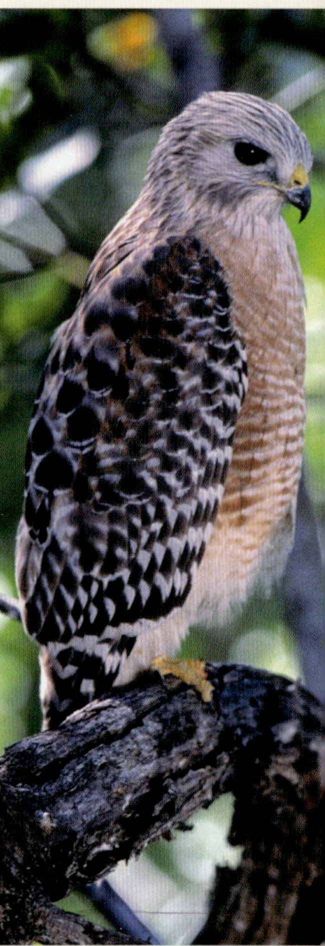

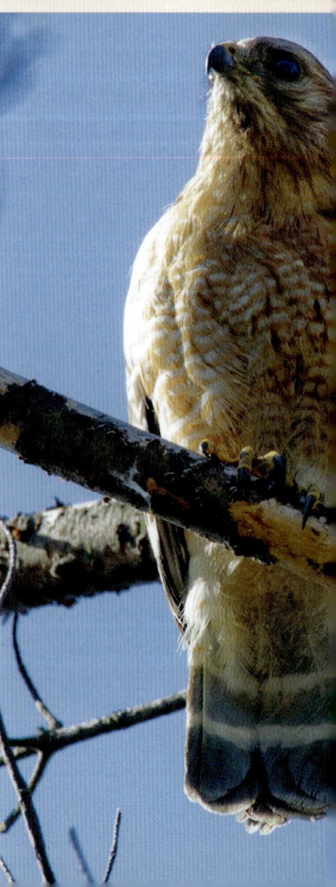

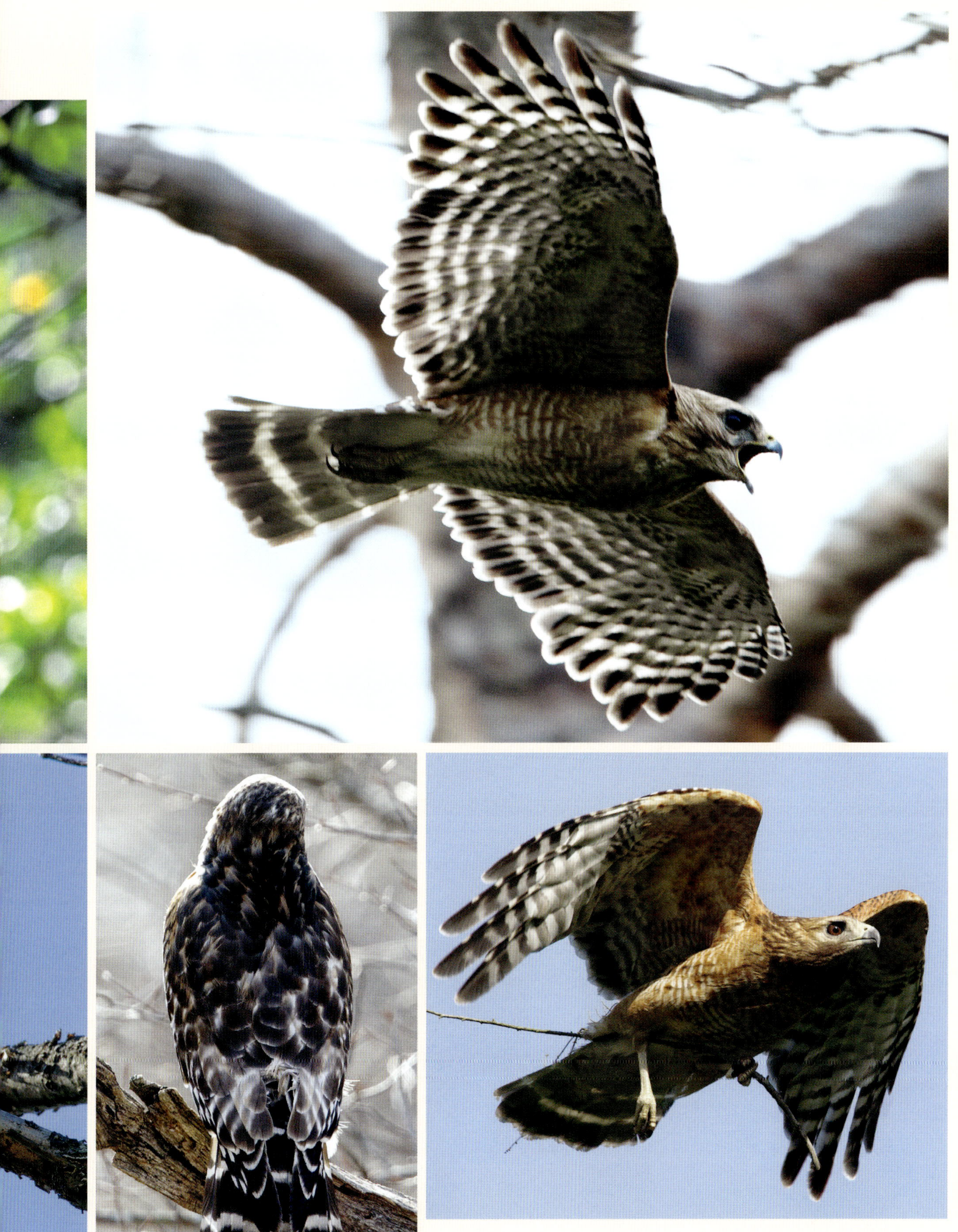

Swainson's Hawk

(Suteo swainsoni)

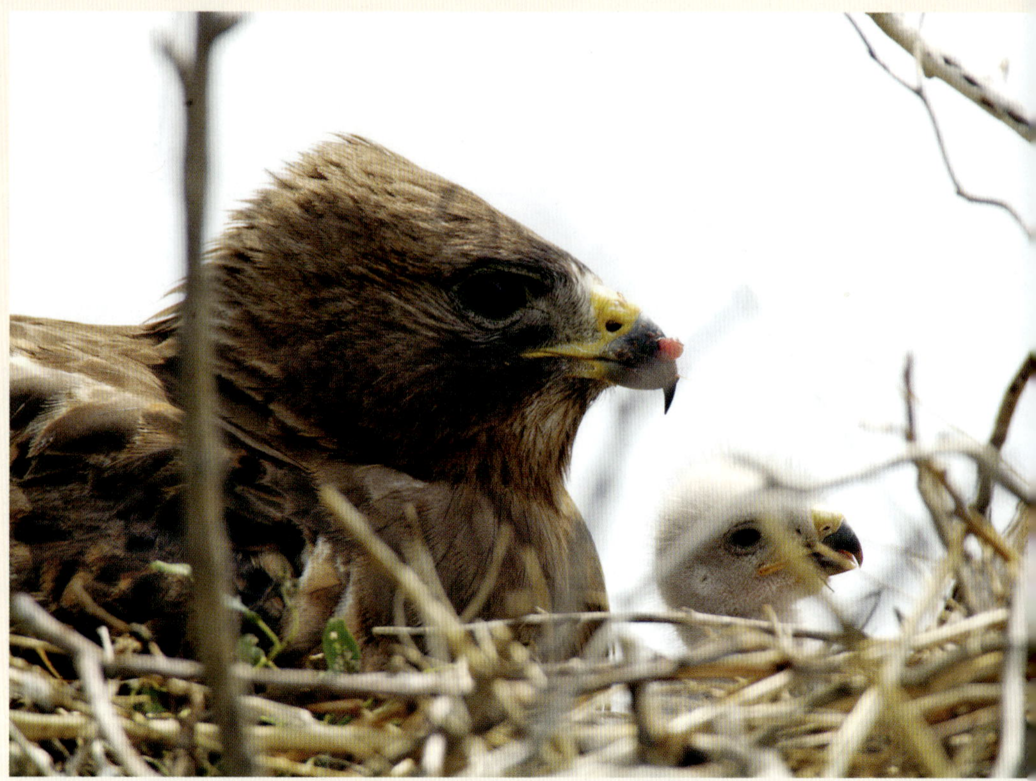

The Swainson's hawk derives its name from English ornithologist William Swainson. It has very long and narrow wings and a long tail. It resides primarily in the western and middle portions of North America, but it migrates for the winter, mostly to South America. This 5,000-mile journey is unusually long in the raptor world. Swainson's hawks will eat rodents, mostly during the breeding season, but they have a special fondness for insects and will chase six-legged quarry while on the ground. Some people call it the locust or grasshopper hawk. Other birds also find themselves on the Swainson's menu. These social raptors like to travel in groups and nest in trees. The female will lay an average of two or three eggs, and the parents start the nestlings out on a diet of mammal after an incubation period of about 35 days.

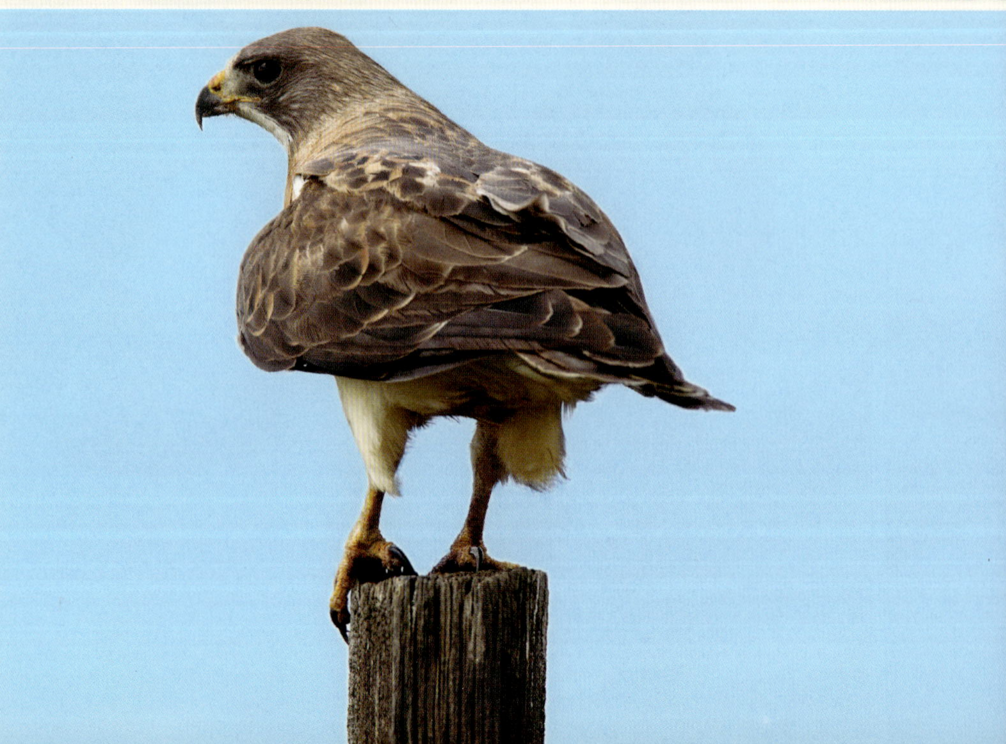

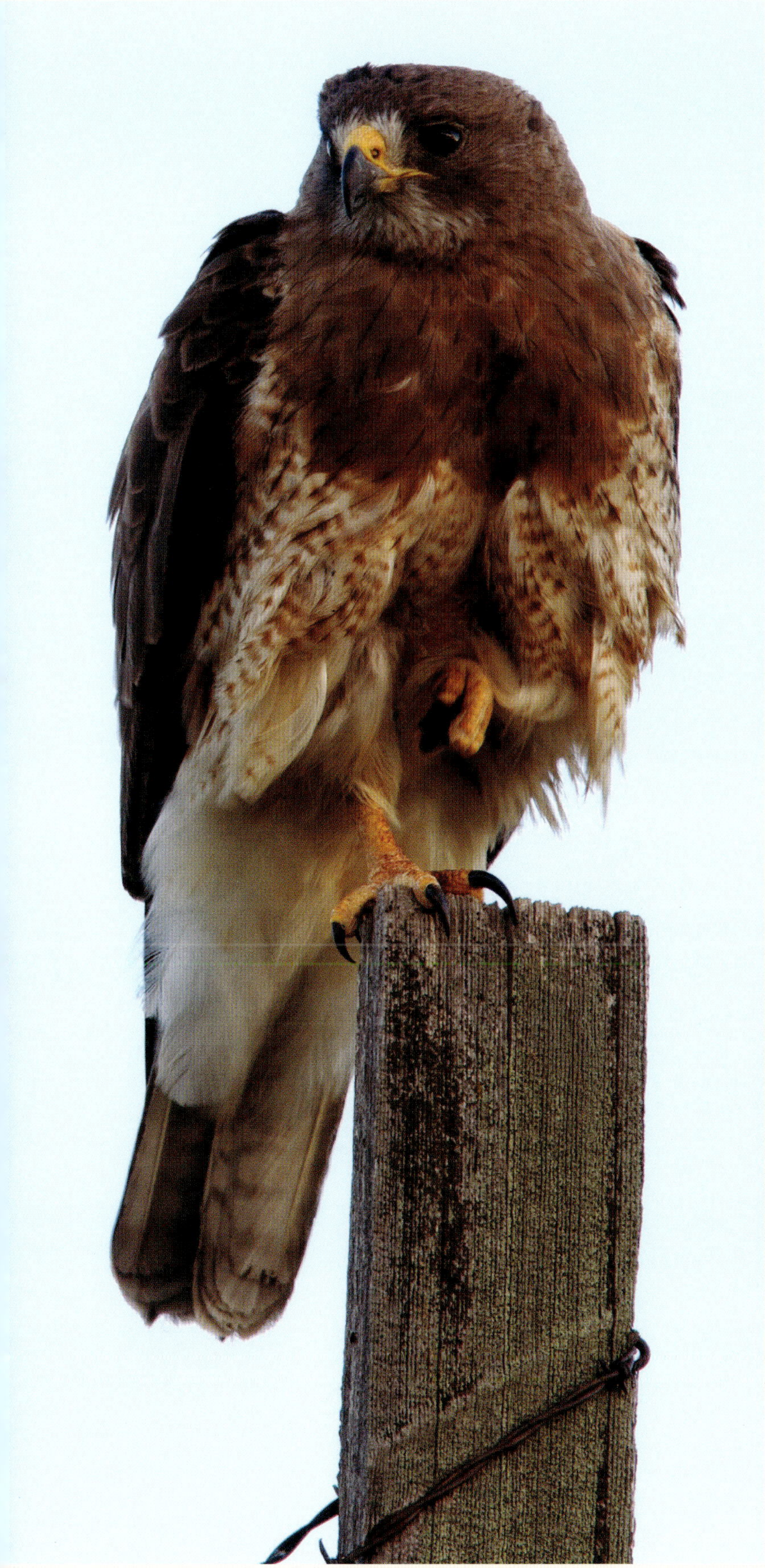

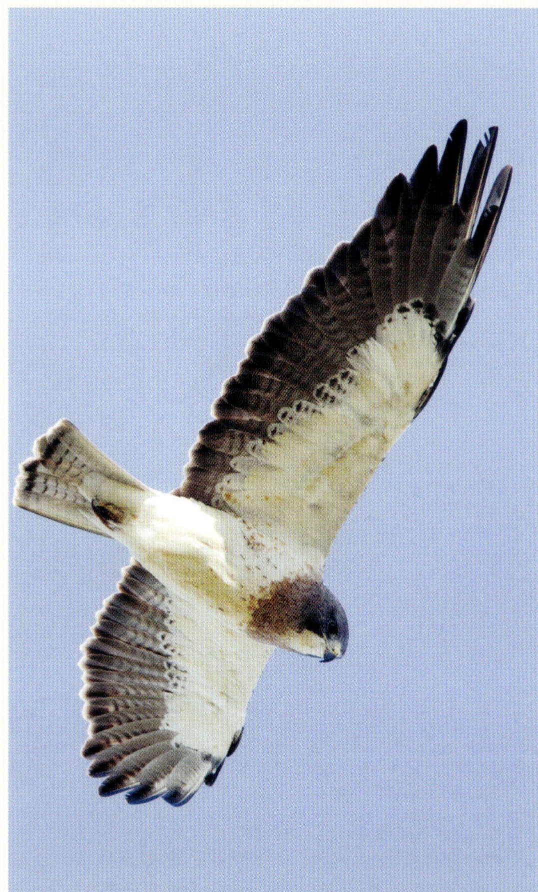

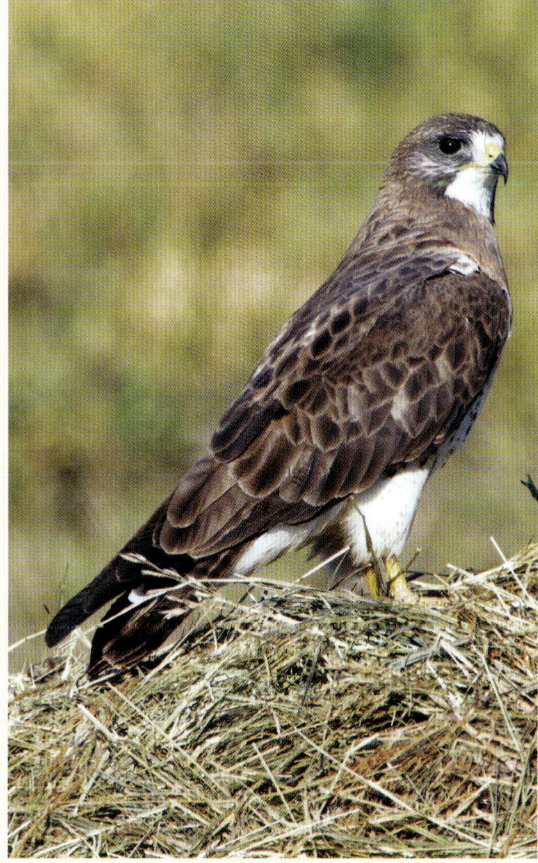

Rough-legged Hawk

(Buteo lagopus)

BY RICK BURKMAN

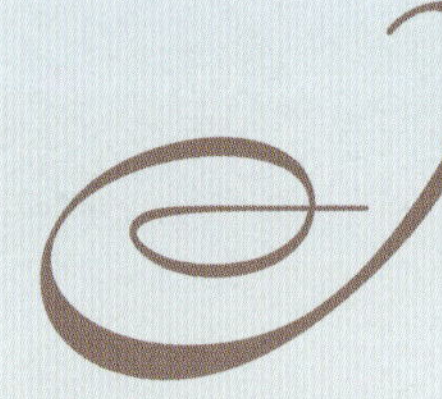

North America's northern states and southern provinces experience winters when temperatures plummet below zero and raging winds pack snow crystals into truck-stopping drifts. Some days have fewer than six hours of full sun, which is often obscured by overcast skies. It is not a place for the weak or the faint hearted. Surprisingly, though, this winter world provides a seasonal refuge for the rough-legged hawk (*Buteo lagopus*), a large arctic predator that considers these lands to be the balmy south.

These arctic vacationers (known as rough-legged buzzards in Eurasia) are regular occupiers of power lines, silos, and the tops of tall trees—anyplace that gives them a wide view of their surroundings. In their summer homes they use cliff faces, hummocks, and large boulders. From these tall perches they watch for their favorite food, which can be anything foolish enough to scurry within view. That includes lemmings, voles, moles, shrews, longspurs, buntings, shorebirds, and game birds.

Daytime hunters, properly known as diurnal raptors, rely on their eyesight to find prey. Some, including the rough-legged hawk, gain a large advantage because they see in ultraviolet light, a wavelength beyond those visible to humans. Urine droplets and scent markings small mammals leave behind them show up remarkably well in this light and apparently the birds can home in on prey by seeing their scent trails.

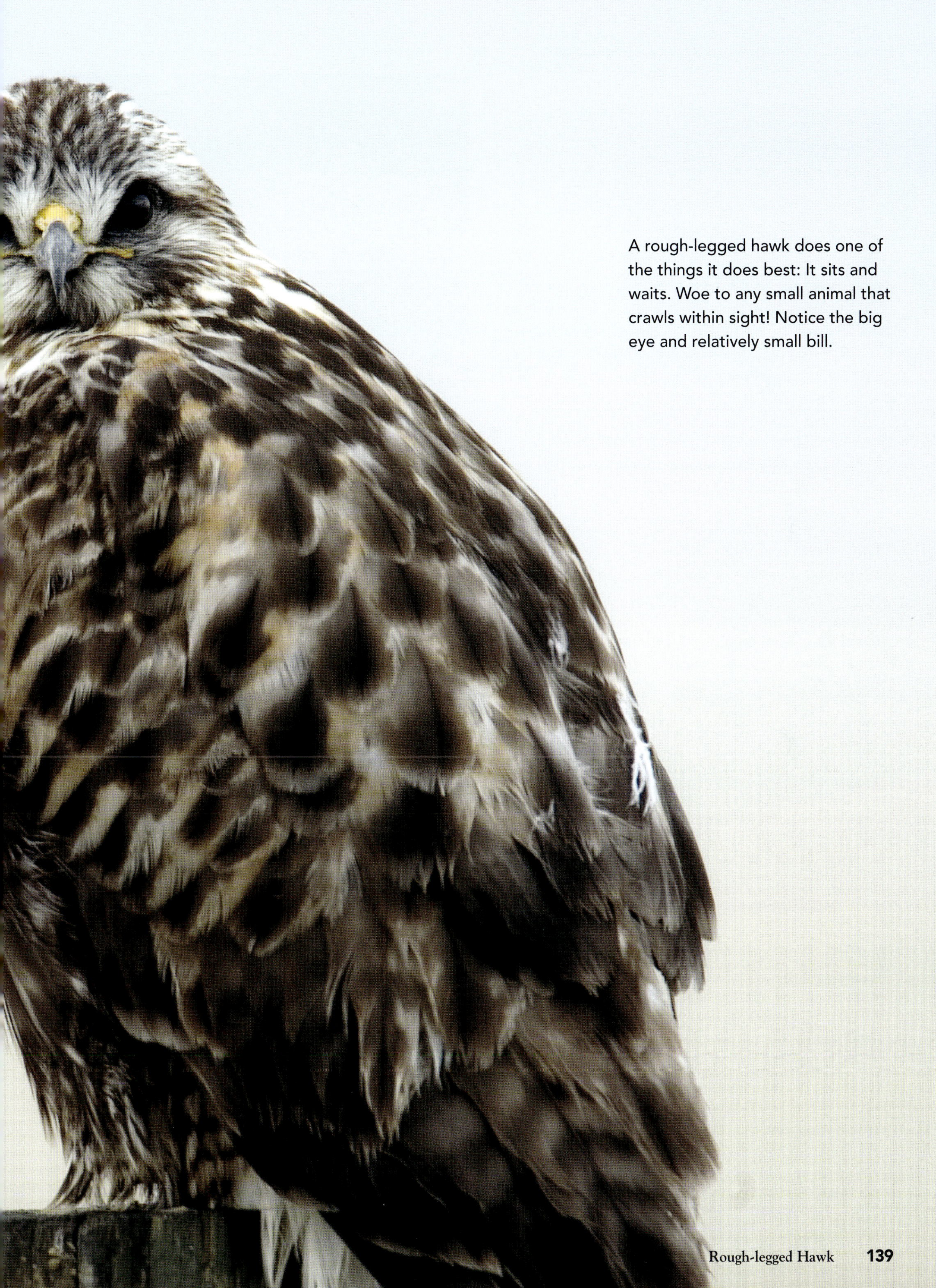

A rough-legged hawk does one of the things it does best: It sits and waits. Woe to any small animal that crawls within sight! Notice the big eye and relatively small bill.

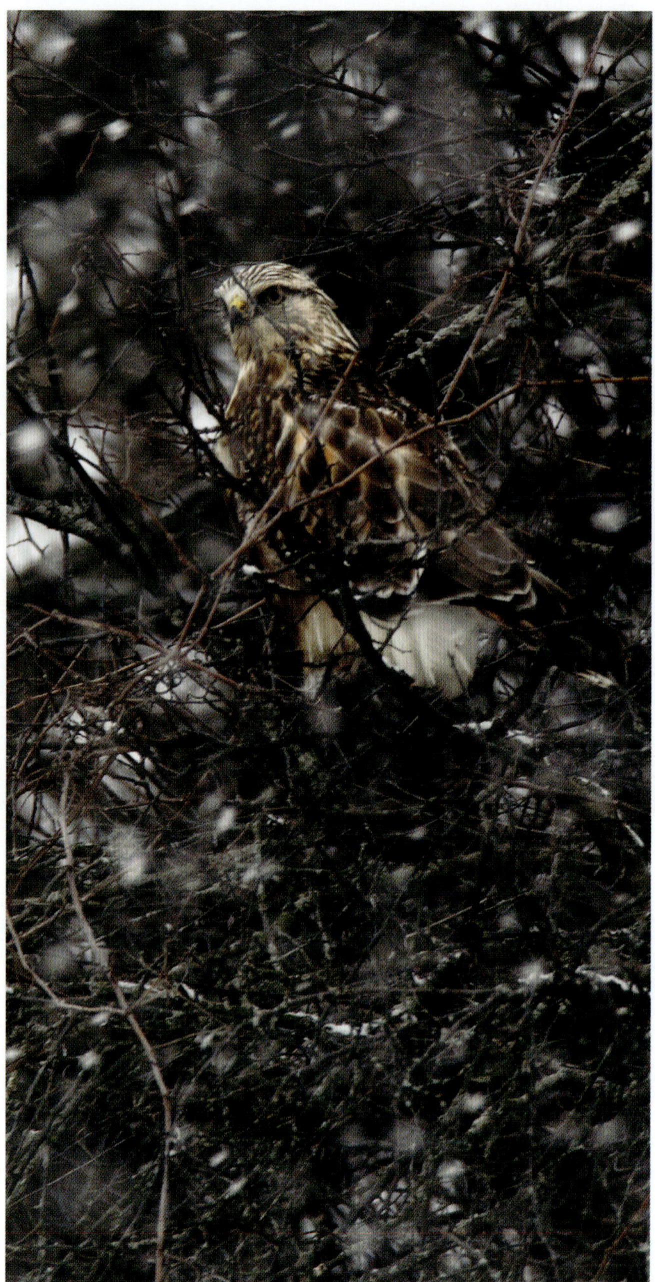

When a hawk spots its prey it flies in a straight line to the target site and hovers over it to pinpoint the unsuspecting meal. Several hawk species are capable of momentary hovering, but the rough-legged hawk, like the ferruginous hawk, kestrel, and kites, can hover for extended periods when hunting. Once the hawk feels assured of its target, it drops from the air, yellow feet spread wide for a quick and silent grab. Black, razor-sharp talons bite deeply and do not let go. These hawks are unusually calm birds, so patient observers with steady binoculars are often rewarded with stunning views as the birds patiently hunt their prey. Still, identifying them can be a challenge. They come in both light and dark morphs, and the birds display a variety of plumages as they mature to adulthood. Although these color phases can appear anywhere, dark morphs are more prevalent in areas with high relative humidity, including the Aleutian Islands, southwest Alaska, and Labrador, Canada. Even in these regions the dark morphs make up less than 20 percent of the population.

The dark morphs are striking, though. The male's jet-black body and narrowly banded tail give this bird an air of dignity and bearing. (Females have only one light tail band and a black terminal band.) Light morphs are stunning, too, but they are much whiter or cream-colored with heavy brown striping, a dark belly band that wraps around the body like a cummerbund, and dark wrist markings on the wings. These hawks have a few other distinguishing characteristics, including rough feathers over bright yellow legs, something they share with ferruginous hawks and golden eagles. (The species name *lagopus* is from an Ancient Greek word that literally translates as "hare footed"). The bills are grayish brown with a blue base and the eye is light brown or gray (yellow in juveniles).

Rough-legged hawks spend their summers, the hectic part of their year, in the taiga and the tundra lands of the north. These areas look like barren wastes in the winter, but the short summers burst with colorful fields of stunted wildflowers, billowing clouds of biting insects, and an abundance of birds and game. The hawks are one of the region's top predators and they stuff themselves from its natural larder. But hawks here do more than feast. This is their breeding ground. Males perform aerial dances over their territories, soaring in ever higher circles before dropping from the sky, sometimes diving, sometimes just letting gravity twist and turn them toward the earth. They spin and flash through their aerial dance trying to lure a female to investigate the territory. If done well, the male gains a mate.

Rough-legged hawks are picky about their nest sites and almost always choose open cliff faces for their summer homes. The breeding season in the north is short and, conversely, rough-legged hawks take a relatively

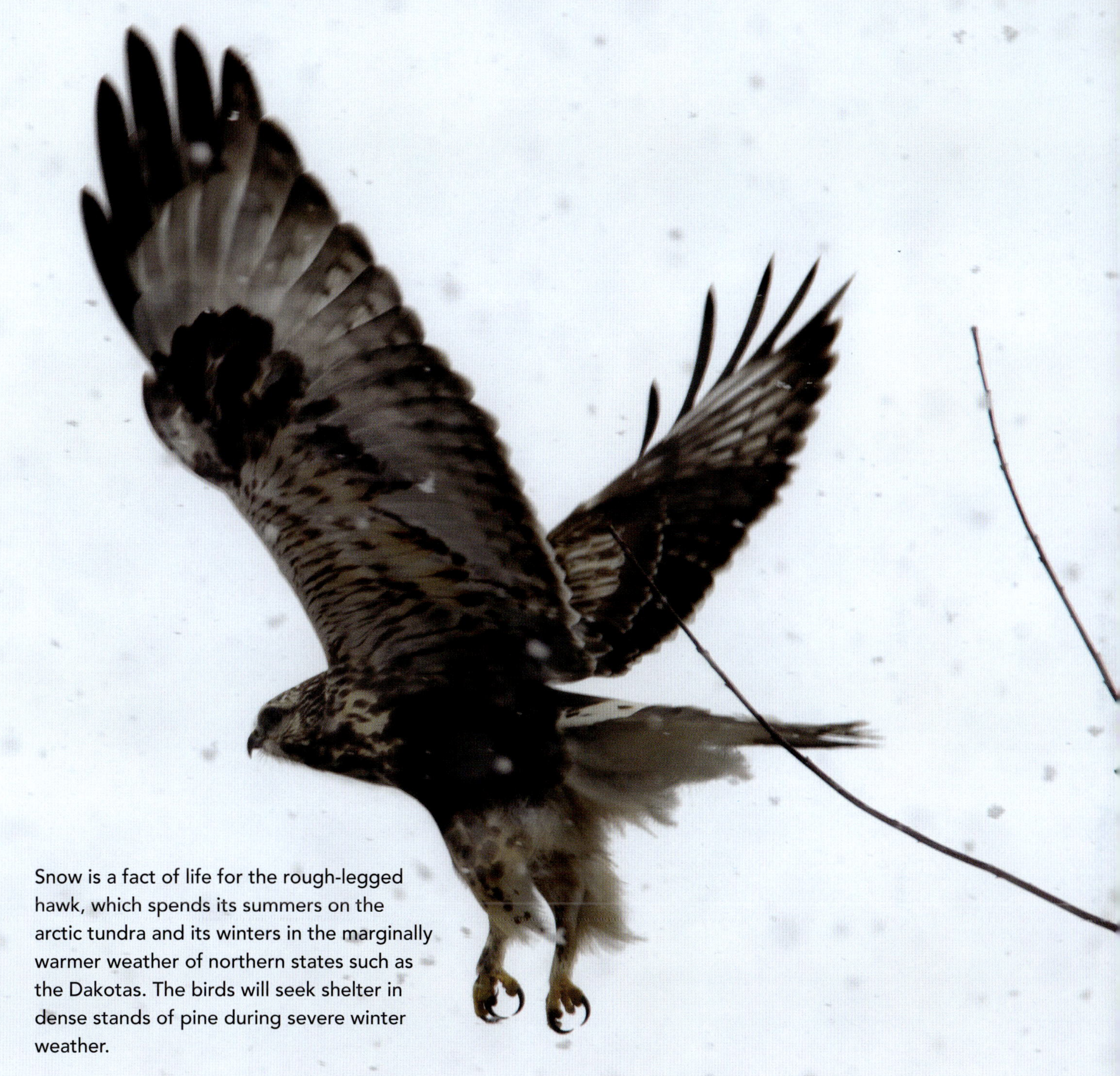

Snow is a fact of life for the rough-legged hawk, which spends its summers on the arctic tundra and its winters in the marginally warmer weather of northern states such as the Dakotas. The birds will seek shelter in dense stands of pine during severe winter weather.

long time to raise their families, so when a pair of birds arrives on their nesting site they waste no time getting the process started.

The male chooses the location and provides the majority of the sticks, twigs, and caribou bones used to form the bulky structure. The female arranges the deliveries in whatever manner suits her best. She lines the nest cup with grasses and other plants and, as the season progresses, feathers and fur accumulate to soften the cup and insulate the eggs.

The birds may take up to 30 days to build a nest. The female will start to lay her clutch of three pale blue eggs once the nest is ready. She lays a new egg every two or three days until the clutch is complete. Birds of prey in the far north start incubating their clutches when the first eggs are laid—the risks of a late spring snowstorm or below-freezing temperatures are too great to leave eggs exposed while the hen replenishes her metabolism. So she lays an egg and then sits tight to keep it warm.

The male is not oblivious to the hen's plight. He provides regular food deliveries so hunger will not drive her from the eggs. He also provides the hen with brief respites by sitting on the eggs himself so she can

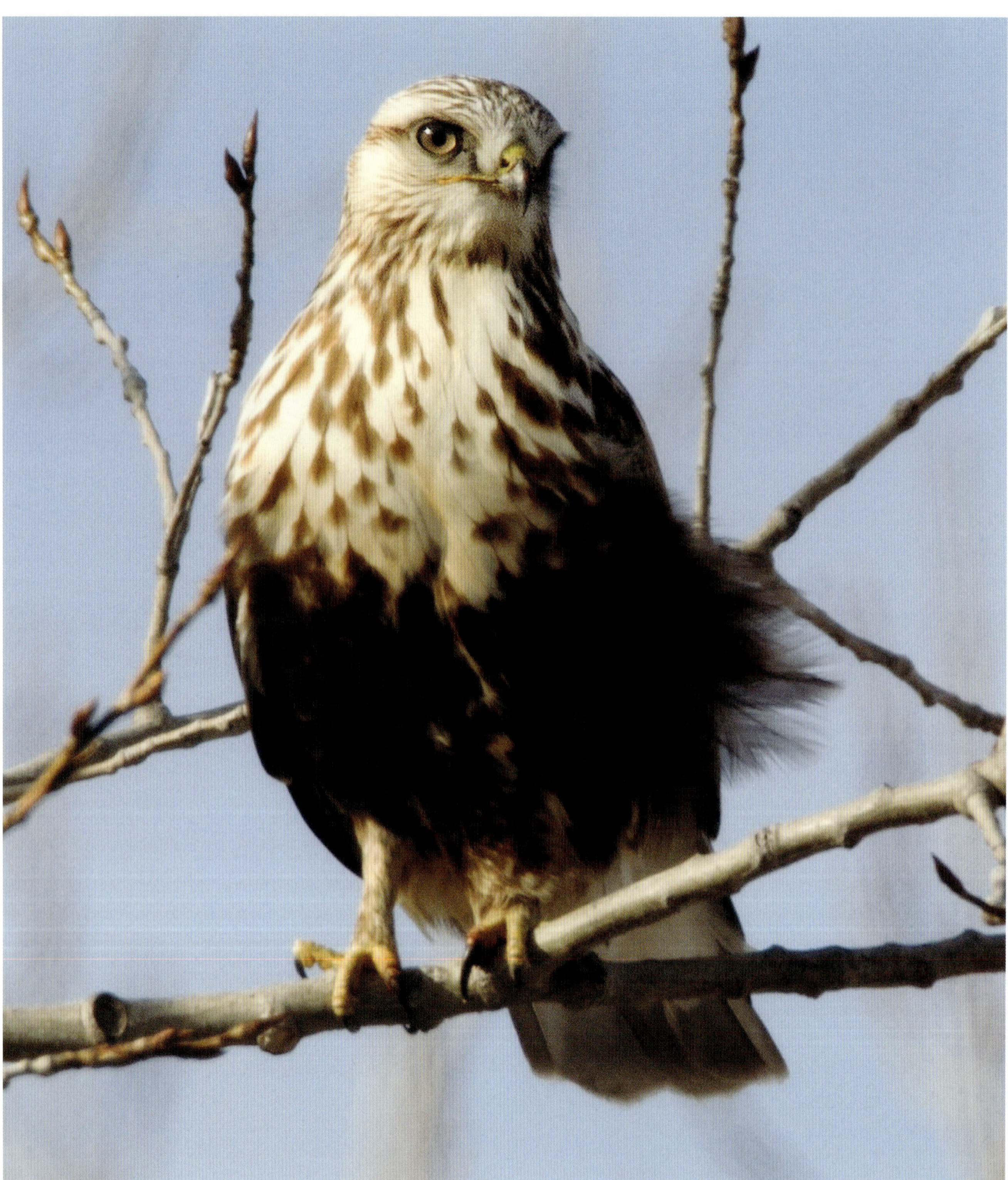

stretch her wings, preen, and keep her hunting skills sharp. Although the male is willing to bring food all the way to the nest, often the female begins her break by intercepting her mate in midair, snatching the food from him in midflight, and landing nearby to eat her meal. The male, meanwhile, quickly replaces her on the exposed eggs.

The first egg hatches after about a month. The process takes two days. The baby hawk pips its shell, forces the cracks larger and larger, and finally gives the shell a mighty push with its feet and curled neck and fully emerges into its new life. The task is so strenuous that the newborn lays in the bottom of the nest for the first few hours after hatching, incapable of even raising its

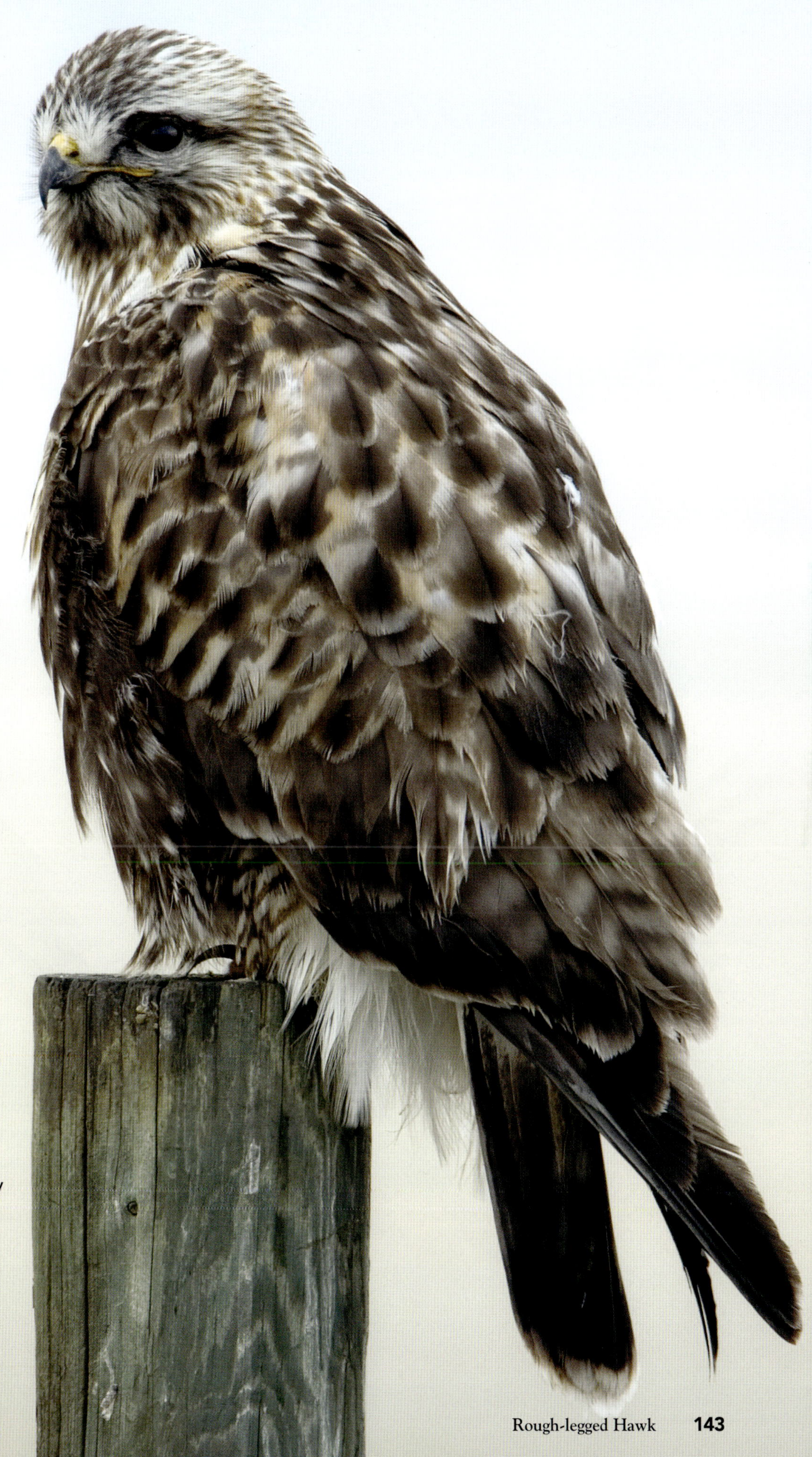

The rough-legged hawk has big eyes but a relatively small bill. A diurnal raptor (meaning it uses eyesight to track its future meals), the hawks are also capable of seeing in the ultraviolet wavelength.

head to open its mouth and beg for food. But after the chicks rest for a time, hunger drives them to the next stage of development. The young birds perk up when the male brings home a meal, knowing that something important is about to happen. They open their mouths and the female tears the meat into small shreds to feed the begging youngsters. The high-protein diet fuels rapid growth. The nestlings can rip off bits of their own food after about two weeks, at the same time their tail and primary feathers first appear. At four weeks the nestlings have increased their weight 20 times. Both parents must keep busy through the long arctic summer days supplying lemmings and voles to the ravenous young.

Although capable of short, clumsy flights a month after hatching, the young birds generally stay in the nest for another 10 days or more. Even after abandoning the nest, the young remain dependent on the parents for food and protection, a dependency that can last another month.

By then the short arctic summer has transitioned to autumn. Even as the daylight hours wane and the birds begin drifting south for the winter, the young follow and beg. But their days of dependency are just about over. Family bonds break. The adults prefer to migrate alone, rarely joining in groups (or kettles), so isolated individuals move south, searching for easy prey and warmer climes.

And once they reach those southern lands, their wintry havens in northern

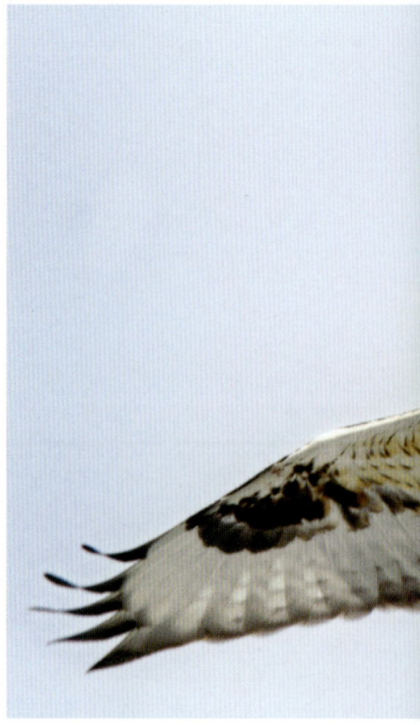

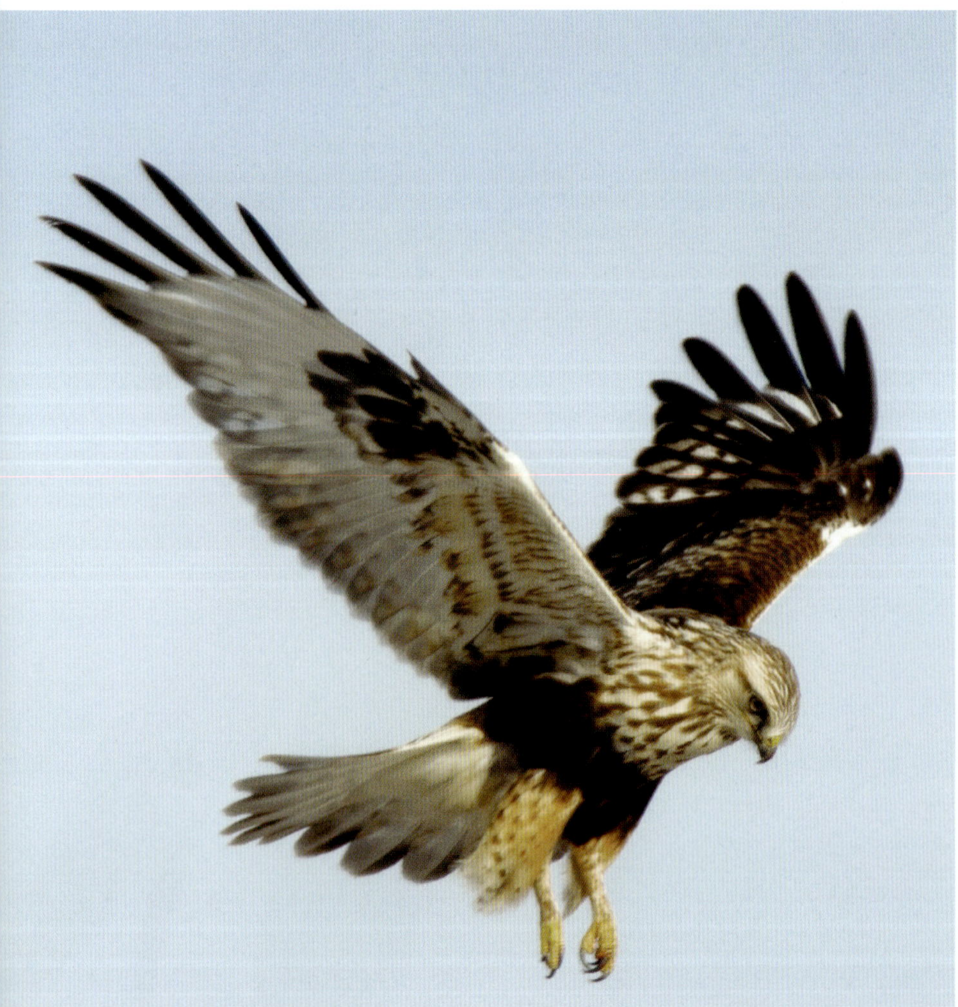

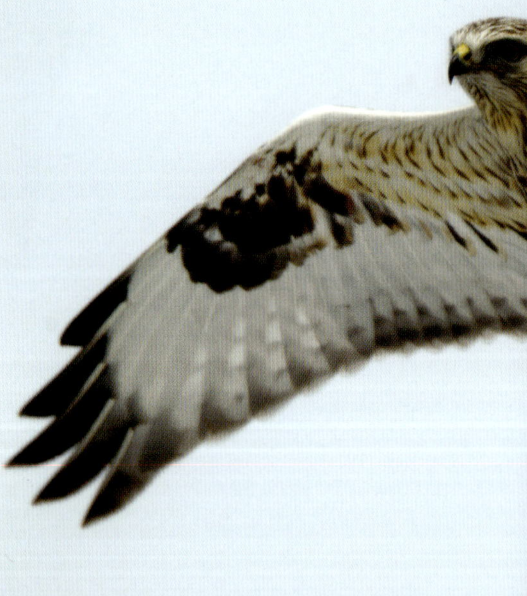

And it's off! The rough-legged hawk will sit patiently on a high perch until it spies prey with its highly developed vision. Once in flight, a hawk can hover over its prey until it feels it has zeroed in on its target. Lemmings and voles are favorites.

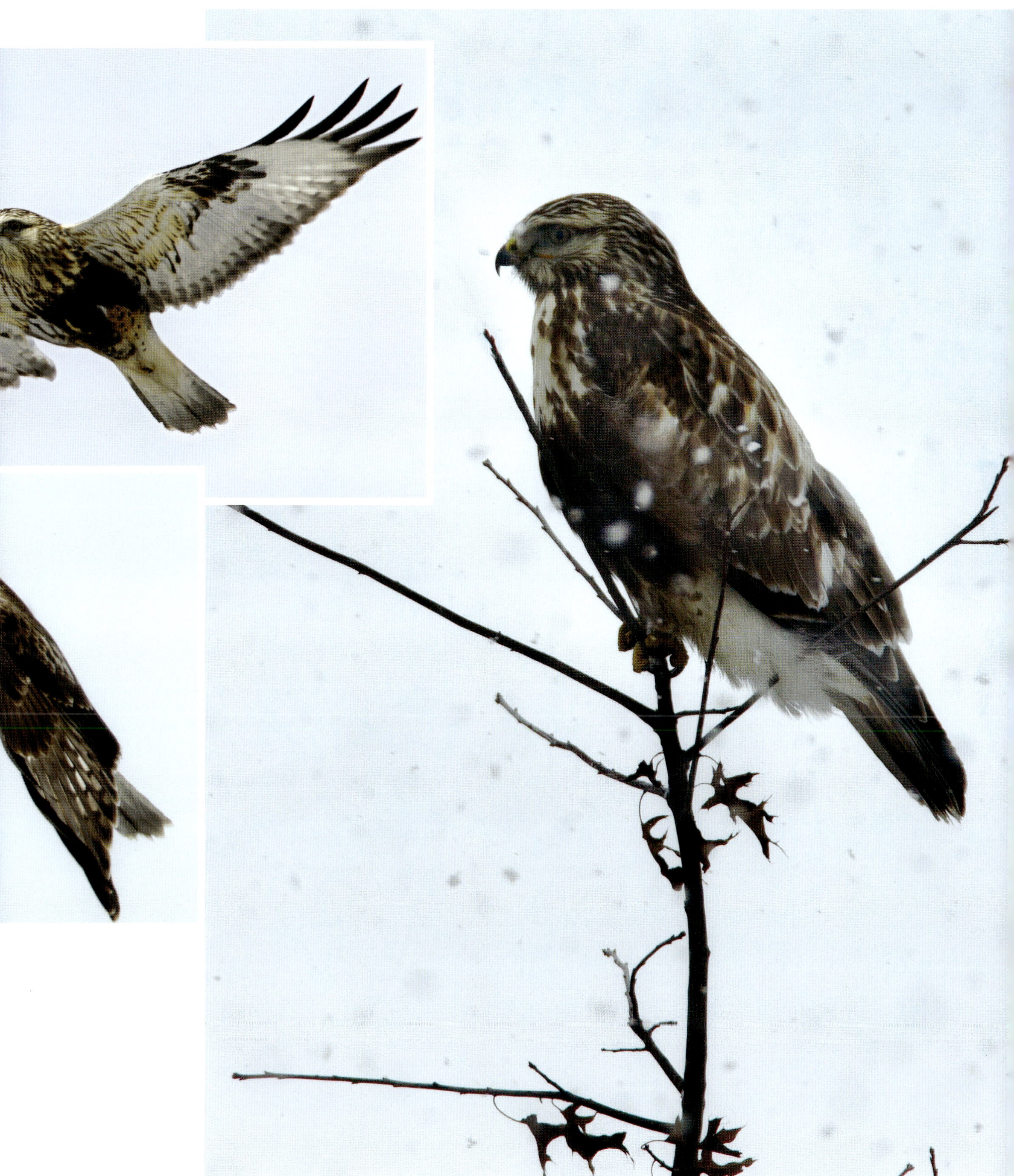

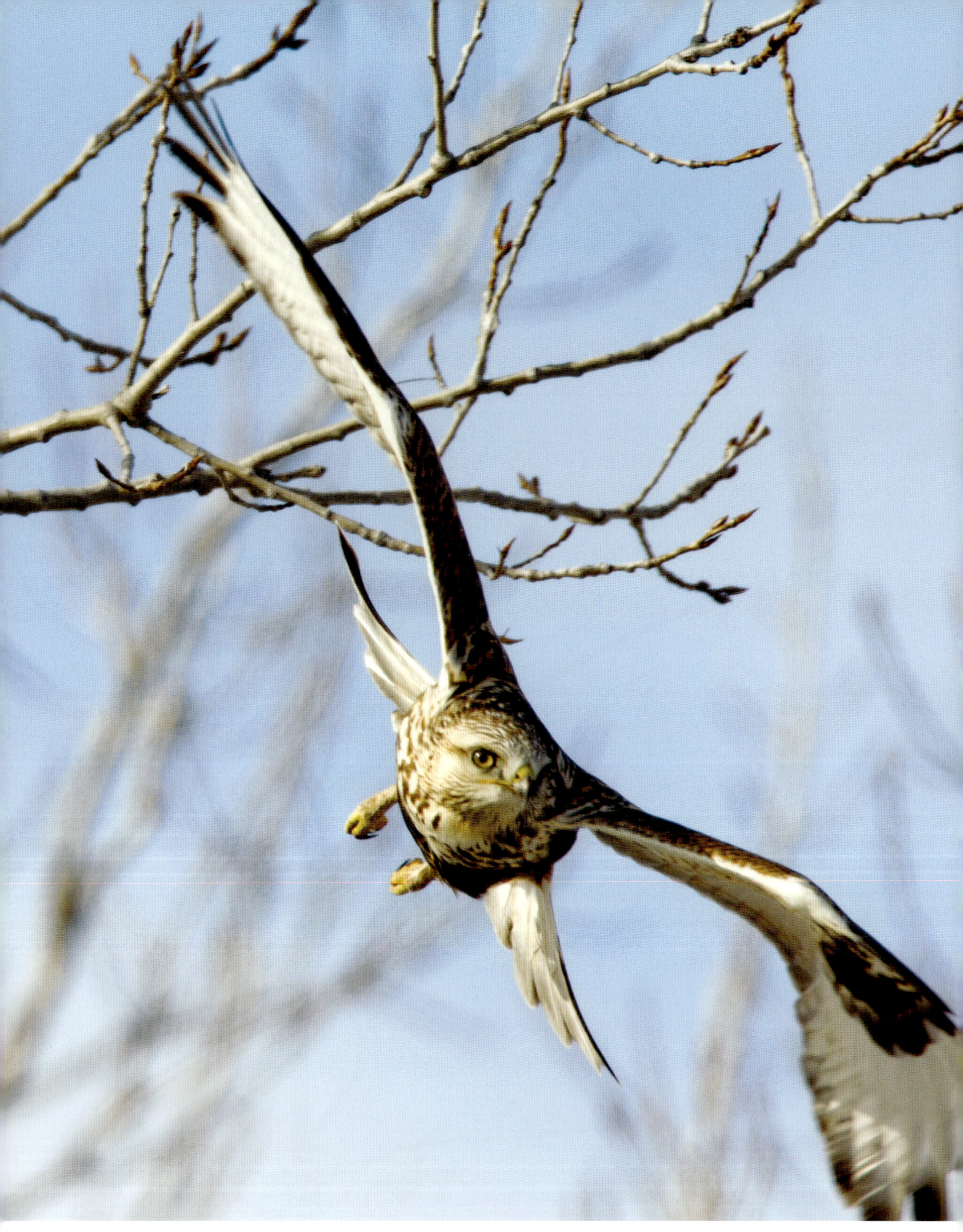

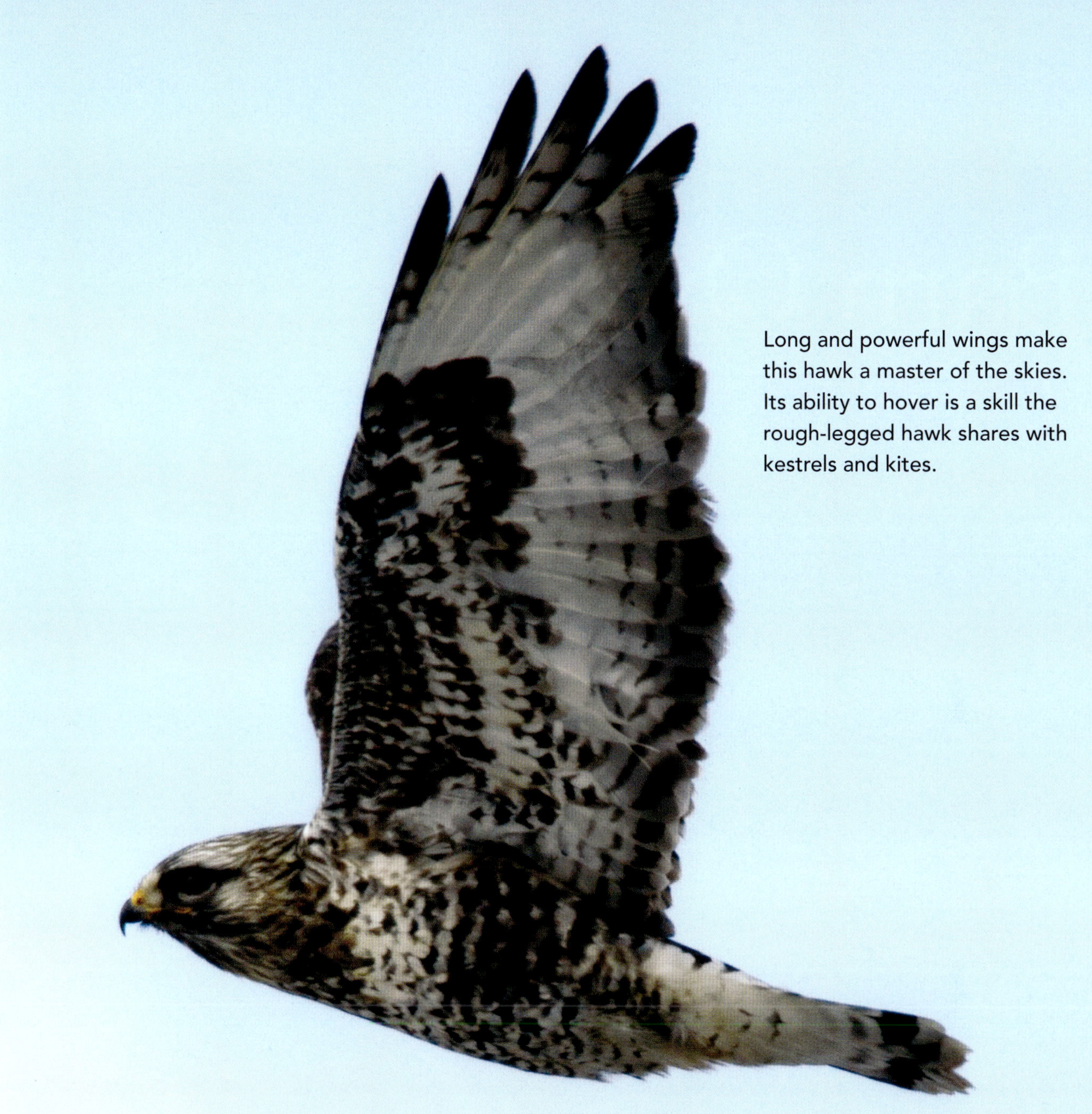

Long and powerful wings make this hawk a master of the skies. Its ability to hover is a skill the rough-legged hawk shares with kestrels and kites.

Wisconsin, Minnesota, the Dakotas, and other storm-prone northern states, they still enjoy their solitude. However, when extreme polar blasts burst into the birds' winter homes, they may choose to roost in dense stands of pine or other vegetation. If the conditions are bad enough, the hawks may form a temporary communal roost to shelter from the weather.

The storms always pass and the rough-legged hawks once again move away, lazily drifting over the land, occasionally hovering to search for a tasty vole or lemming. Solitary and aloof, the Arctic wanderers await their return to spring and the northern summer of endless light.

Measurements (in mm)

	Male	Female
Bill (cere to the tip of upper mandible)	21.4	23.4
Wing Length	410.7	433.7
Tail Length (center rectrix)	215	221
Tarsus Length	70.0	71.4

Barn Owl

(Tyto alba)

BY RICK BURKMAN

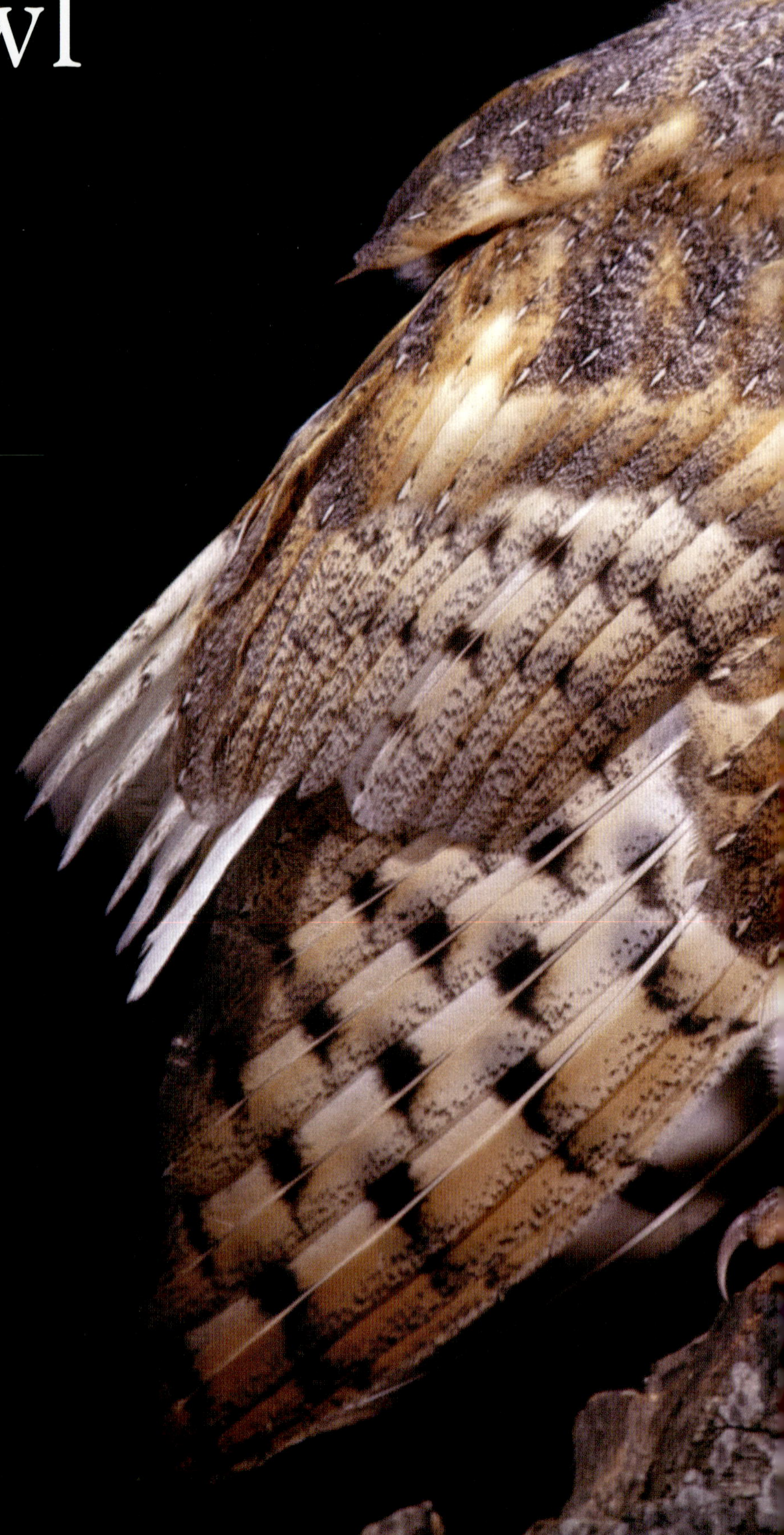

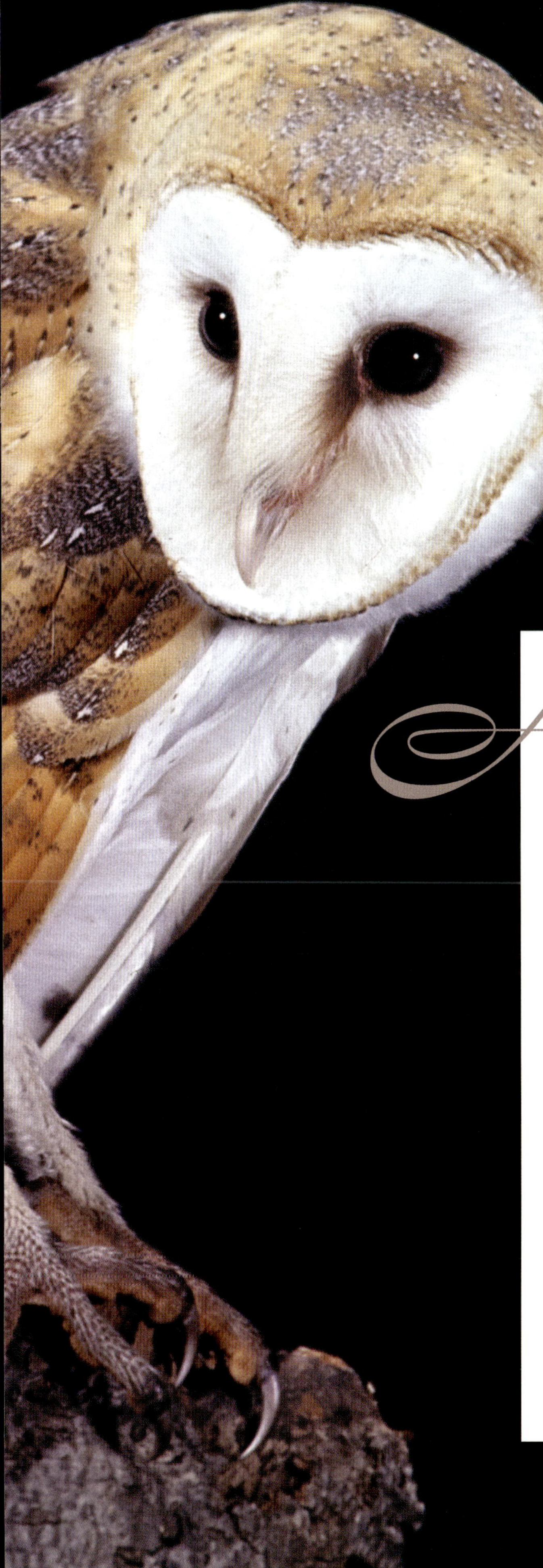

Rodents beware! The nocturnal barn owl can swoop silently from its perch to give its prey a swift and deadly surprise. Voles are a favorite meal, but so are mice, rats, and other creatures that scurry in the night.

A statue of a barn owl (*Tyto alba*) occupies the window ledge above my writing desk. The bird sits atop a fence post. It appears to be just landing, because it has not yet tucked its wings. The left leg supports the bird's weight, while its right leg grips the wood further down. The bird stares outward, alert and aware, with deep brown eyes that sink into a heart-shaped face. The statue leaves no doubt that this light-colored, sleek bird is not only a beauty to behold, but that it also has the body strength, the strong legs, and the sharp bill of a formidable hunter.

Hunters and gamekeepers once despised birds of prey, including owls, for their supposedly wanton killing of game. Many beautiful birds met their ends at the end of a shotgun or rifle barrel—but the barn owl did not. Despite its prodigious hunting skills, the barn owl was one of the few raptors that humans revered. As our ancestors became more adept at agriculture they realized that neatly tended rows of vegetables, along with granaries filled with barley,

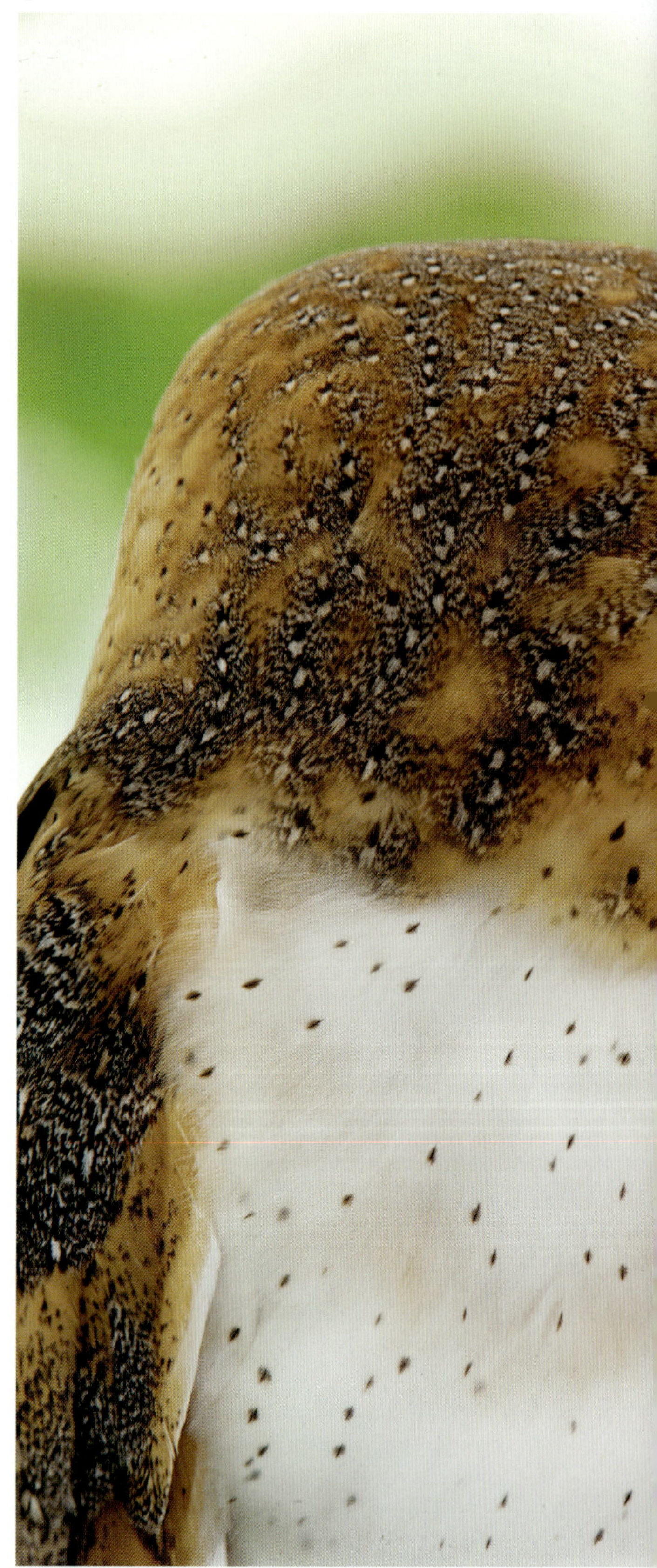

The barn owl has beautiful feather patterns and subtle vermiculation, which makes it a fun but challenging subject for wildfowl carvers. The heart-shaped facial disk and large, dark eyes add to the bird's unique appearance.

rice, wheat, and other cereal staples, offered a paradise for mice, rats, or any small rodents that share our tastes in food. The little rodents destroyed crops, spoiled produce, and sparked a battle for food between man and beast.

Farmers recognized that during a single nesting season, a barn owl family could devour up to 1,000 mice from nearby barns and fields. And the bird's appetites did not abate when nesting time ended, meaning an owl pair could potentially kill and devour many thousands of gophers, mice, rats, and other vermin over the course of a year. So instead of treating the barn owl as an enemy, farmers recognized it as an important ally.

We may like the company of barn owls, but there is no doubt that they are odd-looking creatures. Peer closely at a barn owl and you will see that its deep brown eyes are surrounded by a face that is—there is no other word for it—cute. The owl's facial disk gives its visage the shape of a valentine heart, with the owl's razor-sharp pink bill making up the heart's bottom. Even owl chicks have a long, narrow version of the heart face. This odd facial disk surrounds the eyes, but it has evolved to help direct even the faintest sound to the ears. When cornered, concerned, or interested in something, the barn owl kinks its neck to lower its head, while keeping its eyes focused straight ahead. Then the barn owl bobs and weaves its head like a heart-faced snake charmer.

The barn owl is not, of course, trying to charm snakes. It is trying to identify what it hears or sees by focusing sound waves to its ears. Barn owls are so adept at this they can hunt in total darkness—flying, avoiding obstacles, landing on perches, and, most importantly, snatching unsuspecting prey. In one experiment designed to test the hearing skills and abilities of a barn owl, researchers placed one bird in a completely darkened room. (An owl's

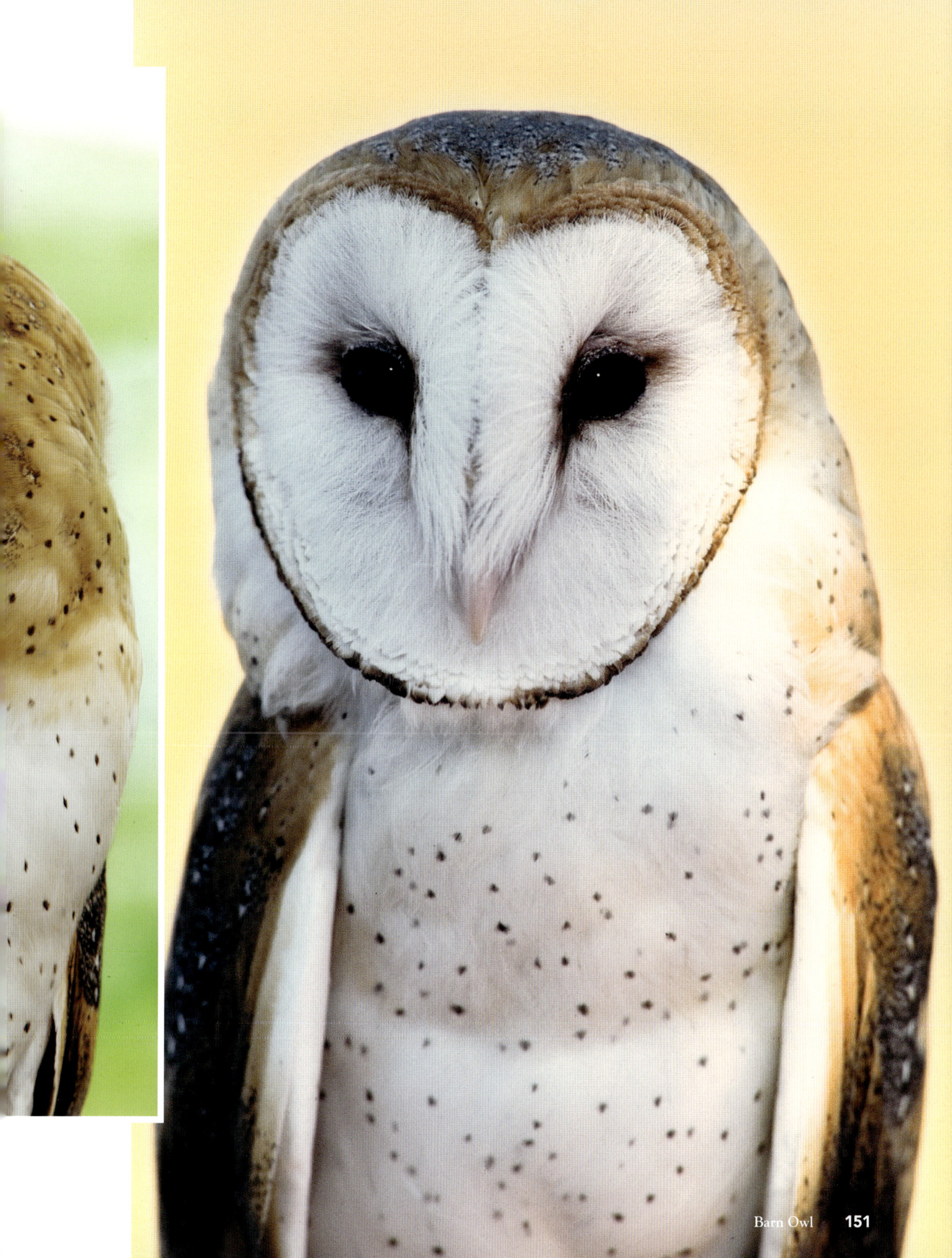

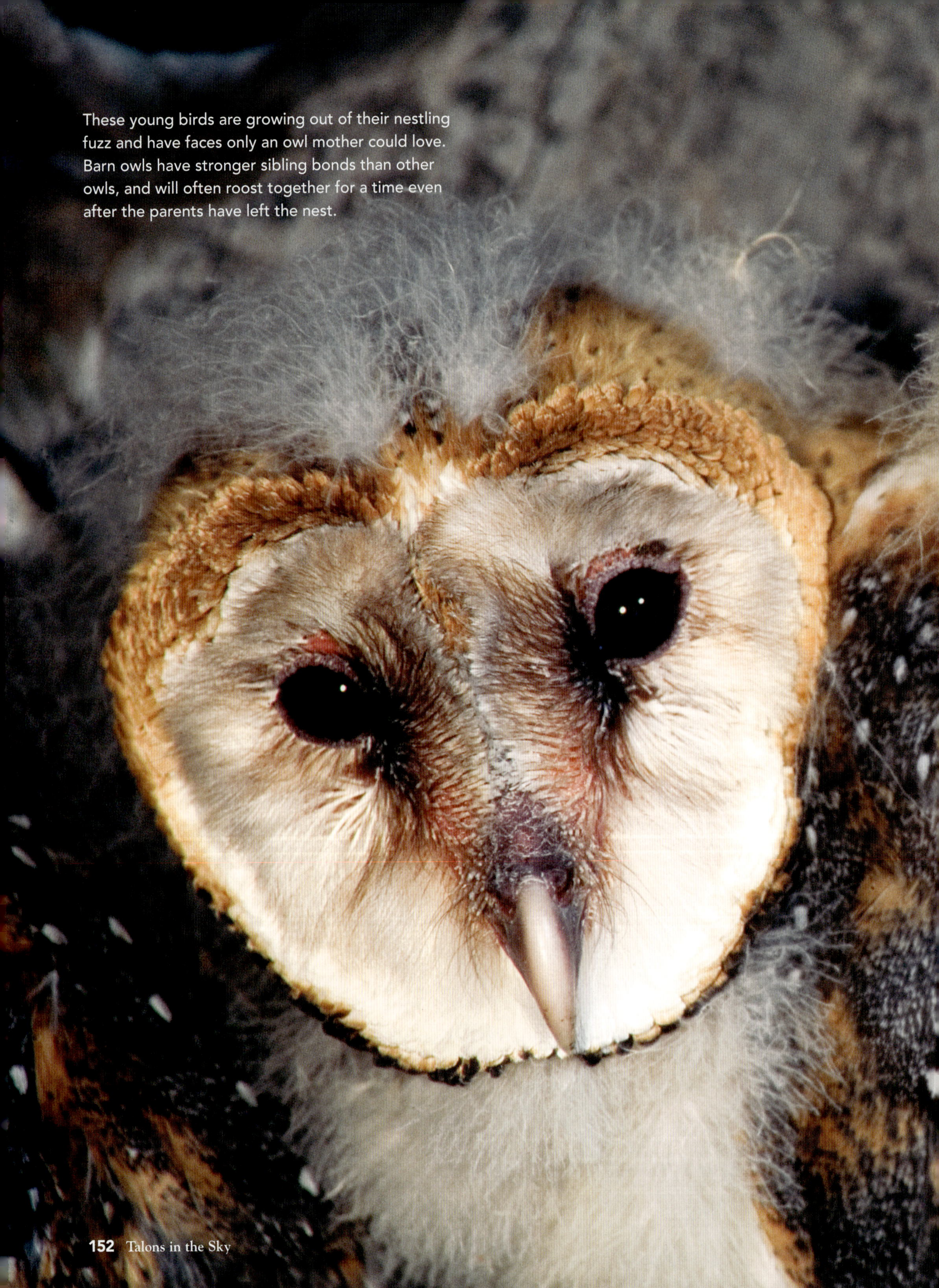

These young birds are growing out of their nestling fuzz and have faces only an owl mother could love. Barn owls have stronger sibling bonds than other owls, and will often roost together for a time even after the parents have left the nest.

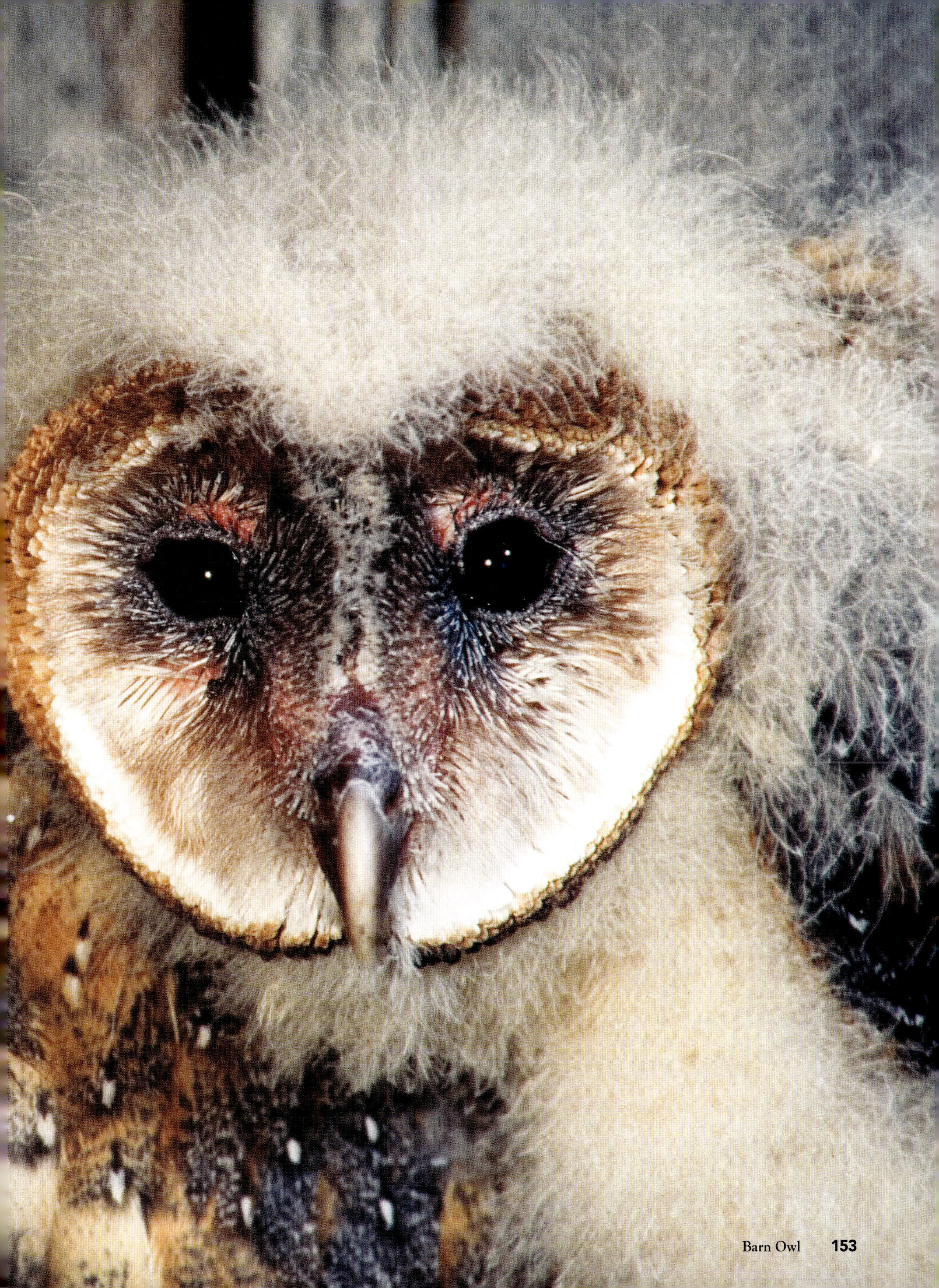

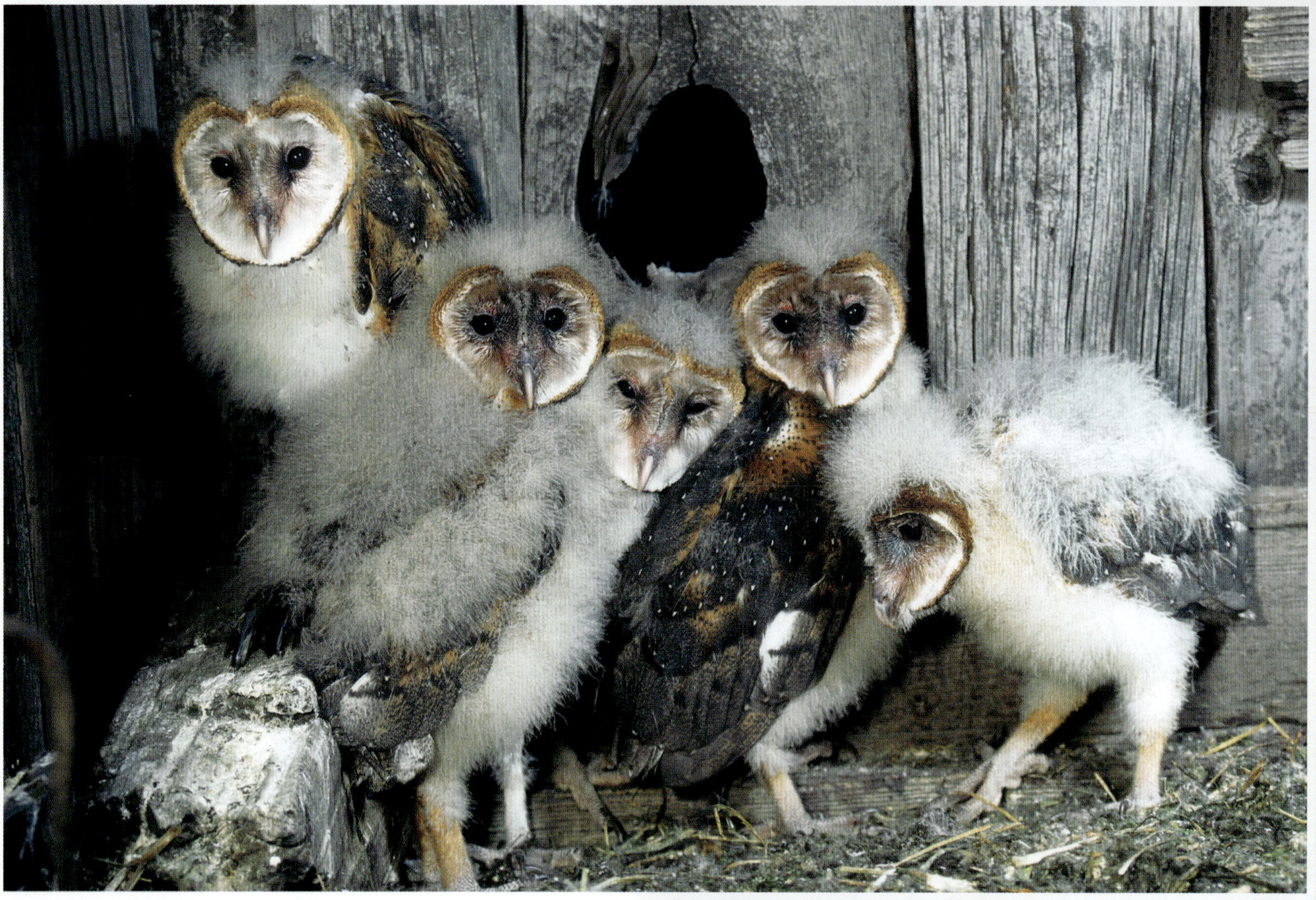

night vision is about 100 times better than ours, so to run a legitimate experiment the room had to be sealed against all light intrusion.) They then released 17 mice into the room. Thirteen of them never had a chance, and the few misses the barn owl made were close ones. Barn owls manage such feats not only by pinpointing their prey by sound, but also by creating a mental map of their environment based entirely upon sound and sound reflection.

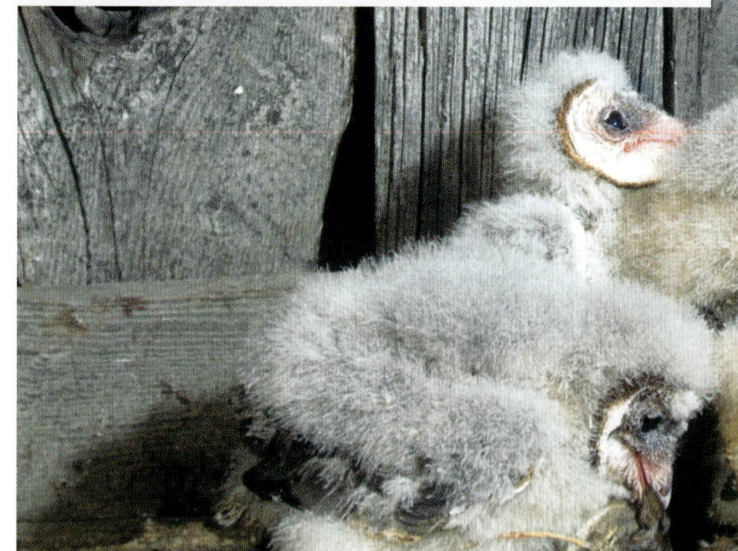

Male barn owls turn their prodigious skills at hunting into part of their mating ritual. After the male captures a juicy morsel, he utters a series of clicks, hisses, squeals, screeches, and other assorted non-owl-like sounds (barn owls do not hoot like other owls), and then drops the prey at his mate's feet. A male barn owl demonstrates his prowess by capturing more prey than his mate can consume in one sitting, but barn owls are patient. The female will sleep and digest for a while and wake up to eat again. To further enchant his mate,

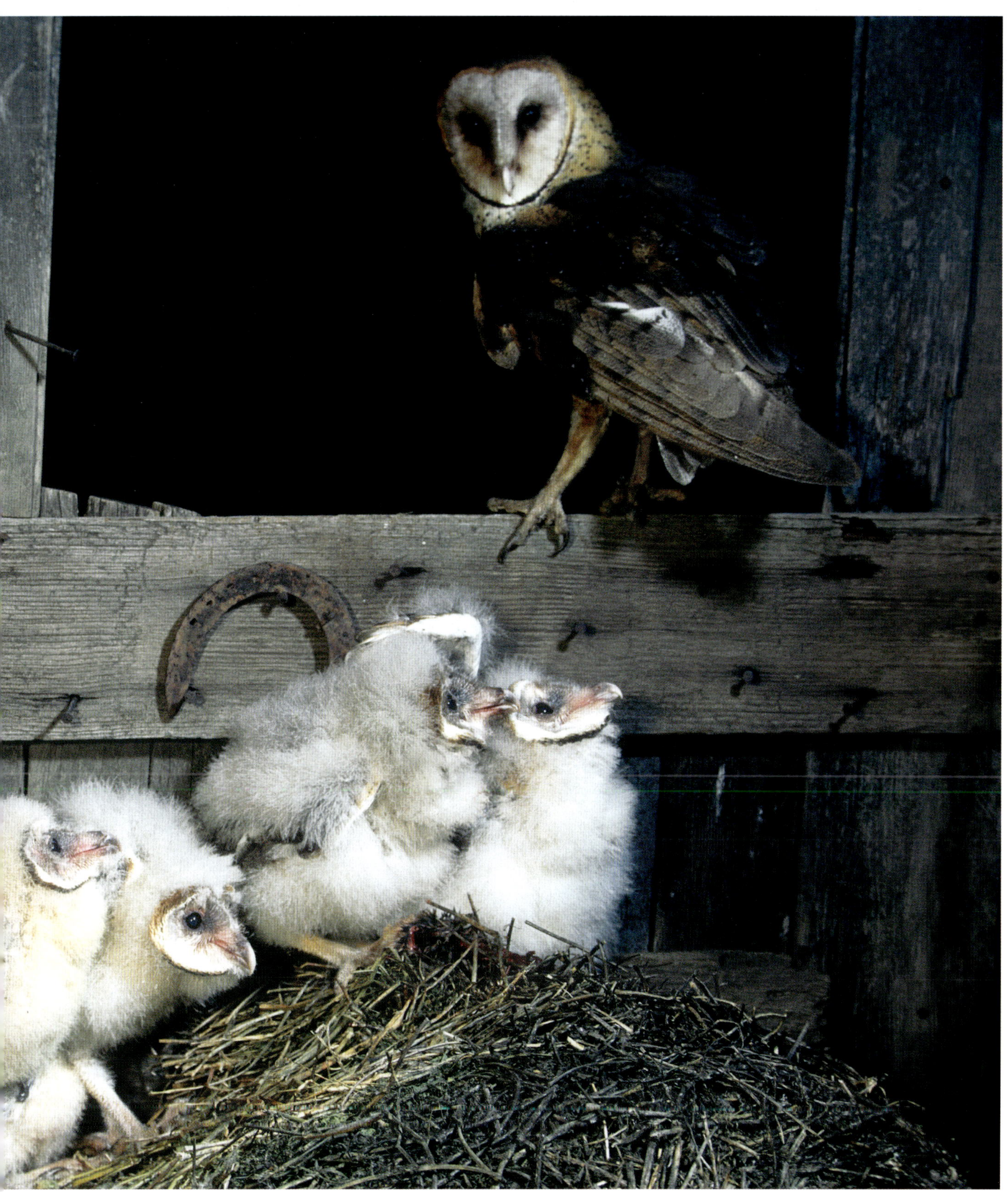

We call them barn owls for a reason, and many farmers owe these birds thanks for putting a check on local rodent populations. The female is responsible for incubation, while the male will bring her food. Her regurgitated pellets become part of the nest.

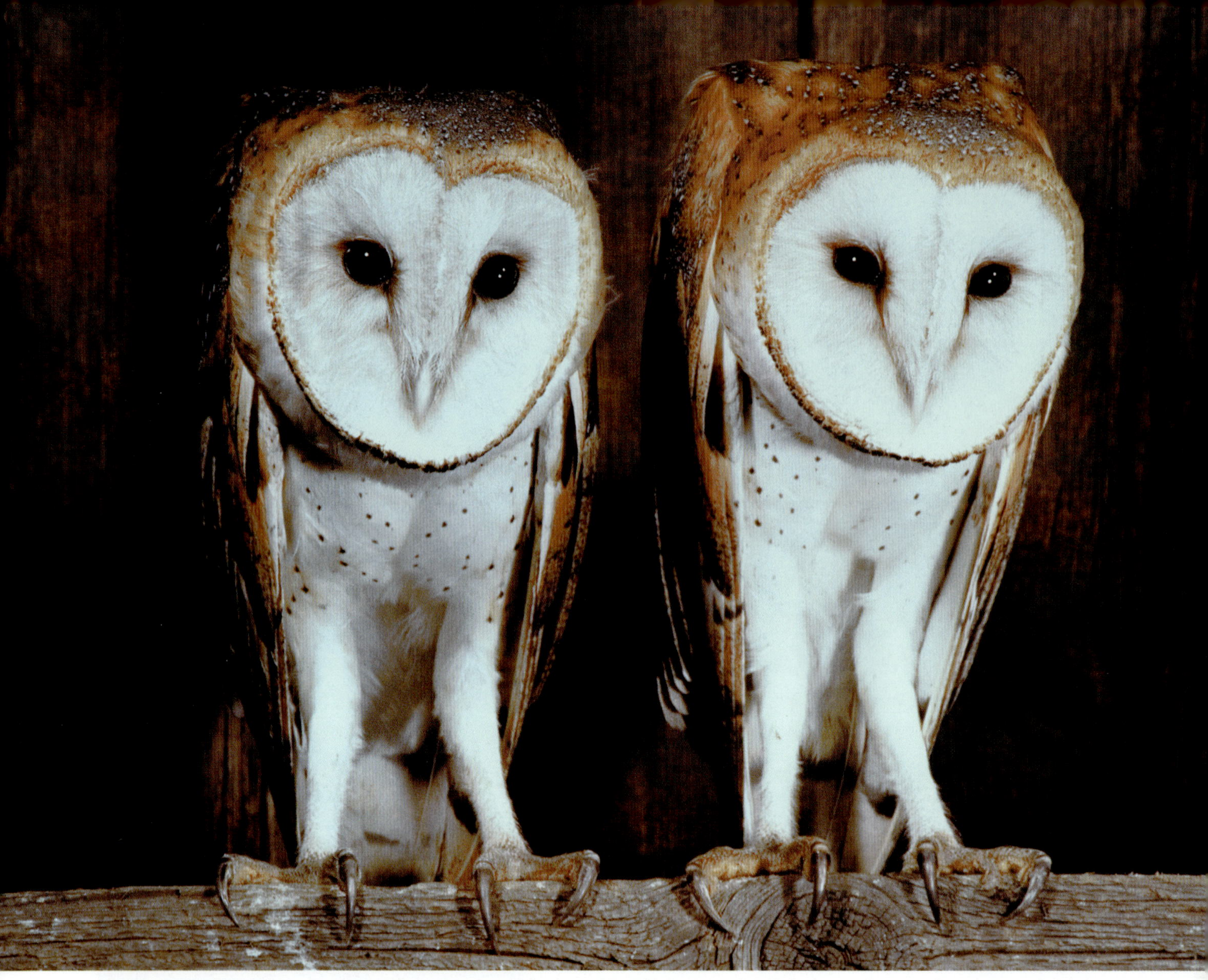

The barn owl's striking appearance isn't merely cosmetic. The strong beak has an obvious function, while the owl can manipulate its facial disk to channel sound to its ears. Its hearing is very acute, allowing the owl to pinpoint prey in the darkness.

the male will often engage in a "moth flight," where he hovers in front of the female with his feet dangling below him for several seconds, bobbing almost magically, as if bouncing on invisible strings.

Eventually, the barn owl pair chooses a nest site. The owls nest in tree cavities, nest boxes, rock ledges, church steeples, haystacks, barns, silos, and other natural and man-made sites. The male makes the initial searches for a nest site and he may show several candidates to his mate, but ultimately the female determines the best place for her eggs. The birds do not build a nest in the traditional sense (although some southwestern birds scrape small burrows in arroyos and dried river beds for their nests). Instead of gathering grass or sticks, the owls simply expel pellets, those bits of indigestible bone and fur. The female then gathers the pellets into a pile and uses this furry and soft, if somewhat macabre, nest for her eggs.

Depending on the area of the country and the severity of the winter conditions in the bird's habitat, nesting can occur at any time, although it usually takes place during the spring and summer months. Despite the fact that barn owls are at the apex of the predatory ladder, they apparently lead challenging lives with a high mortality rate. The average life span is only 21 months (although one Methuselah-like wild bird lived to the ripe old age of 34 years) so most pairs have only one or two broods in their lifetimes. When the hen is ready she will lay three to five dull white eggs. Incubation lasts for about 31 days and starts once the hen lays the first egg. The female alone is responsible for incubation, but her dutiful mate provides her

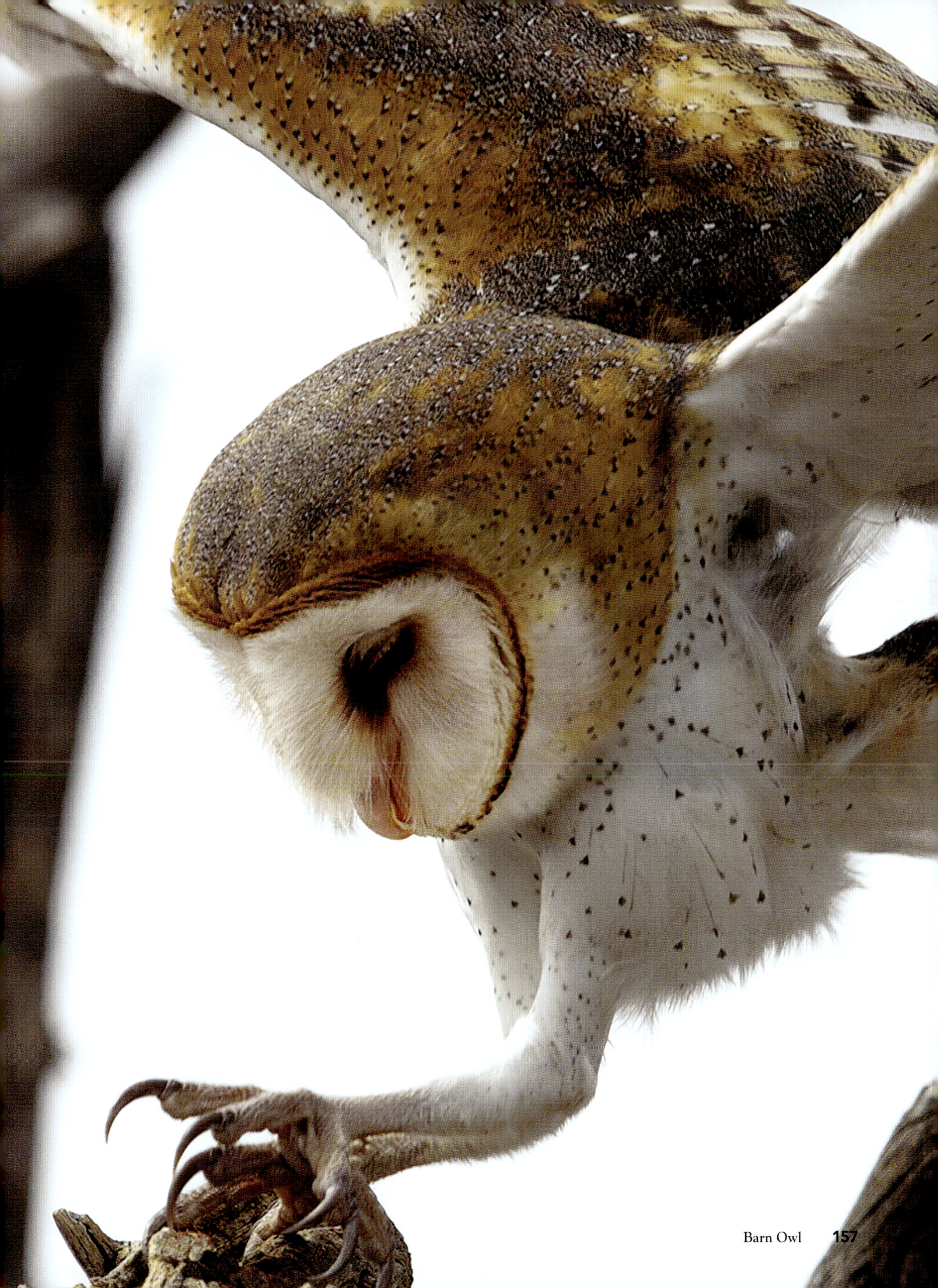

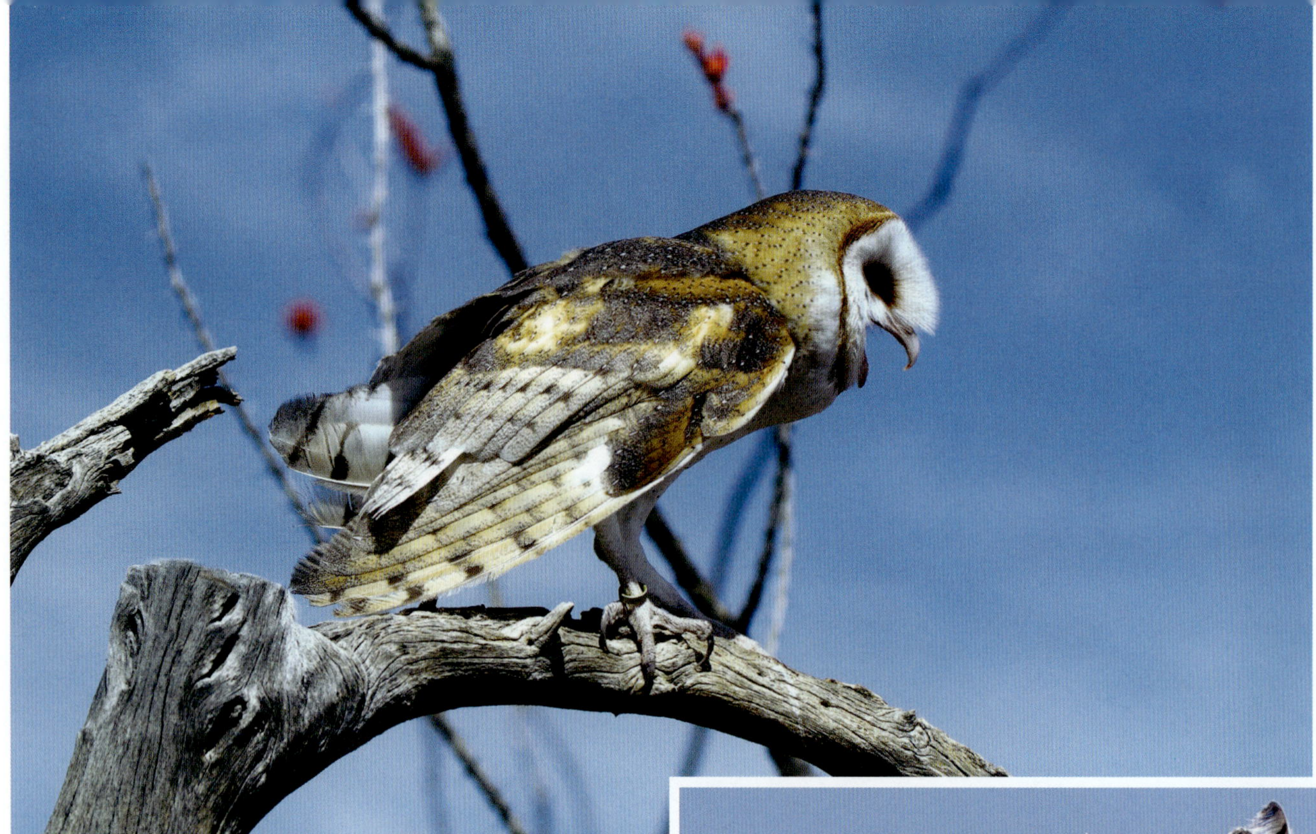

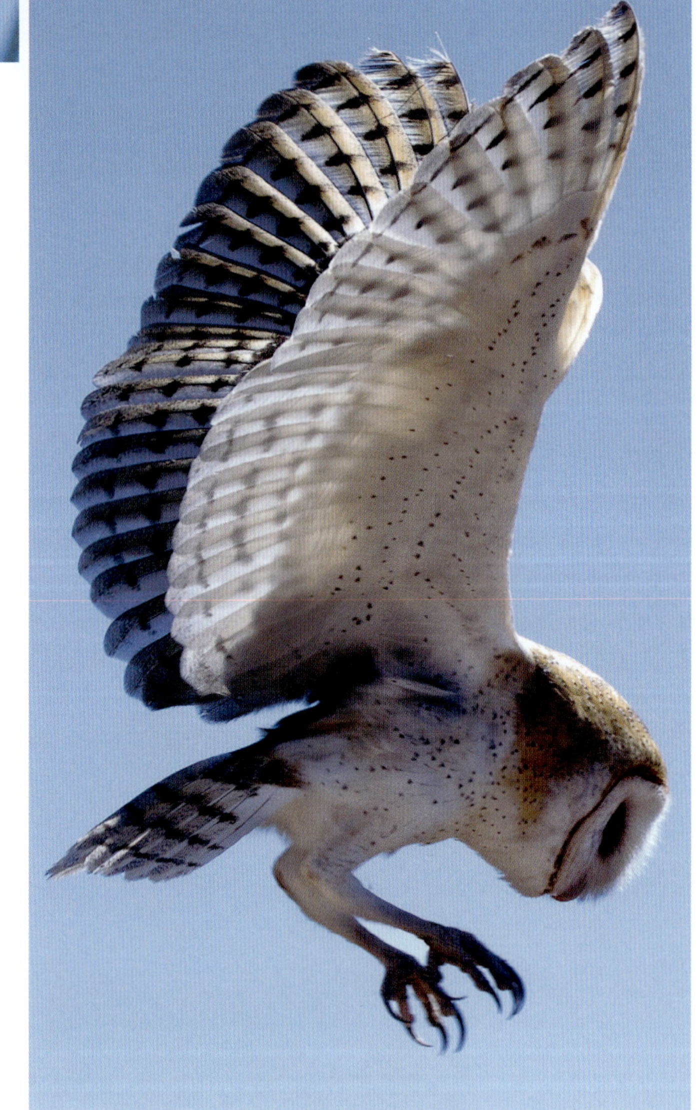

Since the barn owl is largely nocturnal, the sight of one flying during the day is something of a rarity. Strong leg muscles can flex the powerful talons—bad news for potential meals. **OPPOSITE:** Detail of an immature barn owl's wing reveals the subtle coloring that makes this such a striking bird.

with food while she sits on the nest. Each time she regurgitates a new pellet, she adds it to the nest or its surroundings.

Eggs hatch at different times. The first eggs laid are the first to hatch, so it is possible that the oldest chick will be fully fledged and ready to leave the nest while the youngest bird is still covered in fuzzy white downy feathers. Unlike some raptors, whose older nestlings will harass and even eat the younger ones, barn owls are amazingly docile and cooperative. Older chicks may even feed their younger brothers and sisters excess bits of food. The sibling bond lasts past their first flight, and young birds will often roost together in the nest for up to two months after fledging, even as the parents move to outdoor roosts.

Eventually the young birds lose their fuzzy downy coats and replace them with adult plumage. The subtle colorations of an adult barn owl make it one of the truly beautiful birds of the world and a challenging subject for the artist. The backs of adult birds show fawn-colored tan with gray from the top of the head and include a series of fine vermiculations that add subtle changes to the feather patterns. The abdomen, chest, and underwings of the barn owl are a soft pearlescent white, which gives the bird one of its numerous common names, the white owl. Males are usually lighter-colored and smaller than the females.

Barn owls are studies in balance and composition. Sharp, strong toes at the ends of bare pink legs ensure a firm and steady grip on whatever perch they are using. Oddly enough, the barn owl looks knock-kneed because its visible leg joints bend inward, giving it an unstable, unwieldy look. The knock-kneed look is normal for this bird and it does not decrease their strength or abilities. Their legs contain strong muscles that can flex the talons at the end of its equally strong toes into a fatal grip on any other small creature unlucky enough to cross the owl's path. Like other owls, this bird can rotate its head to view its complete surroundings. Considering its inward-bending leg joints, its normal owl ability to rotate and lift its head in large arcs, and its lithe, strong body, it is easy to see why this owl can contort itself into fantastic positions and provide a serious challenge for any carver.

The young birds leave the nest area as soon as they are ready for independence. There is no definitive pattern to their dispersal. They fly in any direction that pleases them and will continue traveling until they find a suitable territory to call their own, one with plenty of prey and little competition. Dispersal often coincides with migration, which is still a bit of a mystery with this bird, in part because they are highly nocturnal (they sleep heavily during the day, almost in a state of torpor). Although migrants are occasionally observed in typical migrant traps (areas where migratory birds are funneled into a narrow area based on land formations) and there are early records of large numbers of barn owls being shot in migration hunts, there is little current evidence of migratory behavior. Whether or not some populations migrate regularly while others stay put is still unknown.

All owls are secretive by nature and barn owls are no exception. Nevertheless, the ghostly white owl-size apparition that occasionally appears over farm fields and prairie lands provides a thrill to anyone lucky enough to see it, and it is a reminder that the wilderness sometimes creeps up to our doors, and sometimes those wild things are our best friends.

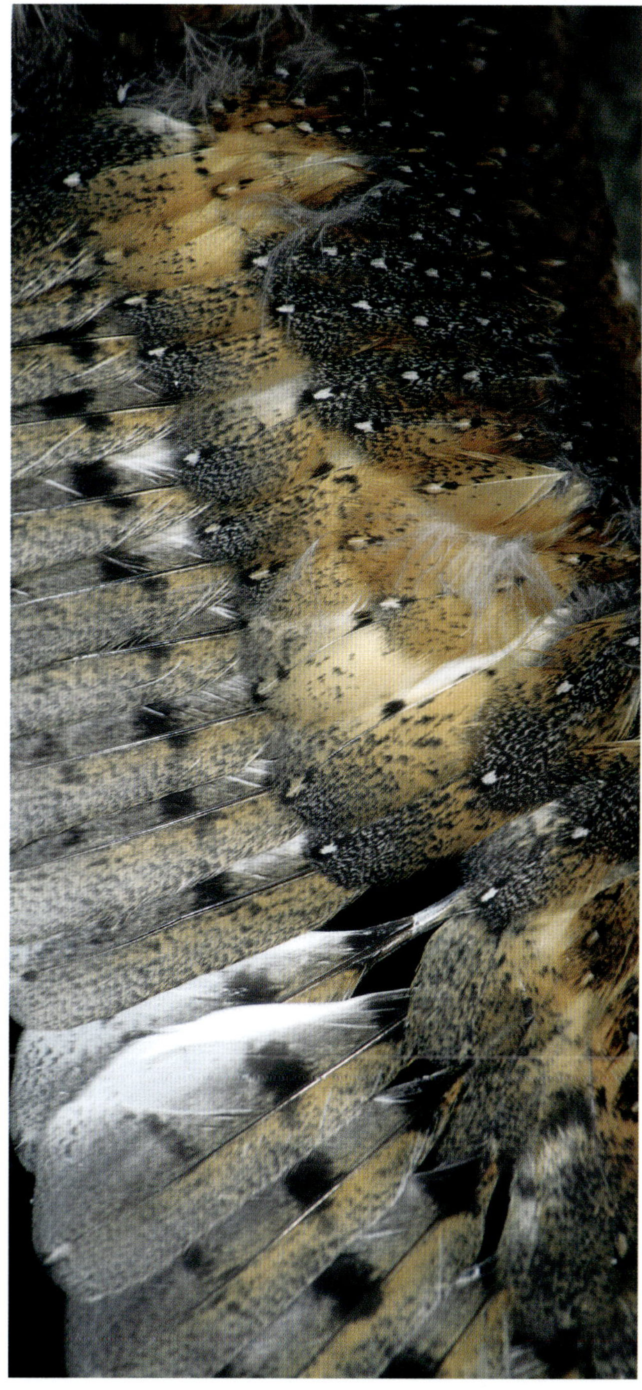

Measurements (in mm)

	Male	Female
Bill Length	21.8	
Wing Length	327.8	337
Tail Length	140	139
Tarsal Length	71/7	
Longest Toe	33	

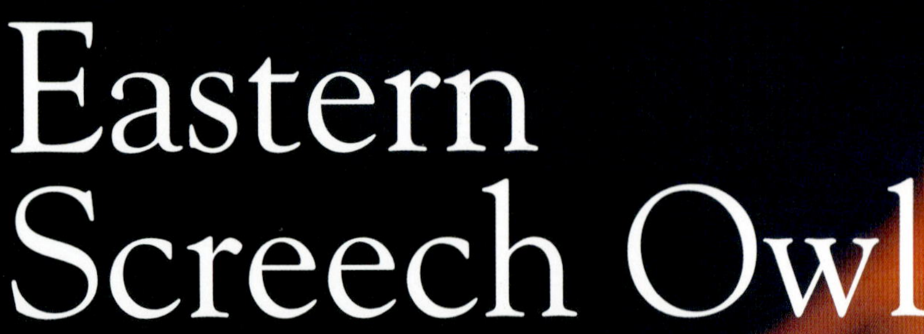

Eastern Screech Owl

(Megascops asio)

BY DR. FRANCES HAMERSTROM

For this screech owl, swooping through the twilight hours as night approaches, the day is probably just beginning. This little owl is a creature of the night, and its big yellow eyes are well adapted to seeing in the dark.

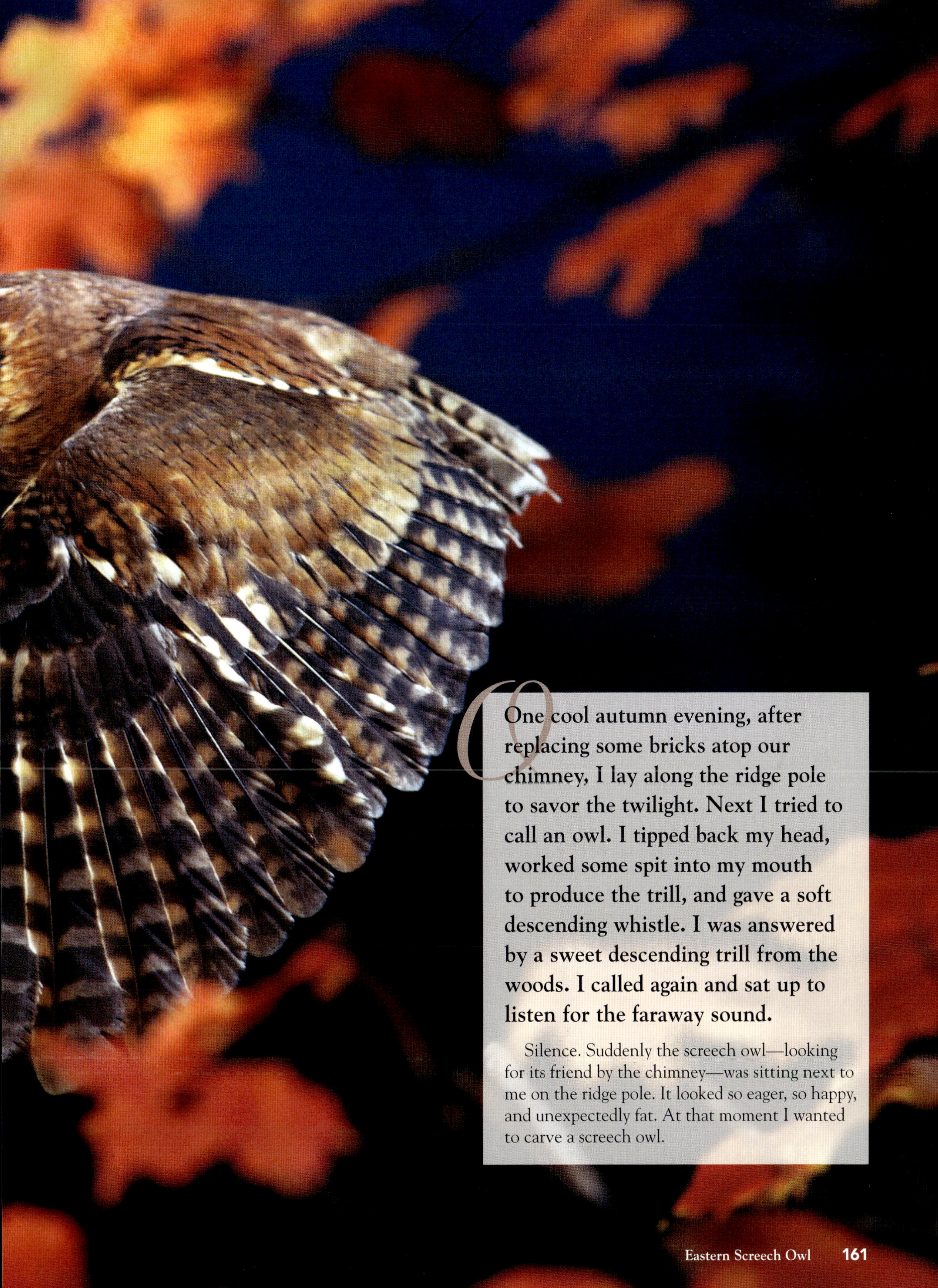

One cool autumn evening, after replacing some bricks atop our chimney, I lay along the ridge pole to savor the twilight. Next I tried to call an owl. I tipped back my head, worked some spit into my mouth to produce the trill, and gave a soft descending whistle. I was answered by a sweet descending trill from the woods. I called again and sat up to listen for the faraway sound.

Silence. Suddenly the screech owl—looking for its friend by the chimney—was sitting next to me on the ridge pole. It looked so eager, so happy, and unexpectedly fat. At that moment I wanted to carve a screech owl.

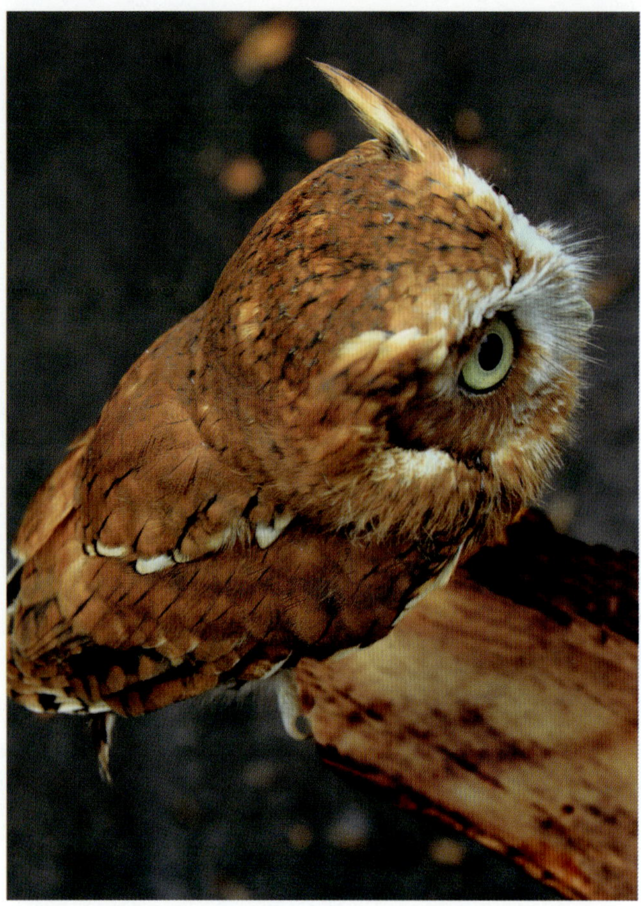

LEFT: This view from above provides a somewhat rare perspective on the screech owl. **OPPOSITE:** They may look cute, but this red-phase bird shows that screech owls are tough and tenacious hunters. No doubt the white-footed mouse would agree.

Screech owls are widely distributed. You could carve a bird to sit upon anything from the spiny tip of a cactus to a branch of northern spruce. The screech owl has nine species: two, the Eastern and the Western, occur in the United States, and seven species live in Mexico, Central America, or the Caribbean. Our eastern screech owl, *Megascops asio*, has 13 subspecies, so all in all, the screech owls have quite a variety of both Latin and common names. I find this good because some of these populations are rarer than others, and every rare bird needs a name so we can do something to save it.

From the standpoint of the artist, I find the differences between these species and subspecies miniscule compared to the enormous differences in pose and mood that any one individual owl can project at a moment's notice; the happy owl versus the scared owl, the drowsy owl versus the wide awake, the alert owl versus the inattentive.

Screech owls are seven to nine inches long. Such measurements are taken from the top of the head to the tip of the tail with the specimen laying on its back. Live owls are almost like contortionists and their movements, masked by feathers, keep shifting their apparent dimensions.

There are two color phases of the screech owl, red and gray, and in Wisconsin I have also seen an intermediate brownish individual. The red owls and the gray owls caused a lot of confusion once upon a time. It was first thought that they belonged to different species, and later, that the red birds were the young of the gray birds. The red owls and the gray owls belong to the same species just as much as brown-eyed and blue-eyed people do. The geographic distribution of the red owls and gray owls has not been well documented. A.W. Schorger picked up 235 car-killed screech owls on 639 trips between Madison, Wisconsin, and Freeport, Illinois, a distance of 70 miles. The gray phase predominated (61.3 percent), while the red phase owls were less common (38.7 percent).

Gray screech owls often mate with red ones. It is said that the offspring may be all red, all gray, or of both phases, but that a gray phase pair apparently produces only gray young. As to the number of young, there are usually four or five. Eggs are not laid every day; every other day is more usual, often resulting in a pronounced disparity in size of owlets. The littlest one sometimes gets trampled underfoot and may get eaten by its older brothers and sisters. Young owlets strike me as more puny and peaked than attractive.

The anatomy of adult owls has a good deal to do with their charm. The eyes of owls are in front, rather like humans'. They are essentially in a fixed position, and owls cannot roll their eyes as horses and people do. Those big eyes—yellow in the screech owl—in that round, flat face (with the strong beak held downwards and almost hidden in feathers) give the adult owl an engaging, babyish look. It is a look that Walt Disney accentuated in some of his Bambi-type mammals; makers of Kewpie dolls have made money off this look; and greeting card artists frequently delight in big eyes, round faces, and small mouths.

Any attempt to make an adult screech owl cuter than life is apt to be just too sweet. The same cannot be said for their young. I cannot improve upon what Miss Althea Sherman wrote in 1911:

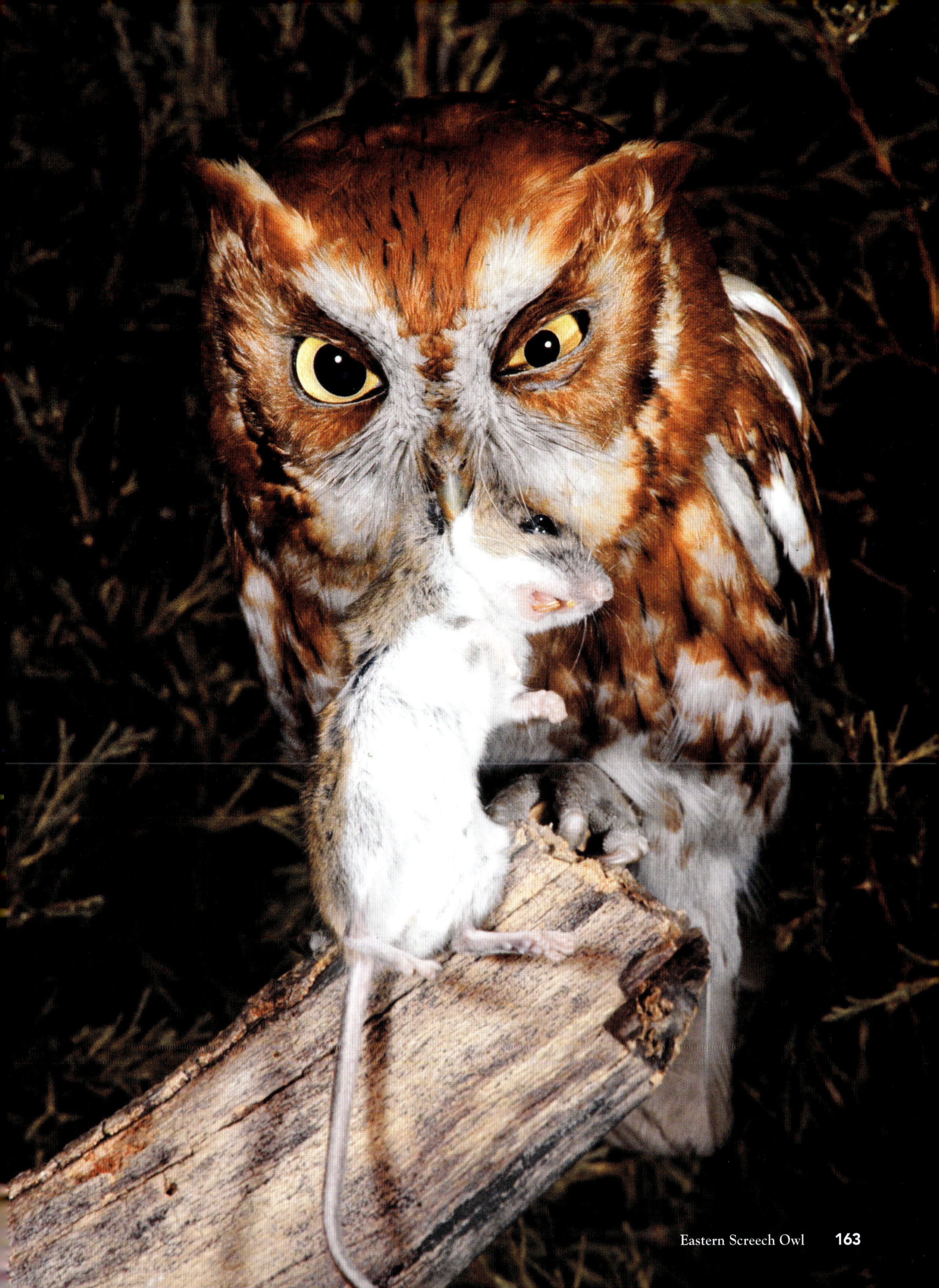

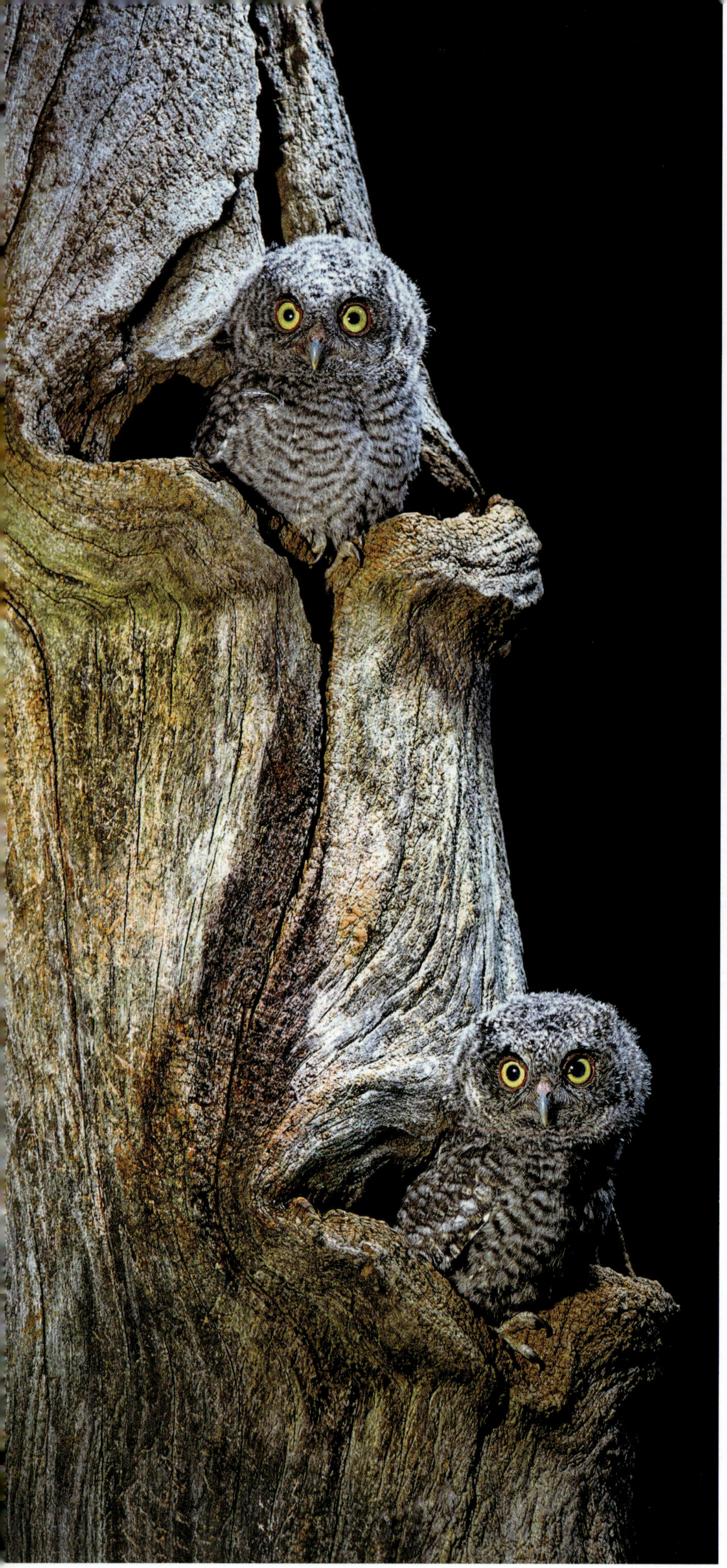

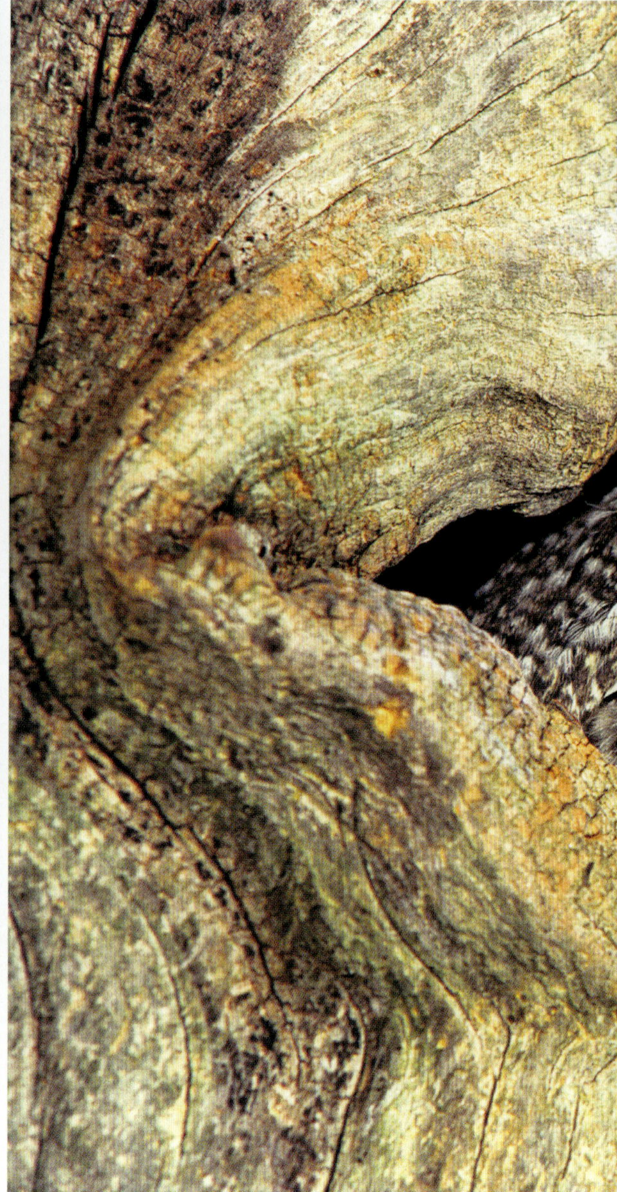

Screech owls don't build nests. They find tree hollows and make their homes there. Like their parents, the nestlings are little birds with big attitudes, and it is not uncommon for a young owl to kill a younger sibling. **FAR RIGHT:** A gray-phase screech owl blends well into its surroundings.

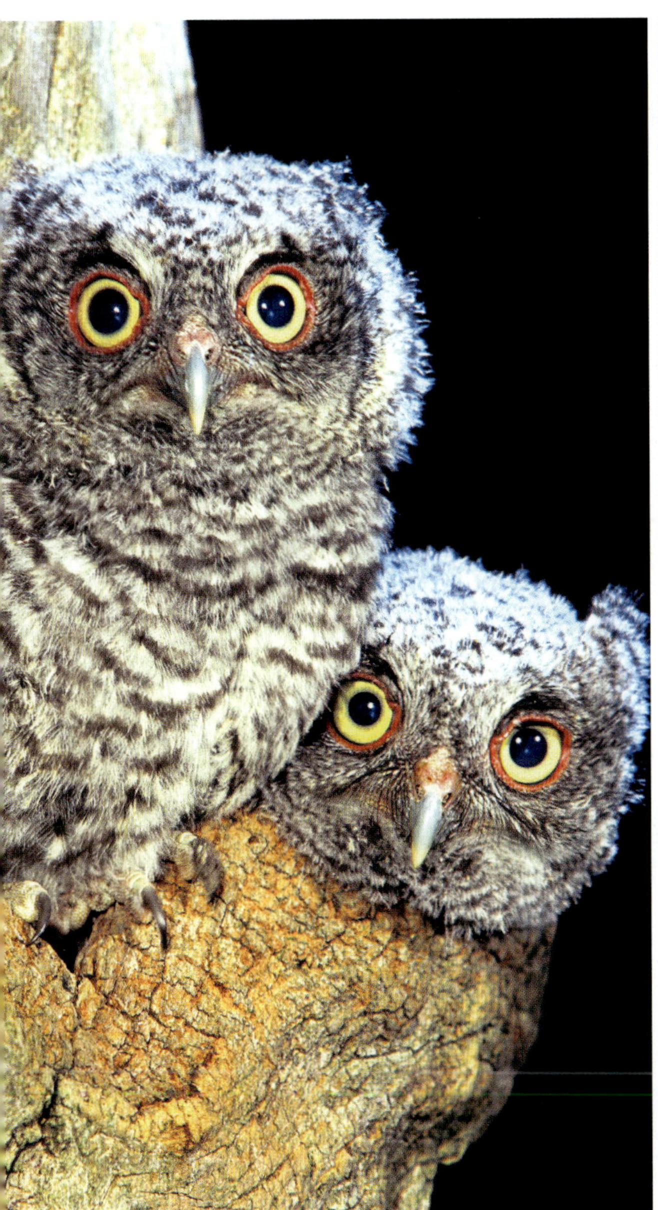

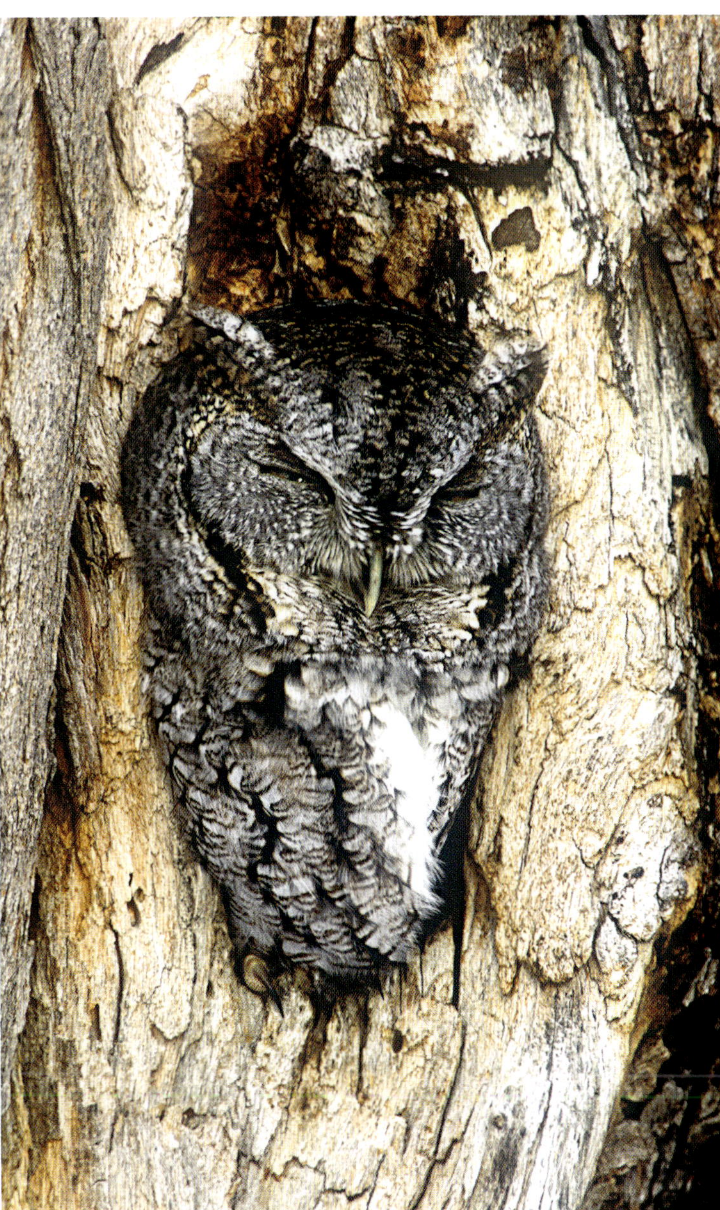

"As they tumbled about in their nest they very forcibly suggested human babies in fleecy white cloaks that are learning to creep. Held in the hand with their beaks downward and out of sight they looked like diminutive blind kittens; perhaps the most noticeable thing about them at that age was their large heads. But this winning aspect of the nestlings was of short duration. In a few days pin feathers began to show in the white down which soon turned to a dirty gray color. By the time they were twelve days old they had become almost repulsive, exceedingly filthy to handle with an appearance that was decidedly repellent. Perfect miniatures were they of a doddering, half-witted old man; the blue beak was prominent and suggested a large hooked nose, while the down below it took the shape of a full gray bread, and that on top of the head looked like the gray that covers a low, imbecile forehead; the eyes not fully open were bluish in color, and had a bleared and half-blind appearance. This loathsome semblance lasted no longer than ten days by which time the eyes were full and bright and yellow, the bird was covered with a thick gray down, and looked as if a facsimile of it could very easily be made from a bunch of gray wool devoid of any anatomy."

I believe it was Bernard Shaw who said, "It is nice that the young are so good-looking; they have so little else to recommend them." He was plainly not talking about screech owl babies.

On the other hand, when an owlet pulls at its

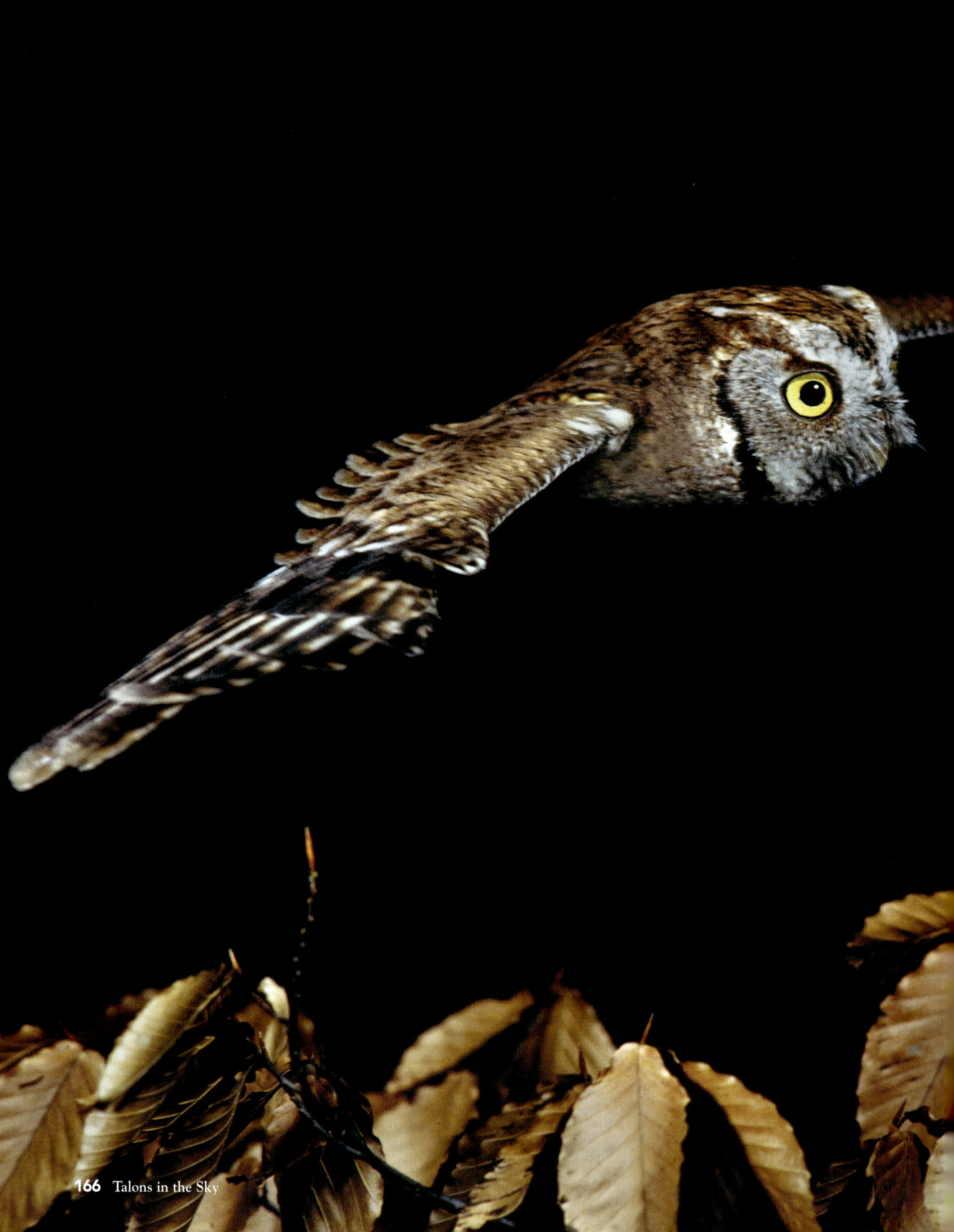

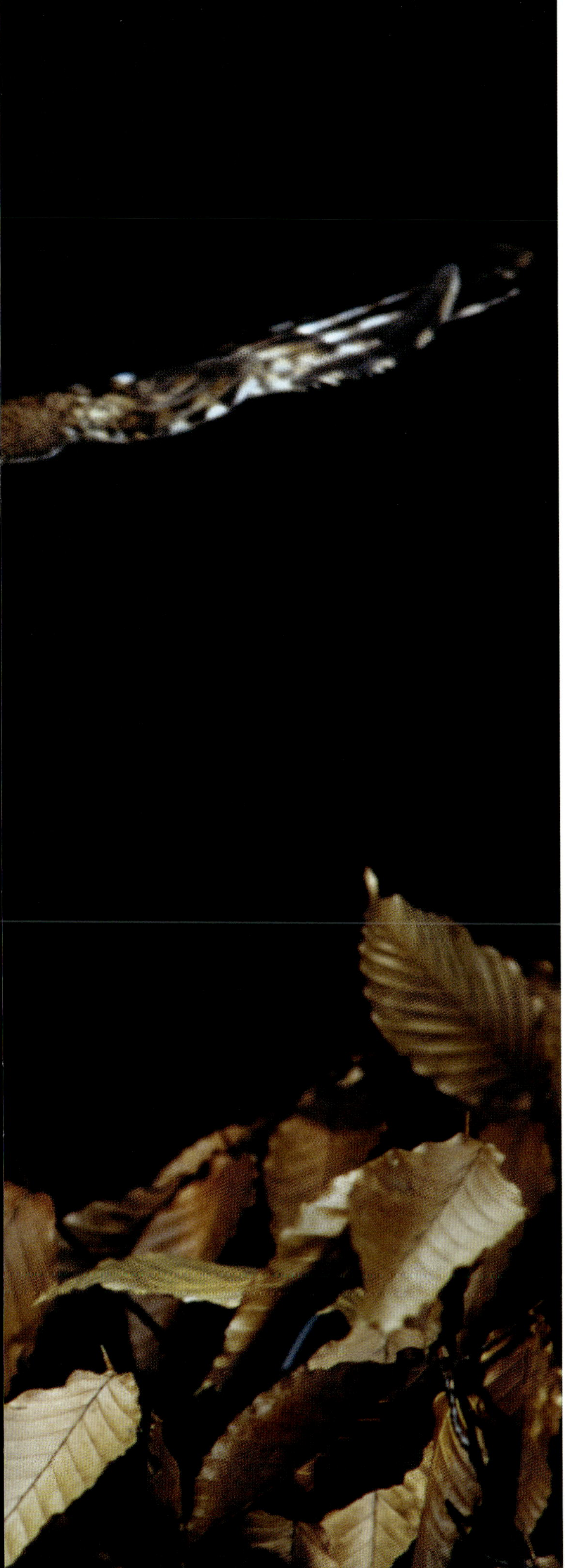

For the screech owl, the nighttime is the right time for hunting, and it has a varied menu. It will eat rodents, many kinds of birds, all sorts of insects, and any reptiles or amphibians it can catch and subdue. It won't turn up its beak at worms or fish, either.

mother's beak, perhaps begging for food, or it if pulls at my fingers with the same idea in mind, I get fond of the little creature—and I have reared numerous young owls.

Young owls eat the same animals that their parents do, except that the morsels of mouse, fish, or bird are presented to them by the adults. Insects are swallowed whole at an early age. According to Arthur Cleveland Bent, screech owls eat whatever is most easily obtained and what they eat is largely a matter of chance:

> *"The long list of items in the food of the screech owl includes the following mammals: mainly mice of various species, but also shrews, rats, moles, flying squirrels, chipmunks, and an occasional bat. . . .*
>
> *"Although birds do not form so large a proportion of the food as mammals, the list of species is a long one, as follows: domestic pigeons, quail, ruffed grouse, woodcock, sparrow hawk, screech owl, downy woodpecker, kingbird, phoebe, wood pewee, horned lark, blue jay, starling, blackbirds, Baltimore oriole, goldfinch, junco, canary, indigo bunting, English and various other sparrows, cedar waxwing, swallows, scarlet tanager, vireos, water thrush and various other warblers, house wren, chickadee, nuthatches, brown creeper, catbird, bluebird, and various thrushes.*
>
> *"In addition to mammals, birds, and insects, the screech owl has been known to eat snakes, lizards, frogs, toads, various fishes, crayfishes, snails, spiders, millipedes, and earthworms."*

Insects eaten are "beetles, cutworms, grasshoppers, locusts, crickets, cicadas, katydids, noctuid moths, caterpillars, and hellgrammites."

These little owls attack creatures much larger than they are. Hungry individuals have been known to bind to a hen, and to attack a ruffed grouse. Screech owls

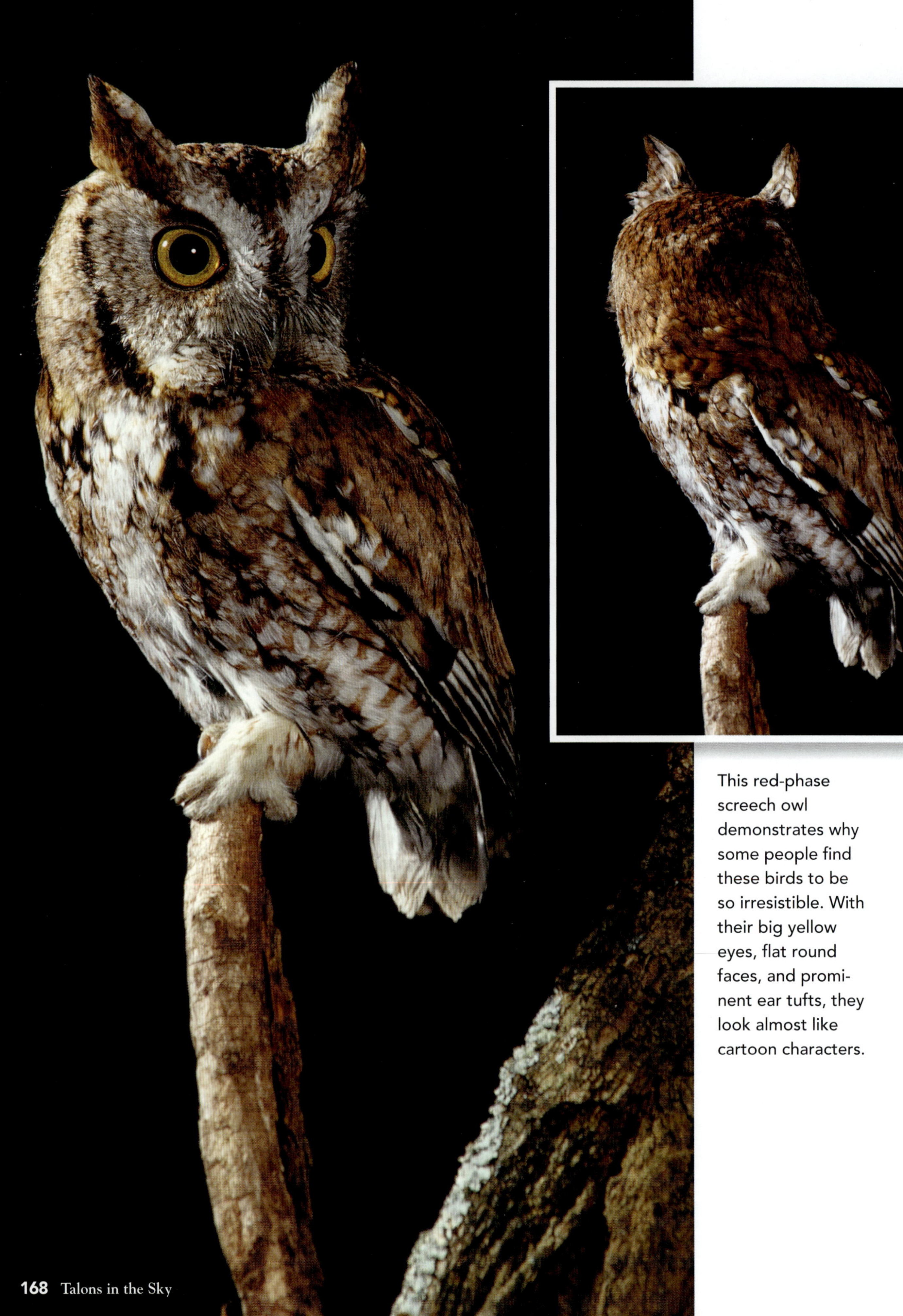

This red-phase screech owl demonstrates why some people find these birds to be so irresistible. With their big yellow eyes, flat round faces, and prominent ear tufts, they look almost like cartoon characters.

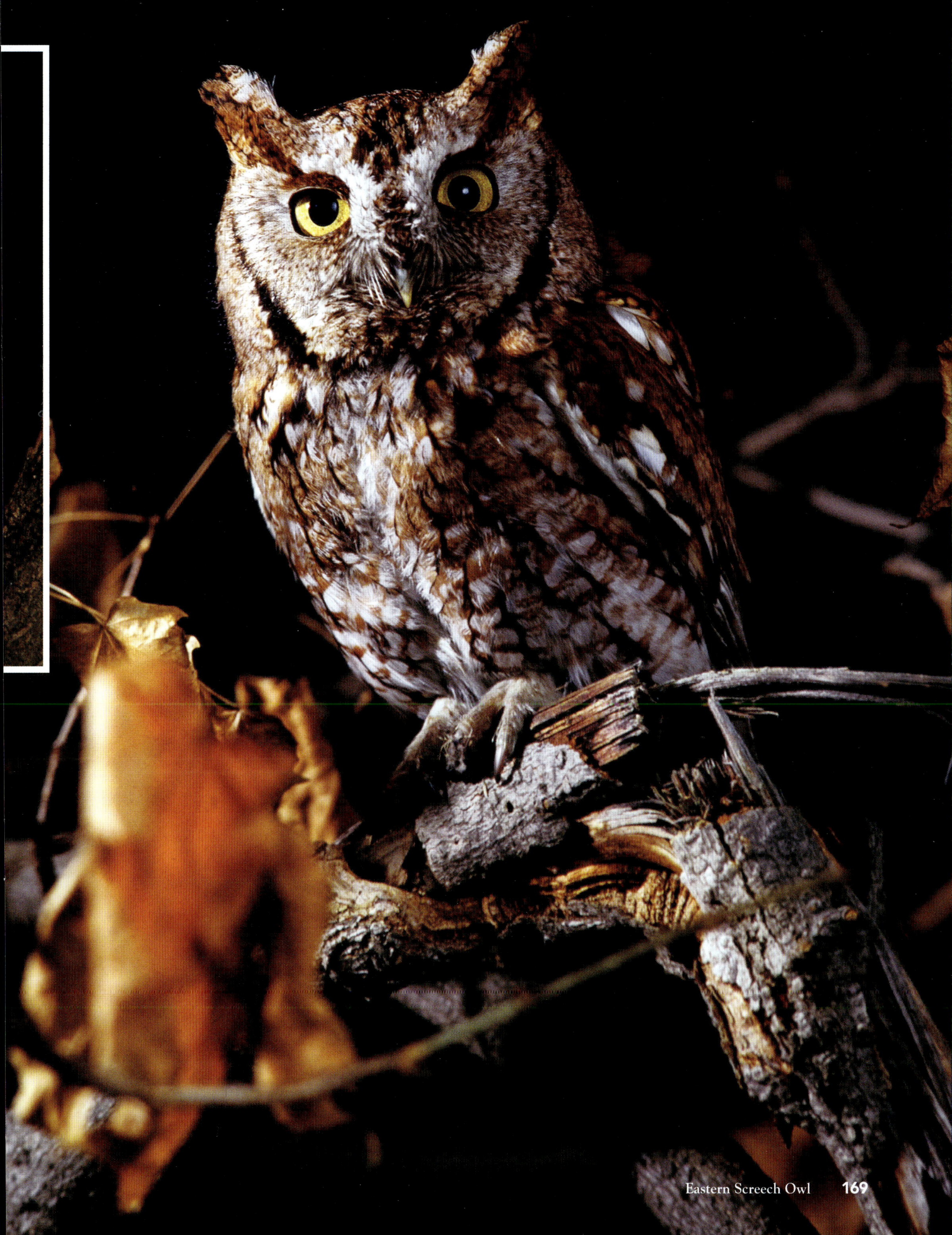

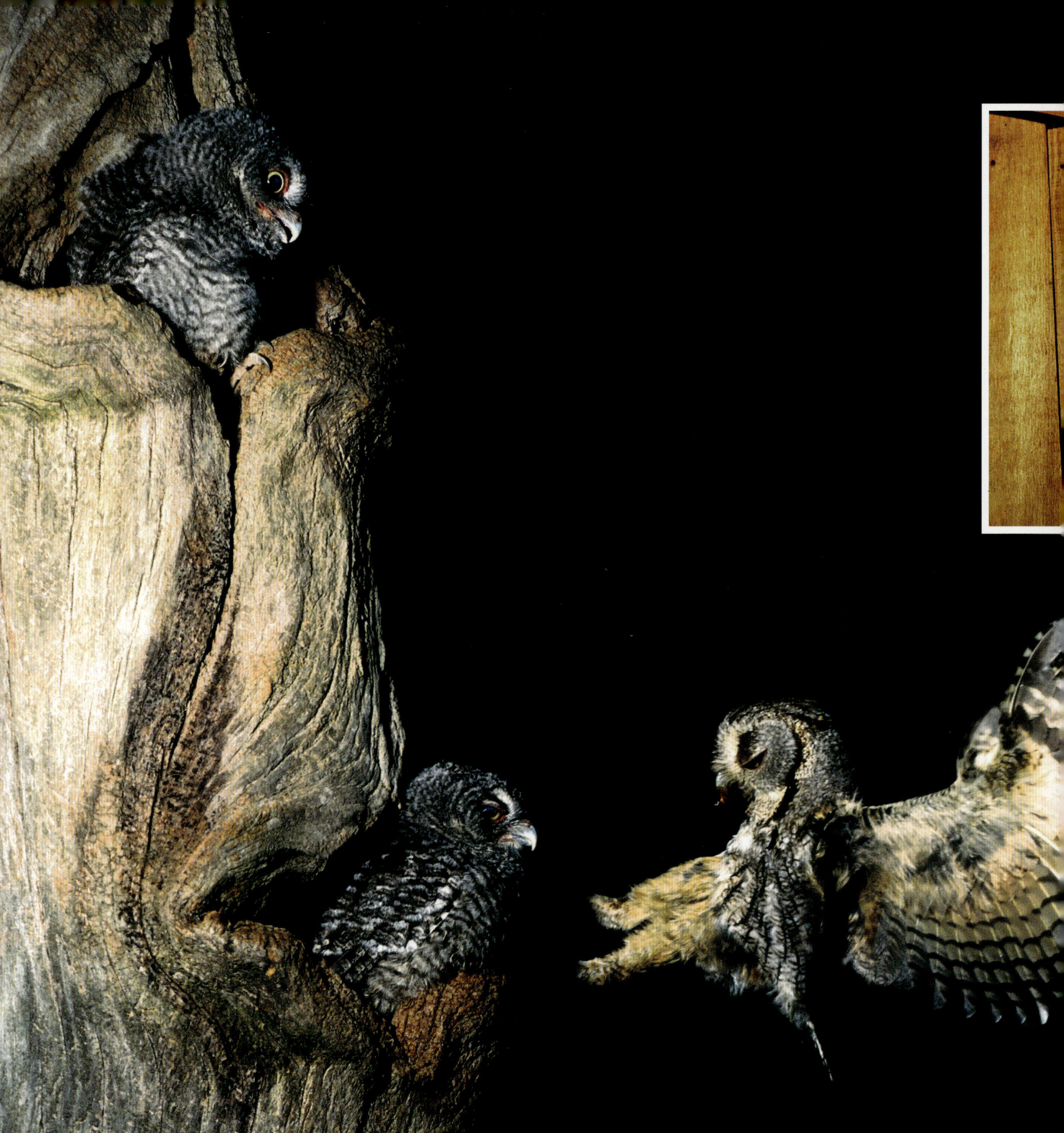

have also attacked college students that have passed too near to their nest on campus, and, furthermore, attacked the policeman who was sent out to shoot them for molesting students.

Screech owls do not build nests; they have to *find* a suitable nest site. They like to nest in old gnarled trees where hollows give them good places to hide and to lay their eggs. They like to nest in old apple orchards, in abandoned buildings around farms, and even in nooks in city buildings. They readily adapt to nesting in houses put up for them, and they are not averse to nesting in houses put up for other species, such as wood ducks.

Most screech owls live in rural areas where there tend to be many opportunities for roosting, so if I wanted to find a screech owl I would head for the city and visit cemeteries. Owls like to spend their days hid-

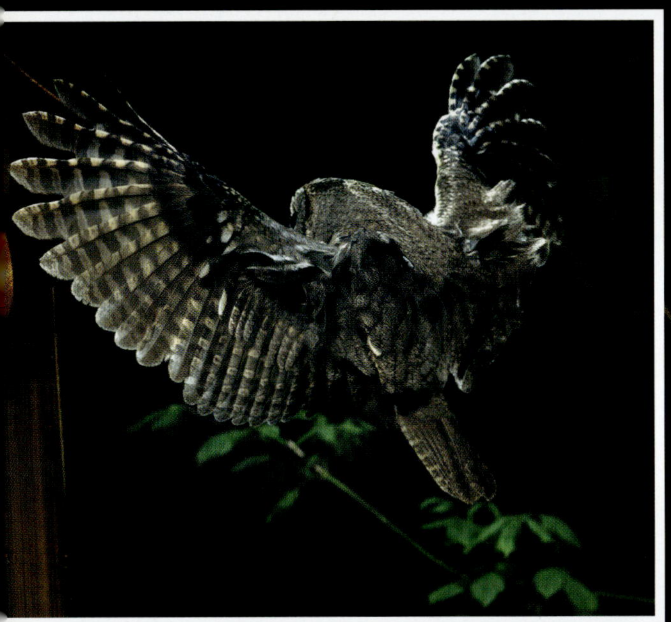

Measurements (in mm)	
Length	16–250
Wingspan	480–610
Head Width	76

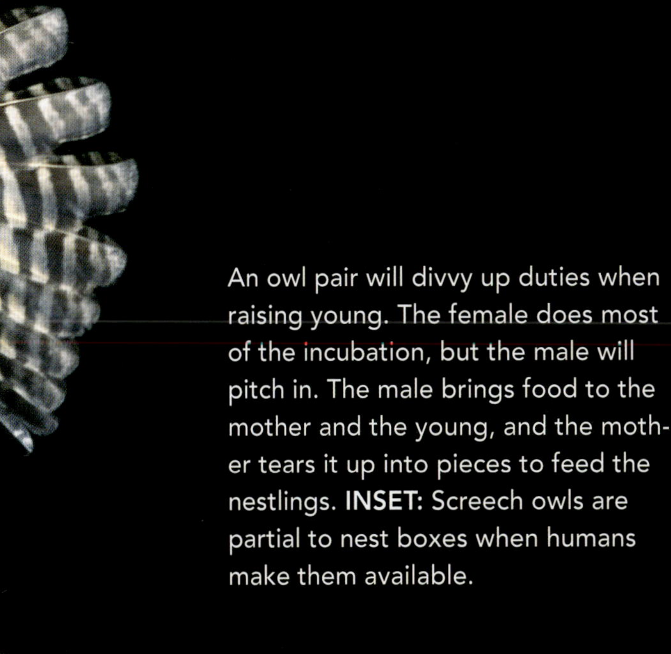

An owl pair will divvy up duties when raising young. The female does most of the incubation, but the male will pitch in. The male brings food to the mother and the young, and the mother tears it up into pieces to feed the nestlings. **INSET:** Screech owls are partial to nest boxes when humans make them available.

den by the somber, dark foliage of graveyard conifers. To find owls, I set forth in daytime and look for pellets and whitewash on the ground. If I peer upwards and find a small owl with ear tufts rather far apart, like a kitten's ears, it is a screech owl. If the owl is slightly larger and its ear tufts are close together, it is a long-eared owl.

The pellets, which I have mentioned, are the result of the owls' eclectic method of eating. Prey is swallowed whole; indigestible matter is regurgitated—actually coughed up—some hours after the meal in the form of rather large pellets consisting of fur, feathers, bones, chitin, and scales. Beneath a screech owl's roost, I have found not only pellets and prey remains but, if the roost had been used a long time, an enchanted garden of bones: the tiny jaws of shrews with their red-tipped teeth; the carrot-colored incisors of meadow mice; the curvaceous solid bones of small mammals, and the relatively straight, hollow bones of little birds. The long bones of frogs feel like fish bones, but have smoothly rounded projections at their ends. And if the owls have been catching crayfish, the ground is scattered with brick-red fragments of what appear to be the remains of a glorious feast of miniature broiled lobsters.

During the mating season, the sweet, descending whistle of the screech owl turns up at dusk, and may be heard well into the night. I have never heard the strange sounds described by Thomas Roberts in *Birds of Minnesota*. After the young have left the nest, Roberts wrote, "The old birds show much concern, flying about immediately over one's head, uttering a short hoo-hoo-hoo and uncanny mysterious sounds like the hissing of cats and the snarling of puppies."

Owls are more courageous during the darker hours than they are in daytime. Screech owls can see well during the day. They don't seem to mind bright light. Dr. Arthur Allen put floodlights up near a nest and watched the birds go about their business in a seemingly normal manner.

Recordings of the screech owl's call have coaxed owls forth from their lairs with astounding success. Excessive use of such recordings could well disrupt the owl's breeding cycle, but limited use of recordings enables one to pinpoint territories without much fuss. I have lived with owls, of one sort or another, most of my life and, for screech owls, prefer to lie on my back and just give them their sweet, falling whistle. The reward of seeing a wild, natural owl looking for the source of the whistle is unforgettable.

Elf Owl

(Micrathene whitneyi)

BY RICK BURKMAN

Everyone is familiar with owls, those quiet denizens of the night with piercing eyes, needle-sharp talons, and a reputation for wisdom. They are mysterious predators, popular in folklore and art. One of the strangest members of this family is the elf owl, which makes its home in the harsh southwestern desert lands of North America. As its name suggests, the elf owl is the world's smallest owl. No larger than a house sparrow, this desert dynamo makes its home in the forests of saguaro cacti, mesquite bosques, and tangles of palo verde shrubs. It comes in a little package, but these tiny birds nonetheless are fully equipped with all the traditional owl parts—a sharp beak, deadly feet, and large, yellow eyes placed in an oversized head.

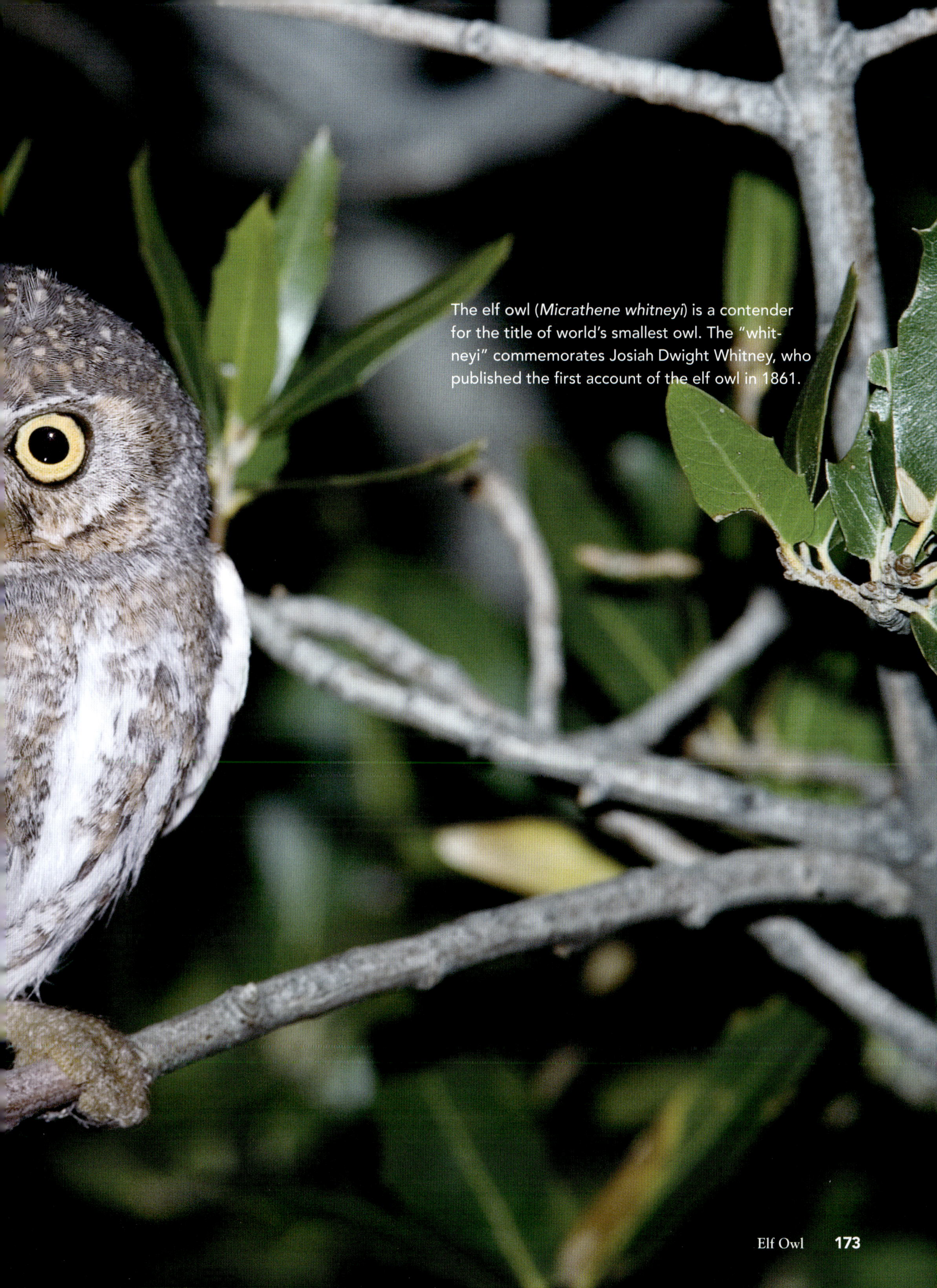

The elf owl (*Micrathene whitneyi*) is a contender for the title of world's smallest owl. The "whitneyi" commemorates Josiah Dwight Whitney, who published the first account of the elf owl in 1861.

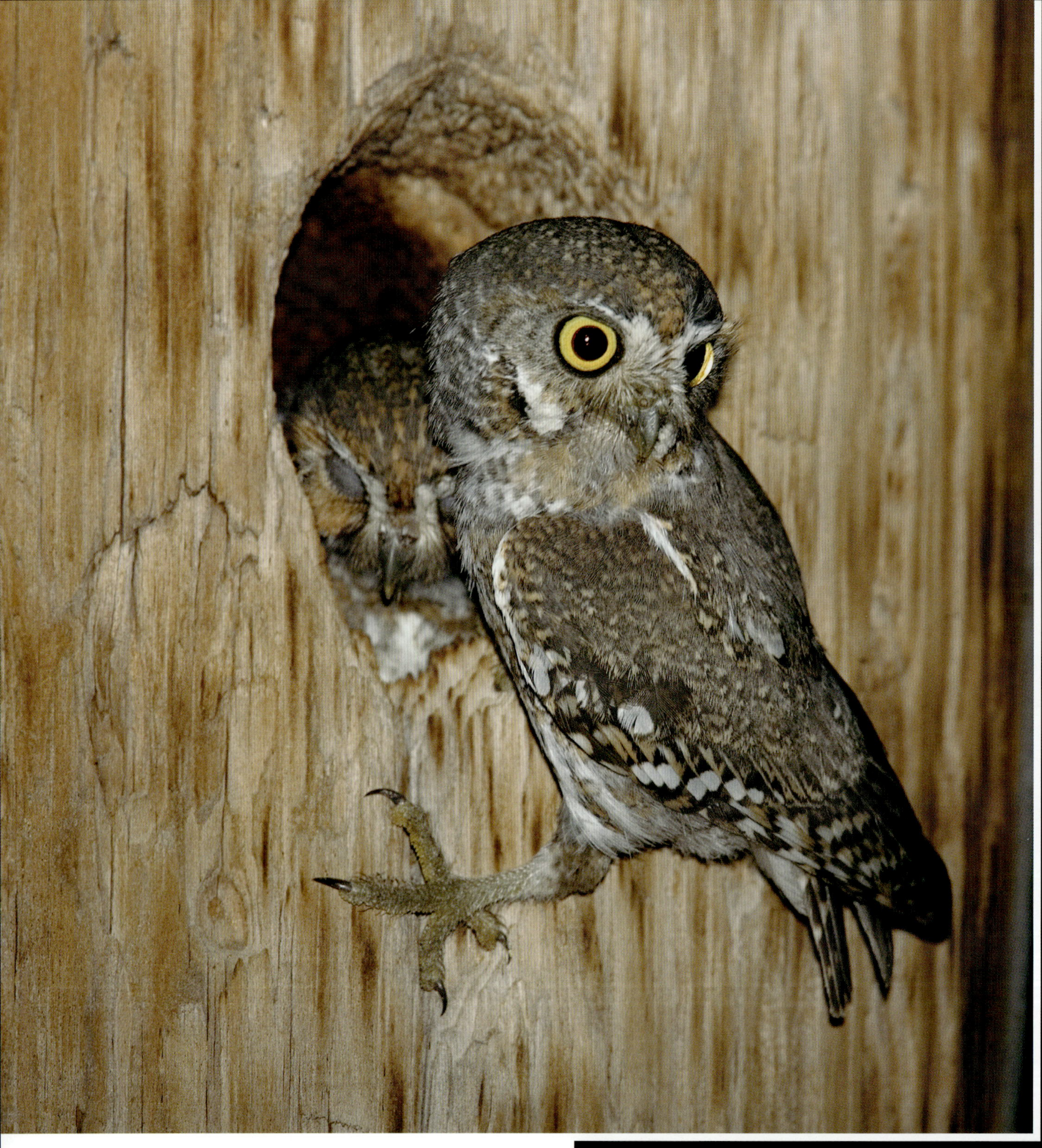

The elf owl hunts prey appropriate to its size. It does not feed on rabbits, rats, and bats like many of its larger cousins do. Instead, it sits and waits for beetles, centipedes, moths, and other night-prowling arthropods. When desert flowers are in bloom, the owl hunts large sphinx moths. It sits in flower bushes or on trees, posts, and cacti, and waits for an unsuspecting moth to bury its head in a flower in search of nectar. Then the owl launches from its perch,

Like most owls, the elf owl is a creature of the night. The extreme temperatures of its desert habitat provide one good reason for avoiding the daylight hours. At night, the male owls break the desert silence with a characteristic "yip" call.

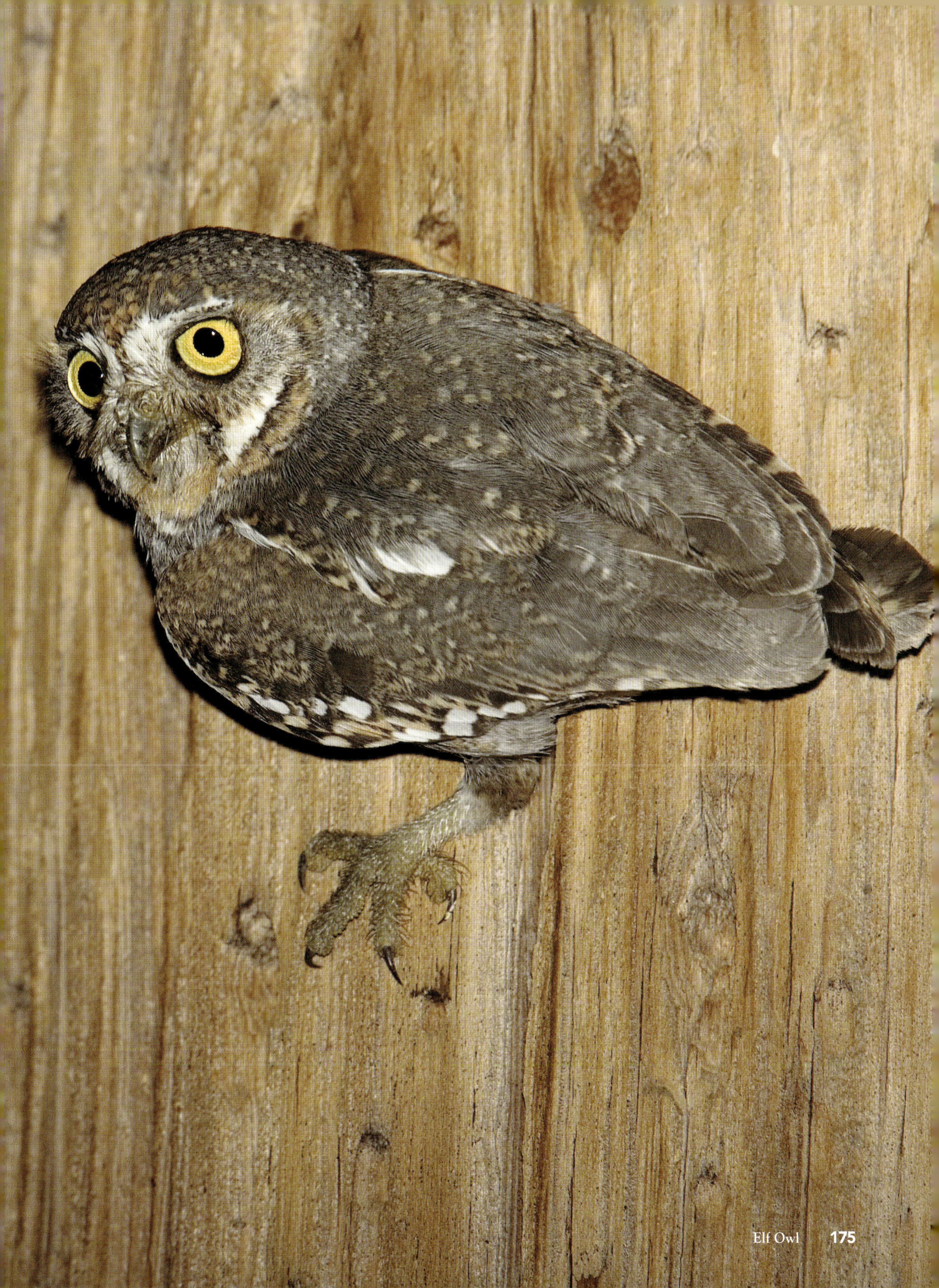

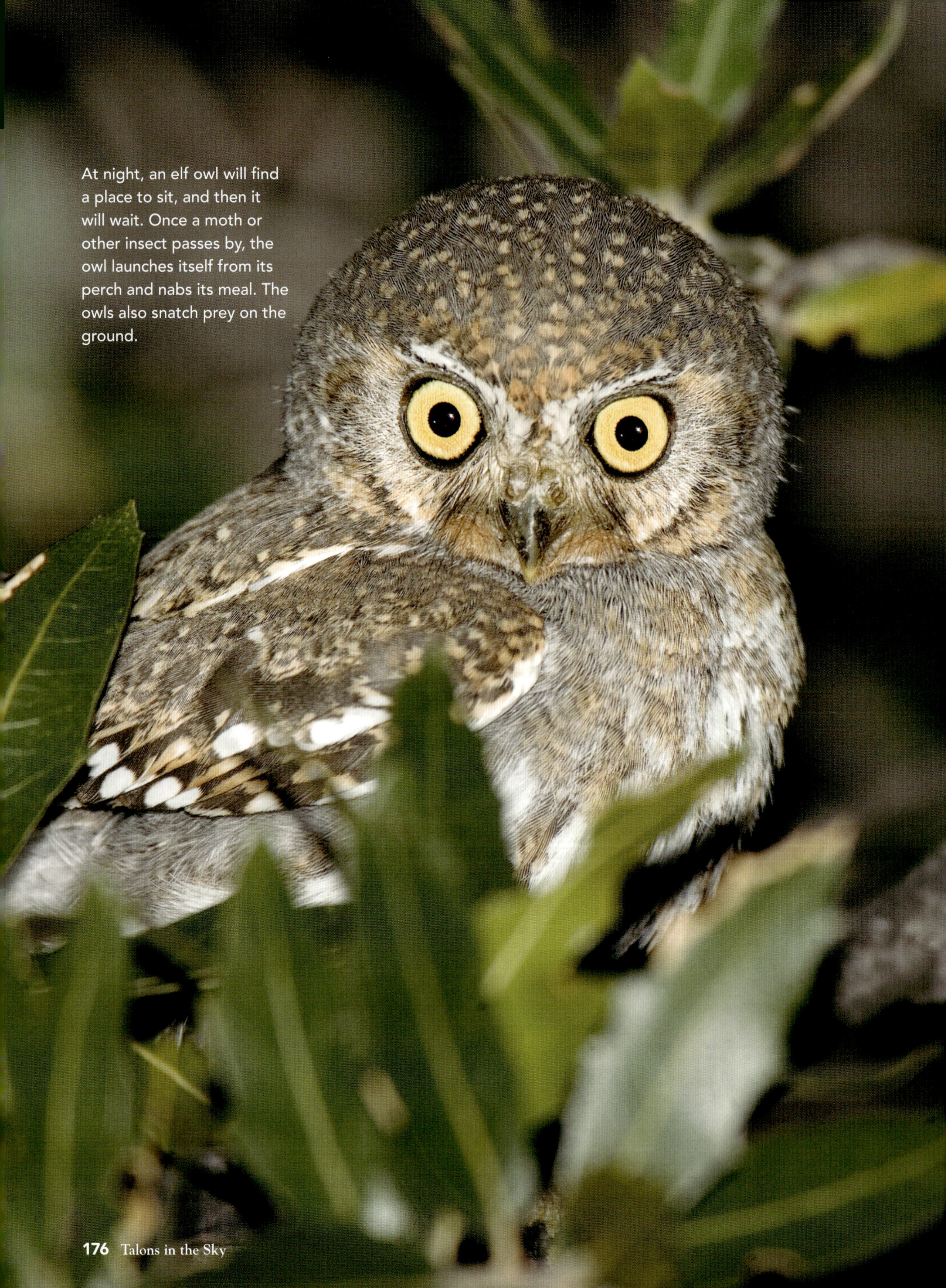

At night, an elf owl will find a place to sit, and then it will wait. Once a moth or other insect passes by, the owl launches itself from its perch and nabs its meal. The owls also snatch prey on the ground.

flying in a straight line toward its unsuspecting prey. It captures large insects with its sharp talons and carries them to a nearby perch where it can deliver a death bite to the neck. The owl then pulls off the insect's wings and eats its meal. It may capture smaller insects with its bill and swallow them whole.

When the flowering plants lose their blooms for the season, the elf owl switches its sights to ground-dwelling insects that come out at night. It grabs iridescent scarab beetles and eats them on the spot, and will also readily consume desert centipedes, some of them as long as the owl itself. The little owl will even eat poisonous scorpions, but only after nipping off the dangerous tail with a sharp bite. By running or hopping, an owl may chase particularly juicy prey that skitters along the ground, but usually it will scoop up even the ground dwellers in a quick nighttime attack. Beetles, scorpions, spiders, small lizards, and other tiny creatures must walk the nighttime sands carefully, lest they become the prey of this tiny owl.

As springtime approaches, the elf owl's thoughts turn to family matters. The owls fly north from Mexico to their breeding grounds in southern Arizona and Texas. Males arrive first and scout out potential nesting cavities along river bottoms, in the montane forests of the mountains, or among the towering saguaro cacti that populate the landscape. The owl takes advantage of work done by birds such as the gila woodpecker, gilded flicker, and ladder-backed woodpecker, which excavate cavities in saguaro cacti. The holes they leave behind ooze sap that dries to a hard finish and results in tubes or gourds inside the cactus that make rigid cavities ideal for elf owl nests.

When the females arrive on the breeding grounds, the males take them on tours of possible homes. Most trees and cacti in a nesting area contain multiple holes, so the owls may nest in an apartment community where flycatchers, sparrows, or woodpeckers use other cavities. These other birds are too large for the owl to prey upon, and they forage during the day while the owl roosts, so there appears to be no interspecies conflict in these desert condos.

The elf owl hunts prey appropriate to its size. It does not feed on rabbits, rats, and bats as many of its larger cousins do. Instead, it sits and waits for beetles, centipedes, moths, and other night-crawling arthropods.

Once the owls choose a nest cavity, they begin site preparation. Unlike other nesting birds, elf owls prefer to nest on bare floors. They don't bring sticks and bits of fur or feathers to the cavity as nest lining, and are instead more likely to remove any nesting remnants left by previous occupants. After the nest cavity is bare, the female begins laying. A typical clutch consists of three glossy white eggs slightly over one inch long, with the owl laying one egg every two days until the clutch is complete. Incubation begins after the second egg is laid. The mother owl is a devoted parent that warms her eggs day and night with only brief respites to stretch her wings at dawn and again at dusk. Although he does not incubate eggs, the male is equally devoted to his mate. He hunts throughout the night and provides food to the brooding hen every few minutes as she maintains her vigil.

After three weeks of incubation, the eggs crack and a prehistoric-looking, large-footed, pink-skinned, down-covered baby owl spills to the floor of the nest. The first two eggs hatch at about the same time and the third owl pops free a day later. Now the male parent gets busier and busier. For the first couple of weeks after hatching, he provides the brooding female and the young with their food. The female moves carefully in the nest with toes curled inward so that she does not accidentally impale one of her young.

Nestlings face other dangers, even in their needle-studded homes. Gopher and rat snakes can prey on the eggs or the nestlings, while ringtails may try

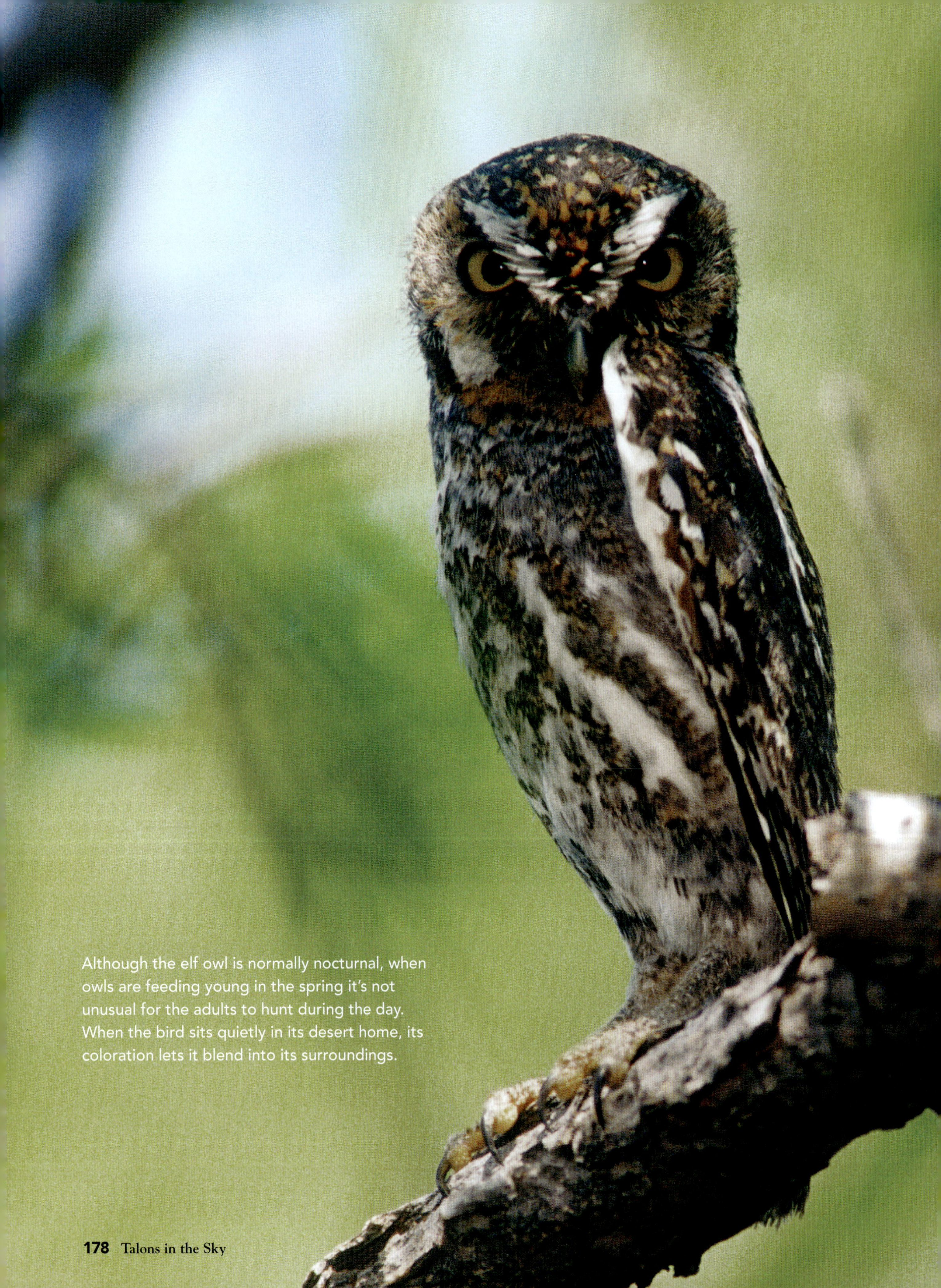

Although the elf owl is normally nocturnal, when owls are feeding young in the spring it's not unusual for the adults to hunt during the day. When the bird sits quietly in its desert home, its coloration lets it blend into its surroundings.

The smallest of all the owls may live in a harsh environment, where daytime temperatures can soar over 110 degrees Fahrenheit and nighttime temperatures can drop below freezing, but this strange little bird with the heart of a hunter and the wisdom of an owl thrives as it thrills all who are lucky enough to find it.

to scoop the owlets from within the nest cavity. Even family squabbles can prove lethal. Occasionally, older and larger siblings will kill and even eat a younger brother or sister. And, because of their small size, even the adult elf owls can become an unwilling meal for a hunting great horned owl. But elf owls are not completely at the mercy of the desert's predators. Elf owls from adjacent territories will respond to a neighbor's distress cries and attack the heads of the predators intent on an owl meal. These persistent mobbing attacks can wound and chase away the larger antagonists.

Elf owl parents may be great protectors and providers, but they will never win awards for housekeeping prowess. They remove nothing from the nest once egg-laying begins, and as a result the nest's interior quickly fills with uneaten portions of insects, lizards, and scorpions as well as feces and even dead nestlings. Luckily, after 24 days the young are ready to fledge. If they don't leave willingly, their parents will lure them out. The young birds are weak fliers but they can move about their home and their immediate surroundings and can even feed themselves by catching crickets shortly after leaving the nest. Like most youngsters, they still beg to be fed by their hard-working parents.

The young birds grow quickly, feathers continue to emerge, and eventually they begin to resemble their parents more and more. Like most owls, the head is large in proportion to the body. The facial disks are made of gray feathers tinged with cinnamon. Whitish eyebrows begin above the gray beak and arch over the large yellow eyes. The top of the head is gray-tinged with cinnamon or buff and lighter spots, and the nape has a diffuse white line. The back is grayish brown with rust or cinnamon mixes, and the belly is covered in soft, light-gray feathering with vertical streaking of cinnamon-brown and white. The wings are long and have white and cinnamon bars on the primary and secondary feathers. When the owl perches, the wings extend beyond the short tail. Grayish or yellowish legs and feet end in sharp black talons. Like all owls, the body coloration of the elf owl is a study in camouflage. When an owl sits still in shrubs, cacti, or trees, its perfect color lets this nighttime hunter blend with its surroundings.

As the young birds grow and learn to thrive on their own, the breeding and growing season comes to a close. The bugs of summer decrease in numbers and the owls migrate to their southern winter homes in the Mexican deserts.

The smallest of all the owls may live in a harsh environment, where daytime temperatures can soar over 110 degrees Fahrenheit and nighttime temperatures can drop below freezing, but this strange little bird with the heart of a hunter and the wisdom of an owl thrives as it thrills all who are lucky enough to find it.

In the wild, elf owls take advantage of holes that other birds—primarily woodpeckers—have dug into a spongy cactus or drilled into a sycamore. Though small, the elf owl can present an intimidating visage from within its prefab home.

Measurements (in mm)

	Male	Female
Total Length	133	133
Wing Chord	107	105
Tail	50	49
Culmen	8.7	8.8

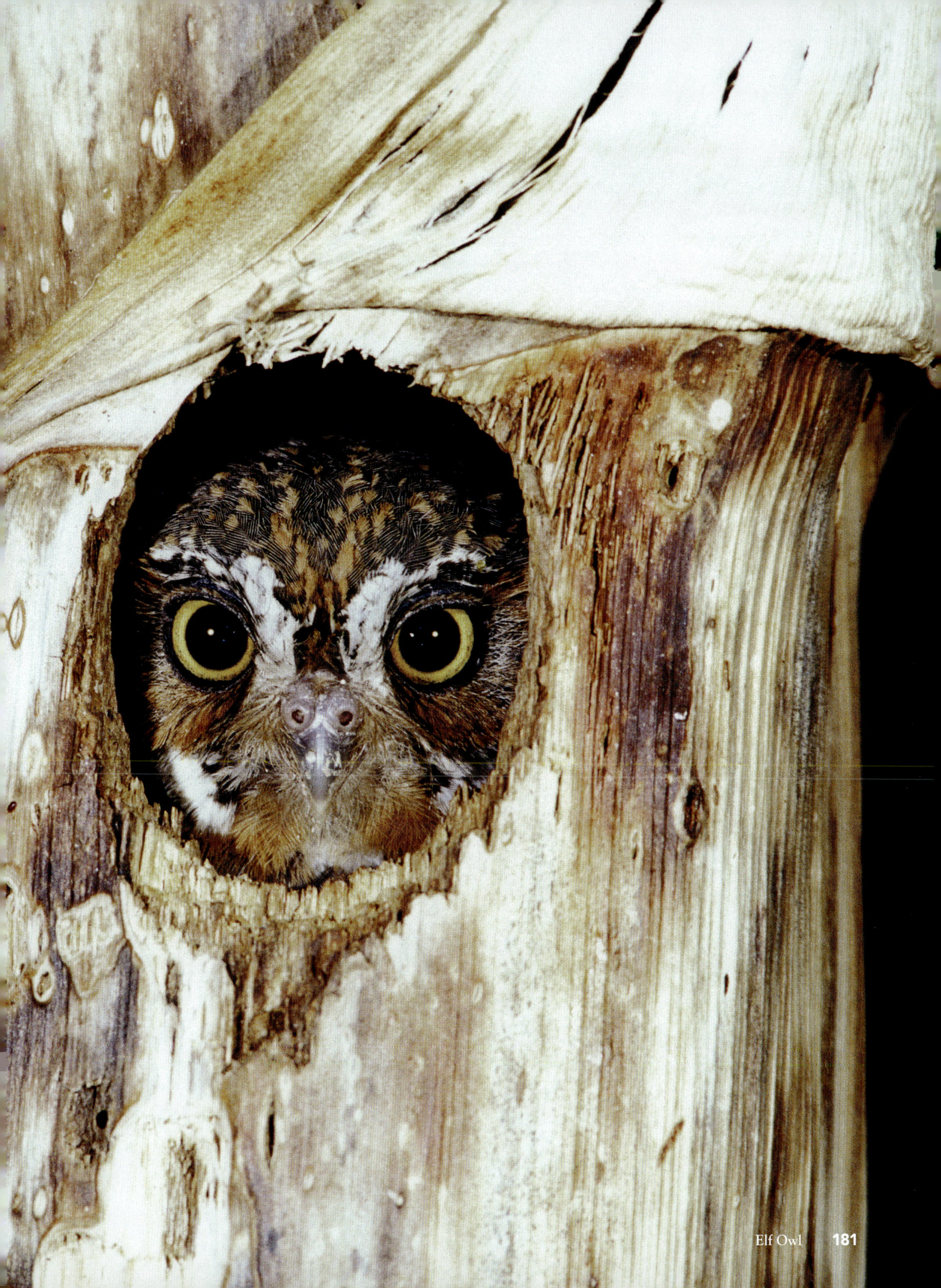

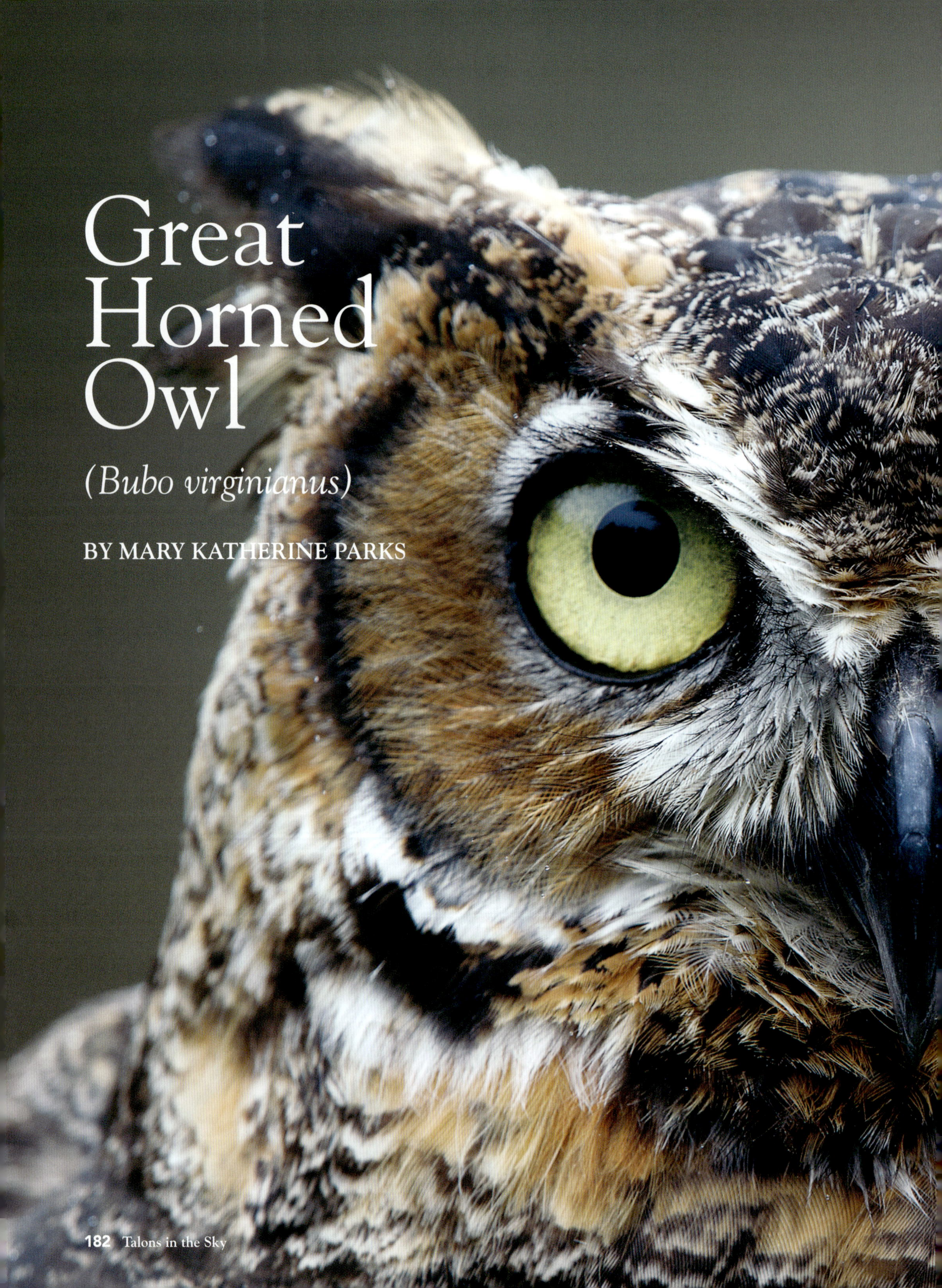

Great Horned Owl

(Bubo virginianus)

BY MARY KATHERINE PARKS

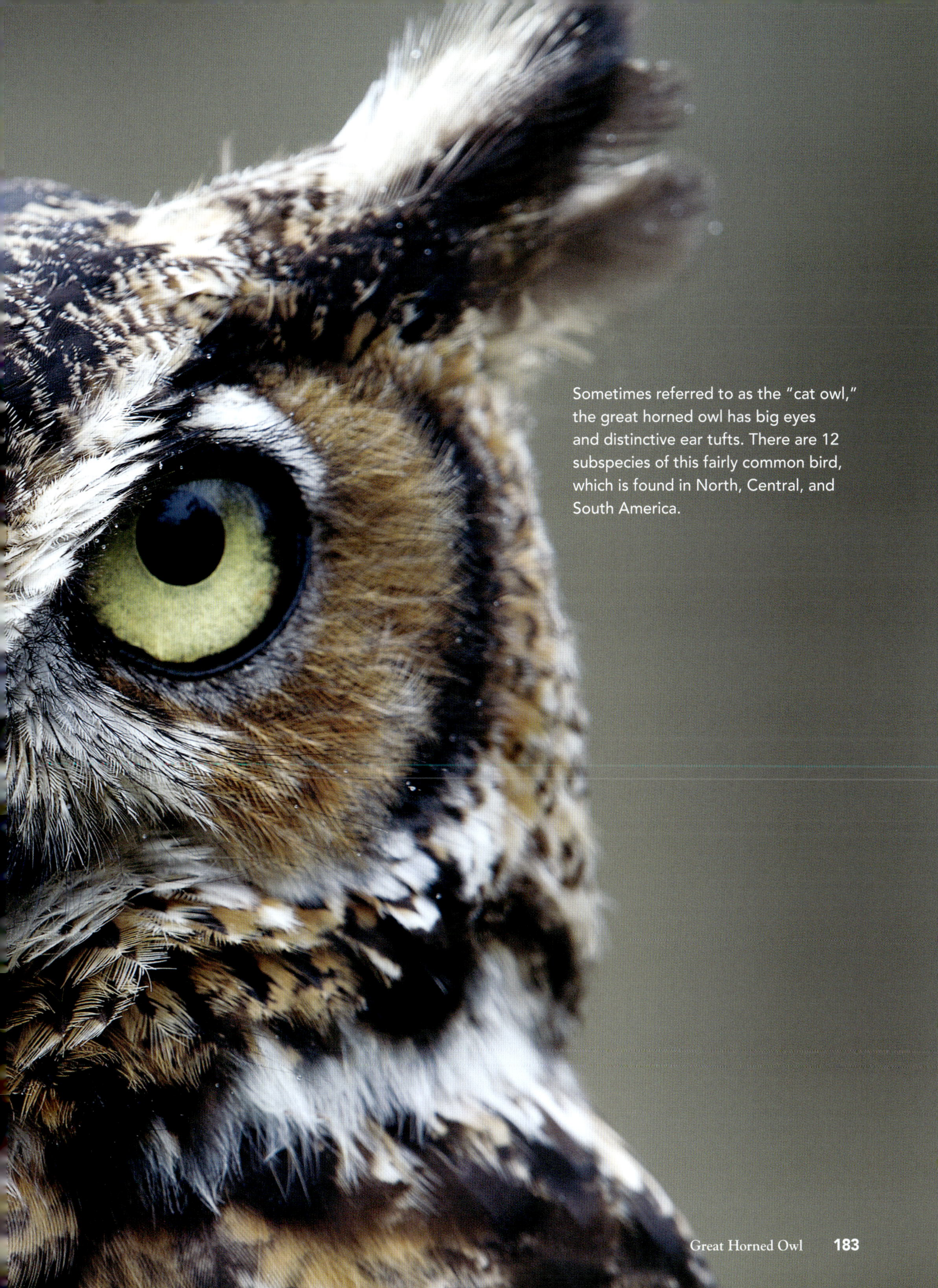

Sometimes referred to as the "cat owl," the great horned owl has big eyes and distinctive ear tufts. There are 12 subspecies of this fairly common bird, which is found in North, Central, and South America.

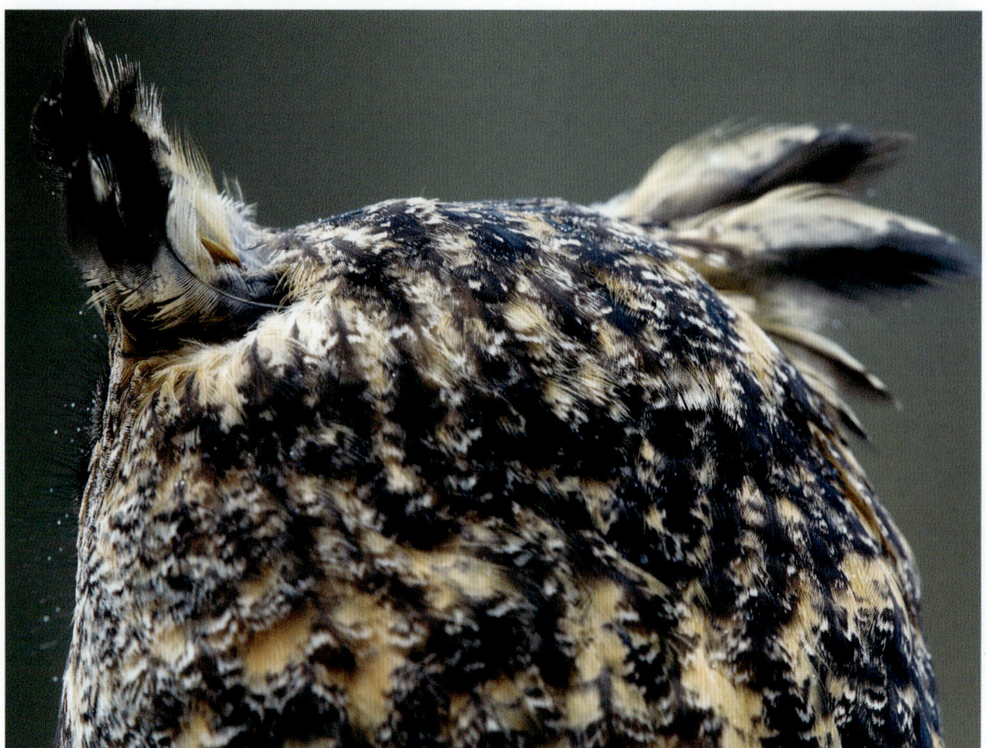

ABOVE: The owl's "horns," or tufts, may serve as short-range recognition markers, or they may help camouflage the owl as it perches. **OPPOSITE**: The great horned owl has binocular night vision, but its eyes are not very mobile. It must turn its head to follow movement, as this owl is doing.

Found in an amazing variety of habitats across North, Central, and South America, the great horned owl could truly be called "America's Owl." When adoring American grandmothers ask their grandtoddlers, "What does the owl say?" the toddlers reply, "Whooo, whooo"—proof that even kids know that when you say "owl" you mean "great horned."

The rich, deep, mellow hoot of the great horned owl is one of the best-known bird sounds, though it is by no means the bird's only vocalization. These large, powerful owls vocalize to communicate anger, to keep track of each other, to express excitement or contentment, and to strengthen pair bonding.

The call is comprised of three to eight deep, loud hoots, with the second and third hoots being short and quick. Paired owls begin hooting with increasing frequency as early as December; the female initiates the call and response. The six-note female call is uttered every 15 to 20 seconds and lasts for about three seconds. The male's call, which consists of about five notes, is more elaborate; it interrupts the female's on occasion or follows her by only a few seconds.

The owl's enemies (man being by far the most pernicious) are met with *krooo-ooo* growls or screams. During times of intense excitement, the owls' back-and-forth, rapid hooting sounds something like frantic apes in a Tarzan movie.

When defending their nests, females have been known to make short, *wha-whaart* sounds. Both parents communicate with recently fledged young through rising whistles. The young communicate their hunger with screams.

The owl's "horns," or ear tufts, and scowling brows over wide-spread eyes make it look perpetually teed off. With swept-back "hair," white "cravat," long, off-the-shoulder "cape," and light-colored "spats," the bird reminds this observer of an ill-tempered maestro.

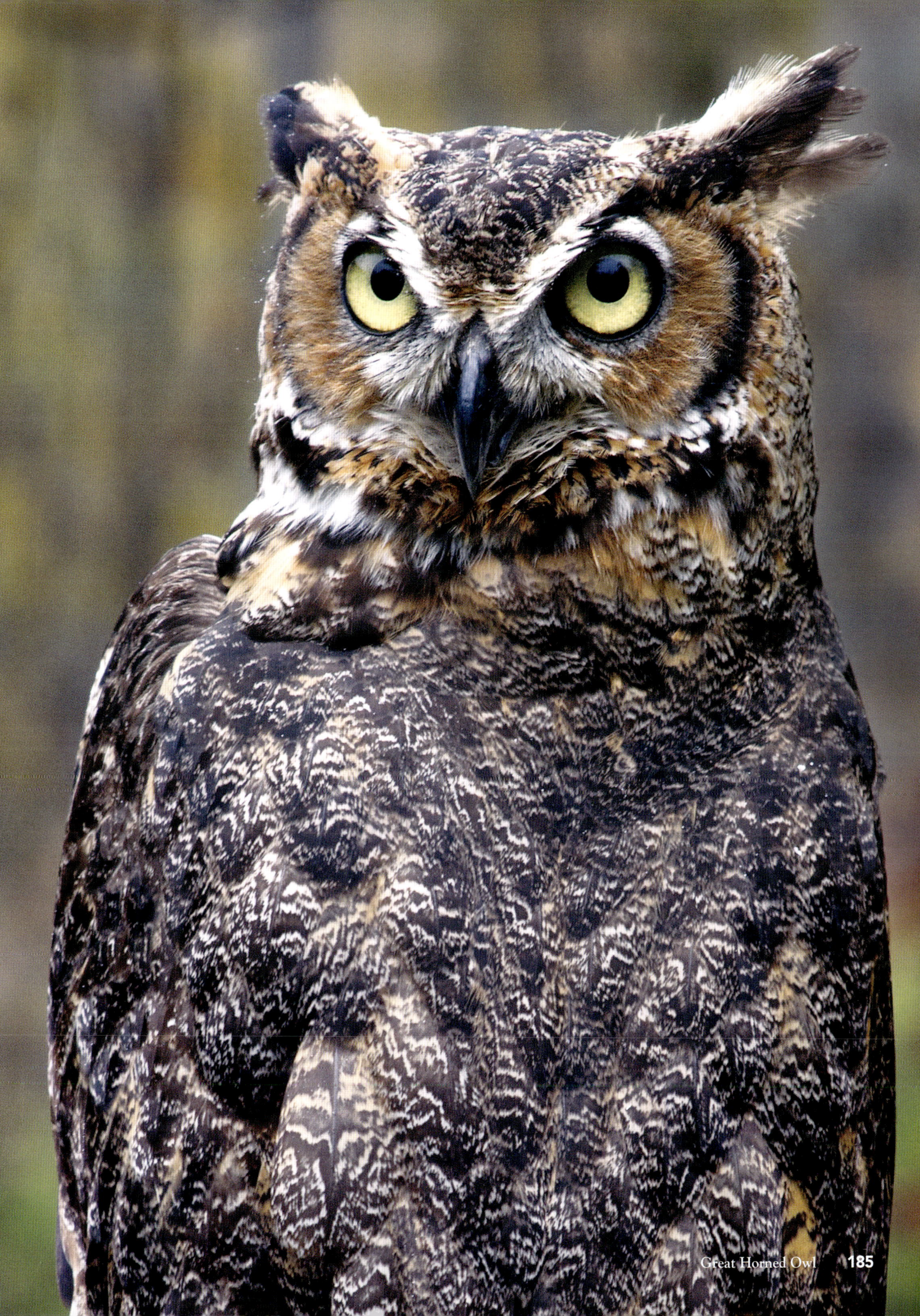

Great Horned Owl

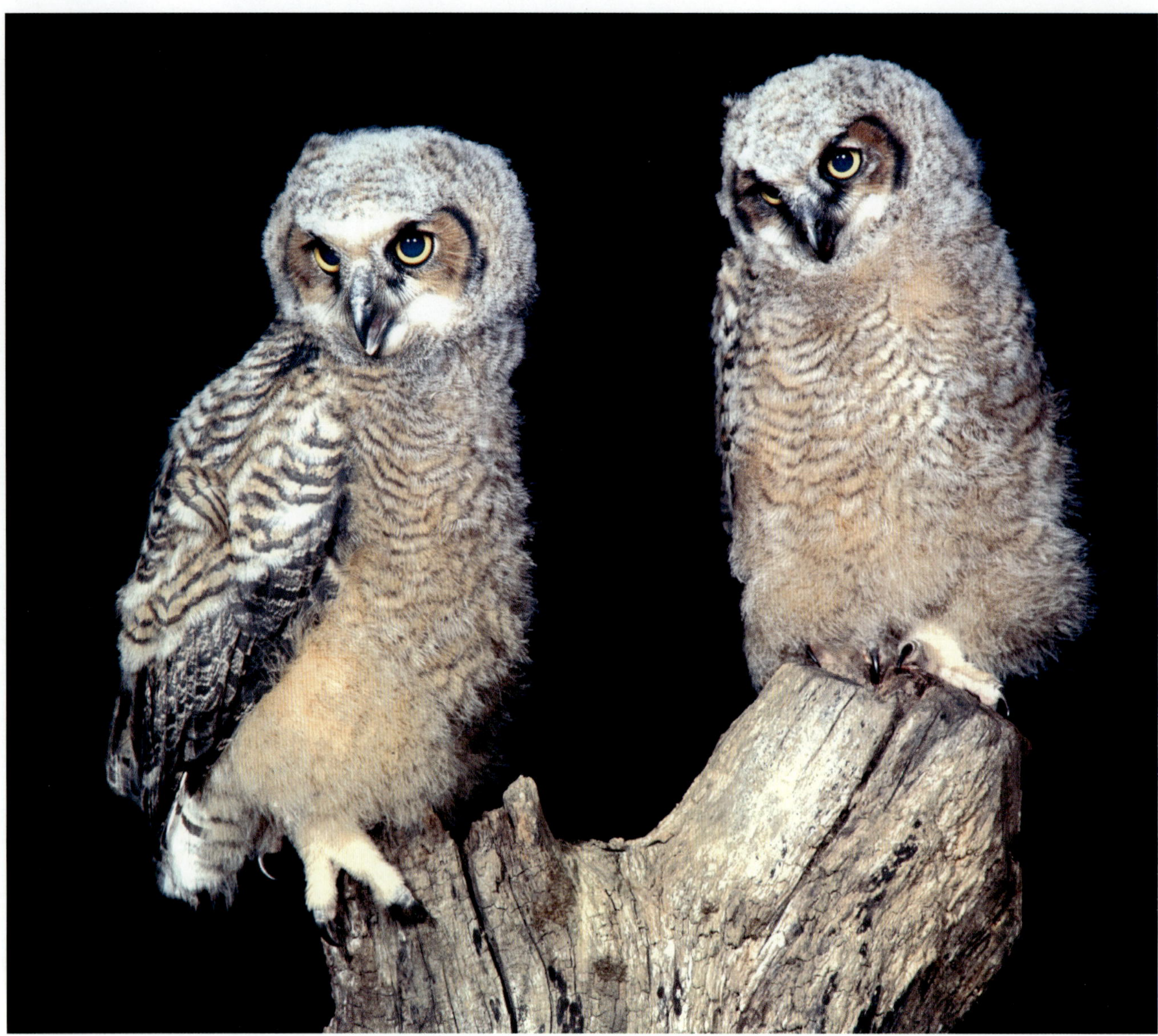

Fifty of the world's 131 owl species have tufts, which may function as short-range recognition marks. (They are certainly a definitive field mark for birders.) It is also believed that the tufts act as camouflage for the birds, which sit motionless for long periods of time on broken or splintered stumps.

Females of most owl species are larger than the males, with the greatest difference in size seen in the larger species. Some ornithologists theorize that the larger size of the great horned owl females relates to her responsibilities as sole egg incubator and primary nest defender.

The tan, orange, and black-and-white markings of the great horned owl resemble those of the calico cat—hence the nickname "cat owl." At its base, the bird is primarily tawny or ocher-colored. Its upper parts are dusky or dark brown, broken by a mottling of gray-white; the crown and hind neck are primarily dusky, forming into wide stripes that come together on the forehead. Light-colored blotches are visible on the outermost scapulars and some of the larger wing coverts. There is some mottling on the secondaries, which are crossed with a mottled, dusky color. The primary coverts are darker, with three or four sooty bands. The ear tufts have black outer webs and ocher-colored inner webs. The face is a dull tan, with a dusty white around the eyes. Dark "cheek lines" run from the chin to the ear tufts. The legs and feet of this owl are covered in light-colored feathers that protect against the cold in winter and biting insects in the warmer months. As is the case with most owls, sexes are similar.

The great horned owl's "mad, marigold eyes," as Bernd Heinrich described them, are larger than human eyes, but less mobile. Though some horizontal

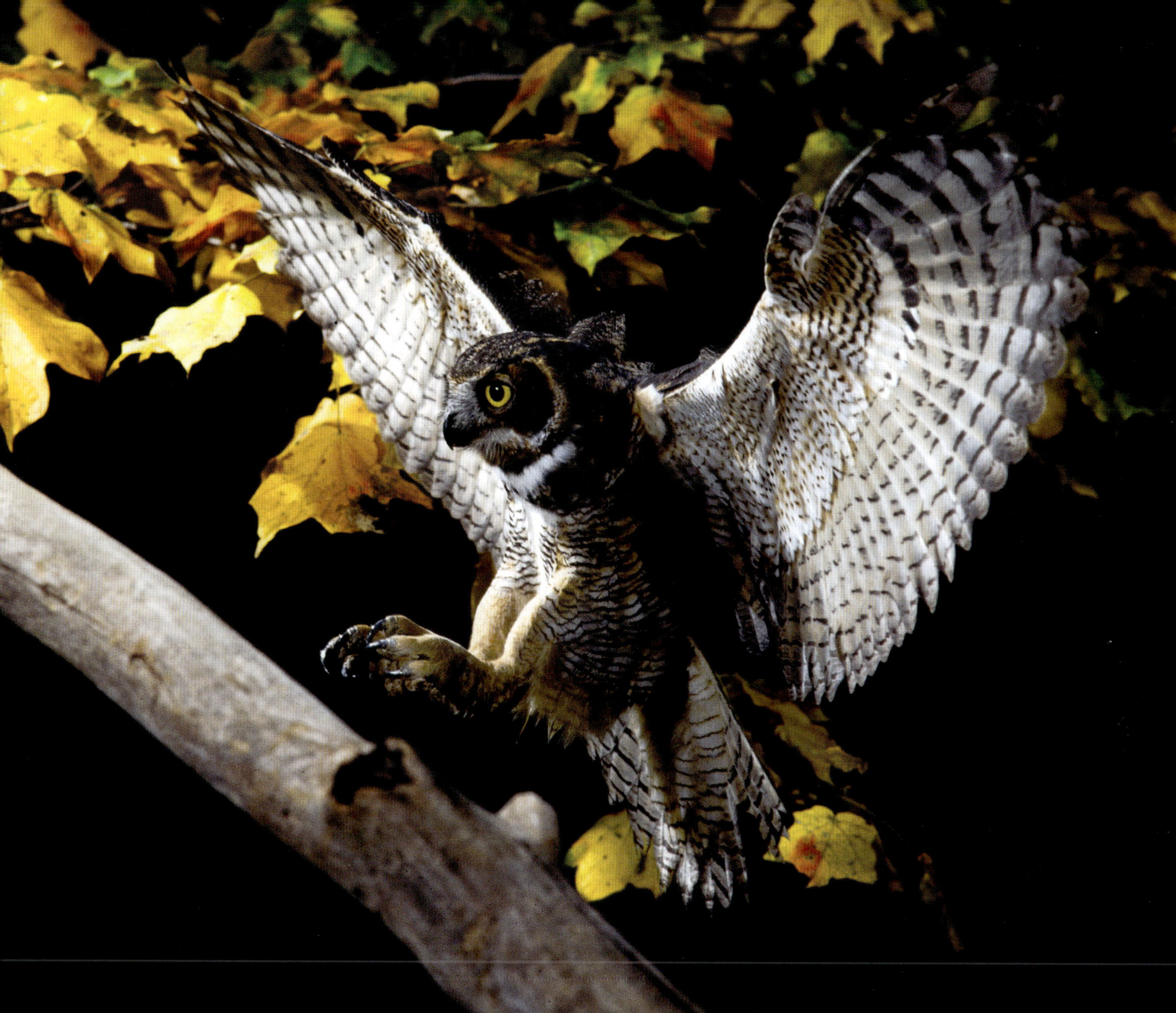

OPPOSITE: The female incubates up to five but usually two eggs. The young are born with a pure white down that is replaced within a week or two by a thicker, gray covering. **ABOVE:** The tips of the owl's primaries are "fluffy," which serves to muffle the downward stroke during flight.

and vertical movement has been detected (primarily for fine tuning of a visual image), the owl must turn its head to follow a movement. Owls, like humans, have binocular vision, which helps them with depth perception, but Heinrich posits that head bobbing, combined with the rapid dilation and contraction of the pupils, provides the birds with information for judging distances.

The owl's eyes are so large that the margins extend beyond the skull and must be protected with a bony sheath. Great horned owls blink in the same way humans (but few other birds) do: by moving the top lid down across the eye. For sleeping, the owl draws its bottom lid up. Both top and bottom lids are feathered. An owl can draw a milky-white nictitating membrane, or inner eyelid, diagonally across the eyeball from the upper inside corner.

Great horned owls may not be quite as large as snowy or great gray owls, but they are more powerful. A great horned owl has been known to tear the wings off a northern harrier it was pursuing, or to take full-size tomcats or skunks as prey, proving itself to be neither cowardly nor particularly discriminating.

The fact that the great horned owl is relatively common can probably be attributed to its ability to adapt to a wide variety of environments, from swamps to city

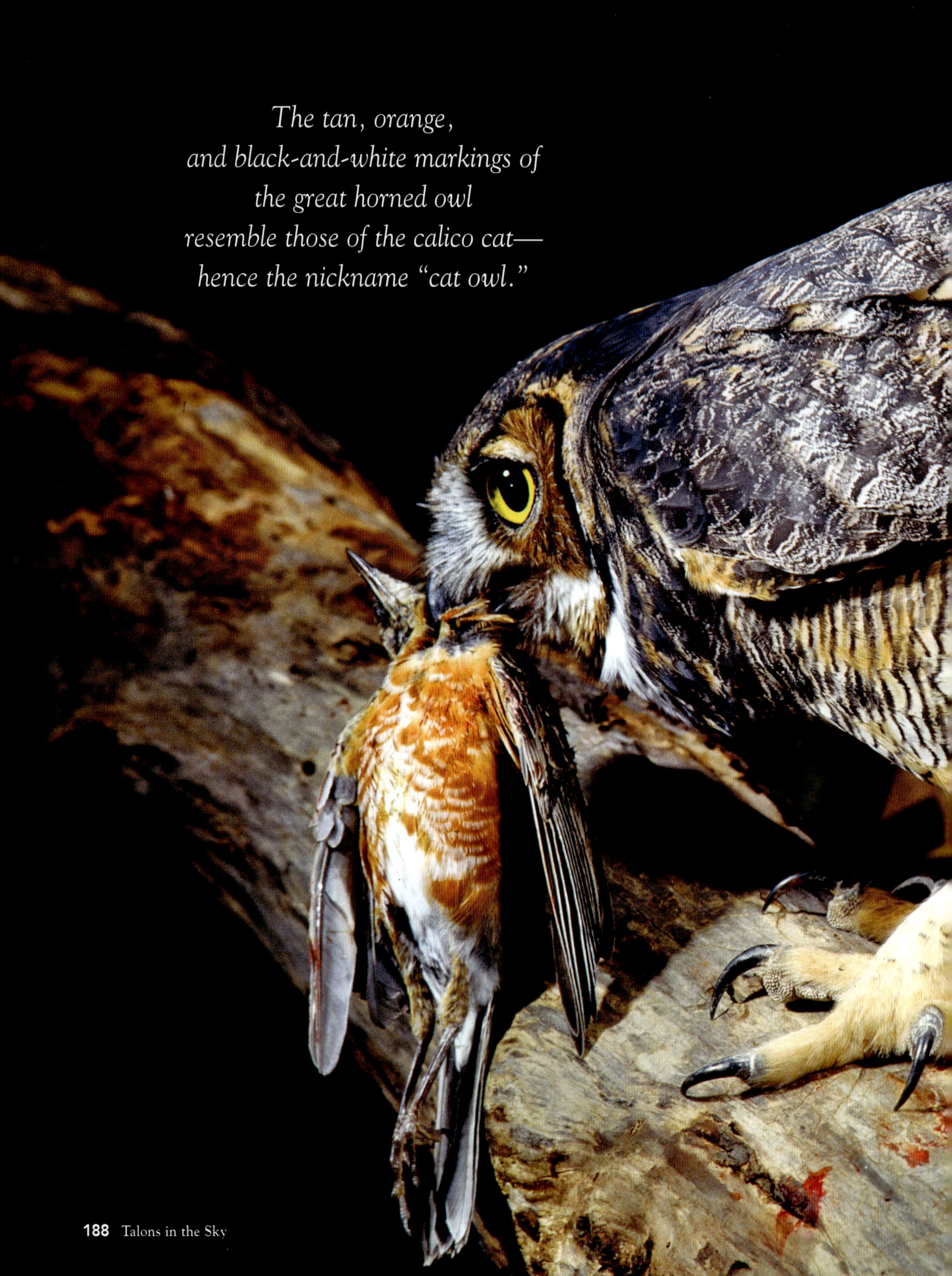

The tan, orange,
and black-and-white markings of
the great horned owl
resemble those of the calico cat—
hence the nickname "cat owl."

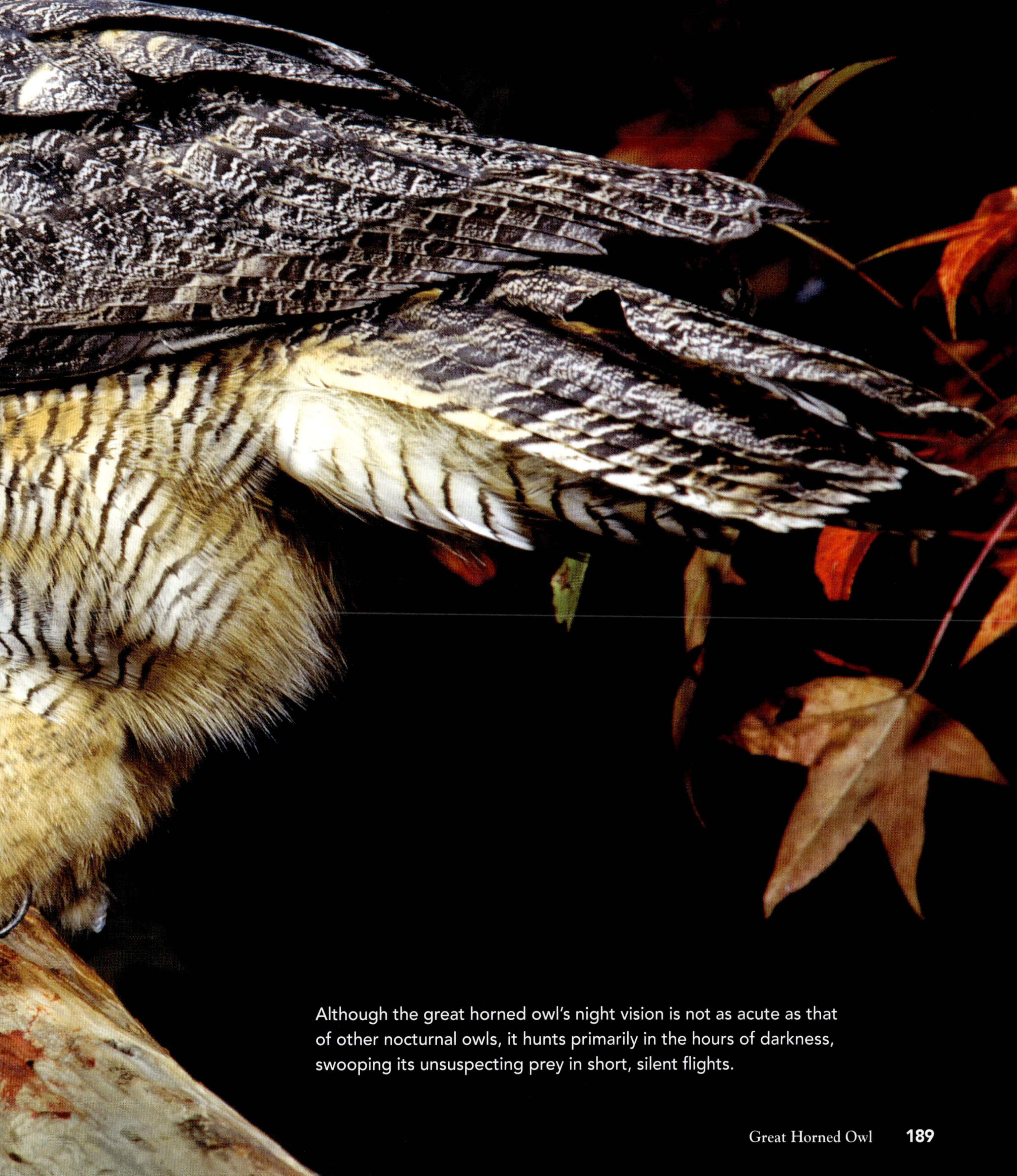

Although the great horned owl's night vision is not as acute as that of other nocturnal owls, it hunts primarily in the hours of darkness, swooping its unsuspecting prey in short, silent flights.

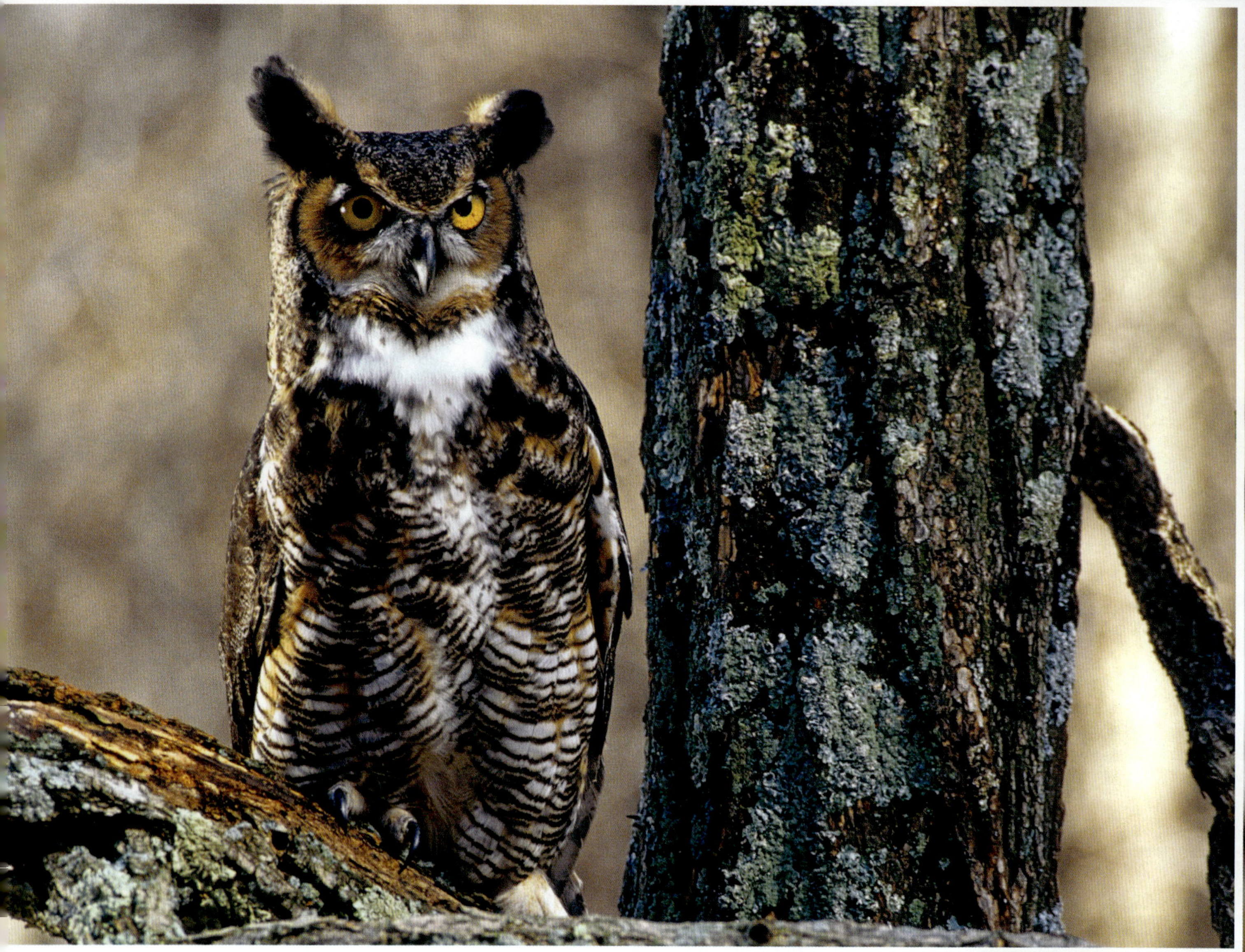

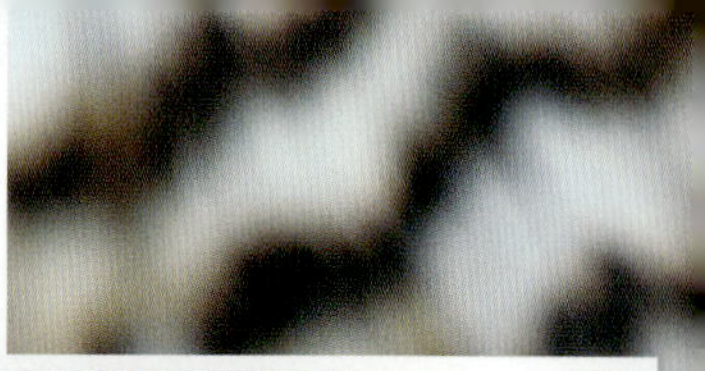

ABOVE: The owl's eyes are so large they extend beyond the skull and are protected by a bony sheath. **RIGHT:** The owl uses its incredibly powerful talons and its equally dangerous beak to dispatch prey. Note how the feathers on the feet look almost like fur.

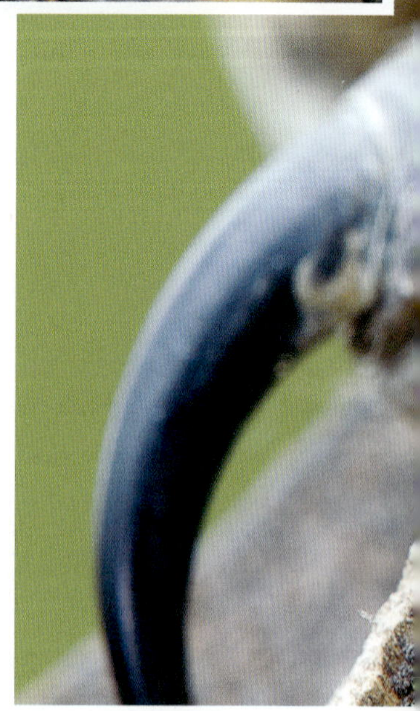

parks, canyons to farms. In the Northeast, the great horned inhabits thick forests; in the deserts of the Southwest, it adjusts to cliffs and rock crevices. Wherever it lives, the great horned owl takes advantage of those who went before, appropriating the nests of red-tailed hawks, squirrels, ospreys, crows, or great blue herons, or just taking what comes—crevices, hollow trees, or even a simple scrape—with very little renovation.

The species' relative health can also be attributed to its cosmopolitan palate. Arthur Cleveland Bent, writing in his *North American Birds of Prey*, describes the owl's diet as "almost any living creature that walks, crawls, flies or swims except larger mammals." From skunks to songbirds, rabbits to herons, insects to woodchucks, great horned owl prey ranges in weight from 1 to 3,000 grams. Though research indicates that the owl will adapt to available food sources, rabbits and hares seem to be the preferred meal.

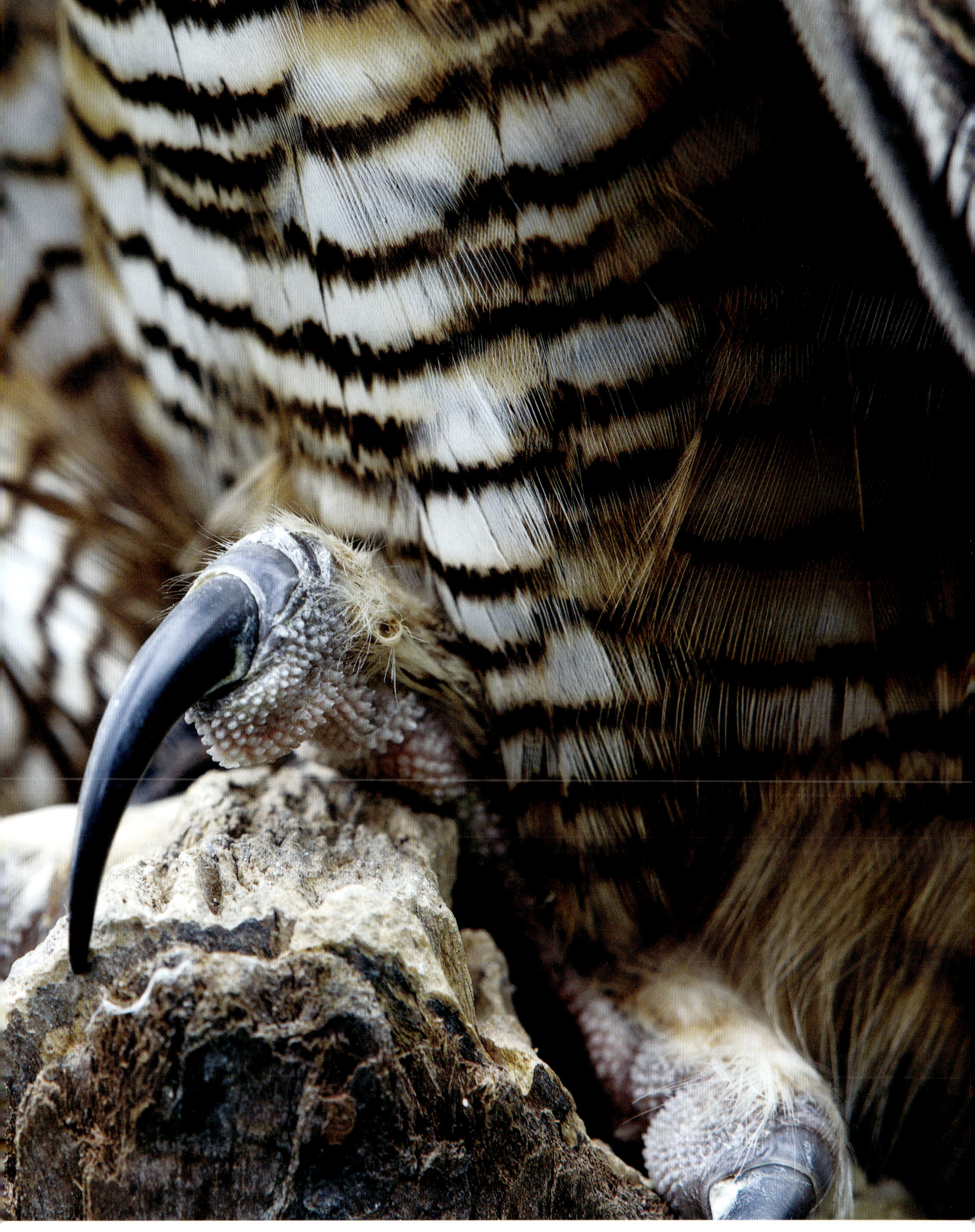

The great horned owl hunts primarily at night, though its night vision is not as acute as that of some other nocturnal owls. The great horned's method of hunting consists primarily of perching at a vantage point, waiting to detect prey, and then launching out on short flights. Incredibly powerful talons and beak make quick work of unfortunate victims, which the owl may cache in underbrush for consumption at a later time.

According to the American Ornithologists' Union, great horned owls breed from western and central Alaska, throughout much of Canada, into North, Central, and South America as far south as Tierra del Fuego. Twelve different subspecies of *Bubo virginianus* have been identified throughout this territory: *B. v. subarcticus*, *scalariventris*, *heterocnemis*, *virginianus*, *occidentalis*, *algistus*, *lagophonus*, *saturats*, *pacificus*, *pallescens*, *elachistus*, and *mayensis*.

Courtship gets underway as early as December. Although great horned owl courtship and copulation have not been well documented, apparent courtship behavior includes bowing, drooping the wings, cocking the tail upward, and hooting. The pair may also rub their beaks together after a prolonged bout of calling.

According to Paul Johnsgard, "copulation in this species is evidentially brief and is stimulated by the soliciting call of the male." The female can begin laying eggs as early as January, making the species the earliest nesting raptor. In the Northeast, one can sometimes find determined incubating females and their nests under a layer of snow. Preferred nest sites are those furthest from the haunts of humans, with live trees preferred over dead. The female incubates the eggs continuously from 28 to 35 days. The male roosts within 75 meters of the nest and supplies the female with food, both while she is incubating and when she is brooding.

The female can lay from one to five eggs (several days apart), although two is the usual number. Clutch size is thought to be dependent on availability of prey, and an owl may make second and even third attempts if the original clutch is destroyed. The eggs weigh approximately 64 grams and average 56 millimeters long and 47 millimeters wide. The hatchlings sport pure white down, but lose this in a week or two to a thicker, gray down.

A single owlet requires 300 grams of food per day. The nestlings' meals are very similar to those of its parents, though in the beginning the fare tends to be smaller mammals and birds. The young experience a rapid increase in weight during the first 25 to 28 days. They start to lose their down by their third week, becoming well-feathered on the wings at six weeks. The young owls fledge at their own pace—though they do not become proficient fliers until they are almost three months old.

Juveniles rely on their parents for survival lessons and food throughout the summer, but must eventually move off the territory by the onset of fall. Mortality is high: only about 50 percent survive their first year, most probably succumbing to starvation.

Great horned owls can live up to 14 years. Habitat destruction and encounters with automobiles are two of the more serious threats to owl longevity. Though in general considered sedentary, these owls do exhibit some significant movement in times of decreased food supplies, particularly in the northern part of their range. By and large, however, they prefer to stay close to their territories throughout the year.

Two great horned owls, somewhat gaudily rendered in orange and black plastic, scowl sternly over the doorway of a local steel spring factory and the roof of a Michigan yacht club. No doubt they are placed there to scare away "pest" birds. We can only hope that the real-life models will be around to scare skunks and tomcats and humans for a long time to come.

Measurements (in mm)

Length	508–584
Wingspan	890–1400
Tail Length	200–230
Eye Width	19
Upper Mandible	1.7–44.4 (following top curvature, including cere
Head Width	125

Great horned owls have a plethora of eyelids—one each on the top and the bottom, and a nictitating lid that slides across the eye from the side for protection.

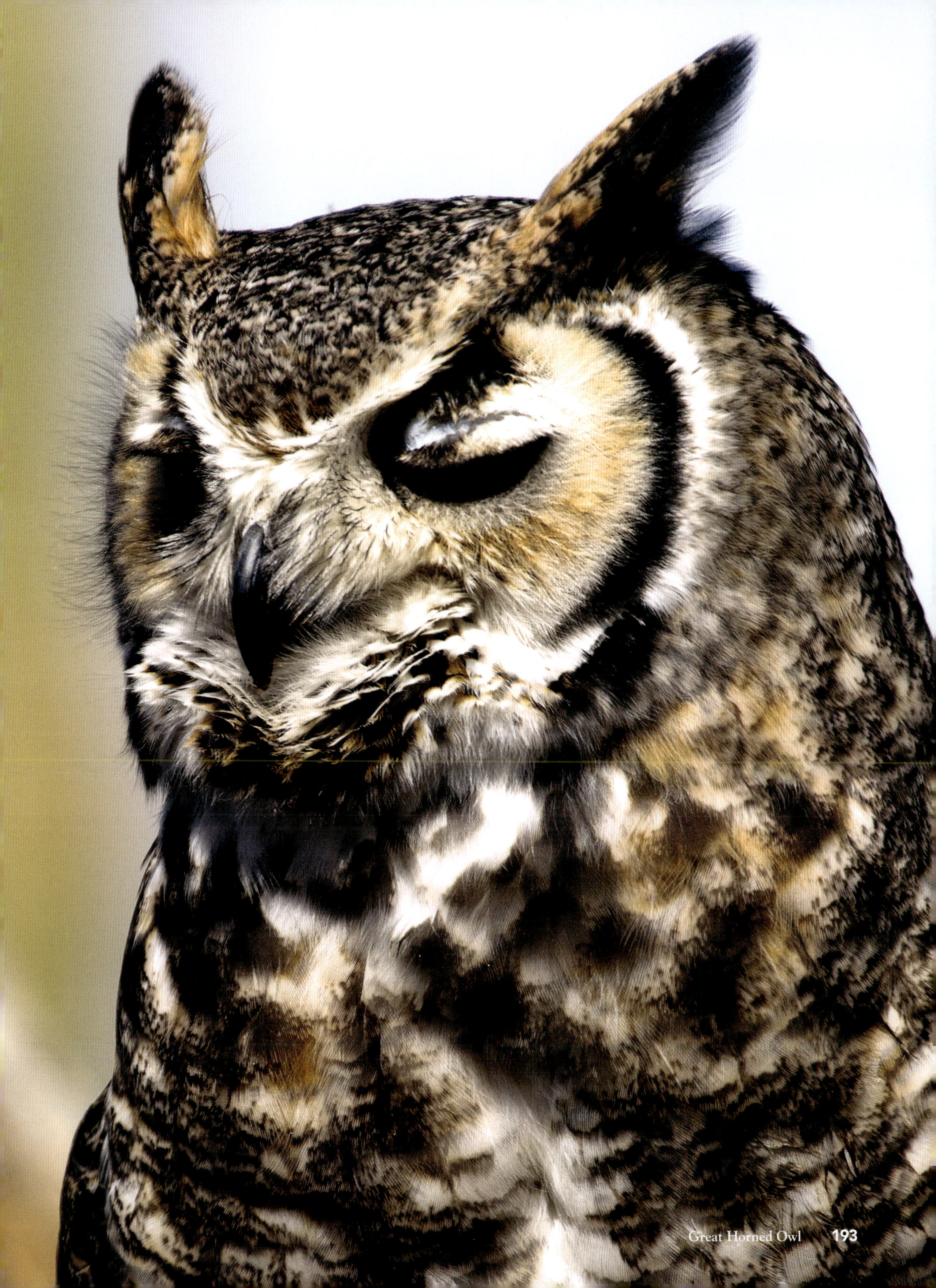

Long-eared Owl

(Asio otus)

Short-eared Owl

(Asio flammeus)

BY RICK BURKMAN

Don't stay in a house when an owl hoots above the roof—it means someone in that house will die before sunrise.

Although that bit of folklore is obviously not true, it does capture the feelings we have for owls, those mysterious creatures of the night. These birds can remain absolutely silent in a world that is filled with hums, buzzes, and chirps. They have a mystical ability to disappear into their surroundings, using natural camouflage that perfectly matches their environment. It is not uncommon for owls to live unseen and unheard in our woodlots and barns, practically under our noses, because we live in the daylight and the owls' realm is darkness.

No owl is better at disappearing before our eyes than North America's long-eared owl (*Asio otus*). This odd, medium-sized owl looks like a shrunken version of a great horned owl, but when it pulls its feathers into its body and lifts its ear tufts (which are located above the eyes and not near the ears) it almost disappears against its background. The long-eared owl has a close relative, the short-eared owl (*Asio flammeus*). Its forehead feathers stick up like the long-eared owls', but they are small and—like the owl itself—often overlooked.

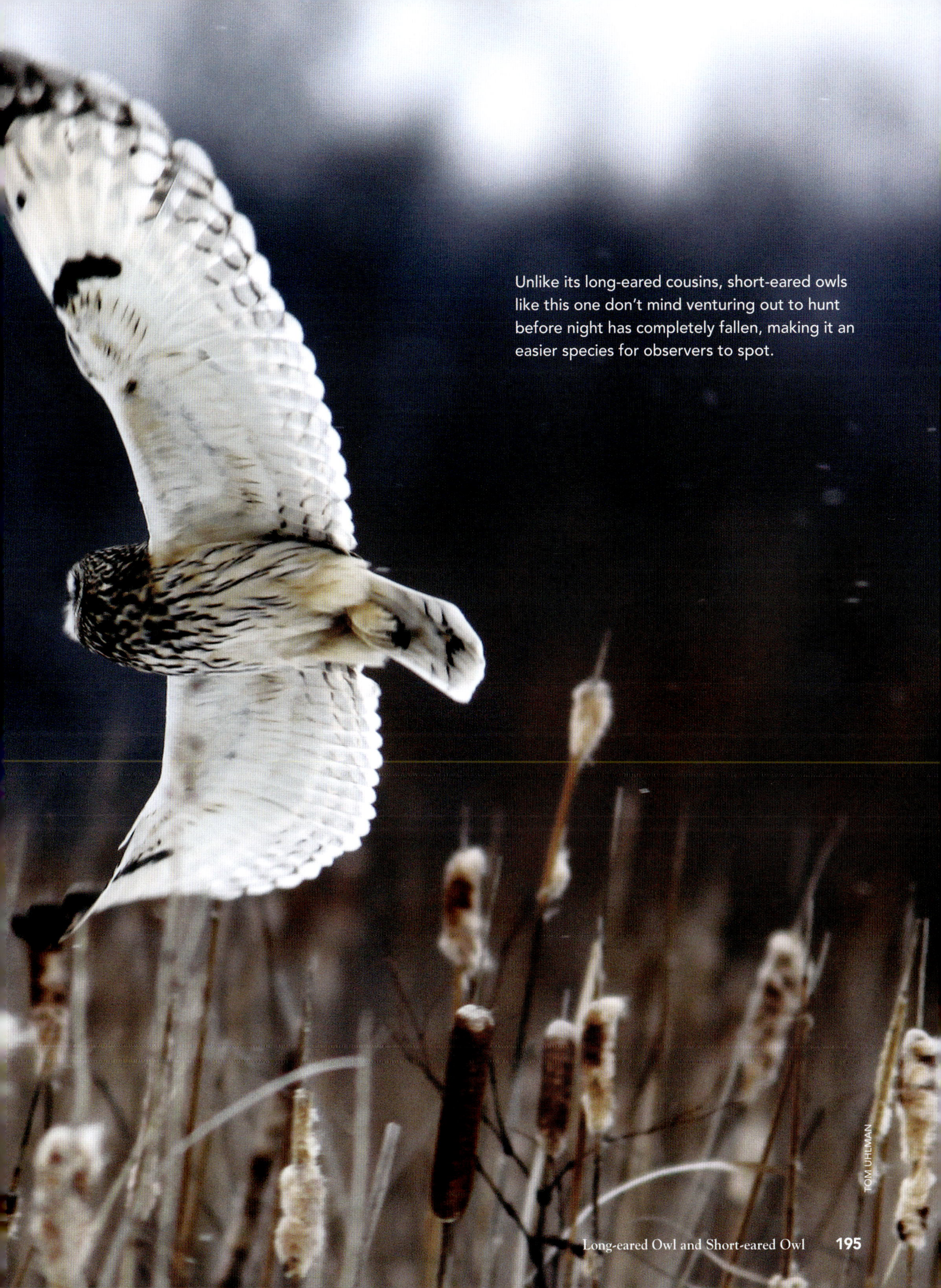

Unlike its long-eared cousins, short-eared owls like this one don't mind venturing out to hunt before night has completely fallen, making it an easier species for observers to spot.

TOM UHLMAN

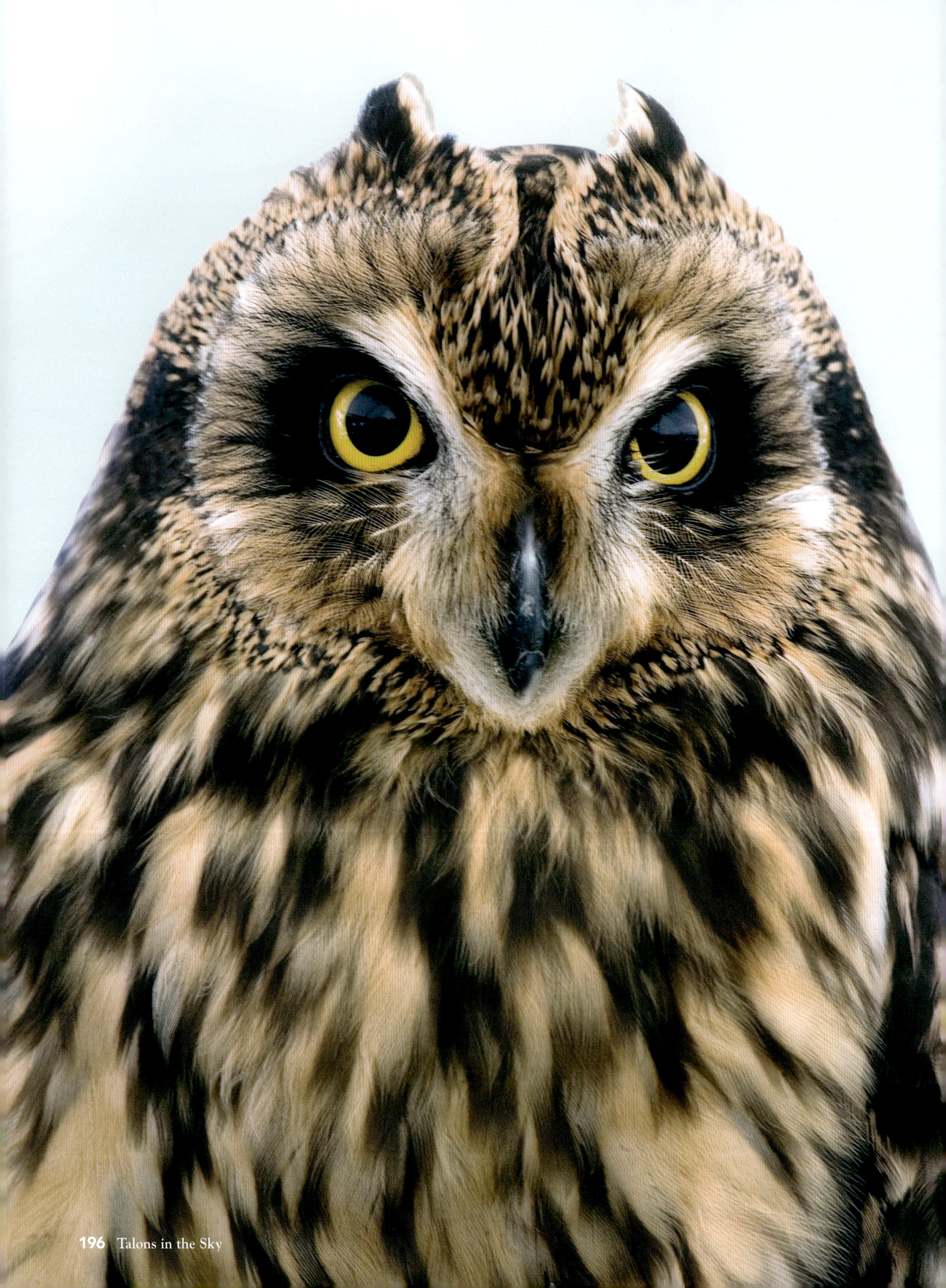

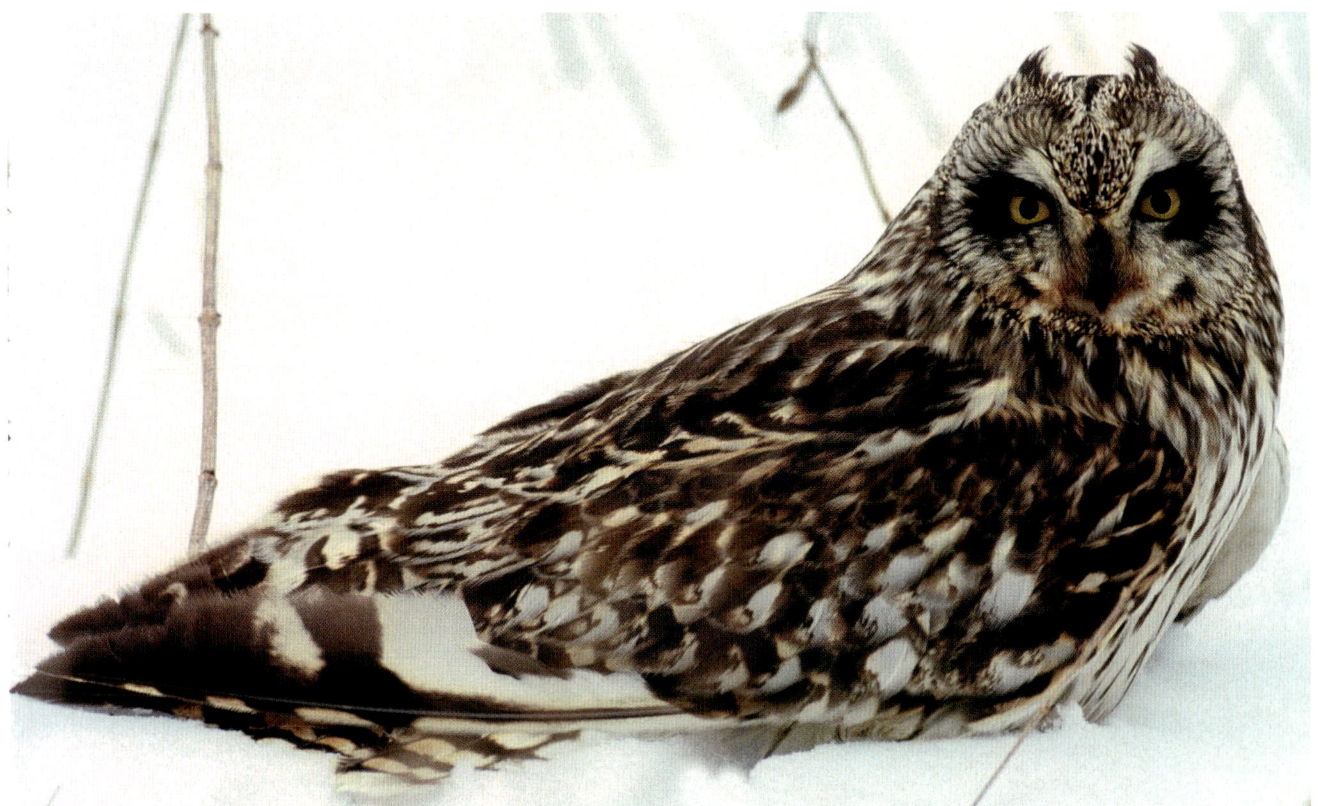

Like other owls, the short-eared variety have developed features especially suited for hunting in the dark. The facial disks help direct sound waves to the ears so the bird can locate prey it can't see. Strong bills and talons mean more bad news for the target, which is usually a vole.

Because owls are nocturnal, their survival depends on their hearing ability. Evolution has given them heads with large facial disks (a scruffy tan or grayish color in the short-eared owls and a dirty orange in the long-eared owls) that work a little like satellite dishes, gathering sound waves and directing them towards the ears. The ear openings are at the outer edge of their facial disks. Typically, the left ear opening is higher than the right and shaped differently. As a result, sound waves reach the ears at different times, allowing the owl to finely discriminate what they hear and making them capable of "seeing" the world in three dimensions through sound alone. Controlled experiments in a perfectly darkened room showed that a long-eared owl can launch from a perch several feet above the ground, pluck a mouse from the floor by homing in on the sounds it makes, and return to its perch to swallow its prey. Short-eared owls are also adept at using sound but overall use their vision more than their long-eared cousins. Short-eared owls will start hunting near sundown, so observers sometimes spot the birds searching for prey in the fading light.

Both long-eared and short-eared owls favor small mammals for food. They have a special affinity for voles, and local population numbers depend almost exclusively on the availability of these small animals. The owls will opportunistically target birds and other small prey but rarely make them a specialty. For the most part their lives are intimately entwined with the voles.

When hunting, long-eared owls flatten their pseudo-ears, so their heads resemble that of their short-eared owl kin. During reconnaissance flights, both types of owls float and bob on outstretched wings, twisting and turning when they think they have located something worth eating. An owl pinpoints its prey by hovering like a dragonfly and adjusting its aerial position from side to side. Then the owl drops suddenly, sinking its sharp talons into the small animal. Sadly for the owl, but luckily for the voles, even skilled owls miss their prey up to 70 percent of the time.

The owls generally eat the entire vole, but during the breeding season males will deliver the prey to the nest for his mate to eat, or piece it out to the growing young. Very small hatchlings will get bits of shredded meat; otherwise the rule is to swallow fast and swallow whole

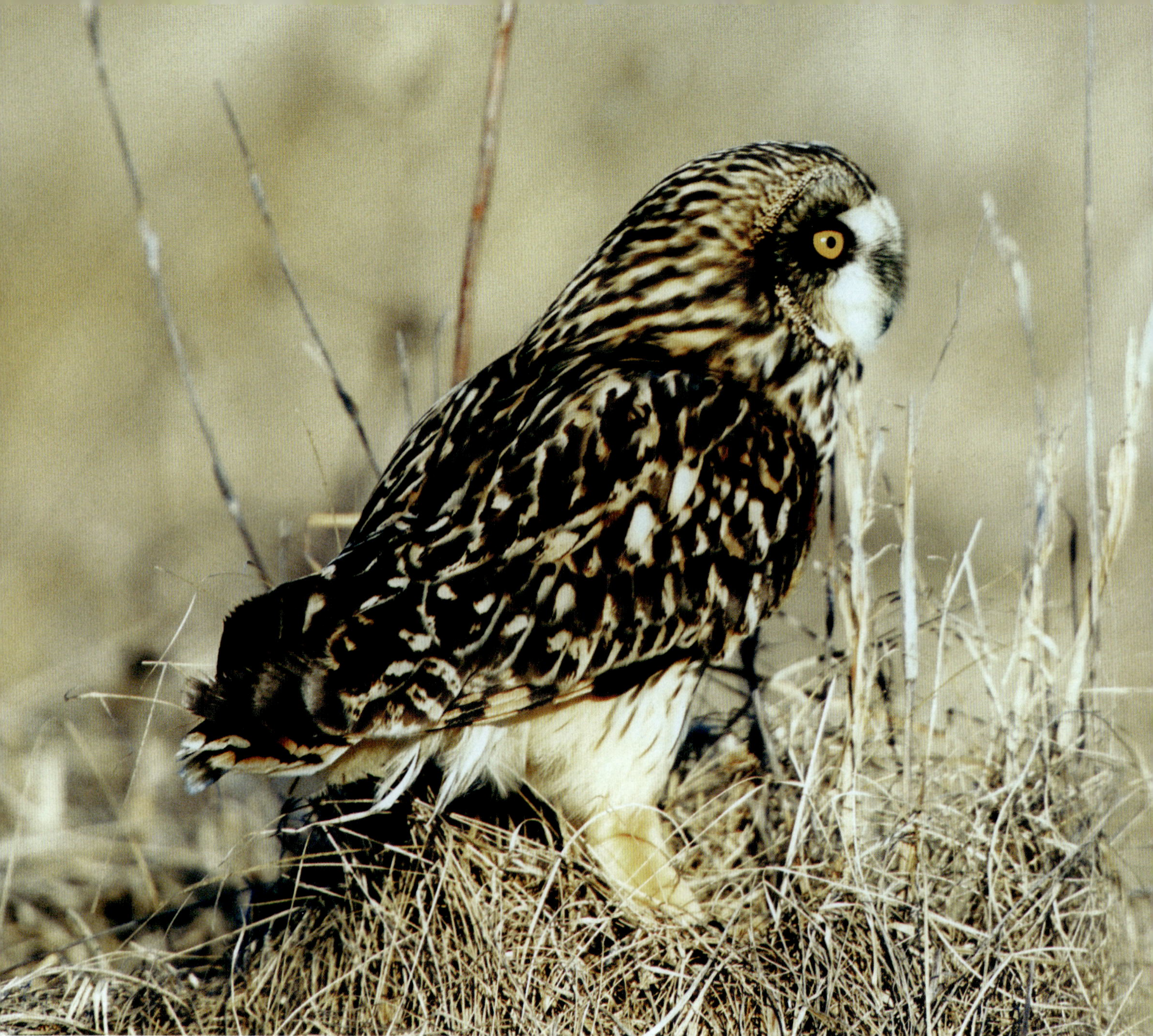

before someone else decides to share or steal the meal. Owls lack a gizzard to grind and mush their food so, while the digestible parts move toward the intestines, the owl spits out the indigestible remnants—fur, claws, teeth, and bones—in the form of an elongated pellet.

Both long-eared and short-eared owls like similar habitats, woodlands on the edges of open marshes or fields. Short-eared owls live their lives in the openings, but the long-eared owls like to spend their days in the dense forests.

The two owl types can be difficult to tell apart in flight when the long-eared variety lays its ear tufts back. The long-eared owl has a set of facial feathers that make an X of the eyebrows and the mustache space on either side of the bill. Piercing yellow eyes surrounded by a dirty orange facial disk complete the facial picture. Short-eared owls sport buffy-white to brownish-gray facial disks framed with white feathers. They also have white eyebrows and a mustache in the shape of the letter X, but their facial feathering is not as extreme as that of the long-eared owl. Darker feathers rim the short-eared owls' yellow eyes, making them look like they are sporting a pair of perpetually "black eyes." They also have a light-colored leading edge to their wings and a lighter abdomen.

When mating season arrives, a male of either species will perform aerial dances as it tries to lure a willing female. Both use wing clapping as part of their flight display, slapping their feathered appendages together below their bodies as they fly through their territory. The sound is akin to slapping your hand against your thigh. The male long-eareds also hoot to attract mates,

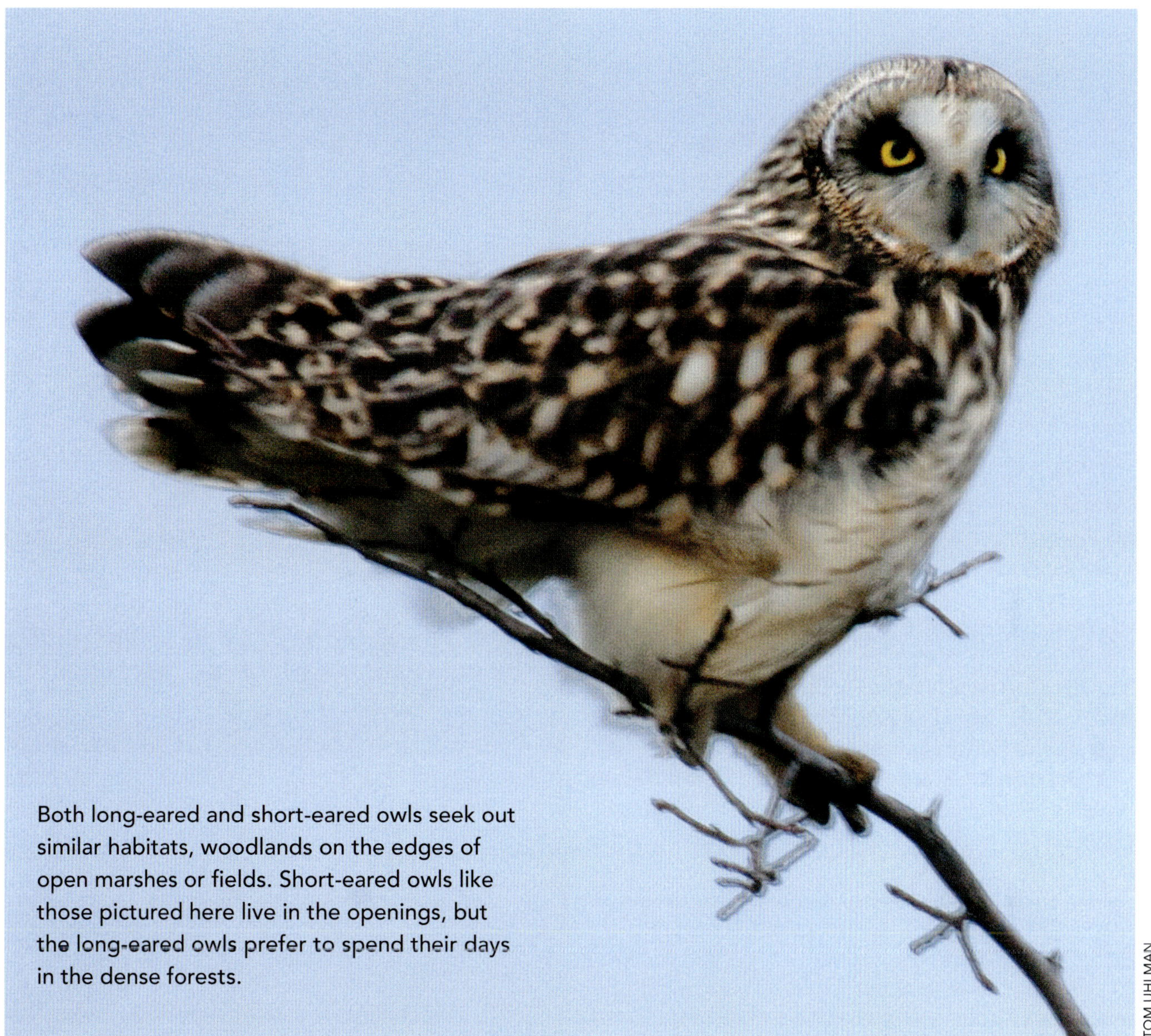
Both long-eared and short-eared owls seek out similar habitats, woodlands on the edges of open marshes or fields. Short-eared owls like those pictured here live in the openings, but the long-eared owls prefer to spend their days in the dense forests.

TOM UHLMAN

a repetitious sound that can be heard for about a half mile.

Long-eared and short-eared owls do not mate for life although, if the nesting area is a good one, the male will return to the same territory year after year. Females of both species are more nomadic and rarely return to nest with their partner from the previous year, which may help them to more successfully ensure that their genes pass to future generations.

After pair bonding, the male takes his paramour on a tour of the local countryside. Long-eared owls check out old forest structures to see which one will make an ideal spot for raising a new family. The long-eared owls never build nests. Instead they commandeer existing crow, hawk, or squirrel nests. The female just plops on the pile and, other than the occasional breast feather that falls out as she preens, adds nothing to the nest.

Short-eared owl males show their mates the grassy hummocks and small elevations of their fields and marshes. A male may point out likely spots, but he does not incubate the eggs and the female chooses the nest site. Short-eared owls are one of the few owls that actually build nests. The structure begins with the hen scraping away debris and vegetation until reaching the underlying soil on a small hummock in the grasslands. She piles grasses, vegetation, and occasional twigs in the depression, creating a built-up mat of vegetation that is relatively easy to see, unlike the nests of most other grassland birds.

Owls are a little erratic when it comes to egg laying. Many species of birds lay an egg each day until a clutch is complete. An owl, on the other hand, may lay one egg a day like normal birds, or it may lay two eggs consecutively, or it may skip a couple of days between eggs. A female continues erratically laying its slightly elliptical, creamy-white eggs until it has a clutch of four to six.

Once incubation starts a female will sit tightly on her nest, almost never leaving her eggs exposed during the day and only rarely at night. Her first response to danger, even when a predator lurks nearby, is to hunker down, partially close her eyelids so they do not blink, and stay as still as possible. If all goes well, the intruder will pass her by. If the owl does leave the nest, she will do it with an explosive burst of wingbeats and feathers. She defecates on the eggs as she leaves, splashing them with a noxious wash of urates and waste that may further deter predators. In the flurry of escaping she might even knock an egg out of the nest. A short-eared owl will later use its curved bill in an attempt to hook the egg and roll it back into the nest. Long-eared owls are tree nesters, so retrieving a lost egg is not an option.

Males do not sit on the nest, but they do patrol the territory, hunting and providing food for their mates. If a potential predator enters the territory, a male will feign injury by flopping on the ground just out of the pursuer's reach. If that doesn't work, the defenders may attack with razor-sharp talons in an effort to drive the intruder away.

Long-eared owls take territory protection a step further by nesting in a loosely based community, unusual behavior in the owl world. If threatened by a potential predator, the neighbors may gather together to mob the creature. During the winter months, long-eared owls occasionally roost together in "owl parliaments" that can total 200 birds.

Male duties extend beyond territory defense. The hen must eat while she sits on her nest, so the male supplies her with sustenance. When the eggs are near hatching, he redoubles his efforts and creates a

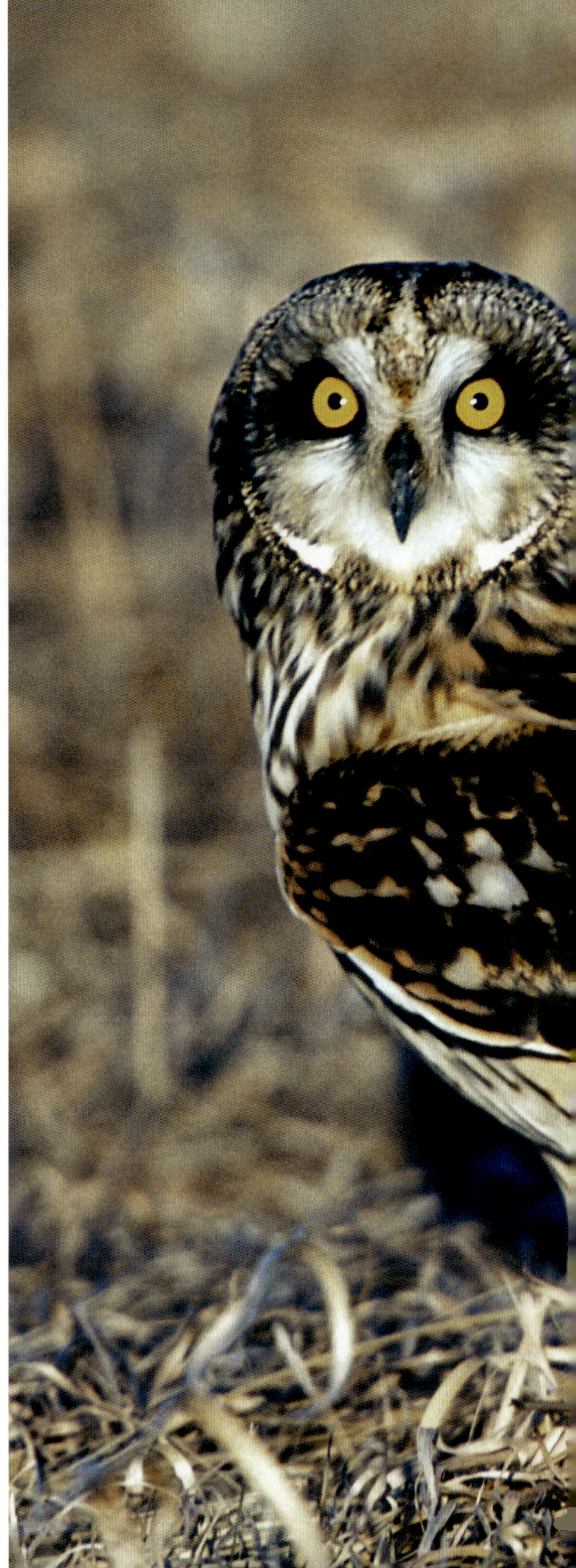

Because eared owls can fold their ear tufts down, this short-eared specimen might appear to be a no-eared owl. Typically, one ear opening will be higher than the other and shaped differently, which allows the owls to better analyze the sounds reaching them.

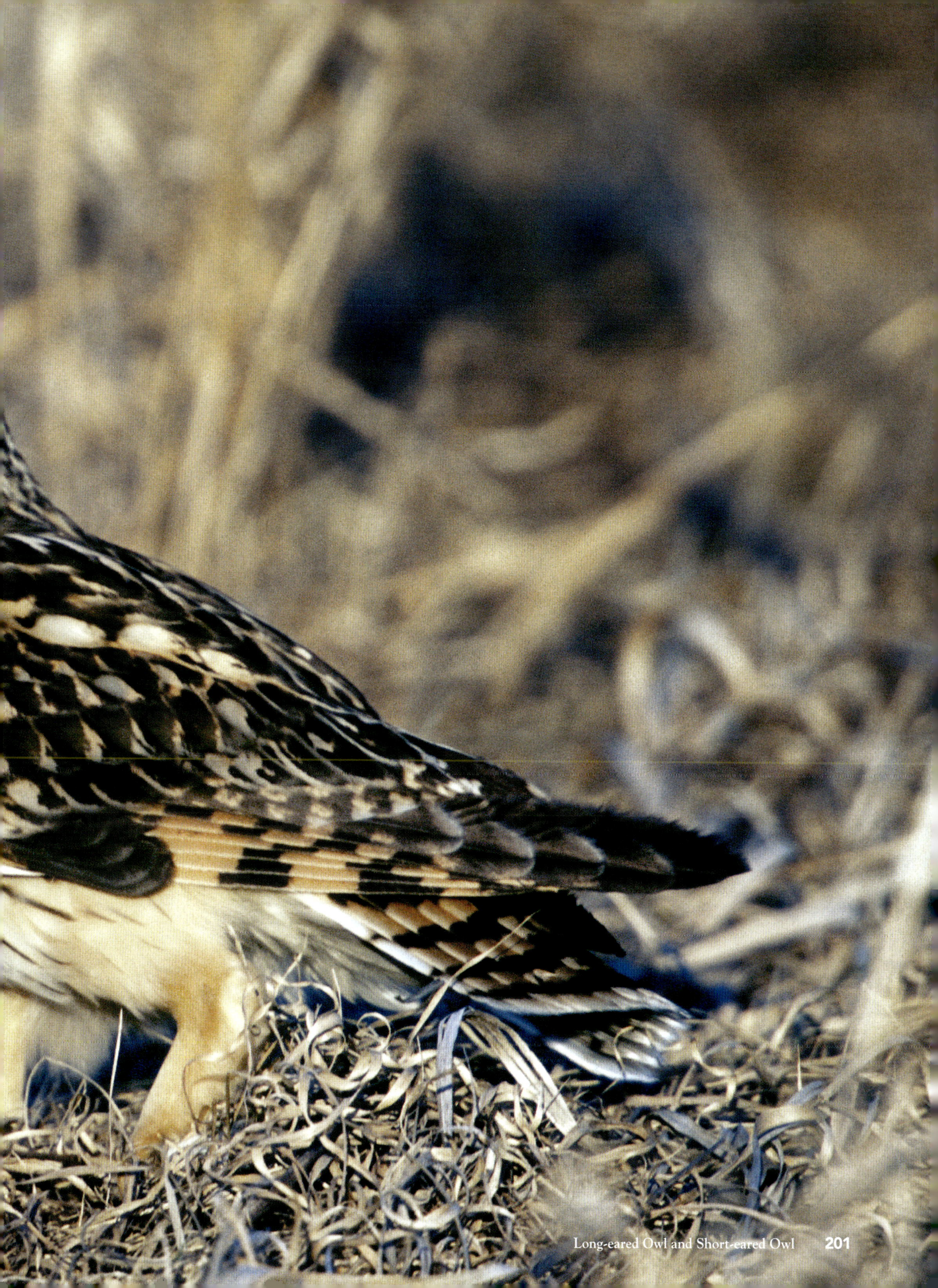

stockpile of food for his mate and young. Owls have learned that stocking the larder provides a buffer in case hunting is difficult or food is stolen by kleptoparasites, like harriers.

Owls begin nesting early in the season, when cold and even snowy weather is still expected. Because of this early nesting, the hen begins incubating her clutch as soon as she lays the first egg. This, of course, results in nestlings of widely varying ages and sizes in an owl's nest. The firstborn grabs all of the food until a sibling hatches. Even after the other eggs hatch, the firstborn is large enough to grab any food that the adults bring to the nest. Sharing with siblings is not in their nature.

As the young birds grow, brooding becomes less and less important and the maternal bond starts to weaken. The female, who up until now has worked diligently to keep her nestlings warm and dry, leaves the nest for longer and longer periods. She uses this time to stretch her wings, to hunt for herself, and, probably, to just sit someplace that does not contain a nest full of squabbling nestlings.

Soon the nest is too crowded for the young birds. Three weeks after hatching, the long-eared owl fledglings sit on the edge of their nest, become restless, and venture forth to explore their home tree. When they get brave enough, they combine walking, hopping, and pulling themselves along with bill and wings to explore nearby trees. Because these owls will occasionally nest in close proximity, young from different broods may find one another and roost together while on their exploratory trips.

Short-eared owls, because they are ground nesters rather than tree nesters, move through the grasses and shrubs of their open lands after about 18 days in the nest. They explore and shelter in the forbs and dense concentrations of vegetation.

Moms may not brood their young birds any longer, but both parents still work diligently to feed and protect their offspring, especially now that they are venturing out to explore the dangers of the world. Like teens around the world, these young birds want to stretch their wings and experience freedom, yet they lack all the skills needed to survive in the wild where everything from larger species of owls plus hawks, eagles, coyotes, and raccoons will willingly eat them. After about four weeks, they are testing their flying skills, the next important stage to adulthood. These young birds are already well-adapted hunting machines, with pointed claws, exquisite hearing, and sharp-focused eyesight. Learning the skills of controlled flight will finish the transition.

When old enough and wise enough, young birds disperse from the nesting grounds. They scatter out into the world, following the voles and congregating in areas with abundant food sources. If the youngsters manage to avoid larger predators, extreme weather, and the other trials and tribulations of life in the wilderness, they will raise their own families, beginning another tale in the cycle of life.

Wily or wise, prescient or not, owls are a fascination. Because they are seldom heard and rarely seen, every encounter is a delight, one that fills the senses with awe and the feeling that we have been allowed to peek into a wild world close to, but maybe not quite in synch with, our high-tech, busy one.

The ear tufts of the long-eared owl are one of the bird's most striking features. Note the X formed by the eyebrows and "mustache."

Measurements (in mm)

	Male	Female	Unsexed
Long-eared Owl			
Bill	15.7	16.2	
Wing Chord	281	283.5	286.2
Wing (flat)			302.8
Tail			146.2
Tarsus	38.2	39.9	
Short-eared Owl			
Bill	16.4	16.6	
Wing Chord	295.7	297.1	
Tail	n/a	157.3	

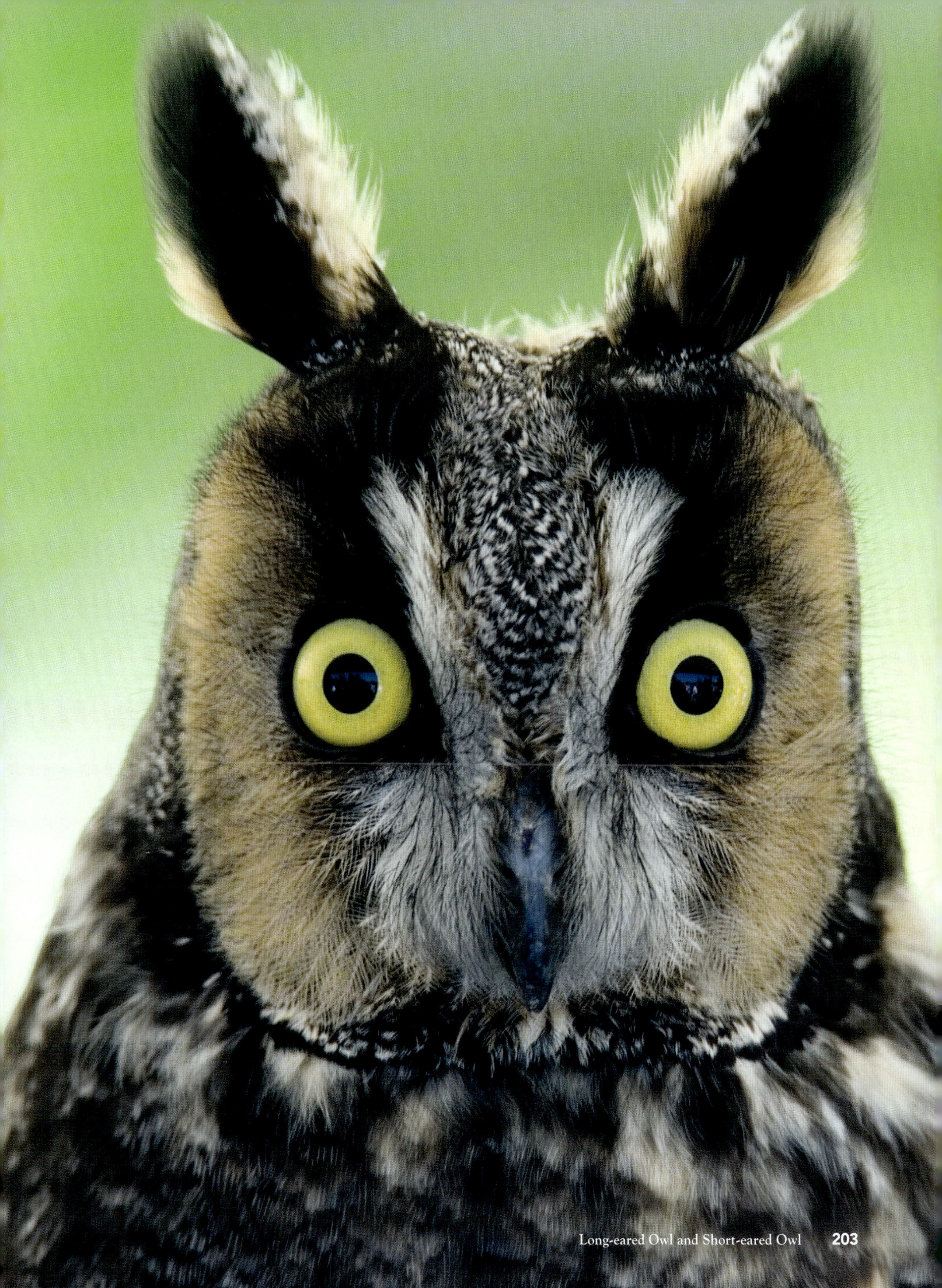

Northern Saw-whet Owl

(Aegolius acadicus)

BY RON AUSTING

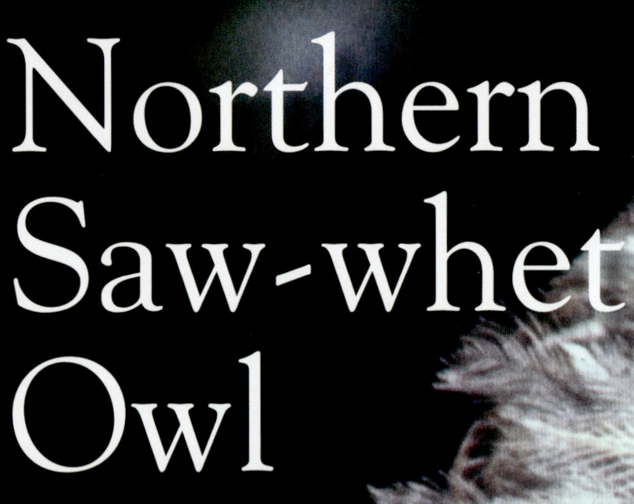

A saw-whet owl may have several roosting sites within its one-square-mile range, and it will visit them regularly for short periods. Its name describes its song, which has been compared to a mill saw being sharpened.

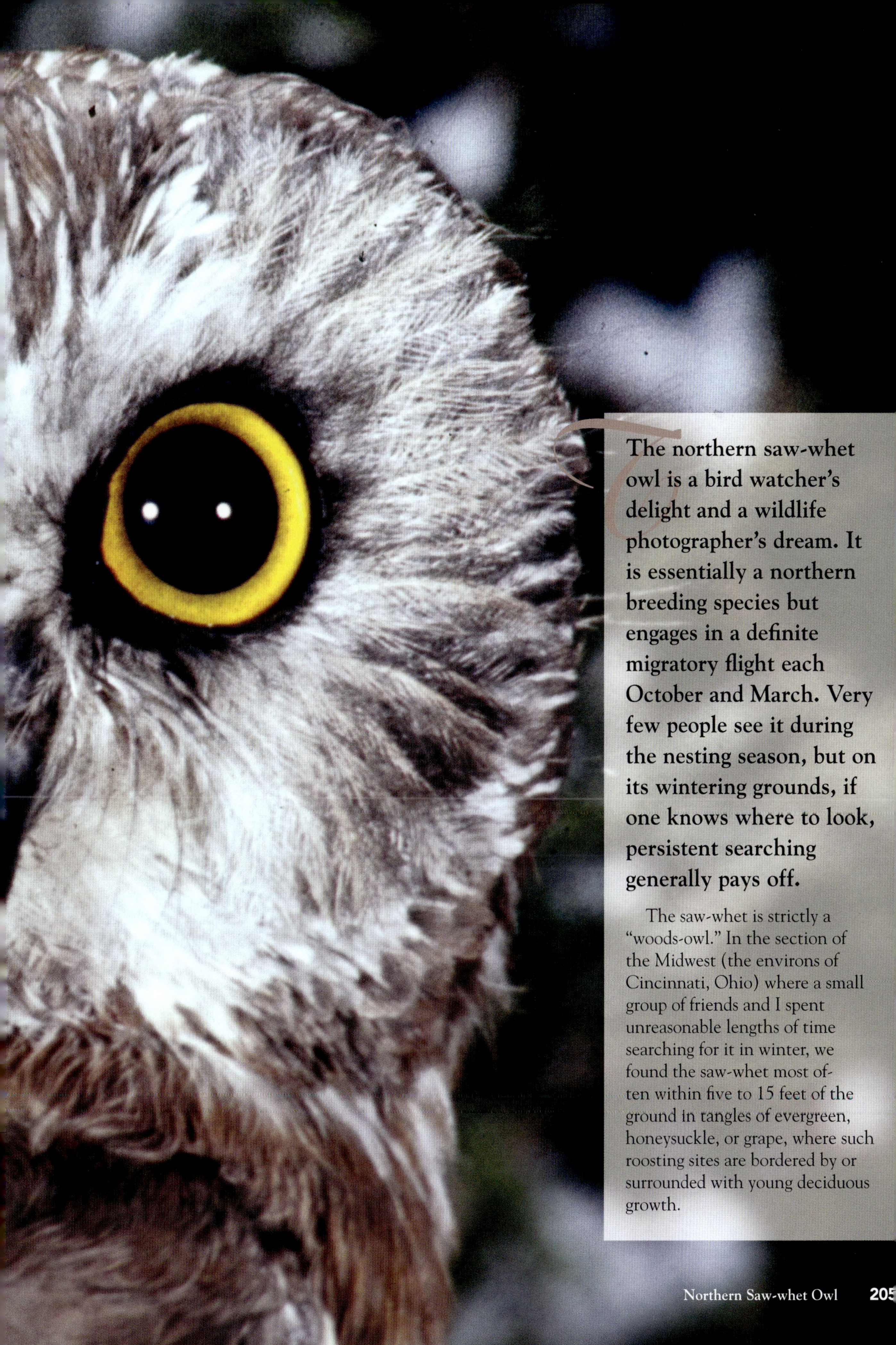

The northern saw-whet owl is a bird watcher's delight and a wildlife photographer's dream. It is essentially a northern breeding species but engages in a definite migratory flight each October and March. Very few people see it during the nesting season, but on its wintering grounds, if one knows where to look, persistent searching generally pays off.

The saw-whet is strictly a "woods-owl." In the section of the Midwest (the environs of Cincinnati, Ohio) where a small group of friends and I spent unreasonable lengths of time searching for it in winter, we found the saw-whet most often within five to 15 feet of the ground in tangles of evergreen, honeysuckle, or grape, where such roosting sites are bordered by or surrounded with young deciduous growth.

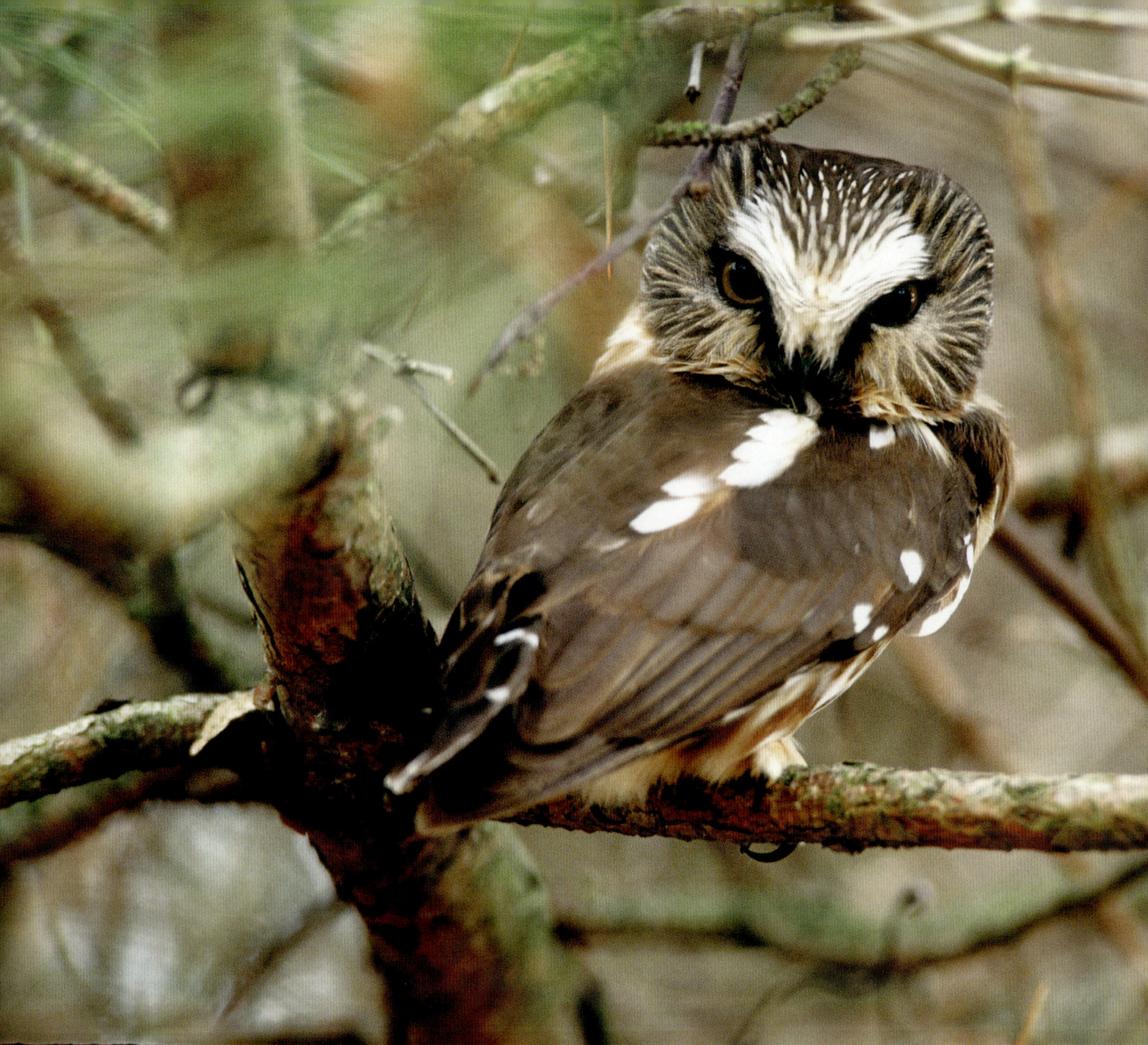

Saw-whets usually roost in the tangles of evergreen, honeysuckles, or grape. Like most owls, they have big eyes that can make them seem very expressive.

My first encounter with a saw-whet owl took place on a seasonable mid-December afternoon in the area around Cincinnati. A fellow raptor enthusiast and I were in the midst of one of our daily after-school hikes, during which we would record as many hawks and owls as we could find. I recall the day as being rather uneventful—perhaps a Cooper's and a red-shouldered hawk and maybe a barred owl—when we paused at the pond to interpret the scoldings of various titmice, juncos, and chickadees. Their attention seemed to be focused on the interior of the large honeysuckle tangle just across the water. Woods-wise in spite of our years, we knew they had encountered a predator but couldn't imagine what it might be. We hurried to the other side to scrutinize the thicket and immediately laid eyes on one of the cutest creatures we had ever seen: a northern saw-whet owl. At the time, we weren't quite sure about the identification; we recalled that the boreal owl looked rather similar. But all that mattered at the moment to two 15-year-olds was capturing this charming little gnome of owldom.

It wasn't to be. Despite our best efforts, the tiny

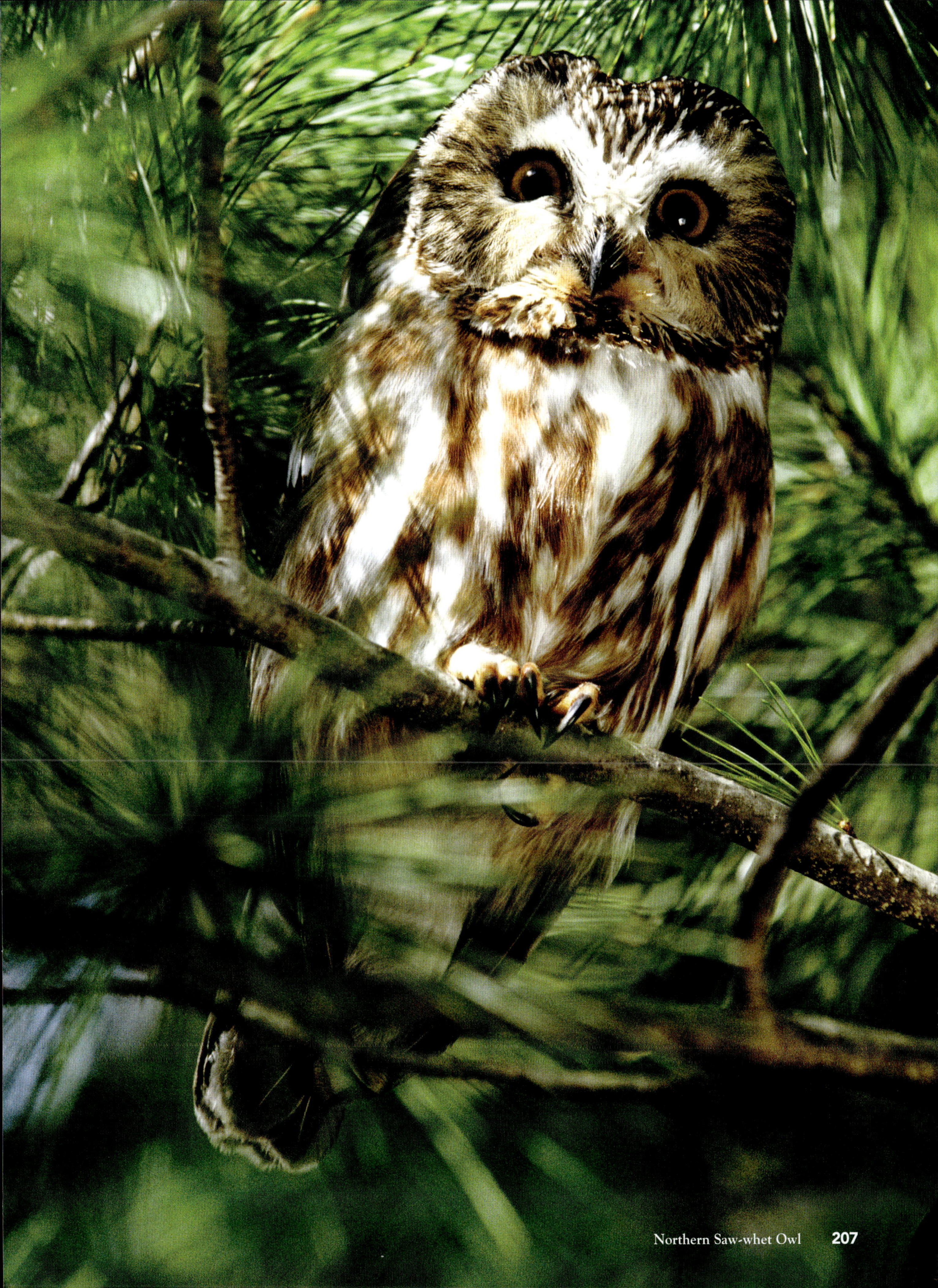

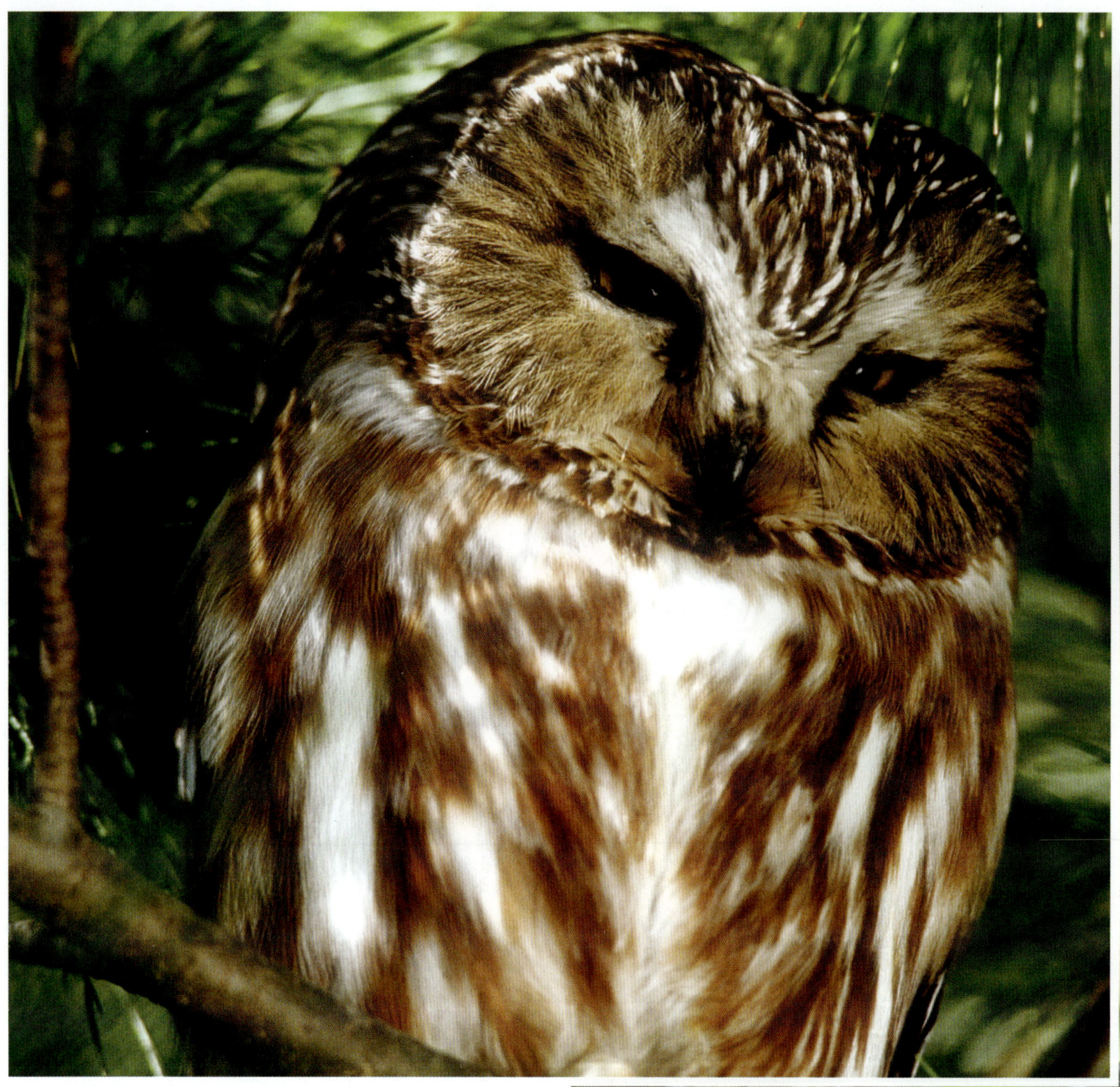

predator would always manage to avoid our eager hands and flush at the last moment, only to alight again 30 or so yards distant, usually within arm's reach of the ground. I was impressed with its swiftness of flight and its agility as it threaded its way through the maze of understory. Darkness soon prevailed and our little bird became a planet lost among the stars. We spent many succeeding afternoons hoping to find him again, but without success.

Whenever we would encounter a new bird on our hikes, raptor or otherwise, my friend and I would research all of the available literature in an effort not only to correctly identify our new discovery, but to learn as much as we could about the habits and life history of the bird.

Saw-whets, like the closely related boreal owl, lack ear tufts. Their beaks are black, and their heads are streaked with white.

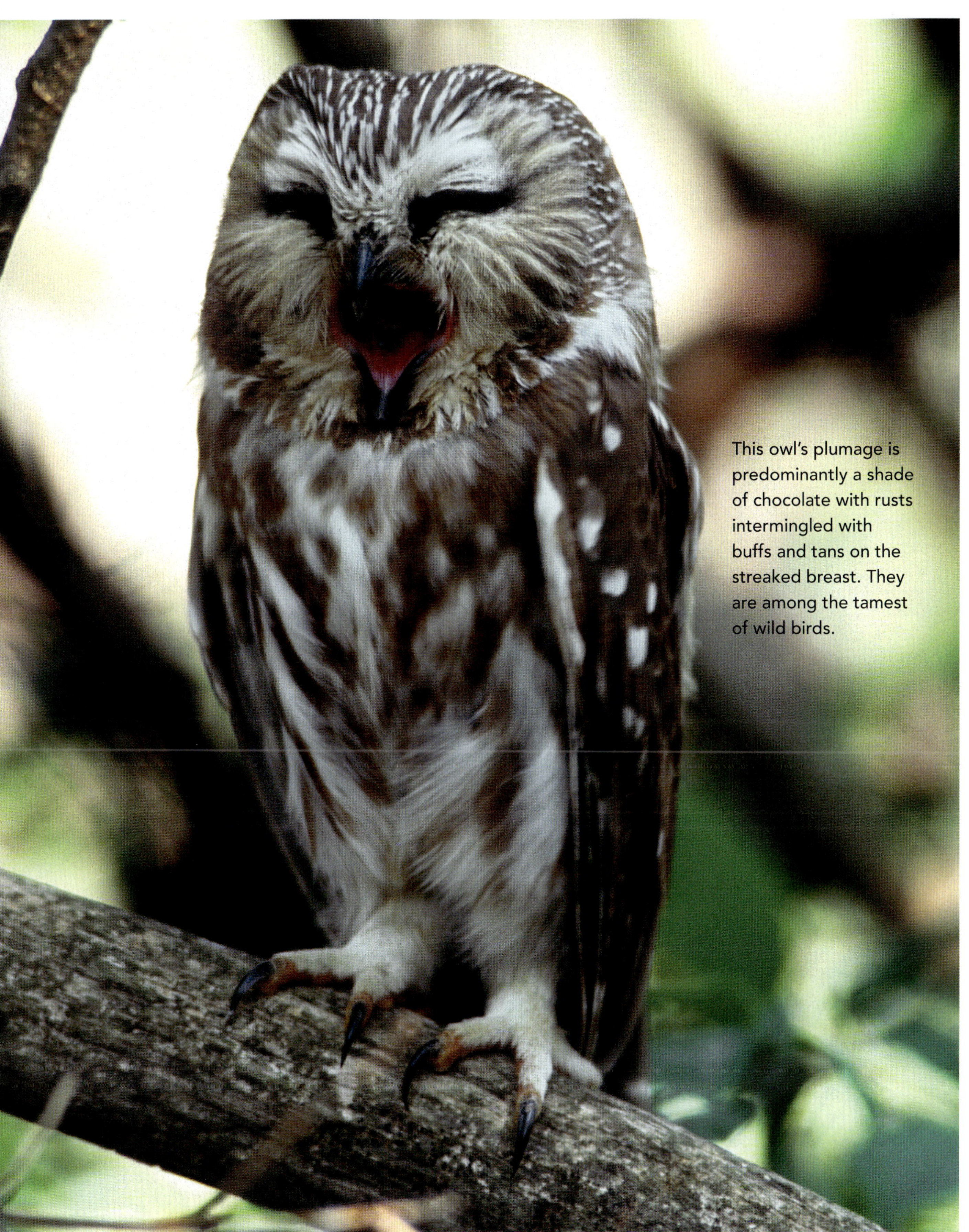

This owl's plumage is predominantly a shade of chocolate with rusts intermingled with buffs and tans on the streaked breast. They are among the tamest of wild birds.

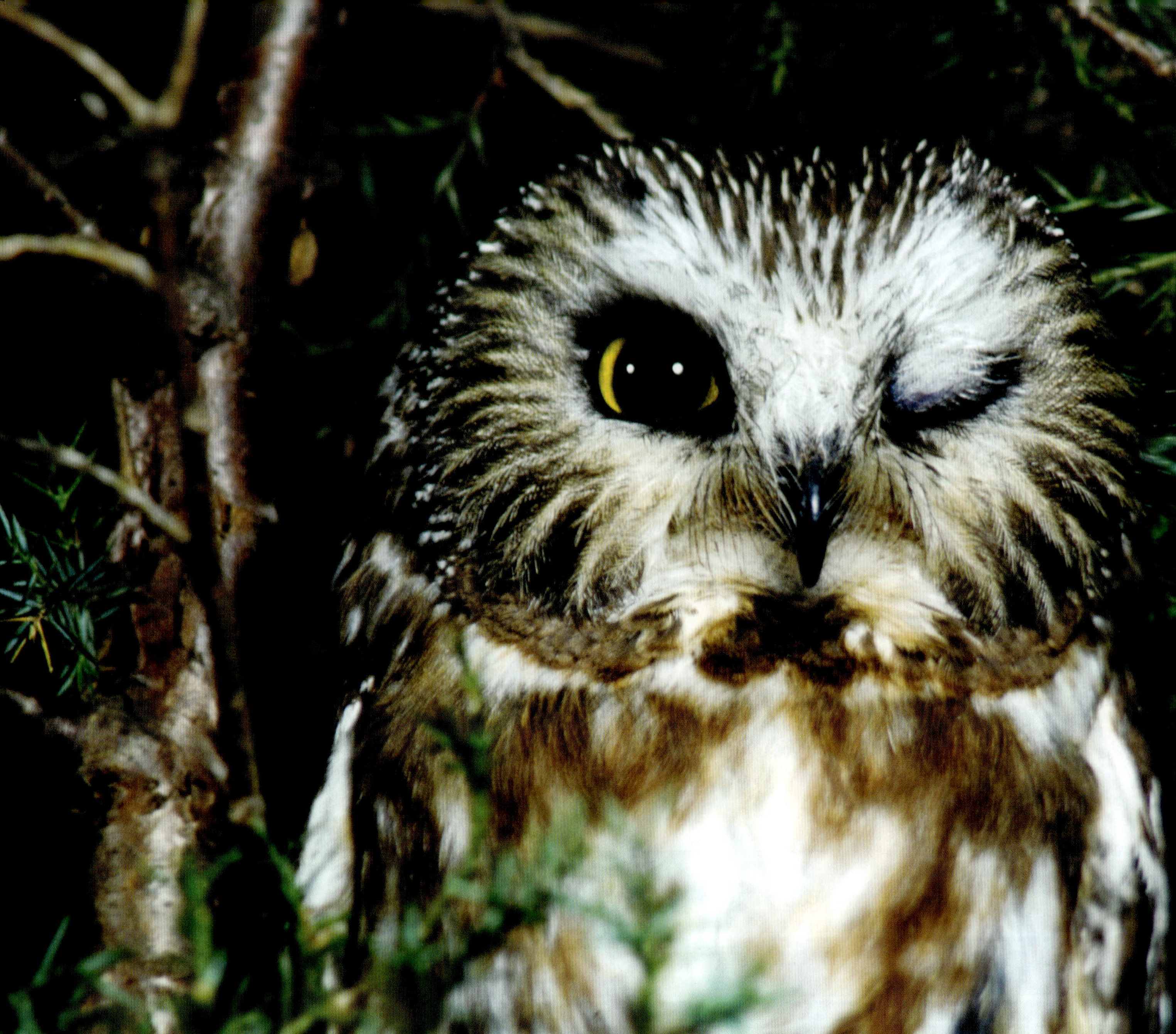

More than a half century later I remained engrossed in the natural history field. That first encounter with a saw-whet owl sparked an intense desire to learn first-hand all I could about this secretive little creature. Even as a teenager probing the journals of the time, I was quick to question the credibility of many of the accounts set to type describing the behavior and habits of the saw-whet owl.

Over the years, living in the same general area around Cincinnati, I devoted much of my time and career to the saw-whet. I have studied saw-whets on their wintering grounds here, captured and banded several hundred individuals, kept several dozen in captivity for closer study for varying lengths of time, and rigged 10 with transmitters for a telemetry study in the late 1960s and early 1970s. On a few occasions, I kept one all winter as a house guest, allowing it free roam of my rambling farmhouse, then releasing it in time for the spring migration. I gradually got to know the saw-whet owl pretty well, and it didn't take long to confirm what I had suspected from early on—that not much was known about the species, and many of the reports were often misinterpreted and even the products of misidentification.

Perhaps the most endearing of all the saw-whet's attributes is its apparent tameness. Upon discovery by a person, many individuals allow such a close approach they can actually be captured in the hand. Such a unique characteristic in a wild bird has prompted the question: "Why?" Some of the standard answers, which have been repeated for decades, speculate that the owls sleep so soundly that they are unaware; that

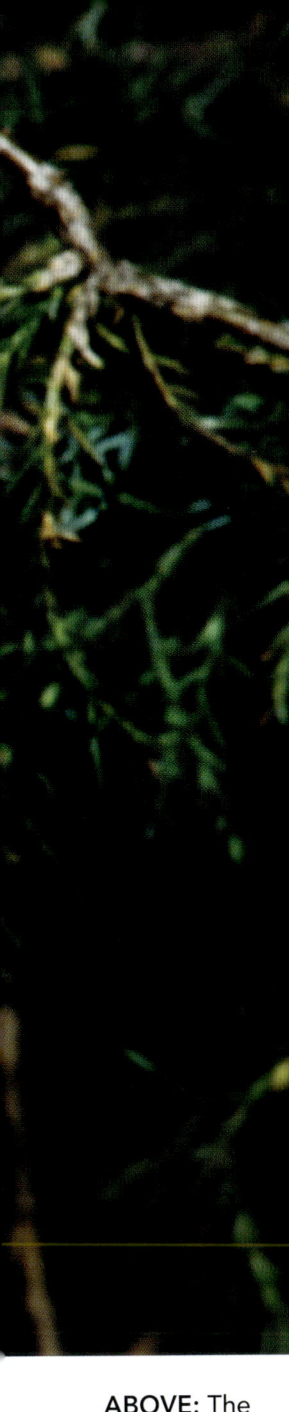

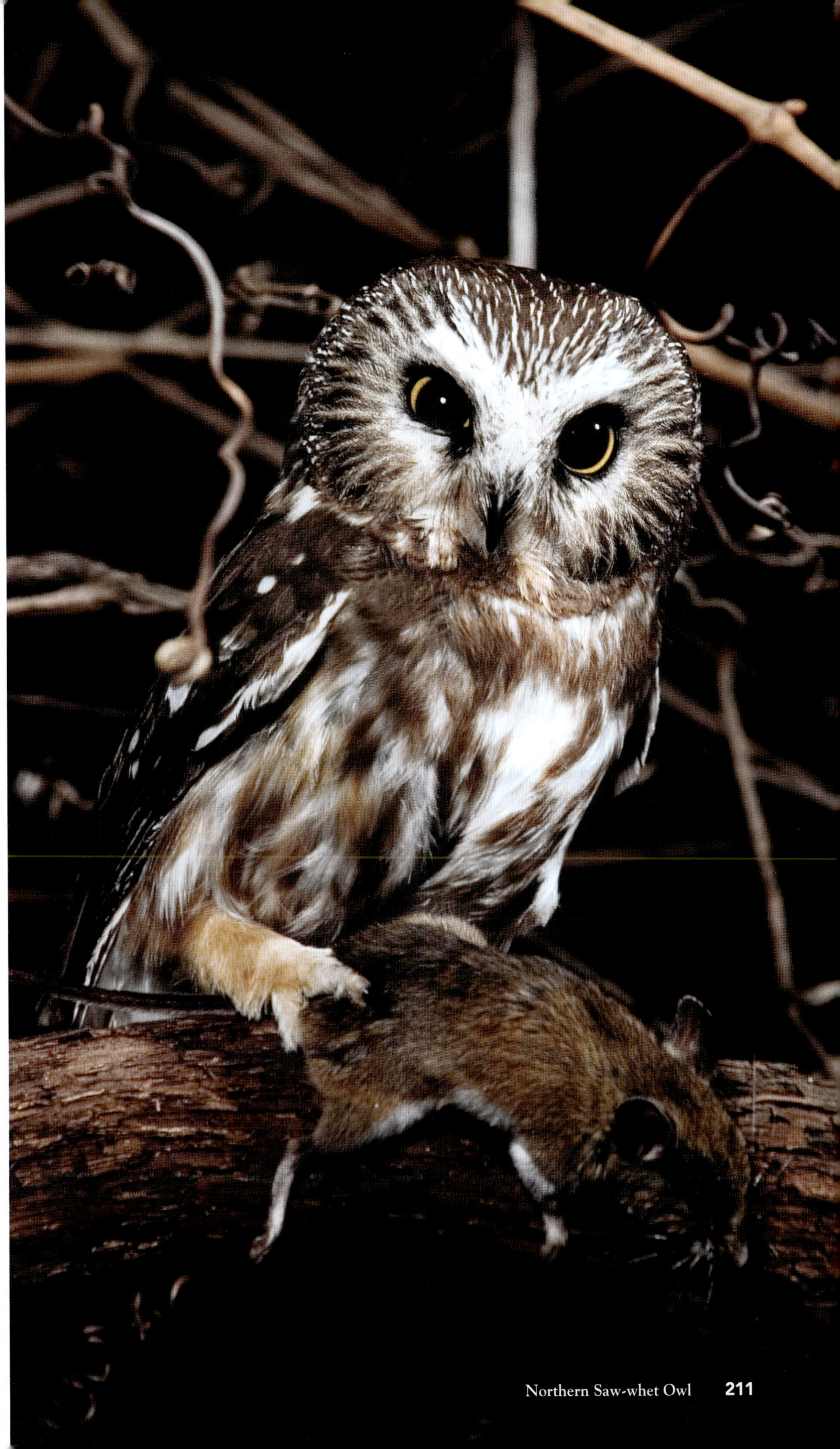

ABOVE: The saw-whet is the smallest owl in the eastern United States. **RIGHT:** Mice are the saw-whet owl's favorite food and it will eat one or two a day.

they do not see very well in daylight or that they are stupid! (The theory of presumed stupidity, as far as I'm concerned, doesn't even merit further discussion.)

I'm not certain why saw-whets allow such a close approach, but I do know it is not because they sleep so soundly. I have never, ever seen one sleeping, including my captive charges. I suspect that, like many other northern species, their lack of association with the dark side of human behavior toward wildlife has instilled no fear of people.

The saw-whet owl is six or seven inches high and weighs a mere three ounces. Like most owls, females are a bit larger than the males. Color varies according to the season and feather wear but is predominately some shade of chocolate with shades of rust on the streaked breast, and buffs, tan, and ocher subtleties intermingled. The pad of the foot is bright yellow. Eye color is usually rich yellow, and occasional birds approach orange-yellow.

Saw-whets, like the closely related boreal owl, lack ear tufts. Their beaks are black, and their heads are streaked with white. Good color photos are obviously a prime reference in reproducing a saw-whet, maybe better even than a bird in the flesh. Natural history museums and ornithological departments of many universities maintain study skin collections or even mounted specimens that could be available to the serious woodcarver.

Contrary to the theory that saw-whets allow close approach because of poor eyesight, the saw-whet (like other owls) sees perfectly well by day, even in the brightest light. During the telemetry studies, I sometimes found them actively hunting during daylight hours. Most often, this daylight hunting was associated with very cold weather and probably relates to the need to consume more food to maintain body heat.

During a recent discussion, Dr. Fred Alsop of East Tennessee State University told me that graduate students monitoring saw-whet nest boxes at the higher elevations of the southern Appalachians found males occasionally delivering food during daylight hours.

The saw-whet's principal food source is woodland mice, especially the white-footed mouse or the deer mouse. Food requirements per day vary between one and two full-grown mice. Quite often, an owl will be found roosting with the hindquarters of a mouse or other prey, which probably represents its second kill of the night, one that it was unable to consume. The saw-whet must now await the digestive process; it will not be able to consume the prey until it regurgitates the indigestible remains of the first meal—fur and bones—in the form of a small pellet. Most raptors habitually cache excess food for later consumption, but the saw-whet is the only one I know of that regularly roosts with it. Such a habit ensures thawed meat in times of severe weather.

On their winter ranges, saw-whets commonly use a half dozen or so favorite roosting sites, and it isn't long before the conspicuous white droppings that accumulate beneath the bird betray its otherwise nearly invisible presence. The pellets accumulate beneath the roost at a rate of one per day.

The telemetry study confirmed one aspect of saw-whet behavior I had long suspected: they do not roost in holes, in spite of the fact that they are reared in such situations. But I was surprised to find some individuals occupying such extensive winter ranges, a square mile or more. However, it appeared that the birds utilized only narrow corridors within such areas. An owl might be for several days in succession found on Roost A, then for the next week be discovered on Roost E, a half mile away. Then perhaps back to Roost A again for a few days, before off to Roost C. (Although, I once found a bird on the same roost for nearly 70 days.) The transmitters also revealed that saw-whets occasionally roosted high up, in retained foliage of mature oaks or beeches, instead of the more usual low elevations. Without the transmitters, such behavior could not have been recorded because the owls would never have been located.

Despite some of the writings that describe the saw-whet as a fierce and aggressive predator with such an insatiable appetite that it must eat all night long, it is one of the most delicate and fragile of the raptors. When I read some of the commonly repeated myths about its depredations, I feel like casting a pellet

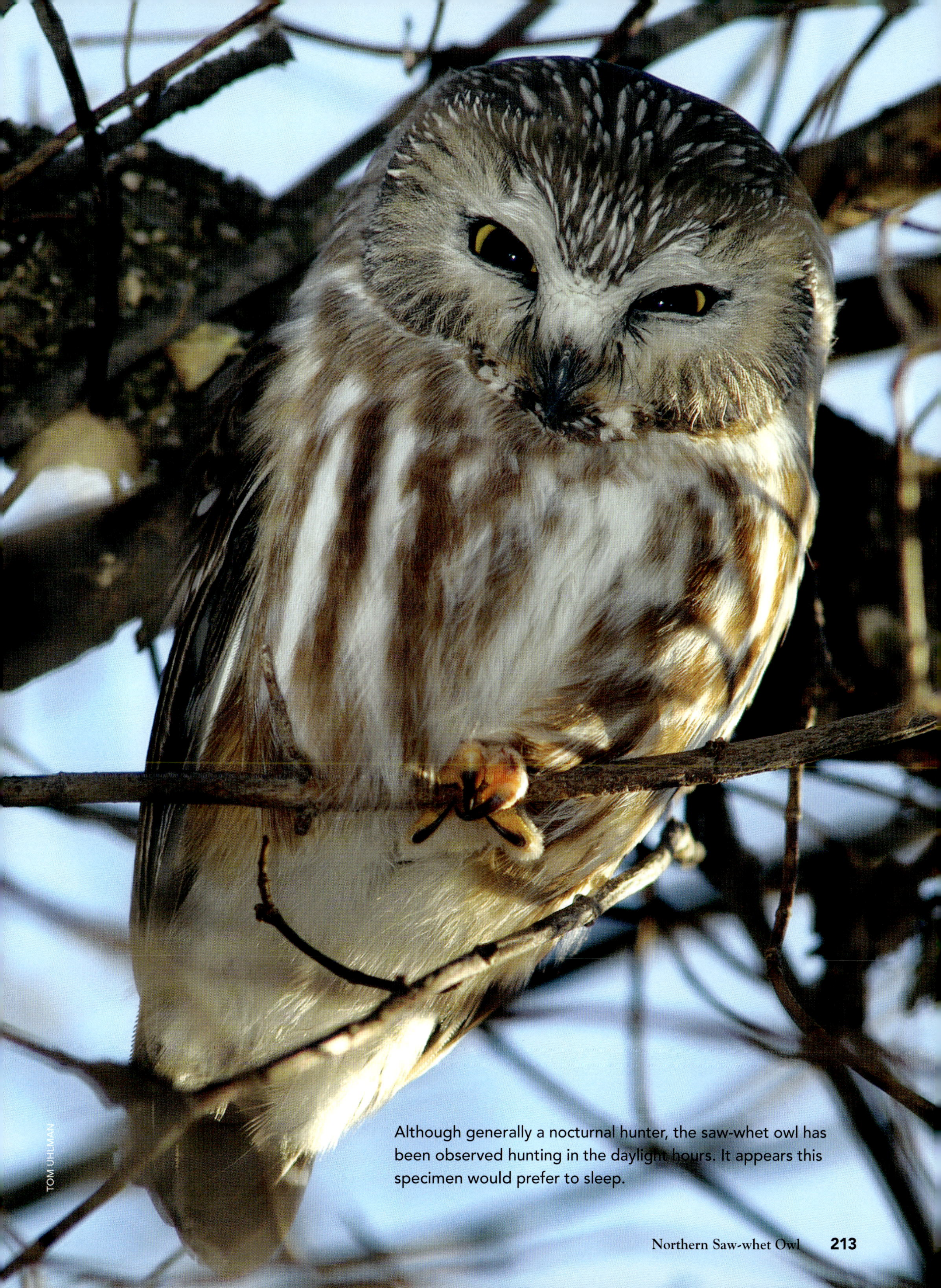

TOM UHLMAN

Although generally a nocturnal hunter, the saw-whet owl has been observed hunting in the daylight hours. It appears this specimen would prefer to sleep.

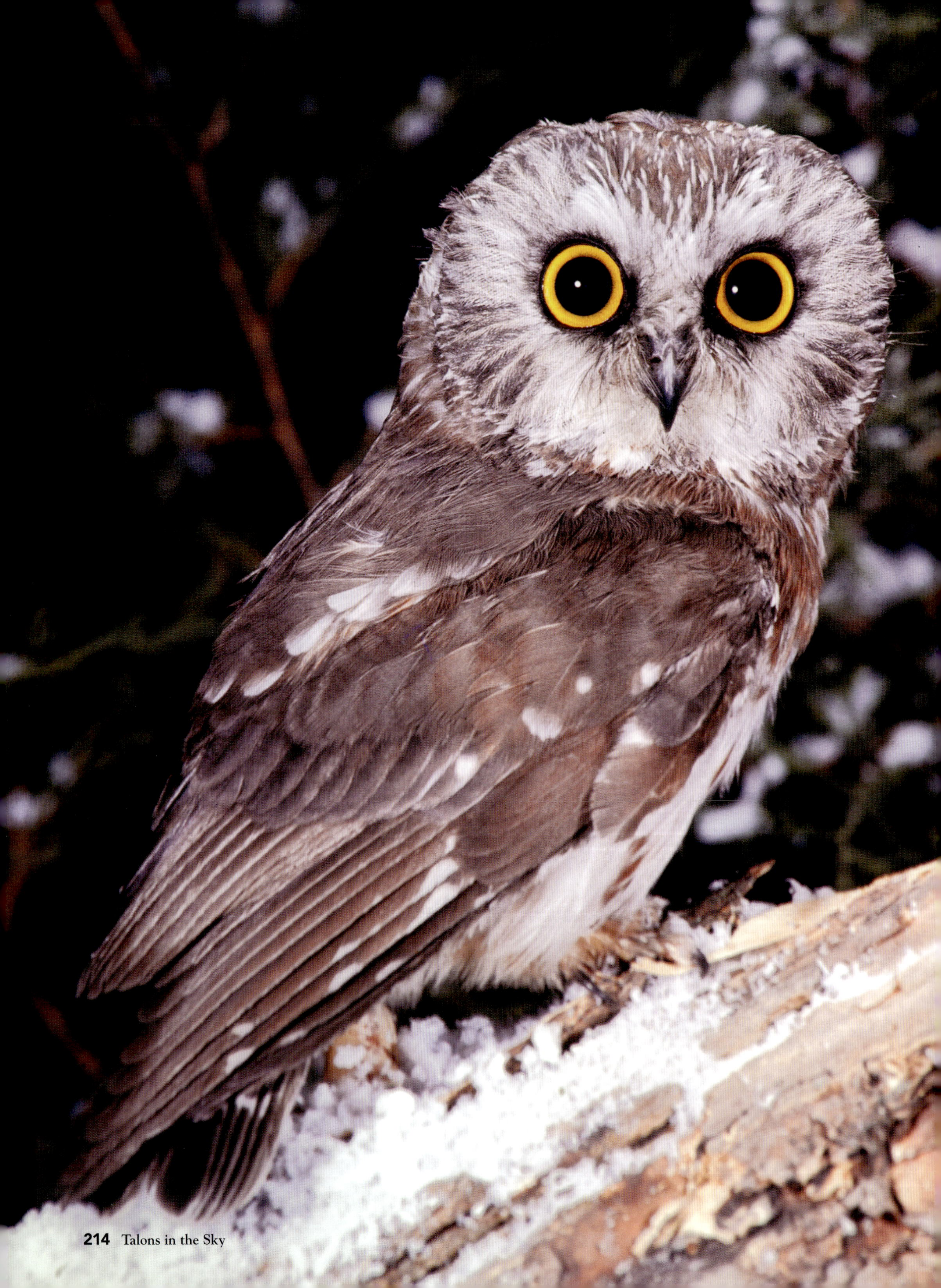

myself! Especially when I see pigeons, young rabbits, and flying squirrels listed on its bill-of-fare. Much of this misinformation stems from misidentification by the early observers, some from the nineteenth century, many of whom were pioneers and farmers making casual observations as best they could. Unfortunately, many modern writers, lacking sufficient field experience, tend to accept at face value anything they find in their research.

As a bird photographer, I have always enjoyed shooting raptors. The regal bearing of the hawks and eagles and the intense, scholarly stare of the owls tend to command the instant attention of even a casual observer. The owls, especially, exhibit the ability of modifying their appearance to suit the occasion. Saw-whets are especially animated. Fear, anger, and contentment are all expressed in the various contortions of the face and the body plumage.

When roosting in its "hiding pose," a saw-whet is likely to have body plumage moderately compressed, facial area drawn and eyelids closed to mere slits, as it sits motionless on one foot, apparently asleep. But walk around behind it and wait a few seconds. The head will gradually, ever so slowly, revolve 180 degrees to face you. Retreat some distance and remain motionless or watch from a blind, and the owl will gradually revert to a more relaxed attitude. The plumage will be more expanded, and on very cold days the bird may appear almost the shape of a softball as it insulates itself. Defense or fear is expressed in the same way as other owls: with beak snapping and wide-eyed swaying back and forth with wings spread and presented in such a way as to make itself appear much larger and more formidable than it really is.

The saw-whet has been misidentified, mislabeled, and misaligned, but for me it will always be the subject of great fascination and admiration.

Measurements (in mm)

	Male	Female
Length	170–210	170–210
Wingspan	460–560	460–560
Wingspan	460–560	460–560
Weight	2.6 oz.	3.5 oz.

Aegolius acadicus's colloquial names include Acadian and Kirtland's owl, saw-flier, and sparrow owl. It has good vision day or night, and lacks ear tufts.

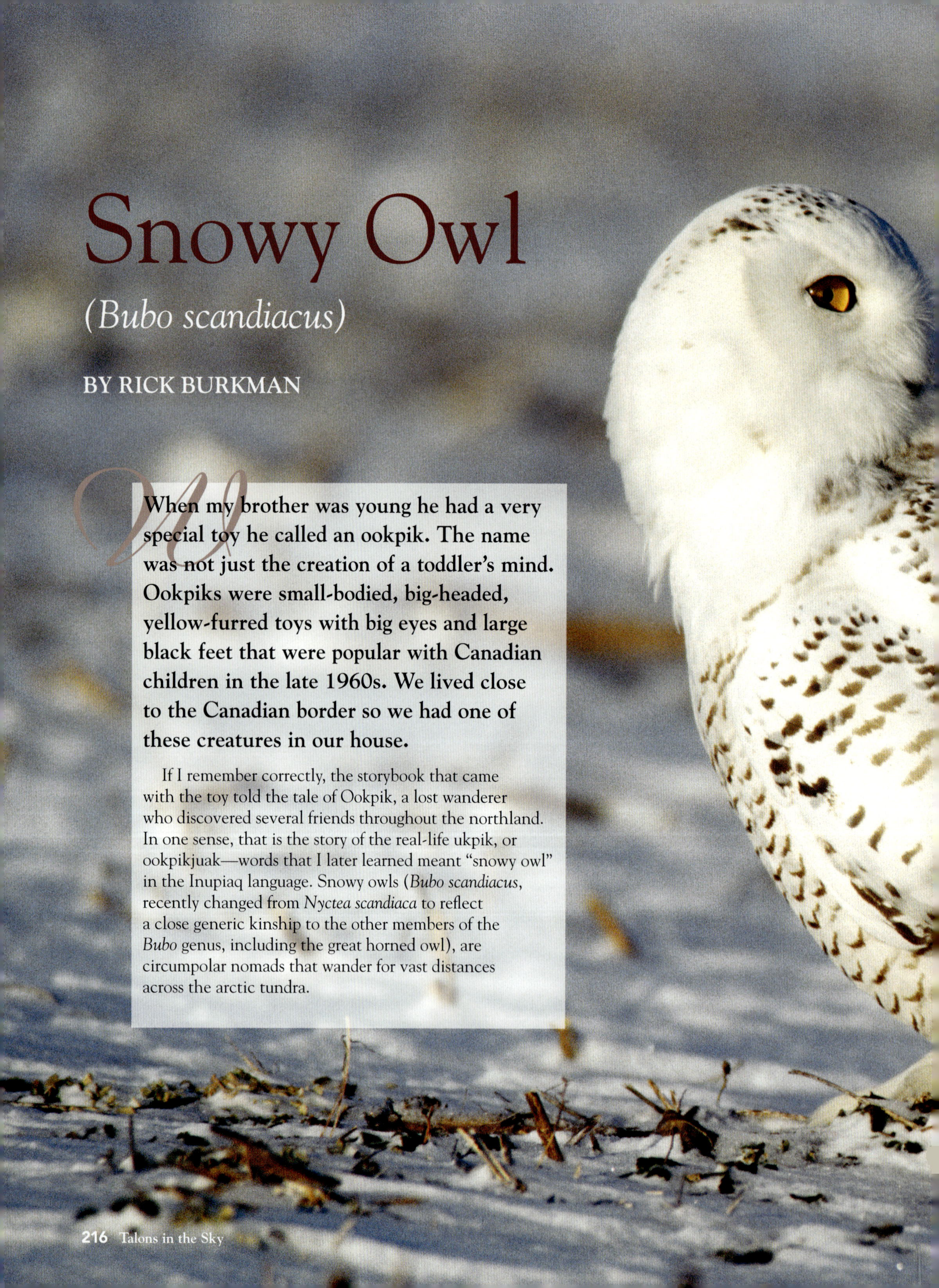

Snowy Owl

(Bubo scandiacus)

BY RICK BURKMAN

When my brother was young he had a very special toy he called an ookpik. The name was not just the creation of a toddler's mind. Ookpiks were small-bodied, big-headed, yellow-furred toys with big eyes and large black feet that were popular with Canadian children in the late 1960s. We lived close to the Canadian border so we had one of these creatures in our house.

If I remember correctly, the storybook that came with the toy told the tale of Ookpik, a lost wanderer who discovered several friends throughout the northland. In one sense, that is the story of the real-life ukpik, or ookpikjuak—words that I later learned meant "snowy owl" in the Inupiaq language. Snowy owls (*Bubo scandiacus*, recently changed from *Nyctea scandiaca* to reflect a close generic kinship to the other members of the *Bubo* genus, including the great horned owl), are circumpolar nomads that wander for vast distances across the arctic tundra.

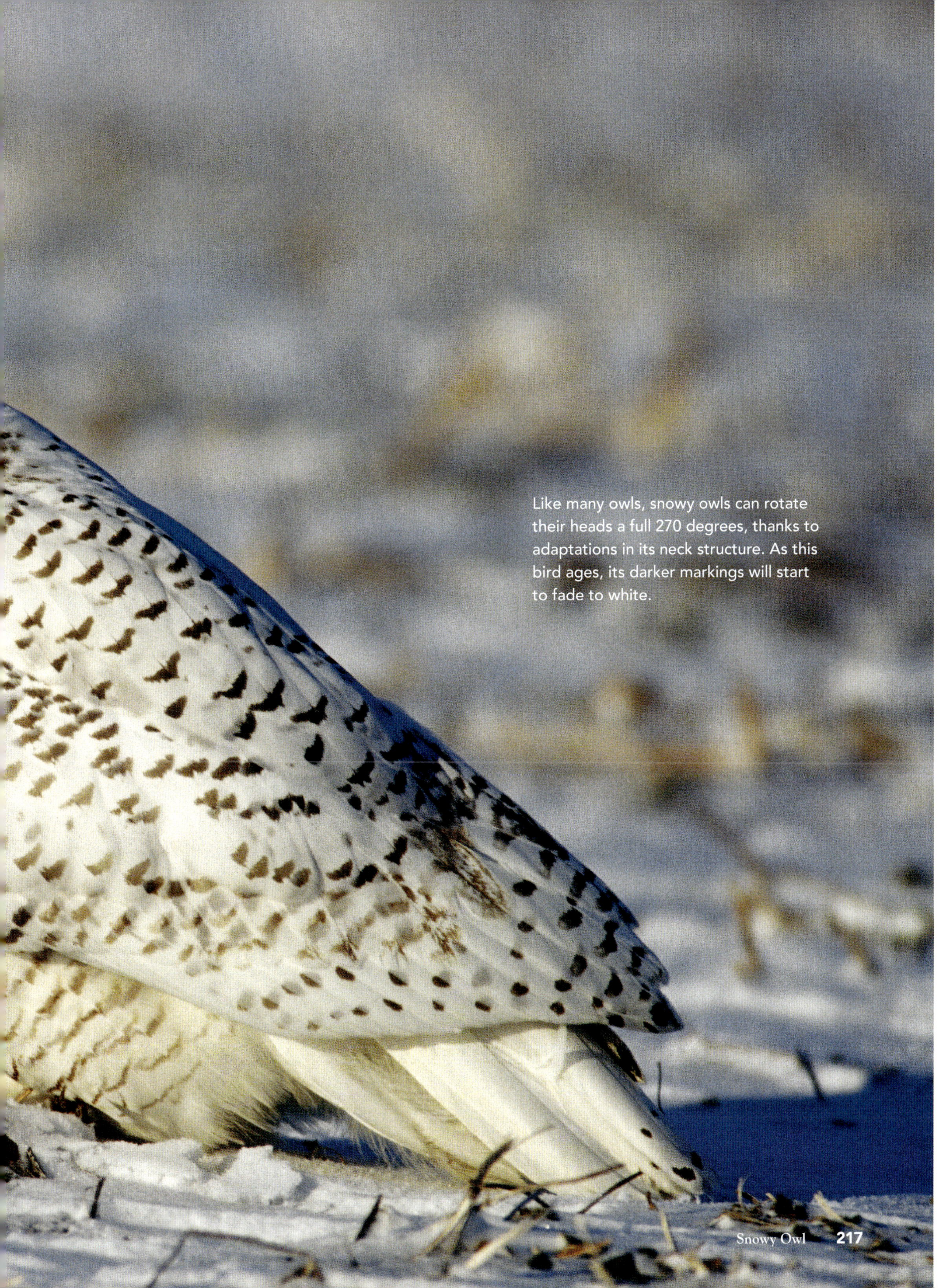

Like many owls, snowy owls can rotate their heads a full 270 degrees, thanks to adaptations in its neck structure. As this bird ages, its darker markings will start to fade to white.

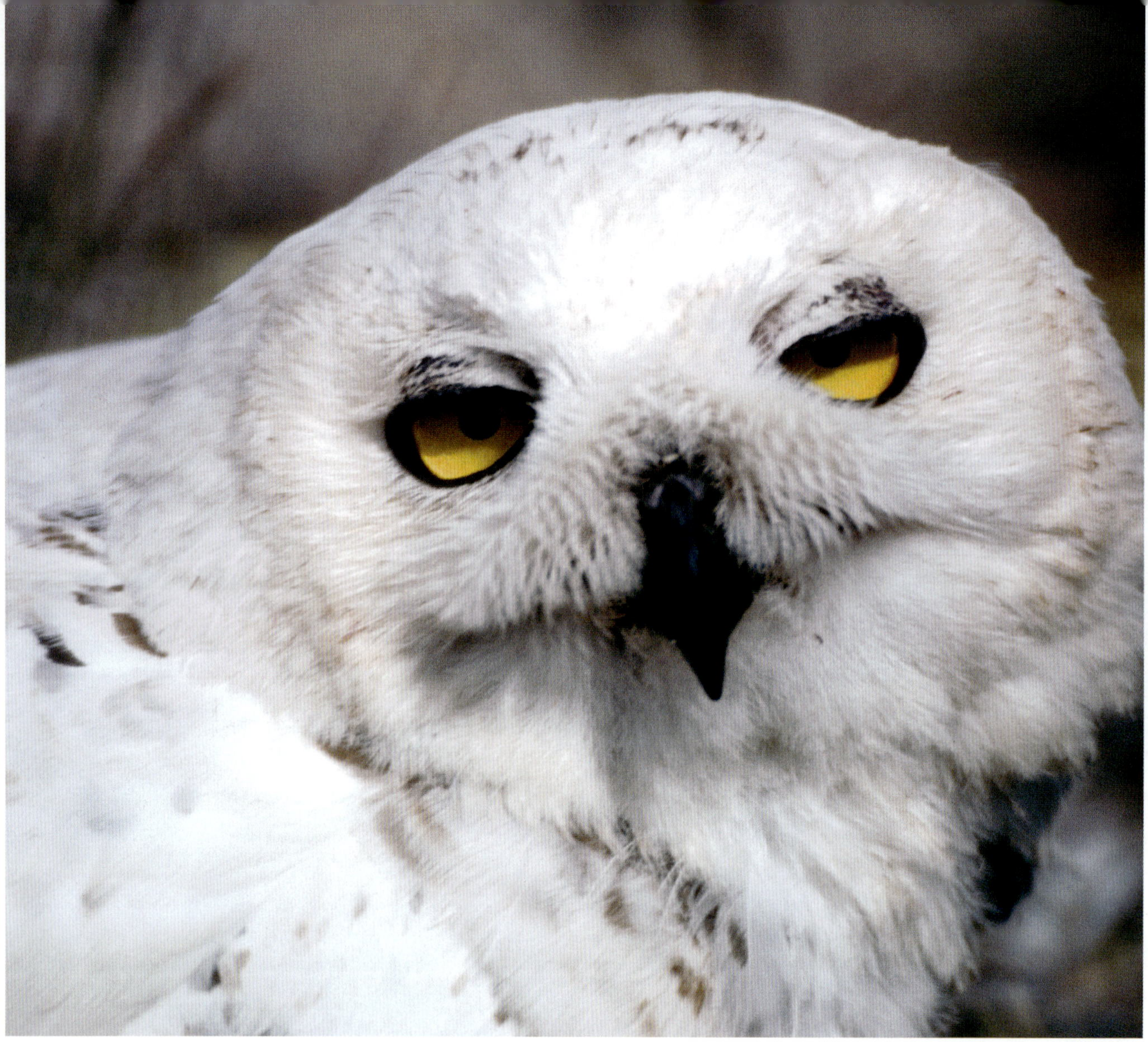

The snowy owl's prominent upper eyelids serve as protection from the bright arctic sun. **OPPOSITE:** An owl will often perch conspicuously on the ground or on low stumps, fence posts, or buildings. Then, with a strong flap of its wings, it will speed toward its next victim.

Snowy owls have intrigued and mystified humans since prehistoric times. A depiction of a pair of snowy owls surrounding a downy nestling found in the mysterious Le Trois Frère caves of France is the oldest known artistic interpretation of any bird species. Snowy owl bones have been found in archeological digs, and findings indicate that they were not only venerated by Paleolithic hunters, they were probably eaten by them as well.

Snowy owls themselves, on the other hand, like to eat rodents. Lemmings make up the largest part of their diet, but few creatures living in an ookpik's territory are safe when hunger pangs strike. The owl will sit quietly for long periods until a likely meal makes an appearance. Then, with a strong flap of its wings and its crisp golden eyes holding steady on its prey, the owl will speed toward its victim. Pointed talons on the ends of feathery toes with the ability to rotate make a trap that few targets can escape. Arctic hares are plucked in mid-bound, ducks are snatched from the air, and fish are scooped from cold, ice-filled waters. Geese and plovers are plucked from shorelines and ptarmigans are eagerly captured when available. Occasionally, crows or ravens mob a sitting owl in a dangerous game of chicken—more than one mobbing corvid has become lunch for a hungry, irritated owl.

At the start of a meal, a snowy owl swallows small prey head first. An owl may consume several lemmings this way before it begins to be sated, and then, like a kid at a dinner table, it will start to pick apart the remaining elements of its meal. Several hours later, the owl will expel a large pellet that contains a bundle

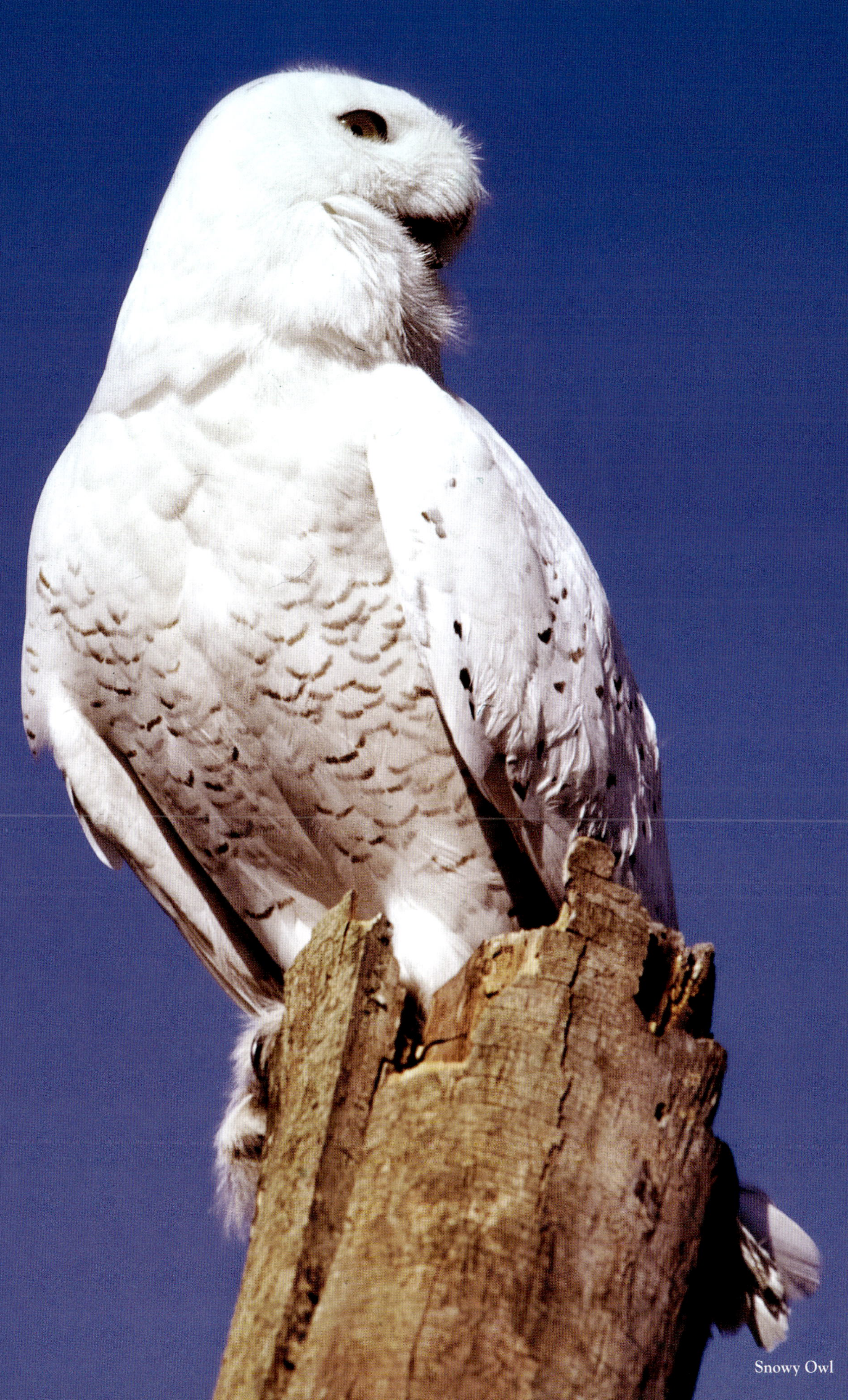

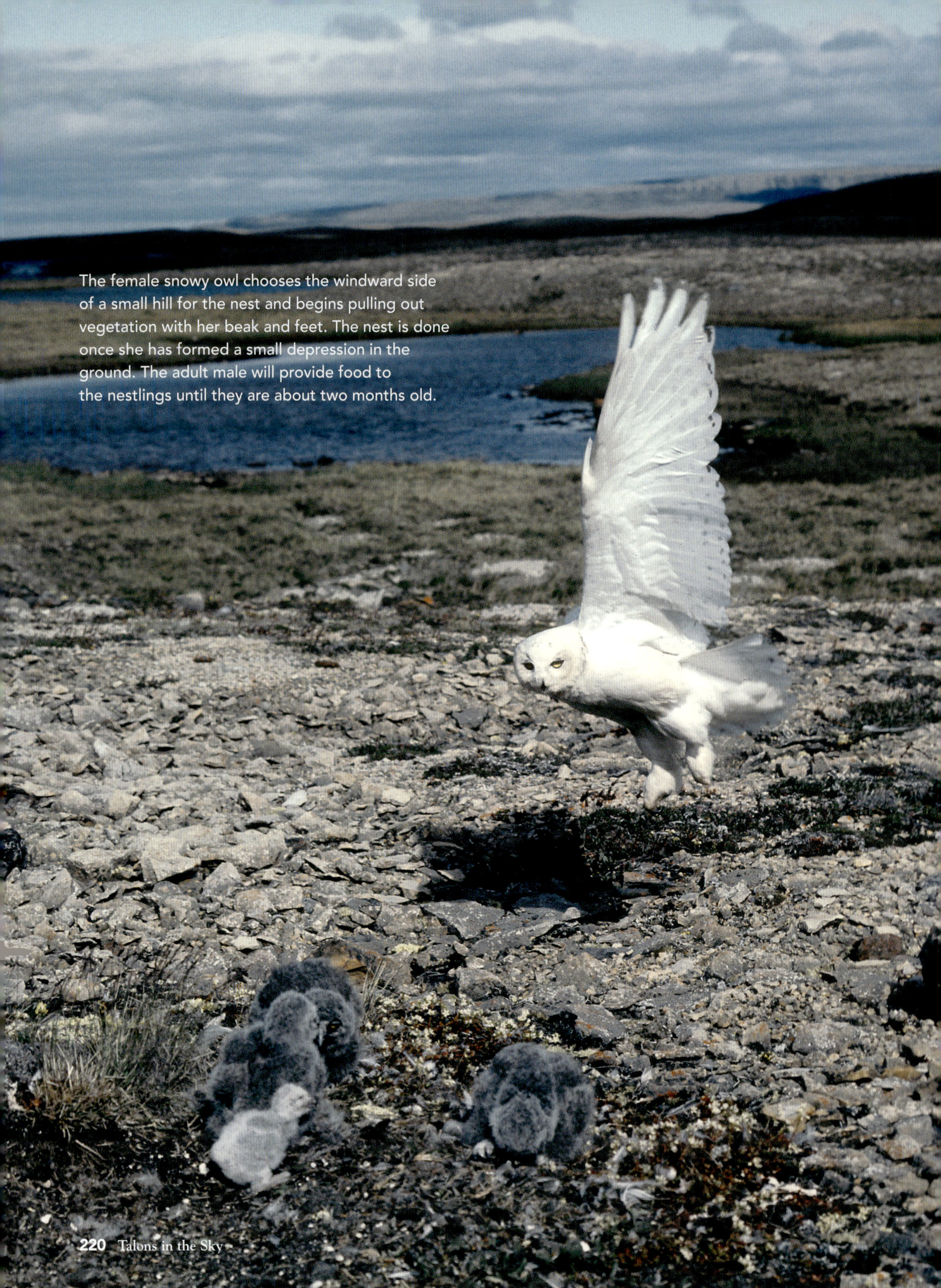

The female snowy owl chooses the windward side of a small hill for the nest and begins pulling out vegetation with her beak and feet. The nest is done once she has formed a small depression in the ground. The adult male will provide food to the nestlings until they are about two months old.

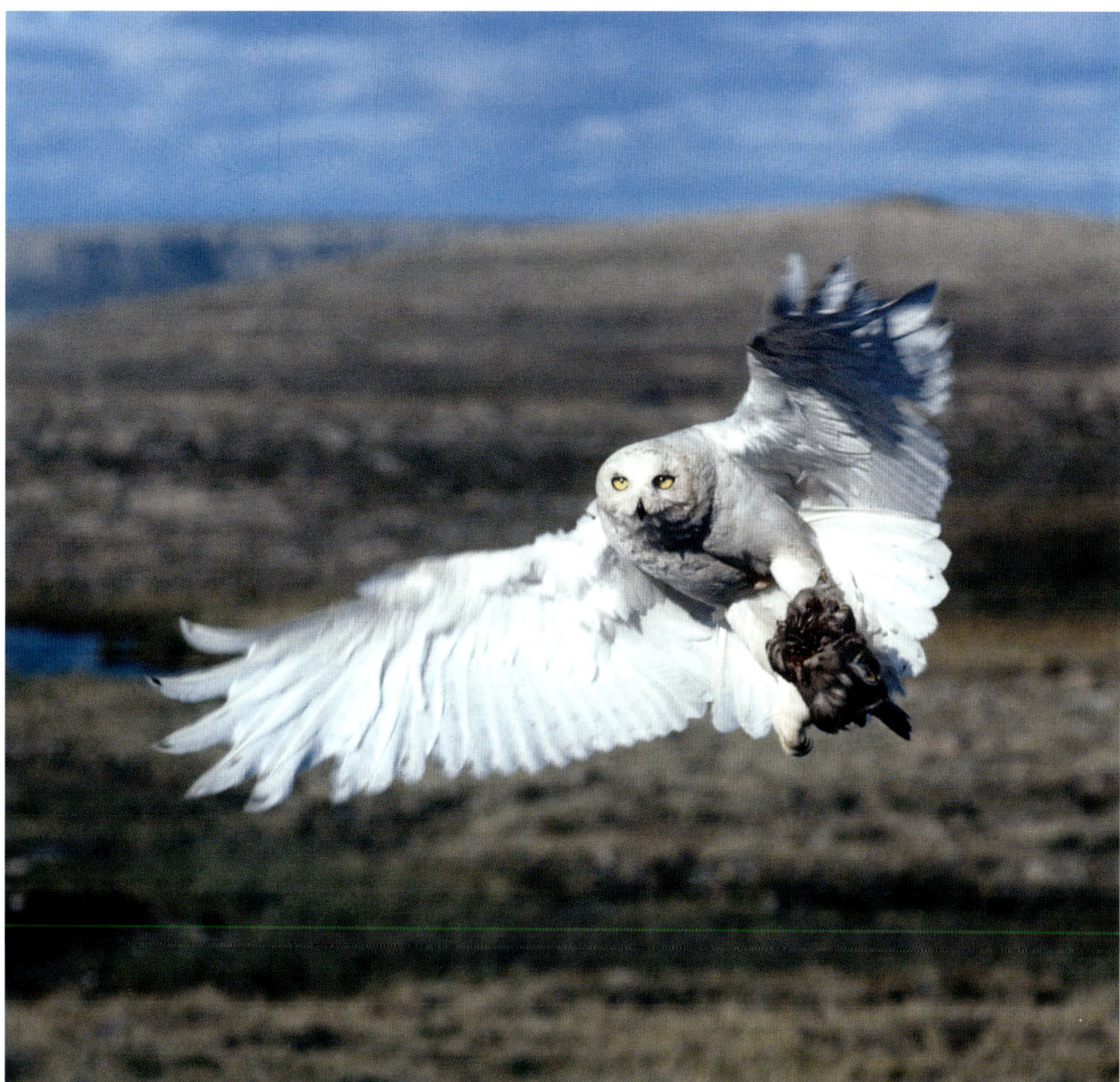

of fur, crushed bones, and tiny teeth—the indigestible remnants of its last supper.

These large, sometimes aggressive birds are gentle when it comes to pair bonding and nesting. A male shows his interest in a female by flying past her perch with powerful wingbeats. At the peak of each upstroke, he pauses momentarily and then quickly regains altitude with a deep, exaggerated down stroke. The resulting display flight is undulating and showy, not the direct line of attack used when hunting. Like any good suitor, the owl brings a gift to his would-be lover—a freshly killed lemming is the preferred delicacy for seducing snowy owl females.

He drops his treat on a small hill, sometimes the site of an old nest, and then stands tall over the prize. He spreads his wings slightly with his wrists held high so that he looks like a white signal flag beckoning in the distance. As the female approaches his hilltop, the male drops his head and lowers his body closer and closer to the ground. Sometimes the two will take to the air and the male will present the lemming to the female during the paired flight. This final symbol of betrothal apparently seals the deal. The male has shown that he will be a good provider and the female accepts him as her mate.

After bonding and copulation, the pair settle down to create a home for the next generation of owls. The female is responsible for the nest building and mainte-

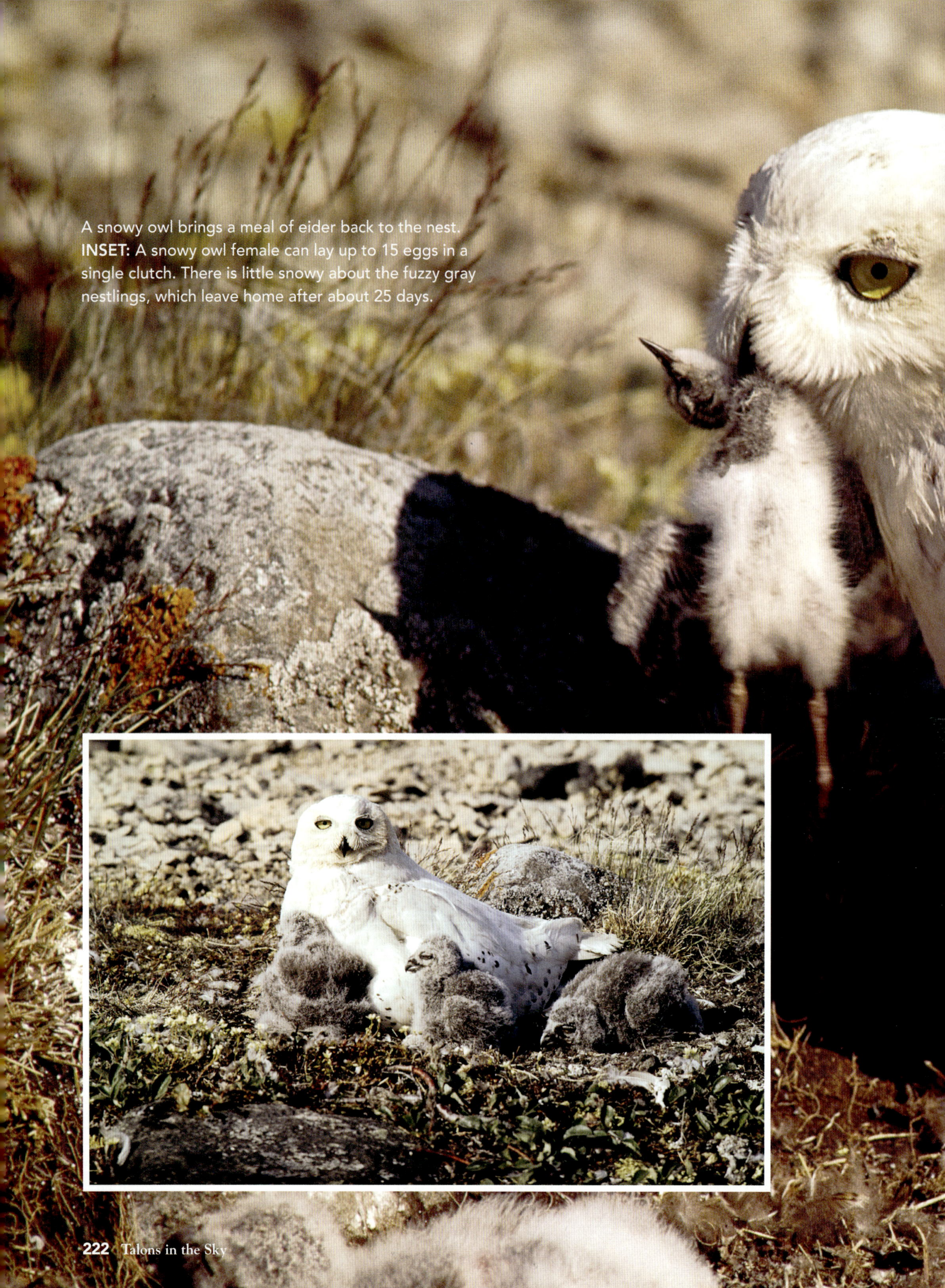

A snowy owl brings a meal of eider back to the nest. **INSET:** A snowy owl female can lay up to 15 eggs in a single clutch. There is little snowy about the fuzzy gray nestlings, which leave home after about 25 days.

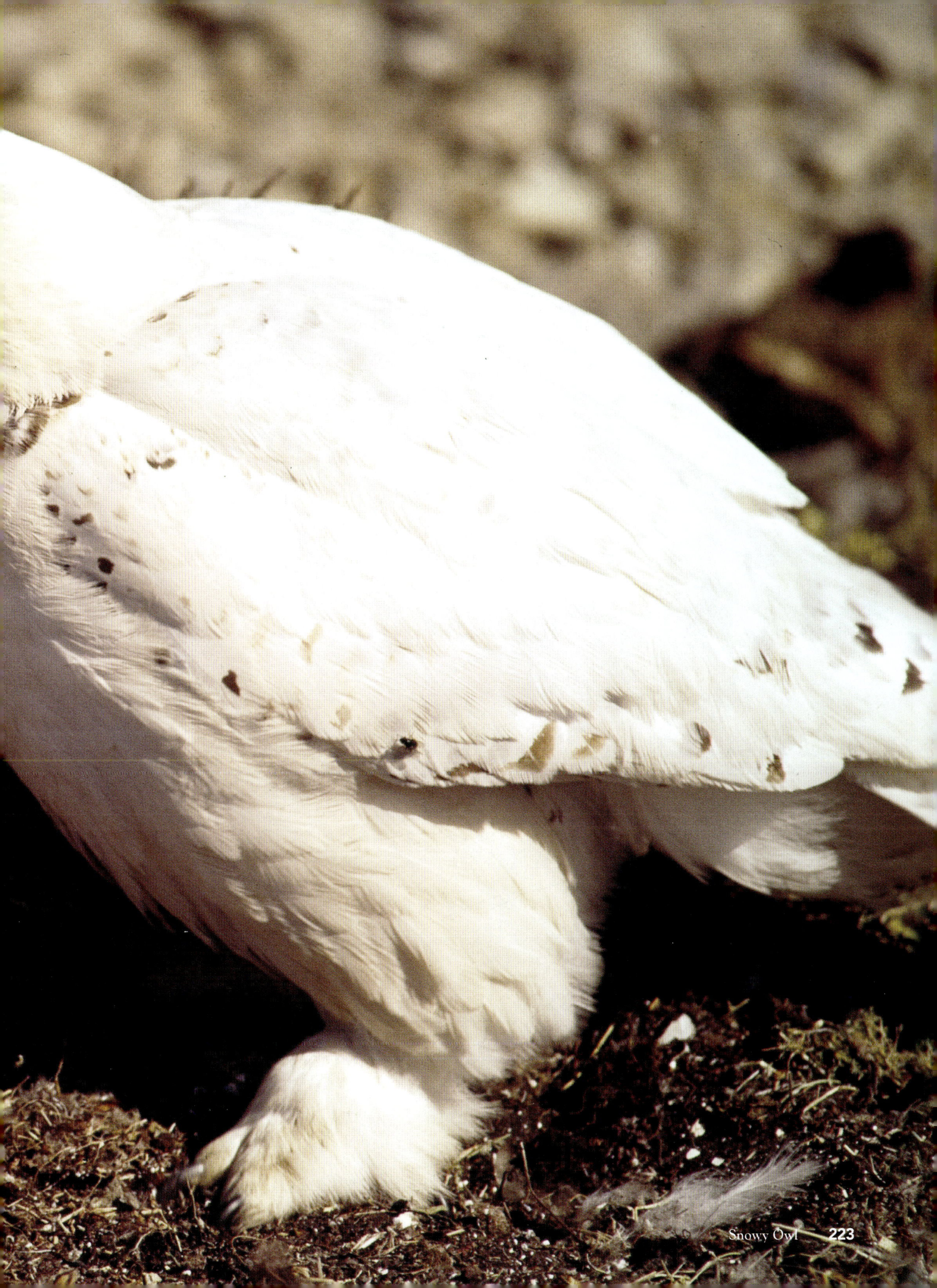

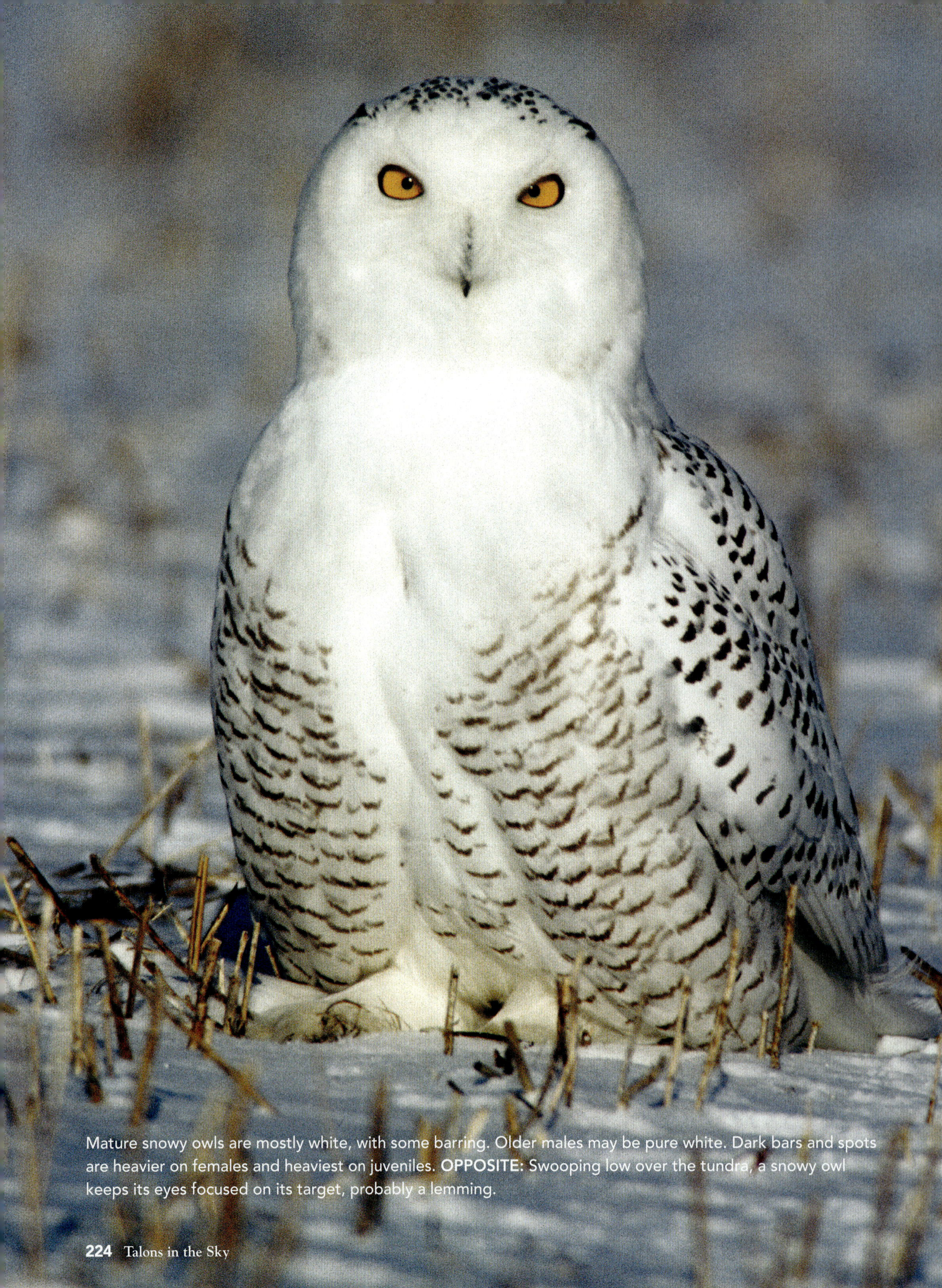

Mature snowy owls are mostly white, with some barring. Older males may be pure white. Dark bars and spots are heavier on females and heaviest on juveniles. **OPPOSITE:** Swooping low over the tundra, a snowy owl keeps its eyes focused on its target, probably a lemming.

nance, but she does not do very much. She chooses the windward side of a small hill, the side with the least snow, and begins pulling, twisting, and turning vegetation with her wide, strong beak and large, powerful feet until she exposes bare earth. As soon as a little depression forms in the soil, the nest is done. The ground is frozen with year-round permafrost and provides no insulation to the nest, but apparently the body heat of the incubating female is sufficient to keep the eggs warm.

When the nest is complete, the female begins laying her short, elliptical, creamy-white eggs. Even in the spring and summer, when the sunlight bathes the land 24 hours a day, weather conditions can be extreme around the Arctic Circle, so the female begins incubating after she lays the first egg. Every two days she lays another egg until a clutch of seven or eight is complete. She lays fewer eggs in low lemming years and more eggs during years with high lemming populations; as few as three and as many as 15 eggs have been recorded. By the time the female is done laying, she may have produced a mass of eggs totaling more than 40 percent of her body weight—an unusual expenditure of energy in the raptor world.

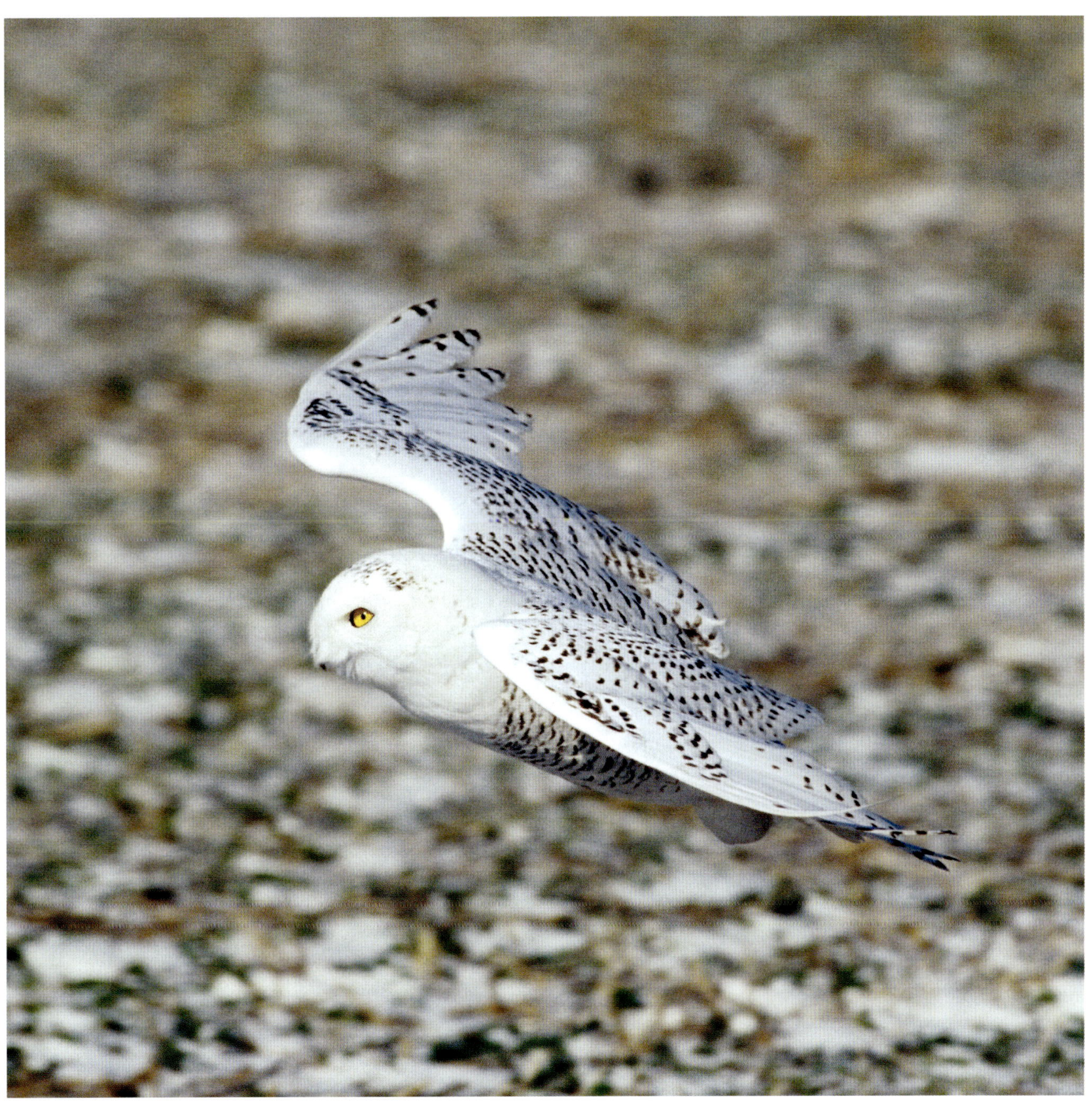

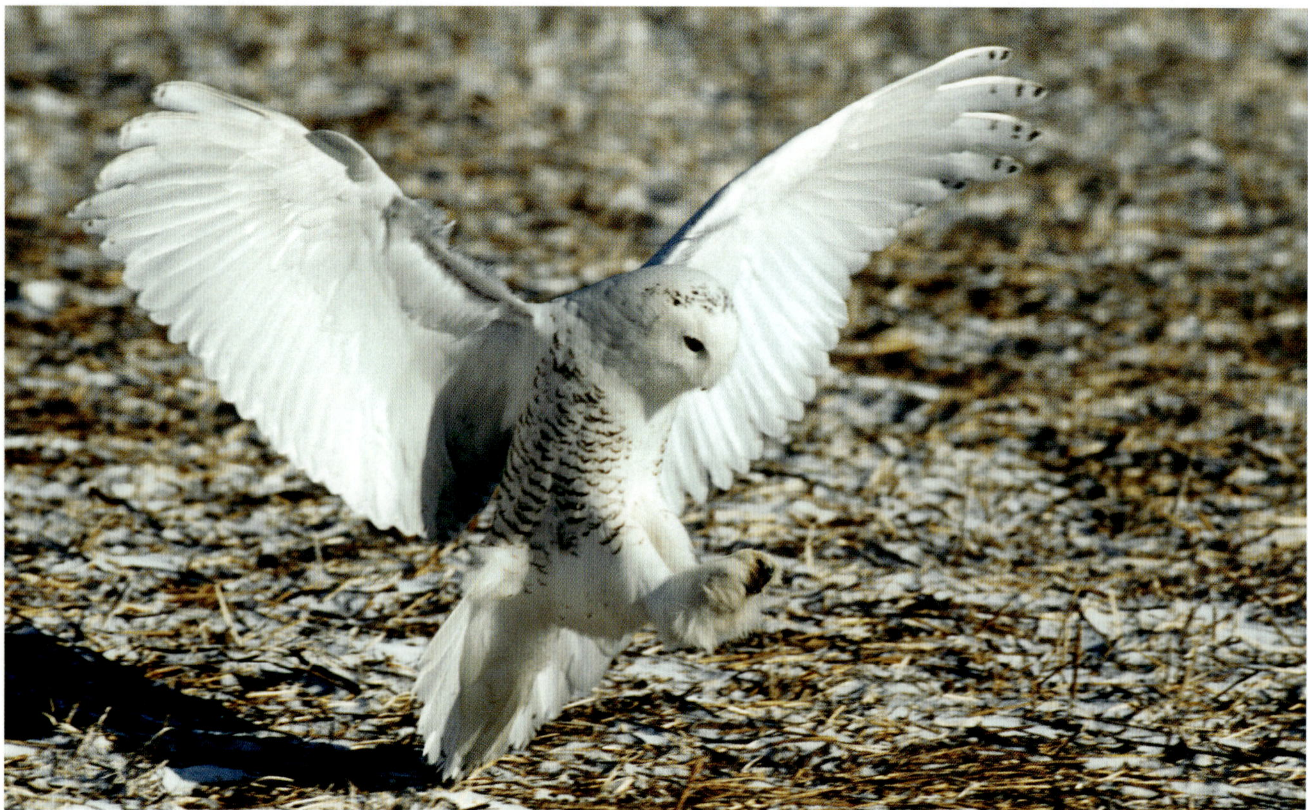

ABOVE: A snowy owl swoops down on prey. Lemmings are the owl's favorite meal, and when lemming populations decline in the arctic, the owls may wander as far south as northern Alabama, Oklahoma, and central California. **OPPOSITE:** Pointed talons on the ends of feathery toes create a trap that few targets can escape.

Hatching, like egg laying, happens at two-day intervals. After 32 days inside an egg, the snowy owl chicks are ready to break free and begin their lives. Blind, wet, helpless, and small, the owlets push their way out of their dirty white shells. The short downy feathers that cover their bodies dry rapidly, turning the owlets into little white fuzzy balls with gaping black beaks. Their eyes open within a week and by the time they are two weeks old their white neonatal down has changed to an ashy gray fluff that blends with the surrounding landscape.

Active owl nests are attractive to other birds, even birds that are potential prey animals for the owls. Black brants, common eiders, and greater and lesser snow geese will all nest around a knoll that supports an owl's nest. The protection the owl provides against arctic foxes and other predators is apparently worth the risk of being added to the menu.

After living in the nest for about 25 days, young owls begin to abandon their homes. Younger birds remain in the nest until they, too, are about 25 days old. Depending on the size of the clutch, more than 100 days can pass from the time the first egg is laid until the last juvenile bird leaves the nest. When the nest is empty, the trampled eggshells, decomposing pellets, lemming leftovers, and other nest debris provides a quick seasonal flash of fertilization to the nutrient-poor soil, turning the nest hill into a brief oasis of greenery in the short arctic summer.

The recently departed nestlings are still too young to fly, so they hop, jump, and run through the sedges and mosses of the tundra. The adult male is a good provider and will hunt through the light of a 24-hour day to bring food to the young birds until they are about two months old. By that time, the owlets have practiced short flights and are starting to hunt on their own. It is estimated that a nest of nine owlets can consume up to 1,500 lemmings—almost 125 pounds of small rodents—before dispersing from the nest territory.

After leaving their natal home, the young birds begin their nomadic lifestyle. Tagged birds have been recorded moving for thousands of miles across the frozen Chukchi and Bering Seas, as they travel from

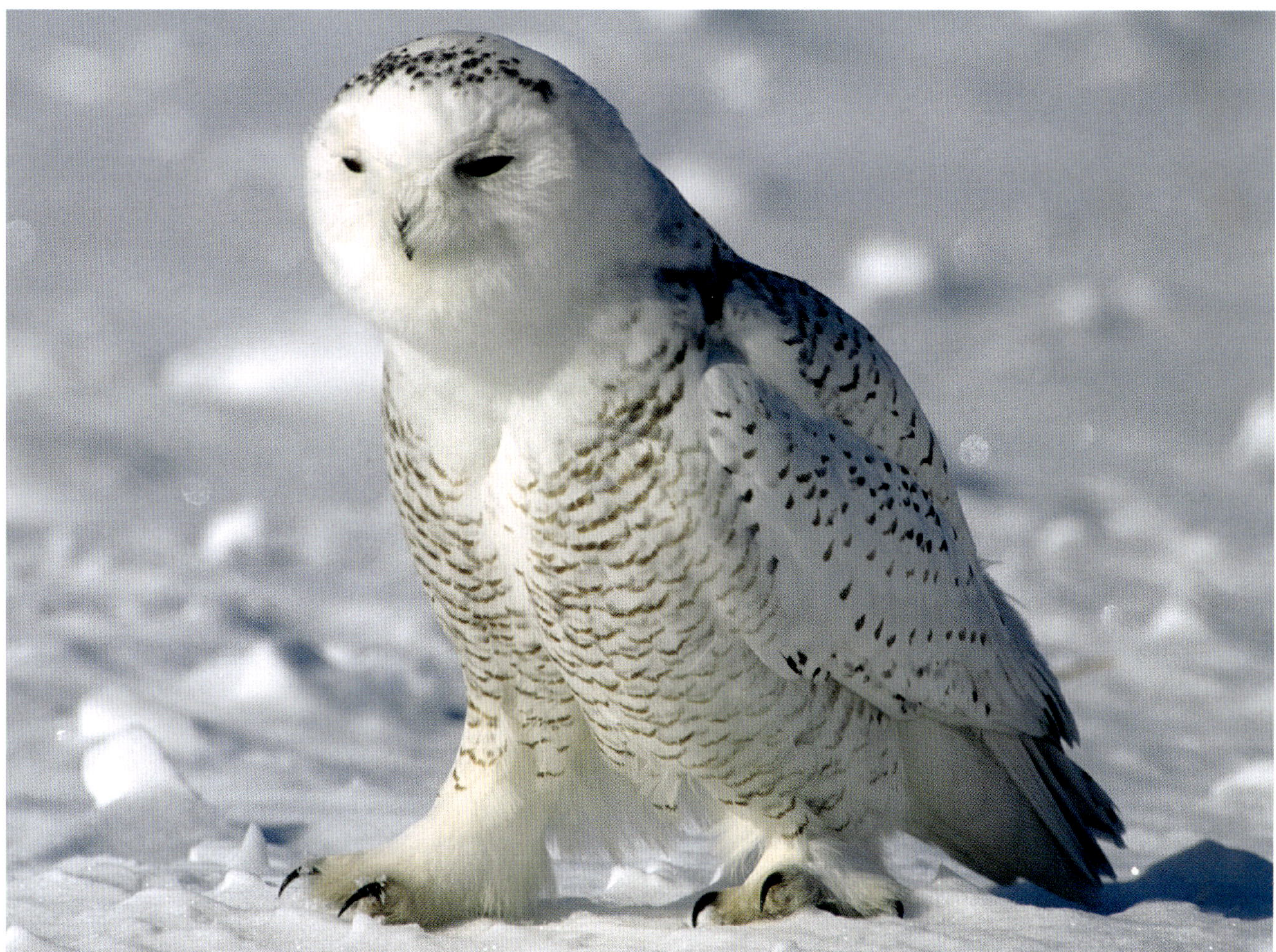

North America to Eurasia and back. It is probably safe to assume that Eurasian birds engage in their own version of circumpolar sojourning and make visits to North America. While some of the North American youngsters are on the snowy owl version of a walk-about, others are migrating to their southward retreat on the wintry, windswept Great Plains or the farm fields and marshes of the northeast, northwest, and north-central portions of Canada and the United States. Snowy owls like a good view of their world, so they can often be spotted surveying their winter territories from church steeples, silo roofs, fence posts, and small hills.

Snowy owl populations irrupt southward every three to five years, closely following the rise and fall of the arctic lemming populations. When these small mammal populations crash, the owls search for better hunting grounds. During irruption years, they move as far south as South Carolina and northern California, sitting patiently, watching and waiting for a small mouse, lemming, or vole to pop its head out of a burrow.

By February or March many of the migratory birds are feeling the urge to return north. Like silent white ghosts, they float and drift and flap their way back home to the land somewhere between the tree line and the edge of the polar seas. There the males will find and defend new territories—small in good lemming years, immense when lemming populations drop—and the females will raise new families. The nomadic life cycle will begin again.

Next winter, snowy owls will again rest on the Great Plains of North America, ride ice floes to Siberia, and survey the manicured winter fields of northern Europe. Ookpiks truly are white winter wanderers.

Measurements (in mm)

	Male	Female
Bill	26.6	28.4
Wing Chord	416.5	455.9
Tail	235.3	246.2
Tarsus	68.0	68.0

Barred Owl

(Strix varia)

Great Gray Owl

(Strix nebulosa)

BY RICK BURKMAN

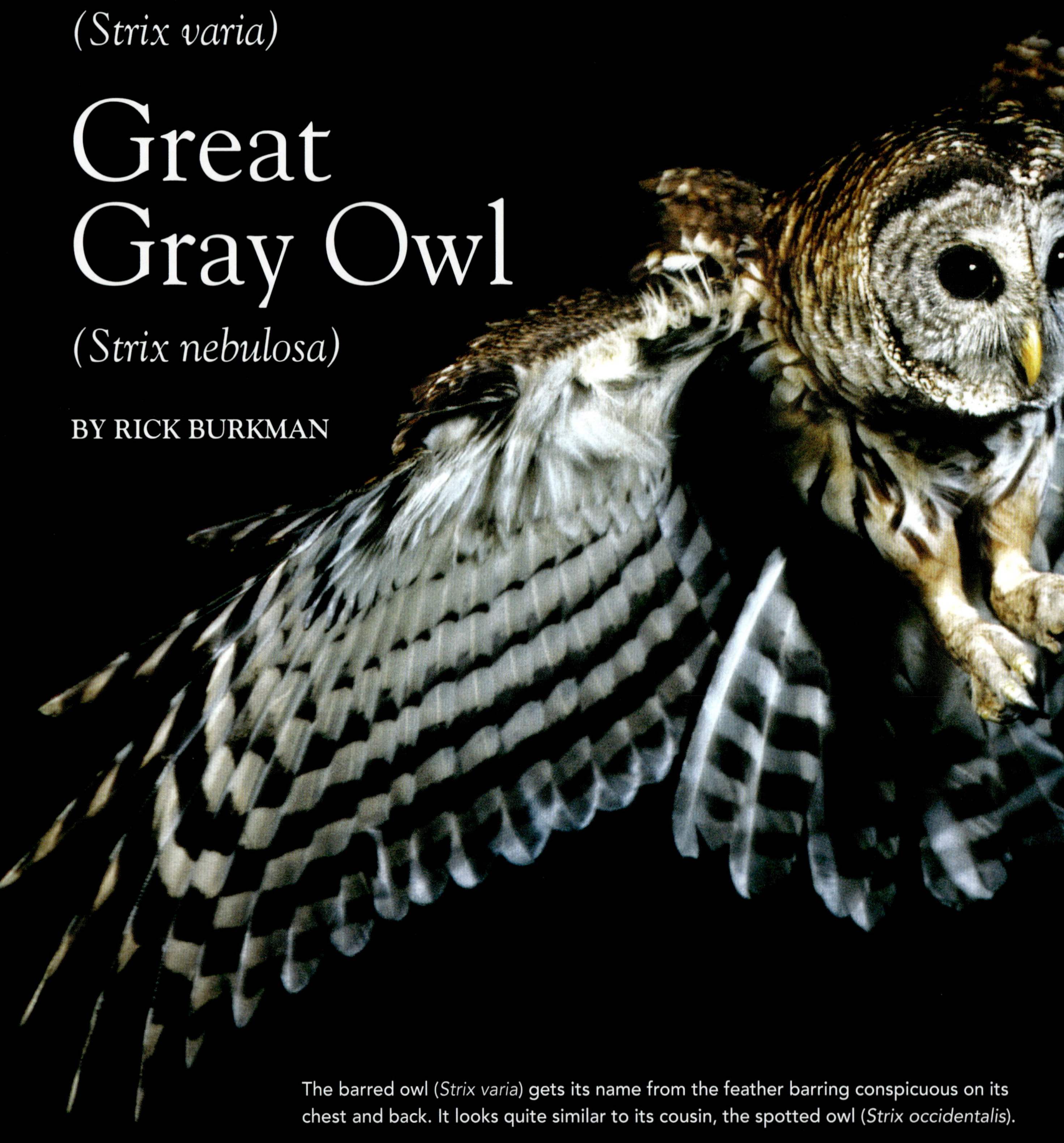

The barred owl (*Strix varia*) gets its name from the feather barring conspicuous on its chest and back. It looks quite similar to its cousin, the spotted owl (*Strix occidentalis*).

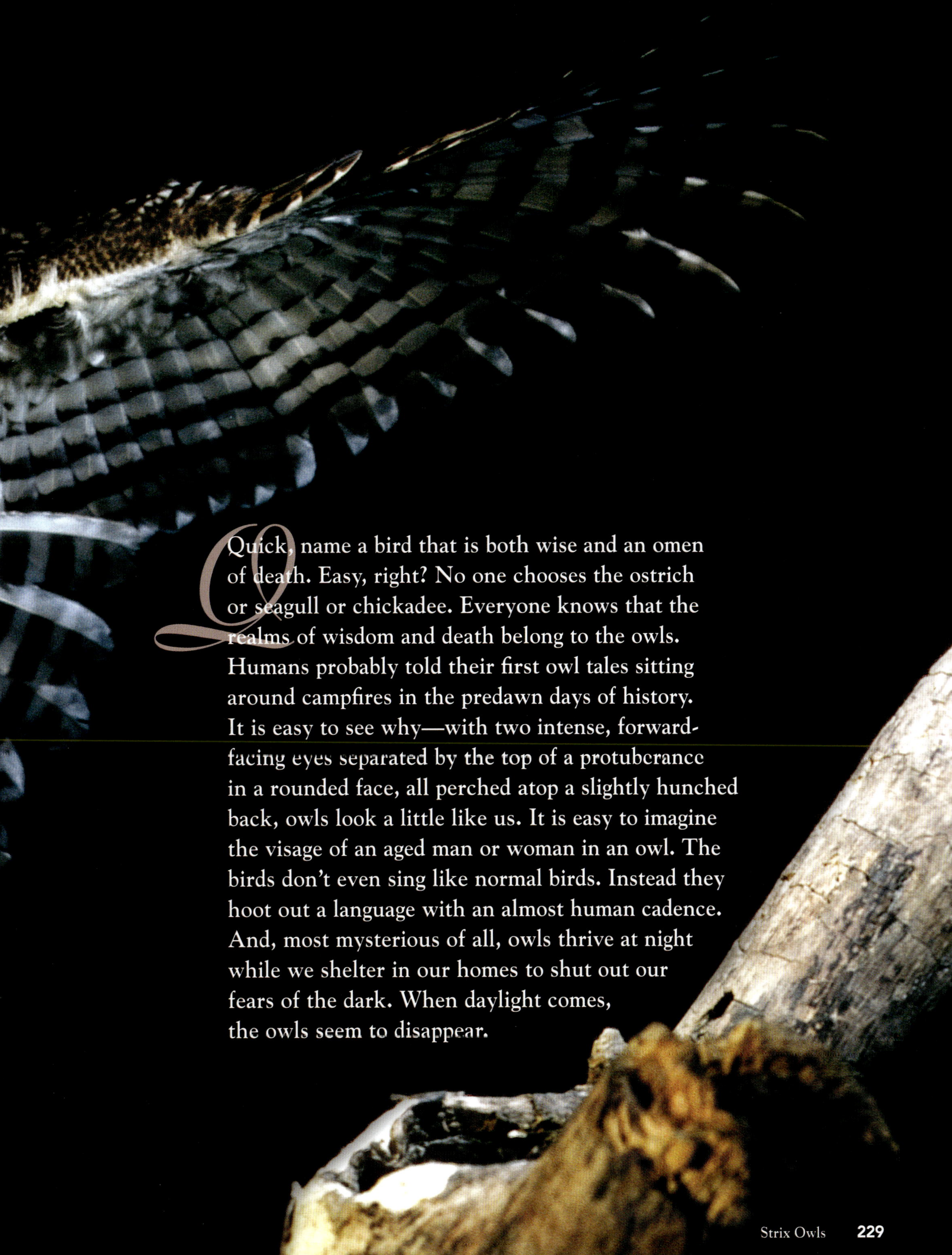

Quick, name a bird that is both wise and an omen of death. Easy, right? No one chooses the ostrich or seagull or chickadee. Everyone knows that the realms of wisdom and death belong to the owls. Humans probably told their first owl tales sitting around campfires in the predawn days of history. It is easy to see why—with two intense, forward-facing eyes separated by the top of a protuberance in a rounded face, all perched atop a slightly hunched back, owls look a little like us. It is easy to imagine the visage of an aged man or woman in an owl. The birds don't even sing like normal birds. Instead they hoot out a language with an almost human cadence. And, most mysterious of all, owls thrive at night while we shelter in our homes to shut out our fears of the dark. When daylight comes, the owls seem to disappear.

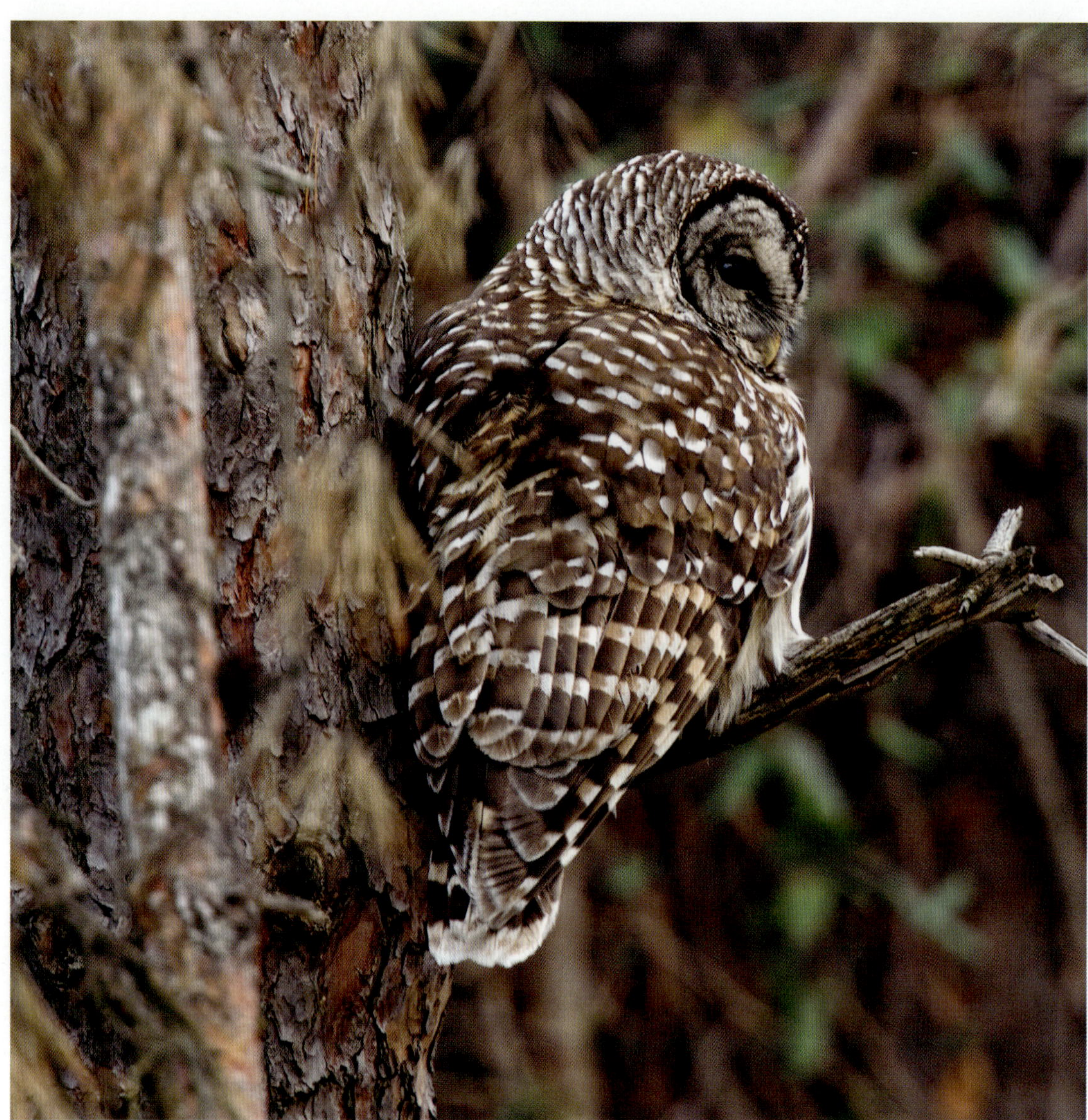

One of the barred owl's striking features is its large, dark eyes, something it shares with its spotted owl cousin, which is a little smaller. The feathered facial disks highlight the eyes, but their real purpose is to direct sound to the ears.

Today, of course, we know that owls are neither harbingers of doom nor mysterious messengers of ancient wisdom. They are hunters that have evolved to become the top avian predator of the night, supremely adapted to stalk their prey in quiet, low-light conditions, while their cryptic camouflage lets them rest undisturbed during the day.

Because they are so rarely seen, however, identifying owls even to the species level can be a challenge. The Strix owls—the barred (*Strix varia*), spotted (*Strix occidentalis*), and great gray owl (*Strix nebulosa*)—are considered non-eared owls because they lack the ear tufts found in some of their cousins, such as the great horned, long-eared, and screech owls. The names of the Strix owls are good clues to their looks: the barred owl has transverse brown barring on its chest and vertical barring on its belly; the spotted owl's front is dotted with hues of brown and white; and the great gray owl is large and ghostly. (Its scientific name, *nebulosa*, means "foggy plumage.")

When viewed face-on, the rounded heads of the Strix owls seem to take up a significant portion of their body size, but the head appears more flattened or sloped when viewed from the side, especially in the great gray owl. Despite the unusual body proportions, the eyes are the most striking feature. The intent, dark

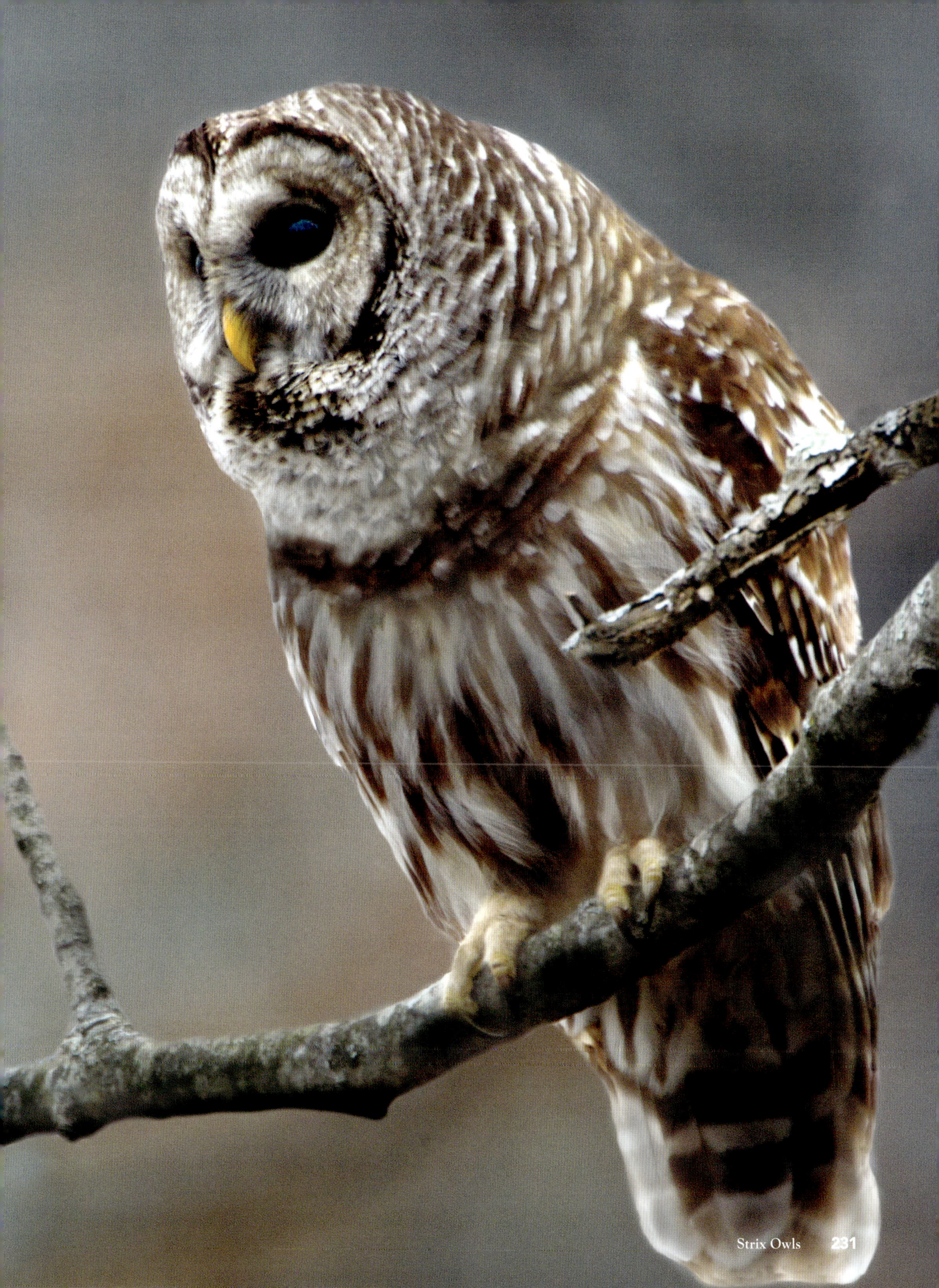

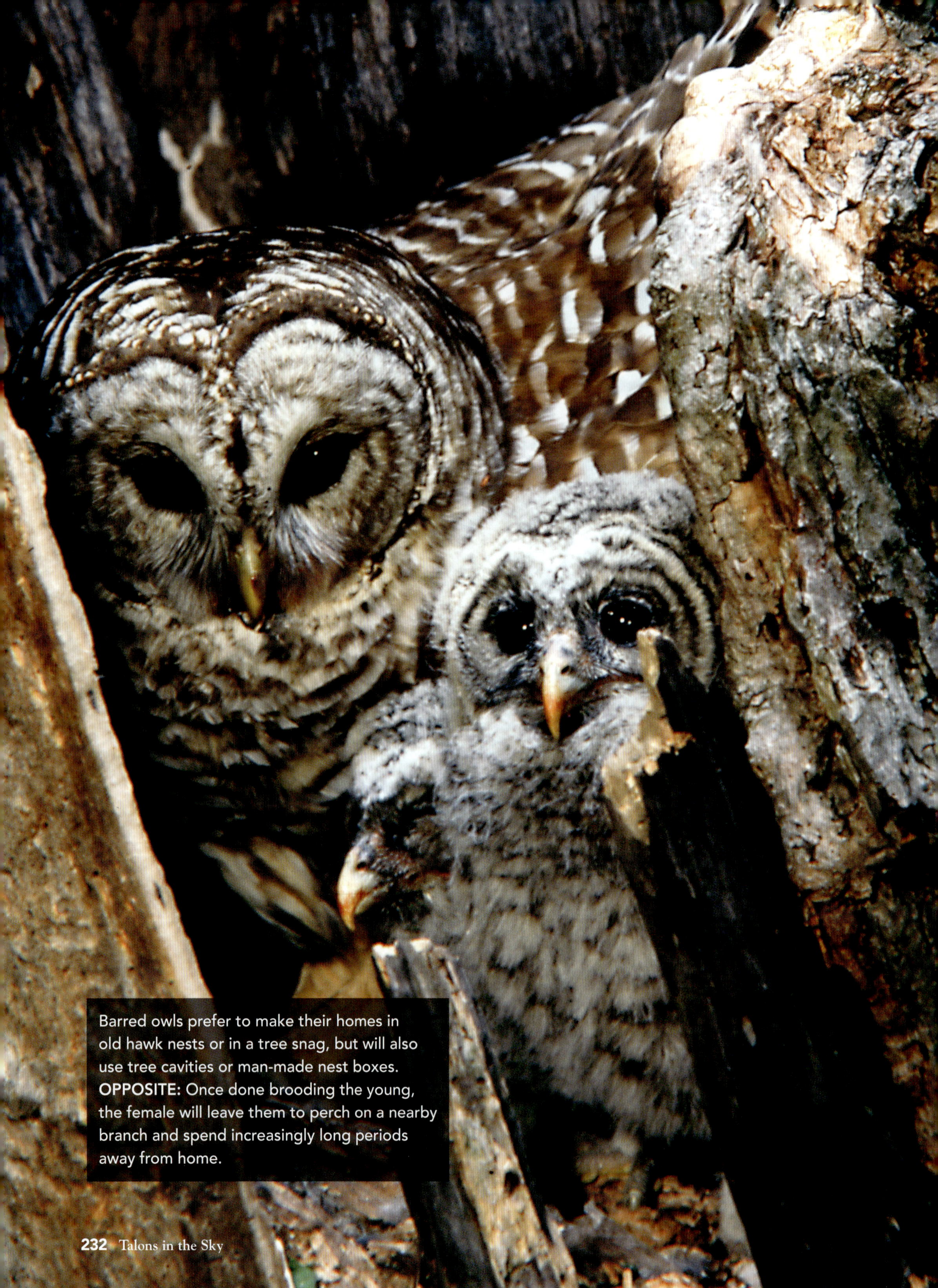

Barred owls prefer to make their homes in old hawk nests or in a tree snag, but will also use tree cavities or man-made nest boxes. **OPPOSITE:** Once done brooding the young, the female will leave them to perch on a nearby branch and spend increasingly long periods away from home.

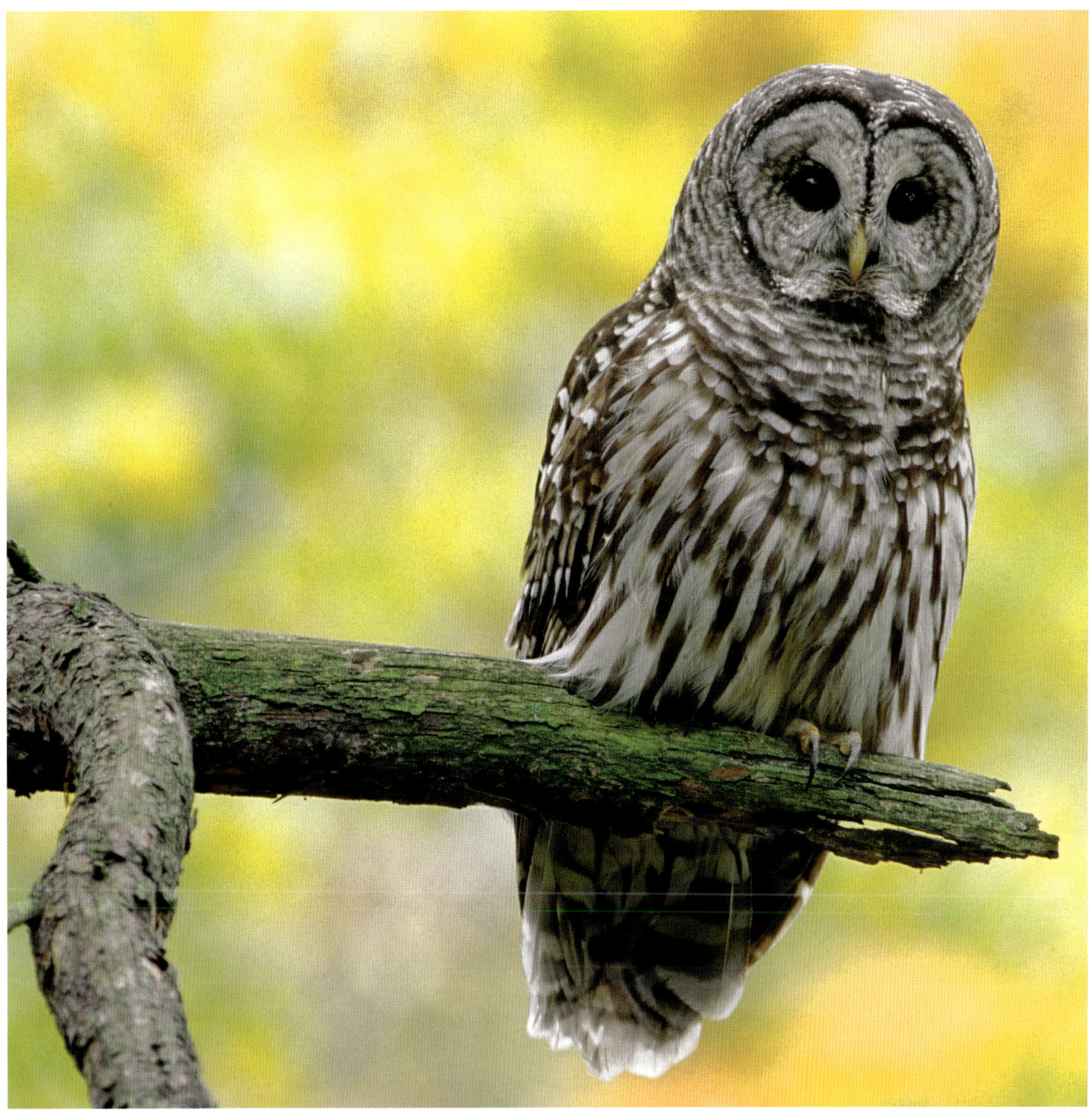

staring eyes of the barred and spotted owls and the bright yellow eyes of the great gray owls are highlighted by a group of fluffy, whitish, X-shaped feathers that form a bushy mustache and eyebrows. The eyes and the central X are surrounded by large facial disks lined with concentric rings of deeper color, which only accentuate the intense gaze.

The feathered facial disks highlight the eyes, but their purpose is to direct sound to the ears. Owls have ear openings on either side of the head, with one opening always higher than the other. This allows them to pinpoint the sources of sounds without using their eyes. The huge disks of the great gray owl are especially suited for this task, and the bird can detect the scratching and chewing of a meadow vole when the rodent is below 18 inches of snow a hundred yards away.

Good hearing is essential to the owls' survival. They are predators that require a diet of fresh meat. For spotted and barred owls, that means hares, skunks, and grouse. However, the largest bird of this group, the

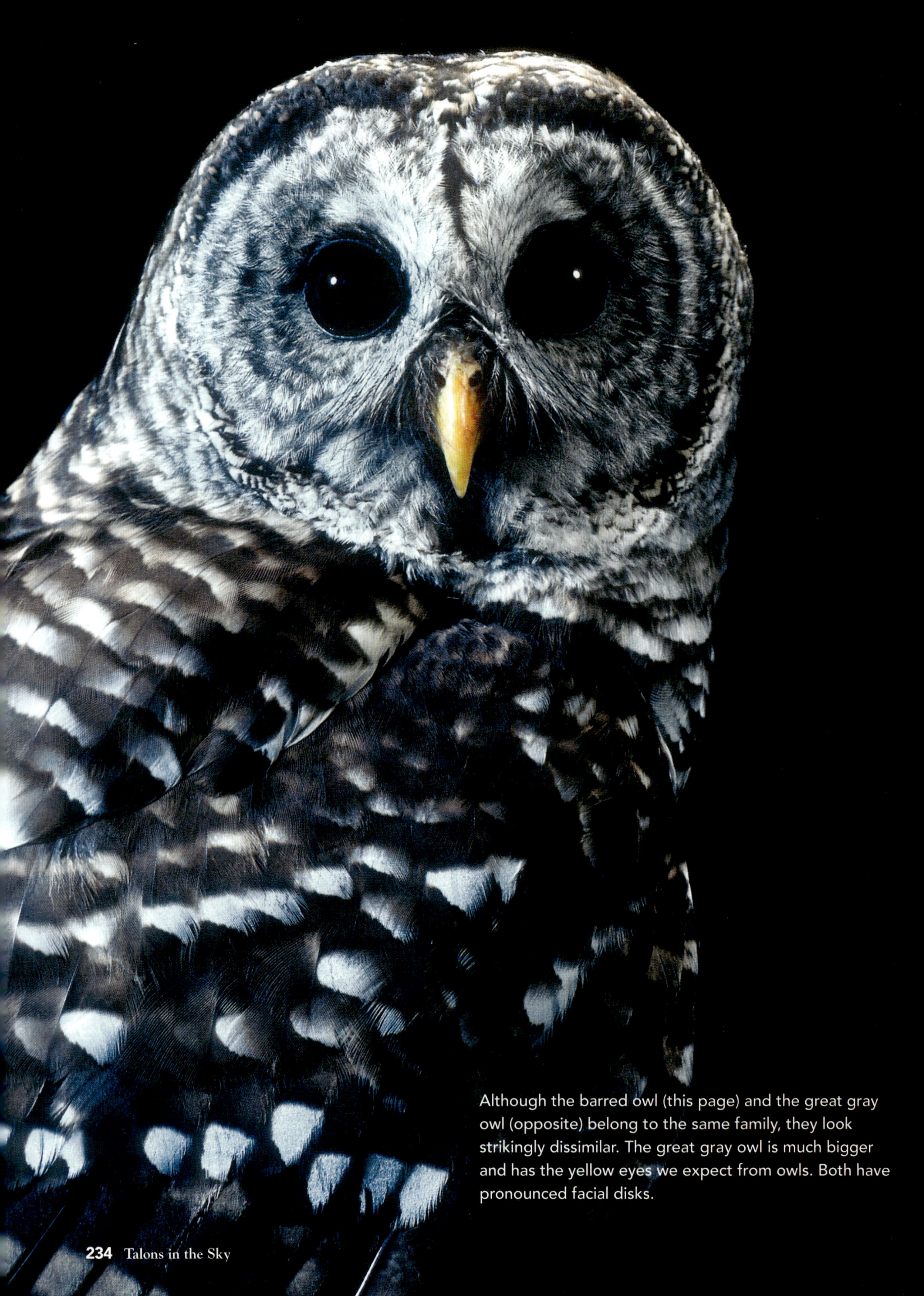

Although the barred owl (this page) and the great gray owl (opposite) belong to the same family, they look strikingly dissimilar. The great gray owl is much bigger and has the yellow eyes we expect from owls. Both have pronounced facial disks.

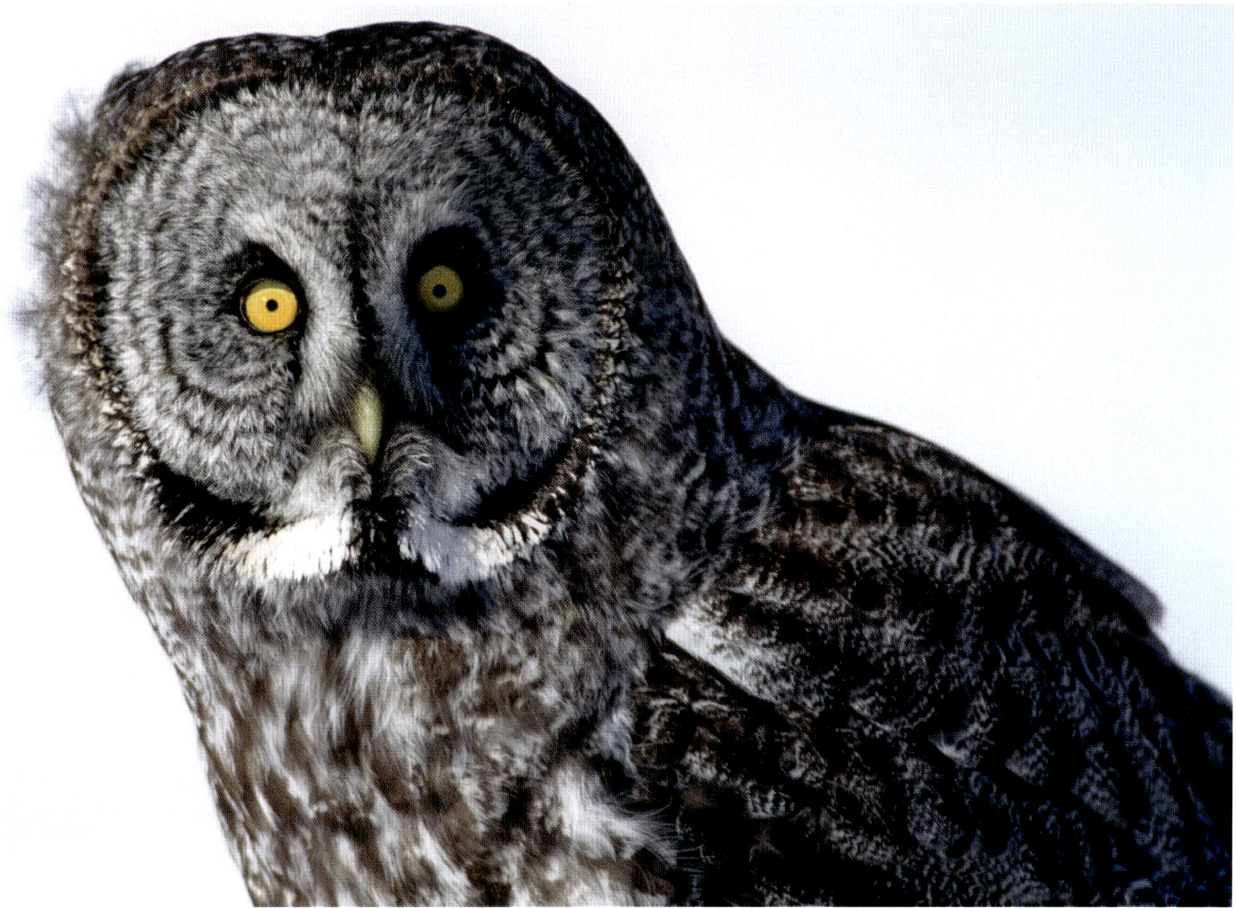

great gray owl, is satisfied with tiny voles. Despite the great gray's fluffy structure, it can pounce with enough force to break through an icy snow crust that could support a 180-pound human.

It's a little surprising that great gray owls are so powerful, because much of their size is just fluff. The great gray is the world's longest owl and it hoots in deep sonorous blasts like a big owl should, but under the feathers the owl has a smaller body than its cousin the great horned owl.

Strix owls are no strangers to the national news. Occasional irruptions of the great gray owl, normally a far-northern boreal species, catch the interest of local television broadcast stations every year. Even more prominent are the stories about the future of the spotted owl, a species found along the western edges of North America. (Its scientific name actually means "Western owl."). Spotted owls need mature, late-stage coniferous forests to survive. Humans use late-stage coniferous forests for homes, tools, and supplies for daily living. Today the two sides seem to keep creeping closer to a compromise, but it is a challenging task to balance the needs of wild creatures with human demand for shelter, tools, and luxury. The owls, oblivious to the uproar, do what they have done for eons—eat rodents, lay eggs, huddle in snowy weather, and scritch and hoot in the darkness.

Owls are not nest builders. They prefer to commandeer an old hawk's nest, settle in on top of a squirrel nest, or blend in on the jagged platform atop an old tree snag. The barred and spotted owls will use tree cavities and occasionally set up housekeeping in man-made nest boxes. The great gray owl is too big to bother with tree cavities, so its nests are always a platform of some type. All the owls start looking for nest sites in the same way. Because adults generally defend a territory year-round, they are already familiar with the local woodlands and know the best spots. The adults begin visiting favored sites several weeks before the actual nesting begins. No matter the species, the owls' knowledge of nest construction ends with choosing the site. A few feathers may fall and line the nest as the hen comes and goes, or she may pull a few while brooding and preening, but that is the extent of the building process. When the time is right, the female lays her eggs on the platform of her choosing. Clutch

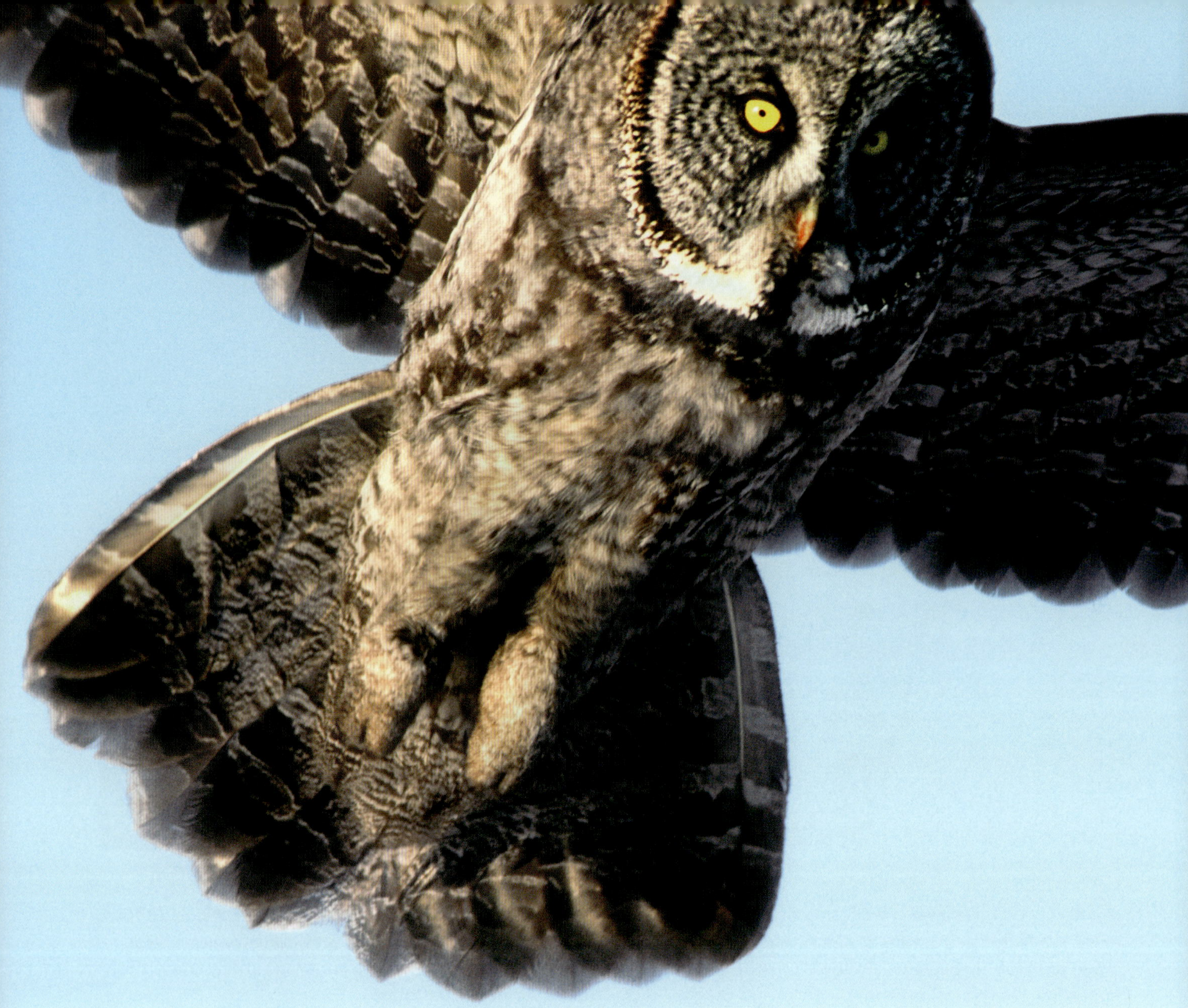

sizes vary from one to four whitish eggs, and it can take the female a long time to get that clutch. She usually lays eggs at the rate of one per day, but it is not unusual for three days to pass between eggs.

Brooding starts with the first egg. These owls live in cool climates and nesting starts early in the year, often while there is still snow on the ground and daytime temperatures are well below freezing. Barred owl eggs can come as early as mid-December, but March is a much more common nesting time for all three owls.

The hen sits on the eggs for about a month before they hatch. She suffers through cold, pelting sleet, and rain, and patiently waits as snowstorms pile powder on her back. It does not seem like an auspicious time to start a family, but the mother is diligent and the male does his fair share by capturing enough food to keep them both fed. He may not know it yet, but this is good practice for the days to come. After about 30 days of egg warming, the chicks begin to emerge. The first egg laid is the first to hatch and the others follow in order, sometimes several days apart. It is still winter when the young burst into the world, so protecting the downy nestlings from cold is as important as defending them from predators. Because the hen stays on the chicks during these early post-hatching days, the male is still the family's only source of food.

Nestlings huddle under mom for warmth and protection for varying amounts of time. Spotted owls continuously warm their nestlings for as little as eight days in California, but the great gray owl hens will brood their chicks for up to 21 days in the far North. Eventually the young birds can regulate their own body temperatures, and the first of their real feathers begin poking through their fluffy down. As the end of brooding time nears, the hen leaves the nest for short periods, sitting on nearby branches and preening, but still keeping an

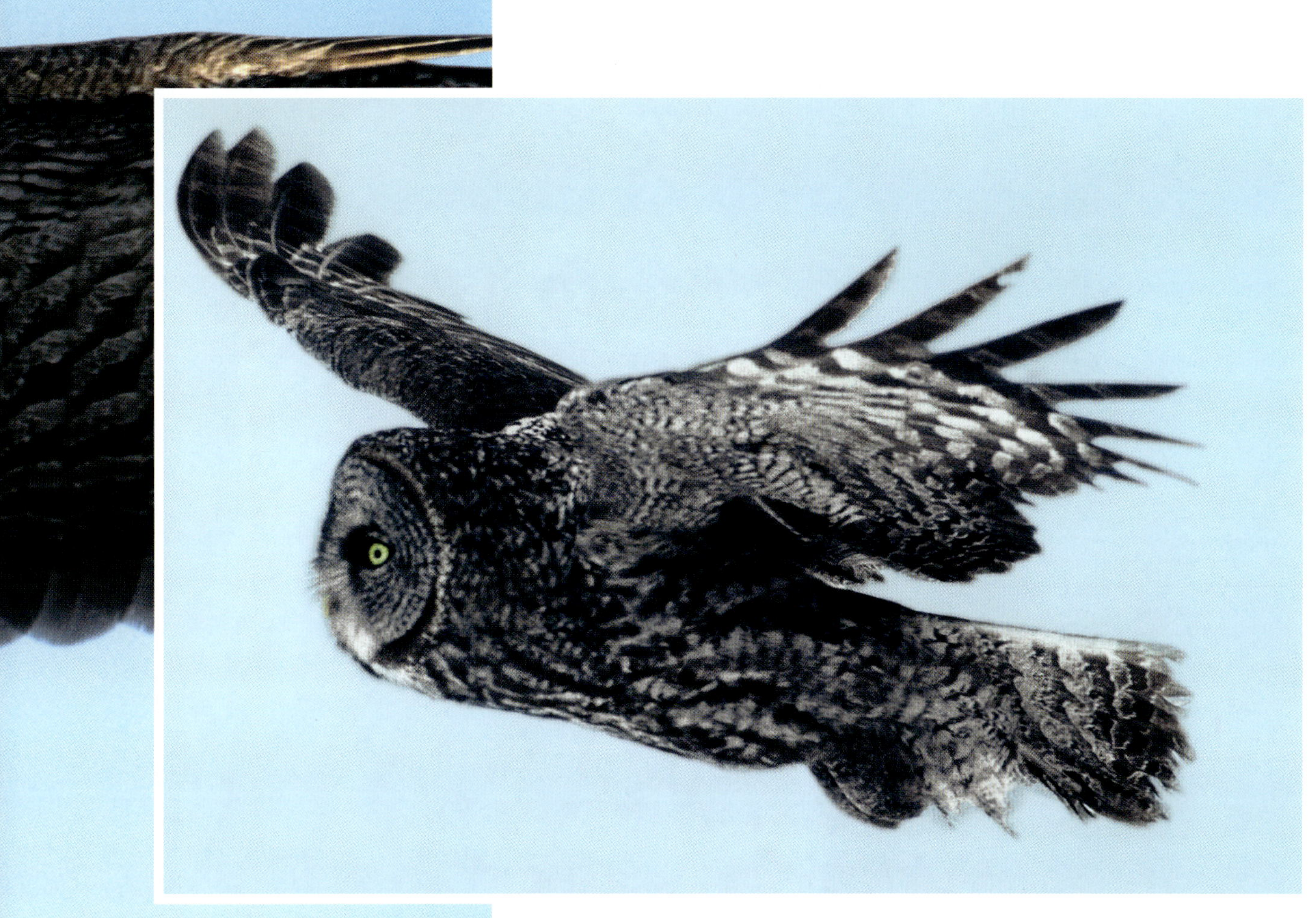

The great gray owl (*Strix nebulosa*) is North America's longest owl, but its size is mostly feathers. Other owls, such as the great horned and the snowy, are smaller, but they weigh more. Despite its featherweight rating, the great gray owl is an effective hunter.

eye on her precious brood. Before long she is making longer forays away and begins hunting again. Eventually, the hen gives up the nest completely, preferring to roost in a nearby branch or tree, leaving the crowded nest to the growing nestlings.

Nestlings are not sanitary creatures. Early in life they defecate in the nest. As they get a little older and more mobile, they perform their daily duties by squirting over the nest edge. Nestlings also produce pellets, regurgitated clumps of bone, feathers, and hair, as soon as they start eating. Some pellets make it over the nest edge to accumulate on the forest floor, but many don't. Before long, the nest area is an aromatic place, a scent beacon for predators such as raccoons, bobcats, foxes, and wolverines. Although the parents are diligent and dangerous nest defenders, nest predation occurs, especially when both parents are off hunting.

To make hunting more difficult for the predators, the nestlings waddle away from home within a few weeks of hatching. They creep through tree branches and totter across the ground, looking for another tree to climb and explore. They have no flight feathers at this stage, so they use a combination of firm talon grips, a stiff bracing tail, and a strong beak to pull and climb their way through the trees. Once they find a spot, they sit there throughout the daylight hours. Even if a predator happens upon the area, the fledglings are now separated and well hidden away from the nest. Fledged owlets are as well camouflaged as the adults and, even though the parents know where their young are, predators will pass them right by, unaware.

While the owlets are crawling through the brush and trees, they are growing stronger and stronger feathers. A few weeks after the young leave the nest, their mother's interest begins to wane. She spends less and less time caring for the young birds, and drifts farther

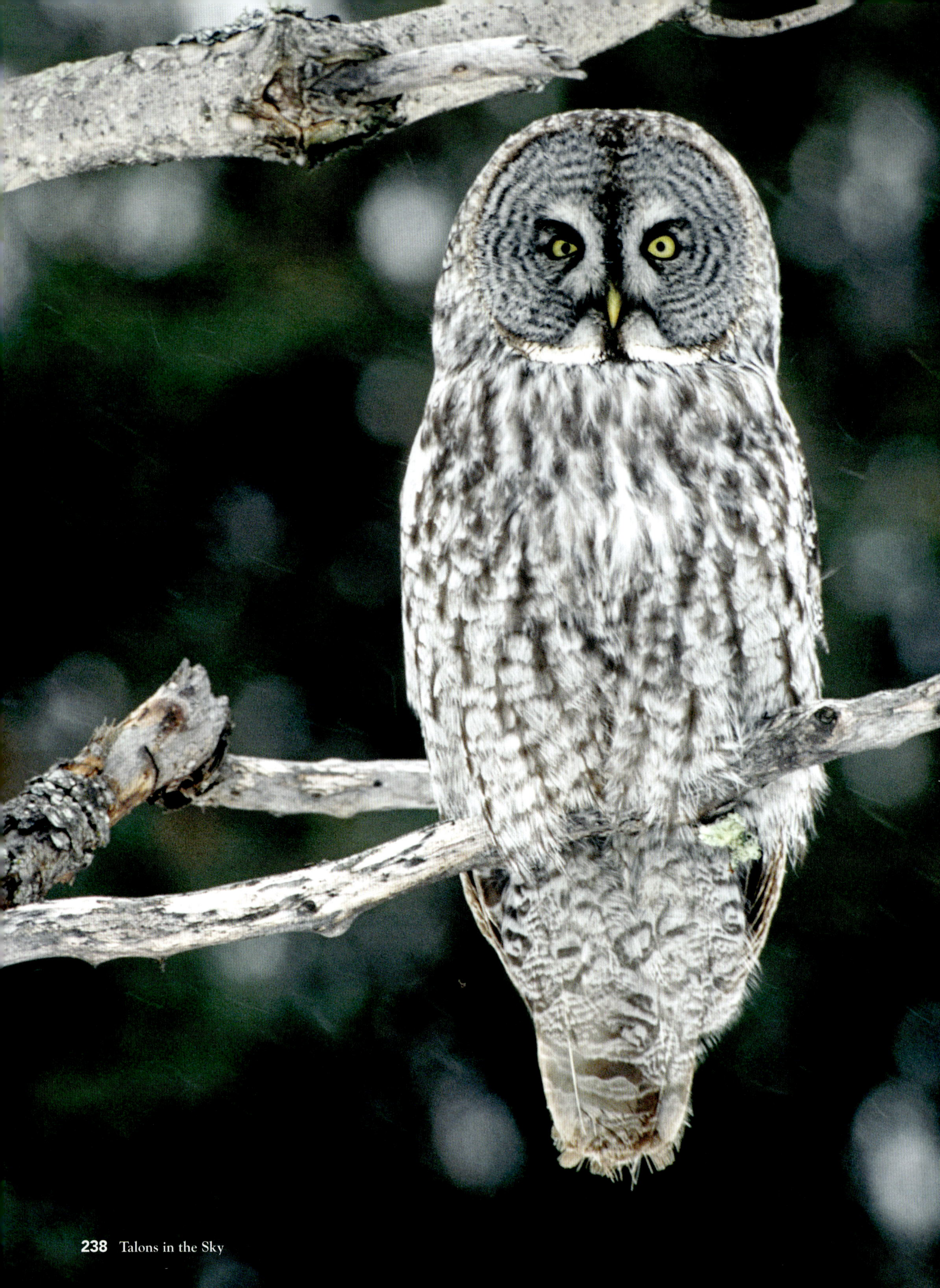

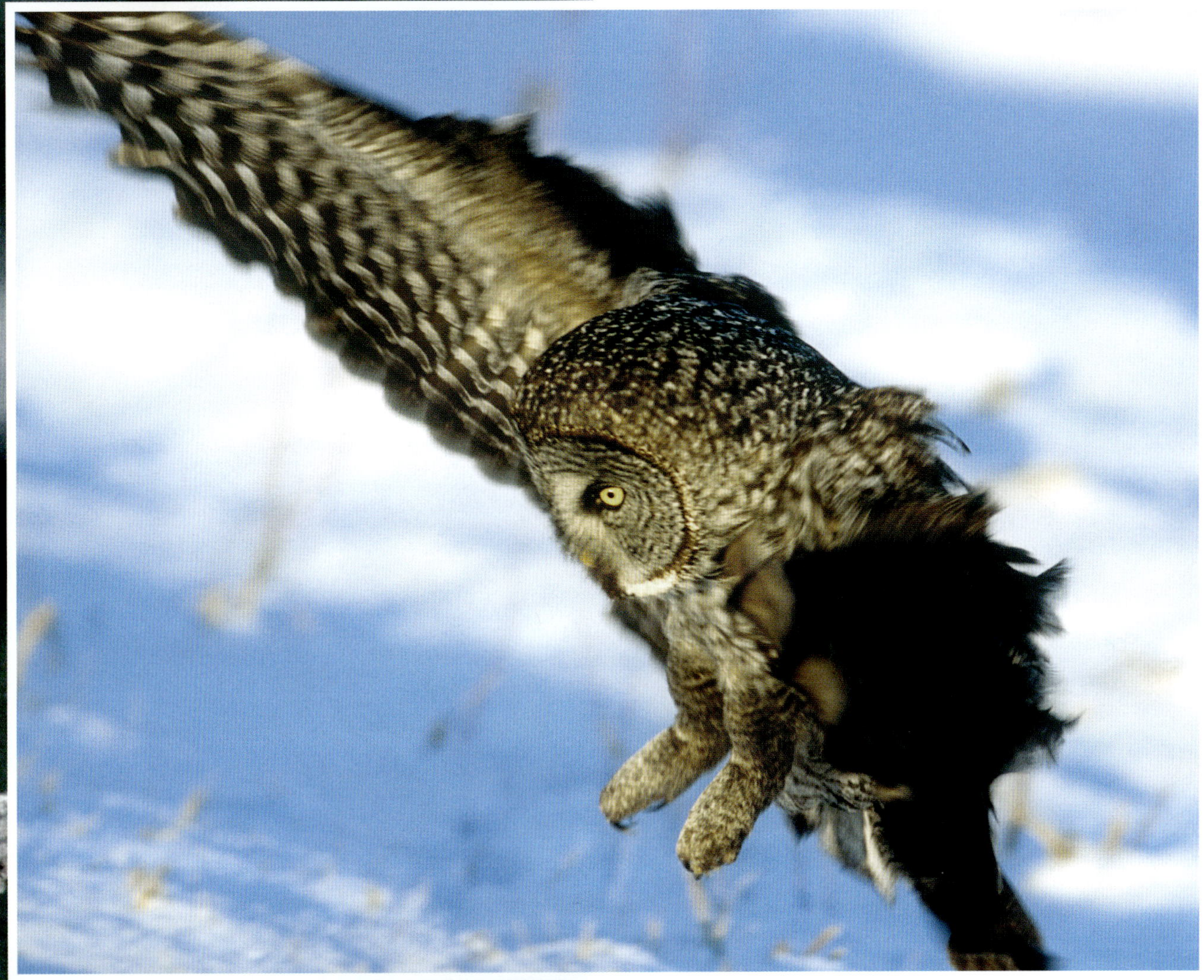

The great gray owl is a seriously strange-looking bird, which only adds to its air of mystery. Its scientific name, *nebulosa,* means "foggy plumage."

and farther away to hunt. She shares less of the food she finds. Great gray owl mothers may even visit other nesting territories and check on a neighbor's brood for a while before returning to her own territory. The males continue to feed their young birds during this period, and will supply any fledgling they come across.

Before long, the young birds have their first new set of feathers and they become more independent with each passing day. Some will stay in their parents' territory for a few months, but many will drift away to set up their own homesteads in vacant territories. There they will reign as the supreme raptor of the night and the new harbinger of death—but only if you are a rabbit or shrew or something equally small.

The great gray owl is normally a northerner, but the owls will occasionally stray south in irruptions when their food sources become limited.

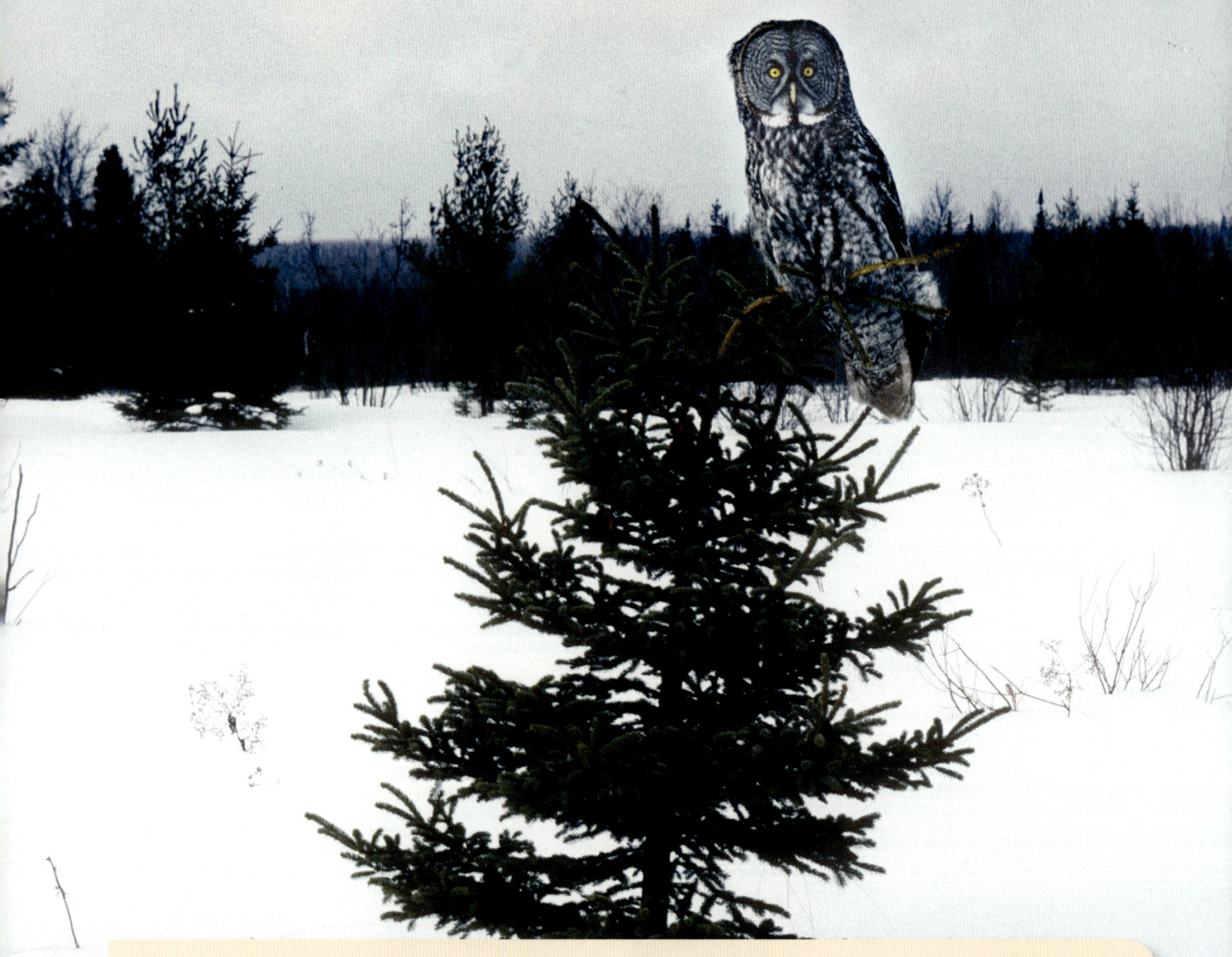

Measurements (in mm)

	Male	Female
Barred Owl		
Culmen	25.1	25.8
Wing	332.8	338.3
Tarsus	63.8	68.6
Tail	225.4	230.3

	Male	Female
Great Gray Owl		
Culmen	40.4	40.6
Wing	404.5	424.7
Tarsus	63.5	69.2
Tail	289.5	298